THE BEST PLAYS OF 1931-32

THE BEST PLAYS
OF 1931-32

AND THE
YEAR BOOK OF THE DRAMA
IN AMERICA

EDITED BY
BURNS MANTLE

ARNO PRESS
A New York Times Company
New York — 1975

THE BEST PLAYS OF 1931-32

"OF THEE I SING"

The Candidates: John P. Wintergreen for President. Alexander Throttlebottom (left) for Vice President.

(*Victor Moore and William Gaxton*)

THE BEST PLAYS
OF 1931-32

AND THE
YEAR BOOK OF THE DRAMA
IN AMERICA

EDITED BY
BURNS MANTLE

With Illustrations

DODD, MEAD AND COMPANY
NEW YORK   -   -   -   1932

INTRODUCTION

THE American theatre last year rode through storms and came to nothing resembling a clearing. It was, commercially, the worst year the theatre has suffered in its recent history, and it would be silly to attempt any blinking of that fact.

But the theatre did ride through, and is still riding through, and there should be some encouragement in that. Also the theatre, shaken by the economic elements, is settling back on its foundations and taking stock of its problems and possibilities as it never has done before.

If you had told any seasoned and experienced showman even so recently as a dozen years ago that the time would shortly come when the Erlanger lions and the Shubert lambs would permit themselves to be bedded together to conserve such covering as the times permitted you would have been hooted out of the hall.

And yet here we have the organization of the American Theatre Society and a combined booking office for the mutual protection of these rivals and the coöperative development of new circuits and systems that shall benefit theatre-goers everywhere.

I don't suppose we can go so far as to intimate that the theatre is, like many another shaken individual and institution, finding its soul in this widely advertised depression. Certainly not without inviting lawfter and raucous cheers. The theatre, commercially considered, is as soulless as a public utility corporation and twice as dumb. But the commercial theatre has discovered that high-handed policies involving trickery and greed are no longer workable and that there is not only mutual protection but a compensating mutual satisfaction to be found in a fair amount of honest coöperation.

Inflated salaries are tumbling down. Inflated egos are suffering a wholesome compression. It is easier, as the accumulated evidence of the season will show, to get a bad play produced now than it was when costs were up. But the search for good plays has also been notably stimulated because only good plays can live even a little while.

I have headed the list of ten plays selected to represent the theatre season of 1931-32 in this volume of the year book with

George Kaufman's, Morrie Ryskind's and the brothers Gershwins' "Of Thee I Sing."

First, because "Of Thee I Sing" was the winner of the Pulitzer award of the year as being "the original American play performed in New York that shall best represent the educational value and power of the stage," and, second, because it serves as a sort of overture to the dramatic list that follows.

You may debate, if you like, the wisdom or the right of the Pulitzer committee in making this award. Is a musical comedy a play in the commonly accepted sense of the term? Or is it just a musical comedy? Is a musical comedy a success because of its music or in spite of it? Can a musical comedy be stripped of its score and still be played straight as a series of related episodes that combine in the telling of a connected and coherent story? Would Joseph Pulitzer, were he alive, consider "Of Thee I Sing" a proper entrant in the competition he created?

As to that last supposititious query in debate I believe he would. J. P. was a crusading rebel among the journalists of his day, and he was pretty consistently agin the government. I think he would have adored this satirical fling at our political system and the breed of self-seeking politicians it has developed. The Kaufman-Ryskind javelins of wit flung at our sentimental and nose-ringed citizenry, and its hysterical following of every hokumeer who can catch the public attention, would probably have delighted his soul.

It is my own conviction, too, that whether "Of Thee I Sing" can legitimately be classified as a play within the meaning of the Pulitzer restrictions or not, the action of the committee in hurdling the question and giving the prize to the most intelligent entertainment of the year, whatever its form, will do great good in stimulating the ambitions of those authors who work from choice in other than the dramatic play medium.

The conviction is strong that had the committee passed "Of Thee I Sing" as ineligible the prize would have gone to Eugene O'Neill's triple distilled tragedy of a New England House of Atreus, "Mourning Becomes Electra." True, Mr. O'Neill has previously had the prize three times, with "Beyond the Horizon," "Anna Christie" and "Strange Interlude," but it would have been quite as awkward for the committee to explain why his "Electra" should be barred for that reason as it was for it to take what it concedes to be the "unusual" course of selecting a musical satire as the winner.

"Mourning Becomes Electra" inspired its reviewers to such a marshaling of shouting superlatives as no other play in our time has called forth. The public response was somewhat less hysterical, but steadily and consistently approving. The trilogy was voted, in general comment, a work of power and dignity which confirmed its author's position as America's greatest dramatist by revealing him as the one native writer for the stage who has developed the courage to attempt the classic Greek model or has indicated the ability to achieve it.

It has not been easy to reduce this tremendous work to such space limits as the year book exacts. Mr. O'Neill, I feel, is entitled to an engraved vote of thanks for permitting the digest to be made. Despite the sacrifice of most of the text, I have tried to preserve something of the spirit of the tragedy and the quality of its writing.

Robert Emmet Sherwood's comedy, "Reunion in Vienna," meets the Continental dramatists on their own ground and likewise improves upon its model. His story, which reassembles a group of exiled Austrian royalists in Vienna to celebrate the 100th anniversary of Emperor Josef's birth, might have been taken from a Freudian case history. In its retelling a former mistress of a wild Hapsburgian crown prince, now the wife of an eminent psychoanalyst, is frankly advised by her husband to cure an old infatuation by renewing contact with its inspiration, which she does with results both amusing and romantically stirring. It was the Theatre Guild's second hit of the season, and was unquestionably greatly aided by the personal and professional gifts brought to it by its leading players, Lynn Fontanne and Alfred Lunt.

Paul Green's "The House of Connelly" is one of that author's sensitively fine and dramatically authentic studies of Southern character about which he is so well informed and sympathetically concerned. It is, I think, a more appealing play than it appeared to be in performance. It was cast to fit the player material of a particular group of drama enthusiasts rather than according to suggested type. Performances were technically proficient but frequently out of key. The story, which follows the disintegration of a once-proud Southern family through the defeats immediately preceding its fall, is somewhat emotionally depressing and the play may reasonably fail of a wide popularity because of that. But I expect to see it revived in later years with added honor to its author.

"The Animal Kingdom" was the Philip Barry entry of the year, and one of his finer achievements in character analysis and plausible story building. In mood it is companion to last year's

Barry entry, "Tomorrow and Tomorrow." In place of the modernized miracle of Elisha and the Shunammite woman we have an adaptation of the Samson and Delilah theme applied to a story in which a man, shorn of spiritual strength in a physical mating with the woman he married, thinks to recover his soul by returning to the mistress who was, he concluded, his truer wife. An appealing and understanding performance by Leslie Howard added to the play's popularity.

Elmer Rice wrote and produced two of his own plays during the season, and both proved popular. One was "The Left Bank," the other "Counsellor-at-Law." In selecting "The Left Bank" for this record I was actuated by the wider appeal of its theme. This is a story of two American college radicals who move to Paris to escape the "spiritual vacuum" which is America. After six or eight years of illuminating experiences in Paris the wife, convinced of the failure of the experiment, so far as she and her child are concerned, recovers the child from the control of a modern psychiatrist engaged in correcting its alleged maladjustments and returns to America to continue its upbringing among the wholesome crudities of her native land. The fuming father remains behind, which provides a happy ending for the audience, as well as the stage family.

"Counsellor-at-Law" told of the rise of an East Side New York Jewish boy to a commanding position among the criminal lawyers of his day. A breach of ethics of which he was guilty during the climb catches up with him and threatens his future until he is able to prove the moral laxity of his chief Gentile persecutor. This was a stronger dramatic theme than that of "The Left Bank," but the play is fairly local to New York in situation and written with a racial consciousness that minimizes its appeal.

Rose Franken's "Another Language" was a quick success of the spring season. A simple domestic drama, its strength lies in the honesty of its writing and the recognizable truth of its character reactions. The story has a Candida background in that it tells of a youthful aunt who is the only one of a large family who expresses an understanding sympathy with an adolescent boy of artistic ambitions. The boy falls desperately in love with his aunt, but circumstances and her good common sense are equal to a reasonable solution of the resulting problem.

S. N. Behrman's "Brief Moment" seemed to me to be peculiarly reflective of the times in which we live. Being admittedly based on the recent adventure of a wealthy art patron's son who sought to balance his social budget and appease his general restlessness by marrying a musical comedy actress, it commands timeliness of theme and a keen observation of the modern generation in action. It is, as a piece of writing, brightly superficial. In real life the boy's adventure was a widely forecasted failure. In the play both the boy and the girl work through to a clearer and cleaner understanding of their individual obligations, which could easily have been the author's smiling concession to the demands of his star, his producer, and box office appeal.

There are two plays of English authorship at the end of the list, placed there, however, with no intention of suggesting that that is where they belong. This happens, after all, to be a year book of the American theatre in which the work of American authors is, I think, reasonably given precedence.

"Cynara" is a popular romantic play made from R. F. Gore-Browne's novel, "An Imperfect Lover," by Mr. Browne and H. M. Harwood, a veteran British dramatist. It shows with convincing plausibility the trouble a perfectly good, upright, clean-living, clean-minded British barrister can get into when his wife leaves him for five weeks and circumstances throw him into pleasant association with a sympathetic and lonely manikin. His effort to reëstablish his respectable routine results in the suicide of the girl and the dragging of the eminent sinner through a coroner's inquiry to eventual forgiveness by the wife. Philip Merivale, playing the barrister, made much of the fairly conventional material.

Benn W. Levy's "The Devil Passes" (called "The Devil" in London, where it fell under the ban of the official censor) has two virtues to commend it: Exceptionally well-written dialogue and an imaginative and provocative theme. Herein the Devil, assuming the pleasing shape of a youthful curate, passes through an English parish and assists in the readjustments of several lives by revealing to a group of dissatisfied humans their sounder virtues in place of stimulating their desire to capitalize their weaknesses. This is doing God's work as this Devil sees it, and makes for interesting discussion and the projection of varied philosophies.

There were several other plays of perhaps equal claim to recognition on a tentative list that I carry through the season. These included John Van Druten's "There's Always Juliet," Maxwell Anderson's "Night Over Taos," Denis Johnston's "Moon in the Yellow River," Mary Axelson's "Life Begins," Ferenc Molnar's "A Good Fairy." For one reason and another these were finally put aside in favor of the list as you have it.

The book's features have not otherwise been changed. I have, through the courtesy of John Chapman, who compiled them, included the titles of the principal song hits of those musical comedies which boasted song hits. I trust you will find this new bit of information interesting, and that you continue to find satisfaction in those features that have previously been included.

B. M.

Forest Hills, L. I., June, 1932.

CONTENTS

xi

ILLUSTRATIONS

THE BEST PLAYS OF 1931-32

THE BEST PLAYS OF 1931-32

THE SEASON IN NEW YORK

THOSE things this particular theatre season has given us to remember it by are in no especial way significant. We will, being put to it, probably recall it as the season of Eugene O'Neill's "Mourning Becomes Electra." That was an event in the theatre which inspired not only the comment of thousands but the use of many, many columns of newspaper space by the drama's critics in a concentrated effort to do the event justice.

In this connection also there is the correlated incident of the season's most sensational dramatic success being lightly set aside by the Pulitzer play committee when it awarded its annual prize to a musical comedy, "Of Thee I Sing." That caused a deal of comment also.

The season is likely to be catalogued as that one which brought about the downfall of many producers, including the Shubert Theatrical Company, and put several of them, including A. H. Woods, in the debtors' court with a plea in bankruptcy.

But, by this very fact, it was also a season in which probably a hundred or more newcomers were drawn into the fascinating business of play producing. Many of these newcomers were bankers, trying to protect their investments in the theatre, and it was well that they were forced into the open. Their stockholders may not have been properly impressed with their judgment as financiers, but they know now what happened with at least a part of those funds they had intrusted to the keepers of the vaults.

This situation in turn brought about one reform that is very likely to mean more to that touring territory known as the road than anything that has happened in the theatre in the last fifty years. When the receivers of the Shubert enterprises met the directors of what was left of the Erlanger enterprises it became apparent that the only hope of bringing good out of the situation which both companies were facing lay in the burying of their ancient grudge and the cessation of their continuous acts of reprisal.

There were conferences and agreements that resulted, first, in the combining of those subscription audiences organized in twelve key cities of the country by the New York Theatre Guild and the Shubert Professional Players, and, second, in the organization of an American Theatre Society which is to have charge of the selection and assignment of the plays that are to be sent out to entertain these combined audiences.

This means that for the first time since the formation of the so-called Theatre Trust thirty years ago there will be no cut-throat competition in the booking of plays sent on tour. If the society holds out, a committee will decide upon the best plays to be toured, and these will be routed in such a way as to avoid conflict and unfair competition. Playgoers will not be asked to choose between two popular dramas in one week, nor will they be forced to make their choice between a musical comedy and a revue, both of which have become nationally famous through their New York successes, and both of which are booked in Detroit, say, the same night or the same week.

Incidents of a playgoing year that add to the romantic legends of the theatre included the return of Maude Adams to the stage after she had been away thirteen years. Miss Adams wisely determined not to risk all on the report of her return by the New York critics. Or to let them have the first say as to the wisdom of her returning in that Shakesperian rôle to which she probably is as little fitted as any. Having elected to play Portia, which would at least assure her the support of an established classic, and having engaged Otis Skinner to play her Shylock, thereby adding the strength of that actor's very considerable road following to the guarantee, she came no closer to New York with "The Merchant of Venice" than Newark, N. J.

Those reviewers who had known and loved this popular actress of old made the journey across the river to see her, and wrote sympathetically and in praise of the performance. The others did not take the trouble. There were subtle intimations that the creation was mostly Adams and very little Shakespeare, but there were no such stings as might have greeted the revival had those younger critics unfamiliar with and without interest in the Adams tradition sought to justify their disappointment in extended columns.

Also that incident in the season that took the Earl Carroll Theatre in New York away from Mr. Carroll and gave it to his leading rival, Florenz Ziegfeld, as the Casino, was not without its touches of a romantic gambler's luck that plays so prominent a part in show business.

Mr. Carroll had, from a standing start some years ago and

without a dollar in his pocket, built a theatre at Seventh Avenue and Fiftieth Street, New York. The success of that venture inspired his backers to erect a second Carroll theatre on the same site. Into this enlarged and expanded playhouse Mr. Carroll had put every comfort for both his players and his audiences that he could think of, from automatic powder sprays, mirrored dressing rooms and recreation halls for the players, to spacious lounges, open ticket racks, concealed amplifiers and tiny electric lights on the backs of seats to aid in the locating of names and numbers of the players during the dark changes, for the audience. There were tall Swiss guards to serve as ushers and ticket takers, and a corps of handsome dress-suited young men to outdo movie theatre attachés in helping a lady locate her lost pocketbook or recover her dropped kerchief. Probably the opening night of the new Carroll theatre was the most satisfyingly emotional adventure of the entire Carroll career.

And then, it transpired, Mr. Carroll could not meet those obligations he was expected to meet and the theatre was taken from him. A few months later it was leased to Ziegfeld, who chiseled and painted out the Carroll name wherever it appeared and replaced it with his own. The Carroll became the Casino; the Ziegfeld "Show Boat" was revived with most of the original cast and Paul Robeson singing "Ol' Man River." Broadway history flowed back into its normal channels, and "Show Boat" did an enormous business, at, as the showmen say, a three-dollar top.

This 1931-32 season was also the season in which Representative Sirovich of New York arose in the House of Representatives and dignified all dramatic critics, and those of New York particularly, as a menace to the peace of the land and the prosperity of its theatres. The drama critics were unduly flattered but the House decided there was nothing much to do about the situation. There was enough unemployment as it was.

This was the season that the burlesque theatres began to creep into the Times Square district in New York. The late William Minsky, having made a success of the so-called lower forms of stage art, took over the Central Theatre on Broadway and the Republic Theatre on Forty-second Street and introduced there samples of those legomania entertainments that were considered the last word in boldness and a depraved public taste thirty years ago. The public in general, having been trained to accept a burlesque quality of humor in most of its revues and many of its musical comedies the last several years, and to have grown completely calloused to the exposure of female figures, paid but little attention to the Minsky invasion. Property owners in Forty-second Street, however, decided that real estate values were being depressed and the moral standards of the neighborhood appreciably lowered. Suit was brought to oust the Minskys and their nudes. The case, at this writing, is still in court.

The summer of 1931 was normally active in the playhouses, following mid-June, when we closed last year's year book. Nothing of consequence, however, was produced until Mr. Ziegfeld, having duly sworn never to do another, brought in a new "Follies" on July 1. It was his first in four years. Headed by numerous stars the favorite revue ran on for a hundred and sixty-five showings. In mid-July Heywood Broun, popular columnist and Socialist candidate, thought to lessen actor unemployment by staging a competitive revue entitled "Shoot the Works." It was a coöperative affair in which Mr. Broun contributed his all, including an appearance under a surprised wife's bed in a black-out. "Shoot the Works" made a good living for a hundred or more entertainers for eleven weeks.

Early August had nothing to offer tourists and stay-at-homes, except some very good Gilbert-Sullivan and old-favorite revivals, "Robin Hood," etc., by the dependable Milton Aborn. Late August, on the other hand, brought one well-staged and fairly interesting drama called "After Tomorrow" to the John Golden Theatre, and an Earl Carroll "Vanities" to that producer's new theatre. The "Vanities" played there for nearly three hundred performances. The opening was quite gala.

George M. Cohan suffered one of his few quick failures with a drama extolling the virtues of understanding parents called "Friendship"; Owen Davis suffered one of his comparatively few quick failures with a dramatic preachment called "Just to Remind You," in which the gangster menace was a bit too obviously exposed, and a smarter-generation comedy, "Cloudy with Showers" failed to duplicate for Floyd Dell and Thomas Mitchell, its authors, the success they had won the year before with "Little Accident." It did, however, last through nine weeks and passed out with unexpected suddenness.

The first Arthur Hopkins production of the year, the first of the satires on American hero worship, a comedy entitled "The Man on Stilts" by Edwin and Albert Barker of Chicago, also proved a quick failure. This was unfortunately discouraging to that producer. Seeing that most of us look to Mr. Hopkins as one of the sturdier hopes of the theatre, this adventure was quite generally depressing. The Barkers' story was of an alert young

American who grabbed a steam-roller in lieu of salary when he was working on a street paving job in San Francisco. He started with it for the suburbs. A wild newspaper reporter announced that he had started a trans-continental tour with it. Ballyhooers got after him and pushed him on. By the time he reached New York he was a Lindbergian hero plus. In the end he quit his exploiters in high disgust.

Raymond Moore, who helps the summer visitors up Cape Cod way through the summer with a variety of stock company productions, brought a play in which he had confidence to Broadway in early September. It was a piece called "Ladies of Creation," written by Gladys Unger and well played in its chief rôle by Chrystal Herne. It enjoyed eight light weeks.

By mid-September George White was ready to challenge with another "Scandals" the current success of the Ziegfeld "Follies" and the Carroll "Vanities." As in former years there seemed plenty of business for all three. "Scandals," being better than usual, set the White crowd cheering and kept it cheering all winter.

Mae West, again representing the harlots' hope in one of her own dramas called "The Constant Sinner," created enough excitement to play eight weeks, after which, I believe, she started West and ended in Hollywood.

Failures being common, the Theatre Guild began its season with one. A comedy written by Alfred Savoir, called "He," hopefully imported, failed to satisfy as many of the Guild subscribers as usual and did not quite last out the six-week subscription period. It was Savoir's amiable conceit that a man who claimed to be God could temporarily fool a group of free thinkers in convention in Switzerland. Thanks to the aids of circumstance and accident, they accepted him for a time. Then guards came and took him back to the sanitarium where, he claimed, God would most likely be found if ever he decided to walk the earth a natural man.

Messmore Kendall brought from London a Somerset Maugham comedy called "The Breadwinner." It had been fairly successful on the other side, but New York would have none of it. Maurice Schwartz, the Yiddish Art star, decided to have another try at establishing himself on Broadway, this time as an English-speaking actor. Mr. Schwartz had come to believe that he had lost his older Jewish public because the younger East Side generation was not interested in Yiddish plays. His first play was "If I Were You," an adaptation from the Yiddish of Sholem Aleichem, which he was able to play ten weeks. He followed this with two other foreign plays done into English, "Bloody Laughter" from the German of Ernst Toller and "Wolves" from the French of Romain Rolland. His season, however, was not the success commercially that Mr. Schwartz had hoped it would be and he has decided, I understand, to return to the Yiddish drama this year, leasing a roomy Broadway playhouse which will permit him to lower his prices of admission considerably.

An important and satisfying late September adventure was that of the Group Theatre, Inc., an organization of former Theatre Guild associates which had previously produced "Roar China" successfully. The Guild, having bought the rights to a Paul Green drama named "The House of Connelly," turned it over to the Group and the Group, rehearsing it all summer in a barn theatre up Westchester way, made a splendid production of the play at the Martin Beck Theatre. The reviewers were quite thrilled, and for a matter of eight weeks "The House of Connelly" was reasonably well supported. Around holiday time business was poor and the play was closed. Later it was revived for an additional three weeks, but it never could quite be listed with the successes. I have included excerpts from "The House of Connelly" in this volume of best plays.

Gilbert Miller, long impressed during his London adventures with the skill of Charles Laughton as a character actor, brought that player to America in a murder drama called "Payment Deferred," in which Mr. Laughton played with skill the rôle of a murderer haunted by the knowledge that he had buried his victim in his garden and must forever after hang about for fear another tenant would take to digging. The actor was wildly praised, but the play did not take firm hold of the public's interest. "The Good Companions," another London success, being a scattered adaptation of an extremely popular novel of the same title by J. B. Priestley, also failed of popular support and was gone after nine weeks.

In early October Elmer Rice, recently arrived from a long stay in Europe, where he went shortly after his "Street Scene" won the Pulitzer prize in 1929, determined to be the producer of his own works in the future. He took over the Little Theatre and there staged an interesting domestic comedy called "The Left Bank," which is also included in this volume. The play ran for 240 performances. A few weeks later Mr. Rice made his second production, that of a melodrama called "Counsellor-at-Law," which dramatically details the rise of a young Jew from New York's East Side to a foremost position among the city's great criminal

lawyers. "Counsellor-at-Law" proved the greater popular success
of the two and ran on through the summer. The chief part was
played originally by Paul Muni. Later Otto Kruger, who had
been successful with a Chicago "Counsellor-at-Law" company,
followed Muni in New York and Harry Mervis succeeded Kruger
in the Chicago cast.

Lawrence Langner, of the Theatre Guild directorate, feeling an
urge for more freedom of action in the producing of plays, organized a Westchester stock company for the summer and gave trial
performances to several promising plays. One was a revival of
Dion Boucicault's ancient and amusingly artificial "The Streets
of New York," which, with a little forcing, was played for eleven
weeks. A second Langner offering was a revival of Ibsen's "Pillars
of Society," which lasted for no more than two performances, and
a third was a bright comedy by Will Cotton called "The Bride
the Sun Shines On," in which Dorothy Gish and Henry Hull
played the leads. This one got fifty-five performances but not
much money. Then the Langners closed shop and waited for the
summer to resume their practicing in the country.

William A. Brady, Sr., who previously had taken little part in
the season's activities, now came forward with a fairly trivial
comedy, "A Church Mouse," which Ruth Gordon and Bert Lytell
did much to save for 160 showings. The Shuberts, not yet with
their backs against the wall, but standing close to it, had a
musical comedy made from the Hackett-Goodrich comedy, "Up
Pops the Devil." They called it "Everybody's Welcome" and
did only fairly well with it. Oscar Shaw, Frances Williams and
Ann Pennington were in the cast.

The first outstanding musical comedy success of the year turned
out to be Jerome Kern's and Otto Harbach's "The Cat and the
Fiddle," which boasted a frankly romantic plot and a tuneful
Kern score. It ran the season through and deserved to.

Then, in late October, Eugene O'Neill's long and impressive
"Mourning Becomes Electra" startled the town and thrilled the
critics into a release of all their choicest superlatives. Not everyone bowed down before this rather tremendous work (it was
originally written as three full length plays and then reduced to
one play in three divisions, fourteen scenes and a required playing
time of approximately six hours), but the playgoing majority
were for the first time in agreement as to O'Neill's rightful standing as America's greatest dramatist. The play, with six showings
a week, ran for 145 performances.

Further indication that it was a good season for romantic plays was found in the immediate success of "Cynara," in which Philip Merivale detailed with moving sincerity the misery a perfectly well-meaning husband created for himself when he drifted into a too intimate friendship with a sympathetic manikin. This drama also lasted through the season, and is included among those from which I have taken excerpts for this book.

A second early November success was that of "The Laugh Parade," written, staged, financed and played by Ed Wynn. This favorite comedian further strengthened his grip upon the affections of the people with this success. "Brief Moment," the Behrman comedy that made an actor of Alexander Woollcott, the critic; "The Social Register," which Leonore Ulric kept in the popular-priced success class for a hundred performances; Ethel Barrymore's three-week visit with "The School for Scandal," which she had been playing on tour, and an amusing light comedy satirizing the activities and scandals of the Metropolitan Opera Company, written by Murdock Pemberton and David Boehm and called "Sing High, Sing Low," were other November features.

The agreeably successful "Reunion in Vienna," which the Guild's first acting company, headed by Alfred Lunt and Lynn Fontanne, played for thirty-four weeks, or from November to July, and Gilbert Miller's hit with Molnar's "The Good Fairy," with Helen Hayes as the star, also raised the November average. One of the minor disappointments was the failure of a biographical drama written around the career of Florence Nightingale as "The Lady with a Lamp." Edith Evans, the creator of the rôle in London and a fine actress, came over to play it here but was ready to go home again after two bad weeks.

The December satisfactions included the quick success of a light and saucy farce, "Springtime for Henry," with Leslie Banks and Nigel Bruce, English players, adding their weight of personable likeableness to a thin but amusing story. This one was written by the Benn W. Levy whose "The Devil Passes" came in later and which is contained in skeletonized form in this volume. Christmas week saw the triumphant New York showing of the Pulitzer prize winner, "Of Thee I Sing," the first musical comedy ever to win the theatre's honor ribbon and the thousand dollars that go with it. You will find more of that elsewhere.

"The Bride the Sun Shines On," previously noted as a feature of the Lawrence Langner season, was a Christmas present, and the week following Constance Collier revived Noel Coward's "Hay Fever," playing the part of the actress heroine which had fallen originally in America to Laura Hope Crews. Miss Collier's personal following, plus the increased interest in Coward's works, kept the revived "Hay Fever" playing to fair returns a matter of twelve weeks.

The early weeks of the new year uncovered a success or two. Levy's "The Devil Passes," before mentioned, did well for a time, and on the twelfth Philip Barry's "The Animal Kingdom" jumped into immediate favor. Leslie Howard was an important factor in this success and also a co-producer with Gilbert Miller and Mr. Barry himself. "The Animal Kingdom" was freely spoken of as a logical runner-up for the Pulitzer prize, and in excerpt form is included herein.

Basil Sydney and Mary Ellis tried to make something out of "The Jewel Robbery," but without the success frequently attending their joint efforts. On the other hand Ernest Truex did a good deal personally to make "Whistling in the Dark" one of the jolliest melodramatic farces of the winter. In this Gross-Carpenter comedy Ernest plays a captive novelist who is held by a gang of killers until he thinks up a plot to cover a fancy murder.

Interesting failures in mid-season included a play written by Walter Damrosch's daughter Gretchen, "The Passing Present," which detailed the disintegration of an old New York family of social distinction, and "1931—," an intensely earnest criticism of the failure of civic and social forces to grasp the problems of the depression. This play by the Paul Siftons dealt notably with the problem of unemployment and its devastating effect upon human souls. "Lost Boy," a study of those criminal-breeding influences stemming from poverty-stricken homes, plus reform school methods, also disappointed its audiences. It was written by T. C. Upham, a new playwright with an old crusader's spirit. The public's refusal to support these plays voiced again its human determination to buy happiness in the theatre, and to avoid contact with civic and home problems, publicly exploited, as completely as possible.

Guthrie McClintic, directing the destinies of the Belasco theatre, which he and his wife, Katharine Cornell, had under lease, was greatly disappointed, as were we, in the failure of a Dan Totheroe piece called "Distant Drums," with Pauline Lord playing its heroine. McClintic had given the drama every advantage of cast and production and the story was historically significant in picturing the hardships of the early pioneers who fought their way through to the Pacific coast, but the public could not be interested, either in the play or in Miss Lord's performance.

Another interesting failure was that of a prize play, "If Booth

Had Missed," written by Arthur Goodman and first played by the Morningside Players of Columbia University. It was Mr. Goodman's experiment to add the main facts of Andrew Johnson's term as President, following Lincoln's death, to Lincoln's career, proving that if the martyred President had lived, and had continued his fight against his political enemies, he probably would have been impeached in place of Johnson. Goodman had Lincoln assassinated finally just after his stirring conduct of his own defense in the impeachment proceedings. The play received frequent endorsement from its reviewers but little from the public.

"Blessed Event" brought the modern Broadway columnist into the theatre in a biographical farce written by Manuel Seff and Forrest Wilson. It was the story of a town tattler who got a dance hall girl into trouble by reporting her expectant motherhood and who was thereafter threatened by her gangster protector.

In February Herbert Marshall and Edna Best, two widely popular players of both West End theatres in London and Broadway in New York, came in with a John Van Druten whimsy entitled "There's Always Juliet" and played on through the spring. It could have continued indefinitely but moving picture magnates, who were eager to have Mr. Marshall appear in a screen drama, bought off the last weeks of the engagement and sent the Marshalls (Miss Best being Mrs. Marshall off-stage) to Hollywood.

"There's Always Juliet" revealed a pleasantly romantic episode relating the meeting of an American architect and an English débutante in London and the intensive three-day campaign which finally won the young woman for the architect. There were but four characters in the play, which may have had something to do with its success. Too many actors frequently spoil the froth.

Now, with predictions rife that the season was practically over, there appeared two or three other sizable hits. The first of them was a second satirical musical comedy called "Face the Music." This one was written by the Moss Hart who had laid out the original plot scheme for last season's immensely popular "Once in a Lifetime," and Irving Berlin, Mr. Berlin doubling also as composer of the music. The story revolved about both the depression and the recently exposed vice squad grafters. The tin boxes in which they and their higher-up contacts kept their ill-gotten wealth furnished backing for a musical comedy within this musical comedy. This play within a play, it was promised, would help the grafters get rid of large packages of their troublesome currency. "Face the Music" was a ruthless exposure and rough in spots, but it inspired laughter that was both hearty and free and ran well into the summer.

John Golden found a good comedy by Daniel Rubin, "Riddle Me This," which Frank Craven staged and cast for him. Craven and Thomas Mitchell played the leads, one a tough police reporter and the other a tougher police captain, and were successful in building up a run of a hundred performances.

William A. Brady stepped forward again with a revival of two Barrie plays, "Alice Sit-by-the-Fire" and "The Old Lady Shows Her Medals," in which he induced Laurette Taylor to come back to the stage after a retirement of four years. The start was fine but the finish, five weeks later, found Miss Taylor unable physically to stand the strain.

The Theatre Guild suffered another artistic failure with a drama of the Irish revolution sympathetically and often beautifully written by Denis Johnston and called "The Moon in the Yellow River." The story was the placid recital of a German materialist's attempt to build a power plant on an obscure portion of the Irish coast and the opposition he met from the rebellious citizens' army. The reformers resented all so-called progressive enterprises that carried with them the threat of further unemployment to native workmen and blew up the plant. After which the village settled back more or less calmly into its older routines.

Florenz Ziegfeld, having a script and score for a musical comedy called "Hot-Cha," which did not seem to be a particularly good idea in titles at the time, engaged a cast that included Bert Lahr, one of the rougher and funnier burlesque comedians; Lynn Overman, Buddy Rogers and Lupe Velez of the cinema. "Hot-Cha" indirectly was George White's gift to Mr. Ziegfeld. Mr. White had quarreled violently with Lew Brown of the firm of Brown and Henderson, composers and lyricists, the year before, and they, in retaliation, had written this score for his rival. Its success was great for a matter of ten or twelve weeks. After that the overhead began to bear down upon the receipts. "Hot-Cha" was closed after a hundred and nineteen performances.

The Group Theatre, after its not very heartening experience with two good plays, "The House of Connelly" and "1931—" turned to another of America's first dramatists, Maxwell Anderson, for a third play. This was "Night Over Taos." Beautifully written and staged there was again the question of a proper judgment in casting to handicap what chances the play had. However, it probably was too casual a story, too unexciting a tragedy to stir anything resembling mass interest.

An honest drama of the maternity wards was Mary McDougal

Axelson's "Life Begins," but the scene was embarrassingly intimate and the public was unhappily repelled rather than attracted. In contrast "The Warrior's Husband," a farcical treatment of a classic legend, the attempt of Hercules to recover the girdle of Diana from Hypolyta, Queen of the Amazons, and thus strip the fighting ladies of their physical prowess, proved sufficiently strong to last out eleven weeks, though to no better than fair business.

In early April the Theatre Guild made its last production of the season, that of Bernard Shaw's latest play, "Too True to Be Good." The subscribers, or a goodly majority of them, took to it with avidity during the first weeks of the run and it proved sufficiently popular with the general playgoing crowd to run a week past its allotted six, even though the weather was becoming muggy. The play was a collection of Shavian preachments on a variety of Shavian themes, making intelligent and good-natured sport of the human race.

Still seeking a play for Pauline Lord, Guthrie McClintic revived Milne's "The Truth About Blayds," with O. P. Heggie playing his old part of the monogenarian poet who lived fifty years on the reputation of a dead writer whose work he had published as his own. Again a splendid production but little public response.

A group of earnest young adventurers in the theatre took over the Provincetown Playhouse in late April and there produced a vicious exposure of organized politics (New York politics by inference) entitled "Merry-Go-Round." It revealed a Mayor and a Governor who were willing to connive at the framing of an innocent boy for murder to save such an organization as New York's Tammany and preserve its standing with a notorious gangster.

The play attracted enough attention to warrant a transfer to an uptown theatre, but when the move was suggested as many political barriers as possible were put in the way. When these were finally hurdled the play was given a chance at the Avon Theatre, but died of its own extravagances in five weeks.

Practically the last flare of the season was the quick success of a comedy entitled "Another Language," written by Rose Franken and produced by an independent, Arthur J. Beckhard, who had tried it first the summer before with a summer stock company. "Another Language" was one of those mysterious overnight hits and was still running when this compilation was finished in late June. It is also included among the best plays in this volume. In May Mr. Ziegfeld took over the Carroll, as reported, with Paul Robeson succeeding Jules Bledsoe in the cast of the revived "Show Boat."

Statistically the season was practically a duplicate of last season's depression record.   There were something like one hundred and ninety-five plays and important revivals, a hundred and thirty-four of which were new.   Of new plays this is ten more than the former season offered.

There were four failures produced for every success, on a box-office basis, and that certainly is a new low in averages.   It is accounted for by the fact that with cheap theatres, cheap actors and cheap costs of production a good many plays were produced by those professional theatrical hangers-on who are willing to take a chance with any kind of play so long as there is sufficient money forthcoming to pay them a salary and cover their "office expense," even for a few weeks.

Many an angel-group, made up of relatives and friends, financed the promising work of a young hopeful who, as they told each other, "certainly could write a better play than "Abie's Irish Rose," but didn't.

THE SEASON IN CHICAGO

By Charles Collins
Dramatic Editor of the *Chicago Tribune*

THE Chicago stage struggled through the season of 1931-1932 like a wounded stag with the remorseless hounds of the economic depression in close, menacing pursuit. It ended its long, heartbreaking run in a state of exhaustion. Observers of the chase, however, felt that the stricken thing won honors for its gameness.

The season began late and feebly, and after spurts of speed and strength through the fall and winter months reached the finishing line of summer in rags and tatters, limp and dejected. Its offerings for a rounded year, from June 1, 1931, to May 31, 1932, have numbered 74 titles, and when this total is compared with that of the preceding year, a shrinkage of 10 may be noted. This is not much of a loss, at first glance; and indeed, when the general business condition of the period is taken into consideration, one feels that it might have been much worse. However, it continues the ebbing trend that the statistics of the Chicago stage have shown for several years past.

These 74 titles may be classified as follows: Plays, 50; operettas and musical comedies, 9; revues, 11; miscellaneous entertainments, 4. In the department of drama, only 18 productions deserved to be rated as possessing superior quality. The operettas and musical comedies contained nothing of distinguished merit, although this group as a whole can be called satisfactory. Among the revues, 6 were outstanding affairs.

The dramatic productions to which I have attached blue ribbons were: "The Green Pastures," "The Silent Witness," with Lionel Atwill; "Private Lives," with Donald Brian and Edith Taliaferro; "Once in a Lifetime," "The School for Scandal," with Ethel Barrymore; "The Admirable Crichton," with Walter Hampden and Fay Bainter; "Mrs. Moonlight," with Edith Barrett and Sir Guy Standing; "The Vinegar Tree," with Mary Boland; "Tomorrow and Tomorrow," with Zita Johann and Glenn Anders; "Payment Deferred," with Charles Laughton; "Grand Hotel," with Eugénie Leontovich, Sam Jaffe and the others of the New York cast; "As Husbands Go," with Catherine Calhoun Doucet;

16

"Counsellor-at-Law," with Otto Kruger; "Cyrano de Bergerac," with Walter Hampden; "The Barretts of Wimpole Street," with Katharine Cornell; "The Devil Passes," with Arthur Byron and others; "The Good Fairy," with Helen Hayes; "Mourning Becomes Electra," with Judith Anderson, Florence Reed and others; and "The Merchant of Venice," with Maude Adams and Otis Skinner.

The better operetta and musical comedy companies were: "Blossom Time" (revival); "Marching By," with Natalie Hall and Guy Robertson; "The Chocolate Soldier," with Vivienne Segal and Charles Purcell; and "Everybody's Welcome," with Frances Williams and Oscar Shaw.

The revues of importance were: "The Third Little Show," "Three's a Crowd," "The Wonder Bar," with Al Jolson; "The Ziegfeld Follies, 1931"; "The Band Wagon," with the Astaires and Frank Morgan; and George White's "Scandals," with Rudy Vallee, Everett Marshall, Willie Howard, etc.

In order to tell the story completely, it might be well to call the roll of the other shows, for which cheers have been omitted. They were, in more or less chronological order:

Plays—"High Hat," with Edna Hibbard; "A Modern Virgin," with Roger Pryor and Margaret Sullavan; "Salt Water," with Taylor Holmes and Fiske O'Hara; "In the Best of Families," "Unexpected Husband," "Surf," with Walker Whiteside; "The Venetian"; "The Merchant of Venice," "Julius Cæsar," and "Hamlet," as produced by the Chicago Civic Shakespeare Society; "The Blue Ghost," "Against the Wind," with Mrs. Fiske; "The Unknown Warrior" (matinées); "Ten Nights in a Barroom" and "East Lynne" as staged by Billy Bryant's show boat company; "Tonight or Never," with Fritzi Scheff; "Strange Interlude" (provincial cast), "This Weaker Sex," "Broken Dishes," "The House Beautiful," "Elizabeth the Queen" (provincial company); "Samson and Delilah," with Jacob Ben-Ami; "Fata Morgana," "Zombie," with Pauline Starke; "Louder, Please," "A Church Mouse," with Louise Groody and Ernest Glendinning; "Confidential Service," with George M. Cohan; "Experience Unnecessary," with Walter Woolf and Verree Teasdale; "The Sandy Hooker," with Edna Hibbard; "Death Takes a Holiday" (provincial company); and "Hay Fever," with Constance Collier.

The other musical comedies and operettas were: "You said It," with Lou Holtz; "Girl Crazy," "The Beggar's Opera," "The Blue Mask," with Guy Robertson; and "Smiling Faces," with Fred Stone.

The revues not already given honorable mention were: "Crazy Quilt," with Phil Baker, Fannie Brice and Ted Healy; Earl Carroll's "Vanities," eighth edition; "Rhapsody in Black," with an all-Negro cast; Balieff's "Chauve-Souris," and Yascha Yushny's "Blue Bird."

These miscellaneous entertainments were offered as regular theatrical attractions: "Pearly Gates," a Negro cantata based on the repertory of "spirituals"; Maurice Chevalier in songs and impersonations; Cornelia Otis Skinner in her character sketches called "The Wives of Henry VIII," and the Tatterman Marionettes.

The downtown district of Chicago contains twenty playhouses that may be used for legitimate stage productions. Some of them are obsolete and idle; some of them are only in occasional operation; eleven may be regarded as forming the main body of the Chicago stage. This survey includes the magnificent Civic Opera House, which made a début into theatrical life last spring by sheltering Mr. White's "Scandals."

A listing of these playhouses, with the number of bookings each has had during the year 1931-1932, will present a cross-section view of the Chicago theatrical scene. So here you have them, with the number of their engagements, in alphabetical order:

Adelphi, 7; Apollo, 5; Blackstone, 8; Cort, 3; Civic Opera, 1; Civic Theatre, 0; Erlanger, 6; Eighth Street, 1; Goodman, 1; Garrick, 3; Grand Opera House, 6; Great Northern, 3; Harris, 8; Illinois, 3; Majestic, 1; Princess, 0; Playhouse, 3; Selwyn, 7; Studebaker, 5; Woods, 1.

These figures, which more or less parallel the showing of several years past, point to the fact that since the advent of the talking pictures, Chicago cannot keep its twenty theatres filled, either with shows or with audiences. Its source of supply from New York (the city creates practically nothing for the stage) has been dwindling; and its appetite for the legitimate stage, as evidenced by box-office returns, has been waning. These are distressing facts, but they must be faced.

However, certain things happened in the course of the past theatrical year which suggest that the playgoers of Chicago, in multitudes, are eager to worship at the ancient altar of the drama, whenever the proper kind of fire is touched off there. These incidents were the engagements of Walter Hampden in his revival of "Cyrano de Bergerac" and of Katharine Cornell in "The Barretts of Wimpole Street." They came late in the season, and the town that had been indifferent, even antagonistic, to many highly

acclaimed Broadway hits—"Once in a Lifetime," for example—
went crazy in its ticket-buying ardor.

Mr. Hampden, who had visited Chicago earlier in the year
in a revival of "The Admirable Crichton" without stirring up
much excitement, brought his cross-country touring production
of Rostand's famous drama into the Blackstone Theatre for a single week. It was no novelty; Chicago had seen his characterization of the Chevalier of the Wonderful Nose eight years before.
But to the surprise of everyone, including Mr. Hampden, it
wanted to see the play and the performance again, in a feverish
kind of way. There was a whirlwind demand for tickets; and the
Blackstone was sold out for every performance. When the box-office statements were added up, it discovered that this week of Mr.
Hampden in "Cyrano de Bergerac" was a close second in receipts
to the banner week in the Blackstone's history, which covers
nearly thirty years. It was surpassed only the Christmas week
of Frank Bacon's famous engagement in "Lightnin'."

Katharine Cornell's Chicago triumph in "The Barretts of Wimpole Street" was less surprising. Here was an actress on the crest
of her vogue, in her most recent and most popular vehicle. It
was, however, no less emphatic. Miss Cornell remained at the
Harris Theatre for four weeks, and the demand for tickets was
furious. Her first week, incidentally, coincided with that of Mr.
Hampden's harvest. The play and the star, with her brilliant
company, were the talk of the town.

At the end of her engagement Miss Cornell gave, on two days'
notice, a special Sunday matinée performance of "The Barretts"
in the Civic Opera House, which can seat 3,800 people. She
offered any and every seat in the house for one dollar, first come
first served, and decreed that the box-office would not be opened
until 10 A.M. on the day of the performance, in order to baffle
the ticket speculators. Every ticket was sold inside of two hours,
and 5,000 potential buyers were turned away.

All of which goes to prove that a passion for the drama still
survives in Chicago.

The traditional date for the start of the playgoing season, Labor
Day, brought "The Green Pastures" into Chicago. This was an
auspicious opening, but not until a month later were the other
theatres in line with their fall bookings. The famous Negro religious fantasy of Marc Connelly's authorship was received with
enthusiasm, and won long-run honors for the year with its nineteen weeks. Strict score-keeping gives "Counsellor-at-Law" a tie
in this competition, but "The Green Pastures" should receive the

medal, for Elmer Rice's play was compelled toward the end of its run to resort to that vice of the Chicago box-offices known as the "two-for-one" ticket.

Maude Adams' return to the footlights as Portia in "The Merchant of Venice," with Otis Skinner as her co-star, marked another brightening of the old glamour of playgoing. Her stay was brief but prosperous; the elder generation rallied to welcome her, and the young people of the cinema epoch also manifested a decided curiosity concerning the Maude Adams tradition.

"Grand Hotel" also captivated the attention of the town, although its run was comparatively short—some six or seven weeks. "Payment Deferred" aroused much cheering for the acting of Charles Laughton. "Mrs. Moonlight" pleased the sentimentalists tremendously; "The Devil Passes," with its array of major and minor celebrities, caught Chicago's fancy; "As Husbands Go" had a happy run; and Billy Bryant's troupe of show boat mummers, in their manglings of "Ten Nights in a Barroom" and "East Lynne," were accepted as a civic lark.

The subscription drama programs offered by the Theatre Guild and the Dramatic League of Chicago suffered, to some extent, by a drying up of the source of supply. The Guild gave only one production of its own—"Mourning Becomes Electra"—and lent its blessing and its subscription audience to two others—Gilbert Miller's "Tomorrow and Tomorrow" and John Golden's "As Husbands Go." The season died with the Guild owing Chicago two plays.

The Dramatic League, under Shubert direction, made a closer approach to the fulfillment of its prospectus. It promised eight plays and gave seven, as follows: "The Silent Witness," "The Venetian," "Mrs. Moonlight," "Payment Deferred," "The House Beautiful," "Fata Morgana," and "Experience Unnecessary." The last two plays were obviously stop-gaps.

At the end of the season the formation of the American Theatre Society, as a merger of Guild and Shubert subscription activities in Chicago and other cities outside of New York, was announced. The news was received as a promising step toward the correction of manifest weaknesses in both systems.

The appearance of "Mourning Becomes Electra" was regarded, of course, as an event of the first magnitude. The Theatre Guild's cast for the tour of O'Neill's trilogy was in line with this organization's high ideals of interpretation, and could be called a "second company" only in point of time. Judith Anderson won new laurels in the rôle of Lavinia.

The Chicago Civic Shakespeare Society made its final bid for recognition by adding Tyrone Power, Helen Menken and William Faversham to Fritz Leiber's faithful band. "The Merchant of Venice," "Julius Cæsar" and "Hamlet" were staged, in three ghastly weeks; then the company went to New York to meet with similar neglect and disband. This gallant but ill-directed adventure in classic revivals is now dead, and beyond the hope of resurrection.

Another unhappy episode of the stage year in Chicago was Mrs. Fiske's last production—almost a case of death-bed activity. She had found a comedy by Carlos Drake, a young Chicagoan, which seemed to contain a rôle for her. "Against the Wind," it was called, and she came to its première against her doctor's orders. Her physical weakness was pitiful, and after a few performances, during which it seemed that she might die in harness, she surrendered. Three months later she was dead.

During the month of June, 1932, all the roads of the nation led toward Chicago; the two great political parties were in convention to nominate the next President of the United States. But the Chicago stage could contribute nothing to the entertainment of these many pilgrims. Only three of the city's legitimate playhouses were open, offering items of utter insignificance. The withering away of the theatre arts was almost total. Furthermore, the month brought announcements of the abandonment of summer opera at Ravinia, and the cancellation, following the collapse of the Samuel Insull financial structure, of the Civic Opera Company's plans for next season. The managers of the theatres, moreover, were curiously silent about their bookings for the fall.

The year 1933 will find Chicago with its Century of Progress Exposition in full swing. What part the stage will take in this great entertainment project remains to be seen. To peer into the future is, at the moment, an unrewarding practice. The motto of the times seems to be: Fog ahead!

THE SEASON IN SAN FRANCISCO

By George C. Warren

Drama Editor of *The San Francisco Chronicle*

THE year from June 1, 1931, to May 31, 1932, had many high spots in the theatres of San Francisco, and more than the usual number of organizations came from New York with more or less original casts. In one or two cases the productions were a bit bedraggled with much traveling. There were also several American premières during the year, and several movie actors made their re-entry on the stage after years of screen work.

Early in the year Ethel Barrymore offered her fine performance of Lady Teazle in "The School for Scandal," and played to large business. Billy Rose's "Crazy Quilt," with Fannie Brice, Ted Healy and Phil Baker drew packed houses, and Earl Carroll's 1931 "Vanities" somewhat denuded of its array of revue stars, played to crowds.

One of the unfortunate episodes of the season was the duplication of Edmond Rostand's "Cyrano de Bergerac." Belasco and Curran made a handsome production with Richard Bennett as Cyrano and Kay Johnson as Roxanne. Bennett was unhappy in the title rôle, and the production suffered in patronage because of the fact that Walter Hampden had already been announced in the play. Bennett played at the Curran Theatre; Hampden at the Columbia. Hampden's engagement was hurt by the Bennett production, but played to comfortable business.

Al Jolson, on home ground—he began his career in the music halls of San Francisco—was seen in "Wonder Bar" with the New York cast fairly represented in the company. He prospered but the engagement was not the overwhelming triumph he used to have before his appearances on the screen.

Maude Adams and Otis Skinner in "The Merchant of Venice" at the Columbia were well received and played to good-sized audiences, but the impression was that Miss Adams made a mistake in coming back to the stage as Portia.

"The Green Pastures" with the complete cast and production seen in New York prospered mightily. Both of these attractions played the Columbia Theatre.

Of new plays the first in point of time was the American première of Frank Harvey's melodrama, "Three Men and a Woman,"
which was known in London as "Cape Forlorn." Walker Whiteside, Florence Reed, Guy Bates Post and Barrie O'Daniells acted
the play, which ran two weeks at the Columbia, where also the
Nugents, J. C. and Elliott, produced their tennis play, "A Fast
One," both acting in the comedy with Elliott's wife, Norma Lee,
also in the cast. This play had a brief run in New York later
under another title.

Dr. Hans Siegfried Linne's operetta, "Love Time," which ran
200 nights in Berlin and was seen in continental Europe for three
years, had its American première at the Geary Theatre with Dr.
Linne conducting, and ran two weeks. The score runs to waltzes,
two-steps and marches, with an occasional touch of jazz.

Jane Cowl came from New York to play Marguerite Gautier in
Dumas's "Camille" for Belasco and Curran. The production was
handsome, and Roland Gilbert, the young Mexican screen actor,
was the Armand Duval. This was Miss Cowl's first appearance in
the famous old play.

Mrs. Fiske made her final appearances in "Mrs. Bumpstead-
Leigh" under Henry Duffy's management at the Alcazar Theatre,
performances that were almost the last she gave anywhere, her
brief engagement in Chicago in Carlos Drake's "Against the
Wind," bringing her great career to an end shortly afterward.
Mrs. Fiske made her first appearance at the same San Francisco
theatre more than forty years ago in "Caprice."

Henry Duffy brought Bebe Daniels to the stage from the screen
for a very successful engagement in Lonsdale's "The Last of Mrs.
Cheney." Reginald Denny also came back from the talkies for
an appearance as the brassy columnist in "Blessed Event," and
Colleen Moore made an appearance for Duffy in the Cinderella
play, "A Church Mouse."

At the Alcazar, too, Perry Askam, the operetta star, made an
essay in spoken drama, appearing in Prince Antoine Bibesco's
naughty comedy, "Ladies All."

Laura Hope Crews came from Hollywood to direct and act in
Rachel Crothers' comedy, "As Husbands Go," and in Sidney Coe
Howard's "The Silver Cord," both done at the Columbia Theatre.

Dorothy Hall, who since has achieved stardom in "Child of
Manhattan," came to San Francisco to play Schatze in Zoe Atkins'
"The Greeks Had a Word for It," with Wanda Lyon and Elda
Vockel as the other girls of the trio of gold diggers, and Edgar
Walter's "On the Spot" was done at the Curran with Crane Wil-

bur, Anna May Wong and Glenda Farrell of the New York cast.

Belasco and Curran presented "Tonight or Never" with Helen Gahagan and the principals of the New York cast, excepting Melvyn Douglas, his rôle being taken by Anthony Bushell, who came from the films to play the lead. Lionel Atwill was seen in "The Silent Witness," and I. J. Golden's propaganda play, "Precedent," the play written around the Mooney case, was done at the Curran with Robert Warwick as the Prosecuting Attorney.

Billie Burke came to in "The Vinegar Tree," with Warren William in his original rôle, and William Morris playing the husband. "Tomorrow and Tomorrow" was done with Kay Johnson, Henry Daniell and Leon Waycoff in the leads, and Vina Delmar's "Bad Girl" had Wallace Ford and Marjorie Paterson as Eddie and Dot.

The Stratford-upon-Avon Festival Players had three and a half weeks of very large business at the Columbia, presenting nine of Shakespeare's plays, including the seldom acted "Measure for Measure," "A Winter's Tale" and "King Lear." At the same house William Gillette was seen in his farewell to the stage as the protagonist in "Sherlock Holmes," his engagement drawing tremendous audiences.

"Grand Hotel" had a six weeks' run at the Geary with Olga Baclanova, Ian Keith, Arnold Korff, Christian Rub and Dorothy Tree in the five top parts, and Grace George came to the Curran in "The First Mrs. Fraser," with A. E. Matthews, Reginald Mason and John Halloran in the cast.

Ruth Chatterton made her début as a producer, presenting her husband, Ralph Forbes, in Gilbert Wakefield's comedy, "Let Us Divorce," which had its first American performance at the Geary Theatre April 12. Rose Hobart was co-starred with Forbes.

Edward Everett Horton, who had played in Los Angeles for ten years, made his San Francisco début in Benn W. Levy's "Springtime for Henry," with Laura LaPlante, from the screen, and Ruth Weston in the cast. The play ran four weeks at the Curran Theatre.

Amateur organizations were active, but did not make so many productions as in former years. The Dramatic class at the University of San Francisco, under the direction of J. J. Gill, gave a first performance of a new play by Paul Dickey. It is called "The Brass Rail" and shows a dipsomaniac hiding in the wilds of the Canadian Northwest trying to conquer the drink habit, but having a complete bar with its brass rail in his hut. This same organization made a production of William Bolitho's "Overture," which caused much comment. Harold Helvenston, head of dramatics at Stanford University, gave one of the few productions of Saki's "The Mistress of Briony," and a new adaptation by Edwin Duerr and Theodore Bowie of Molière's "Tartuffe" was acted by the dramatic students at the University of California, with Edwin Duerr directing.

Professor Charles D. von Neumayer of the same university directed a performance of Euripides' "The Bacchæ" in the Greek Theatre on the campus and Professor Sara Huntsman Sturgess presented her class on the platform stage of Wheeler Hall at the University in Leonid Andreyev's "The Life of Man."

The Wayfarers, a subscription organization, offered Edmond Rostand's "The Last Night of Don Juan" in their tiny theatre, and the Playmakers of Berkeley made a production of a full length original play, "The Gravy Train," by Edna Higgins Strachan.

THE SEASON IN SOUTHERN CALIFORNIA

By Monroe Lathrop

Dramatic Editor, Los Angeles *Express*

AS the dramatic season of 1931-32 limped to its close (June 30) theatre devotees looked back upon a year of high tide and low tide in Southern California—high for the public in one of the best of many years in variety and quality of plays, and low for the courageous producers who carried on in the face of flattening purses.

To the fortitude of a few managers who refused to haul down the flag we owed a consistent succession of interesting events while the high record of bull market times, when more than a dozen stages shared in the activity, was shrinking to a brave three or four. Of Mr. Mantle's selections of the Ten Best for this volume none reached the coast, but one, "Brief Moment," had been seen here in a previous season, and three, "Reunion in Vienna," "The Cat and the Fiddle," and "Cynara," are on the threshold for the beginning of the new season.

But many Manhattan hits of the past two seasons made their appearance, including "Grand Hotel," "Carroll's Vanities," "Springtime for Henry," "A Church Mouse," "Whistling in the Dark," "Blessed Event" and "The Unexpected Husband." That the public is concentrating its favors was made evident in the enormous success of engagements of "Green Pastures," "The Barretts of Wimpole Street" and "Wonder Bar" while other merely good shows languished for proper support.

The season was spiced by a sensational court fight upon the classic "Lysistrata" and its performers, with the noted star Nance O'Neil as one of the asserted malefactors. The case collapsed in court because of the pitiful showing of the police raiders, while it meantime afforded the wits of the press a fine chance to lampoon the cops as boob detectives with a warrant in baffled search of the lewd author, one Mr. Aristophanes.

A different side of the season, which gave it distinction, was the 1000th performance of "The Green Pastures," celebrated at the Biltmore Theatre, with almost every member of its original New York cast participating in the exceptional event. Only two or three of the personnel of 125 which launched this extraordinary artistic and financial success have left the play.

Another unusual incident of the season was the coincident rivalry on two stages of elaborate productions of "Cyrano de Bergerac." Mr. Walter Hampden brought his version in, en tour, as Belasco and Curran brought in from the north their long-planned production with Mr. Richard Bennett as the title character. The incident paralleled the historic original American presentation of "Cyrano" when Augustin Daly and Richard Mansfield rushed the Rostand semi-classic to the footlights as rivals. As Mr. Daly yielded to Mansfield, so Mr. Bennett, after a brief engagement, gracefully bowed out and left the field on the coast to Mr. Hampden.

The season was marked by the advent of Miss Maude Adams and Mr. Otis Skinner playing "The Merchant of Venice," in the former's return to the theatre after her long retirement. It failed to deliver promised revivals of the Gilbert and Sullivan operettas by De Wolf Hopper and of "The Copperhead" by Ian Keith, owing mainly to the stressful times. It did give us one notable performance of "Hamlet" in which Mr. Keith, in the title rôle, gathered about him many actors of note resident on the coast for the other parts.

Few premières of new plays marked the year in the "commercial" playhouses, the managers preferring to lay their chances upon tested drama rather than untried material, however hopeful. Four exceptions justified their caution. "The Mad Hopes," a new comedy by Romney Brent, starring Miss Billie Burke; "Let Us Divorce," a revised version of a comedy produced in England as "Counselor's Opinion," presented here by Ruth Chatterton with Ralph Forbes and Rose Hobart featured, and "Dinner Is Served," produced and starred in by the author, Alan Mowbray, received scant favor. "The Bad Penny," by William Anthony Maguire, starring Henrietta Crosman, met with like fate.

Upon Belasco and Curran, Henry Duffy and Edward Everett Horton the public depended chiefly for their new theatre diversion. To the first it was indebted for such high-grade things as "Tonight or Never," with Helen Gahagan; "The First Mrs. Fraser," with Grace George; "Camille," with Jane Cowl; "The Greeks Had a Word for It," with Ina Claire; "The Silent Witness," with Lionel Atwill; "Grand Hotel," "Cyrano de Bergerac," and "Whistling in the Dark," with Ernest Truax.

Mr. Duffy offered an unbroken string of attractions which included such notable things as "The Silver Cord," with Laura Hope Crews; "A Church Mouse," marking the stage début of Colleen Moore; "The Last of Mrs. Cheney," with the début of Bebe Daniels; "Ada Beats the Drum," with Irene Franklin; "Blessed Event," with Reginald Denny; "House Beautiful," with Charles Ray; "The High Hatters" ("Ritzy" in New York); "Square Crooks," with Joe Brown; "The Fall Guy," with the Gleasons, and a revival of "Topsy and Eva," with the original authors and stars, the Duncan sisters.

With the exception of a revival of Boucicault's "The Shaughran" under the title of "The Scamp," the season of Edward Everett Horton as producer and star was very successful. He gave us "Springtime for Henry," "The Unexpected Husband," and Noel Coward's "Private Lives."

The Biltmore Theatre (Erlanger) after a tardy start gave us such things as "The Barretts of Wimpole Street" with Katharine Cornell and her original cast; "Green Pastures," "Crazy Quilt," with Phil Baker and Ted Healy; Carroll's "Vanities"; Hampden's "Cyrano"; Maude Adams' return as Portia; William Gillette in "Sherlock Holmes"; Al Jolson in "Wonder Bar"; "Three Men and a Woman," with Florence Reed, Guy Bates Post and Walker Whiteside; "The School for Scandal," with Ethel Barrymore; Cornelia Otis Skinner in dramatic recitals, and a season of Shakespeare's plays by the players from the Memorial Theatre at Stratford-upon-Avon.

The Pasadena Community Theatre, steadily growing in repute for its high quality productions and drawing heavily from all the surrounding country, had a notable season in its fine theatre. It included the 200-year-old "Marriage of Figaro," by Beaumarchais; the classic "Damon and Pythias"; revivals of "When Knighthood Was in Flower," "The Three Musketeers" and "A

Pair of Spectacles"; Shakespeare's "Twelfth Night"; "The Play's the Thing," with Guy Bates Post; "Berkeley Square," "Saturday's Children," "Once in a Lifetime," "Passing Brompton Road" (English and new in America); Lonsdale's "Canaries Sometimes Sing"; "Black" and "Censored," by Conrad Seiler, both premières; "Hullabaloo," a new revue by Paul Gerard Smith; Gilbert Emery's "Episode"; Shaw's "Apple Cart"; Coward's "The Young Idea," first time in America; "Green Grow the Lilacs," "The Constant Nymph" and Laszlo Fodor's "I love an Actress."

Other Los Angeles houses showed "Girl Crazy," a Louis Macloon production; the "Bluebird" revue from Russia; Pollock's "The Enemy"; Pirandello's "The Living Mask," with Arnold Korff, its original star; the Tom Mooney play, "Precedent"; a new drama, "Modern Morals," by Ethel Dolson; "Lucky Day," a new negro revue; Prince Bibesco's "Ladies All"; "Sons o' Guns," with Ethelind Terry; "Shining Blackness," with Lucille La Verne; "Vengeance," by Hugh Weldon (new), and "Hoodooed," a colored revue.

The little theatres were never more active. Southern California has more of these, probably, than any other section in the world. The year saw the formation of the Los Angeles County Dramatic Association, with more than sixty groups and 10,000 active members. From these came "The Perfect Alibi," "The Wisdom Tooth," "In the Spirit," by Alan Mowbray (new); "Life in New York," a sixty-year-old melo.; "Alison's House," "Anathema," by Andreyev; W. S. Gilbert's "Engaged"; "Hotel Universe"; "The Passion Flower," with Nance O'Neil; "The Mad Seeress" (new); "In the Red," by Mary Flanner (new); Galsworthy's "The First and the Last"; "Mostly David," by Paul Gerard Smith (new); "The Broken Heart," an Elizabethan drama; "Promiscuous," by John Craig and John Watts (new); "The Truth About Eve"; "Modern Wives," by J. C. McMullip (new); "Lovely Lady," by Ruth Cole (new); John Galsworthy's "The Mob."

"The Mission Play" had its twenty-first season and the "Pilgrimage Play" its twelfth.

OF THEE I SING
A Music Play in Two Acts

By George S. Kaufman and Morrie Ryskind

Music and Lyrics by George and Ira Gershwin

THE outstanding event of the New York theatre in midseason was the production at the Music Box on Saturday evening, December 26, of the long-heralded musical satire, "Of Thee I Sing." The entertainment had been first revealed in Boston, and there its reception so stirred even the sacred cods as to result in an engagement nothing less than sensational.

This sensation was duplicated in New York, and climaxed three months later when the committee in charge of recommendations for the Pulitzer play prize boldly decided to hurdle all previously accepted precedents and award this musical play the $1000 that annually is given to "the original American play performed in New York which shall best represent the educational value and power of the stage."

The award created considerable discussion. Could "Of Thee I Sing" properly, or even fairly, be classed as a play in any generally accepted sense, or in the sense that inspired the writing of that particular paragraph in the late Joseph Pulitzer's will? Or couldn't it?

There were many debates, but in general the prize committee's award was heartily endorsed. The nation's genius for playing dumb politics with the dumber politicians, as well as a growing native predilection for sentimentalizing anything remotely resembling a heart romance, in state house or state prison, was due for the correction that intelligent satire inspires.

"In 'Of Thee I Sing,'" George Jean Nathan writes in the foreword of the edition published by Alfred Knopf, "I believe that we discover the happiest and most successful native music-stage lampoon that has thus far come the way of the American theatre. With it, further, I believe that American musical comedy enters at length upon a new, original and independent lease of life."

Later he adds: "The music show is not for pundits in their punditical moments, but for pundits, if at all, in such rare

29

moments as they think and argue with laughter. I accordingly invite the more sober species of reader to engage this script with his top hat cocked saucily over his mind, with his ear filled with the hint of gay tunes and with his eye made merry by the imagined picture of all the relevant and appropriate clowns in the persons of actors, of madly painted canvas, and of appetizing femininity. Only by so approaching it will he get from it what its authors wish him to."

George S. Kaufman and Morrie Ryskind, authors of the book, had worked together on a former satirical success called "Strike Up the Band." At least the book of that entertainment had first been written by Mr. Kaufman, and then revised by Mr. Ryskind when the verdict of the minor theatre centers where it was first tried found it a bit too sharply pointed.

"Of Thee I Sing," as a political satire should, starts with a political parade. "The marchers," report the authors, "with their torchlights and banners, move against a shadowy background of skyscrapers, churches, and—almost certainly—speakeasies. Across this background is thrown a huge election banner on which are Gargantuan reproductions of the faces of the party's candidates. Highlit and prominent is the party's battlecry:

"FOR PRESIDENT
"JOHN P. WINTERGREEN

"The name of the vice presidential candidate, however, is lost in shadow. As for the countenances of the candidates it is a little hard to pick them out in the general blur, and the chances are that that's a break for the party."

It is a shambling, singing procession and there are many banners. "Vote for Prosperity and See What You Get!" is one. "A Vote for Wintergreen Is a Vote for Wintergreen!" boldly asserts another. "Wintergreen—A Man's Man's Man!" "Wintergreen —The Flavor Lasts!" "The Full Dinner Jacket!" are some that follow.

"He's the man the people choose—
Loves the Irish and the Jews."

Such is the burden of the marchers' song. The excitement mounts and then dies away as the procession is swallowed up in the darkness and probably turns a corner.

A rising curtain reveals a shabby room in a hotel. This is where the National Campaign Committee is about to meet. "It's not that they couldn't afford a better hotel, for the party is notoriously rich, but somehow this room seems thoroughly in keeping with the men who occupy it."

There are two committeemen present. Francis X. Gilhooley obviously represents the Irish and Louis Lippman the Jews of the song. Mr. Gilhooley is playing solitaire and drinking what might be White Rock. Mr. Lippman is taking his newspaper sprawled out on the bed, but disengages himself long enough to answer the telephone and inform the party at the other end, looking for a Mr. Throttle-something, that he is wrong.

The convention is over. The delegates are practically prostrated after sixty-three ballots, but the ticket has been put over. Mr. Gilhooley, however, is now inclined to worry about the election to come. It is just possible the people are getting wise to the old party.

No such fears assail Mr. Lippman. "If they haven't got wise to us in forty years they'll never get wise." That's the Lippman idea.

"We've got a great ticket, haven't we?" demands Mr. Lippman. "For President: John P. Wintergreen! He even sounds like a President."

"That's why we picked him," agrees Gilhooley.

"And for Vice President—" Mr. Lippman hesitates. "What's the name of that fellow we nominated for Vice President?"

"Ah—Pitts, wasn't it?"

"No, no—it was a longer name."

"Barbinelli?"

"No."

"Well, that's longer."

"You're a hell of a National Committeeman. Don't even know the name of the Vice President we nominated!"

The other committeemen are gathering. First comes Matthew Arnold Fulton, owner of a string of newspapers. Mr. Fulton is also unable to recall the name of the vice-presidential candidate. At the moment he is worried about other things. He has been talking with his editors all over the country and the election isn't going to be anything resembling a cinch.

Senators Carver Jones of the West and Robert E. Lyons of the South join the meeting, which, it transpires, has been called by Mr. Fulton. The newspaper king is trying to get what is known as a line on the ticket's chances. Senator Jones is confident the West can be depended upon. John P. Wintergreen is one of the greatest men the party has nominated since Alexander Franklin—

"And Robert E. Lee," quickly adds Senator Lyons.

JONES—Unfortunately, however, while the people of the West admire our party, and love our party, and respect our party, they don't trust our party. And so, gentlemen, in the name of those gallant boys who fought overseas, and the brave mothers who sent them, we must not, we cannot, we dare not allow Russian Bolshevism to dump cheap Chinese labor on these free American shores! Gentlemen, I thank you. (*He finishes his drink and sits.*)

FULTON—Thank *you*, sir. And now, Senator Lyons, tell us about the South.

LYONS (*who doesn't need to be asked twice*)—Gentlemen, you ask me about the South. It is a land of romance, of roses and honeysuckle, of Southern chivalry and hospitality, fried chicken and waffles, salad and coffee.

LIPPMAN—No dessert?

FULTON—Thank you, gentlemen. That just about confirms what my editors have been telling me. The people of this country demand John P. Wintergreen for President, and they're going to get him whether they like it or not. And between you and me, gentlemen, I don't think they like it. (*There is a knock on the door.*) Come in. (*The door is slowly opened. Enter a timid little man—hopefully smiling. His name, believe it or not, is* ALEXANDER THROTTLEBOTTOM.)

THROTTLEBOTTOM—Hi, gentlemen!

FULTON—Yes, sir. What can we do for you?

THROTTLEBOTTOM—Hello, Mr. Fulton.

FULTON—I'm afraid I don't quite place you. Your face is familiar, but—

THROTTLEBOTTOM—I'm Throttlebottom.

FULTON—What?

THROTTLEBOTTOM—Alexander Throttlebottom.

JONES (*pushing him right out*)—We're very busy, my good man. If you'll just—

THROTTLEBOTTOM—But I'm Throttlebottom.

FULTON—I understand, Mr. Teitelbaum, but just at present—

GILHOOLEY—You come back later on.

LIPPMAN—After we're gone.

THROTTLEBOTTOM (*insistent about it*)—But I'm Throttlebottom. I'm the candidate for Vice President.

Now they remember Throttlebottom. At least they remember there was some such person nominated. But they have a hard time conquering the name, even after Throttlebottom spells it out for them.

Throttlebottom is there with a mission. He has come to ask a favor of the committee. He doesn't want to be Vice President. He wants to be let off. What if his mother were to find out?

Of course, the committee is agreed, it would be like Throttlebottom to remember his mother after it is too late. But he need have no fear. His mother will never hear about his candidacy. He will have forgotten it himself in three months.

"Besides," suggests Mr. Lippman, "suppose something should happen to the President. Then you become President."

"Me?"

"Sure."

"President! Say!"

They are about to drink a toast to "Our next President" as further cheer for Mr. Throttlebottom when in walks Candidate John P. Wintergreen himself, quite in a mood to join them. He is a handsome young man, smartly turned out by a progressive tailor. Reaching for a glass to join the toast he mistakes Throttlebottom for a waiter, takes his drink, and sends him back for a dill pickle. Then he is ready to say a few words.

WINTERGREEN—Well, gentlemen, it certainly was a great convention. I never expected to get the nomination. Didn't want the nomination. Never was so surprised as when my name came up. (*Takes pickle from* THROTTLEBOTTOM, *and gives him the empty glass.*)

GILHOOLEY—Who brought it up, anyhow?

FULTON—Yah. Who was that in the back calling "Wintergreen?"

WINTERGREEN—That was me. Most spontaneous thing you ever saw. So here I am, gentlemen—nominated by the people, absolutely my own master, and ready to do any dirty work the committee suggests. (*In one quick movement he takes the full glass* THROTTLEBOTTOM *has finally succeeded in getting for himself, and replaces it with the pickle.*)

LYONS—*Mr.* President—

WINTERGREEN—I'll drink to that too! Anything else, gentlemen? Anything at all! (FULTON, *meanwhile, is nervously pacing.*) What's the matter, Fulton? Something wrong? You're not sober, are you?

FULTON (*his tone belying his words*)—No, no! I'm all right.

WINTERGREEN—Must be something up. (*A look at the others.*) What's the matter?

LIPPMAN (*deprecatingly*)—A lot of schmoos.

FULTON—Well, it's this way. Begins to look as though there may be a little trouble ahead.

WINTERGREEN—Trouble?

FULTON—I don't think the people are quite satisfied with the party record.

WINTERGREEN—Who said they *were?*

FULTON—Well, you know what Lincoln said.

WINTERGREEN—Who?

FULTON—Lincoln.

GILHOOLEY—What did he say?

WINTERGREEN—Was it funny?

FULTON—"You can fool some of the people all the time, and you can fool all of the people some of the time, but you can't fool all of the people all of the time."

WINTERGREEN—Was that Lincoln?

THROTTLEBOTTOM—Abraham J. Lincoln.

WINTERGREEN—It's different nowadays. People are bigger suckers.

The first time Wintergreen becomes Throttlebottom conscious, he would throw the intruder out. Is this or is it not a closed meeting? But when he realizes that Throttlebottom is not only the candidate for Vice President, but also the man who brought him the dill pickle, his attitude changes.

Mr. Fulton is worried about a lot of things that have happened the last four years. Mr. Wintergreen suggests that perhaps it would be just as well if they were to stick to the party record of 1776 or, even, as Mr. Lippman suggests, 1492. A combination of the two would give them pretty nearly three hundred years to count on. And if it seems wise, as it does to Senator Lyons, to bring in something about the Civil War, which must have been around 1812— No, on second thought, it would probably be better to put the Civil War back to 1776. Which is perfectly all right with both Senator Jones and Senator Lyons.

Still, that isn't enough. What they need, as Mr. Gilhooley points out, is a good live issue.

"Yes! That's what we need—an issue," repeats Mr. Fulton. "Something that everybody is interested in, and that doesn't matter a damn. Something the party can stand on. . . . We've got to get something that'll take hold of the popular imagination— sweep the country."

"The country could stand a good sweeping," admits Lippman.

The chambermaid, who has made several ineffectual efforts to turn down the bed, is in again. She, to Mr. Fulton, represents the people. She's a good American citizen, though, of course, she has never voted.

FULTON—What do you care more about than anything else in the world?

CHAMBERMAID—I don't know. Money, I guess.

GILHOOLEY—That's no good.

WINTERGREEN—Brings up Rhode Island.

FULTON—Of course, money. We all want money. But there must be something else, isn't there?

CHAMBERMAID—No—I like money.

FULTON (*exasperated*)—But after money, what?

CHAMBERMAID—Well, maybe love.

FULTON—Love?

CHAMBERMAID—Yeh. *You* know, to meet a nice young fellow that's crazy about you, and you're crazy about him, and you get engaged, and then you get married, and—*you* know—love.

THROTTLEBOTTOM (*a trifle fussed*)—Sure.

FULTON (*rather thoughtful*)—Oh, yes. Thank you. Thank you very much.

CHAMBERMAID—Shall I turn the bed down now, sir?

FULTON—Not now. Come back later on.

CHAMBERMAID—Yes, sir. (*Starts to go.*)

FULTON—Ah—here you are. (*Starts to give her a coin.* THROTTLEBOTTOM *reaches for it.*) No, not you.

CHAMBERMAID—Thank you, sir. (*Goes.*)

LIPPMAN—Well, you got a lot out of that.

WINTERGREEN—Put women into politics and that's what you get. Love!

GILHOOLEY—Love!

FULTON (*slowly*)—What's the matter with love?

THROTTLEBOTTOM—I like love!

FULTON—People *do* care more about love than anything else. Why, they steal for it, they even kill for it.

WINTERGREEN—But will they vote for it?

FULTON—You bet they will! If we could find some way to put it over—why, we could get every vote. Everybody loves a lover; the whole world loves a— (*Stops as he gets an idea; looks fixedly at* WINTERGREEN.)

WINTERGREEN—What's the matter?

FULTON—I've got it!

THROTTLEBOTTOM—He's got it!

FULTON—You've got to fall in love!

WINTERGREEN—You're crazy!

FULTON—You've got to fall in love with a typical American girl! . . . You make love to her from now till Election Day as no girl was ever made love to before! . . . My God, are you blind? You do ᵗhis right and you'll get elected by the greatest majority that the American people ever gave a candidate! You'll get every vote! . . . You'll go down in history as the greatest lover this country has ever known! You'll be the romantic ideal of every man, woman and child in America! . . . A hundred million hearts will beat as one; they'll follow your courtship in every State in the Union! You meet the girl, you fall in love with her, you propose, you're accepted, and you're swept into the White House on a tidal wave of love!

Candidate Wintergreen, moved in spite of himself, still objects that he is not in love with anybody. Fulton meets that objection with a further burst of ideas.

"We'll have a contest—a nation-wide contest to select Miss White House—choose the most beautiful girl from every State— get them all together at Atlantic City, pick the winner and you fall in love with her!"

"But suppose I don't fall in love with her!" protests Wintergreen.

"Then *I* get her!" cries Throttlebottom, exultantly.

Another minute and Fulton has his chief editor on the wire. "Stop the presses!" he orders that worthy. "John P. Wintergreen will run for President on a one-word platform: Love! National Beauty contest in Atlantic City to select Miss White House! Now listen! I want a love cartoon on the front page of every one of my papers from now till Election Day! Right! And call up Coolidge and tell him I want a thousand words on love to-morrow morning!"

The scene changes to Atlantic City, where the beauty contest is in full swing. A line of candidates for First Lady in three-quarter piece bathing suits is strung along a section of the board-walk. "It is notorious, of course, that the prime requisite for a First Lady is that she should look well in a bathing suit."

The girls are singing right lustily and swaying in restless, if not agitated, rhythms as they sing—

"Who is the lucky girl to be?
Ruler of Washington, D. C.?

Who is to be the blushing bride?
Who will sleep at the President's side?
Strike up the cymbals, drum and fife!
One of us is the President's future wife!

"We're in Atlantic City
To meet with the committee,
And when they've made their mind up
The winner will be signed up.
The prize is consequential—
Presidential!
Our bodies will bear witness
To our fitness.

"If a girl is sexy
She may be Mrs. Prexy!
One of us is the President's future wife!"

A string of reporters, cameras in hand, file in. They, too, are lyrical, and revealing, as follows:

"More important than a photograph of Parliament,
Or a shipwreck on the sea—
What'll raise the circulation
Of our paper through the nation
Is the dimple on your knee."

The girls are briefly worried for fear they may have to go back to cafeteria dish-washing if they fail of election, but the newspaper boys, ever friendly to girls with dimpled knees, are generously reassuring.

The girls are now gathered in Committee headquarters in one of the grander boardwalk hotels. Newsmen and newsreelers are there to record their smiles. The award is shortly to be made. Outside, Mr. Fulton reports, there must be ten thousand people milling about.

Mary Turner, secretary of the contest, is present to greet Mr. Fulton. "She is chiefly distinguished from the other girls by the fact that she is dressed." Also by the fact, to a lay observer, that she appears alertly intelligent as well as beautiful.

The committee gathers slowly. Mr. Throttlebottom is one of the last to arrive but one of the most interested in both the proceedings and the girls.

"Is your mother down here with you?" Mr. Throttlebottom inquires of the blonde near the end of the line.

"Yes, sir," she answers.

"Oh! Well! Never mind!" continues Throttlebottom, losing interest.

Both Fulton and Gilhooley are a little worried about having Throttlebottom there. He should know that Vice Presidents don't usually go around in public. They're not supposed to be seen.

THROTTLEBOTTOM—But I'm not Vice President yet. Couldn't I go around a little longer?

GILHOOLEY—That isn't the point. If you're going to be Vice President you've got to practice up for it. You've got to go in hiding.

THROTTLEBOTTOM—But I came up the back way.

FULTON—You shouldn't have come at all. Suppose somebody sees you?

GILHOOLEY—We'd lose the election.

THROTTLEBOTTOM—You mean you want me to hide from everybody?

JONES—That's it!

FULTON—Right!

THROTTLEBOTTOM (*gets an idea*)—I could go back to my old business.

FULTON—What's that?

THROTTLEBOTTOM—I used to be a hermit.

FULTON—Great!

GILHOOLEY—That's the idea!

THROTTLEBOTTOM—The only thing is, I thought you might want me to make some speeches.

FULTON—No, no!

GILHOOLEY—You just go and sit in your cave.

THROTTLEBOTTOM (*thinks it over*)—I know. I could go back to the cave and write my speeches there.

FULTON—That's the idea!

JONES—Perfect!

GILHOOLEY—And make them there, too!

JONES—Don't let anybody find you—don't let anybody see you.

THROTTLEBOTTOM—I won't. I won't even come out in February to cast my shadow.

Diana Devereaux, one of the most beauteous of the candidates, is from the South. Her accent indicates as much and Senator

Lyons's personal assurance that she is, indeed, "just a breath of the old Southland," confirms it. Newspaperman Fulton, observing Miss Devereaux in the flesh, is a little disappointed that he had not run for President himself.

The first prize, as the girls know, is Mr. Wintergreen. The second prize is a season pass to Coney Island and the third prize is an autographed photograph of Clara Bow, or ten cents in gold.

John P. Wintergreen himself is glad to meet all the girls and quick to assure them that they are really the only girls he ever loved. But to Fulton, John P. is forced to confess that he doubts his ability to go through with the program as outlined. Then he meets Diana Devereaux.

"Mr. President," coos Diana, with her thickest Southern accent, "I'm mighty happy to meet you! I hope we're going to see a lot of each other."

"Any hope of yours, Miss Devereaux," Wintergreen gallantly replies, "is a hope of mine, I hope."

Now the time has come for the final test. There is great agitation among the girls, and considerable primping.

"It has been a grueling contest—you have been under a great strain," agrees Chairman Fulton. "And we of the committee want to thank you—and through you the three million others who took part in the contest, only ninety-eight percent of whom had to be sent home for misbehavior. And now, ladies, the judges await you. And may the best girl win."

The girls have retired singing, "Who is the lucky girl to be ruler of Washington, D. C.," when Candidate Wintergreen first notices Mary Turner seated at her desk. She is small, attractive, becomingly gowned and serious about her work. Wintergreen immediately has a feeling that he can confide in Mary, which he does. Wintergreen admits that he is nervous, though Mary can't understand why.

"Twenty-four of the most beautiful girls in the country—and you get the winner," she reminds him. "Lots of men would like to be in your shoes."

"Yeah, but it's my bedroom slippers I'm worrying about . . ." protests Wintergreen.

Mary has a feeling that of all the girls Miss Devereaux probably stands the best chance of winning, which does not excite Wintergreen at all. He thinks it probable that that Southern dialect would be terrible if he had to listen to it all the time. Besides, when a man marries he wants a home and a mother for his children.

As for children, Mary thinks it likely that Diana would listen to reason, and as to her qualifications as a housekeeper, he does not have to worry about that. The White House is full of servants. Besides, every girl can cook. Anyway, Mary can.

"I can cook, and sew, and make lace curtains and bake the best darned muffins you ever ate! What do you know about that?" boasts Mary.

To prove it she produces a corn muffin from her lunch. It is a marvelous corn muffin, Wintergreen discovers when he tastes it. Fairly melts in his mouth. A girl who can cook like that is worth knowing.

"Say, why in God's name didn't you get into this contest?" demands Wintergreen.

"One of the three million?" suggests Mary.

WINTERGREEN—Well, you know what the first prize is?

MARY—Yeah, can you imagine!

WINTERGREEN—And you get your picture in the paper.

MARY—Having tea on the lawn with the Filipino delegation. And you throwing the medicine ball at the cabinet.

WINTERGREEN—Oh, do we have a cabinet?

MARY—What would you throw the medicine ball at? Me?

WINTERGREEN (*suddenly sobered*)—Gosh, it'd be fun with you. We could have a grand time.

MARY (*the Southern accent*)—Why, Mr. Wintergreen—

WINTERGREEN—No, I mean it! Listen—I've only got a minute —maybe less than that! I love you! I know it's awful sudden, but in a minute it'll be too late! Let's elope—let's get out of here!

MARY—But—but wait a minute! You don't know me!

WINTERGREEN—I know you better than those girls! (*A gesture.*) You can make corn muffins, and—you're darned cute-looking, and I love you!

MARY—But I don't know *you!*

WINTERGREEN—What's there to know? I'm young, I'm a swell conversationalist, and I've got a chance to be President! And besides that you love me!

MARY—But it's absurd! Why, you can't—

WINTERGREEN—The hell I can't! (*He seizes her and starts kissing her.*) It's fate, Mary, that's what it is—fate! (*Kisses her again.*) Why, we were meant for each other—you and me!

MARY—You and I!
WINTERGREEN—All right, you and I!

There is a burst of music and the doors are thrown open. In troop the girls and the committee, headed by Fulton, who sings—

"As the chairman of the committee,
I announce we've made our choice;
Every lover from Dubuque to Jersey City
Should rejoice."

To which the committee responds—

"We rejoice!
When the angels up there designed her,
They designed a thoroughbred;
And on March the fourth the President will find her
Worthy of his board and bed."

"And now it thrills me to introduce the rarest of American beauties," thrills Chairman Fulton, "the future first lady of the land—a fit consort for the ruler of our country. Gentlemen—Miss Diana Devereaux!"

There is much rejoicing in song and Miss Devereaux is properly exalted, until John P. Wintergreen offers objection.

"Stop! No!" he trills, dramatically. "Though this be a blow, I simply cannot marry Diana Devereaux! Please understand—it isn't that I would jilt or spurn 'er: It's just that I love someone else!"

They are all quite excited. Who is this someone else? And why does Mr. Wintergreen love her?

What's to be done? The committee is agitated. Although Diana has won, though she has signed up, Wintergreen seems to have made his mind up—"his love he'd ruther give to the other." A statement Diana meets with a lyrical protest. Sings she:

"He will do nothing of the sort;
First we'll settle this thing in court.
(*To* WINTERGREEN.)
You seem to think Miss Turner hits the spot;
But what has she got that I haven't got?"

"My Mary makes corn muffins!" proudly replies Wintergreen. "Can you make corn muffins?"

Diana is forced to confess sadly that she cannot make corn muffins. So Wintergreen goes on:

> "Some girls can bake a pie,
>   Made up of prunes and quinces;
>   Some make an oyster fry—
>   Others are good at blintzes.
>   Some lovely girls have done
>   Wonders with turkey stuffin's,
>   But I have found the one
>   Who can really make corn muffins."

Out of Mary's lunch Wintergreen passes muffins to the committeemen. They are quite overwhelmed. Surely it must be fate! "We must declare these muffins the best we ever ate! There's none but Mary Turner could ever be his mate!"

Practically everybody has broken into a wild dance of rejoicing as the curtain falls.

We are now at the very height of the Wintergreen campaign and just outside of Madison Square Garden which is decorated with a huge banner bearing the pictures of John and Mary. Beneath the banner runs the campaign slogan:

"Lovers! Vote for John and Mary!"

There is no mention of Mr. Throttlebottom. A crowd has gathered and is pushing its way through the doors of the Garden, singing and cheering. Inside the place is packed to the rafters and there is even more cheering and singing, punctuated by the calls of cold drink vendors and hot dog salesmen.

The rostrum is built high in the center of the Garden and over it hangs a cluster of amplifiers. Members of the committee are conspicuously on the rostrum, seated either side of two chairs placed thronelike and awaiting the candidates. Chairman Fulton is addressing the crowd with considerable passion—

". . . Seventeen hundred and seventy-six, eighteen hundred and twelve, eighteen hundred and sixty-one, eighteen hundred and ninety-eight, and nineteen hundred and seventeen!" He pauses for a sip of water and there is loud applause. "And so, my friends, on Tuesday next yours is a great privilege. You will cast your ballots for the greatest cause and the greatest emotion known to the heart of mankind! Love! (*Applause.*) Yes, my good friends, for love! For love and for the greatest of all lovers! John P. Wintergreen!"

Mr. Fulton sits down. Through the loud speaker it is announced that on the following Wednesday night Jack Sharkey, American champion of the world, will meet Max Schmeling, German champion of the world, for the championship of the world! And probably Jack Sharkey will win. There is also a message for a Dr. Kristmacher. The doctor's wife has telephoned the box office asking the doctor not to come home that evening.

The next speaker is none other than the silver-tongued orator of the West, Senator Carver Crockett Jones, who has for many years "waged a great and single-handed fight for what he considered his own interests." Chairman Fulton announces that while Senator Jones is speaking entertainment will be furnished by two of the world's greatest wrestlers, Vladimir Vidovitch, the Harlem Heaver, and Yussef Yussevitch, the Terrible Turk.

The wrestlers appear, their mountainous bulk concealed by bathrobes, which they drop at the side of the arena. At the sound of a gong the wrestlers go into action in front of the stage. At the same signal the Senator begins speaking.

"My friends!" shouts the Senator, confidently, despite the competition of the wrestlers, "we have arrived at a great moment in our history. Magnificent though our past has been, it dwindles into utter insignificance beside the brilliance of our future destiny. Gaze into that future, my friends, and what do you see? What do you see? (*At this moment what one chiefly sees is the rear elevation of* VIDOVITCH, *which is being stared at by something akin to admiration by* YUSSEVITCH.) There it is, my friends, for all the world to envy. (*The wrestlers reverse, and it is now* YUSSEVITCH *that is starred. They break, and resume wrestling as* JONES *resumes talking.*) Not for us the entangling alliances of Europe, not for us the allying entanglances of Asia. (*A burst of applause. The wrestlers, at the moment, have a complicated double scissors hold on each other, but their arms are free. Pausing in their labors, they join in the applause.*) Here then we stand, alone in our strength, solitary in our splendor, the greatest and most glorious country that God Almighty put upon earth—the United States of AMERICA!!!"

As Senator Jones reaches what might have been a second peroration one wrestler makes a sensational dive for the other wrestler's legs. They fall to the floor with a crash. The audience, including the members of the committee, cranes forward. Excitement is a shade better than intense. As one wrestler finally gets the other down, and wins the bout, there is a second commotion at the entrance. The crowd again rises excitedly to its feet. There is a scuffle and much shouting. Out of the mess Alexander Throttlebottom emerges considerably mussed.

Fortunately, as he comes through the crowd, Throttlebottom is able to produce a banner bearing his name as candidate for Vice President and this serves as his means of identification. He is permitted to take a place on the rostrum. But Chairman Fulton is not pleased. Why did Throttlebottom leave his cave? Because, the vice presidential candidate explains, the other hermits objected.

As an unexpected surprise for the audience Chairman Fulton would now like to introduce Mr. Throttlebottom, which, with some little difficulty in remembering the name, he proceeds to do. But Alexander has no chance to speak. First the baseball scores are given over the loud speaker. Then an intermission is called. Finally, with excited cheering and a great milling of a crowd of flashlight men, camera men and reporters, John P. Wintergreen and Mary Turner, preceded by a police escort, enter the hall and take their places on the platform. Mr. Throttlebottom is violently ejected by an over-zealous policeman during this excitement.

Chairman Fulton is able to still the tumult with upraised hand and introduce the next speakers—"the most beloved couple that have ever run for the highest office in the gift of the American people."

"There have been many great lovers in history," admits Mr. Fulton. "But Romeo never loved Juliet, Dante never loved Beatrice, Damon never loved Pythias, as John P. Wintergreen loves Mary Turner. (*Applause.*) My friends, the issue of this campaign is a simple one. We do not talk to you about war debts or wheat or immigration—we appeal to your hearts, not your intelligence. It is the old, old story, yet ever new—the sweetest story ever told. John P. Wintergreen, candidate for President of the United States of America, loves Mary Turner. Mary Turner, the most beautiful, the loveliest example of typical American womanhood—and I defy our opponents to say otherwise—loves John P. Wintergreen. He has proposed to her in 47 States of the Union, and in 47 States she has accepted him. Tonight she will give him her answer in the great Empire State of New York! John and Mary, stand up! (*They do so.*) Can you look at them and not be thrilled by their youth, their charm, their passion? Ladies and gentlemen, I give you John P. Wintergreen and Mary Turner!"

Fulton has sat down. The Garden is in an uproar. It is a good half minute before John, who has advanced with Mary to the front of the platform, can begin speaking.

WINTERGREEN—My friends, I come before you in this final rally of the campaign not as John P. Wintergreen the candidate, not as John P. Wintergreen the statesman, but as a simple man in love. So I beg you to bear with me for a moment while I ask the girl of my dreams if she will be my heart's delight. (*There is applause as he turns to* MARY.) Miss Turner, there has been something on my mind for a long, long time.

MARY—Yes, Mr. Wintergreen?

WINTERGREEN (*the hesitant lover*)—May I not call you—Mary?

MARY—I wish you would—John.

WINTERGREEN—Do you remember that night we first walked together, on the boardwalk in Atlantic City?

MARY—With the moon shining overhead?

WINTERGREEN—And the lights rippling on the water. Do you remember what I said to you, Mary, as I took your dear hand in mine?

MARY—You said—(*She drops her eyes.*) that I reminded you of your mother, who had been dead these many years.

WINTERGREEN—And in the cornfields of Kansas, on the plains of Arizona, in the mountains of Nebraska, I whispered to you how much you were beginning to mean to me.

MARY—Our friendship has been a wonderful thing to me.

WINTERGREEN—And in the cave in Kentucky—(*Two photographers dash on.* WINTERGREEN *stops until the picture is taken.*) when you were frightened of the darkness, I put my arm around your trembling shoulder and drew you to me.

MARY—You were so brave, so strong.

WINTERGREEN—Mary, I can conceal it from you no longer. Look at me, darling. (*He tilts her face up.*) I love you. (*The crowd breaks into great cheers and applause.* WINTERGREEN stops them with a gesture.) Yes, Mary, I love you. (*A gesture to halt applause that has not come.*)

MARY—Why, John! I hardly know what to say.

WINTERGREEN—Say that you love me, Mary, and that you will be mine.

MARY—I do love you, John. (*Applause. The crowd on its feet.* WINTERGREEN *again checks them.*)

WINTERGREEN—And if I am elected President, you will marry me?

MARY (*with simple determination*)—I will.

WINTERGREEN (*turns quickly to the crowd, his arm still around* MARY)—Citizens, it is up to you! Can you let this glorious romance end unhappily?

MARY—Can you tear asunder two loving hearts whom God hath joined together?

WINTERGREEN—I put my faith and trust in the American people! Go then to the polls on Tuesday and show the whole world that the United States of America stands first, last and always for Love! Are you with me?

ALL (*on their feet*)—YES!

FULTON—Sing 'em the campaign song, Jack! Sing the campaign love song!

WINTERGREEN—

> Of thee I sing, baby,
> Summer, autumn, winter, spring, baby.
> You're my silver lining,
> You're my sky of blue,
> There's a love light shining,
> All because of you.
> Of thee I sing, baby,
> You have got that certain thing, baby—
> Shining star and inspiration,
> Worthy of a mighty nation,
> Of thee I sing!

(*The crowd yells itself blue in the face. When they are good and blue, the curtain falls.*)

It is Election Night. The scene is, as usual, indescribable. "The roar of the crowd, the blowing of horns, the tooting of sirens. A band plays furiously. The voice of a Nation is speaking, and the results are being thrown upon a motion picture screen. Faster and faster they come—bulletins from here, there, and everywhere; photographs of the candidate, photographs of Mary Turner, photographs of people that have nothing to do with anything. And returns, returns, returns:

Whiteside, Vt., is 154 strong for Wintergreen! Waterville, Mass., gives Wintergreen 12 and Scattering 1! Atlanta, Ga., gives Wintergreen a majority of 1000 over Jefferson Davis, and Landslide, Neb., votes twelve thousand times for Wintergreen and only once for "A Man Named Wilkins."

In Hollywood, Cal., the contest is close. Wintergreen gets 160,-000 to 159,000 for Mickey Mouse and 84,638 for Gloria Swanson's First Husband.

There are pictures of John P. Wintergreen casting Ballot No. 8 at Public School 63, and Ballot 168 at Public School 145! There is a picture of Alexander Throttlebottom's shoes being shined before the vice presidential candidate enters the election booth! There are pictures of Patrick Henry, Primo Carnera, Benjamin Franklin, Babe Ruth and Man o' War!

Lexington, Ky., with practically all election districts heard from, gives Wintergreen 27,637, Light Wines and Beer 14, and Straight Whiskey 1,850,827! In Manchester, Eng., the vote is heavily Wintergreen, with only a couple for King George and one for Queen Mary! But in Rome, Italy, Mussolini gets 828,638 and Wintergreen none!

There are more pictures. One of the White House! One of the Capitol! One of the Roxy! One of a Friend of Roxy's! One of "An Unidentified Man. (*Who looks suspiciously like the vice presidential candidate.*)"

In conclusion there is a flash indicating the Wintergreen election! Followed by a flash announcing that Wintergreen needs but four more votes and finally a picture of Wintergreen casting the necessary four!

Then there are two bulletins:

"Heartily congratulate you on your splendid victory," the defeated candidate wires Mr. Wintergreen, "and charge fraud in Indiana, Illinois, Nebraska, Montana, Washington, Ohio and Massachusetts." And

"At midnight tonight Alexander Throttlebottom refused to concede his election as Vice President!"

"Next Week

NORMA SHEARER

In

'THE LOVE GIRL' "

"And to finish off, the Metro-Goldwyn lion. It opens its mouth! It crows!" The curtain falls.

Inauguration Day finds the usual crowd on the steps of the Capitol at Washington, D. C. "The scene is one of flashing uniforms and surging crowds. . . . The steps are packed with diplomats, Army and Navy attachés, Cabinet members, Senators, Congressmen and anyone else who could get a ticket."

The nine Judges of the Supreme Court of the United States file in in order, in black robes and in whiskers that make them all look "astonishingly like a certain Chief Justice who shall be nameless."

In song the Judges announce their position and their mission:

> "As the super-Solomons of this great nation,
> We will supervise today's inauguration,
> And we'll superintend the wedding celebration,
> In a manner official
> And judicial."

There is a fanfare of trumpets in the distance, followed by song and considerable hail, hailing. Wintergreen and the Campaign Committee high-hatted and frock-coated, are received with much shouting and song. After which, at the request of the Chief Justice, President Wintergreen recites his inaugural address to appropriate musical accompaniment.

WINTERGREEN—

> "I have definite ideas about the Philippines,
> And the herring situation up in Bismarck;
> I have notions on the salaries of movie queens,
> And the men who sign their signatures with *this* mark!
>   (*He makes a cross.*)
> But on this glorious day I find
> I'm sentimentally inclined,
> And so—
> I sing this to the girls I used to know:

> "Here's a kiss for Cinderella,
> And a parting kiss for May;
> Toodle-oo, good-by! This is my wedding day!
> Here's a final smile for Della,
> And a lady known as Lou;
> Toodle-oo, good-by! With bach'lor days I'm through!"

(*And the girls in question, believe it or not, parade tantalizingly by him.*)

Now the crowd turns to welcome Mary Turner, who appears on a platform at the head of the stairs, gorgeous in her bridal finery. Mary joins John before the Chief Justice.

CHIEF JUSTICE—Do you, John P. Wintergreen, solemnly swear to uphold the Constitution of the United States of America and to love, honor and cherish this woman so long as you two shall live?

WINTERGREEN—I do.

CHIEF JUSTICE—Do you, Mary Turner, promise to love, honor

and cherish this man so long as you two shall live?

MARY—I do.

CHIEF JUSTICE—Therefore, by virtue of the power that is vested in me as Chief Justice, I hereby pronounce you President of the United States, man and wife.

WINTERGREEN—Mary!

MARY—John! (*They embrace; the crowd yells its head off.*)

WINTERGREEN AND MARY—

Is it true or am I dreaming?
Do I go to Heav'n to stay?
Never was a girl so happy on her wedding—

(*Enter, of all people,* DIANA DEVEREAUX. *And is she annoyed!*)

DIANA—Stop! Halt! Pause! Wait!

ALL—Who is this intruder?
There's no one could be ruder!
What's your silly notion
In causing this commotion?

DIANA (*recitative, and with highly operatic interludes*)—I was the most beautiful blossom in all the Southland. I was sent up North to enter the contest, with the understanding that the winner was to be the President's wife. The committee examined me. My lily white body fascinated them. I was chosen. It was the happiest moment of my life.

ALL—Yes, yes, go on! Yes, yes, go on!

DIANA—Suddenly the sky fell—suddenly for no reason at all, this man rejected me. All my castles came tumbling down. And so I am serving him with a summons—for breach of promise!

Consternation follows. The crowd is terribly excited. The Chief Justice thinks it outrageous for Diana, on John's wedding day, to put him on the spot, and the crowd quickly figures that it's a communistic plot.

The crowd is inclined to be fair. At least sopranos and altos agree that Diana may have her rights,

"And if it's true she has a claim
You should be called a dirty name,"

they inform John, who is considerably perturbed despite Mary's assurance that "no matter what they do to hurt you the one you love won't desert you."

John again brings up the matter of the corn muffins and after the Nine Judges of the Supreme Court have gone into a football

huddle they emerge to announce the decision of the Court to be
in favor of corn muffins!   This naturally excites the crowd to
another song.

ALL
Great!   Great!
It's written on the slate!
There's none but Mary Turner
Could ever be his mate!

DIANA
It's I, not Mary Turner
Who should have been his mate;
I'm off to tell my story
In ev'ry single state!

CHIEF JUSTICE
Be off with you, young woman,
He's married to his mate!
Be off with you, young woman,
He's married to his mate!
(DIANA *goes but she'll be heard from again.*)

ALL
There's none but Mary Turner
Could ever be his mate!
There's none but Mary Turner
Could ever be his mate!

WINTERGREEN
Of thee I sing, baby,
Summer, autumn, winter, spring, baby—
Shining star and inspiration,
Worthy of a mighty nation,
Of thee I sing!

'THE CURTAIN FALLS

ACT II

The President's office in the White House is now also the
President's Wife's office.   The Presidential desk is divided.   One
side is piled high with state papers and the other lined with per-
fumes and cosmetics.

Two secretaries, Sam Jenkins and Mary Benson, are busy at their appointed tasks, but not too busy to sing a song, with rows of other secretaries who join them for the choruses.

A White House guide, followed by a group of ten or twelve typical sightseers, passes through the room, the guide explaining the uses to which the room is now put and those to which it has been put in the past. During the coal strike of 1912, for instance, it was used as a garage. "We are now entering the room from which, on an historic occasion, the Spanish Ambassador jumped out of the window, in the very nick of time."

It is, to accept it from the secretaries, going to be a busy day. There will be a delegation from South America to see if something can't be done about cleaning up Hollywood; a delegation from the Camisole Indians, who want scalping restored, and a delegation from the cotton growers, who want Mrs. Wintergreen to go back to cotton stockings.

Another crowd of sightseers includes, at its tailend, none other than Alexander Throttlebottom, who is just wandering around on a private tour of investigation. The guide, finding Alexander straying a little too far from the rest of the group, cautions him politely to get back. A moment later, however, he proves of help to the guide. One of the sightseers would like to know where the Vice President lives. Throttlebottom can tell him that. The Vice President lives at Mrs. Spiegelbaum's boarding house, in Z Street, which is a great place if you like kosher cooking.

The guide is naturally interested in any friend of the Vice President's and glad to hear that Alexander Throttlebottom is really a very decent sort of chap when you come to know him. One confidence leads to another and the guide in turn is able to help Mr. Throttlebottom by clearing up in his mind a matter that has been puzzling him a good deal. Just what does the Vice President do when he works? The Vice President, explains the guide, presides over the Senate.

"Over what?" demands Mr. Throttlebottom.

"The Senate. You know what Senators are, don't you?"

"Sure—I saw them play yesterday."

"No, no! The Vice President presides over the Senate. It meets in the Capitol."

This is news to Throttlebottom, and as soon as he finds out how to get to the Capitol he is on his way. . . .

The Wintergreens arrive in the Presidential office together, take their places at the desk, and plunge into the day's work.

The President must order the scrapping of two battleships and the building of four others in the cause of disarmament. Mrs. Prexy dictates a letter to Queen Marie of Roumania congratulating her on the soap she is selling.

The President would politely inform the Liberian minister that he is still twelve dollars and forty-five cents shy from Friday night's poker game. Which will add something to the Liberian National Debt.

When Mary comes to her ordering for the day she finds it difficult. If the President is sure there will be only the Chief Justice, the Attorney General, Jackie Cooper and three paroled judges, that will be eight in all, and sixteen lamb chops will be sufficient. But if it should happen that an expected dirigible from Germany gets in there will be at least sixty-four passengers and two stowaways on that. Mary ends by ordering a hundred and forty-eight lamb chops, a carload of asparagus and seventy-five loaves of rye bread.

Secretary of Agriculture Lippman and Secretary of the Navy Gilhooley are in for a conference.

WINTERGREEN—Well, what's on your mind, Louis? How's agriculture?

LIPPMAN—That's what I came to talk to you about. Listen, Jack! I don't know anything about agriculture. I told you I wanted the Treasury.

WINTERGREEN—What's the matter with agriculture?

LIPPMAN—Agriculture's all right—it's those farmers. Wheat, wheat! All they know is raise wheat! And then they raise hell with me because nobody wants it.

WINTERGREEN—Why do you let them raise so much?

LIPPMAN—How can you stop 'em? I did all I could. I invited the seven-year-locusts, but they didn't come. Even the locusts don't want their lousy wheat. And they're always complaining about being in one place all the time—they want to travel.

GILHOOLEY—You call that trouble? How'd you like to have a lot of sailors on your neck?

WINTERGREEN—What do *they* want—*two* wives in every port?

GILHOOLEY—Yeah. And any port in a storm. And no storms. And they won't stand for those bells any more. They want to know what time it is the same as anybody else. But that's not the big thing.

WINTERGREEN—Well?

GILHOOLEY—It's the ocean. They don't like the ocean.

WINTERGREEN—Which ocean don't they like?

GILHOOLEY—All of them. They say it's a nice place to visit, but they don't want to live there. It's no place to bring up a family.

WINTERGREEN (*thinking it over*)—The farmers want to travel and the sailors want to settle down. . . . I've got it! Have them change places!

LIPPMAN—What?

WINTERGREEN—It'll solve the whole problem! Sailors don't know anything about farming—in two years there won't *be* any wheat! You'll have a wheat shortage!

LIPPMAN—And I'll get hell again!

WINTERGREEN—And look what it does for business! You get the farmers on the boats; the traveling salesmen will come back to the farmhouses—*you* know, to stay over night! Why, I haven't heard a good story in years.

Secretary of State Fulton is full of party trouble when he arrives. Principally it is concerned with Diana Devereaux and the campaign to get justice for her. There always has been a crowd that insisted that Devereaux did not get a square deal. Now the New Jersey Woman's club has come out solid for Diana, and the Kansas City Elks have taken similar action.

Senator Jones reports the West to be up in arms. Senator Lyons insists the South is on fire. Nebraska has declared martial law and Louisiana is rioting. Mary is quite upset by the news. It is, she feels, all her fault. But John will not listen to that. He had much rather have Mary than any number of recalcitrant states.

"We carried forty-eight states in the campaign, didn't we? Mary and I?" demands John. "And there was Devereaux propaganda then. We licked it before and we can do it again!"

When the reporters are shown in for the daily press conference they find the Wintergreens standing solidly back of their old platform of true love. The reporters, growing melodious, frame their queries in verse. There are a lot of things they don't care to know about, moratoriums and beer and the League of Nations, but—

> "Here's the one thing that the people of America
> Are beside themselves to know:
> They would like to know what's doing
> On the lady who is suing
> You—Diana Devereaux? . . .

WINTERGREEN
It's a pleasant day—
That's all I can say!

MARY
Here's the one thing we'll announce:
Love's the only thing that counts!

WINTERGREEN
Who cares what the public chatters?
Love's the only thing that matters.

The Committee is inclined to congratulate President Wintergreen on his success with the reporters, and a campaign is hurriedly outlined. Again a feature shall be Mary's corn muffins—
corn muffins for the unemployed!

"That's my girl!" chirrups John. "You feed 'em and I'll sing
to them! We'll get the country back! Give us a week and
they'll forget that Devereaux ever lived!"

The threatened trouble is not long in arriving. A squad of
French soldiers, singing, is followed by the French Ambassador
himself, also with song, beginning in recitative:

"I am the Ambassador of France! And I have come here to
see a grievous wrong righted. My country is deeply hurt. Not
since the days of Louis the Seventh, the Eighth, the Ninth, the
Tenth, and possibly the Eleventh have such a thing happen!"

WINTERGREEN—What's troubling you?

FRENCH AMBASSADOR—You have done a great injustice to a
French descendant—a lovely girl whose rights have been trampled
in the dust!

ALL—Who is she? What's her name?

FRENCH AMBASSADOR—Her name is Diana Devereaux.

ALL—Diana Devereaux! Diana Devereaux! Since when is
she of French descent?

FRENCH AMBASSADOR—
                I've been looking up her family tree,
                And I've found a most important pedigree!
                She's the illegitimate daughter
                Of an illegitimate son
                Of an illegitimate nephew
                Of Napoleon!

ALL (awed)—Napoleon!

FRENCH AMBASSADOR—
>She offers aristocracy
>To this bizarre democracy,
>Where naught is sacred but the old simoleon!
>I must know why
>You crucify
>My native country
>With this effront'ry,
>To the illegitimate daughter
>Of an illegitimate son
>Of an illegitimate nephew
>Of Napoleon!

Soon Diana is there to plead her own cause, also in song. "I might have been First Lady, but now my path is shady; oh, pity this poor maidie!" melodiously laments Diana.

Still, President Wintergreen will not give way. Leave his Mary? Never! Let them do what they will!

What they do at the moment is to march away with the warning that France shall be told.

Senator Fulton is again convinced that something will have to be done. Perhaps John had better resign. That John also refuses to do. Then it may be necessary, the party leaders believe, to impeach him. Even that does not frighten John and Mary. They are singing cheerfully that life is one long jubilee, "So long as I care for you and you care for me," as the lights dim and the curtains close.

In a Capitol corridor, just outside the United States Senate, the committee composed of Fulton, Lippman, Jones and Gilhooley has met informally. They are considerably distressed at the thought of having to do what they are about to do to President Wintergreen, but there is no other way.

They are also slightly set back when it is suggested that if Wintergreen is impeached the Vice President will be President, and everyone has again forgotten who the Vice President is.

Fortunately Alexander Throttlebottom arrives at that moment and is able to renew their recollection of him. Alexander is much thrilled when they tell him he is to be President. He is still there when President Wintergreen and his secretary, Jenkins, arrive. The President is so agitated that he does not recognize the Vice President, excepting as the man who gave him the dill pickle at campaign headquarters. Still, he would be friendly.

"What are you doing now?" he asks Throttlebottom.

"I'm Vice President."
"You don't say? Lost your other job, huh?"

THROTTLEBOTTOM—Well, I'm going to have a good job now, because I'm going to be President.

WINTERGREEN (*realizing it*)—Say, that's right! If they kick me out that makes you President.

THROTTLEBOTTOM—Say, I wonder if you'd mind doing me a favor?

WINTERGREEN—Sure!

THROTTLEBOTTOM—You see, I don't know anything about being President. I just found out today how to be Vice President.

WINTERGREEN—Well, that's something.

THROTTLEBOTTOM—Isn't there some book I could read?

WINTERGREEN—Yes. I'm writing one. "What Every Young President Ought to Know."

THROTTLEBOTTOM—Has it got pictures?

WINTERGREEN—It's got everything! Tells you just what to do! Of course the first four years are easy. You don't do anything except try to get reëlected.

THROTTLEBOTTOM—That's pretty hard these days.

WINTERGREEN—It looks that way. The next four years you wonder why the hell you wanted to be reëlected. And after that you go into the insurance business and you're all set.

THROTTLEBOTTOM—Well, couldn't I save a lot of time and go right into the insurance business?

WINTERGREEN—No, you've got to work yourself up.

THROTTLEBOTTOM—Yeah, but it's a pretty hard job, being President. You've got to keep on writing those Thanksgiving proclamations, no matter what—and then there's that other bunch, Congress. I guess there isn't anything you can really do about Congress, is there?"

WINTERGREEN—Take my advice and keep them out of Washington.

THROTTLEBOTTOM—Can you do that?

WINTERGREEN—St. Patrick did it. Keep them out if you have to quarantine the place. Get the measles.

THROTTLEBOTTOM—I had measles once.

WINTERGREEN—Yeah, but you never had Congress. That's worse.

THROTTLEBOTTOM—Oh! What about those messages that the President is always sending to Congress—who reads those, anyway?

WINTERGREEN—The fellow who prints 'em.

THROTTLEBOTTOM—Well, wouldn't everybody read them if you made them funnier?

WINTERGREEN—No, we've had some pretty funny ones.

THROTTLEBOTTOM—Couldn't you make a speech instead? Then they'd *have* to listen.

WINTERGREEN—No, no! You've got to be careful about speeches. You only make a speech when you want the stock market to go down.

THROTTLEBOTTOM—What do you do when you want the stock market to go up?

WINTERGREEN (*fairly falling on his neck*)—Oh! wouldn't I like to know!

Inside the Senate Chamber the great chair of the presiding officer is mounted on a high dais. In front of the desk, seated in semi-circular rows, are the Senators themselves—all kinds of Senators with all kinds of whiskers. When the curtain rises Vice President Throttlebottom is calling the roll to a musical accompaniment, which he continues to do until he runs out of rhymes.

After roll call the Senators are still in singing mood. Their theme song runs—

"There's action ev'ry minute when this happy group convenes:
        To get business into tangles
        We can guarantee more angles
Than the town of Boston guarantees in beans!
        If you think you've got depression
        Wait until we get in session
And you'll find out what depression really means!"

Now Vice President Throttlebottom would get right to the business of impeaching the President, but the clerk insists that the first order of the day must be unfinished business. There is, for instance, a little matter the Senator from Massachusetts insists on bringing up. It concerns the famous ride of Paul Revere and the injustice done Jenny, the horse that Paul Revere rode. Jenny, the Senator from Massachusetts contends, is at least entitled to a pension.

But, as Senator Jones points out, Jenny is dead and has been dead since 1805. This comes as a great surprise to Vice President Throttlebottom and he immediately moves that the Senate shall rise for one minute in silent tribute to the departed horse from Massachusetts. That finishes Jenny.

Senator Lyons would next crave the indulgence of the Senate while he says a few words in honor of his wife's birthday. He also moves the appropriation of $5000 for flowers to be sent the wife on this historic occasion. It is so ordered.

The Senate gets to the matter of impeachment shortly. The President has arrived and the Committee proceeds to intone its charges in harmony—

COMMITTEE—Whereas—

LYONS—At a meeting of the Senate at which a quorum was present a motion was made and it was proposed that—

COMMITTEE—Whereas—

LYONS—John P. Wintergreen had undertaken to marry the winner of a contest held at Atlantic City—

COMMITTEE—Whereas—

LYONS—His subsequent refusal to marry the winner, Miss Diana Devereaux, will lead to dire international complications—

COMMITTEE—Whereas—

LYONS—Now therefore be it resolved that President John P. Wintergreen be, and he hereby is, impeached from the said office of President of these United States.

JONES—I second the nomination.

FULTON—Our first witness—the French Ambassador.

The singing French soldiers precede the French Ambassador into the Senate and the Senators welcome them with appropriate exercises. The French Ambassador repeats his charge that they have "dealt a lovely maid a blow that is injurious; a very dirty trick was played, and France is simply furious."

"Ambassador, please explain why France should be concerned about the plaintiff." And the Ambassador sings with feeling—

> "She's the illegitimate daughter
> Of an illegitimate son
> Of an illegitimate nephew
> Of Napoleon!"

> "She's contemplating suicide
> Because that man he threw aside
> A lady with the blue blood of Napoleon.
> What sort of man
> Is this who can
> Insult my country
> With this effront'ry?"

The Ambassador then introduces the Atlantic City witnesses in the persons of the bathing beauties. These are followed by Diana Devereaux, who, having exchanged her Southern accent for a French accent, sings the story of her jilting and the devastation it has caused. There is practically nothing now for Diana to do but to lay her down and dee.

Called upon for his defense, President Wintergreen is again defiant. "Impeach me! Fine me! Jail me! Sue me!" he shouts, dramatically. "My Mary's love means much more to me!"

"Enough, enough! We want no preachment!" cries Throttlebottom, proving that he can do it too. "It's time to vote on his impeachment!"

A roll call produces a succession of "Guilty!" votes. At which moment Mary Turner appears suddenly upon the scene and stops the proceedings.

"Before you go any further, with your permission," pleads Mary, "I must tell you of my husband's delicate condition." Which she proceeds to do in a gay little song.

MARY—

> I'm about to be a mother;
> He's about to be a father;
> We're about to have a baby:
> I must tell it,
> These doings compel it!
> Oh, I'm about to be a mother;
> He's about to be a father;
> We're about to have a baby—
> A baby to love and adore—

WINTERGREEN—Mary, is it true? Am I to have a baby?

MARY—It's true, John, it's true!

WINTERGREEN—It's wonderful, it's wonderful—water! Water! (*He faints.*)

DIANA—It eez a fine countree—I am compromised and she has zee babee!

THROTTLEBOTTOM—Gentlemen, gentlemen—this country has never yet impeached an expectant father. What do you say?

SENATORS—Not guilty!

The French Ambassador storms out to make his report by cable, dragging Diana Devereaux after him. The Senate is jubilant.

"Great work, Jack!" congratulates the Senator from Massachusetts. "You'll be reinstated in the hearts of the American people."

"You're doing your duty by posterity," chimes in Senator Jones.

"Posterity—" echoes Wintergreen, "why, Posterity is just around the corner." And this, sounding like a music cue, leads him to sing it lustily while the Senators find their tambourines and riot in a joyful dance.

From somewhere Alexander Throttlebottom produces a bass drum and leads a march about the room, everybody singing and dancing, as the curtains close.

Months later, in a corridor of the White House, Secretaries Jenkins and Benson are counting up the months and agreeing that it will be great to have a baby in the White House. The child should be born in December. The country is stirred. The voters have lined up solidly behind the President. Of course France may still make trouble, but—

The President comes dancing in. He has just finished *such* a breakfast! And he never felt more fit. Mrs. Wintergreen is well, too.

Senator Fulton has arrived, even more full of congratulations than he was before.

A moment later the French Ambassador is announced. He comes this time without his singing bodyguard, and he comes with good news.

"France consents to your having the child!" he reports to the President.

"France consents?" Wintergreen finds the news hard to credit.

"Freely," insists the Ambassador.

WINTERGREEN—Why, that's wonderful of her. Good old France! Do you mind if I tell my wife, so she can go ahead? (AMBASSADOR *bows.*) You've no idea how this will please her. Won't take me a minute—I'll be right back.

FRENCH AMBASSADOR—But one moment, Monsieur. (WINTERGREEN *pauses.*) France consents, but on one condition.

WINTERGREEN—Yeah?

FRENCH AMBASSADOR—France must have the baby!

FULTON AND WINTERGREEN—WHAT?

FRENCH AMBASSADOR—Do not be hasty, Monsieur. You must understand the desperate condition of my country. For fifty years the birth rate of France has been declining, declining, declining.

WINTERGREEN—What's that got to do with me?

FRENCH AMBASSADOR—You must see, Monsieur. If you had married Mlle. Devereaux, as you have promise, the baby she is French. But now you have taken away from France one baby, and she demand replacement.

WINTERGREEN—Never!

FULTON—I should say not!

FRENCH AMBASSADOR—It is the old law, Monsieur; an eye for an eye, a tooth for a tooth, and a baby for a baby.

WINTERGREEN—You'll get no tooth from my baby!

FRENCH AMBASSADOR—The tooth, the whole tooth, and nothing but the tooth!

WINTERGREEN—Not one tooth!

FRENCH AMBASSADOR—That is your final word?

WINTERGREEN—It is! Good day, Monsieur!

FRENCH AMBASSADOR—Good day! (*Clicks his heels; salutes; turns and starts out.*) Lafayette, we are coming! (*Goes.*)

FULTON—What do you think France'll do?

WINTERGREEN—What's the worst she can do? Sue us for what she owes us?

FULTON—But that other thing! France is awful touchy about her birth rate!

WINTERGREEN—What are you worrying about? I fixed *this* up, didn't I?

FULTON—What?

WINTERGREEN—Well, Mary's going to have a baby, isn't she?

FULTON—Yes!

WINTERGREEN—Well! Next year I make a tour of France! Lafayette! (*He salutes.*)

The famous Yellow Room of the White House is this day "an endless vista of hallway, and polished floor, and chandeliers, and ladies in evening clothes, and men in magnificent uniforms."

White-wigged flunkies move in and out, bellowing the names of foreign diplomats, and wheeling in an almost endless line of baby carriages. They come with the compliments of Ecuador, and Bolivia, of Spain and Lithuania, and a little one from Scotland.

There is a grand burst of song in celebration of the expected event. "Oh, trumpeter, trumpeter, blow your golden horn. A White House baby will very soon be born. . . . With a hey nonny nonny, and a ha cha cha!"

The Doctor is in, but without definite news. The crowd besieges him for an opinion. Will the baby be a girl or a boy?

As to that the Doctor will not venture an opinion, reminding his questioners that—

> "On that matter no one budges
> For all cases of the sort
> Are decided by the judges
> Of the Supreme Court."

Now the Judges have arrived in order. Followed by the members of the Cabinet. They, too, would know the sex of the expected infant. All the sailors in the Navy, all the cowboys on the prairies, are eager to know. "For baby boy or girl they are keen, but they want nothing in between," carols Senator Jones.

When President Wintergreen arrives he is frightfully nervous. Whenever he thinks of Mary, in there, alone, he gets even more nervous. He has to have a drink. Every man produces a flask.

Now the Supreme Court has retired for consultation, and the French Ambassador has arrived with another proposition from France.

"Will you surrender the baby?" demands the Ambassador.

"Never! Give my baby to France and have it eat snails and get ptomaine poisoning! Never!" answers Wintergreen.

FRENCH AMBASSADOR—Then, sir, I am instructed to say that with the birth of the child France severs diplomatic relations!

WINTERGREEN—Hurray!

FRENCH AMBASSADOR—And that is not all, sir. I wish furthermore to report— (*Two flunkies enter and blow a fanfare on their trumpets. The Supreme Court reënters.*)

JUDGES—Whereas—

CHIEF JUSTICE—A child has been born to the President of the United States and his consort—

JUDGES—Whereas—

CHIEF JUSTICE—The Supreme Court of the United States has been called upon to determine the sex of the aforesaid infant—

JUDGES—Whereas—

CHIEF JUSTICE—By a strict party vote it has been decided that—

JUDGES—It's a boy! (*The Committee and guests press around* WINTERGREEN *to congratulate him.*)

WINTERGREEN—A boy! That makes me a father! Thank you! Thank you very much! I certainly am a lucky man! Boy, the cigars! Smoke up, everybody! Here you are, ladies and gentlemen! Have a cigar, Frenchy!

FRENCH AMBASSADOR—My thanks, Monsieur. On behalf of France permit me to offer my felicitations.

WINTERGREEN—Attaboy! Let bygones be bygones! Have another cigar!

FRENCH AMBASSADOR—And permit me also to inform you that France hereby severs diplomatic relations! (*He reaches for a cigar.*)

WINTERGREEN (*closes the humidor with a bang*)—Then the hell with you!

FRENCH AMBASSADOR—You understand what this means, Monsieur?

WINTERGREEN—I do! (*Takes back the first cigar.*) It means no smoke!

Again there is a fanfare of trumpets, followed by the reappearance of the Judges. They have come, with another set of whereases, to announce the arrival of a second child. It's a girl this time, which, as Wintergreen sees it, makes him a father and a mother, too. Twins are a little more than he counted on, but he bears up bravely.

The French Ambassador is irate. This sort of thing is certain to lead to war. Taking not one, but two, babies away from France! What they have done to Mlle. Devereaux!

But Diana is taking her disappointments better than most. In the distance she can still be heard singing, "I was a beautiful blossom—" Her entrance might have been more dramatic, but at the moment the Vice President is announced.

Alexander Throttlebottom arrives knitting a baby's sweater. Fortunately he has an extra one in his pocket, so the news of the twins does not disturb him. The French Ambassador, however, is still upset.

FRENCH AMBASSADOR—Once and for all, Monsieur, what are you going to do? What are you going to do about Mlle. Devereaux and her babies?

WINTERGREEN—Well, she can have her own babies.

DIANA—But I am not married, Monsieur.

WINTERGREEN—What's that got to do with it?

FRENCH AMBASSADOR—Everything. The family has been illegitimate long enough.

WINTERGREEN—Then let her get married!

FRENCH AMBASSADOR—Exactly! But it was agreed, Monsieur,

that she was to marry the President of the United States.

WINTERGREEN—But she can't have me! I'm married!

FRENCH AMBASSADOR—Then it is war, sir! When the President of the United States fails to fulfill his duty—

WINTERGREEN—That's it! I've got it!

ALL—Got what?

WINTERGREEN—It's in the Constitution! When the President of the United States is unable to fulfill his duties, his obligations are assumed by—

THROTTLEBOTTOM—The Vice President! (*Gleefully.*) I get her!

CHIEF JUSTICE—Article Twelve!

FRENCH AMBASSADOR—Monsieur, you are a genius!

THROTTLEBOTTOM (*to* WINTERGREEN)—I could throw my arms right around your neck!

WINTERGREEN—Oh, no, you don't! Hers! (*The Trumpeters reënter. Another fanfare.*) Oh, my God!

CHIEF JUSTICE—It's all right. The boys are merely practicing. (*There is a great burst of music, and from the more intimate quarters of the White House there comes into the room a great canopied bed, hung with gold, and silver, and bald-headed eagles. In it is* MARY TURNER WINTERGREEN, *a twin on each arm.* WINTERGREEN *advances to greet her; the crowd bursts into song. And of all the songs in the world, you'd never guess what they pick out. It's "Of Thee I Sing, Baby."*)

THE CURTAIN FALLS

MOURNING BECOMES ELECTRA
A Trilogy in Fourteen Scenes

By Eugene O'Neill

IT was in the spring of 1926 that Eugene O'Neill made his first note on the work that five years later became the dramatic trilogy produced under the embracing title of "Mourning Becomes Electra."

"Modern psychological drama using one of the old legend plots of Greek tragedy for its basic theme," that first note ran. "The Electra story? The Medea? Is it possible to get modern psychological approximation of Greek sense of fate into such a play, which an intelligent audience of today, possessed by no belief in gods or supernatural retribution, could accept and be moved by?"

By the fall of 1928, when the idea recurred, O'Neill had decided on the story of Electra and family as being psychologically the most interesting. Through 1929 in France he worked fairly steadily on the play, which soon assumed the heroic proportions of three full-length dramas.

The first draft he finished in the spring of 1930. It was, he wrote, "scrawny stuff, but serves purpose of a first draft." He thought in the rewriting he might use half-masks and a technique similar to that he had employed in "Strange Interlude."

By July he had finished a second draft, and abandoned the masks. Through August and September and part of October he rewrote the play twice. In January it was typed. In February it was revised. By April he was satisfied, and the mighty script was on its way to the New York Theatre Guild.

O'Neill followed "Electra" to America and there were many summer conferences with the Guild directorate. A generous cutting was agreed upon, to bring the three plays within six hours of playing time, with a dinner interval following the completion of "Homecoming," the first play.

The first performance was given at the Guild Theatre the night of October 26, 1931, before a typically expectant audience of Guild subscribers and an anxious producing organization. If failure were to be added to the existing depression, it might easily mean the temporary abandonment of all Guild plans!

But there was no failure. The morning editions of the New York papers, in their dramatic columns, carried such shouting superlatives of praise as no other dramatic production has called forth in the history of the native theatre. Columns, carefully written, lovingly, excitedly edited by the leading critics, proclaimed the birth of a literary and dramatic masterpiece. For the playwright, for the producers, for the director (Philip Moeller), for the acting company—headed by Alice Brady as Electra and Alla Nazimova as Christine—there was nothing but extravagant praise.

Eugene Gladstone O'Neill had come at last into general acknowledgment as America's greatest dramatist; the living theatre had risen to justify itself completely and undeniably. For months thereafter the public filled the Guild Theatre at every performance, of which six were given each week.

A special curtain has been painted for "Mourning Becomes Electra." It shows the Ezra Mannon residence in New England as it is seen from the street. It is "a large building of the Greek temple type that was in vogue in the first half of the nineteenth century. A white wooden portico with six tall columns contrasts with the walls of the house proper, which is of gray cut stone." A somber, fascinating picture, and one likely to put an audience in a proper mood for unusual happenings.

HOMECOMING

When the curtain rises the front of the house is revealed. "It is shortly before sunset and the soft light of the declining sun shines directly on the front of the house. . . . The white columns cast black bars of shadow on the gray walls behind them."

In the distance a village band can be heard faintly playing "John Brown's Body." Nearer a man's voice is heard singing the sea chanty, "Shenandoah." The singer is Seth Beckwith, the Mannon's gardener and man of all work; "an old man of seventy-five with white hair and beard, tall, raw-boned and stoop-shouldered."

Seth, serving as a sort of guide, is bringing in Amos Ames, Louisa Ames, his wife, and Minnie, a cousin. "These three are types of townsfolk rather than individuals, a chorus representing the town come to look and listen and spy on the rich and exclusive Mannons."

Photo by Vandamm Studio, New York.

"MOURNING BECOMES ELECTRA"

Christine: What are you moon-gazing at? Puritan maidens shouldn't peer too inquisitively into spring. Isn't beauty an abomination and love a vile thing?

(Alla Nazimova and Alice Brady)

Seth is in jubilant mood. There has been report of Lee's surrender and it is Seth's opinion that it will be the patriotic duty of every man in town to celebrate. But he is not forgetting his duties as guide.

"I promised Amos I'd show ye the sights when you came to visit him," he tells Minnie. " 'Tain't everyone can git to see the Mannon place close to. They're strict about trespassin'."

MINNIE—My! They must be rich! How'd they make their money?

SETH—Ezra's made a pile, and before him, his father, Abe Mannon, he inherited some and made a pile more in shippin'. Started one of the fust Western Ocean packet lines.

MINNIE—Ezra's the General, ain't he?

SETH (*proudly*)—Ayeh. The best fighter in the hull of Grant's army!

MINNIE—What kind is he?

SETH (*boastfully expanding*)—He's able, Ezra is! Folks think he's cold-blooded and uppish, 'cause he's never got much to say to 'em. But that's only the Mannons' way. They've been top dog around here for near on two hundred years and don't let folks fergit it.

MINNIE—How'd he come to jine the army if he's so rich?

SETH—Oh, he'd been a soldier afore this war. His paw made him go to West P'int. He went to the Mexican war and come out a major. Abe died that same year and Ezra give up the army and took holt of the shipping business here. But he didn't stop there. He learned law on the side and got made a judge. Went in fur politics and got 'lected mayor. He was mayor when this war broke out but he resigned to once and jined the army again. And now he's riz to be General. Oh, he's able, Ezra is!

AMES—Ayeh. This town's real proud of Ezra.

LOUISA—Which is more'n you kin say fur his wife. Folks all hates her! She ain't the Mannon kind. French and Dutch descended, she is. Furrin-lookin' and queer. Her father's a doctor in New York, but he can't be much of one 'cause she didn't bring no money when Ezra married her.

SETH (*his face growing grim—sharply*)—Never mind her. We ain't talkin' 'bout her. (*Then abruptly changing the subject.*) Wall, I've got to see Vinnie. I'm goin' round by the kitchen. You wait here. And if Ezra's wife starts to run you off fur trespassin', you tell her I got permission from Vinnie to show you round.

Seth has left them staring gawkily at the house. Christine Mannon comes through the front door to the top of the steps. "Christine is a tall, striking-looking woman of forty, but she appears younger. She has a fine, voluptuous figure and she moves with a flowing animal grace. . . . Her face is unusual, handsome rather than beautiful. One is struck at once by the strange impression it gives in repose of being not living flesh but a wonderfully life-like pale mask, in which only the deep-set eyes, of a dark violet blue, are alive. . . . She stands and listens defensively, as if the music held some meaning that threatened her."

Christine, with a shrug of disdain, has walked off into the garden. Immediately there is much buzzing in awed whispers among the watchers. Christine is handsome, they allow; Christine is too furrin-lookin'; Christine's mask-like face is the Mannon-look.

"They don't want folks to guess their secrets." That's Ames's opinion. "And they got a lot of skeletons in the closet," adds Louisa. There's a story about Abe's brother David marryin' a French Canuck nurse girl after he'd got her into trouble—

The appearance of Lavinia Mannon in the doorway stops that bit of scandal. Lavinia, at twenty-three, is tall, like her mother. "Her body is thin, flat-breasted and angular, and its unattractiveness is accentuated by her plain black dress. Her movements are stiff and she carries herself with a wooden, square-shouldered, military bearing. She has a flat, dry voice . . . but in spite of these dissimilarities one is immediately struck with her facial resemblance to her mother."

Lavinia stands at the edge of the portico, watching her mother in the garden with eyes that "are bleak and hard with intense, bitter enmity." She, too, hears the music of the distant band. Her eyes "light up with a grim satisfaction, and an expression of strange, vindictive triumph comes into her face." She is quite oblivious to Seth and his friends until Seth, sending the others into the orchard to wait for him, speaks to her.

Seth brings news. According to the telegraph feller, Lee's a goner sure, this time. Which means that Lavinia's father will be coming home soon now. Good news for Lavinia, Seth takes it. Also he is inquisitive. Where's she been gallivantin' the last couple days? New York? There's where he thought she was, though she'd told the servants different.

Seth also would like to warn Lavinia about something which may be nothin' and again may be somethin'. It has to do with Captain Brant— Peter and Hazel Niles have come up the drive. Seth's warning must wait.

The Niles are brother and sister. Hazel "is a pretty, healthy girl of nineteen . . . frank, innocent, amiable and good." Peter is very like Hazel in character—straightforward, guileless and good-natured. "A heavily built young fellow of twenty-two . . . he wears the uniform of an artillery captain in the Union Army."

Peter and Hazel's call is casual. Peter has time to stay, if that would please Lavinia, but Hazel has come principally to learn if there is news of Lavinia's brother, Orin. Hazel has not heard from Orin in ages, and she is worried. He should be home soon, now, in view of the good news. And Peter, his wound healed, will not have to go back.

Hazel, without much subtlety, decides she had better be going to give the embarrassed Peter a chance to talk with Lavinia. But even alone Peter can make little headway. Lavinia is in no mood to talk of love, which would be Peter's subject.

"I don't know anything about love," declares Lavinia, brusquely. "I don't want to know anything! I hate love! . . . I can't marry anyone, Peter. I've got to stay at home. Father needs me."

"He has your mother," suggests Peter.

"He needs me more," Lavinia answers, sharply.

Lavinia is fond of Peter. She hopes earnestly that nothing will be permitted to spoil the long friendship that has existed between the four of them—Lavinia, Peter, Hazel and Orin. Nor is she at all interested in anyone else. Certainly not in that—that clipper ship Captain Brant. She fairly hates the sight of Brant.

PETER—Gosh! I'm glad to hear you say that, Vinnie. I was afraid—I imagined girls all liked him. He's such a darned romantic-looking cuss. Looks more like a gambler or a poet than a ship captain. I got a look as he was coming out of your gate— I guess it was the last time he was here. Funny, too. He reminded me of someone. But I couldn't place who it was.

LAVINIA (*startled, glances at him uneasily*)—No one around here, that's sure. He comes from out West. Grandfather Hamel happened to meet him in New York and took a fancy to him, and Mother met him at Grandfather's house.

PETER—Who is he anyway, Vinnie?

LAVINIA—I don't know much about him in spite of what you think. Oh, he did tell me the story of his life to make himself out romantic, but I didn't pay much attention. He went to sea when he was young and was in California for the Gold Rush. He's sailed all over the world—he lived on a South Sea Island once, so he says.

PETER (*grumpily*)—He seems to have plenty of romantic experience, if you can believe him!

LAVINIA (*bitterly*)—That's his trade—being romantic! (*Then agitatedly.*) But I don't want to talk any more about him.

PETER (*with a grin*)—Well, I don't either. I can think of more interesting subjects.

Christine Mannon comes from the garden with a large bunch of flowers. Sensing her presence Lavinia whirls and faces her. "For a moment mother and daughter stare into each other's eyes. In their whole tense attitudes is clearly revealed the bitter antagonism between them. But Christine quickly recovers herself and her air resumes its disdainful aloofness."

Christine has been wondering where Lavinia has been. She is pleased to see Peter and surprised that Lavinia lets him go so casually. A rude way, thinks Christine, for Lavinia to treat her most devoted swain.

Christine is also in doubt as to Lavinia's treatment of her. On returning from New York, the night before, Christine had found that Lavinia had locked herself in her room. This convinced Christine that her daughter had been intentionally trying to avoid her. There were later reports that Lavinia was suffering from a headache.

No, Lavinia was not suffering from a headache, she admits. She wanted to be alone—to think things over. Did her mother find Grandfather better in New York? He seems to have been sick a good deal the last year.

Yes, Christine reports, Grandfather is much better. He'll soon be going his rounds again. And then, as if anxious to change the subject, she draws attention to the flowers.

"I've been to the greenhouse to pick these," she says. "I felt our tomb needed a little brightening. (*She nods scornfully toward the house.*) Each time I come back after being away it appears more like a sepulchre! The 'whited' one of the Bible— pagan temple front stuck like a mask on Puritan gray ugliness! It was just like old Abe Mannon to build such a monstrosity—as a temple for his hatred. (*Then with a little mocking laugh.*) Forgive me, Vinnie. I forgot you liked it. And you ought too. It suits your temperament."

CHRISTINE— . . . By the way, before I forget, I happened to run into Captain Brant on the street in New York. He said he was coming up here today to take over his ship and asked me if he might drop in to see you. I told him he could—and stay to supper with us. (*Without looking at* LAVINIA, *who is staring at her with a face grown grim and hard.*) Doesn't that please you, Vinnie? Or do you remain true to your one and only beau, Peter?

LAVINIA—Is that why you picked the flowers—because he is coming? (*Her mother does not answer. She goes on with a threatening undercurrent in her voice.*) You have heard the news, I suppose? It means Father will be home soon!

CHRISTINE (*without looking at her—coolly*)—We've had so many rumors lately. This report hasn't been confirmed yet, has it? I haven't heard the fort firing a salute.

LAVINIA—You will before long!

CHRISTINE—I'm sure I hope so as much as you.

LAVINIA—You can say that!

CHRISTINE (*concealing her alarm—coldly*)—What do you mean? You will kindly not take that tone with me, please! (*Cuttingly.*) If you are determined to quarrel, let us go into the house. We might be overheard out here. (*She turns and sees* SETH.) See. There is your old crony doing his best to listen now! I am going in and rest a while.

LAVINIA (*harshly*)—I've got to have a talk with you, Mother —before long!

CHRISTINE (*turning defiantly*)—Whenever you wish. Tonight after the Captain leaves you, if you like. But what is it you want to talk about?

LAVINIA—You'll know soon enough!

CHRISTINE (*staring at her with a questioning dread*)—You always make such a mystery of things, Vinnie.

Christine has gone into the house. Lavinia has motioned to Seth to sit beside her on a bench at the left of the porch. She would know what it is about Captain Brant against which Seth would warn her.

"I want to know all I can about him because—he seems to be calling to court me," explains Lavinia.

"Ayeh," says Seth, managing to convey his entire disbelief of this statement in one word.

Seth's further interest in Captain Brant is inspired by his discovery that the Captain bears a striking resemblance to Lavinia's

father, and an even more striking resemblance to her grandfather's brother, David. Seth also recalls that there was a scandal
in which David Mannon figured which caused the speaking of
his name in the Mannon house to be forbidden by the General.

"I've heard that he loved the Canuck nurse girl who was taking
care of Father's little sister who died, and had to marry her because she was going to have a baby," admits Lavinia, "and that
Grandfather put them both out of the house and then afterwards
tore it down and built this one because he wouldn't live where
his brother had disgraced the family. But what has that old
scandal got to do with—"

"Wait. Right after they was throwed out they married and
went away. There was talk they'd gone out West, but no one
knew nothin' about them afterwards—'ceptin' your grandpaw
let out to me one time she'd had the baby—a boy. He was
cussin' it. (*Then impressively.*) It's about her baby I've been
thinkin', Vinnie."

Captain Brant is about thirty-six years old, Seth goes on, which
would make it right. And his name of Brant might easily be a
contraction of the French girl's name of Brantôme. Brant would
have good reason not to use the name of Mannon around that
house.

Seth is distressed that Lavinia should feel so violently about
the possibility of Brant's family relationship, but he is convinced
she owes it to her father to make sure.

"Catch him off guard sometime and put it up to him strong—
as if you knowed it—and see if mebbe he don't give himself
away. . . ."

When Captain Brant enters from the drive he starts perceptibly at seeing Lavinia, but immediately "puts on his most polite,
winning air."

"One is struck at a glance by the peculiar quality his face in
repose has of being a life-like mask rather than living flesh. He
has a broad, low forehead, framed by coal-black straight hair
which he wears noticeably long. . . . His wide mouth is sensual
and moody. . . . In figure he is tall, broad-shouldered and powerful. . . . He is dressed with an almost foppish extrava-
gance. . . . There is little of the obvious ship captain about him,
except his big, strong hands and his deep voice."

Captain Brant apologizes with exaggerated politeness for walking in on them without ceremony. He counts himself in luck to
find Lavinia and is glad her mother is not there to watch over
them. The Captain is eager to renew a conversation he had with

Lavinia on a certain moonlight night. The recollection is apparently less pleasing to Lavinia.

The news of Lee's surrender being mentioned, Lavinia admits she will be glad to see her father soon again.

"I love Father better than anyone in the world," she declares, intensely. "There is nothing I wouldn't do—to protect him from hurt."

"You care more for him than for your mother?"

"Yes."

"Well, I suppose that's the usual way of it. A daughter feels closer to her father and a son to his mother."

Captain Brant is surprised, however, that Lavinia does not take more after her mother, they are so much alike in many ways. Their hair, for instance. Never, on but one other woman's head, has he seen such hair—that was his mother's.

Looks, insists Lavinia harshly, amount to nothing. Everybody knows she takes after her father and is not a bit like her mother. The Captain is startled that she should apparently feel so deeply in the matter. He finds Lavinia most puzzling. What is it, if he may come straight out, what is it she is holding against him? He wouldn't have bad feeling come between them for anything in the world. Ever since the night of their walk in the moonlight he had been nursing the hope that she liked him. Has she forgotten?

"I haven't forgotten," Lavinia answers, coldly. "Did Mother tell you you could kiss me?"

"What—what do you mean?" The Captain is momentarily worried, but quickly recovers. "Oh! I see! But, come, now, Lavinia, you can't mean, can you, I should have asked her permission?"

"Shouldn't you?"

"Well, I wasn't brought up that strictly," Brant goes on, uneasily. "And, should or shouldn't, at any rate I didn't—and it wasn't the less sweet for that."

Other memories of the night of the moonlight and the walk along the shore assail Captain Brant. He is afraid now he gabbed too much—Lavinia was quite interested, he thought, in his account of his life on the islands of the South Seas.

"I remember your admiration for the naked native women," says Lavinia, in a dry brittle tone. "You said they had found the secret of happiness because they had never heard that love can be a sin."

"So you remember that, do you?" Brant's surprise is plain.

He still finds Lavinia puzzling. "Aye! And they live in as near
the Garden of Paradise before sin was discovered as you'll find
on this earth! . . . The Blessed Isles, I'd call them! You can
forget there all men's dirty dreams of greed and power!"

"And their dirty dreams of love?"

The Captain is startled by Lavinia's attitude. The more so
when she violently repulses his further attempt to recall their
walk and to follow up its attendant excitements. He stands
stunned before her as she all but shouts:

"Don't you touch me! Don't you dare—! You liar—!
You—" As he starts back "she seizes the opportunity to follow
Seth's advice, staring at him with deliberately insulting scorn."

"But I suppose it would be foolish to expect anything but
cheap romantic lies from the son of a low Canuck nurse girl!"

"What's that?" bellows Brant, leaping to his feet. "Belay,
damn you!—or I'll forget you're a woman—no Mannon can
insult her while I—"

"So—it is true— You are her son! Oh!"

Now Brant, fighting to control himself, faces Lavinia with
harsh defiance. He is proud of being his mother's son! His only
shame is his dirty Mannon blood! So, it was because he was
the son of a servant that Lavinia had drawn away from him!
Well, let her know that it was her grandfather's jealousy of his
brother David's love of the Canuck girl that caused him to send
David away and cheat him out of his rightful share of the
Mannon inheritance.

There are other things Lavinia should know, he goes on: Of
how David Mannon had taken to drink, "a coward, like all
Mannons, once he felt the world looked down on him"; of how
David sank down and down, letting his wife support him, until
finally, racked by his own disgrace, he had killed himself.
"They found him hanging in a barn," says Brant. "The only
decent thing he ever did."

"You're lying!" shouts Lavinia. "No Mannon would ever—"

"Oh, wouldn't they?" answers Brant, his anger flaring fresh
and strong. "They are all fine, honorable gentlemen, you think.
Then listen a bit and you'll hear something about another of
them—"

He tells of his mother; of how she sewed for a living and sent
her son to school; of how she was bound to make a gentleman
of him at any cost; of his running away to sea at seventeen,
taking only a part of his mother's name as his own, for he'd have
nothing to do with the name of Mannon. For years he had no

contact with his mother, or news of her, and then he came back to New York to find her dying. She had, in her last desperate trouble, asked Lavinia's fine father for a loan and he never answered the letter.

"She died in my arms," he says, with vindictive passion. "He could have saved her and he deliberately let her die. He's as guilty of murder as anyone he ever sent to the rope when he was a judge."

That he would be revenged on Lavinia's father Brant had sworn on his mother's body. Lavinia, now that she knows, springs to her feet and faces him furiously.

"She is only your means of revenge on Father, is that it?" she cries. ". . . I've found out all I want from you. I'm going to talk to her now. You wait here until I call you."

". . . I don't know what you mean, Lavinia. I swear before God it is only you I—"

From the top of the steps Lavinia stares down at him with such a passion of hatred that he is silenced. Her lips move but she does not speak. She turns stiffly and goes into the house as the curtain falls.

The Ezra Mannon study "is a large room with a stiff, austere atmosphere. The furniture is old Colonial. . . . Above the fireplace, in a plain frame, is a large portrait of Ezra Mannon himself, painted ten years previously. One is at once struck by the startling likeness between him and Adam Brant. . . ."

Lavinia, come directly from her scene with Brant, is standing by the table, "fighting to control herself, her face torn by a look of stricken anguish." For a long moment she stares at her father's portrait.

Christine Mannon comes into the room. "She is uneasy underneath but affects a scornful indignation." Lavinia has sent for her mother. She feels that she has to talk to Christine and she prefers doing it in her father's room. Lavinia knows what has taken her mother to New York; knows, because she has followed Christine—followed her from Grandfather Hamel's New York house to Brant's room. She had talked with a woman in the basement of that house and she knows Christine had been there with Brant many times the last year.

"It was the first time I had ever been there," cries Christine, desperately. "He insisted on my going. He said he had to talk to me about you. He wanted my help to approach your father—"

"How can you lie like that?" Lavinia is furious. "How can you be so vile as to try to use me to hide your adultery?"

"Vinnie!"

"Your adultery, I said."

"No!"

LAVINIA—Stop lying, I tell you! I went upstairs! I heard you telling him—"I love you, Adam"—and kissing him! (*With a cold bitter fury.*) You vile—! You're shameless and evil! Even if you are my mother, I say it! (CHRISTINE *stares at her, overwhelmed by this onslaught.*)

CHRISTINE—I—I knew you hated me, Vinnie—but not as bitterly as that! (*Then with a return of her defiant coolness.*) Very well! I love Adam Brant. What are you going to do?

LAVINIA—How you say that—without any shame! You don't give one thought to Father—who is so good—who trusts you! Oh, how could you do this to Father? How could you?

CHRISTINE (*with strident intensity*)—You would understand if you were the wife of a man you hated!

LAVINIA (*horrified—with a glance at the portrait*)—Don't! Don't say that—before him! I won't listen!

CHRISTINE (*grabbing her by the arm*)—You will listen! I'm talking to you as a woman now, not as mother to daughter! That relationship has no meaning between us! You've called me vile and shameless! Well, I want you to know that's what I've felt about myself for over twenty years, giving my body to a man I—

LAVINIA (*trying to break away from her*)—Stop telling me such things! Let me go! (*She breaks away, shrinking from her mother with a look of sick repulsion.*) You—then you've always hated Father?

CHRISTINE (*bitterly*)—No. I loved him once—before I married him—incredible as that seems now! He was handsome in his lieutenant's uniform! He was silent and mysterious and romantic! But marriage soon turned his romance into—disgust!

LAVINIA (*wincing again—stammers harshly*)—So I was born of your disgust! I've always guessed that, Mother—ever since I was little—when I used to come to you—with love—but you would always push me away! I've felt it ever since I can remember—your disgust! (*Then with a flare-up of bitter hatred.*) Oh, I hate you! It's only right I should hate you!

CHRISTINE (*shaken, defensively*)—I tried to love you. I told myself it wasn't human not to love my own child, born of my body. But I never could make myself feel you were born of any body but his! You were always my wedding night to me—and my honeymoon!

LAVINIA—Stop saying that! How can you be so—! (*Then suddenly—with a strange jealous bitterness.*) You've loved Orin! Why didn't you hate him too?

CHRISTINE—Because by then I had forced myself to become resigned in order to live! And most of the time I was carrying him, your father was with the army in Mexico. I had forgotten him. And when Orin was born he seemed my child, only mine, and I loved him for that! (*Bitterly.*) I loved him until he let you and your father nag him into war, in spite of my begging him not to leave me alone. (*Staring at* LAVINIA *with hatred.*) I know his leaving me was your doing principally, Vinnie!

LAVINIA (*sternly*)—It was his duty as a Mannon to go! He'd have been sorry the rest of his life if he hadn't! I love him better than you! I was thinking of him!

If Orin had not gone to war what has happened never would have happened, Christine insists. With Orin away there was nothing left to her but hate, a desire to be revenged—and a longing for love. It was then that Adam came—

Lavinia is scornful. Adam, she insists, has never loved Christine. He is only being revenged on General Mannon. The son of a low nurse girl—

Christine knows that too. Adam had told her about his mother. Nor does it worry her. But she must know what Lavinia purposes to do. Tell her father?

Lavinia will save her father that disgrace, if she can. She won't tell him anything if Christine will agree to give up Brant, never see him again and become a dutiful wife to General Mannon to make up for the injury she has done him.

Christine can see through that reasoning. It is not to spare her that Lavinia would be so generous, but because she wants Adam Brant for herself.

"If you told your father, I'd have to go away with Adam," she shrills. "He'd be mine still. You can't bear that thought, even at the price of my disgrace, can you?"

"It's your evil mind."

"I know you, Vinnie!" the older woman continues, accusingly. "I've watched you ever since you were little, trying to do exactly what you are doing now! You've tried to become the wife of your father and the mother of Orin! You've always schemed to steal my place!"

Wildly Lavinia denies the charge, and refuses to hear more of it. Again she would know what her mother proposes to do. She can't go away with Adam. If she did her husband would follow them and use all his influence to have Adam blacklisted. He'd lose his command and in the end he'd come to hate the woman who was "an anchor around his neck," a woman five years older than he.

"You devil," Christine shouts, her arm raised threateningly; "you mean little—"

"I wouldn't call names if I were you," answers Lavinia, calmly. "There is one you deserve."

Christine has recovered her calm. She can answer Lavinia now, she says, as a sinister expression comes to her face. She will agree to give up Adam Brant, and to do all Lavinia has demanded, after she has seen Adam once more.

For a moment Lavinia is suspicious. Her mother appears to be giving up her lover rather easily. But Christine had better not try breaking her promise. Both Orin and General Mannon have been put on their guard by letters that Lavinia has already written. She has not told them much—only that Captain Brant had been around a good deal and there had been gossip—

Brant is waiting outside. Let her mother call him and tell him what she has to do. Lavinia will be in the village for half an hour. When she returns she wants to find Brant gone. Otherwise she will not wait even for her father to come home. . . .

Christine, arrived at a decision, finds a bit of paper on the table and writes two words on it. Then she goes to the window and calls Brant. A moment later she has drawn him quietly into the room and closed the door carefully behind him.

Brant is not surprised to hear from Christine that Lavinia knows about them. He had suspected she did. For the moment he is more excited by the discovery of the portrait of General Mannon. "Instantly his body shifts to a fighting tenseness; it is as if he were going to spring at the figure in the painting."

"Does Orin by any chance resemble his father?" demands Brant.

"No! Of course not," Christine is quick to answer, staring at him in some agitation. "What put such a stupid idea in your head?"

"It would be damned queer if you fell in love with me because I recalled Ezra Mannon to you," muses Brant. ". . . I remember that night we were introduced and I heard the name of Mrs. Ezra Mannon! By God, how I hated you then for being his! I thought, by God, I'll take her from him and that'll be part of my revenge! And out of that hatred my love came! It's damned queer, isn't it?"

"Are you going to let him take me from you now, Adam?" she asks, hugging him to her. ". . . You swear you won't, no matter what you must do?"

"By God, I swear it!"

They are agreed that some decision must be made as to what they shall do. The time for skulking and lying is over, Brant is agreed. Christine has a plan. She has made one blunder after another; she has waited patiently hoping, praying, that General Mannon would die. Now that chance is finished.

Brant, uneasy at the inference, suggests that he wait until the General comes home from the front and then confront him with the truth—that Christine, his wife, loves and is going to belong to Marie Brantôme's son! If the General so much as lays a hand on him Brant will kill him.

Nor would he be hanged for murder. Not if he could catch the General alone, where no one would interfere, and let the best man come out alive. Or openly insult him on the street and let him have the first shot. Then he could kill in self-defense.

He could not propose such things, insists Christine, if he were to stop thinking of his revenge and think of her. If he were to attack the General he would only be arrested. If he were to carry her off triumphantly aboard his ship, providing he could keep his ship, her husband would never divorce her, for spite. Her life would be ruined and soon he, her lover, would grow to hate her.

"If he had only been killed, we could be married now and I would bring you my share of the Mannon estate," calculatingly suggests Christine. "That would only be justice. It's yours by right. It's what his father stole from yours."

"That's true enough, damn him!"

"You wouldn't have to worry about commands or owners' favors then. You could buy your own ship and be your own master!"

To own his own clipper! That has always been Brant's dream. With his own ship what a honeymoon he could take Christine on—to China, and through the South Pacific—

"Yes—but Ezra is alive!" Christine reminds him.

"I know it's only a dream," he admits, gloomily.

"You can have your dream—and I can have mine," she says slowly. "There is a way."

General Mannon has written from the front complaining of pains about his heart, Christine hurriedly reports. Among the neighbors she has let it be known that her husband has heart trouble. She has even consulted the Mannon's family doctor. Ever since she has realized her husband must soon be coming home Christine has been thinking of what, she feels, she would fatefully be moved to do.

"If he died suddenly now, no one would think it was anything but heart failure," she whispers. "I've been reading a book in Father's medical library. I saw it there one day a few weeks ago—it was as if some fate in me forced me to see it! (*She reaches in the sleeve of her dress and takes out the slip of paper she had written on.*) I've written something here. I want you to get it for me. (*His fingers close on it mechanically. He stares at it with a strange, stupid dread. She hurries on so as not to give him time for reflection.*) The work on the 'Flying Trades' is all finished, isn't it? You sail for Boston tomorrow, to wait for cargo?"

"Aye."

"Get this at some druggist's down by the water-front the minute you reach there. You can make up some story about a sick dog on your ship. As soon as you get it, mail it to me here. I'll be on the lookout, so Vinnie will never know it came. Then you must wait on the 'Flying Trades' until you hear from me or I come to you—afterward!"

"But how can you do it—so no one will suspect?"

"He's taking medicine. I'll give him his medicine. Oh, I've planned it carefully."

Vinnie will not suspect anything, Christine insists. Nor Orin. Orin will believe anything she wants him to. Everybody will think the excitement of coming home and the reaction were too much for a weak heart.

Brant is still reluctant. Poison is a coward's trick. But soon his remembered revenge and his hatred of the Mannons, and now his jealousy, have been stung into action by Christine's tauntings.

"I'm a damned fool to have any feeling about how Ezra Mannon dies," Brant concludes.

"Now you're the man I love again, not a hypocritical Mannon," exultantly declares Christine, throwing her arms about his neck and kissing him passionately.

The boom of a cannon is heard. It may be a salute from the fort in honor of the General's homecoming. . . .

Brant has hurried away. Christine has watched him from the window as he disappears down the driveway.

"You'll never dare leave me now, Adam—for your ships, or your sea, or your naked Island girls—when I grow old and ugly!" she mutters.

"She turns back from the window. Her eyes are caught by the eyes of her husband in the portrait and for a moment she stares back into them, as if fascinated. Then she jerks her glance away and, with a little shudder she cannot repress, turns and walks quickly from the room and closes the door behind her." The curtain falls.

A week later, still dressed severely in black, Lavinia is sitting stiffly upright on the top step of the Mannon portico. It is around nine o'clock at night. "The light of a half moon falls on the house, giving it an unreal, detached, eerie quality."

Down the drive Seth Beckwith can be heard singing his favorite sea chantey as he approaches. Doing his patriotic duty by historical events has kept Seth busy. First he celebrated Lee's surrender, then he drowned his sorrow over Lincoln's assassination, and soon he will be celebrating General Mannon's return, the General being expected any day now. . . .

Back of them in the door, Christine Mannon appears. "She is dressed in a gown of green velvet that sets off her hair. . . . She closes the door and comes into the moonlight at the edge of the steps. . . . Lavinia does not turn or give any sign of knowing her mother is behind her."

"What are you moongazing at?" Christine demands, her tone dry and mocking. "Puritan maidens shouldn't peer too inquisitively into Spring. Isn't beauty an abomination and love a vile thing?" She laughs tauntingly. "Why don't you marry Peter? You don't want to be left an old maid, do you?"

"You needn't hope to be rid of me that way," answers Lavinia, quietly. "I'm not marrying anyone. I've got my duty to Father."

"Duty! How often I've heard that word in this house," answers Christine. "Well, you can't say I didn't do mine all these years. But there comes an end."

"And there comes another end—and you must do your duty again." Lavinia's tone is grim.

There is further understanding between them, and added warnings against attempted trickery. There is talk of the possibility of General Mannon's imminent return. He probably is the beau for whom Lavinia is waiting in the moonlight, Christine suggests. And then the sound of footsteps on the drive excites them. A moment later General Mannon walks into the yard, pausing in the shadows.

"He is a tall, spare, big-boned man of fifty, dressed in the uniform of a Brigadier-General. One is immediately struck by the mask-like look of his face in repose, more pronounced in him than in the others. He is exactly like the portrait in his study . . . except that his face is more lined and lean and the hair and beard are grizzled. . . . His air is brusque and authoritative."

Lavinia, with a cry of joy, has rushed forward and thrown her arms about her father. Her eyes fill with tears that will not be controlled, though the General reminds her that she has been taught never to cry.

Mannon's exchange of greetings with Christine is formal and embarrassed, though he gallantly finds his wife younger and prettier, even, than he had remembered her.

Both Christine and Lavinia are solicitous for the General's comfort. Christine suggests that he may like to rest a time on the porch. Lavinia is sure the dampness is not good for her father. He must be hungry. Let him go inside while she finds food for him.

Mannon, "really reveling in his daughter's coddling, but embarrassed before his wife," decides on the porch for a spell. He has leave for only a few days, he explains. Then he must go back to dismiss his brigade.

"The President's assassination is a frightful calamity," he says. "But it can't change the course of events."

"Poor man! It is dreadful he should die just at his moment of victory," declares Lavinia.

"All victory ends in the defeat of death. That's sure. But does defeat end in the victory of death? That's what I wonder."

Christine is eager to have news of Orin. The news is not good. Orin has been wounded. He is in a hospital, but his condition does not warrant the hysteria with which Christine is threatened the moment she hears "her baby" is hurt.

"He's no baby now," Mannon declares, with proud satisfaction. "I've made a man of him. He did one of the bravest things I've seen in the war. He was wounded in the head—a close shave but it turned out only a scratch. But he got brain fever from the shock. He's all right now. He was in a rundown condition, they say at the hospital. I never guessed it. Nerves. I wouldn't notice nerves. He's always been restless. (*Half turn-*

ing to CHRISTINE.)   He gets that from you."

Orin will be able to come home in a few days, according to the doctors.   He has been out of his head a little, acting as though he were a child again and talking to "Mother."

"I don't want you to baby him when he comes home, Christine. It would be bad for him to get tied to your apron strings again."

"You needn't worry.   That passed—when he left me."

Lavinia would know about her Father's heart trouble.   It has been bad, he reports.   The doctor has given orders for him to avoid worry or any over-exertion or excitement.

CHRISTINE (*staring at him*)—You don't look well.   But probably that's because you're so tired.   You must go to bed soon, Ezra.

MANNON—Yes, I want to—soon.

LAVINIA (*watching him jealously*)—No!   Not yet!   Please, Father!   You've only just come!   We've hardly talked at all! (*Defiantly to her mother.*)   How can you tell him he looks tired? He looks as well as I've ever seen him.   (*Then to her father, with a vindictive look at* CHRISTINE.)   We've so much to tell you.   All about Captain Brant.   (CHRISTINE *is prepared and remains unmoved beneath the searching, suspicious glance of* MANNON.)

MANNON—Vinnie wrote me you'd had company.   I never heard of him.   What business had he here?

CHRISTINE (*with an easy smile*)—You had better ask Vinnie! He's her latest beau!   She even went walking in the moonlight with him!

LAVINIA (*with a gasp*)—Oh!

MANNON (*now jealous and suspicious*)—I notice you didn't mention that in your letter, young lady!

LAVINIA—I only went walking once with him—and that was before—

MANNON—Before what?

LAVINIA—Before I knew he's the kind who chases after every woman he sees.

MANNON (*angrily to* CHRISTINE)—A fine guest to receive in my absence!

LAVINIA—I believe he even thought Mother was flirting with him.   That's why I felt it my duty to write you.   You know how folks in town gossip, Father.   I thought you ought to warn Mother she was foolish to allow him to come here.

MANNON—Foolish!   It was downright—!

CHRISTINE (*coldly*)—I would prefer not to discuss this until we are alone, Ezra—if you don't mind! And I think Vinnie is extremely inconsiderate the moment you're home—to annoy you with such ridiculous nonsense. (*She turns to* LAVINIA.) I think you've done enough mischief. Will you kindly leave us?

LAVINIA—No.

MANNON (*sharply*)—Stop your squabbling, both of you! I hoped you had grown out of that nonsense! I won't have it in my house!

LAVINIA (*obediently.*)—Yes, Father.

MANNON—It must be your bedtime, Vinnie.

LAVINIA—Yes, Father. (*She kisses him—excitedly.*) Oh, I'm so happy you're here! Don't let Mother make you believe I— You're the only man I'll ever love! I'm going to stay with you!

MANNON (*with gruff tenderness*)—I hope so. I want you to remain my little girl—for a little longer, at least. (*Then suddenly catching* CHRISTINE'S *scornful glance.*) March now!

LAVINIA—Yes, Father. (*Behind her mother.*) Don't let anything worry you, Father. I'll always take care of you. (*She goes in the house.*)

General Mannon is pacing up and down self-consciously. Christine would have him sit beside her and tell her quite frankly what it is of which he suspects her. She has felt his distrust from the moment he arrived. It must be all on account of a stupid letter Vinnie had no business to write.

It is true, admits Christine, that she had met Adam Brant at her father's. When he had later called at the Mannon home she could not, out of respect to Father, be rude to him. There had been no gossip. All the talk in town was that he had come to see Vinnie.

General Mannon is regretful now that he has been unjustly suspicious. Awkwardly he would try to make up for his gruffness. He finds Christine's interest in him, her fear something might have happened to him, quite touching.

"I've dreamed of coming home to you, Christine!" His voice is trembling with desire and a feeling of strangeness and awe. He touches her hair with an awkward caress. "You're beautiful! You look more beautiful than ever—and strange to me. I don't know you. You're younger. I feel like an old man beside you. Only your hair is the same—your strange, beautiful hair I always—"

But Christine, with a start of repulsion, draws away from his hand. She doesn't mean to be unappreciative—but she is ner-

vous. Later, as he would explain his feelings, Christine sits with
eyes closed. Some strangeness he feels about her keeps him from
touching her. Perhaps it is because he can't get used to home,
after the feel of camps, with thousands of men around.

"Don't keep your eyes shut like that," he cries, suddenly.
"Don't be so still!" Then, as she opens her eyes, he continues,
explosively. "God, I want to talk to you, Christine! I've got to
explain some things—inside me—to my wife—try to, anyway!
(*He sits down beside her.*) Shut your eyes again! I can talk
better. It has always been hard for me to talk—about feelings.
I never could when you looked at me. Your eyes were always
so—so full of silence! That is, since we've been married. Not
before, when I was courting you. They used to speak then.
They made me talk—because they answered."

Christine would stop these confessions, but General Mannon is
determined to go on. It was probably seeing so much of death
in the war that set him thinking. Queer, too, that death should
make him think of life. But that has always been the Mannons' way of thinking. "They went to the meeting house on
Sabbaths and meditated on Death. Life was a dying. Being
born was starting to die. Death was being born."

CHRISTINE (*staring at him with a strange terror*)—What has
this talk of death to do with me?

MANNON (*avoiding her glance—insistently*)—Shut your eyes
again. Listen and you'll know. (*A note of desperation in his
voice.*) I thought about my life—lying awake nights—and about
your life. In the middle of battle I'd think maybe in a minute
I'll be dead. But my life as just me ending, that didn't appear
worth a thought one way or another. But listen, me as your
husband being killed, that seemed queer and wrong—like something dying that had never lived. Then all the years we've been
man and wife would rise up in my mind and I would try to look
at them. But nothing was clear except that there'd always been
some barrier between us—a wall hiding us from each other! I
would try to make up my mind exactly what that wall was but
I never could discover. (*With a clumsy appealing gesture.*) Do
you know?

CHRISTINE (*tensely*)—I don't know what you're talking about.

Doggedly General Mannon blunders on. Probably she has
always known that she didn't love him; he had had a feeling that
she had grown to hate him. When he went to the Mexican war,

maybe she was hoping he would get killed! When he came back she had turned to her new baby, Orin. She had driven him to depend on Vinnie. But a daughter is not a wife. In time he had turned to his work in the world and left her alone. That's why he had become a judge, and a mayor, "and such vain truck." All to keep his mind from dwelling on what he had lost—her love as he had known it before they were married. Now he has come home—

"I came home to surrender to you—what's inside me." Mannon protests. "I love you. I loved you then, and all the years between, and I love you now."

"Ezra! Please!"

"I want that said! Maybe you've forgotten it. I wouldn't blame you. I guess I haven't said it or showed it much—ever. Something queer in me keeps me mum about the things I'd like most to say—keeps me hiding the things I'd like to show. . . . You'll find I have changed, Christine. I'm sick of death! I want life! Maybe you could love me now! (*In a note of final desperate pleading.*) I've got to make you love me!"

"For God's sake, stop talking!" Christine has pulled her hand away from him and leaped to her feet. "I don't know what you're saying," she cries. "Leave me alone! What must be, must be! You make me weak." Then abruptly, she adds: "It's getting late."

Mannon is terribly wounded. Again he is the stiff soldier, in armor. Mechanically he ascends the steps. It is, he agrees, time to turn in.

Christine is worried. Now she would explain that it was only his waste of words that she would stop. There is no wall between them. She loves him. That is something he would give his soul to believe. He is holding her convulsively to him when Lavinia appears in the doorway.

Lavinia wears a dressing gown over her nightdress. She shrinks from the sight of her father's embrace. When he curtly questions her coming she pleads wakefulness and her thought of taking a little walk on so fine a night.

"We are just going to bed. Your father is tired," explains Christine, as she draws General Mannon after her, up the stairs.

The door has closed upon the General's good-night. Soon there is a streak of light beneath the shutters of the bedroom on the second floor. Lavinia turns toward that light.

"I hate you!" she cries in anguish. "You steal even Father's love from me again! You stole all love from me when I was

born! (*Then almost with a sob, hiding her face in her hands.*)
Oh, Mother! Why have you done this to me? What harm had
I done you? (*Then looking up at the window again—with passionate disgust.*) Father, how can you love that shameless har-
lot? (*Then frenziedly.*) I can't bear it! I won't! It's my duty
to tell him about her! I will!"

Desperately she calls to her father. The shutters open and
General Mannon, leaning out, sharply demands to know what
it is she wants. Lamely she stammers that she had forgotten to
say good night. The General is exasperated. Then again his
mood grows gentle.

"Oh—all right—good night, Vinnie. Get to bed soon, like a
good girl."

"Yes, Father. Good night."

"He goes back into the bedroom and pulls the shutter closed.
She stands staring fascinatedly up at the window, wringing her
hands in a pitiful desperation." The curtain falls.

In Ezra Mannon's bedroom a big four-poster, head against the
rear wall, is conspicuous in the shadows of early dawn. "Christine's form can be made out, a pale ghost in the darkness, as she
slips slowly and stealthily from the bed."

General Mannon has not been able to sleep, either. He has
raised himself in the bed, sits with his back against the head-
board, and would have Christine light a candle that they may
talk.

Christine prefers the dark, though not, as he charges, so she
cannot see her "old man of a husband."

General Mannon is eager to explain, apologetically, that he
has not meant things that he has said. He feels strange, but not
about his heart, if that is what she was hoping for. It is something troubling his mind—"as if something in me was listening,
watching, waiting for something to happen." . . . "This is not
my house. This is not my room nor my bed. They are empty—
waiting for someone to move in! You are not my wife! You are
waiting for something!"

"What would I be waiting for?" demands Christine shrilly.

"For death—to set you free."

Christine will have none of his crazy suspicions. She resents
his nagging. It has not been so long since he was satisfied with
her as his wife.

"You were lying to me tonight as you have always lied," Mannon charges, "as if all the bitterness and hurt in him had sud-

denly burst its dam." "You were only pretending love. You let me take you as if you were a nigger slave I had bought at auction! You made me appear a lustful beast in my own eyes!— as you've always done since our first marriage night! I would feel cleaner now if I had gone to a brothel! I would feel more honor between myself and life!"

Christine's voice grows strident as she answers him, working herself gradually into a passion and becoming deliberately taunting. "You want the truth?" she cries. "You've guessed it! You've used me, given me children, but I've never once been yours! I never could be! And whose fault is it? I loved you when I married you! I wanted to give myself! But you made me so I couldn't give! You filled me with disgust!"

With calculating cruelty Christine continues, ignoring Mannon's almost pleading demand that she be quiet. Yes, she has lied—lied about everything; lied about Adam Brant; lied about her trips to New York. It was Adam she had gone to see. It was she, not Vinnie, Adam had come to visit. Adam is her lover! She loves him! Now he knows the truth!

"He's what I've longed for all these years with you—a lover!"

"You—you whore—I'll kill you!"

Mannon has struggled out of bed, his face distorted in frenzy. Suddenly he falls back, groaning, doubled up. Christine, "with savage satisfaction, hurries through the doorway into her room and immediately returns with a small box in her hand." Now he has called for his medicine. Pretending to look for it Christine takes a pellet from the box, hands it to him with a glass of water and, when he opens his mouth before her, puts the pellet on his tongue and presses the glass of water to his lips.

Suddenly a wild look of terror comes over Mannon's face. "That's not my medicine!" he cries. Christine, the hand with the box held out behind her, shrinks back from him until she can drop the medicine on the table top, and hold both hands before his eyes, "fixed on her in a terrible accusing glare."

"Help! Vinnie!" he calls, wildly, and falls back in a coma, breathing heavily. Christine in terror snatches up the bottle of pellets from the table.

At that moment Lavinia, a dressing gown over her nightdress, appears suddenly in the doorway. She is dazed and frightened.

"I had a horrible dream—I thought I heard Father calling me —it woke me up—"

"He just had—an attack," stammers Christine, trembling with

guilty terror.

Lavinia has hurried to her father's side. Her arms about him give him sufficient support to straighten up in a sitting position. He is glaring at Christine as he laboriously raises an arm and points an accusing finger at her.

"She's guilty—not medicine!" he mutters, and falls back limply.

Frightened, Lavinia feels his pulse and puts her ear against his heart.

"He's dead!" she says.

"Dead?" repeats Christine, mechanically, and adds, in a strange flat tone: "I hope—he rests in peace!"

The women are facing each other, hatred and suspicion in Lavinia's eyes. Now she has become accusing. Why did her father point at Christine as he did? Why did he say she was guilty?

Because she had told him that Adam was her lover, explains Christine. Then she murdered him, Lavinia cries. She did it on purpose. And that other accusing charge: "Not medicine?" What did that mean? Christine doesn't know. Surely Lavinia is not accusing her mother—

Christine, her strength gone, muttering that she feels faint, tries to make her way to her own room. Suddenly her knees buckle under her and she falls in a dead faint. As her hand strikes the floor the box of pellets slips out onto the rug.

Lavinia bends over Christine until she is satisfied her mother has only fainted. Her anguished hatred has returned and she speaks with strident denunciation as she starts to her feet:

"You murdered him just the same—by telling him!" she repeats. "I suppose you think you'll be free to marry Adam now! But you won't! Not while I'm alive! I'll make you pay for your crime! I'll find a way to punish you!"

She starts to her feet. Her eyes fall on the little box. "Immediately she snatches it up and stares at it, the look of suspicion changing to a dreadful, horrified certainty. Then with a shuddering cry she shrinks back along the side of the bed, the box clutched in her hand, and sinks on her knees by the head of the bed, and flings her arms around the dead man. With anguished beseeching—"

"Father! Don't leave me alone! Come back to me! Tell me what to do!"

THE CURTAIN FALLS

THE HUNTED

Two days after the death of Ezra Mannon, the Bordens, the Hills, and Dr. Blake, townsfolk, are calling at the Mannon House. It is a moonlight night. There are funeral wreaths, one on the column to the right of the steps, another on the door. "The house has the same strange eerie appearance it had before."

The neighbors call their good nights to Mrs. Mannon and pause at the foot of the steps to compare notes on their call. The women, Mrs. Borden and Miss Hill, are agreed there is something queer about Christine Mannon and always has been. Yet, in her grief, they find her a more sympathetic figure than she had been, and there is general agreement that she has always seemed a dutiful wife.

As to Lavinia, her taking her father's death as she does, appearing "as cold and calm as an icicle," is no surprise to anyone who knows the Mannons. That's the Mannon way.

The men feel the loss of Ezra Mannon, and the town is certain to feel it. Yet his passing, as Dr. Blake points out, was to be expected. From what Mrs. Mannon had told him of Ezra's symptoms while he was at the front it could not have been anything but angina. Dr. Blake didn't have to examine Ezra to know that much.

"The minute they sent for me I knew what'd happened. And what she told me about waking up to find him groaning and doubled with pain confirmed it. She'd given him his medicine— it was what I would have prescribed myself—but it was too late. And as for dying his first night home—well, the war was over, he was worn out, he'd had a long, hard trip home—and angina is no respecter of time and place. It strikes when it has a mind to."

The women have gone on ahead. Dr. Blake holds Borden back to explain more intimately his reasons for concluding that Ezra Mannon's death was easily traceable to natural causes. Love is what killed Ezra, Dr. Blake suspects. "Leastways love made angina kill him, if you take my meaning," the doctor explains. "She's a damned handsome woman and he'd been away a long time. Only natural between man and wife—but not the treatment I'd recommend for angina. He should have known better, but—well—he was human."

"Can't say I blame him," confesses Borden. "She's a looker! I don't like her and never did, but I can imagine worse ways of dying!" They are chuckling as they start after the women.

Christine Mannon comes from the house to stand at the top of the steps. "She is obviously in a terrible state of strained nerves. Beneath the mask-like veneer of her face there are deep lines about her mouth, and her eyes burn with a feverish light."

Hazel Niles follows Christine from the house. Hazel would be sympathetic and helpful. Christine is breaking under the strain of the stream of people come to stare at the dead. Yet she feels she must not appear old and haggard to Orin when he comes. Christine knows that Hazel loves Orin, too, and she is glad. She will do all she can to help Hazel marry Orin. She is eager to get Orin away from Vinnie's possessiveness and she knows Vinnie has always been jealous of Orin's interest in Hazel. They must work together to keep Orin from coming again under Vinnie's influence. Hazel never suspected that of Vinnie. She can't believe it now.

"You are genuinely good and pure of heart, aren't you?" says Christine, staring at Hazel, strangely. "I was like you once— long ago—before—" There is a note of bitterness and longing in her voice. "If I could only have stayed as I was then! Why can't all of us remain innocent and loving and trusting? But God won't leave us alone. He twists and wrings and tortures our lives with others' lives until—we poison each other to death! (*Seeing* HAZEL'S *look, catches herself—quickly.*) Don't mind what I said! Let's go in, shall we? I would rather wait for Orin inside."

A moment later Orin Mannon, with Peter Niles and Lavinia, comes up the drive. Orin closely resembles both Ezra Mannon and Adam Brant. "There is the same lifelike mask quality of his face in repose, the same aquiline nose, heavy eyebrows, swarthy complexion, thick, straight, black hair, light hazel eyes. . . . He is about the same height as Mannon and Brant, but his body is thin and his swarthy complexion sallow. He wears a bandage around his head high up on his forehead. . . . When he speaks it is jerkily, with a strange, vague, preoccupied air. But when he smiles naturally his face has a gentle boyish charm which makes women immediately want to mother him."

Orin is hurt and disappointed not to find his mother waiting for him. He had dreamed so often of coming home through the endless months of war. He was out of his head so long he thinks perhaps he is still dreaming. Did the house always look so ghostly and dead—like a tomb? It is a tomb, now, Lavinia reminds her brother.

For the moment Orin had forgotten his father. It is not easy for him to get used to the thought of his being dead. "You wouldn't understand unless you had been at the front," Orin explains. "I hardened myself to expect my own death and everyone else's, and think nothing of it. I had to—to keep alive! It was part of my training as a soldier under him. He taught it to me, you might say! So when it's his turn he can hardly expect . . . My mind is still full of ghosts. I can't grasp anything but war, in which he was so alive. He was the war to me— the war that would never end until I died. I can't understand peace—his end! (*Then with exasperation.*) God damn it, Vinnie, give me a chance to get used to things!"

Orin is sorry for that outburst—but war doesn't improve a man's manners. There is something that Orin wants to know. All that stuff Vinnie had written about Captain Brant. And there is something that Lavinia must tell him, too. But there is no time now. Their mother will be coming in a moment.

"All I want to do is warn you to be on your guard," says Lavinia, grimly. "Don't let her baby you the way she used to and get you under her thumb again. Don't believe the lies she'll tell you! Wait until you've talked to me! Will you promise me?"

"You mean—Mother?" demands Orin, staring at her bewilderedly, and then breaking forth angrily: "What the hell are you talking about, anyway? Are you loony? Honestly, Vinnie, I call that carrying your everlasting squabble with Mother a bit too far! You ought to be ashamed of yourself! (*Then suspiciously.*) What are you being so mysterious about? Is it Brant—?"

Christine can be heard in the hall protesting angrily to Peter that she should have been told Orin had come. Now she has run down the steps and thrown her arms about her son, with a wild cry, "My boy! My baby!"

"Mother! God, it's good to see you!" All Orin's suspicions have been forgotten. Suddenly he pushes her from him. "But, you're different! What's happened to you?"

"I? Different? I don't think so, dear. Certainly I hope not— to you!" A forced smile has disappeared. She touches the bandage on his head, tenderly. "Your head! Does it pain dreadfully? You poor darling, how you must have suffered! (*She kisses him.*) But it's all over now, thank God. I've got you back again! Let's go in. There's someone else waiting who will be so glad to see you."

"Remember, Orin!" calls Lavinia, harshly, from the foot of the steps. A look of hate flashes between mother and daughter.

Christine has led Orin into the house, but immediately reappears again to face Lavinia. "For a moment mother and daughter stare into each other's eyes. Then Christine begins haltingly, in a tone she vainly tries to make kindly and persuasive."

"Vinnie, I—I must speak with you a moment—now Orin is here. I appreciate your grief has made you—not quite normal—and I make allowances. But I cannot understand your attitude toward me. Why do you keep following me everywhere—and stare at me like that? I had been a good wife to him for twenty-three years—until I met Adam. I was guilty then, I admit. But I repented and put him out of my life. I would have been a good wife again as long as your father had lived. After all, Vinnie, I am your mother. I brought you into the world. You ought to have some feeling for me. (*She pauses, waiting for some response.*) Don't stare like that! What are you thinking? Surely you can't still have that insane suspicion—that I— (*Then guiltily.*) What did you do that night after I fainted? I—I've missed something—some medicine I take to put me to sleep— (*A grim smile of satisfaction forms on* LAVINIA's *lips.*) Oh, you did—you found—and I suppose you connect that—but don't you see how insane—to suspect—when Doctor Blake knows he died of—! (*Then angrily.*) I know what you've been waiting for—to tell Orin your lies and get him to go to the police! You don't dare do that on your own responsibility—but if you can make Orin—isn't that it? Isn't that what you've been planning the last two days? Tell me!"

Lavinia, her body rigid, her eyes staring into those of her mother, turns finally and walks off into the yard.

Christine, "trembling with dread," hears Orin's voice calling her. By an effort of will she mounts the steps.

"Here I am, dear!" she mutters, as she shuts the door behind her. The curtain falls.

The sitting-room of the Mannon house is "a bleak room without intimacy, with an atmosphere of uncomfortable, stilted stateliness. Portraits of ancestors hang on the walls, . . . one of a grim-visaged minister of the witch-burning era; . . . another of Ezra Mannon's father in the uniform of an officer in Washington's army."

Hazel and Peter are there. Orin's voice can still be heard in the hall, calling, "Mother! Where are you?" Hazel and Peter are agreed that the Mannons have been pretty hard hit.

Now Orin has found his mother and they come to the sitting-room together. Christine is all right again and will not listen to their advice that she go to bed. Orin is in much greater need of rest than she, Christine insists.

Again Orin is reminded that they have forgotten the General. Yet, strangely, to him everything, everybody in the house, seems changed except his father. General Mannon still seems to be the same—and still there.

They would talk to Orin of his own experiences and his own feelings. At first he is inclined to be interestingly reminiscent, but soon the war memories are horrible and he is on the verge of hysteria. The next minute he is apologetic and calm.

Lavinia appears quietly in the doorway. She would have Orin come and see his father. So firm and deep is her voice that Orin jumps to his feet, his hand automatically going to the salute. It is as though the dead man had spoken.

Christine would interfere with Lavinia's plans. Orin is all worn out. He should have a minute to rest. He should stay with her a little. Then he will come.

Lavinia has returned to her vigil. Hazel and Peter have gone. Christine and Orin are alone. Christine "stands for a moment looking at Orin, visibly bracing herself for the ordeal of the coming interview, her eyes full of tense, calculating fear."

Orin's suspicions will not down. Why has his mother suddenly taken a new interest in Hazel? Why does she now seem eager to marry him off? By her own admission she used to be jealous of Hazel. If his mother has been lonely for him, as she says, why is it she found time to write but twice? How could her letters have been lost, as she suggests, when he received all of Hazel's and all of Vinnie's? Who is this Captain Brant who has been calling on her?

That, insists Christine, is a silly idea. Vinnie must have written him the same nonsense she wrote his father. His father had seen through it plainly enough. Vinnie was jealous of her mother and always had been. Little he knew in what sly ways his sister proved her jealousy.

"I think you will discover before you are much older," ventures Christine, "that there isn't anything your sister will stop at—that she will even accuse me of the vilest, most horrible things!"

"Mother! Honestly, now! You oughtn't to say that!"

"I mean it, Orin. I wouldn't say it to anyone but you. You know that. But we've always been so close, you and I. I feel you are really—my flesh and blood! She isn't! She is your father's! You are a part of me!"

"Yes, I feel that, too, Mother!"

With so much sympathy between them, with memories of the old game they used to play, in which "No Mannons allowed!" was their password, Christine hopes that Orin will be prepared for what lies he is likely to be told by Vinnie. He will find it hard to believe that Vinnie has changed as much as she has since he has been away; she has really gone a little out of her head. Surely he has noticed how queerly his sister acts?

"And her craziness all works out in hatred for me!" explains Christine. "Take this Captain Brant affair, for example— A stupid ship captain I happened to meet at your grandfather's who took it into his silly head to call here a few times without being asked. Vinnie thought he was coming to court her. I honestly believe she fell in love with him, Orin. But she soon discovered he wasn't after her at all!"

"Who was he after—you?"

"Orin! I'd be very angry with you if it weren't so ridiculous!"

After her? An old married woman with two grown children? No, indeed. Captain Brant had hoped to insinuate himself as a family friend in the hope of having General Mannon give him a better ship. And that was all there was to the great Captain Brant scandal.

Orin thinks perhaps he has been a fool, thinking of things as he did. The war has got him silly.

It was Vinnie's fault that he ever went to war, recalls Christine. But, to get back to Captain Brant—Vinnie has it all worked out that he is the son of the nurse girl, Brantôme. Isn't that crazy? And more than that, Vinnie actually accuses Christine of being in love with such a man, and of going to New York to meet him—like a prostitute. Vinnie has even followed her to New York and when she saw her meet a man—her crazy brain immediately decided it was Brant.

"Oh, it's too revolting, Orin! You don't know what I've had to put up with from Vinnie, or you'd pity me!"

ORIN—Good God! Did she tell Father that? No wonder he's dead! (*Then harshly.*) Who was this man you met in New York?

CHRISTINE—It was Mr. Lamar, your grandfather's old friend who has known me ever since I was a baby! I happened to meet him and he asked me to go with him to call on his daughter. (*Then, seeing* ORIN *wavering, pitifully.*) Oh, Orin! You pretend to love me! And yet you question me as if you suspected me, too! And you haven't Vinnie's excuse! You aren't out of your mind! (*She weeps hysterically.*)

ORIN (*overcome by remorse and love*)—No! I swear to you! (*He throws himself on his knees beside her.*) Mother! Please! Don't cry! I do love you! I do!

CHRISTINE—I haven't told you the most horrible thing of all! Vinnie suspects me of having poisoned her father!

ORIN (*horrified*)—What! No, by God, that's too much! If that's true, she ought to be put in an asylum!

CHRISTINE—She found some medicine I take to make me sleep, but she is so crazy I know she thinks— (*Then, with real terror, clinging to him.*) Oh, Orin, I'm so afraid of her! God knows what she might do, in her state! She might even go to the police and— Don't let her turn you against me! Remember you're all I have to protect me! You are all I have in the world, dear!

ORIN (*tenderly soothing her*)—Turn me against you? She can't be so crazy as to try that! But listen. I honestly think you—you're a little hysterical, you know. That—about Father— is all such damned nonsense! And as for her going to the police —do you suppose I wouldn't prevent that—for a hundred reasons—the family's sake—my own sake and Vinnie's, too, as well as yours—even if I knew—

CHRISTINE (*staring at him*)—Knew? Orin, you don't believe—?

ORIN—No! For God's sake! I only meant that no matter what you ever did, I'd love you better than anything in the world and—

CHRISTINE (*pressing him to her and kissing him*)—Oh, Orin, you are my boy, my baby! I love you!

ORIN—Mother! (*Staring into her eyes—with somber intensity.*) I could forgive anything—anything!—in my mother—except that other—that about Brant!

CHRISTINE—I swear to you—!"

ORIN—If I thought that damned—! (*With savage vengefulness.*) By God, I'd show you then that I hadn't been taught to kill for nothing!

Christine is now filled with a new terror for Brant's safety. On her knees she again swears her innocence. For a moment Orin is contrite and soothing. He is sitting on the floor at her feet and remembering again how hungry he was for word from her when her letters were so few and seemed so cold. Orin would dream of his mother then—wonderful dreams of the two of them on South Sea Islands. All of the time he was out of his head the dream would recur.

"There was no one there but you and me," recalls Orin. "And yet I never saw you—that's the funny part. I only felt you all around me. The breaking of the waves was your voice. The sky was the same color as your eyes. The warm sand was like your skin. The whole island was you."

"Oh, if only you had never gone away!" Christine cries out in agonizing tenderness. "If you only hadn't let them take you from me."

"But I've come back," he answers. "Everything is all right now, isn't it?"

"Yes! I didn't mean that. It had to be."

"And I'll never leave you again now. I don't want Hazel or anyone. You're my only girl!"

Christine is stroking Orin's hair tenderly, remembering him as a little boy in his nightdress hiding in the hall to get another good night kiss; trying to agree with him that everything will be all right now, after they get Vinnie married to Peter and there is no one left but the two of them, when the doors open a little and Lavinia steps into the room. She has come to ask Orin again if he is not coming to see their father. And Orin, hastening past her, leaves Lavinia and Christine staring at each other.

They are standing arm's length apart, Lavinia's eyes bleak, her mouth tightened to a thin line; Christine speaking in a low voice, defiantly, almost triumphantly.

"Well, you can go ahead now and tell Orin anything you wish," says Christine. "I've already told him, so you might as well save yourself the trouble. He said you must be insane. I told him how you lied about my trips to New York—for revenge!—because you loved Adam yourself!"

Lavinia shudders faintly, but is immediately stiff and frozen again. Christine smiles tauntingly and goes on, with increasing vehemence—

"So hadn't you better leave Orin out of it? You can't get him to go to the police for you. Even if you convinced him I poisoned your father, you couldn't! He doesn't want—any more than you do, or your father, or any of the Mannon dead—such a public disgrace as a murder trial would be! For it would all come out! Everything! Who Adam is and my adultery and your knowledge of it—and your love for Adam! Oh, believe me, I'll see to it that comes out if anything ever gets to a trial! I'll show you to the world as a daughter who desired her mother's lover and then tried to get her mother hanged out of hatred and jealousy!"

She laughs tauntingly. Lavinia is trembling but her face remains hard and emotionless.

"Go on! Try and convince Orin of my wickedness!" Christine goes on, defiantly. "He loves me! He hated his father! He's glad he's dead! Even if he knew I had killed him, he'd protect me!"

Then all her defiant attitude collapses and she pleads, seized by an hysterical terror, by some fear she has kept hidden.

"For God's sake, keep Orin out of this! He's still sick! He's changed! He's grown hard and cruel! All he thinks of is death! Don't tell him about Adam! He would kill him! I couldn't live then! I would kill myself!"

Lavinia starts and her eyes light up with a cruel hatred. Again her pale lips part as if she were about to say something but she controls the impulse and about-faces abruptly and walks with jerky steps from the room like some tragic mechanical doll.

Christine stares after her—then as she disappears, collapses, catching at the table for support—terrifiedly.

"I've got to see Adam! I've got to warn him!" she mutters as the curtain falls.

The body of General Ezra Mannon, dressed in full uniform, is laid out on a bier in his study. The bier is placed lengthwise directly beneath the portrait of him over the fireplace. Table and chairs have been moved back.

Orin Mannon is standing in back of the bier. He is staring straight before him, the thoughts racing through his mind evidently disturbing. He does not hear Lavinia follow him into the room. He turns his gaze to the face of his father.

"Who are you?" he muses, wonderingly. "Another corpse! You and I have seen fields and hillsides sown with them—and they meant nothing—nothing but a dirty joke life plays on life." He smiles dryly as he continues: "Death sits so naturally on you! Death becomes the Mannons!"

Lavinia's voice startles Orin and stops his ruminations. She must talk with him. To bar interruptions she quietly closes the door. She is amazed that Orin could have grown so calloused. If she had been at the front she would have known why, he answers. He must "grin with bitter mockery" when she reminds him of the pride his father took in his son's bravery. Brave? Heroic? Because he was always volunteering for extra danger

for fear anyone would know he was afraid. Brave? Because
sneaking through the enemy lines he had stabbed two Rebs to
death and forever after thought of war as meaning that you
murdered the same man over and over, and that he finally turned
out to be yourself! Brave? Because in a kind of delirium he
decided to treat war as a joke and walk boldly toward the enemy,
with hand extended, and a lot of fools followed him and cap-
tured a part of the enemy line?

Let Lavinia be proud of him if she wants to. But let her not
waste her breath making charges against his mother. Orin has
been warned. What the hell has got into Lavinia? How can she
think such things?

Lavinia would remind Orin that he knows she never has lied
to him. Even if he thinks she is lying now he will not be able to
doubt the absolute proof. If he will not listen she will go to the
police—as a last resort.

"It would mean that Father's memory and that of all the honorable Mannon dead would be dragged through the horror of a
murder trial! But I'd rather suffer that than let the murder of
our father go unpunished!"

"Good God, do you actually believe—"

"Yes! I accuse her of murder!"

From the bosom of her dress Lavinia produces the box of pellets she had found. She repeats her father's words. She is willing
to swear, her hand on the body of their father, that she is telling
Orin the truth.

Still Orin doubts the story. He would have Lavinia declared
insane. He admits, under her charging, that his mother means a
thousand times more to him than his father ever did.

Lavinia changes her attack. If Orin will not help her punish
the murderer of their father, perhaps he is not so great a coward
he will let his mother's lover escape. That story, too, is a lie, insists Orin.

Proof will be forthcoming very soon, Lavinia is certain. Christine, she says, is frightened out of her wits. She will try to see
Brant the first chance she gets—

There is a knock at the door. Christine's voice, terrified when
she finds the door locked against her, demands that they let her in.

As Orin goes to the door Lavinia lays the box of poison on the
body of General Mannon, over the heart. "Watch her when she
sees that if you want proof!" she says.

Orin opens the door. Christine all but falls into the room.
"She is in a state bordering on collapse. She throws her arms

about Orin as if seeking protection from him." Soon she has sensed from their attitudes what has happened. Lavinia has told her vile lies. Perhaps Lavinia has also threatened to go to the police. Orin must not let his sister do that. Now, with fascinated horror, Christine has turned her eyes toward the corpse.

"No—remember your father wouldn't want—any scandal—he mustn't be worried, he said—he needs rest and peace—" Her voice has taken on "a strange tone of defiant scorn" as she addresses the dead man directly. "You seem the same to me in death, Ezra! You were always dead to me! I hate the sight of death! I hate the thought of it!"

Her eyes have shifted and she sees the box of poison. "She starts back with a stifled scream and stares at it with guilty fear."

ORIN—Mother! For God's sake, be quiet! (*The strain snaps for him and he laughs with savage irony.*) God! To think I hoped home would be an escape from death! I should never have come back to life—from my island of peace! (*Then staring at his mother strangely.*) But that's lost now! You're my lost island, aren't you, Mother? (*He turns and stumbles blindly from the room.* LAVINIA *reaches out stealthily and snatches up the box. This breaks the spell for* CHRISTINE, *whose eyes have been fixed on it hypnotically. She looks wildly at* LAVINIA'S *frozen, accusing face.*)

LAVINIA (*in a cold, grim voice*)—It was Brant who got you this—medicine to make you sleep—wasn't it?

CHRISTINE (*distractedly*)—No! No! No!

LAVINIA—You're telling me it was. I knew it—but I wanted to make sure. (*She puts the box back in the bosom of her dress and walks woodenly from the room.*)

CHRISTINE (*stares after her wildly, then her eyes fasten again on the dead man's face*)—Ezra! Don't let her harm Adam! I am the only guilty one! Don't let Orin—! (*Then, as if she read some answer in the dead man's face, she backs to the door and rushes out.*)

The curtain falls.

Adam Brant's clipper ship, the "Flying Trades," is moored alongside a wharf in South Boston. Unloaded, "her black side rises nine or ten feet above the level of the wharf."

"Only the part aft of the mizzenmast is visible with the curve of the stern at the right." It is the night following Ezra Mannon's funeral.

Adam Brant, dressed in his merchant captain's uniform, is standing by the rail, when Christine, heavily veiled, moves stealthily out of the shadows. A moment later, weakened by the adventure of finding the ship, and him, she lets him hold her close until she is able to explain her errand.

Vinnie knows, Christine tells Adam. Vinnie had come into the room when Mannon was dying— Now, Vinnie and Orin have gone to spend the night with a cousin, hoping the change will do Vinnie good. Christine and Brant must plan what they are to do—

Brant, shaken with the news, takes Christine below decks into his cabin. A moment later Orin and Lavinia come stealthily along the deck. Orin wears a long coat over his uniform and a slouch hat pulled down over his eyes. In the light that comes from a skylight above the cabin his face "becomes distorted with jealous fury." Lavinia has a restraining hand on his arm as the light fades.

When the cabin is lighted the interior is visible through the side of the ship. It is a small compartment, newly painted, a table, a sideboard against the wall, a long narrow couch, like a bunk.

Brant and Christine are seated at the table. She is just finishing her account of General Mannon's dying, and of Vinnie's unexpected interference— How could Christine have foreseen that? There is sweet revenge for Brant in the knowledge that General Mannon knew who he was before he died, but deep dejection, too—

"It serves me right, what has happened and is to happen," he says. "It wasn't that kind of revenge I had sworn on my mother's body! I should have done as I wanted—fought with Ezra Mannon as two men fight for love of a woman!"

It is Christine's idea that they should get away as soon as possible. If not on Brant's ship, as passengers on another. However suspicious Vinnie and Orin might be they would lie to save the family. Once away, thinks Christine, she and Adam can find happiness somewhere. She will make everything up to Adam, in those Blessed Isles he loves so well . . .

Now the hour is late and Christine must go. Her parting with Brant is pitifully intense. A strange feeling assails her, a feeling that she will never see her lover again. Nor does his confidence reassure her. Brant will walk to the end of the wharf with her. Beyond that they might be seen.

On deck Orin has pulled a revolver from under his cloak and

would start furiously after them if Lavinia did not throw herself in his path. Let him run no unnecessary risk. The cabin is the place. Everything must be done as they had planned if there is to be no suspicion—

"Do you think I'm a fool?" protests Orin. "I'm not anxious to be hanged—for that skunk! (*Then with bitter anguish.*) I heard her asking him to kiss her! I heard her warn him against me! (*He gives a horrible chuckle.*) And my island I told her about—which was she and I—she wants to go there—with him! (*Then furiously.*) Damn you! Why did you stop me? I'd have shot his guts out in front of her!"

Lavinia has hidden herself in the cabin. Outside in the alley-way Orin is waiting. A moment later Brant has returned to the cabin. He is standing blinking at the light when Orin steps in the door, and "with a pistol almost against Brant's body, fires twice." When he would fire a third bullet into the prostrate form Lavinia stops him. There is more to do. Let him be breaking into Brant's stateroom and smash things as though robbery were the motive. Let him take anything valuable and throw it overboard later. . . .

They have turned the dead man's pockets inside out, taken his watch and money. Orin still stands over the body, peering into Brant's face—

"This is like my dream," he says. "I've killed him before—over and over."

"Orin!"

He stares at the face of the dead man, fascinated. Lavinia has difficulty in pulling him away. The curtain falls.

The front door of the Mannon house stands open, the night following. Christine is pacing the drive nervously, expectantly.

Lavinia and Orin come up the drive. Christine would escape if she could. They find her with her back against a pillar at the top of the steps. "Lavinia is stiffly square-shouldered, her eyes hard, her mouth grim and set. Orin is in a state of morbid excitement."

Orin would do the talking. He carries a newspaper in his hand. In answer to Christine's stammering inquiry Orin reports his and Vinnie's trip to Boston—not to Blackridge as planned. They had followed Christine to Brant's ship. She need not lie. Orin had seen his mother meet her lover; had heard her warning Brant against him. Let her read the newspaper. It is only a few lines. It tells of the discovery of Brant's murder and the conclusions of the police.

The paper has slipped through Christine's nerveless fingers; she has sunk to the lowest step, moaning and wringing her hands. Orin savagely resents his mother's grief. How can she grieve for "that servant's bastard"? He must have hypnotized her; he must have had her under his influence. How else could she have said or done the things she did?

"I heard you planning to go with him to the island I had told you about—our island—that was you and I!" he wails. . . . Her moaning has begun to exhaust itself. Suddenly Orin has stopped before her. Now he is kneeling beside her, pleadingly. "Mother! Don't moan like that!" he cries. "You're still under his influence! But you'll forget him! I'll make you forget him! I'll make you happy! We'll leave Vinnie here and go away on a long voyage—to the South Seas—"

"Orin!" calls Lavinia, sharply.

Orin does not hear her. Now he is pleading for further understanding at his mother's hands, for her forgiveness. After all that has happened, Lavinia charges, with bitter scorn, he is becoming her crybaby again. Into the house with him—

Meekly, automatically, Orin obeys his sister. It is as though he again heard the voice of his father.

Lavinia turns to her mother. "He paid the just penalty for his crime," she says. "It was the only way true justice could be done."

The words have awakened Christine to agony again. "She springs to her feet and stands glaring at her daughter. . . . In spite of her frozen self-control Lavinia recoils before this. Keeping her eyes on her daughter Christine shrinks backward up the steps. . . . Lavinia suddenly makes a motion as if to hold her back. . . . 'Mother!' she calls wildly, 'what are you going to do? You can live!'"

"Live!" cries Christine, in tones of strident mockery and a burst of shrill laughter. "She raises her hands between her face and her daughter and pushes them out in a gesture of blotting Lavinia forever from her sight," and rushes into the house.

Lavinia, fighting an impulse to follow her, is standing "square-shouldered and stiff, like a grim sentinel in black," when Seth's voice singing his favorite chantey down the drive is punctuated by the sharp report of a pistol. With a shuddering gasp Lavinia has started up the steps. "It is justice!" she mutters. "It is your justice, Father!"

Orin's horrified cry is heard in the house as he finds his mother's body. Now he has rushed wildly to the porch, reproaching himself hysterically for having driven his mother to her death. Why didn't he let her believe that burglars had killed Brant?

"She would have forgotten him! She would have turned to me!" Orin wails, in a frenzy of self-denunciation. "I murdered her!"

"For God's sake, will you be quiet?" demands Lavinia, putting her arms about him. And a moment later she would still his weeping. "Shhh! Shhhh! You have me, haven't you?" she says. "I love you. I'll help you to forget."

Seth, still singing, has come from the drive. He is curious about the shot he has heard. Did Lavinia hear it?

"I want you to go for Dr. Blake," says Lavinia. "Tell him Mother has killed herself in a fit of insane grief over Father's death!"

Seth stares at her, dumbfounded and wondering.

"Will you remember to tell him that?" demands Lavinia, more sharply.

"Ayeh," answers Seth, slowly. "I'll tell him, Vinnie—anything you say."

Seth has gone. Lavinia, stiffly erect, follows Orin into the house as the curtain falls.

THE HAUNTED

It is just after sunset of a summer day two years later. "The afterglow of the sky still bathes the white temple portico of the Mannon house in a crimson light." The shutters are closed and the front door is boarded up.

Five men from the village, led by Seth Beckwith, have just entered the drive. They include Amos Ames, Abner Small, Joe Silva and Ira Markel. As in the first acts of "Homecoming" and "The Haunted" these five are "a chorus of types representing the town as a human background for the drama of the Mannons."

They are all drunk, and Seth carries a stone jug in his hand. "There is a grotesque atmosphere of boys out on a forbidden lark about these old men." They are full of song as well as liquor. Presently it appears from their conversation that a wager has been made.

There is a report in the village that the Mannon house is haunted. Seth has bet Abner Small ten dollars and a gallon of liquor that he (Abner) dare not enter the house and stay there alone until moonrise at ten o'clock. He is to stay in the dark and not even light a match. He is supposed to go in sober, and if he comes out before ten he loses. Still, Seth would not make the conditions too hard. Abner can have one good drink.

Seth has taken the screws out of the temporary door and Small follows him into the house, whistling, as the others laugh and jeer at him. Now talk of ghosts has sent the three back to the jug for more courage.

A moment later Seth reappears. Abner, he reports, "is shying at the furniture covers and his teeth are clickin' a'ready." Seth is shakin' a bit himself, though he denies that charge fiercely.

Peter and Hazel Niles arrive unexpectedly a moment later, and Seth is at some pains to explain that he is just showing a few of his friends around.

Suddenly, with a yell of terror, Abner Small comes crashing out the front door. His face is chalky white.

"God A'mighty," screams Abner, "I heard 'em comin' after me and I run in the room opposite; an' I seed Ezra's ghost— Here's your money, durn ye!"

Seth hurriedly explains the wager to Hazel and Peter. He was hopin' Abner's experience would stop the gossipin' in town. But Seth himself wouldn't stay in the house all night if they'd give him the town.

" 'Tain't bosh, Peter," Seth insists, defensively. "There's been evil in that house since it was first built in hate—and it's kept growin' there ever since, as what's happened there has proved."

Peter and Hazel are there to open the house. They have word that Vinnie and Orin will be home next day, and they want to get the rooms aired out and a fire built. Seth is mystified at the sudden call, but goes dutifully for lanterns. . . .

Lavinia and Orin come quietly in from the drive. Lavinia is the first. "One is at once aware of an extraordinary change in her. Her body, formerly so thin and undeveloped, has filled out. Her movements have lost their square-shouldered stiffness. She now bears a striking resemblance to her mother in every respect, even to being dressed in the green her mother had effected."

Lavinia calls to Orin. There is nothing to be afraid of. Hesitatingly Orin moves forward. "He carries himself woodenly erect now, like a soldier. His movements and attitudes have the statue-like quality that was so marked in his father. He now wears a close-cropped beard, in addition to his mustache, and this accentuates his resemblance to his father."

"You must be brave!" Lavinia warns Orin. "This is the test! You have got to face it. Do you feel you can, now we're here?"

"I'll be all right—with you," Orin answers.

"That's all I wanted—to hear you say that!" Lavinia has taken her brother's hand and is patting it encouragingly. She sees the light through the shutters and suspects Peter and Hazel are there.

Orin still keeps his eyes averted. Lavinia has some trouble getting him to look at the house. There are no ghosts there. Let him be sure of that. He admits that much obediently. But when they reach the spot where his mother had sat moaning the last time he had seen her alive he stops with a shudder.

"That is all past and finished," says Lavinia, quickly. "The dead have forgotten us! We've forgotten them! Come!"

He obeys her woodenly. She gets him up the steps and they pass into the house as the curtain falls.

The living-room of the Mannon house is dimly lighted by two candles that Peter has placed on the mantel. It is a room full of shadows and has "the dead appearance of a room long shut up."

Coming in from the hall Lavinia pauses briefly at the door. Again the change in her appearance is marked. She could easily be mistaken for her mother. "She seems a mature woman sure of her feminine attractiveness."

Lavinia is standing before the portraits of the Mannons. She suddenly addresses them in a harsh resentful voice. "Why do you look at me like that?" she demands. "I've done my duty by you. That's finished and forgotten!"

Orin has followed his sister into the room. His movements are slow, "his face wears a dazed expression, his eyes have a wild, stricken look." Orin has been in the study, thinking to find his mother there. But she was not there. "She's gone forever. She'll never forgive me now," he wails.

Only Lavinia's firmness can calm Orin, his nerves shattered, hysteria assailing him. He must pull himself together, Lavinia insists. He must appear at his best when they meet Peter and Hazel. Lavinia is depending on the love and friendship of their old friends to help them forget. . . . Orin must conquer his spells of morbidity. He must never talk nonsense again, as he promised. Let him remember those long, terrible months on the ship. Let him remember that this homecoming was what he had wanted—this chance to face his ghosts and rid himself forever of the silly guilt about the past. Let him not disappoint her now and become strange again.

"Listen, Orin! I want you to start again—by facing all your ghosts right now!" demands Lavinia, her eyes fixed upon his. "Who murdered Father?"

"Brant did—for revenge—because—"

LAVINIA (*more sternly*)—Who murdered Father? Answer me!
ORIN (*with a shudder*)—Mother was under his influence—
LAVINIA—That's a lie! It was he who was under hers. You know the truth!
ORIN—Yes.
LAVINIA—She was an adulteress and a murderess, wasn't she?
ORIN—Yes.
LAVINIA—If we'd done our duty under the law, she would have been hanged, wouldn't she?
ORIN—Yes.
LAVINIA—But we protected her. She could have lived, couldn't she? But she chose to kill herself as a punishment for her crime —of her own free will! It was an act of justice! You had nothing to do with it! You see that now, don't you? (*As he hesitates, trembling violently.*) Tell me!
ORIN (*hardly above a whisper*)—Yes.
LAVINIA—And your feeling of being responsible for her death was only your morbid imagination! You don't feel it now! You'll never feel it again!
ORIN—No.
LAVINIA (*gratefully—and weakly, her strength gone*)—There! You see! You can do it when you will to!

As Lavinia kisses Orin he breaks down, and sobs against her breast. Again, to distract his mind, Lavinia becomes suddenly busy with the clearing of the furniture covers and the straightening of the room.

Orin is at the window staring into the darkness when Peter comes into the living-room and finds Lavinia. At first Peter is startled. He thinks she is the ghost of her mother. He is delighted with the change in her, when it is confirmed a moment later, and more than delighted to find Lavinia now willing, even eager, to accept his love.

Now Orin has been dragged from the shadows. It is an effort for him to rouse himself, to assume a friendly manner toward Peter, but he makes the effort. The effort carries him into a mood that is sly, insinuating and mocking as he agrees with Peter on the great change that has come over Lavinia. Imagine Lavinia becoming romantic! Imagine Lavinia succumbing to the influence of the "dark and deep blue ocean"—and of the islands! They turned out to be Vinnie's islands, not his, Orin reports. Peter should have seen her with the men—the handsome, romantic-looking men, "with colored rags around their middles and flowers

stuck over their ears!" Vinnie was a bit shocked at first by the
Islanders' dances, but if they had stayed a month—

"I know I'd have found her some moonlight night dancing
under the palm trees—as naked as the rest!"

"Orin! Don't be disgusting!" protests Lavinia.

Lavinia, flustered by such "fibs" would shut Orin up if she
could. When she sends him to look for Hazel she would explain
to Peter the strange moods and fancies that sometimes attack her
bother. He has not yet overcome the shock of the war, his
father's death and his mother's suicide, following so closely
after. . . .

Lavinia is nestling gratefully against Peter's shoulder now, admitting freely her love for him and the growing desire to be near
him that she has felt ever since she and Orin had left the islands.
It was all foolishness—the stuff Orin talked about the islands—
but the natives had reminded Lavinia of Peter—they were so
simple and fine—

Peter is glad at the change in Lavinia, glad that now she wants
love, and finds it beautiful; glad to hear her say that she is eager
to be married soon, and to settle in the country where they can
make an island for themselves on land and have children, "and
love them and teach them to love life so they can never be
possessed by hate and death!"

But there's Orin, Lavinia suddenly remembers. She can never
leave Orin until he is all well again. Orin still feels guilty about
his mother's killing herself. Peter must explain to Hazel, Lavinia
prompts, so Hazel may understand any crazy thing Orin may
say—

"I'll warn her," agrees Peter. "And now don't you worry any
more about him. We'll get him all right again, one way or another."

Lavinia is in Peter's arms, kissing him, when Orin and Hazel
appear in the doorway. "Hazel is a bit shocked, then smiles happily. Orin starts as if he'd been struck. He glares at them with
jealous rage and clenches his fists as if he were going to attack
them."

"I'm afraid we're interrupting, Orin," laughs Hazel, as Peter
and Vinnie jump apart. Orin quickly pulls himself together. His
savage mood vanishes.

"Don't be so solemn—Fuss Buzzer," he calls to Peter. "I was
only trying to scare you for a joke." He holds out his hand, his
smile becoming ghastly. "I suppose congratulations are in order.
I—I'm glad—"

Peter takes Orin's hand awkwardly. Hazel is plainly bewildered, as she moves toward Lavinia. "Lavinia stares at Orin with eyes full of dread" as the curtain falls.

A month passes. The scene changes. Orin is sitting at the left of the table in his father's study under the painting of General Mannon in his Judge's robes. He is intent on his writing and there is a stack of manuscript at his right hand. He has aged noticeably, increasing his resemblance to his father. Sardonically he addresses the portrait of his father:
"The truth, the whole truth and nothing but the truth! Is that what you're demanding, Father? Are you sure you want the whole truth?" . . .
Lavinia's knock at the door disturbs Orin. He hides the manuscripts before he lets her in. He is casual in his answers to her queries. He is newly interested in the study of law, he insists, when she would know what it is that has kept him locked in the study so much of the time. Her anxiety over his health interests but does not impress Orin.
Orin would turn questioner. Why is it that Lavinia, now that he has asked Hazel to marry him, in response to his sister's urging, will never leave him alone with Hazel? Is she afraid of accidental revelations? Yet, he, too, is afraid of being to much alone with Hazel. "When I see love for a murderer in her eyes my guilt crowds up in my throat like poisonous vomit and I long to spit it out—and confess!"
"Oh, God!" cries Lavinia. "Over and over and over! Will you never lose your stupid guilty conscience? Don't you see how you torture me? You're becoming my guilty conscience, too! (With an instinctive flare-up of her old jealousy.) How can you still love that vile woman so—when you know all she wanted was to leave you without a thought and marry that—"
"Yes!" answers Orin, with fierce accusation, "exactly as you're scheming now to leave me and marry Peter! But, by God, you won't! You'll damn soon stop your tricks when you know what I've been writing!"
It is the history of the Mannon family, Orin tells her, that he has written. A true history of all the family crimes, beginning with Grandfather Abe's—
"I've tried to trace it to its secret hiding place in the Mannon past the evil destiny behind our lives— . . . Most of what I've written is about you, Vinnie. I found you the most interesting criminal of us all—. . . So many strange, hidden things out

of the Mannon past combine in you—"

There was, Orin recalls, the first mate Wilkins on the voyage to Frisco, whom Lavinia favored, doubtless because he reminded her of Brant? That's why she discarded mourning and adopted her mother's colors. She had wanted Wilkins as she wanted Brant. It was her jealous hatred that had inspired her mother's murder. It was Brant's influence that had taken her to the islands—Adam Brant's islands. It was there, with the handsome men staring at her, that she suddenly took on the beauty of her mother. What had she done with the native Avahanni? Kissed him good night because he was so innocent and good? Was that all?

Lavinia's anger flares at the accusation. Furious, she would defiantly admit the truth of any evil in Orin's mind. "I'm not your property! I've a right to love!" she cries. And then, shaken and trembling as he would grab her by the throat, Lavinia sobs out an admission that she has been lying to let him think so of her. It was an evil spirit, a ghost from the past, that rose up and made her lie to him.

"I believe you about Avahanni," Orin admits, slowly. "I never really suspected, or I'd have killed him—and you, too. I hope you know that! . . . But you are guilty in your mind, just the same!"

"Stop harping on that! Stop torturing me!" demands Lavinia distractedly. "I warn you again, I can't bear any more! I won't!"

"Then why don't you murder me?" taunts Orin. "I'll help you plan it, as we planned Brant's, so there will be no suspicion of you! And I'll be grateful! I loathe my life! . . . Can't you see I'm now in Father's place and you're Mother? That's the evil destiny out of the past I haven't dared predict! I'm the Mannon you're chained to! So isn't it plain—"

"For God's sake won't you be quiet—" Lavinia's hands are over her ears to shut out his answers. . . . Now, again, her horror has turned to violent rage and she would warn him of her desperation—

"Take care, Orin! You'll be responsible, if—" She stops abruptly.

ORIN (with a diabolical mockery)—If what? If I should die mysteriously of heart failure?

LAVINIA—Leave me alone! Leave me alone! Don't keep saying that! How can you be so horrible? Don't you know I your sister who loves you, who would give her life to bring you peace?

ORIN (*in a harsh threatening tone*)—I don't believe you! I know you're plotting something! But you look out! I'll be watching you! And I warn you I won't stand your leaving me for Peter! I'm going to put this confession I've written in safe hands—to be read in case you try to marry him—or if I should die—

LAVINIA (*frantically grabbing his arm*)—Stop having such thoughts! Stop making me have them! You're like a devil torturing me! I won't listen! (*She breaks down and sobs brokenly. Orin stares at her dazedly.*)

ORIN (*strangely*)—Don't cry. The damned don't cry. (*He slumps down heavily.*) Go away, will you? I want to be alone —to finish my work. (*Still sobbing, her hand over her eyes, Lavinia feels blindly for the door and goes out. Orin unlocks the table drawer, pulls out his manuscript, and takes up his pen as the curtain falls.*)

Lavinia has come from the study to the sitting-room. Here, too, candles on the mantelpiece shed their flickering light on the portraits of the Mannon ancestors.

Lavinia, "in a terrific state of tension," is twining and untwining her fingers, pacing the room and muttering to herself: "Why does he keep putting his death in my head? He would be better off if— Why hasn't he the courage—?" A moment later, "in a frenzy of remorseful anguish," she is unconsciously pleading forgiveness of the Mannon portraits. "O God, don't let me have such thoughts. You know how I love Orin! Show me the way to save him! I couldn't bear another death!"

Peter and Hazel are back, though none too willingly. Hazel has come to hate the Mannon house. And to question Vinnie's influence over Orin. Vinnie's changed so. Hazel has asked her mother if Orin cannot visit the Niles for a time. Vinnie has opposed that, but Hazel has not given up. Peter, too, is willing to use his influence. He will do anything to get Orin well—so Vinnie will be free to marry him.

Now Peter has gone on to a Council meeting and Orin has joined Hazel. He has brought a big sealed envelope with him. Eagerly, nervously, he wants Hazel to keep the envelope for him, to keep it in a safe place and never let anyone know she has it. She must promise never to open it unless something happens to him.

"I mean if I should die—or—but this is most important, if she tries to marry Peter—the day before the wedding—I want you to make Peter read what's inside."

"You don't want her to marry Peter?"

"No! She can't have happiness! She's got to be punished!"

Beyond that Hazel must also agree to give Orin up. He cannot love her any more; he can only love "guilt for guilt which breeds more guilt." Hazel will not listen. She is tender with Orin and soothing. There is something troubling him, she knows that, and if he would tell her what it is, that would relieve his mind. With sudden desperation Orin is pleading that Hazel help him get away from the Mannon home, away from Lavinia.

Lavinia has appeared in the doorway. She senses a conspiracy between them. She is suspicious of Hazel's awkward efforts to keep Orin's letter behind her. What is it they are hiding? And what is this plan for Orin to go to the Niles'? Lavinia will not hear of that.

Now Lavinia has caught sight of the envelope Hazel is trying to conceal and fiercely demands that it be turned over to her. Barring the door, she will not let Hazel pass until she has given up the letter. Let Orin, too, consider what it is he is putting into the hands of another. No Mannon could do this thing. Still Orin is not moved.

"For my sake, then!" pleads Lavinia, desperately. "You know I love you! Make Hazel give that up and I'll do anything—anything you want me to!"

"You mean that!" Orin is staring at his sister with morbid intensity.

"Yes," answers Lavinia, shrinking back from him.

There is a crazy triumph in Orin's laughter as he takes the letter from Hazel. . . . "Forget me," he abjures her, with a twisted smile. "The Orin you loved was killed in the war. Remember only that dead hero and not his rotting ghost!"

Orin gives the envelope to Lavinia when they are alone. She knows, she agrees, that her promise means giving up Peter. But she doesn't know all that it means, protests Orin, "a distorted look of desire" coming over his face. She doesn't seem to realize all that she means to him now, since they murdered their mother.

"I love you now with all the guilt in me—the guilt we share," cries Orin. "Perhaps I love you too much, Vinnie. . . . There are times now when you don't seem to be my sister, nor Mother but some stranger with the same beautiful hair. . . . Perhaps you're Marie Brantôme, eh? And you say there are no ghosts in this house?"

"For God's sake— No! You're insane! You can't mean—"

"How else can I be sure you won't leave me? You would never dare leave me—then! You would feel as guilty then as I do. You would be as damned as I am—"

Now the mood is broken. Orin is pleading hysterically that Lavinia go with him, and confess, and pay the penalty for their mother's murder and find peace. Briefly Lavinia wavers. Then, again, her will is strong. She will make no compromise with a coward. There is nothing to confess. There has been only justice! She turns on Orin as he taunts the Mannon ancestors to break her. She hates Orin! She sees him as too vile to live! If he weren't a coward he would kill himself!

For a second Orin stands stunned before her, a pitiful, pleading look in his eyes. Then, wildly, he is shouting again that she would drive him to suicide, as he had driven his mother! Now she *is* his mother! Now his mother is speaking through her.

"Yes," he cries, "it's the way to peace—to find her again—my lost island—Death is an Island of Peace, too—Mother will be waiting for me there—"

Orin has turned and is striding toward the door. Lavinia, rousing herself, stricken with remorse, would throw her arms about his neck, but is cast roughly aside. "Get out of my way, can't you?" he shouts. "Mother's waiting!"

Orin is going to the study to clean his pistol, he tells Peter, as he passes him in the doorway. Now Lavinia is in Peter's arms, trying nervously to recall her vision of their happy marriage that is to be, with a home and garden and trees.

"I love everything that grows simply—up toward the sun—everything that's straight and strong," Lavinia is saying. "I hate what's warped and twists and eats itself and dies for a lifetime in shadow. I can't bear waiting—waiting and waiting and waiting—!"

From the study a muffled shot is heard. Peter releases Lavinia and runs to the door. Lavinia supports herself weakly against the table. "Forgive me, Orin!" she mutters. "Her mouth congeals into a frozen line. Mechanically she hides the sealed envelope in a drawer of the table and locks the drawer. 'I've got to go in—' She turns to go and her eyes catch the eyes of the Mannons in the portraits fixed accusingly on her—defiantly— 'Why do you look at me like that? Wasn't it the only way to keep your secret, too? But I'm through with you forever now, do you hear? I'm Mother's daughter—not one of you! I'll live in spite of you!' She squares her shoulders, with a return of the abrupt military movement copied from her father which she had of old—as if by the very act of disowning the Mannons she had returned to the fold—and marches stiffly from the room." The curtain falls.

Again, three days later, the façade of the Mannon house is bathed in a soft, golden sunlight that "shimmers in a luminous mist on the Greek temple portico." The shutters are now fastened back, the windows open.

Seth, puttering in the shrubbery, is still singing bits of "Shenandoah." Across the yard he catches sight of Lavinia in the flower garden. Seth had hoped Lavinia would stop pickin' flowers now the funeral's over—

Lavinia is carrying a large bunch of flowers when she comes. Three days have effected a remarkable change in her. "Her body, dressed in deep mourning, again appears flat-chested and thin. . . . Her lips are bloodless, drawn taut in a grim line." The flowers she has brought are for the house. Peter is coming. . . .

Seth's been noticing things. Every morning he has found Lavinia sitting on the steps, drawn and sleepless. Wouldn't she like him to bring out a couch?

"You understand, don't you?" mutters Lavinia. "You've been with us Mannons for so long! You know there's no rest in this house which Grandfather built as a temple of Hate and Death!"

"Don't you try to live here, Vinnie!" Seth blurts out. "You marry Peter and git clear!"

Vinnie is going to do that. She will close up the house and leave it in the sun and rain to die. "The portraits of the Mannons will rot on the walls and the ghosts will fade back into death. And the Mannons will be forgotten. I'm the last and I won't be one long. I'll be Mrs. Peter Niles. Then they're finished! Thank God!"

Hazel Niles has come. Hazel has not been fooled by the report that Orin killed himself. She knows. Lavinia drove him to it. She can't prove that, but she knows. There was something that was driving Orin crazy—

When Hazel can control her sobs it is not Orin she wants to talk about. It is Peter. She is not going to have Lavinia marry Peter and ruin his life. "You'll only drag him into this terrible thing and make him share it," she charges Lavinia. . . . "Oh, Vinnie, you've got to be fair to Peter. You've got to consider his happiness, if you really love him."

Already Peter has changed, says Hazel. He has fought with his mother when she tried to talk with him. He has gone to a hotel to live. Does Lavinia want to take the risk of driving Peter to do what Orin did?

Now Lavinia, wildly, as one at the end of a tether, is defiant before Hazel. She *will* marry Peter! Let Hazel leave her alone, leave the house before she gets Orin's pistol and kills her—

Hazel is frightened but not beaten. The least Lavinia can do is to let Peter read what Orin had in that envelope. Orin had wanted Peter to read it before he married Lavinia, and Hazel has warned Peter.

"The dead! Why can't the dead die?" mutters Lavinia, as if to herself. . . .

Peter has come. His greeting is cheerful. He is worried about Lavinia, about the way she looks. But soon they will be married—

"You'll love me and keep me from remembering?" she asks, longingly.

"You bet I will! And the first thing is to get you away from this darned house! I may be a fool, but I'm beginning to get superstitious about it myself."

"Yes. Love can't live in it. We'll go away and leave it alone to die—and we'll forget the dead."

Peter is pleased with that program. They cannot go too far from the house and the town to suit him. . . .

Lavinia is worried. Peter has never been so bitter before. His eyes have a hurt look. Is it because he is suspicious of her? Is he wondering what Orin wrote?

Peter is sure of himself. Doesn't he know Orin was out of his mind? Why should he ever suspect Lavinia of anything? What does she think he is?

Then, demands Lavinia, desperately, is he ready to marry her at once, that night?

Peter is shocked at the suggestion. It wouldn't look right. Out of respect to Orin. Was there anything in what Orin wrote that would stop them?

"The dead coming between," laughs Lavinia, a wild beaten laugh. "They always would, Peter! You trust me with your happiness! But that means trusting the Mannon dead—and they're not to be trusted with love."

No, the risk is too great for Lavinia. She loves Peter too much. She has thrown her arms about him now, pleadingly, wildly. Why should they worry about marriage? Let them be happy for a little while despite all the dead. "I want a moment of joy—of love—to make up for what's coming," cries Lavinia. "I want it now! Can't you be strong, Peter? Can't you be simple and pure? Can't you forget sin and see that all love is beautiful? (*She kisses him with desperate passion.*) Kiss me! Hold me close! Want me! Want me so much you'd murder anyone to have me! I did that—for you! Take me in this house of the dead and love me! Our love will drive the dead away! It will shame them back into death! (*At the topmost pitch of desperate, frantic abandonment.*) Want me! Take me, Adam! (*She is brought back to herself with a start by this name escaping her—bewilderedly, laughing idiotically.*) Adam? Why did I call you Adam? I never even heard that name before—outside of the Bible! (*Then suddenly with a hopeless, dead finality.*) Always the dead between! It's no good trying any more!"

"Vinnie! You're talking crazy!" Peter is both shocked and repelled. "You don't know what you're saying! You're not like that!"

The end has come. Lavinia's voice has gone dead. She can never marry Peter. Let him go home and make it up with his mother and sister. Let him marry someone else.

Yes, she agrees wildly, it is something Orin wrote that has changed her! It was something about the islands, as he suspects. Something about the native! Why should she lie any more? Orin suspected she had lusted with that native, and she had!

"Why shouldn't I?" she cries. "I wanted him! I wanted to learn love from him—love that wasn't a sin! And I did, I tell you! He had me! I was his fancy woman!"

"Then Mother and Hazel were right about you—you are bad at heart—no wonder Orin killed himself—God, I—I hope you'll be punished—I—I—"

Peter has gone. With a desperate cry Lavinia starts after him, calling, "Peter! It's a lie! I didn't—"

Now she has stiffened into her old square-shouldered attitude. Seth has come from the garden and is watching her. To attract Lavinia's attention he begins singing the chantey. He is frightened as he sees her start toward the house.

LAVINIA (*grimly*)—Don't be afraid. I'm not going the way Mother and Orin went. That's escaping punishment. And there's no one left to punish me. I'm the last Mannon. I've got to punish myself! Living alone here with the dead is a worse act of justice than death or prison! I'll never go out or see anyone! I'll have the shutters nailed closed so no sunlight can ever get in. I'll live alone with the dead, and keep their secrets, and let them hound me, until the curse is paid out and the last Mannon is let die! (*With a strange cruel smile of gloating over the years of self-torture.*) I know they will see to it I live a long time! It takes the Mannons to punish themselves for being born!

SETH (*with grim understanding*)—Ayeh. And I ain't heard a word you've been sayin', Vinnie. (*Pretending to search the ground again.*) Left my clippers around somewheres.

LAVINIA (*turns to him sharply*)—You go now and close the shutters and nail them tight.

SETH—Ayeh.

LAVINIA—And tell Hannah to throw out all the flowers.

SETH—Ayeh. (*He goes past her up the steps and into the house. She ascends to the portico—and then turns and stands for a while, stiff and square-shouldered, staring into the sunlight with frozen eyes. SETH leans out of the window at the right of the door and pulls the shutters closed with a decisive bang. As if this were a word of command, LAVINIA pivots sharply on her heel and marches woodenly into the house, closing the door behind her.*)

THE CURTAIN FALLS

REUNION IN VIENNA

A Comedy in Three Acts

By ROBERT EMMET SHERWOOD

COUNTING "Mourning Becomes Electra" as two plays which, in its subscription list, the Theatre Guild did, "Reunion in Vienna" was the fourth production of the Guild's season, Alfred Savoir's "He" having been the first.

The play was a considerable departure for Robert Emmet Sherwood, gifted author of "The Road to Rome" and "The Queen's Husband." It is written quite in the Continental manner, could easily have been builded on a base by Ferenc Molnar, or adapted from something by Lazlo Fodor. In fact, in its perfect approximation of the spirit and atmosphere of Viennese comedy this play is a distinctly clever achievement.

"Reunion in Vienna" was also greatly helped by the appearance in its chief rôles of Alfred Lunt and Lynn Fontanne, leaders of the Guild's first acting company. They had been some months away from New York and were heartily welcomed home this November opening night.

The play was received rapturously by a majority of the newspaper reviewers and the Guild subscribers flocked enthusiastically to its support. The larger public outside the subscription lists endorsed the early success, and the comedy easily ran the season out.

Considered a bold piece by many playgoers, the play's success outside the more sophisticated theatre centers may be a little less positive. But it gains so much in the exuberant playing of Mr. Lunt and Miss Fontanne, that its lack of those conventional moralistic and romantic values to which older and more conservative playgoers are still definitely attached is likely to be generously overcome.

As the play begins the drawing-room in the house of Herr Professor Doctor Anton Krug, in Vienna, is decorated in the most ultra-modernistic style. As we enter it this bright May morning there is a small American-made radio turned on and playing a Brahm's concerto. Kathie, a stout elderly maid, is calling her mistress, Elena, to check over the laundry which has just been

118

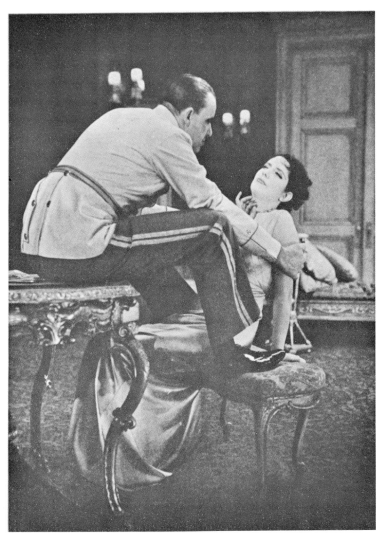

Photo by Vandamm Studio, New York.

"REUNION IN VIENNA"

Rudolf: Good God, that wedding ring! Of all the bourgeois adornments! On you it is a gross anachronism! Like a brassiere on the Venus de Milo. We must remove it. It offends me.

(*Alfred Lunt and Lynn Fontanne*)

delivered.

Frau Krug is an attractive woman probably in her early thirties. At the moment she is wearing a severely plain housedress and apron and is thoroughly intent on her housekeeping duties. Her count of the laundry is precise and complete, nor can it be interrupted even by the Herr Doctor Anton himself, a solid man some years older than Elena and of settled, professional appearance.

The Doctor, a specialist in psycho-analysis, is eager that Elena shall stop whatever she is doing and entertain briefly two of his young students. The students have heard of Elena, have visioned her as both glamorous and regal, and Dr. Anton is eager they shall see her.

The students are Emil Loibner and Ilse Hinrich, "very young, earnest, confident of their ability eventually to right all the manifold wrongs that are about them. Emil is dark, bespectacled, poorly but neatly dressed. Ilse might be blondly beautiful if she cared to be."

"I have one more patient to see before we can begin our work," Anton explains, as he deposits them in the drawing-room. "A dreadful woman! She came all the way from—where is it?—Pennsylvania, to learn about the more elementary facts of life. She's married too, now. What sort of husbands do you suppose they have in Pennsylvania that their wives must come all the way to Vienna to learn the facts?"

Emil and Ilse, who are at some loss to know what they shall talk about, are helped out by Herr Krug, the Doctor's father, a fussy old gentleman who breaks into the conversation whenever opportunity offers, and occasionally when it doesn't.

Father Krug is quite proud of the position to which his son's success has raised the family, though he is not so sure they would not all have been better off if Anton had followed his father's footsteps and become a good shoemaker. But Anton was bound to be a scientist.

"They sent for my boy all the way from America," reports Herr Krug, "and he went across the ocean to tell those Americans how to live. They didn't know. And when he came back he brought me a present—that wireless machine, there. Did you ever see one so fine as that? It's mine—but they won't let me play it."

Frau Krug, beautifully dressed now, is back and eager to entertain Emil and Ilse. Pleased to hear that they approve the decorations of her home and interested in their enthusiastic reports of their work with Anton.

"He makes us understand that if you'll only think right you'll live right," Ilse explains. "I mean if you can bring what's in your subconscious to the surface—then you'll know what it is— and you'll know what to do about it."

"No. No. It's infinitely more than that," insists Emil. "He's gone far beyond psychoanalysis. He teaches us the gospel of the better life—the life that is seen through the microscope and the changing colors of the test tube. He teaches us to banish from the world all false fear of God—to know Him, and recognize Him only as a measurable force in cosmic technology. He teaches us not to look to the vague hills of mysticism, but into ourselves, our bodies, our minds, for the knowledge that will set us free."

"Well—that covers about everything, doesn't it?" ventures Elena.

"You see, Madam," Emil continues a moment later, "hardly more than ten years ago we were living under conditions of medievalism."

"Ten years—ten years ago?"

EMIL—When I look at the decaying relics of the old order, the empty palace of the Hapsburgs, and the silly monuments they erected to their own glory—I bless the revolution that delivered us from the tyranny of ignorance.

ELENA—And what do you say when you look at me?

ILSE—At *you*, Frau Krug? What connection has that . . .

ELENA—I'm one of the relics of the Middle Ages, of ten years ago.

EMIL—But you are the wife of the most enlightened scientist in Austria. (DR. KRUG *comes in.*)

ANTON—Emil! I overheard that last remark.

EMIL—Yes, sir!

ANTON—I'm afraid you must have misunderstood me. I told you to flatter her, not me.

ELENA—They've been charming, both of them.

ANTON (*casually looking for book*)—I'm glad to hear it. Is that copy of "Sons and Lovers" here?"

ELENA—I think it's there—somewhere.

ANTON—I want to give it to that Pennsylvania woman. It might help her.

ELENA—What's the trouble with her?

ANTON—The usual complaint. Another frustration! For twenty years she's been measuring her poor husband in terms of her first love—the one that got away. . . . (*He comes inti-*

mately to ELENA *with book.*)

ELENA—And what are you prescribing, beside that book?

ANTON—She must find her first lover, and have a good look at him as he is now. He's a manufacturer of dental supplies. I think she'll be cured. . . . (*He goes out.*)

ELENA—I hope he does cure her. It must be awful to be always unsatisfied, and puzzled. . . .

EMIL—He'll cure her—if she has the capacity to understand.

From their questioning it is apparent to Father Krug that Emil and Ilse would be most interested in having Elena tell them something about the Hapsburgs. Nor is Elena displeased at the suggestion. They are, after all, studying to be psycho-analysts, and should do a considerable amount of research work, in the drawing-room as well as in the laboratory. And, as a matter of fact, she (Elena) is a peculiarly interesting specimen. Even Dr. Anton will admit that. "He'll tell you that most of his vast knowledge of human frailty comes from observation of me," declares Elena.

Emil is content to take Dr. Anton's word for it that the world has improved, but Ilse, having had an experience, is beset with doubt. The experience came to Ilse while she was in Nice on her vacation. She had one day called a taxi and, looking in the mirror above the driver's seat, was startled to see the driver staring at her openly and insolently. She tried not to look at him, but his queer eyes kept drawing her back. Finally, when the driver had taken her along a most precipitous road, and had frightened her terribly, she had screamed to him in German to stop. With this he had stopped the taxi, got in beside her and a moment later was kissing her passionately.

"I tried to tell myself that he was nothing more than an emotional extravert. Possibly with a womb complex, but that didn't seem to help me," Ilse explains. "Then he said: 'Permit me to introduce myself: I am the Archduke Rudolf Maximilian von Hapsburg.' "

As it turned out Ilse's Archduke was quite real. He was well known in Nice. And, after the kissing interlude, he had taken her right back to her hotel and would accept no fee. "Nonsense, my dear," he had said. "On *this* ride you have been my guest."

That, chuckles Herr Krug, would be like the Archduke. Like all of them, in fact. Emil thinks if he had been there he would have punched the Archduke in the nose, but the women are not so sure.

Ilse, naturally, is disturbed. She cannot analyse her own emotions and she has lacked the courage to confess her adventure to Dr. Krug.

"You don't have to consult him," Herr Krug insists, still chuckling. "Elena, you know more about these things than Anton ever will, with all his experiments. Tell them about that time when the old Emperor caught you and Rudolf Maximilian posing on the fountain at Schonbrunn, both naked as the day you were born."

Before Elena can decide upon what to say Anton is back. Nor will she be lured into continuing before him, though she does tell him that Ilse has had an experience in a taxicab with Rudolf Maximilian. She would have Ilse seek further advice from Anton.

"Tell him about it," Elena insists, with some fervor. "He'll analyze your emotional reactions, as he analyzed mine. He cured me, and I delivered myself, body and mind, to the new god."

Anton is about to take his students into his office when callers are announced for Elena. They are Count and Countess Von Stainz, Frau Lucher and the Baron Povoromo. They have come, Herr Krug is amused to announce, because they want Elena to attend a party that night at Lucher's Hotel, a celebration in honor of the hundredth anniversary of Franz Joseph the First. Frau Lucher has bribed the police to avoid a rumpus, Herr Krug reports, but, in his estimation, there is going to be a rumpus just the same.

Anton, being slightly startled by the news, Elena is ready to turn the callers away. But Anton can see no reason why she should do that. They are her old friends—is she afraid of meeting them because of memories of associations they will revive? Is she afraid to go to a party at the Hotel Lucher because it had been the scene of many of her meetings with Rudolf? However, let her decide for herself. Anton has gone back to his students when Elena's friends are shown in.

"Frau Lucher is a formidable old party, absurdly dressed in ancient clothes, but imposing. Her voice is gruff, her expression unchangeably hostile, her manner toward all arrogant and despotic. The Count is about fifty-five. He hasn't enough flesh left to fill his clothes. He is just the least bit drunk—which is his normal condition. The Countess, about fifty, is dowdy and excessively emotional."

The greeting of her friends is effusive and a little embarrassing to Elena. They have had great trouble, they report, getting back to Vienna from their various places of exile. When they finally get to the business of their call it is, as Herr Krug predicted, to ask Elena to come to their party. Frau Lucher had been brought to do the pleading, but Lucher is not particularly interested one way or the other. She is giving the party because she has her sentimental moments. "When I realized that this was the hundredth anniversary I thought that we might have a revival of the old insanity at my expense," she explains. "However, I have decided that I was over-optimistic."

"You really can't disappoint us, Elena," pleads Count Von Stainz. "We've looked forward so to this, and to having you there, laughing in the way you always laughed."

"But, that's just it, Franz. I couldn't laugh. I'd probably weep."

"Splendid," agrees the Countess. "We'll all weep together and have a glorious time."

"And when you've become gloomy enough you'll start throwing bottles through the windows, I know!" predicts Frau Lucher.

There is to be quite a party, according to the Count. Everybody is coming who can afford to get there: Old General Hoetzler, who is now a train announcer at Erfurt; the two Koeppkes, who are running a lodging house in Zermatt; the beautiful Gisella Von Krett—

Now Anton has returned. He finds them in the midst of a hearty laugh because someone has just recalled the night Rudolf, drunk, had ordered a jeweler out of bed at two in the morning, bought a diamond necklace for Elena, threw it into her lap and insisted that they go on with the dance.

Anton is pleased to meet Elena's friends, and quite in agreement with them in their enthusiastic endorsement of his wife's charms. Also, Anton is perfectly willing that Elena should go to their party. Even Elena has about decided that it might be great fun, when "Poffy" Povoromo has a twinge of conscience.

"Elena, I know why you're changing your mind," says Poffy. "Why?"

POFFY—Because you realize this party will be nothing more than a gathering of broken down old outcasts, like myself—with no one to give us animation, no one to give us the illusion of youth—but—I'm afraid that it may not be quite what you expect—

LUCHER—What are you talking about?

POFFY—I received a message this afternoon.

ELENA—Yes?

POFFY—I was commanded to say nothing about it to anyone—but, Elena, I think you should know about it before you go

to that party; and you too should know, Herr Professor— If
I could have a word with you in private.

COUNTESS—In private?

POFFY—You'll forgive me—

COUNT—Rudolf?

ELENA—He's to be there?

LUCHER—Great God!

POFFY—He left Nice yesterday on his way to Vienna.

COUNTESS—Rudolf!

LUCHER—Great God!

ANTON—Will they allow him to cross the border?

LUCHER—No. They'll never let him in after all the things
he's said and done. The officials are so stupid that the smaller
fry can sneak past them, begging your pardon, Count and Countess, but they're not so stupid as to allow the most violent member of the Hapsburg faction to get back into Austria.

POFFY—Regardless of all that, Elena, I thought you should
know. I ask your pardon, Herr Professor, for having mentioned
the subject.

ANTON—Not at all. There's nothing I can say. It's for
Elena to decide.

ELENA—I can't go.

COUNTESS—But, my little angel—what Lucher said is true.
He couldn't possibly come into the country—

ELENA—I can't go.

COUNT—You can't change your mind, Elena. We need you.
You've always made things go. Have you forgotten all those
times when—

ELENA—Yes. I have forgotten. And I advise you to forget
too.

COUNTESS—You're asking a great deal of people who have
nothing but memories to live on.

ELENA—That's just it. You're trying to live on something that
doesn't exist. That's why you're all so hopeless and degraded.
That's why you have to drug yourselves with such infantile
pretense as this reunion. Wallowing in sentiment. Weeping into
your beer!

COUNTESS—I never hoped to hear a more brutal statement.

Elena is willing to admit the brutality of her statement, but
no one can deny its truth. She is apologetic but firm. She is
thankful to Poffy for having warned her about Rudolf, but it
would have made no difference. Things have changed with

Elena.

Now the party has left and Anton has taken up the argument. Elena did not come off so well in her encounter, insists Anton. It might be a good thing for her to go to the party. In fact Anton favors her going.

"I suppose you consider that it will be good for me to go there and feel wretched and out of place, merely to assure myself that I'm right."

"That's just the point. . . . If you take my advice, Elena, you'll go. You're not the calm superior being that you fancy yourself."

ELENA—Are you prescribing for me as you prescribed for that last patient of yours?

ANTON—Yes, that's exactly what I'm doing. The tender spot has been uncovered. Now we can take measures to cure it. Elena, as your family physician as well as your husband, I order you to go to Lucher's tonight, and do the inane things you used to do, and that you still secretly think were gloriously romantic.

ELENA—I know you've been subjecting me to treatment ever since we were married. But you've at least been subtle about it. Now your methods are a little too obvious to be effective.

ANTON—I've revised my methods because I learned something myself when I saw you with your old friends. You deliver all this fine talk about the old days and the new—the woman who was reborn after the revolution. And now some pitiable specters appear to you and you can't bear to face them.

ELENA—I can face anything, Anton, including your vast overpowering intelligence.

ANTON—Yes, you can do that. But there are some things you can't face because you can't see them. You're still in a state of emotional bondage. You're tied to those people by a cord that's strong. You've got to cut that cord and here's the chance to do it.

ELENA—When I require your professional services I shall make an appointment and come to your office.

ANTON—The appointment is now.

The situation, they are agreed, is a silly one and they both are able to laugh about it. But Anton is still convinced. There has always been some lack of understanding between them, he feels. There has always been the specter of Rudolf between them. Anton would have Elena know Rudolf as he is.

"You've seen what ten years have done to the Count and Countess Von Stainz," he reasons. "Ten years is a long time. Go to that party. Have a good look at him, and then come home and admit that I'm right."

"You're always right, Anton. That's your only fault," admits Elena.

It is agreed that Elena shall go to the party and let herself go completely. That is Anton's prescription. Let her wear the white dress she got in Paris. She is beautiful in that. . . .

Anton has gone. Father Krug is back fooling with his radio. From the air the instrument picks up excerpts from "The Dollar Princess!" The band at the Bristol always plays the old tunes a half hour before dinner. . . .

Now Elena has called Anton to fetch her diamond necklace from the safe. She has grabbed Herr Krug and is dancing him around wildly to the tune of a waltz as the curtain falls.

ACT II

The sitting-room of the one-time Imperial Suite of the Hotel Lucher is a somewhat stuffy place, but still eloquent of an old-time grandeur. There are at back folding doors that give into the royal bedchamber. When the doors are opened a canopied bed may be seen. The furniture is heavy with brocaded upholstering.

To this room Frau Lucher has summoned Strup, her aging maître d'hôtel, and Bredzi, the faithful orchestra leader, to acquaint them with her plans for the evening's anniversary celebration. Her message to Bredzi, after looking over his program, is that he has included too much Mozart and too few waltzes apassionata. The guests will want many waltzes apassionata, Frau Lucher is convinced, both before they are drunk and after, when they will want to cry on each other's shoulders.

As for Herr Strup's wine list, she will have him know that they are not to waste their Cliquot 1911 on any crowd that hasn't known what a palate is since any of them can remember. Let the maître d'hôtel serve a half bottle of Tizane to each person with the roast, and after that nothing but beer—Vienna beer, not Muenchner.

Also, they are to remember, and this includes waiters and busboys, that they are to show the guests every courtesy and deference, to "treat them as if they were still lords of creation and as if you expected heavy tips for your services, which I promise you won't get," warns Frau Lucher. "All the old formalities, the old nonsense, from all of you—until they start breaking the furniture—then, a firm hand! If you can't manage them by yourselves, send for me."

A large policeman has arrived, sent by the Inspector, to have a look around. He is particularly interested in the list of those expected, which the Baron Povoromo has brought. As he can see, there is no one on it that could reasonably cause the police the least apprehension.

The policeman has just retired to start his look around in other parts of the hotel when Archduke Rudolf Maximilian unexpectedly arrives. "In face and bearing he is unquestionably a Hapsburg of the Hapsburgs, but he is dressed as though he has just come from a walking tour in the Tyrol. . . ."

Rudolf greets Frau Lucher with a hearty "Good evening, venerable strumpet," as well as a saucy slap. He finds her utterly unchanged and that amuses him.

He has come, he tells her, by various means of conveyance to Vienna and through her smelly kitchen to her presence. He will again occupy the Imperial Suite, and so far as the servants are concerned, he is traveling incognito. He is not worried by Frau Lucher's report of the police, and he finds it incredible that so many things have remained unchanged about the old place.

"Does this city realize that it is hopelessly defunct?" he demands. "It is like a corpse that twitches with the reflexes of life—a grewsome spectacle. I don't envy you, Lucher, having to abide here among the remains. They drained the blood from Vienna when they removed us—and now observe the results! Serves the swine right."

His Highness is interested in the expected guests, but greatly surprised to find that Elena Vervesz is not to be among them. His surprise gives way to amazement when he learns that not only is Elena in Vienna and aware that there is to be a party but that she still refuses to come. Something tells him that when she knows that he is to be there Elena will find a way quickly to change her plans. He would have Frau Lucher send for her immediately, nor will he admit the possibility of Elena's refusing to come, however happily married she may be.

"If by any chance she should not be here when I am ready," warns Rudolf, as he takes playful but earnest hold of Frau Lucher's throat, ". . . but you know the consequences, don't you—old filthy? You know!"

"There is something else in Vienna that is not changed," protests Frau Lucher, sputteringly. "You! You are the same maniac—like all your wretched family."

"No—not a maniac," corrects Rudolf. "It is only that I am constantly intoxicated with my own charm. . . . Tell her to take all the time she wants. I don't approve of women who jump into their clothes like fire horses. She must make every possible effort to look alluring."

Rudolf has bounded into the bedroom to change his clothes and Frau Lucher has barely time to direct Strup to change the wine order back to Cliquot 1911, and be sure and serve caviar, when the policeman returns. He has heard reference to a list of nine in place of eight guests and he would like to know about the unexpected one for whom a gold chair is being ordered at the head of the table.

That place, Frau Lucher assures him, is for herself. It is her hotel and her party. Why not? With the notes she takes from her pocketbook the policeman is content to return to his Inspector and report that he has discovered nothing at all suspicious at the Hotel Lucher. . . .

Now the party is beginning to assemble. General Hoetzler has already started on his war reminiscences, with particular reference to the incident in which Von Hindenberg had practically stolen the Hoetzler campaign plans and thereby prevented Austria from virtually winning the war.

They have swung freely into the spirit of the preliminaries with the cocktails when Elena, in her beautiful white satin, walks in upon them and throws them into sentimental ecstasies. Immediately there is a demand for more drinks and the reception is noisy and happy.

Elena explains that she changed her mind suddenly, about coming, largely because of a selfish desire that had come over her to see them all again. . . .

After the party has filed into the dining-room, there is some commotion in the royal bedchamber. A moment later a valet is cast forth, followed by an angry Rudolf. Rudolf objects strenuously to being dressed by a stable-boy who has clumsily scratched his ear when he tried to brush his uniform. His Highness is now resplendently arrayed and more eager than ever to see Elena. Let them bring her forth. He will not join the party until he has seen Elena, and probably not for some time after that. Let them bring Elena and champagne. And let them be quick about it.

"She isn't the same one you used to make free with!" warns

Lucher. "Her husband is a very fine man—a big man, too—and
. . . I tell you you had better not try any of your old tricks on
her. She's different."

Elena opens the dining-room door in time to save Frau Lucher
from being thrown rather heavily from the room. She stands for
a moment returning Rudolf's wide-eyed stare. Then he crosses
quickly to her, slaps her face resoundingly and kisses her "with
avid ferocity." Still, Elena is quite unmoved.

"How long has it been since you were kissed like that?" Rudolf
would know. "Ten years? More than ten years! Think of it!
Come, we'll have a drink."

He has followed her to a bench and they look, then laugh, at
each other.

"You know," Elena confesses, "I realize now that I had completely forgotten you."

RUDOLF (*pouring drinks*)—Yes. It's too bad. We're not
equipped with the power to recall sensations. One of our Creator's most serious mistakes . . . However—tonight we will both
refresh our memory. That's a very graceful tribute, Elena. I'm
referring to the necklace. But— Good God! (*He is looking
at her left hand, seizes it and examines her wedding ring.*) That
wedding ring! (*Laughs uproariously.*)

ELENA—There is nothing to laugh at. (*She is trying to pull
her hand away but he has a tight grip on her wrist.*)

RUDOLF—Of all the bourgeois adornments! On you, it is a
gross anachronism. Like a brassière on the Venus de Milo. We
must remove it. It offends me. (*He pulls off the ring.*)

ELENA—Don't do that, Rudolf.

RUDOLF—I told you it offends me.

ELENA—Are you going to give me back my ring?

RUDOLF—Yes, my darling. I'll give it back, cheerfully, in the
morning. But in the meantime—well—surely you can understand my point. That heavy gold band on your finger would
strike a discordant note.

ELENA—I'm not planning to be in communication with you tomorrow morning. I want it now. (*She tries to get it.*)

RUDOLF—I must ask you to be more careful, Elena. Refrain
from irritating me. You will recall that the members of my
family are subject to epileptic rages—sheer exuberance you know
—which invariably result in one form or another of physical
violence . . . I should not care to send you back to your hus-

band with your lovely nose broken, and minus one or two conspicuous teeth. . . .

ELENA (*staring at him*)—It can't be true!

RUDOLF—On the contrary, I can assure you that one more allusion to that detestable ring will prove that it is true. . . .

ELENA—I wasn't thinking about that. I was thinking of what ten years have failed to do to you.

RUDOLF—That's only natural. Any alteration in my character would have implied dissatisfaction with myself as I was.

ELENA—Ten years of exile, and humiliation—and poverty—they haven't shaken the conviction that Franz Joseph is still reigning in Schonbrunn.

RUDOLF—No—I admit that I have occasional qualms. There are moments when I suspect that the Hapsburgs are not what they once were. But when I see you, my eternally beloved, and realize that you have had the pride to preserve your figure against the day of my return . . . then I know that there has been no revolution. (*Now bending over her.*)

ELENA—Don't come near me.

RUDOLF—You don't want to be kissed?

ELENA—I do not!

RUDOLF—Very well—if you feel that you need the inspiration of a little more champagne, you shall have it . . . (*He goes to the table to pour out another glass for her, but finds that she has had none. He empties her glass into the ice bucket, and refills it.*)

ELENA—We must go in there and join the others.

RUDOLF—We must do nothing of the kind.

ELENA—I came here tonight to be with them. . . .

RUDOLF—Whereas I came here to be with you. That collection of relics is of no interest whatever to me. . . . Come now—drink!

ELENA (*refusing*)—I'm going in there.

RUDOLF—No, you're not.

ELENA—Rudolf, let me tell them you're here. It's all that's needed to send the poor things into a complete state of delirium. Think of the excitement when they see you looking as young as ever, and as handsome, in your lovely uniform, with all the medals. Think how pleased he'd be (*pointing to portrait*) if he knew that a Hapsburg was again holding court in Vienna.

RUDOLF—Very well—I'll show myself to them for his sake. (*Tries to open door but it is locked.*) Lucher has locked us in. The tactful old bawd!

When the guests come from the dining-room, their excitement mounting at the discovery of their Archduke, Rudolf is standing immediately under the portrait of Franz Joseph. The orchestra has started the national anthem. One by one the guests enter, the women kneeling before Rudolf, the men formally acknowledging his nods of recognition. But Rudolf has little time for them at the moment. As soon as he has greeted the last one he waves them all back into the dining-room and resumes his campaign for the subjugation of Elena. . . .

So, she loves her husband! That's all right. And her husband is a psycho-analyst—"a practitioner of Vienna's sole remaining industry"—and a writer of books? Good! If he has already done one book in eight volumes, as Elena boasts, after Rudolf meets him he should have material enough to do eight more.

And there are no children! Well, with a purely intellectual husband children were hardly to be expected, though Elena assures Rudolf the fault is hers and not her husband's.

As for Rudolf's own story, his life has been varied the last ten years. He has had an occasional good run at baccarat. He has played one or two engagements in the cinema studios. He has created a great scheme for mulcting American tourists, but the government took it away from him and used it themselves. He has also, on occasion, driven a taxi, but only to carry people he knows.

"And if you don't know them before you start the drive, you do before it is finished," suggests Elena, significantly.

That, laughs Rudolf, is only gossip. As a matter of fact, his life has been a good deal of a bore. He has been lonely. Desperately lonely for Elena. Still Elena is unmoved.

"Your heart wasn't always cold," Rudolf protests.

"You have never been lonely—never deserved one atom of sympathy from anyone," Elena insists.

RUDOLF—You don't understand me. No one has ever understood me. I suppose it's because I'm inscrutable.

ELENA—Perhaps. But I remain unimpressed by your appeal for pity.

RUDOLF—Pity! Have you the effrontery to suggest that I'm asking you to pity me?

ELENA—Yes!

RUDOLF—I see. . . . Then I shall have to abandon that tack. (*He laughs.*) You know, Elena, it has always seemed miraculous to me that anyone could be as intelligent as you are, and still alluring. You are alluring. . . .

ELENA—Thank you.

RUDOLF—And that's not intended as a tribute to you; it's a tribute to my own flawless taste. I'm proud to think it was I who first realized you; and the sight of you now tells me that, by God, I was right! You're so beautiful, my darling. You—you glow. You delight me—you refresh me. And I am speaking nothing less than the truth when I tell you that refreshment is what I most urgently need.

ELENA—What tack are you off on now?

RUDOLF—None. I am driving straight to the point. . . . My room is in there.

ELENA—How convenient!

RUDOLF—Yes. It's a room that we have occupied before.

ELENA—I suppose we've occupied all of them.

RUDOLF—We have indeed, my darling. We have made history in this hotel.

ELENA (pause)—Rudolf . . .

RUDOLF—Yes?

ELENA—I think it's time for me to announce that I'm not going to bed with you.

RUDOLF—Very well. (He rises.) I can wait. A few moments. Who's playing in there?

ELENA—Bredzi.

RUDOLF—No? Bredzi?

ELENA—Bredzi.

That gives Rudolf an idea. He has Bredzi and his accordion player in. He orders them to play for him "Over the Waves" and "Vienna Beauties." He waltzes with Elena, around the room, around the pillar, into the bedroom. But Elena is out again a second later, not visibly impressed by Rudolf's impatience over her reluctance nor his confident acceptance of her challenge.

The musicians have stopped the waltz and swung into a livelier tune, "Kek a Kokeny." And from that into something more passionate, the Hungarian song, "Majus ejarakajau." That is reminiscent. That reminds them of a night when, it being too warm indoors, Rudolf took an entire symphony orchestra with them into the forest, and then beat poor Bredzi over the head with a cane because his musicians could not play blindfolded.

The memory is overpowering to Rudolf. He has again returned to kissing Elena passionately, and the musicians break joyously into a tango, singing as they play. Then Bredzi and the accordion player are banished as superfluous stimulants.

It is time, Rudolf asserts, for bantering to cease. He knows now that Elena is the only woman he has ever really loved, though he is free to confess that there have been many women in his life—women of all shades and all nationalities, including the Siamese. But they have been no more than incidental interludes, and his enjoyment of them purely vicarious. All have been proxies for Elena, creating for him the image of the one he loves.

Elena's experience has been different. Memory, to her, has been kind enough to withdraw discreetly. If, for a time following her marriage, she had remembered Rudolf, it was not long before she had forgotten him in the awakened love she felt for her husband. Now her determination is fixed. She is now going back to the dining-room.

Elena has made the start but finds herself held tightly in Rudolf's arms. That, he suggests, is her cue to shriek. But Elena has no intention of shrieking. She is not, as Rudolf is pleased to remember, the shrieking kind. She always knew when she was beaten. As he kisses her now, on eyes, and ears, nose and throat, Elena offers neither resistance nor response, but listens calmly to his impassioned pleading.

RUDOLF—Ah, Elena, my own darling—it isn't easy for you to yield, is it? You keep on thinking of that wedding ring in my pocket. You are loyal to him, because you have the courage to be decent. You were always loyal, always brave. But with me, it isn't as it would be with anyone else. Can't you see that? I loved you first. And you loved me. You weren't lying when you said you loved me. You never knew how to lie. And I'm only asking you to love me again, for a little while, reminiscently, not as a rival of your husband, but as the echo of a voice that enchanted you when you were innocent and impressionable and young. You can't tell me that those things have changed. I can see that they haven't. You have not grown old. You can still make me adore you, and I can still make you love me! (*He is holding her tightly.*) Why not admit it, Elena? Don't maintain that formidable rigidity, as though you were a pure-minded school girl in the clutches of an avid gorilla. Relax, my darling. Let yourself go. (*She has begun to laugh.*) Have I happened to say something witty? (*She continues to laugh.*) There is something in the quality of that laughter which suggests that

I'm wasting my time wooing you.

ELENA—Rudolf, you told me to let myself go.

RUDOLF—I did, but it was not intended as a pleasantry. (*She seizes his face and kisses him as ferociously as he had kissed her.*) Great God, Elena, I didn't expect. . . .

ELENA—No, you didn't expect me to take your advice so quickly. (*She slaps him.*) Did you? (*She slaps his other cheek and she kisses him again.*) You thought I'd keep up the pretense of frigidity forever, didn't you? Am I frozen now?

RUDOLF—No, there's been an unaccountable thaw.

ELENA (*starts to kiss him again*)—Am I restraining myself now? Am I being subdued, repressed, coldly unresponsive? Am I? (*She starts to slap him again.*)

RUDOLF—No, but, my God, Elena, there is such a thing as going too far.

ELENA—No, there isn't. Let's open the doors.

RUDOLF—No.

ELENA—Yes, I want them to see that I haven't changed, that there are some things that never change.

Elena has thrown open the doors and both guests and musicians crowd into the room. She leaps now upon the sofa and is standing there smiling when Rudolf joins her. She leans down and kisses him, and slaps him gayly. He picks her up in his arms and waltzes back into the bedroom with her. There is great rejoicing at this audacity and the musicians swing excitedly into "The Merry Widow" waltz.

Now there are toasts drunk and a general excitement. The Countess Von Stainz feels that at last life is complete and she can die happy.

Then Frau Lucher bursts into the room. The police have come back, they are downstairs and they have heard the racket. A bottle thrown out the window in the excitement has hit someone in the street, complicating matters.

Suddenly there is a great pounding heard in the bedroom. Rudolf's voice rises above the clamor. He is shouting Elena's name. Presently he comes through the doors. Elena has eluded him! Let a search for her be started at once.

"I never should have trusted her to go into that bathroom alone," wails Rudolf.

"How did she get out?" demands the Countess. "Did she jump out of the window?"

"No. She went through another door. I wouldn't have trusted

her if it hadn't been for the affectionate way she hit me!"

Elena, it appears, has gone home. And Rudolf excitedly would know where that home is, if he has to beat the address out of the protesting Frau Lucher. What does he care for the police? He may be insane to step foot out of the hotel, but he is going. Let them fetch his cap! Let them get out of his way! Rudolf doesn't give ten thousand damns what happens to him or his uniform.

"She's leading me on. She wants the thrill of the chase. Then, by God, she'll have it." He is shouting now and making for the door.

"If the accommodations at her house are inadequate I'll bring her back here," calls Rudolf. "So see to it that this party is still going on when I return, whether it's tomorrow—or the next day— or whenever! Come on, Poffy!"

Poffy and Rudolf have dashed through the door. The party is stunned. Frau Lucher is distressed.

"You fools!" she cries. "You fools! Don't you see what will happen? They'll catch him. They'll kill him. Tomorrow there'll be another Hapsburg burning in hell."

Poffy has come dashing back, calling for Frau Lucher. "Have they got him?" she asks, anxiously.

"No. . . . His Imperial Highness presents his compliments and wishes you to advance him a few shillings for his taxi fare!"

Lucher, with a fulsome "My God!" is digging into her purse as the curtain falls.

ACT III

We are back in the living-room of the Krug home. Anton is at the radio, trying to extract an interest from it that will allay his anxieties as he listens intently and watches door and window.

A second later Elena has burst into the room, breathless and agitated. She is wearing Rudolf's cloak, and starts immediately for her room.

Her replies to Anton are monosyllabic. The party was neither amusing nor exciting. Not even upsetting, though her manner may indicate that it was. Why, demands Elena, did Anton ask her to go? That she might have a good time? Well, he was wrong. "You know, Anton, your prescriptions are not always in-fallible!"

On the balcony Elena is stopped again by Father Krug, also excitedly awaiting a report of the party. It is the elder Krug who notices when her cloak drops open that Elena has forgotten her

dress! Elena makes no attempt at explanation for that oversight
as she bundles the cloak about her and disappears into her room.

Now Father Krug is excited. To him Elena is certainly acting
strangely. And people do not take off their clothes for no reason.
There's something the matter, that's plain. But Anton is not
interested.

A moment later a furious ringing of the night bell is startling.
Followed by the excited entrance of Kathie announcing a maniac
and his keeper as the callers.

Rudolf is apologetic but determined on entrance. He brushes
by the gently protesting Anton. He permits Baron Povoromo to
satisfy Anton's curiosity as to who he is by introducing him formally as "the former Archduke Rudolf Maximilian."

"The former!" objects Rudolf. "One would think I had already joined my ancestors in their eternal Empire. However, my
dear doctor, you will readily observe that such is not the case. I
am here, in your charming home, and I wish to see your wife."

"I'm very sorry. My wife has gone to bed."

"She will wish to be aroused."

Anton's answer to that is to send his father to bed, much to the
older man's disgust. Poffy, too, is sent away—back to Lucher's
to see that the party carries on.

Briefly Rudolf and Anton stare at each other. Then Anton's
advance is most friendly. He is indeed glad to see Rudolf.

"You're glad to see me?" The idea is fairly startling to Rudolf.

ANTON—I should think you could imagine why. You've been
something of a presence in my home, for a long time, ever since
Elena and I were married. Not an entirely agreeable presence, I
might add. (*He laughs.*) But one that we could never quite get
rid of. At times, you've stalked around this house as if you
owned it.

RUDOLF (*pleased*)—Have I?

ANTON—I naturally resented it, a little. But now that I have
the chance to see you, and talk to you, I can feel much more
friendly toward that presence.

RUDOLF (*delighted*)—Well! I've known husbands in my time
—but you're the first one who ever granted me a kind word. . . .
I'm glad to see you, too, Herr Professor. Your vast reputation
has not done you justice. (*He bows.*)

ANTON—A remarkably graceful compliment! (*Another bow.*)

RUDOLF—Of course I've known you through your books—I've
studied them, carefully.

ANTON—All eight of them?

RUDOLF—You don't believe me, do you? Very well—cross-examine me.

ANTON—No, no. I don't like cross-examinations. I'm only too eager to take your word for it.

RUDOLF—It's very fortunate that you are. Otherwise I should have been proved a liar. (*They both laugh.* ELENA *enters.*) But I'm going to read them. I know now that they're good.

Elena has entered upon this scene. She finds Rudolf and Anton arm in arm and laughing heartily. They are friends, they assure her eagerly.

"As a matter of fact," adds Rudolf, "we're an incredibly happy combination. Your husband represents the sublimity of the intellectual, and I the quintessence of the emotional. You know—between us, just about there (*Pointing to spot on carpet nearer to himself than Anton.*)—there ought to be found the perfect man."

Rudolf is full of conversation. He has many things to say to them, or more particularly to Anton, and he is confident that he can interest Elena sufficiently to keep her awake, although she has protested that she and Anton are both very sleepy.

First, Rudolf is eager to confess to Anton that he has been making advances to Elena and he is there now for the purpose of continuing those advances until his objective has been reached. Fifteen years before, Rudolf recalls, he became intimate with Elena—

"She was then a maiden, exquisitely frail," he reports, despite Anton's assurance that he is familiar with the preface; "standing hesitantly upon the threshold of infinite potentiality—if you will forgive my eloquence. Ah—she was lovely, Herr Professor. You would have adored her!"

"I'm sure of it," agrees Anton.

RUDOLF—As for myself, I was then as now, a rank idealist—and when I first looked upon her, and felt the touch of her hand and saw the virginal invitation in her eyes, I vowed to myself, "This is the ultimate." So I made her my mistress. For four beautiful years, I was devotedly . . .

ELENA—It was hardly more than two.

RUDOLF—Don't interrupt.

ELENA—Don't exaggerate.

RUDOLF (*rising in rage*)—Don't interrupt.

ELENA—Don't exaggerate.

RUDOLF—I do so only because of a desire to flatter you. Our idyllic romance was terminated by the revolution. Austria was compelled to give up most of her treasured provinces and possessions, including my family. We were waltzing that morning at Lucher's when the summons came. I never even had a chance to say good-by. In my exile I concluded that I would never see my darling again and I made an effort to reconcile myself to that dismal realization. The effort was not completely successful. For ten years I have felt the lack of her. So I decided to return to Vienna, have one more look at her, and let my youthful illusions be shattered once and for all.

ANTON—That was a highly intelligent decision, wasn't it, Elena?

ELENA—I'm not quite certain.

RUDOLF—Yes, it was, in theory. For I assumed that she would have become a commonplace, obese, bourgeois housewife.

ANTON—She has resisted the influences surrounding her.

RUDOLF—She has, indeed, and I've been grievously disappointed. I find that my acute want of her was no illusion. It remains a fact. A fact which we all must face.

It may be a bit difficult for Anton to accept the situation at first, Rudolf is prepared to believe. It was not easy for Elena to accept it, even after Rudolf had confessed his complete subjugation to her charms and her constant presence in his memory. But Anton will, Rudolf believes, prove entirely qualified to deal with the situation. If Anton will only subject him to treatment, Rudolf insists, they will all be better off. It may take a long time for a treatment, but Rudolf is prepared to prolong his stay indefinitely.

Anton has no intention of subjecting Rudolf to treatment. Anton is a psychiatrist. Rudolf's case demands the services of a neuropathologist. Let him go to Munich, where there is a good one.

"But I don't want to go to Munich," protests Rudolf. "I want this problem to be settled now."

"I'm not a witch doctor, my friend," answers Anton. "I can't straighten out a mass of glandular complications with one wave of the hand."

"But I'm not complicated—even though I do like to present myself as an enigma— . . . You see, Herr Professor, I'm simply a man who lives on sensations. They're meat and drink and breath of life to me. You must realize that for all my talk the

thing that I most urgently need is nourishment for my self-esteem.
My ego is like the belly of a starving man. It's bloated but
empty."

ANTON—And you imagine that I can furnish the necessary
nourishment?
RUDOLF—Well, if you can't—no one else can.
ANTON—If this could be dealt with in a rational manner, it
would be simple. I'd tell you to look at her to your heart's content—fill your imagination with her. And then see for yourself
that for you she has no substance; she's a dream that you've
explained, and disposed of, and that you can never recapture.
But it isn't so simple as that.
RUDOLF—You're right, my friend. I must do more than just
look.
ELENA—Well, Anton, what have you to say to that?
ANTON—There's nothing for me to say. I don't want to have
anything to say.
RUDOLF—It's a damned awkward situation. It wouldn't have
arisen if it hadn't been for your decency. When I came in here
I was ready to fight and either be dragged out myself or take
Elena with me. But you were so kind. You were so friendly.
You showed me that this dispute should be settled by reason as
opposed to force.

To Anton the dispute is becoming essentially unreasonable.
To Rudolf it is altogether natural. He is not trying to take
Elena away from her husband for good and all. He is merely
proposing that she return to him for one night. On such a
memory he will be able to live for another ten years. In ten
years he will no longer be a serious menace.
Now Anton feels himself being forced into the "hellishly uncomfortable position of a jealous husband." Seemingly the only
way he can extricate himself is to act like a jealous husband and
put Rudolf out of his home.
If that is the only way to settle it Rudolf is ready, though he
is greatly disappointed in Anton. "I have exposed him before
your eyes," he calls exultantly to Elena. "This triumph of civili-
ation is behaving like a vindictive ape."
Elena has perched herself on the bench in front of the fireplace. Nothing could induce her to leave. "I've just realized
that I've been waiting for this moment for years," she cries.
"That's right," excitedly answers Rudolf. "Stay where you

are. When I've had enough I'll call to you and you can drag him off me!"

Rudolf warns them that he has no intention of fighting fair. He does not know how to fight with his fists. He has a handsome offer to make.

"Give her to me for this one night," proposes Rudolf, "and I shall give to you in return my one possession—namely, this carcass that I wear about my immortal soul, these priceless pounds of flesh. Tomorrow I shall go forth upon the Ringstrasse. I will kick and insult policemen. My identity will become known. I shall be beaten to earth and shot, and I shall die gloriously in the gutter, my head pillowed on a pile of excrement. But before I take this suicidal action, I shall sign documents bequeathing my remains, unconditionally, to the eminent Professor Doctor . . . What's the name?

"Krug."

"Krug! All that is left of me will be yours. You will appreciate my value to science. You may lay me out on your operating table, you may probe me, dissect me, discover just what it is about me that has made me what I am, the quality that dominated most of Europe for the past six hundred years. You will be able to say to your students: 'Here, gentlemen, this revolting object that I hold before you is the heart of a Hapsburg.' "

Now Anton is undone. He cannot fight such a man. There are a thousand reasons why he should hit Rudolf, but he can't do it. He could, he feels, finish such a fight, but he cannot start it.

Nor could he finish it, Elena sees now. Only she can do that—

There is a violent ringing of the bell. A moment later Baron Povoromo has dashed in to report that the police are again closing in on Rudolf. They will be upon him any minute.

It is Rudolf's opinion that this would be an easy way to settle everything, but Elena is insistent that he shall not be taken. He must hide. With further persuasion and a little pushing Rudolf is forced into the bedroom.

Now it is the Baron Povoromo's suggestion that Anton should go to the street door and reason with the police. He has great influence with the authorities. He can, if he will, persuade Herr Wreede, the Prefect, who is at Schonbrunn, to permit His Highness to leave Austria quietly. That will be an act of great generosity.

"An act of great generosity," muses Anton, "and, let us hope of great wisdom."

"Have you any doubt of the wisdom, Anton?" Elena asks.

"Yes, I have, but I must not admit it," replies Anton. "I am facing the test of my own principles. You've heard what my students call me: 'The Messiah of a new faith.' Well, to-night I've heard the bitter injunction that is given to all messiahs: 'Physician, heal thyself.' Very well, I'll go out to Schonbrunn and see Wreede. I shan't be back before morning."

"Oh!"

"Yes. You saw the truth, Elena. You're the only one who can settle it. If you can look at him, and laugh at him, and pity him, as you'd pity a deluded child; if you can see him for what he is, and not for what your imagination tells you he was—then you're free. He can never hurt you whatever he does or what-ever you do."

"Very well, Anton."

"Good-by, Elena. And tell him not to worry. Herr Wreede will be glad to do me a favor. His wife is one of my patients."

Rudolf comes dejectedly into the room, carrying his coat. 'Hidden in the bedroom he has been suffering the pangs of self-abasement, resulting from deflation of the ego."

He is perfectly safe now, Elena assures him. Anton has gone to arrange matters with the prefect of police, and Anton has great influence. She is, Elena admits, sublimely trustful of Anton.

"As effective a bit of foul play as I have ever witnessed," sar-donically asserts Rudolf. "He's tricked me into his debt—put me on my honor. He knows that I have that. It runs in the Hapsburg blood—honor and epilepsy. . . . God damn him! He's devitalized me, emasculated me. While I was in there, hiding, waiting for him to protect me from the law, I looked at my coat, and the obsolete medals, and the worn-out lining, and a great truth dawned on me. It came to me in a revelation that I am no longer an archduke, nephew of the Emperor. I am a taxi-driver, dressed up!"

"And did your revelation also disclose to you what I am now?"

"Yes. You're no longer a mistress—you're a wife—and con-sequently unprepossessing."

Rudolf must also have realized, Elena reminds him, that she, Elena, can now face him, laugh at him and pity him as she would a deluded child. . . . Now she thinks he had better go to bed and get some rest against his traveling in the morning.

"I shall rest peacefully, soothed by the knowledge that even I have influential friends in Vienna," agrees Rudolf. "Good night. And when the benevolent doctor returns, please try to

express to him some measure of my gratitude. Assure him that
thanks to his generosity, I shall leave Vienna, forever, and return
to my taxi."

Elena is handing him his coat when she notices a tear in the
lining. She would mend that for him.

RUDOLF—Please don't bother. I'll never wear it again.

ELENA—You will, Rudolf. You'll always wear it, gallantly,
even if it is a little torn. It's something they can never take
from you. It's your coat.

RUDOLF—Yes, one of the meager possessions of Herr Von
Hapsburg! You're very sweet, Elena. I don't quite know why
you should be, in view of the ridiculous trouble I've caused. I'm
sorry.

ELENA—No, Rudolf, you must never be sorry.

RUDOLF—Good night, my dear. (*Kisses her hand.*) Good-by.
(*He goes into the bedroom. Elena picks up his coat and looks
at the medals, hanging limply. Sits on the sofa beside coat,
smiles. After a moment she turns off the light, goes to bedroom
door and opens it. The light from within shines upon her. She
goes in.*) The curtain falls.

Next morning the room is brilliantly sunny. Kathie is completing the breakfast arrangements. There is coffee service for
four and a dish of kidneys for Dr. Krug.

Father Krug is the first to come in. He is in a state of mind
because the morning papers have failed to make any report of
the most exciting happenings at the Hotel Lucher the night before. He would also very much like to know what happened in
the house after he went to bed. But Kathie cannot tell him.

Rudolf is radiantly cheerful when he comes. This, to Rudolf
is probably the most glorious morning of any that has ever
dawned in Vienna, already widely celebrated for the quality of
its mornings.

Elena, also radiant, joins them shortly. She also remarks the
gorgeousness of the morning. When she would pour their coffee
she cannot remember whether Rudolf takes sugar or not. It
doesn't matter. Rudolf doesn't remember himself. The idea is
vastly amusing to Father Krug. To all of them, in fact.

Anton and Baron Povoromo find the three laughing uproariously when they arrive. The Baron is slightly disheveled. He
has been standing outside in the street all night, thinking he

might be of some help if the police should come to take his prince. For that show of gallantry Rudolf is moved to give Poffy one of his medals.

Now, breakfast finished, Rudolf would return to the Hotel Lucher and wake up the celebrants. The party is still on. But Anton is sure there will not be time. By the arrangements he has made Rudolf must start immediately for Passau, where he will be allowed to cross the frontier. There is a government car waiting for him downstairs, and Anton, who has given his word that he will see Rudolf depart from Austria, will go with him.

"It's time to go, Rudolf," says Elena.

"I know it is," he answers, turning to Anton. "But before I depart, Herr Professor, let me say that I call your roof tree blessed. For beneath it a Hapsburg has been entertained—royally entertained—and has been granted into the bargain, a superb demonstration of applied psychology. (*He turns to* ELENA *and kisses her hand.*) Good-by, Elena. No wistful tears, please."

He has said his farewells to Poffy, kissed Herr Krug on both cheeks and is gone. Elena turns to Anton:

ELENA—Anton, there's something I must say to you before you go.

ANTON—Please don't say anything. I have only to look at you . . .

ELENA—But what I wanted to say was; when you get to the frontier ask him to give you back my wedding ring.

ANTON—I shall. And I left a package for you in the hall. Frau Lucher gave it to me. It's your white dress. (*He smiles at* ELENA *and goes out.*)

KRUG (*looking out of window*)—A government car with the shades drawn.

ELENA—Sit down, Poffy, and have some breakfast. You must be famished.

POFFY (*taking place* RUDOLF *has vacated at the table*)—I rather imagine that I am.

KRUG—Wait! They're just starting. And the policeman is saluting them.

ELENA—Oh, all the kidneys are gone. Father, ring the bell and tell Kathie to cook some more.

KRUG—Enough for me too?

ELENA—Of course.

KRUG (*ringing bell*)—Good.

ELENA—Cream, Poffy?

POFFY—No, thanks. I've got out of the habit of cream.

KRUG—You know, Elena, I've never had so much fun in all my life.

ELENA—Neither have I. (*She hands* POFFY *his coffee.*)

THE CURTAIN FALLS

THE HOUSE OF CONNELLY

A Drama in Two Acts

BY PAUL GREEN

THE New York Theatre Guild had been considering the production of this play by Paul Green, "The House of Connelly," for the better part of two seasons, but its directorate had some difficulty making up its collective mind in the matter.

There was a group of newer Guild members, actors and minor executives, variously disposed in the work of the organization, which had been responsible for the production of "Roar, China!" the previous season. Having earned a *succes d'estime* with that venture the leaders of the group were eager to try another production.

The Guild finally gave "The House of Connelly" into their keeping in the spring of 1931. Led by Lee Strasberg and Cheryl Crawford, who were to stage the play, these Guild associates rented a farm in Connecticut, fitted up the barn as a theatre and there, for ten weeks, rehearsed the Green play, as well as several others, preparatory to making their Broadway début in the fall. A part of the time Mr. Green, coming up from his North Carolina home, worked with them.

"The House of Connelly" was presented independently by The Group Theatre, Inc., at the Martin Beck Theatre on September 28, 1931, but also "under the auspices of the Theatre Guild," according to the program. The response on the part of the reviewers was highly favorable, and this endorsement was later confirmed by the public, though the drama never quite reached the popular success hoped for it. It continued at the Martin Beck until the Guild wanted this playhouse for the use of Alfred Lunt and Lynn Fontanne, due with "Reunion in Vienna" in mid-November. The Connelly play was then transferred to the Mansfield Theatre where it was played for an additional six weeks.

"The House of Connelly," like other plays of the South by the author of "In Abraham's Bosom," which won him a Pulitzer prize in 1927, is a vividly human study of the Paul Green neighbors. It concerns the last of a family of proud but decadent aristocrats of the old South brought into conflict with a younger,

145

more vigorous and more definitely democratic new South, represented in this instance by a heroine drawn from the "poor white" tenantry on the disintegrating Connelly estate. The drama has a poetic value common to the Green plays and a sweep of drama in its climacteric episodes that is tremendously moving.

The opening scene is in the fields of the Connelly farm. It is late afternoon, "and across the land to the west a murky cloud creeps up the sky, lighted along its edge by a bluish tinge from the hidden sun." In the foreground "a rail fence grown up with an unkempt hedgerow of dead fennel weeds, poke stalks and sassafras bushes."

"Two old sybil-like Negro women come in from the right, one carrying a hoe and the other a tow sack, and both chewing tobacco in their toothless jaws. They are huge creatures, sexual and fertile, with round moist roving eyes and jowled faces smooth and hairless as a baby's. The mark of ancient strength and procreation still remains in their protuberant breasts and bulging hips. Under old coats their broad shoulders and arms are muscled like men."

These two are Big Sis and Big Sue, and they have come to dig sassafras roots. Big Sue does most of the digging, snarling in simulated anger as she attacks the roots with her hoe, which amuses Big Sis. Three empty stack poles in the nearby field that stand out "lak de gallows whah dey hung Nigger Purvis on," attract their attention, stirring them reminiscently.

"Po' Purvis," sighs Big Sis.

"Po' General," echoes Big Sue.

"Own flesh and blood make no difference. De law say hang."

"De General say hang."

"Purvis can't say 'Pappy'!"

"General can't say 'son.' No, Lawd, no!"

"Umh—po' Purvis—dat nigger twist 'bout lak a worm on a fishhook de day dey hang him."

They are at their digging again. From far off the sound of a shot is heard. They stand for a moment listening. Then they break into peals of laughter.

It is Mr. Will Connelly shooting doves, they are agreed. But Mr. Will ain't hittin' um. Mr. Will ain't the shootin' man old General Connelly was. Nor the hoss man. Nor the heavy ridin' man. Mr. Will can't do nothin'. "Creep about. Let the world rot down. Can't do nothin'."

Their attention is attracted down the road. A new tenant girl is picking pokeberries. A keen-eyed tenant girl. "Been

Photo by Vandamm Studio, New York.

"THE HOUSE OF CONNELLY"

Uncle Bob is both startled and amused by the marked change in Will. "It's rejuvenation," he insists, eyeing Will and Patsy narrowly. "Two weeks ago he couldn't have stood up and faced them," he says. "Now he speaks like an orator."

(*Franchot Tone, Morris Carnovsky and Margaret Barker*)

moved on dis plantation three weeks and sees everything,"
observes Big Sis. "Po' white trash," sneers Big Sue. "Pushing
up in de world—reaching and a-grabbing at de high place of de
quality and de roof over our heads!"

Patsy Tate "is a lithe full-figured girl of twenty or more, with
cheeks pink in the cold and dark gipsy-like eyes—eyes which at
times have a bright, hard look. She wears a cloak buttoned close
up under her throat and a stocking cap pulled down over her
ears."

Patsy, reaching them, is friendly, but critical. She notices
Big Sis and Big Sue have pulled a rail off the fence. The hogs'll
get through that hole. They'd better put the rail back. If
they want firewood there's plenty in the woods.

The women are civil enough, and obedient, but they do considerable disrespectful snickering between answers. Patsy, they
suspect slyly, is looking for the hunter shootin' down in the
cawnfield. The hunter who can't hit nothin'. They hee-haw
with laughter at the thought.

"Us tell yo' fortune 'bout loving," slyly ventures Big Sue,
picking up a handful of damp holly leaves.

"Can you?" Patsy is smiling, but interested.

"Us bofe kin," adds Big Sis.

BIG SUE—Us don't miss 'um neiver. (*Prancing before her and
holding a leaf up.*)   Name one dem p'ints yo' sweetheart's name.

PATSY (*glancing at her sharply*)—Hm—m—

BIG SUE (*sweetly, mammy-like*)—Gwine tell yo' fortune,
honey.

BIG SIS—Yah, name yo' man, honey.

BIG SUE (*shambling away*)—Aw raght den—now listen, folkses,
and ketch de truf.

BIG SIS—Dat's right, speak it, Sister.

BIG SUE—Done made many a match wid a holly leaf. Toodle-
de-doo. And bruk up many one.

PATSY—Oh, yes.

BIG SIS—Yeb'm
          All of us turn and face de west,
          See who de man dat she love best.

(*They turn and face toward the left, and presently* PATSY, *smiling, does likewise.* BIG SUE *brings her arm over in a circle and
touches each point of the leaf.*)

BIG SUE—Heenery-hinery-hikum-ho,
          Answer muh answer dere below,

Speak wid muh finger, say wid muh voice—
Shall dis 'oman have huh choice?

(*Softly.*) None dem p'ints show any u'gement yit. (*Chanting.*)
Slimmery-slissum-slickum-slo,
Answer muh answer dere below,
Who is de man dis 'oman'll wed—

(*She poises her hand in the air, listening.*)

BIG SIS (*grunting*)—Who she gonna keep warm wid in bed?

BIG SUE—Don't heah no answer, sump'n wrong.
Mischief-meevery-miny-mo,
Answer muh answer dere below,
Gimme some motion, gimme some sound—

In back of them Will Connelly appears the other side of the hedge. "He is a gentleman farmer of thirty or thirty-five, with slightly stooping shoulders and thin clean-shaven face. A gun hangs loosely from the crook of his arm."

Big Sue has gone on with the fortune. Suddenly Big Sis cries out—"Death gwine take huh church-wedding bound."

"Dere," Big Sue exclaims, tearing the holly leaf in two; "you name one man an' us tell you anudder—hee-hee." There is malice in her voice.

"Mought's well take yo' mind off'n him," warns Big Sis.

They are still twitting Patsy when Will Connelly steps forward. The Negro women return quickly to their digging. "In a lightning flash they are no other than two obsequious and ignorant old Negro women."

Will gives Big Sis and Big Sue a quarter for Christmas eve. And there may be some drinkin' stuff at the big house. He'll see. They are roaring with laughter as they go.

Will is not altogether at his ease with Patsy. Admits he is not much of a hunter. Killed a dove once. Never wanted to kill another. He hopes Patsy and her father and brothers like the place they've rented. They've fixed it up a lot, he's noticed. Looks nicer.

Another line of flying doves comes within range. Suddenly Patsy grabs the gun out of Will's arm and fires. Two of the birds tumble into the woods. She would go after them, but he stops her. And changes the subject. What is she going to do with the pokeberries?

The young tenant people are going on a Christmas serenade, Patsy tells him. Some of them will stain their faces with the berries and look terribly funny. Won't he go along too?

Jesse Tate, Patsy's father, "a heavy-set farmer of fifty, with swarthy face and iron-gray hair," is walking across the field and finds them.

"Any luck hunting, sir?" Tate inquires of Will, touching the rim of his hat respectfully.

"Your daughter here just shot two doves," Will answers. "No, I haven't killed anything."

TATE (*pecking at the ground with his stick*)—She's about as good as Daniel Boone when it comes to guns. She is that.

PATSY—Pshaw. Father raised me up same as a boy to ride and hunt, Mr. Will.

WILL—Yes. Good training, I reckon. (*Pulling his coat tight.*) Cold weather, like snow.

TATE (*heavily*)—Don't know. The sky's got a sort of glassy glaze to it, don't look like a muggy, thickish snow cold.

WILL—No. (*After waiting for someone to speak.*) Hope you're not too disappointed in the farm.

TATE—Well, no. I been down looking over that tract you spoke of my tending.

WILL—Hope you can handle it.

TATE—I'll have to, won't I? It's washed out and bogged up with briars and bushes, but I'll clean that out by March.

WILL—Well, don't freeze in this cold, Miss Patsy. Good evening. (*He tips his cap in half embarrassment as he starts off.*)

PATSY and TATE—Good evening.

TATE (*presently*)—Seems like a nice sort of landlord.

PATSY (*turning to her berry picking*)—Yes.

TATE—But he ain't no farmer. I knew the Connelly farm when I lived in this neighborhood as a boy. I wished you could have seen it then.

PATSY—I do.

TATE—He's no more like his father than black is white. The old General Connelly was a ripsnorter. Things moved around him. (*Sighing.*) Still he was right much of an ungodly person, and I reckon things even up somehow, I don't know. Yes, I reckon so.

PATSY—They say Mr. Will is one of the best men in the neighborhood.

TATE—But a man old as him ought to have a family and be making things go along.

PATSY—I don't know. Oh, well, that's not our business, is it?

TATE—No, there's nobody good enough for him, and never will be according to his mother—and his sisters. Never was anybody good enough for a Connelly. There they all set in that great house. If I had this farm— Well, no matter, I say.

PATSY—What?

TATE—Walking over these fields today I'd give anything, anything in good honesty to have owned them. (*Half murmuring.*) It's purty land, purty land and level as a table, two thousand acres of it.

PATSY—You'll have your own farm yet—some of these days you will.

TATE (*with a touch of moroseness.*)—No, I won't. I'll die the other fellow's man—a tenant. (*After a moment.*) You will too.

PATSY (*sharply.*) I won't.

TATE—Oh, but you'll come to it.

PATSY—No.

TATE—Let's go home. (*He climbs over the stile and is gone. Patsy stands looking after him a moment. Presently she tosses her head, and, whistling, turns once more to picking berries. BIG SIS and BIG SUE creep back along the hedge and begin digging sassafras roots again, acting as if in ignorance of her presence.*)

PATSY—What do you want now?

BIG SIS (*swinging her hoe*)—Raise her up—hah—bring her down—hah.

BIG SUE—Sink her to de hilt—hah—sink her to de crown—hah.

PATSY (*eyeing them*)—Hope you work like that when chopping cotton time comes.

BIG SUE (*tearing her piece of rail out of the fence*)—I sticks dis up foh a headboa'd at de grave. A'ready I sticks it up, and watch her rouse mad. (*She jabs it into the earth and watches it swaying as if reading some mystic meaning there.*)

PATSY (*bursting into a laugh*)—That's right, tear the old fence down. We'll put up a wire one where it was.

BIG SUE—And de wind and de rain kin write de name. (*PATSY watches them wryly and half-perplexed a moment and then walks away. Just as she goes out she begins jingling her bucket and whistling, apparently in high spirits.*)

BIG SIS (*winking and singing*)—

> De sporrow sot wid her head in huh wing,
> De snake crope up and 'gun to sing—

(*As if with simultaneous understanding they turn and thumb their noses after* PATSY, *then at the sky, wagging their heads and breaking into loud blasphemous laughter. Between their staccato guffaws,* PATSY *is heard whistling in the distance.*)   The curtain falls.

A few hours later, in the dining-room of the old Connelly mansion supper is being laid. "The tall candles and the firelight illumine an interior once pretentious but now falling to decay.

"The walls paneled and decorated in proud Georgian style, are yellowed and cracked, and the portraits of the Connelly ancestors hang moldering in their frames. The furniture is early eighteenth century, with mahogany table, sideboard, chairs, and tapestries here and there. A wide fireplace is set between fluted pilasters and under an ornate mantel. . . . If once the frilled and pompous gentlemen spent many a joyous evening here in the days gone by—when the guests sat to the board and slaves handed on goblets of liquor and wine, as they said—it is so no longer. For now the grace of hospitality is gone, the jovial host is gone, gone is the slave. The dead Connellys, erect in their frames, wait for the end.

"The two surviving daughters of Connelly Hall, now late middle-aged spinsters, are laying supper in this dining-room, fetching dishes of food from the kitchen at the left. Geraldine is tall and somewhat prim, with pallid aristocratic features; Evelyn is a few years younger and less austere."

Geraldine ("Dennie," Evelyn calls her) has heard the gunshots from the field and has seen her brother Will and Patsy Tate standing together. That worries Geraldine, though Evelyn can see no harm in it. Patsy is as pretty a poor-white girl as Evelyn has ever seen.

Now the table is finished and Evelyn turns to the sideboard to strike the gong with measured strokes. "The two women grow still in their tracks listening as the soft musical tones go echoing through the house."

"I never get tired listening to it," says Evelyn. "Something so lonely beautiful in it. For a hundred years it has called our people into this dining-room. A hundred years—"

Geraldine turns quickly and goes to the kitchen. "I was forgetting the coffee," is her excuse.

Evelyn's musing is not discouraged. Now she hears the old gong go calling, calling through the old house and finding no one. She remembers this Christmas eve, and that one, when their father was alive. The fun they used to have—and the friends.

"We have friends now, Evelyn," Geraldine reminds her.

"Yes, Mother and Will, and Uncle Bob and you and me," counts Evelyn. "There were so many more then. Father—Grandfather—Aunt Charlotte and Uncle Henry. Soon there'll be Uncle Bob and Will and you and me; then you and me and Will; then—"

Will Connelly, dressed as he was in the fields, save that he has taken off his hunter's leggings, comes with the mail—what there is of it. "A letter or two—and some circulars, papers and a few Christmas cards." Will has a box for Evelyn, too. Sid Shepherd sent it. A flashy toilet set—

"Thank you and him both," says Evelyn. "In spite of the—the taste, it's nice."

"Taste nothing," hurriedly answers Will. "Sid Shepherd's all right—if he did grow up from poor white folks."

A second sounding of the gong brings Uncle Bob Connelly. "He is a run-down old Southern gentleman of sixty-five or seventy—dressed in moth-eaten evening clothes of the style of the seventies—with a ragged mustache, pointed scraggly beard, and the pale, mottled face of a consistent drinker."

Uncle Bob is in gay spirits. Singing a bit of a song. Wishing everybody a Merry Christmas. Glad to see that old Madeira has been brought out again for this festal occasion.

Now Will helps his mother in and seats her at the head of the table. Mrs. Connelly is near Uncle Bob's age, but appears much older; a shell of a woman, with something of the dignity and strength of the matriarch yet remaining to her. "She is crippled and walks with the aid of a crutch. Her dress of heavy black silk, surmounted by a lace cap, comes down voluminously around her."

Mrs. Connelly is pleased with the way the girls have arranged things. In quavering voice she asks Divine blessing. "On this hallowed evening we bow our heads before Thee. Bless us, bless this food to our use and to Thy name's honor and glory. Bless this house. Teach us to hold sacred its memory and the memory of our fathers. We humbly beg in the name of the Blessed Redeemer. Amen."

Spirits rise. The Madeira is served. There is a brave show of gayety. Uncle Bob would propose his annual toast—

"On this Christmas eve, marking the one hundred and fiftieth year this house has stood," he begins, rising at his place and drawing out the words in deep oratorical sonority, "we lift our cup to the present keeper of its ancient hearth—one who bears the sacred name of Mother, one who has shared her husband's (*With a gesture towards the portrait above the mantel.*) accomplishments and his glory, one who is the proud possessor of all virtues known to womanhood and not one blemish; (*His voice full of real and genuine feeling.*) one whose life has been an inspiration to us all; to you, Ellen, we drink."

There is a slight note of discord when the Negro Duffy comes for meat for his family and there is nothing to give him except the best ham. The thought fills Uncle Bob with sudden anger. If they could only go back to slave days for a little Uncle Bob would teach the lazy Duffy crowd to work for their meat. The damned Yankees—they're responsible.

Now Will has grown solemn and lost his appetite. Must be in love, ventures Uncle Bob. The wine has set Uncle Bob's mind flashing backward and kept his tongue going.

"I fought the battle of the Wilderness—at Gettysburg I fought," he reminds them, whether they would listen or not. "I yielded up my arms at Appomattox. But I never was whipped. I'm not whipped now."

"Of course not," smilingly agrees Mrs. Connelly.

"Our day is not over," persists Uncle Robert, talking through Geraldine and Evelyn's efforts to plan a visit for Virginia Buchanan, who is coming in the spring. "Chance, luck that makes the great, makes success. A heavy rain is what beat the Confederacy. Our guns were stuck below the hill. It happened to rain. But our day will come. (*Drawing up his shoulders.*) And when it does a Jeff Davis won't have to hide in woman's clothes then. Nor will a Robert E. Lee have to pray to God so much. It'll be minnie balls and not prayer."

Mrs. Connelly is still a gracious listener, but Will Connelly rebels. "Talk, talk," he mutters disgustedly, dropping his knife and fork in his plate with a clatter. "God help me! God help us all!"

They all eye him with astonishment. Mrs. Connelly sits up straight and offended.

"God?" protests Uncle Bob. "Thou hast not read the Stoics, son."

"Stoics, Epicureans, Atomists! Cicero, Horace! They don't tell you how to feed hungry niggers, how to meet over-drafts and pay mortgages. Do they?"

In agitation Mrs. Connelly retires from the table. Despite

Will's statement that he is sorry, and Uncle Robert's voluble explanations, she insists upon being helped to her room. Evelyn is quite distressed. Will, when he returns from his mother, is also apologetic. The Connellys are too proud to live in this world, is Uncle Bob's opinion.

"Let's all take poison and die," Uncle Bob suggests. "Burn up the house. Leave the crickets and the field mice to their inheritance."

There is another way, Uncle Bob admits. Let Will turn the farm over to old man Tate and his daughter. Or even to the daughter alone. The Tates are good farmers. Or Will might consider Virginia Buchanan when she comes a-visiting in the spring. Virginia is an heiress—

"Virginia Buchanan," Will breaks in, "and I beg her pardon— never had a thought but for her blue blood and the Confederate flag and something she thinks her folks did on the battlefields of Virginia."

"Ho-ho-ho," laughs Uncle Bob, significantly. "Did you and Miss Patsy kill any game this evening? I saw you banging away together there by the hedgerow. Sweet, ain't she?"

They have cleared the table when the first sounds from the serenaders come floating over the fields. Now they are thick around the house and Big Sis and Big Sue have edged in to ask for their "drinkum stuff."

The music has stopped. The serenaders crowd up on the portico, laughing gaily, pushing in at the doorway, but hesitating about entering the room. "They are dressed in all sorts of outlandish garbs—some wearing their clothes backwards, some with masks or doughfaces on, and others painted like Indians on the warpath."

At Uncle Bob's enthusiastic invitation Mark Lucas brings in his fiddle and fiddles a tune. It is pleasantly reminiscent to Uncle Bob. He grabs Evelyn and rushes her through a step or two of a dance before she can free herself.

Now there are calls for Patsy Tate and she is pushed through the crowd. "She is dressed in the garb of a gypsy with a scarlet band around her head, a flouncy, flowing dress, with stained lips and cheeks and painted eyebrows and lashes."

Will is mildly astonished at Patsy's appearance, but it is Uncle Bob who would lead her into the dance.

"We'd better go, maybe," says Patsy, drawing back. "We all didn't mean to come in and disturb you so."

Uncle Bob has called a general dance, the crowd is clapping

its hands rhythmically, and there is general hilarity, a part of the company coming into the room but still staying close to the door.

"Let her roll!" shouts Uncle Bob, as he thumps about. "Swing your partner! Sachez to the right, sachez to the left! Promenade all! Hands all around!"

Uncle Bob has grabbed Patsy, to the amusement of the crowd, and dances her past Will. "Come on, play, Mr. Will," Patsy shouts. Will does not respond.

Now the music has changed to "Gipsy Davie," the dancing has stopped and Patsy, weaving her hands around her is singing. The crowd joins in the chorus—

> "Last night I lay on a warm feather bed,
> My arms were around my a-baby, O;
> Tonight I'll lie on some cold river bank,
> In the arms of my Gipsy a-Davie, O."

There is more music and more laughter. Suddenly a half-witted fellow dances out into the room and circles Will, giggling and leering. The serenaders roar with laughter. Will grabs the boy by the collar and quiets him, roughly.

Uncle Bob has climbed on a chair. He raises a glass of wine for a toast. The crowd murmurs approvingly and is quiet. Suddenly Mrs. Connelly appears in the inner doorway. The crowd backs away from her, but Uncle Bob goes on with the toast—

"To the blessed memory of a gallant soldier and a great gentleman—the dead husband of our dear lady and erstwhile master of this house—"

Mrs. Connelly has moved farther into the room. She stands with Geraldine and Evelyn looking up at the portrait of the General. "Will has again dropped his head on his chest and is staring at the floor. The serenaders, as if awed by some uncomprehended ritual, begin to steal out of the room one by one. Uncle Bob, oblivious to all around him, slowly continues, his voice deepening with emotion.

"To him we drink who in the face of death mounted the Stars and Bars above the rampart of the enemy; the first at Manassas, last at Appomattox, furthest at Gettysburg—to thee we lift this cup—(*As if addressing a living person.*) To thee, suh, jurist, patriot, soldier, citizen, we drink—General William Hampton Connelly of Connelly Hall!"

There is great shouting outside. Uncle Bob drinks his wine and steps heavily down from the chair. Patsy is the only one of the serenaders left. Mrs. Connelly moves forward solemnly. "Thank you, Robert," she murmurs. Evelyn kisses her uncle with enthusiasm. Geraldine is still gazing at the General's portrait.

UNCLE BOB—*Arma virumque cano.* How great a thing to have an honored name. Ah, we shall not look upon his like again. (*He moves to the fireplace and stands looking closely at the portrait. Lifting his arm, disclosing a wide rip in his coat, he goes on in the voice of one at prayer.*) In our poor way we honor thee. (*Stretching his other hand back towards Will who looks up somewhat sheepishly.*) And may this, thy son, wear the mantle of his father with profit and renown. May he become conscious of the name he bears, and from this day forth determine by the help of God— (*He stops and sits down in an armchair near the fire, his head bent over.*)

VOICES (*outside*)—Come on, Patsy, le's go!

MRS. CONNELLY—We will excuse you.

PATSY—I—All right. Thank you, Ma'm. (*Now ignoring* MRS. CONNELLY.) Come on, Mr. Will, and go with us a-serenading.

WILL (*starting up*)—Me? (*Foolishly.*) Hah-hah-hah!

GERALDINE—You can go out this way.

PATSY—We're going to stop at the millpond and have an eggfry. All of you come.

UNCLE BOB—I'll go.

PATSY (*her eyes glittering*)—The young folks told me to ask you. (*As no one says anything.*) I'm sorry we disturbed you. (*Impetuously.*) Why're you all so—so solemn? (*She turns and walks with dignity from the room.*)

MRS. CONNELLY (*after a long silence*)—Please see to the fire before you go to bed tonight, Will.

WILL—All right, Mother.

MRS. CONNELLY—Help me to my room, will you, Geraldine? (GERALDINE *helps her out.*)

UNCLE BOB—Old and solemn, mournful as whippoorwills. (EVELYN *goes to the kitchen and leaves them. He pours himself another glass of wine and gestures heavily towards the portraits.*) Ladies— (WILL *suddenly picks up his hat and starts out at the rear.*) Where to, Galahad?

WILL—I'll look about the barn a minute.

UNCLE BOB (*staring after him and spanking his thigh*)—Ho,

ho! (*Calling.*) Don't fall in the millpond. By Jesus! (*Gesturing around again at the portraits.*) Gentlemen—
The curtain falls.

It is a night in the early spring several months later. Moonlight bathes the ruined garden of Connelly Hall. In the foreground there "is an old scraggly myrtle tree with a garden seat under it." To the right of the seat "a stone pool grown up into a mush of lilies and flags." In the dim distance "the tombstones of the family burying ground glitter in the moonlight, the sarcophagus of General William Hampton Connelly standing lordly above the rest."

"The garden is partially illuminated through the lighted windows of the mansion. Contrasting with the mournfulness of the decaying garden and the pallid light of the moon are the gay strains of a waltz coming from an orchestra in the house. Once again a ball is being given in Connelly Hall and the rooms are alive with youthful laughter and music. Twinkling feet go up and down the broad staircase, hands are squeezed and hearts are fluttered as was told of in the old days."

Big Sis and Big Sue are viewing the festivities from this vantage point and forming their own opinions of what they see.

"Lawd, dey's cutting up dere," reports Big Sis, standing by the myrtle tree and looking toward the house. "Sho' giving dat Miss Virginia a blowout—uhm!"

"Dat Miss Virginia sho' God is a queen," ventures Big Sue, coming to stand beside her. "Look how she sashay!"

"Sashay her tail off, do huh no good wid Mr. Will," sputters Big Sis.

Worries them a bit to see that "huzzy bitch Patsy . . . hugging up wid de quality." The thought of what's going to happen to Patsy fills them with such glee that they must do a dance.

They scatter when Will Connelly approaches from the house. Reaching the clearing Will walks mournfully, meditatively up and down. Soon he is joined by Virginia Buchanan, who has also come for the quiet of the garden. "Virginia is a tall gracious woman of twenty-five, somewhat irregularly featured, with a girlish giddy voice that goes prattling along like a bubbling brook."

Virginia likes the old garden. She has been there many times and nothing has disturbed her—nothing but her thoughts of Will. Virginia is anxious about Will. He has hardly spoken to her since she came. Certainly something very serious must be worrying him.

If there is, Will cannot or will not tell Virginia what it is. Nor can he exactly explain to her how Patsy Tate, a tenant girl, is dancing at the house, though, of course, not everybody is as proud as Virginia and Geraldine.

Virginia is worried about Will. He doesn't seem happy. He really ought to come to Charleston for a vacation. . . . And isn't Connelly Hall the loveliest place? . . . Isn't the boxwood gorgeous? . . . Why should Will be mournful such a night? . . . And there's Patsy Tate standing by the window . . . a little forward, Patsy, isn't she? . . . And down there is where the race track used to be, isn't it? . . . Wouldn't it be fun to get it in shape again and invite all the people down from Richmond and Washington, Charleston and Virginia?

Will has risen suddenly and a little impatiently at this picture. "Does this place look like there's any money to be spent on racetracks, Miss Virginia?" he asks.

VIRGINIA—"Miss Virginia." Will—I declare, I call you Will like I'd known you all my life.

WILL—Everybody calls me Will—you can. (*He sits down again.*)

VIRGINIA—Shows people like you.

WILL—Really. (*Bitterly.*) Hah?

VIRGINIA—Of course I've known the Connellys through Father for a long time. (*Laughing.*) Didn't you know he used to kind of love Cousin Geraldine?

WILL—Well, I know something about it. He used to come here when I was a little boy.

VIRGINIA—I wonder why it never went any further. I've heard Mother tease him about the aristocratic Miss Geraldine.

WILL—Aristocratic over the dead! That explains a lot.

UNCLE BOB (*calling from off the left*)—Virginia, come in! We want you to sing for us!

VIRGINIA—I don't understand you, Will.

WILL—And your little moon shines on the tombstones. That's the poetry of it. (*As if quoting into the night.*) And all the great past that comes to dust.

VIRGINIA (*with sudden vehemence*)—No.

UNCLE BOB (*calling again*)—Come on and sing, Virginia! (*Other voices call her.*)

WILL—No, you can't tell me anything about it. I've already thought it out. You'd better go in now.

VIRGINIA—Come in and I'll sing for you then.

WILL (*standing up*)—The great Connellys are all dead. The fools and the weak are left alive. Good night.

Will is being quite silly, Virginia thinks, as she leaves him. Nor need he think he's the only one who has had bitter thoughts.

Will is sitting hunched over with his head in his hands when a rustling up the path attracts him. A second later Uncle Bob comes into the clearing dragging Patsy Tate by the hand. Seeing them, Will wanders off beyond the pool.

Uncle Bob, still wearing his ancient dress clothes, and Patsy, dressed up in a dark frock cut low across her bosom, are not agreed as to this rendezvous. Uncle Bob has told Patsy that he has something important to tell her. Patsy insists they have gone far enough for her to hear it. Uncle Bob feels what he had to tell her will keep past a little love making. Patsy is sure it will not. Nor does she care to be made love to. She is struggling to get out of Uncle Bob's amorous clutches when Will suddenly bounds back through the myrtle and helps her. In the next minute he has met Uncle Bob's shrill anger with a blow that sends the old man to the ground. Will would have struck him again if Patsy had not interfered.

"I'll get my gun," sputters Uncle Bob, dragging himself up on his haunches; "I ought to shoot you like a dog for that—I ought to—Will Connelly, are you gone crazy?"

"Get away from here—right quick——"

Will's voice breaks between shame and anger. But he will not let Patsy laugh at a Connelly's discomfiture. Now she is eager to explain that she would not have come to the party if Uncle Bob had not said that Will had wanted her to come. Will knows that. Knows why Uncle Bob wanted her, too. But he is shamed at having struck Uncle Bob.

On the seat under the myrtle Patsy is as comforting as he will permit her to be. She has taken his hands in hers—his big, strong hands. Patsy's hands are cool—Will doesn't mind the caress.

"I feel sorry because you're sad," Patsy explains. "You weren't sad the night you went serenading with us. You had a lot of fun."

WILL (*stammering, as he draws his hands away*)—I stood in the shrubs and heard it all and I was scared. I didn't know what to do. And then something seemed to go all over me—it made me blind of a sudden and the next thing I knew I was out here and had hit him. (VIRGINIA *is heard singing in the house—"After the ball is over, after the break of day."*) Oh, God, what a mess! Let me tell you something. I'm done.

PATSY (*sharply*)—What do you mean?

WILL—I'm going to work in town somewhere. The farm may go to hell and all with it.

PATSY—No.

WILL—Listen there! Fools, fools we are. Borrowing our last cent to give Virginia a big party, having an orchestra and—my God! I'm done—done!

PATSY (*catching his hand in hers*)—Let me help you, Will.

WILL—I wish you could, I do.

PATSY (*in a low voice*)—I can.

WILL (*raising his head*)—No, you're like the rest. You pity me. I am nothing. Even the niggers laugh at me. (*She bends down suddenly and kisses him on the lips. Incredulous, he stands awkwardly up and then sits down again, nervously fingering his coat.*)

PATSY—I could help you. (*Hesitating.*) And you could help me. You'd be running away like a coward if you left. You'll do it. I'll help you—we'll do it—work—work—together. (*Throwing out her hands.*) I know how to work with the earth. (*Gazing at him with intensity.*) I know her ways. I could teach you. (*Bending vehemently over him.*) See, I talk to you—I pour out my heart for you.

WILL—Patsy. (*Murmuring.*) You make it almost real. With you—yes—I might do something—. But I'm numbed, cold, empty. I've stayed in this old house too long—

PATSY—No, you must live—live! Wipe away all these gullies and broomstraw patches—waste—waste. (*In the background the two Negro women are seen creeping softly forward through the trees and watching them.*)

WILL (*staring at her in a sort of stupefaction*)—It seems strange—like a dream. Yes, I could—maybe we could. (*Suddenly starting.*) No, I don't know you. No—

PATSY (*catching him by the shoulders*)—Yes, yes, you do. (*Putting her arms suddenly around his neck.*) I love you, I do, Will. Come with me. We'll walk in the fields.

WILL (*almost with a pleading shout as he sweeps her suddenly into his arms*)—Yes! Out of this death and darkness—into the light! (*PATSY puts her arm around him and with her head upon his shoulder leads him on. The Negro women wobble in by the myrtle trees.*)

BIG SIS—Dis darkness, bless God!

BIG SUE—Dat light, hallelujah!

BIG SIS—Ehp, huh don't know dat Connelly blood huh messing wid mebbe.

BIG SUE—Huh think dat sassafras water.

BIG SIS—Water kin turn to blood.

(UNCLE BOB *comes blundering through the underbrush at the left.*)

UNCLE BOB—O little Moon, what have I seen? Cock-a-doodledo! (*He crows like a rooster.*)

BIG SIS and BIG SUE—Uhp! (*He cuts a goatish step before them.*) Us done see and fo'see.

UNCLE BOB (*like a court-crier*)—William Byrd Connelly is now out farming! Oh, yus! Oh, yus! (*Calling after* WILL *and* PATSY.) Ain't no fences round your crops—ehp! Let the hogs root.

BIG SIS and BIG SUE (*guffawing*)—Uhp—Lawd!

UNCLE BOB (*beginning to pat his hands*)—Go to it, old squealers. (*They begin hopping up and down, their wrappers flopping about.*) Great doings ahead. Amen.

BIG SIS AND BIG SUE (*as they dance*)—

       Mischief-meevery-miney-mo,

       Answer my answer dere below.

(*They begin doing a hoochee-koochee dance facing each other.* UNCLE BOB *rolls around on the ground clapping his hands and peering at their huge flashing legs and joggling bodies.*)

UNCLE BOB—Hurrah! (*He rises to his knees, beating time and reaching out his hands to the night in a drunken blasphemous call.*) Our Father, who art in heaven, hallowed be the sin which now doth flourish forth to salvation. Ecch, set to it, old cows, we'll all go home at milking time. (*He goes on foolishly clapping his hands. Presently, emitting a long sigh, he stretches himself out flat on the ground.*)

THE CURTAIN FALLS

ACT II

When Will Connelly gets around to breakfasting a few days later his sisters Geraldine and Evelyn have already driven Virginia Buchanan to the train. Will's excuse for not being there to say his good-bys is that he has been obliged to consult his tenants on business.

Now he would have Essie, one of the younger house girls, clear everything away so he can use the dining-room for a meeting. Will is getting ready to address his constituency. The thought of his nephew's suddenly becoming a hustling landlord, like Sid Shepherd, is amusing to Uncle Bob.

"Going to labor under the sign of Venus—eh?" suggests the elder Connelly.

"Go to hell," replies the younger, going to the door to invite in the fifteen or twenty tenants who have gathered on the porch.

"With the exception of old Tate they are a scurvy, nondescript crew. Three or four ancient ebony darkies with faces wizened as aged monkeys beneath their flaring white hair. . . . There are a few middle-aged white men with ragged mustaches and beards, thin gaunt fellows, hollow-eyed and hopeless, their faces burnt like leather by the wind and sun. . . ."

Uncle Bob moves cheerfully among them, "like a lord." The older tenants shake his hand "with a dignity that hides all their knowledge of his sins and meannesses." He is still moving from one to another when Will rises to take charge of the meeting.

WILL (*his embarrassment disappearing as he goes on*)—I asked you to come over here so we can talk about the plantation together. Some of you see me now with my work clothes on perhaps for the first time. (*Smiling intimately.*) Ain't it so?

A YOUNG WHITE FELLOW—That's about so, Mr. Will.

WILL (*as several of the men snicker*)—Go ahead and laugh. Well, I'm going to work. I want to talk to you and I want you to talk to me. This is the first time we've ever got together and that's what it's for. What's been the matter with this farm? Somebody tell me. (*Nobody says anything.*) What would you say, Ransom?

RANSOM (*a middle-aged white man*)—I don't know. I don't just know, Mr. Will.

WILL—There's been something wrong, ain't there?

RANSOM—Seems like it.

A NEGRO (*in the rear—softly*)—Sho' God is.

WILL—Who was that?

VOICES—Charlie over here.

WILL—All right, Charlie, what's been wrong?

CHARLIE (*a little dried-up Negro*)—Nothing, Mr. Will. Sho' ain't nothing! Everything fine.

WILL—Don't be afraid to talk out. (*He waits and no one*

says anything.) Well, I'll tell you. We ain't been working. Year after year we've lived from hand to mouth. We've let the soil wash away, bushes grow up in the fields, half-plowed the land. (*With nervous impetuosity.*) I've been a damn poor manager.

VOICES—You been all right, Mr. Will.

A WHITE MAN—You sure have.

OTHER VOICES—Good Lawd, sho' he has!

A NEGRO—Sho' de truth, Mr. Will.

WILL—Maybe I been too good to you, good and no backbone. But that's not all the trouble. We sleep too much on this place.

A NEGRO (*as if in alarm*)—Uh—uh!

WILL (*tapping the table*)—From this day we're going to change. Ransom, you got children—grown boys and girls somewhere in the world. They're working twelve hours a day somewhere in a factory. They couldn't stand this dead place. They oughta be here with us. We oughta make it so they'd stay. And Jodie's got boys, gone from home, he don't know where they are. The young folks run away from this place like partridges from a hen. Why? We got no life here, that's why. I been figuring on all these things and we're going to take a new start. We're going to be real farmers. We got a lot of land broke but we're going to break a lot more and break it deep. Next week I'll have new plows and more stock. The first thing we'll do is to clean up the hedgerows, patch the fences, and shrub the bushes out of the fields. Everybody's got to work. I'm going to work—we're all going to work. Work won't hurt any of us, will it? And everybody works will get rations. I'm going to start a commissary to furnish you. And I'll see who deserves to eat and who don't.

Uncle Bob approves, a little too vociferously. The others have nothing to say. Anything Will suggests they agree to. Tate is the only articulate one among them, and it is his opinion that its a good farm and will yield good crops when it is properly worked. Will, agrees Tate, has his farmers going now. They know he means business.

The tenants have gone back to their tasks. Will is still excited with the possibilities of the new schemes when his mother insists upon seeing him.

Mrs. Connelly's first complaint is against Will's treatment of Virginia Buchanan. Much had been staked on Virginia's visit and Will had done nothing, less than nothing, to help matters. But it is not too late, if he will act quickly. If he will write to Virginia and make it up with her; if he will accept Virginia's invitation to come down for the hunting in the fall—

But Will is obdurate. He will not go on being the same kind of weakling he has always been. If he were to do what his mother plainly wants him to do it would be Virginia's money that did everything. Will wants to do something himself.

Mrs. Connelly has no confidence in Will's new resolutions, and less in their inspiration. She can see what's happening. She can see the designing woman back of Patsy Tate's every move.

"She's set out in cold blood to become Mistress of Connelly Hall, and you're helping her do it!" charges Mrs. Connelly spiritedly.

MRS. CONNELLY—You've been spending more time over at her house—your own tenant's house—the last week than you have here. Haven't you any pride?

WILL—We've been working out plans for the farm— (*He stops in embarrassment.*)

MRS. CONNELLY—Of course she— (*She waits awhile and then —suddenly changing her tone of voice.*) Well, she loves you?

WILL (*after a moment*)—Yes.

MRS. CONNELLY (*smiling*)—You don't know a thing about such women as she.

WILL (*defensively*)—I know she does.

MRS. CONNELLY (*smoothing out her dress.*)—And how do you know?

WILL (*in a low voice*)—I know.

MRS. CONNELLY (*after a moment.*)—Do you mean what I think—

WILL (*looking at her in shamed triumph*)—Well, whatever you think, I know she—loves me.

MRS. CONNELLY—It proves everything I've said if she's gone as far as that.

WILL—It does not.

MRS. CONNELLY—Any honest woman would tell you she's done that to trap you.

WILL—I don't believe it.

MRS. CONNELLY—I'm a woman and I know. (*After a moment, smiling*)—Well, the Connellys are famous for that. You're one of them after all, aren't you? If she wants to play with fire, then let her get burnt. It won't be you for you're not the woman. (*She looks at him telling her meaning in her eyes and finally he turns away and looks again in the fire.*)

WILL (*helplessly*)—I don't know what to say to you, Mother.

Mrs. Connelly—Then let's don't talk about it any more. (*In a changed voice.*)   After all, I do trust you, Will, you see?

Will (*abstractedly*)—Thank you.

Mrs. Connelly—Now let's talk over your plans for the farm—

Will (*dragging forward an answer*)—They're not all worked out yet.

Mrs. Connelly—What was the meeting about?

Will (*mechanically*)—I'm going to put 'em all to work.

Mrs. Connelly—What did you say to them?

Will—That.

Mrs. Connelly (*she waits, but he says nothing more in reply*) —We'll go over it all later, then.   (*Watching his face.*)   Help me out in the sun now, please.

Will—Don't you see, Mother—

Mrs. Connelly (*quietly*)—Yes?

Will—How you're destroying my confidence in—

Mrs. Connelly—In what?

Will—In, well, in myself then.   (Uncle Bob's *teasing voice is heard in the kitchen.*)

Uncle Bob—Good morning, sweet arbutus.

Mrs. Connelly—I haven't said anything about you, Will.

Will (*hastily*)—All right, all right then.   (*Vehemently.*)   But it's me—me she cares for, Mother.

Mrs. Connelly—It's the Connelly land and the Connelly name she wants.   Only selfishness and greed would make a woman violate herself.

Will—My God!

Mrs. Connelly (*almost gently*)—And Geraldine says Big Sis and Big Sue have heard her scheming in the fields with her father.

Will—No! No!   (Uncle Bob *comes in from the kitchen.*)

Uncle Bob—Another farmer in here wants to see you, Will.

Mrs. Connelly—Help me into the garden, Robert.

Uncle Bob—Excuse me for interrupting you.

Mrs. Connelly—We've just finished.   Go ahead with your plans.   We'll talk them over after supper.

The farmer in the kitchen is Patsy Tate.   She is in rough clothes, and wears a shawl over her shoulders.   Her feet are wet from tramping the fields.   She has come to bring Will the tenant plots she has prepared for him, complete with name, acres and all.   She has made changes.   Duffy's plot for an example, she has increased from twenty-five acres to sixty.   "Him and his crowd ought to tend sixty," Patsy argues.

Will is silent. Not until Uncle Bob accepts the obvious and gets out can Patsy get anything from him. Even then Will is difficult. Flares up angrily when Patsy tries to find out what is troubling him. It is something, she surmises, that his mother has said. She would like to know what it is. She does not want Will to be that way with her. Nor roughly affectionate, either, when he tries to kiss her. Clever? She has made no claim to being clever. What she has done is not clever. Any woman would tell him that. That she loves him he knows.

There is nothing for Will to be sad about, repeats Patsy. Mrs. Connelly will feel differently when everything is going fine. Now let him go look after his men. And stop by her place later to report.

"Yes, later," answers Will, with the tone of a servant. "Other orders?"

"I'll see you this evening, then," Patsy replies, calmly ignoring his manner. "There's something I want to talk with you about."

Big Sis and Big Sue have opened the door. Patsy sees them and draws back. It is almost as though they had been following her. But they have only come to borrow a little flour. Will sends them to the kitchen to wait for Geraldine.

Patsy starts for the garden. Will sends her sharply the other way. His mother is in the garden. Patsy does not take kindly to his tone. Nor is she the least unnerved when he grabs her fiercely by the arm to enforce his commands.

He has turned from her, half ashamed, and gone quickly into the kitchen. She starts after him and then stops. She is standing in the middle of the room looking a little defiantly up at the ancestral Connelly portraits. Her laugh is low and nervous as she half whispers to herself:

"Oh, you look mighty grand. But you don't scare me a bit, not a bit. (*She clenches her hand.*) All right, me against you, all of you."

Some of the defiance goes out of Patsy when Geraldine comes quickly upon her. "She pulls her shawl up around her head and leaves through the rear door."

Will Connelly is still moody when he comes back from the kitchen and begins again to go over his notebook. He bids Essie, an attractive mulatto house girl, fetch him a glass of whisky, and Essie, grinning broadly, is interested in being of service. Essie has noticed things. Noticed the way that purty little woman gazes at Mr. Will with them bright eyes.

Essie expects to be married pretty soon. She's eighteen or nineteen. But she ain't terribly interested in Alec.

"Yeah, you'll be wearing his ring pretty soon—say, right on that finger there," ventures Will, touching her hand lightly, and half disgustedly, with his finger.

"I'd ruther have a lavaliere," admits Essie, suggestively. "I'd cook a long time for that, Mr. Will. It'd make me look a lot prettier, too." (*She makes a broad gesture over her abundant bosom.*) "Let it hang down there. You buy me one, Mr. Will."

"Get away from here!"

Will is shouting and backing away from Essie. "He crams his hat on his head and hurries out at the rear. Essie snickers to herself and begins idly polishing the table, her eyes looking off in a dreamy stare" as the curtain falls.

Months have passed. The weather has turned hot. The Connellys have just finished lunch. Evelyn and Geraldine are, with some effort, clearing away the dishes. Uncle Bob, lying on a cot, reading Latin, and Mrs. Connelly, sunk into a big chair near, are trying to keep comfortable with the aid of palm-leaf fans.

From the fields the labor song of the Negroes is heard. "Say, my gal laid her head down, laid her head down and cried. Tears fell on the cold groun', can't be satisfied—"

"The hotter it gets the more they sing about the girl and the gambling man," sighs Evelyn.

Will Connelly is not home. All night he has been in the village. Will has been away a good deal of late. Mrs. Connelly is worried.

Out in the field Patsy Tate is doing her bit with a hoe, working with the Negroes, working as hard as any of them. "What a woman!" The tribute is Uncle Bob's.

The girl Essie is in. She is dressed up and has come to say good-by. She is going to meet Alec. Alec has heard salvation's call, and the call of the crops cannot stand against that. Essie is going to play the organ for Alec. . . .

Word has come from Virginia Buchanan. Virginia has decided to marry old Senator Warfield, old enough to be her father. But she'll be entertained a great deal in Washington. Mrs. Connelly sees compensation in that.

"In Washington, in Washington," muses Uncle Bob. "*Certes ipso facto.* When the almond tree shall flourish and fear shall be in the way. At last it's true. We're old. *In nomine Ecclesiastici.*"

"It's all so strange, now," murmurs Mrs. Connelly, a wistful, girlish note in her voice. "Sometimes it seems it's been a long time and then again just yesterday since—since we were all so young, you with your hopes, me with mine."

"My love and your hopes," answers Uncle Bob, sharply. "If life were but a dream man might hope to wake from its burden."

Patsy Tate is seen coming toward the house across the fields. Quickly Mrs. Connelly is on her feet. She does not wish to see Patsy. Let them call her when Will comes.

Patsy is looking for Mr. Will. She wants to see him and she must see him herself. She is turning to go when Will comes trampling in. "He is dressed in his Sunday clothes, haggard and the worse for sleeplessness and drink. He has grown stouter and coarser."

Will is restless and cross. He calls Essie to fetch him some dinner. There is no Essie. "Lavalieres have cost her her job," smiles Uncle Bob, significantly, as he goes to tell Mrs. Connelly her son is home.

Patsy has come to warn Will that her father is coming to see him. No, she hasn't told her father about herself and Will. But Tate has heard Big Sis and Big Sue gossiping in the fields. Patsy knows Will understands.

WILL (*sneering*)—All right! If you've the Catechism give me a precept.

PATSY (*her face pale and pinched*)—I know what we ought to do. We ought to pull ourselves together and go on the way we planned, and not let everything fall to pieces.

WILL—That's what I'm trying to do.

PATSY (*scornfully*)—You're not. Everybody in the neighborhood knows you're running around like a fool in town. Do you call that trying? Who has stuck in the fields day after day and tried to keep the tenants at work? Not you.

WILL—You've done it all, haven't you?

PATSY (*with growing feeling*)—Yes, I have. Oh, you started out with a great show, making a speech, and saying this and that, and then blow up when your mother won't consent to your marrying me.

WILL (*eyeing her*)—And who smiled so sweet and talked about life and was free with kisses? (*Triumphantly.*) And it was all a trap. I'll not be caught with that bait—hah-hah.

PATSY (*her lips trembling*)—I'm not begging you. I'm trying to reason with you. If you cared about the farm you'd understand.

WILL—Yes, you love the place and not me.

PATSY—I don't, but why shouldn't I? It's a sight more honest.
The land never tricks you. Do your part and she'll do hers. But
you— I did my part by you and what did you do? Tried to
make a—whore out of me.

WILL (*helplessly*)—Ha, ha, you're the wise virgin, clairvoyant
like God.

PATSY—I know what we ought to do, I know that. (*She hesitates and turns away.*)

WILL—Go on and say it again—get married—hah?

PATSY—I'd like to see you go on any other way. (WILL *sits
down and drums on the table, saying nothing.* PATSY *comes softly
up to him.*) You know I'm right, Will. (*Earnestly, her voice
shaken.*) I take the blame on myself, but you've got to fight too.
I'll help you—I'll do anything to help you. (*Putting her hand
gently and now timidly on his shoulder.*) There's no other way
in the world for you nor for me.

WILL (*presently*)—Don't cry. For God's sake, don't cry. I
can't stand any more of that.

PATSY (*looking up, her eyes bright and tearless*)—I know you
don't trust me.

WILL—Sometimes I do.

PATSY—And you must understand the person you love, must
trust her. I understand you and trust you.

WILL—But you don't love me.

PATSY (*thinking*)—Sometimes I do.

WILL—That's not love.

PATSY—How do you know?

WILL—It's not the kind I want.

PATSY (*turning and seizing his hand*)—What kind do you want,
Will? Tell me, I'll try to give it to you.

WILL—Stop that, Patsy.

PATSY (*with almost a cry*)—And what have I done? (*Excitedly.*) You didn't do it, I did it. You're right. I set a trap
to catch you and it's caught me. (*She clutches his hand with
both of hers.*)

WILL—What do you mean?

PATSY—You've got to believe it. All my people have wanted
land, wanted land above everything. When we moved here I saw
all this great plantation going to ruin. I wanted it, wanted to
make something out of it. I loved you because you stood for all I
wanted. I had never cared for any man. Never been interested
in any man. I saw you liked me and I went on and on with you.

(*She clasps her hands together, rocking her shoulders like an old peasant woman grieving.*)

WILL (*starting to put his hand on her bowed head*)—Patsy—(*But he stops and drops his hand to his side.*)

PATSY—And I went on planning. All that mattered was the land, growing crops, great crops, that's all I could think of. And so—I went to you—that night—led you on. (*Shuddering.*) After that I was different. . . . Something, a feeling for you. I think about the farm now and what we can do with it, but always there is something else there, you yourself. I want to belong to you. Then I think about you, and there's always the farm, and I want to rule over everything—make it great and beautiful! I'm all mixed up inside. I want to obey you, be your wife, have your children. I love you now, you yourself, Will. (*Beseechingly.*) You understand me, don't you? I swear it's the truth.

Will watches Patsy uncertainly as she bows her head on her knees, "her shoulders shaking in silent sobs." Weeping distresses Will. He takes another drink of whisky defensively. Presently he is shouting at the girl to go away and leave him.

Patsy is ready to go. She will let him run things for a while. Then he will see what she has been doing. There never has been such a crop on that plantation before.

"Now I'll go away—and I'll wait till you come for me," repeats Patsy. "You will come, won't you? I'll go away today."

"No, you won't!" fiercely answers Will, his mood changing violently.

"Maybe that's the way for us," continues Patsy. "It'll be hard but in the end it'll be all right. Some day you'll realize how hard it is for me to leave—you'll come then."

Patsy has gone. Will has made a movement as to follow her but settled back in baffled indecision. Uncle Bob finds him and twits him about his lady-loves, in town and out, with a prophecy as to what old man Tate will do to him.

"Let him shoot," shouts Will, defiantly. "I can shoot, too. Let him sue me. I'll pay if that is what he means."

Uncle Bob does not subscribe to that program. The Connells are in enough trouble as it is. What Will should do, and Uncle Bob is quite serious about it, is to "throw everything to the devil and marry Patsy Tate." That would be the best thing for them all.

"You don't see what she is," mutters Will, half to himself. "She's queer. She's cunning, full of plans."

"That's a lie and you know it," sharply answers Uncle Bob.

"I can't get her out of my mind," admits Will. "Sometimes I want to catch her by that pretty throat and kill her."

Mrs. Connelly has come to see Will alone, but Will prefers to talk to them all at once. If they have come to condemn him he will do his condemning first.

"I've waked out of my sleep to see it all," Will shouts, his gestures wide, his voice high and strident. "I'm down, whipped, beaten, as low as Uncle Bob there. See, two by two they go up the stairs! Let the cross-eyed woman pound on the organ! Rotten, rotten, I know it! Lamb of God, cut my throat and bury me in the garden with the others. No, bury me apart with Uncle Bob." (UNCLE BOB *puts out a pleading hand*.)

Uncle Bob, Evelyn, Geraldine try to stop him. Mrs. Connelly hangs her head and waits for him to finish.

"Follow in the footsteps of my fathers," continues Will, taking in the portraits on the wall with a sweeping wave of his arm. "The grand old Connellys—General William Hampton Connelly —in the vanguard of the brave—yes, a nigger wench in every fence jamb." He pushes Geraldine away when she springs toward him with clenched hands. "Down, down, sister and brother, cats and dogs! Sisters and brothers?" It is as though he were talking to someone outside the door. "You, Duffy and Harvey and Jenny? All of you come in! Hist, let's set our flesh and blood at the table—a row of mulattoes. 'Brother, sister, forgive us.' Low? But lower still. And, Essie, be seated close at my right. If there's horror we brought it into the world. Who wouldn't vomit and clean out his stomach?"

Geraldine is on her knees before her mother begging that Mrs. Connelly stop Will, but the older woman calmly waits. Even encourages Will with an "And now?"

"As the old family satyr says," Will goes on, turning to Uncle Bob and imitating his uncle's thin womanish voice, " 'Skip to my Lou, skip to my Lou, if you can't get a white gal a nigger'll do.' "

"Have some mercy!" pleads Uncle Bob, weakly.

"Hah, hah, mercy," shouts Will, his voice rising. "I'll cut into this sore. Let innocent Geraldine and Evelyn know the truth if that's it." As the girls would run away he shouts after them: "Run away? Can you run away from your body's blood? No, sir, no, sir, you can't."

"Is that all now?" asks Uncle Bob.

"Not all until you see the niggers thumbing their noses as you pass, you strutting barren peacock! . . . Patsy's right. We're all rotten!"

Now Mrs. Connelly has risen and with an angry cry called a halt. Across the fields the song of the Negroes still floats in: "I put my little finger ring on her little hand. Feel her rolling, tumbling in my arms, loving up her gambling man."

Mrs. Connelly stands looking down at Will. Her voice is gentle, beggingly soft. "There's nothing more to say," she murmurs, standing between Geraldine and Evelyn, accepting their support, as she goes on. "Yes, something—of other things, Will— of sacrifice and forgiveness and human love— Your father—your father was a great man. He had a hard struggle, over himself and the world around him. He failed, struggled again, his face set upward—on— (*She sways with weakness and leans heavily on her daughters.*) no whining—no tears—of weakness. Now I'm old—weak— (*Smiling.*) But do I weep? No. (*Sternly.*) Does Uncle Bob? What do you know of his life? (*Softly.*) I know— Go to him, if you are a man and beg his forgiveness. (*Pleadingly.*) Do it, Will. You've said things too hard for him."

Will is of no mind to apologize. Nor to surrender. His mother knows the truth and will not face it, he charges.

"I have faced it for forty years, Will," Mrs. Connelly answers calmly. "And yet I did my duty to your father."

Mrs. Connelly and the girls have gone. Uncle Bob, beaten under the lashing of his nephew, does not take up the defense of the Connellys. Suddenly, out of a reverie, he rises and begins adjusting the collar of his opened shirt, and his tie. He is standing before the mirror of the sideboard putting on his coat as Will goes on:

WILL—I stood in the courthouse a boy and heard Father sentence poor Purvis, his own son, to—the gallows. You helped prosecute him. (*In a low voice to himself.*) There in the robes of justice he rose up, the power of the law. Why didn't he strip himself and say, "I am the guilty one, judge me"? (*Clenching his fist.*) True, true! There's something right behind all this. (*Triumphantly as if discovering something.*) But he didn't, the coward, and now I'm a coward. (*Thinking, a note of awe finally coming into his voice.*) There's something to search for—find it —a way to act right and know it's right. Father and Grandfather didn't do it, and we're paying for it. All the old Connellys have doomed us to die. Our character's gone. We're paying for their sins. (*Flinging up his hands.*) Words—words— (*He shakes his head in weariness, his mind growing foggy and losing it's sho...*)

trail. Turning, he pours himself another glass of whisky and drinks it, and stands looking at UNCLE BOB.) Dressing for a party? Well, by God, he will have his joke."

UNCLE BOB—Today's the day. Nothing more to be said. She's said it all. My time to speak. Hear her defend me? Forty years she's done so—knowing—knowing what I am—

WILL (*starting up*)—I leave it all to them—to you. I've got enough for my ticket to Texas. Let everything be sold and pay the debts, the rest divided. You're a lawyer, you'll execute. Hah-hah! And tell the pretty girls all hello for me. Tell them I'll not be riding out any more. Hah, hah!

UNCLE BOB—I will if I see them. And so—good-by.

WILL—I'm not leaving till the morning train.

UNCLE BOB (*surveying himself*)—Not much of a garb for a far traveler.

WILL—Where are you going?

UNCLE BOB (*opens the cupboard drawer and puts a pistol in his pocket*)—Try another shot at that hawk in the cypress tree.

WILL—You've never hit him and never will.

UNCLE BOB—In my ancient primer Ben Franklin said, "If at first you don't succeed—" (*He stands silent as if trying to recall something to mind. Presently he goes on in the same dulled voice.*) Marry Patsy Tate, Will. (*Murmuring to himself.*) For now the proud days are ended. (*He pours himself a drink of whisky, looks at it a moment, and then raises his glass to the portraits on the wall.*) Ladies, Gentlemen, *ave vos salutamus.* (*He touches the glass to his lips and then sets it down without drinking.*) *Via ad avernum facilis est—quis—quamquam—mea memoria—nemo—mei—mnemisc*—I cannot remember.

WILL (*chuckling*)—Good, good. An apt joke. A dead language.

Uncle Bob has gone quietly into the garden. Will takes a roll of bills from his pocket, counts them and jots an amount down in a notebook. The single report of a pistol sounds in the garden.

"Valedictorian, silver-tongued orator, most lately nothing," smiles Will. "He shoots at a hawk and away flies—well, ambition."

He pours himself a drink. Suddenly Big Sis and Big Sue burst in at the back, moaning and gesticulating. Will goes to the door and looks out. A shout dies in his throat. Old Tate and Duffy carry in the prostrate body of Uncle Bob, laying him on the cot.

It is hard for them all to believe that Uncle Bob is dead. The

Negro women are still moaning, their aprons over their heads.
Will has run from the room. In the hall Evelyn and Geraldine
are seen weeping. Mrs. Connelly comes hobbling into the room
on her crutch. With a low, convulsive moan she stands above
the couch. "Forgive me!" she cries, crumpling down on her knees
on the floor.

The moaning of the Negro women continues. The labor song
still is heard in the fields. Will is calling loudly for Geraldine as
the curtain falls.

Christmas eve has come round again. A fire is burning low on
the hearth in the Connelly dining-room, but there are no signs
of even a poor attempt at celebrating.

Big Sis and Big Sue are there. They have brought down two
suitcases and are awaiting Miss Geraldine and Miss Evelyn, who
are leaving. Miss Evelyn with "her little heart done broke in
two." Mr. Will's responsible, according to Big Sis. Big Sue
is more tolerant.

"Dis morning he say de truf done come to him an' he gwine
follow it," remembers Big Sue.

"Patsy Tate de truf he gwine follow," sneers Big Sis, spitting
bitterly at the fireplace and half moaning. . . . "And dis heah
de end now. Eigh, Lawd, de House o' Connelly is fell lak de
Great Temple."

Geraldine and Evelyn are in deep mourning when they come
downstairs. "A few months of grief and change and broken ties
have aged the two sisters more than a few months should."
Evelyn has lost her spring and go; Geraldine's hair is grayer and
"the primness and gentility of her nature have grown more hard
and bitter."

The Negro women are sent to tell Jerry to bring around the
buggy. The girls are ready and there is no reason, to Geraldine,
why they should wait to see Will. He has made his choice between his wife and them. The Lord knows, she says, that they
have tried to be good to Will, to sympathize with him, to talk to
him. But—

Geraldine has lifted the corner of the Confederate flag and let
it fall over the face of General Connelly's portrait. Now she decides to set the table and leave it for Will. She wants to remember the room as it's always been.

Evelyn is tearful at the end, but Geraldine is firm. Big Sis
and Big Sue are in tears. Outside a thick snow is falling, and
far away the serenaders are tuning up, "waiting for Mr. Will—

and de wedding party."

Jerry has come, the tearful farewells have been said, and the girls have gone, "deir liddle hands cold and still lak ice," . . . "And nobody in dis great world to warm um."

Big Sis has spied a bottle of wine. That's comforting. Big Sue, too. Between them they drain it. For a minute, in the silence of the great house, they stand listening.

"Everything so still!"

"Heah de snow falling 'gin de windows."

"And on de houses and de fields and on de po' graves."

"And de dead rest saft under it in deir sleep."

"Po' old Missus lie onrestless dere!"

Now the serenaders have broken forth. The sound of fiddles, horns and guitars comes rolling across the snow. A moment later Will and Patsy, "dressed up snug from the cold," come across the portico.

"Will is well-dressed in a dark suit, overcoat, hat and gloves. There is something stronger and more manly in his bearing than before; and though his face shows the harassed signs of what he has been through, there is a certain satisfaction in him of one victorious in a struggle with himself. Patsy is dressed in an attractive brown coat-suit, with a lace collar showing above it, hat and gloves. Her cheeks are pink and her eyes bright from the cold."

The serenaders have followed them to the house and are making merry outside. "Their shouts and calls are loud and joyous and no longer marked with the teasing and derision of the Christmas before."

Old Man Tate pushes through the crowd, awkwardly embraces his daughter, and shakes hands with Will. There are loud calls for a speech. Will demurs, but manages a few words of embarassed thanks. Patsy does better.

"We both thank you for your welcome. We appreciate it from the bottom of our hearts. Mr. Will wants me to tell you he knows how hard it's been on you all this last year. But it won't be any more. You'll have what's been promised you. Won't they, Will?

"We've had death and trouble—you know. But that's past, and now—"

"After trouble comes the good things!"

"That's so," shouts the crowd. "Everything'll be all right. Hurray for Mr. and Mrs. Connelly!"

They step up and shake hands with the bride and groom when Will dismisses them. There is much laughing and yelling. Then they are gone and the music fades out in the distance.

For a little both Patsy and Will are held under the spell of their reception. They cling to each other a little apprehensively, but hopefully. Patsy admits she was like a person dead away from the farm until Will came for her. She is sure of her love for Will. She is hopeful he will learn to love her.

Now with all they have to do, they must be stirring. First, Will would call his sisters. The sound of his voice rumbles through the rooms. There is no answer. He has gone in search of Geraldine and Evelyn when the Negro women return. They eye Patsy narrowly, "with malevolent sassiness." Patsy's smiles for Big Sis and Big Sue are friendly, but she is definitely on her guard. She asks them to build a fire in the stove and to bring in some wood. They make no move. They stand, as though hearing strange sounds—

"De dead folks cry so loud down in de gyarden," mutters Big Sue.

"De old man and de Missus and Uncle Bob—all dere whah Purvis is," moans Big Sis.

"Twell de trumpet sound and rise um up."

"Did you hear me?" demands Patsy, staring straight at them. And when they snicker disrespectfully and move toward her, she shouts: "I'm mistress here now and you'll do what I say!"

Still the Negro women would mock her and remain threatening, until, with her eyes blazing, she turns to the fireplace and snatches up a heavy poker.

"You'll do it, or by God I'll—"

Big Sis and Big Sue, "their eyes rolling in amazement and fear," back hurriedly away from her and are soon clattering through the kitchen and around the stove. That done, Patsy turns to the picture and lifts the flag back from the General's face.

She is standing there when Will comes excitedly back to report that Geraldine and Evelyn are not to be found. The Negro women confirm his fears. The misses had packed deir little things and went to the train with the report that they were not coming back no mo'.

Big Sue (*casting up her eyes*)—Dey cried a little bit and wiped deir eyes and said good-by to everything. Dey gone to Richmond to live wid Cousin Vera.

Will—Stop that!—When did they go?

Big Sis—Jerry took 'em over jest 'fo' you all come.

WILL (*dropping down in a chair*)—I've run them from their own home! (*Springing up excitedly.*) They've got to come back! (*He starts toward the rear door as if to go after them.* PATSY *runs across the room to him.*)

PATSY (*with almost an angry cry*)—No! No! You haven't done it.

WILL (*with half a shout, as he stops*)—We've both done it then.

PATSY (*clinging to him*)—They know their own minds, Will. Please—please—listen—

WILL (*fiercely to himself*)—They must have hated me. My God, the cruelty of it!

PATSY (*hugging him tightly*)—It is cruel, Will—all this suffering—and—

WILL (*with a cry*)—And I thought we were done with death and suffering.

PATSY—But we'll stand it—stand it together—whatever pain and suffering there is. (*Vehemently.*) That's the way it has to be, Will. To grow and live and be something in this world you've got to be cruel—you've got to push other things aside. The dead and the proud have to give way to us—to us the living. (*Her face close against his.*) We have our life to live and we'll fight for it to the end. Nothing shall take that away from us. (*She bows her head against his breast. Then after a moment she goes on more quietly.*) Right now we have to decide it, Will. It's our life or theirs. It can't be both. They knew it—that's why they went away. (*She stops and stands up straight and waiting.*)

WILL (*clinging to her almost like a child*)—Yes—yes—help me —ah, I need you so, Patsy.

PATSY (*after a moment*)—And I'll always be here to help you when you need me.

WILL (*brokenly*)—Aye, you will—you will. Yes, let them go. Let the past die. It's our life now—our house! (*He stands staring out before him. The two Negro women bow their heads in resignation.*)

PATSY (*to* BIG SIS *and* BIG SUE)—Go on back to the kitchen. (*But they remain standing where they are.*) Will looks up, his mind echoing Patsy's command.)

WILL—Miss Patsy's my wife now.

BIG SIS and BIG SUE (*hesitating*)—Yessuh.

WILL (*loudly*)—Then you do what she tells you!

BIG SIS and BIG SUE (*as they take each other by the hand*

and go into the kitchen)—Yessuh, Mr. Will.

WILL (*suddenly sweeping* PATSY *into his arms*)—And with you I'll go on—I'll go on! (*They stand wrapped in each other's embrace. Across the fields the serenaders are heard playing and singing about Fair Elinor.*)

PATSY (*her voice shaking*)—Think of it, you've had no supper. (*She gently moves away from his arms and begins lighting the candles.*)

THE CURTAIN FALLS

THE ANIMAL KINGDOM

A Comedy in Three Acts

By Philip Barry

THE percentage of Philip Barry successes is sufficiently large to inspire an annual season's promise. His first play of any season is awaited, if not impatiently, at least with considerable curiosity and a good deal of confidence.

This season Mr. Barry followed his "Tomorrow and Tomorrow" of last year, which will be remembered as a modernization of the Old Testament legend of Elisha and the Shunammite woman, with a second social comedy somewhat vaguely suggested by the Biblical adventure of Samson and Delilah. At least it is the story of a strong man shorn of spiritual strength by the Delilah type of helpmate.

The title of the new play is "The Animal Kingdom." It was produced by Gilbert Miller and Leslie Howard at the Broadhurst Theatre the second week in January. Mr. Howard played the chief male rôle, and was a co-producer. Both play and star were hailed with enthusiasm, many of the reviewers frankly insisting that it was Mr. Barry's best play to date. The run at the Broadhurst continued until early April, when the play was moved to the Empire Theatre. There it ran out the season.

It is about seven o'clock on an April evening. Tom Collier's house, in the country, not too far from New York, is a partially converted farmhouse. Its library, into which we are ushered, is a fair-sized room. "The furniture of no particular period, is well chosen and, in the case of chairs and sofa, invitingly comfortable. It is a cheerful room, now filled with the late evening sun."

Rufus Collier, "in his early fifties, small, slight and gray"; Owen Arthur, "about thirty-five, well-built, well-dressed, agreeable looking," and Cecelia Henry, "twenty-eight, lovely of figure, lovely of face, beautifully cared for, beautifully presented," are waiting in the library. Waiting and trying, with no particular success, to make conversation.

It is the first time, it transpires, that Rufus Collier has been asked to his son's house. This seems a little strange to Cecelia, and a little regrettable to Owen, who is Tom's close friend and fairly constant companion.

In the near-by village Tom has his publishing business—the Bantam Press. His father did not know that. He did not even know that publishing was the latest thing Tom had turned to. The elder Collier is frank to admit his disappointment in his son.

"Thirty-one—thirty-two in October—and he's wasted his life from the cradle," explodes Rufus.

"It must have been pathetic to see him wasting it at three," suggests Cecelia.

"I assure you his genius for it showed even then. I send him to Harvard and he lasts two years there. I send him to Oxford, and he commutes from Paris. I put him in the bank, and he"— There is a profound sigh at the mere recollection. "The world at the feet of that boy, the whole world. And all he's ever done is to run from it."

"He has his own ideas about what he wants to do with his life," suggests Owen defensively.

Richard Regan, "about thirty-two, with the figure of an athlete and a genial, ugly Irish face that appears at some time to have been thoroughly mauled," brings in a radio message for Tom. Regan is the butler, but a little unlike any other butler either Mr. Collier or Miss Henry has ever seen.

Now their curiosity has reverted to the reason for their being there. Tom's father had been sent for and asked not to let anything prevent his coming. Owen had been asked to pick up Miss Henry in New Canaan and come rushing back. And here they are.

It is the father's opinion that it may have something to do with the girl Tom has been living with the last three years. Both Owen and Cecelia know about that girl, too. At least Cecelia has heard of her and Owen knows her as an extremely nice girl, hard-working and talented, who draws for the fashion magazines and is successful.

Even so, Mr. Collier believes Tom either intends to marry her or has married her already and is bringing her home to meet them.

"In fact, I'm certain that that's why we're here," insists Rufus. "It offers the perfect opportunity to cut himself off finally and completely from the life he was born to. I'm surprised he has missed it as long as he has. . . . Well—I've stood for his rowdy friendships, I've put up with his idleness, his ill-mannered insolence, his—"

"I'm sorry, Mr. Collier, but I'll have to ask you to let it go at that," interrupts Cecelia, ". . . because it so happens that I'm

Photo by Vandamm Studio, New York.

"THE ANIMAL KINGDOM"

Tom is a trifle white and wan when he comes in. His memory of what happened at the party, particularly what happened to Tom, is none too clear.

(*Lora Baxter, C. Albert Smith, Ilka Chase, William Gargan and Leslie Howard*)

why we're here. . . . It's me Tom's going to marry, and I've
heard enough against him to last me quite a while."

The news is startling to both the men. Owen is completely
flustered. Mr. Collier is at first speechless and then rather pleased.
When he discovers further that Cecelia is one of the Baltimore
Henrys and that she is prepared to accept Tom, even though he
has little or nothing of his own, he is convinced that she has what
he calls character. And she'll need it.

Cecelia is content. Tom is the most interesting and the most
attractive man she has ever met. She considers herself "shot with
luck." Also Cecelia is convinced that when Tom has someone who
really understands him to work and care for he will make what his
father would call "a citizen" of himself.

Rufus has picked up the radio message Regan has brought.
Now he unfolds and deliberately reads it. "Darling. Am coming
back. Arrive on *Paris* at eight tonight. Much love. Daisy."

Cecelia is not particularly moved. Her chief concern is for
Owen. She is sorry he had to learn about her engagement to Tom
quite so abruptly. She had intended telling him before, but there
never seemed to be just the time.

Owen is frankly puzzled. Cecelia is not at all the kind of girl
he would have expected Tom to be interested in. Nor can he
understand what Cecelia sees in Tom. Owen, as their one mutual
friend, is convinced that Cecelia and Tom have not one single
thing in common. To Cecelia the situation is quite simple. She
is in love at last. . . .

Cecelia is alone when Tom Collier arrives. He "is in his early
thirties, slim, youthful, with a fine, sensitive, humorous face."

He drops the parcels he carries, gets rid of Regan, (who is a
bit insistent on telling him of the radio message that has arrived,)
and would take Cecelia in his arms. She is hesitant about permitting an effusive greeting. He hardly deserves that, being late.
But she does kiss him lightly and is pleasantly forgiving.

Now Tom would have Cecelia's general impressions. How does
she like the house? What does she think of Rufus?

"Well—" Cecelia hesitates.

"Now, now! Keep a civil tongue in your head," admonishes
Tom. "It may take a little time."

TOM—You can learn to like him and beer together. Mother
was the prize: you missed something, there. Father means well,
but you have to stand him off. Give him an inch, and he takes
you home in his pocket. . . . Did you really say you'd marry me?

CECELIA—I'm afraid I did.

TOM—Heaven help us both.—Just this one marriage please, darling. I haven't been very good about marriage. I was exposed to a very bad case of it as a baby. . . . We must make a grand go of it.

CECELIA—We shall, never you fear.

TOM—Just do everything I say, and it will be all right.

CECELIA—With pleasure.

TOM—C, what a marvelous object you are. (*He picks up her left hand, looks at it.*) Look at those fine small bones in your wrist.

CECELIA—What about them?

TOM—This— (*He kisses her left wrist.*) You're so cunningly contrived.

CECELIA—What?

TOM—I say, you're put together on the very best principles.

CECELIA—I don't see so many blunders in you either, Thomas.

TOM—No. Mine is entirely beauty of soul. Shall I tell you about my soul, C?—With lantern-slides? (*She turns to him.*)

CECELIA (*softly*)—Put your arms around me, Tom. (*He draws her to him and kisses her.*)

TOM—Oh, God, I feel good!

CECELIA (*in a breath*)—So do I.

TOM—Let's have all our good things together. (*He turns and calls loudly.*) Red! Oh, Red! (*Then to* CECELIA.) That's a very good rule of life, darling: all one's good things together.

CECELIA—Is it, dear?

REGAN (*appearing, beaming*)—Hello. Not so loud.

TOM—Glasses with ice, Red, and run all the way.

REGAN—O.K. (*He goes out.* TOM *calls again.*)

TOM—Owen? Father! (*To* CECELIA.) Oh, my lovely C—you lovely thing, you.

CECELIA—Stop it, Tom. You're really embarrassing me. I feel quite naked.

TOM—That's fine. (*He goes to her and draws two fingers gently across her cheek.*) It's such a fine binding, darling—such a good book.

There is nothing much to tell Rufus and Owen when they come. They have already heard Tom's news. Their congratulations are friendly but not exactly enthusiastic. Regan displays a greater show of interest, though he evidently is a little in doubt as to just how familiar he should be with Cecelia.

Now Regan has filled their glasses and the time is ripe for the expected toast. "Well—here's how and why and wherefore—and you know where marriages are made," proposes Tom. They all drink, but none as fast nor as heartily as Regan. That finished the matter of the radio again is brought to Tom's attention. This time he is holding it in his hand when Cecelia, the little matter of a date for the wedding having been settled, smilingly raises her glass to him.

"All right, Tom.—To May first!"

They have all drunk to this and Tom has read his radio message. They are watching him closely as he folds it again. He is frowning as he turns to Owen and suggests that perhaps he would like to show Rufus the new bantam-cock—the one that fights at the drop of a hat, even if you don't drop the hat.

Tom has closed the door after them and turns to face Cecelia. He is looking at her intently and frowning, when she speaks.

CECELIA—Don't tell me if you don't want to, Tom.

TOM—But I do. I intended to at the first opportunity anyhow, and— (*He holds the radio message up.*) and it seems that suddenly here it is.

CECELIA—Am I to be a good soldier?

TOM—No. There's no need to be.—Though I'm sure you would be, if there were.

CECELIA—Thanks, dear.

TOM—C,—for quite a long time I've known—known very intimately—a girl who's been very important to me—

CECELIA—Yes.

TOM—Who always will be very important to me.

CECELIA (*smiling*)—That's harder.

TOM—It shouldn't be. Because it has nothing to do with you and me, not possibly.

CECELIA—I'm relieved to hear that.

TOM—In fact, I think she'll be glad for us.

CECELIA—I hope she will.

TOM—*I'm sure of it.* Daisy has done more for me than anyone in this world. She's the best friend I've got. I believe she always will be. I'd hate terribly to lose her. It's been a queer sort of arrangement—no arrangement at all, really. There's never been any idea of marriage between us. It's hard to explain what there has been between us. I don't believe it's ever existed before on land or on sea. Well—

CECELIA—Is she attractive, Tom?

Tom—To me, she is. She's about so high, and made of platinum wire and sand. You wouldn't like me half so well, if Daisy hadn't knocked some good sense into me.

Cecelia—Well, *someone's* done a good job.

Tom (*laughing*)—I'll tell her that! (*Then seriously.*) I sent her a long cable about us this morning. She couldn't have got it, because this— (*Holds up message.*) this is from the boat. She lands tonight.

Cecelia—I see.

Tom (*putting message in pocket*)—C, I want to be sure that you understand it—understand it both ways. I'd rather not go— terribly deeply into it if you don't mind.

Cecelia—I don't, Tom.

Tom—We've been everything possible to each other of course, and—

Cecelia—Yes.

Tom—But at the same time, free as air. I've never felt any kind of—conventional responsibility—toward her or she toward me.

Cecelia—I can understand that.

Tom—Can you, C? Because I never could.—Anyhow, that's the way it's been. We haven't been what you'd call "in love" for a long time now, so—

Cecelia—Does she know that?

Tom—She knew it first. . . . Well—I don't know what more there is to say about it, except that first you needn't worry about us in the least. And—you won't, will you?

Cecelia—No, Tom. Not if you *tell* me I needn't.

Tom—I do.—And second that I think she ought to know the news about us pretty promptly.

Rufus and Owen have come back from their inspection of the fighting bantam. Rufus did not care for the bantam. Now Regan has gaily announced dinner when Tom startles them by declaring that he must hurry back to town.

Tom had planned a celebration, he admits, but what has happened cannot be helped. Someone he has known for a long time is arriving from Europe and he already has missed the landing. It seems to him important that he should see her at once to tell her his—his good news.

"You have the effrontery, the colossal bad taste," explodes Rufus, "on the night of celebrating your engagement to a fine, trusting, loyal girl, to go from her—your fiancée—to your—to your—"

"The same old difficulty with words, eh, sir?" smiles Tom. "Never mind. None of them would apply to Daisy."

Quite unaffected by his father's flaming temper Tom turns to Cecelia, lifts her hand, kisses it lightly and is gone. "Until tomorrow, my angel," he calls, as the curtain falls.

Daisy's flat is on the top floor of an old house in the Murray Hill section of New York. The sitting-room, which also serves as a workroom for Daisy, "is Victorian in atmosphere, light and cheerful and has been decorated and furnished with an unerring feeling for the period. . . . The sofa and chairs are fine old Victorian pieces, but comfortable in spite of it."

It is an hour or two after Tom Collier had left his guests at home. At Daisy's he and Joe Fisk are idly listening to Franc Schmidt, who is playing the concluding measures of a César Franck sonata on her violin. Joe is "twenty-eight, fine, Irish, nervous, intense, attractive." Franc "is thirty, hard-rugged, in appearance more of a handsome farm girl than a musician."

Daisy is home, but has disappeared. Nor does their frequent calling bring her back. Tom is eager that Joe and Franc should go on home. He wants to talk to Daisy. He has news for her, and he refuses to tell them what it is until he has told her.

Now Daisy has re-appeared. "She is twenty-six, slim, lithe, a stripling, but with dignity beyond her years and a rare grace to accompany it. In contrast to Cecelia's lush beauty, she is plain, but there is a certain style of her own, a presence, a manner that defies description. Instantly and lastingly attractive, like no one else one knows; in short, 'a person,' an 'original.' She wears pajamas that might well be a dress and carries a plate of sandwiches."

Daisy is not at all convinced that Joe and Franc really intend going so early, and as for Tom, he can stay the night if he likes, and have her room. She has loads of work to get out before morning. Work that should have been done on the boat, but wasn't. . . .

It is some trick to get the visitors out, but Tom manages it finally. They would much prefer to go on talking endlessly of the work each is doing, or threatening to do. Joe is a writer whose standards, as Tom sees them, are "slipping like a sophomore's socks." Franc, as a violinist, is certain to get somewhere if she will work. As for himself, he may have done more for people than any other man Joe Fisk knows, as Joe insists, and he would like to believe that his life is his art, but—

"It is good to have you back too, Tom," Franc agrees. "You are better than all of us, but Daisy. She is better than best. Between you, you stir up our lazy bones, you hold us together, you bind our wounds. You two are— Ach! my blood is turned to beer! Auf wiedersehen. Good night."

Daisy has come back from seeing Franc and Joe into the hall, gone straight to Tom and put both arms around him.

"Hello, you dear Tom," she says.

"Hello, Daisy." She kisses him lightly.

"Now it seems I haven't been away at all. Oh, it's grand to be back."

"It's grand having you. Was the trip really all you had hoped it would be?"

The trip, Daisy reports, was even better than that. Or would have been if Tom had only been along. She had got drunk on pictures every day, and come back with loads and loads of sketches and a new enthusiasm for painting. Two very exciting things have happened to Daisy, too, and she has dragged Tom over to the sofa to tell him about them. She is snuggled contentedly against his shoulder as from across the court the sound of Franc's violin can be heard. It is a reminder of happy times together.

"Oh, Tom, God love you," Daisy suddenly exclaims.

"God love you, my dear," he answers. For a moment they are silent. Then, as Daisy lifts her head from the comfortable shoulder, both would speak of the thing that is uppermost in their thoughts. Tom insists that he should have Daisy's story first.

Daisy has a plan. Two plans, in fact. The hardest of her work is over. By the first of May she should be comparatively free. And, if he is, too, why not a month in Mexico together? Daisy thinks she can paint, and she wants awfully to try—with Tom as a helpful critic always close at hand.

As for the second plan—Daisy hesitates to reveal that. Suddenly she feels shy before Tom. Something is wrong. Perhaps he has a new Venus, she says, and then—

DAISY—You're a free man, Tommy. You always have been with me. No questions asked. But please, Mexico in May together, because listen— (*He looks at her.*) No! don't look at me. Look the other way— (*He averts his head. She goes on, rapidly.*) I stayed three days with the Allens at Vevey and they've got the sweetest small boy about two and I got crazy about him and I want one, I want one like the devil. I'm crazy for one, and would you please be good enough to marry me, and— (*He straightens up, dropping the pencil on the table—she continues hurriedly.*) Oh, it needn't be terribly serious!—It's not a life sentence—just for a short while, if you like—it'd be such a dirty trick on him, if we didn't.—After I get my stuff through for the June issue—then Mexico for a month.—I love you so much— I was a fool to ever think I didn't—ah, come on, Tom—be a sport— (*She is breathless.*) Give me a cigarette— (*But he does not.*)

Tom—Daisy—

Daisy (*quickly*)—All right . . . No go. Let's forget about it. What a fool necktie that is. The colors are awful.

Tom—Daisy, I—. Oh, God, God Almighty—

Daisy—Well, what is it? (*He covers her hand with his, leaning over the table.*) You're going to tell me something terrible.— What is it?

Tom—I'm going to be married.

Daisy (*incredulously*)—To be—? (*She averts her head.*)

Tom—Oh, listen to me, darling, listen: you don't really care so much. You can't. It's simply that we—you and I—after all this time, naturally we'd feel—

Daisy—It must have happened pretty quickly.

Tom—It did. A month ago we hadn't even met. It was at—

Daisy—You can spare me the details, please. I don't even want to know who she is.

Tom (*after a pause*)—Her name is Cecelia Henry. (*From the distance the strains of a fiddle are heard.*)

Daisy—It sounds familiar. I've heard or read that somewhere. Where? Well, well, will wonders never cease?—If I'd thought you were in a marrying mood, I might have thrown my own— (*She picks up a small limp hat from the table.*) could you call it a hat?—in the ring a bit sooner.—Behold, the bridegroom cometh—and no oil for my lamp, as usual.—A foolish virgin, me— well, foolish, anyway.—When's it to be? Soon?

Tom—About the first of May, we planned.

Daisy—I see.—Of course, in that event Mexico *would* be out, wouldn't it?

Tom—But I never dreamed you'd—Oh, God, I feel so awful.

Daisy—Does she know about us?

Tom—Yes.

Daisy—Honest, Tom.

Tom—Oh, shut up.

DAISY—Remember me, Tom.

TOM—Oh, my dear—as if ever in this world I— (*Suddenly, fearfully.*) Daisy! There's to be no nonsense about not seeing each other as friends again, or any of that, you know—

DAISY—No?

TOM—No. We're grown-up human beings. We're decent and we're civilized. We—

DAISY—But there *will* be that nonsense. Oh, yes—there'll be that, all right— "Cecelia Henry"—now I know where it was! (*She picks up a magazine and begins to run through it.*)

TOM—But I don't understand it. I don't see why we shouldn't. I thought for a long time we'd been out of danger so far as—well, so far as— (*He cannot finish it, but* DAISY *can.*)

DAISY—Wanting each other goes?

TOM—But haven't we?

DAISY—Speak for yourself, Tom. (*He looks at her, waits a minute, then speaks.*)

TOM—You too, Daisy.—You first, I thought.

DAISY (*slowly, thoughtfully*)—It's true, that side of it was never so much to us, was it? Not in comparison—not after those first crazy months. But I thought that was natural. I was even glad of it—glad to find it was—other needs that held us together; (*She looks away.*) closely—without claims—not a claim—but so closely. Tom—do you have to *marry her?*

TOM—I want to marry her.

DAISY—I was just thinking—perhaps you simply want her—want her most awfully.

TOM—It's more than that, much more.

DAISY—I don't see how you can tell quite yet.—For all our big talk, we still belong to the animal kingd— (*She stops and looks closely at a photograph in the magazine.*) Here she is.—Oh, these neat, protected women! I've drawn so many of them, dressed so many more.

TOM—If you knew her—

DAISY—But I don't, you see. (*She holds the magazine at arm's length, gazing at the photograph.*) Such a pretty face—lovely eyes, Tom. She's a prize, my boy. (*She closes the magazine.*) But look out for that chin.

TOM—Why?

DAISY—Just look out for it. (*Puts magazine on table.*) Does she love you? *Will* she love you, head over heels, regardless, as I—shall I say "as I once did"? Would you rather?

TOM—Daisy—don't—

DAISY—I hold you dear, Tom—*you*—for what you are—just *as* you are. I thought it was my special gift. But maybe she has it too. I hope, I hope— (*He takes her hand, raises it to his lips, kisses it.*)

TOM—There's no one like you—never will be. I know that.— But this—it's the damndest thing—I can't tell you—

DAISY—Don't try.—I'll pray for you every night, Tom, I really will, you know, I do that.

TOM—Oh, my sweet dear—

DAISY—Yes—be good enough to remember me kindly, if you will. .

Daisy has taken up her sketch pad. She wants Tom to pose for her, just a second. Just a memory pose, just a line—that is all she will keep of him. And then good-by to Tom Collier—till doomsday!

Tom will have none of that. Nothing is going to separate two people as important to each other as they are—nothing. That would be ridiculous. Nor will he say good-by. Not to her. Not with all her pleading that the break be "sharp, decent, clean, with no loose ends between us two." Still, Daisy will not listen to any other way.

Let him pack up his things, such as they are. Let him bring them from the other room and say good-by and be gone.

". . . You must grab my hand in yours—one splendid gesture— and murmur, 'Good-by, my Daisy. Thanks very much. A charming association. . . . And may we never, never meet again so long as we two shall live.' You will, won't you?"

"No."

Daisy has gone to bring the things. Tom quickly picks up his hat and goes out. She comes in, calling: "See! The wash is back. Now, do as Daisy says, and say—"

"She sees that he has gone. She moves toward the door, stops against the work-table. The bundle droops in her hand, drops upon the table."

THE CURTAIN FALLS

ACT II

The following January Cecelia Collier and Grace Macomber, a neighbor, are having after-dinner coffee in the Collier living-room. The room has undergone certain changes. "Small, feminine touches, such as new lamps, cretonne curtains at the windows and slip covers of the same material on the chairs and sofa, have made a woman's room of it."

"Grace is just over thirty. Without a single feature to remark upon except a slim and well-kept body, she manages, with the aid of coiffeurs, dressmakers and manicurists, to impress one as an attractive woman."

Tom has left the dinner table to go write some letters, somewhat to the irritation of the dinner guest. He and Cecelia are planning to go into town later to hear Franc Schmidt's concert. It is Miss Schmidt's début, Cecelia explains, and, being an old friend of Tom's, he is most eager to hear her. It is a long, cold ride, however, and Cecelia hints that it is possible they may not go.

There is, also, another thing that may explain Tom's sudden disappearance this evening, Cecelia suggests. He is facing the task of discharging Regan, the butler, and that worries him. Regan, it appears, has been indulging another of his weekly bats, and Cecelia feels that the time has come when something has to be done about him.

When Tom does come Mrs. Macomber makes a noble effort to be chatty and agreeable. She was simply ravished, she reports, by the latest book Tom has published. It happens to be a book that Cecelia recommended. Tom is convinced it is "tripe" and is quite ashamed of it, but Cecelia is convinced it will make enough money to permit him to publish three or four that he does like.

Cecelia has gone to the door with Grace when Regan arrives. His walk is a trifle unsteady, but extremely dignified and he is able to stand and report to Tom a good time in town and a discovered preference for ale rather than beer. Ale, Red admits, is bitter but quicker.

This is, undoubtedly, a good time to talk with Regan, but as Tom faces his butler with that idea in mind he weakens and ends by asking Red to bring in a couple of bottles of beer.

Cecelia is back to protest that Tom has been perfectly terrible to Grace, who is at least a kind and friendly person. But to Tom Grace is nothing more than a "silly, idle, empty, destructive woman." She represents exactly the kind of people he has spent his life trying to keep away from—"people utterly without stature, without nobility of any sort."

Again there is the question of Regan to be decided. Cecelia is determined something shall be done about Regan—for Regan's sake. Aren't they depriving the young man of whatever chance he ever had to make something of himself?

Tom is admittedly fond of Red. Also he thinks that so long as Red does not drink during the week he is entitled to get a little "mellow" on his day off. But, if necessary, he will speak to him.

And about Franc Schmidt's concert. Yes, Tom is quite set on going. An artist's first concert is an occasion. As to his other old friends? The one named Daisy something—? Tom never sees them any more. Not because he is not interested in them, but because they will not see him.

Tom wishes Cecelia would go and get ready for the trip to town. Even if she has a headache, the cool air will help her. He doesn't want to telegraph his best wishes. He wants to go. Franc has been working for years, and—

Regan is in with the beer. This, Cecelia pantomimes, is the time for Tom to speak to his friend. Then she disappears.

Regan is cheerful, if a little ragged. He is glad to stick around and have a little glass of beer with Tom. He would be glad to show Tom a new card trick if Tom were interested. It's a good trick, having cost five dollars, and Red will pass it on for a bargain price of two ninety-eight.

The news from town, which fills in the next lapse in conversation, is that everything is pretty terrible. Men on the corners selling apples. Steel down to two hundred.

Tom is feeling the pinch a bit himself. Red is anxious about that. If there is anything Red can do—? There isn't. On the other hand, if Red should ever be hard up—? That goes both ways, naturally.

More sparring, and finally Tom manages a new approach. "Red," he says, "do you ever think of your future?"

"I guess I'll go to hell, all right," ruefully admits Red, before he realizes what Tom is driving at. "Oh, you mean here. Now, that's a funny thing, because, listen. Tom—"

Tom—What?

Regan—I've been thinking maybe I— Oh, what the hell—

Tom—But what? (Regan *puts his glass down on the table.*)

Regan—Fill her up, will you? (Tom *refills both glasses.*)

Tom—Not much future in buttling, eh, Red?

Regan (*with deprecatory gesture*)—Oh, well— (*He picks up glass.*)

Tom—I'm—I'm certainly very grateful for all you've done.

Regan (*uncomfortably*)—Ahhhhh!—Be still, will you?

Tom—I am, though.

Regan—That's fine, from you.—I'll never forget, when I was—

and you— (*He gulps and picks up glass.*) I'll never forget it. (*He dashes his hand across his eyes, sniffs, and drinks.*)

Tom—Put it there, old man. (REGAN *puts down his glass. They clasp hands across the table.*)

REGAN—You're the top, boy. I don't know what you'll think of me when I— (*He is unable to continue.*)

Tom—When you what?

REGAN—When I—well, what would you say, for instance, if I— (*He looks at him, then looks away.*) Nope, it's no good—

Tom (*anxiously*)—You're not in trouble, are you?

REGAN—Trouble? Me? What trouble?

Tom (*steeling himself*)—Then look here, Regan—

REGAN (*raises his glass almost like a toast and grin*s)—Well, Chief? (Tom *looks at him. The steel melts—he returns* RED's *grin. They enjoy a good laugh.* RED *raises his glass.*) Tom Collier for President. The People's Choice.

Tom—Listen a minute—

REGAN—Wait! Tom, I've just got to tell you. I've—I've— Don't hold it against me, Tom, but I'm quitting you. I've took another job.

Tom—You've—?

REGAN—Oh, I know what you'll say!

Tom—Holy Cats, Red—

REGAN (*confidentially*)—I couldn't stand it any longer. She don't like my ways. I mean the Missus. I get on her nerves.— Last week Moe Winters told me he wanted to open a country gym and would I run it with him, on the order of Muldoon's, but with a little bar attached and . . . Well, God help me—I give him my word.

Tom—What's there in it for you?

REGAN—Don't put it that way, Tom.

Tom—But I really want to know.

REGAN—Two hundred a month, and a smell at the gate, if any.

Tom—It sounds like a good deal.

REGAN (*looking at* Tom)—Aw, the hell with it!—Let's let it go. I'll phone him.

Tom (*alarmed*)—No! When do you start?

REGAN (*rather ashamed*)—He wanted me last Wednesday. I've been trying all week to get up the nerve to tell you.

Tom (*with finality*)—How long will it take you to pack?

REGAN—Well, there's my hat-trunk and my shoe-trunk, and the trunk for my fancy-dress ball-clothes—

Tom (*firmly*)—You leave by noon tomorrow, you hear? Not

a minute later.

REGAN—O.K., Chief. (*Looks at* TOM *and droops.*)   I'm sorry you had to take it this way.

TOM—Don't be a fool.   I'm overjoyed for you.

REGAN (*uncertainly*)—Fact?

TOM—Absolutely.   (*Raises his glass.*)   Here's to the new job.

REGAN—Take it from me, boy, you're the goods.

TOM—You've got your points, too, you know.

REGAN (*raising his glass and swaying slightly*)—Anyhow—

TOM—Anyhow.   (*They drain their glasses, put them down and again clasp hands.*)

REGAN—You'll explain to the Missus?

TOM—Of course.

REGAN—Tell her I'm sorry—hope no inconvenience—but—

TOM—I'll explain.

REGAN—So long, Tom.

TOM—Good-by, Red.

REGAN—I'll give you a ring how it goes.

TOM—Do that.

REGAN—Keep your bib clean.

TOM—I will, old boy.

With a final pat on the shoulder and a heartfelt "Good luck, Tom," Regan is gone.   Tom is dejectedly toying with the deck of cards when Cecelia reappears at the head of the stairs wearing a lovely negligee.

The news of Regan's leaving is pleasant to Cecelia and she would comfort Tom.   She is sitting on the arm of his chair and has drawn him into her arms, his head against her breast.   She hasn't any clothes on, she admits, and she cannot go on with her dressing unless he will come and help her.   But—perhaps that would not be wise.   Amused by the ardor of Tom's advances, Cecelia is in playful mood.

Now the negligee recalls many things to them both.   A funny little French hotel in Quebec; a very cold morning; frost on the window they could not see through, even if they wanted to; a breakfast before the fire that was never finished—

Now it is Tom who is losing interest in the concert, and a trip to town in the cold.   Cecelia appears quite surprised at his change.   She thinks now he had better go on without her.   She will tuck herself snugly in her warm bed—and he will probably need his heavy coat for the ride.   Cecelia will miss Tom—   He must be sure to keep warm—

She has retreated up the stairs "with a provocative smile and an admonitory gesture." As Tom goes slowly toward his heavy coat Cecelia can be heard singing softly to herself a little French song, "La Femme a la Rose."

By the time she reaches the second line of the song Tom has made a decision. He moves swiftly to the light switch. All the lights go out except the desk light and that shining from Cecelia's room. He stands for a moment looking toward Cecelia's room, then moves on to the telephone. He is calling Western Union as the curtain falls.

At Daisy Sage's, one fine bright day the following May. Joe Fisk and Franc Schmidt are waiting for Daisy. The room is much as we saw it last, though there is a great litter of painting materials about and a large easel near the window.

Joe and Franc are nervous, Franc particularly. They are the organizers of a conspiracy and they do not know how it is going to work. Daisy, Franc is sure, will never forgive them. But— Tom Collier had called up Joe and said he wanted to see him. Joe had told Tom to come to his place and then he had left a note on the door saying he had been called over to Daisy's, and for Tom to follow. Now what is going to happen? Tom and Daisy have seen each other but once since Tom's marriage.

Daisy, it appears, has been giving an exhibition of her paintings. They are agreed that there is something lacking in the canvases that Daisy has shown. They just don't do anything to you.

When Daisy comes she is still full of her exhibition, and worried about it. None of her friends will be honest with her. She is glad it is over. And for the moment she would like to talk about something else. How about Nova Scotia? Daisy has heard it is a fine place to go, Nova Scotia. A lot like Maine, but better.

Joe brings up Tom's name. Daisy is not interested. At least not particularly interested. She would like to know if Tom had any explanation for those "eggs" the Bantam Press has been laying lately. And she remembers that Tom always gets colds in the Spring, which probably accounts for his voice sounding sunk. There aren't many people in Nova Scotia—

When the buzzer sounds Franc lets Tom in. He is carrying his brief case and he is excited enough to toss his hat aside and rush to Joe. He is glad to see them, ever so glad to see them all. He loves them, all three of them, he wants them to know. Daisy tries to remain poised and lightly interested. The silence is long and a little embarrassing. Tom breaks it with a sort of joyful cry.

"Holy cats! Talk to me, will you? Am I a leper?" he calls. When they do not answer he goes on: "Now, listen, the lot of you. I've had enough of this nonsense. For months you've been avoiding me like the plague and I won't stand for it. You're important to me and by heaven, I'm going to hang onto your coat tails, dog your footsteps, sit on your doorstep, until you're ready to grant that a man can marry, and go on being a friend.—Is that understood?"

The next minute their words are coming in a rush. Suddenly they have remembered all the things that have been happening: Sandy Patch is doing a war group in bronze for a town in Texas. Joe's book is going fair, but nothing, of course, like the Bantam sensations, "Indian Summer" and "Young Ecstasy." Franc is doing well enough with her music, and Daisy's exhibition—

Tom has seen the exhibition. He thinks Daisy has not been painting long enough to show yet. Painting less than a year and already thirty canvases—

"So you didn't care for any of them?" Daisy demands coldly.

"Oh, yes," Tom answers, frankly. "One I loved particularly; the one of the doorstep with the milk bottles. I want to own that one."

"Number seven. Sorry, it's not for sale."

Daisy's drawing is great, Tom admits. There she has improved marvelously. But she cannot expect, living in cities all her life—fever, rush, hysteria—all day, every day—

Joe and Franc have run out. Daisy is furious—at Tom for his criticism, at Franc and Joe for their desertion. Now she faces Tom defiantly.

DAISY—Well? What more, Teacher?

TOM—All I said and all I'm saying is, you can't expect, the first crack out of the box, to—*you've* got to *work*, Daisy.

DAISY—Sweet Heaven! What else have I been doing? What have I done but?

TOM—But differently—with such pains. You're turning out too much, you know it.

DAISY (*suddenly, the fight going out of her. Woefully*)—May be, may be—. Anything's too much.

TOM—Ah, darling—

DAISY—No— Don't soften on me. Stay tough!

TOM—I do believe that's it, though. I believe it's the whole story: still hung over from the old job. Pressure, pressure all the time. Still rushing countless sketches through against a magazine's deadline.

Daisy—Anyway, against some deadline—

Tom—Daisy—darling—

Daisy—You're cruel, inhuman. You're a brute.

Tom—Oh, Daisy—

Daisy—Thanks for being.

Tom—If you mean it—

Daisy—From my heart. (*She looks at him, smiling now.*) Oh, you skunk—

Tom (*laughs, relieved*)—Worse. Much worse.

Daisy (*serious again*)—Who but you, Tom? (*She points her finger at him as she rises.*) Look: only you and strangers honest with me ever.

Tom—The country's the place to work, Daisy. Listen: There's a grand little house about six miles from us. Woods, hills, meadows—you can get it for almost nothing.

Daisy—That's about my price.

Tom—It could easily be painted up. What about a white roof for it?

Daisy—Oh, lovely idea!

Tom—C discovered it. She can find out all about it. I'll tell her who it's for. (*But at this* Daisy's *mood changes.*)

Daisy—Don't dream of it.

Tom—Why not?

Daisy—I've got other places in mind.

Tom—Anyhow, go somewhere.

Daisy—Sure—somewhere.

Tom—You're going to good, Daisy. Don't think I don't think you're good.

Daisy—I won't. I won't think anything.

Tom—This is a big day for me, do you know it?

Daisy—How?

Tom—Well, I've been seeing the folly of my ways here lately. Poor C—I must have been sweet to live with this past week. She's been grand about it, though.

Daisy—I'm sure she has.

Tom—I—suddenly for some reason, I—saw that somehow I'd got off the track—my track. It was pretty painful— But I'm getting back on, Daisy.

Daisy—I'm glad, Tom. You must, you know.

Tom (*catching her hand*)—Daisy— Have you missed me, Daisy?

Daisy—You? Well, I'll tell you, it's this way: I— (*But she stops and looks at him, drops her bantering tone, and nods dumbly.*)

Tom—Much? (*Again she nods, and adds, under her breath*):

Daisy—Skunk, skunk.

Tom—Oh, and I you!—It's a lot of nonsense, this. It's ridiculous.

Daisy (*looking at her watch*)—It *is* six.

Tom—Hell!

Daisy—You'd better run.

Tom—We need each other, we two do.

Daisy—You think?

Tom—Most terribly. I'm convinced of it. There never were such friends as you and me. It's wicked to give that up, to lose anything so fine for no good reason. Why you, of all people, for a shabby, low-down question of convention, fit only to be considered by shabby, low-down—

Daisy—Wait a minute!

Tom—A hundred times I would have given my eyes to see you, to talk to you—

Daisy—Well—here I am—

Tom (*eagerly*)—Daisy—may I come again?—Just now and then, you know?

Daisy (*after a moment*)—If you like—just now and then.

Tom—Oh—my sweet dear—thanks!

Daisy—But don't say "sweet dear." That belongs to another life, years ago.

Tom—Oh—there are to be rules, are there?

Daisy—One or two. One strict one—

Tom—What?

Daisy—Never secret. Never hidden.

Tom—No, no!

Daisy—Always open, as before.

Tom—But of course, of course!

Daisy—I couldn't go it otherwise.

Tom—Why should a friendship be hidden? What's there to hide?

Daisy—It gets misunderstood.

Tom—It won't, it can't, or the whole world's rotten.

Daisy—It's been pretty ripe for a long time, Tommy.

Tom—"Tommy!" (*He laughs exultantly and draws her into his arms. They stand rocking back and forth, laughing in delight.*) Oh, my darling, how grand this is!

Their moods are playful and happy, now. Daisy notices that Tom is running to tweeds and fears he may be going county. Tom is pleased to admit that he is quite a "lit'ry" and "very artistic" somebody in his very respectable, very dull set. But he and Daisy are not respectable, nor going to be, praise heaven! Just happy! With reservations. Of course, as Daisy points out, they are not in love any more. That makes a difference.

And how about lunch tomorrow? At the old place? At one? . . . And they might have dinner at Donovan's! . . . And next day, Wednesday? Why shouldn't Daisy come along when Tom goes to the country to see poor Pat Atkins, who is ill? . . . And Wednesday night? And Thursday? And Friday—

"Good-by then, darling. Till tomorrow!"

"Good-by, Tom." He has taken her in his arms and his kisses are ardent.

"Sweet dear, sweet dear—" He has grabbed up his hat and is at the door.

"One o'clock!"

"One o'clock!"

"Ten minutes of one—"

He is gone. For a moment Daisy stands rigid, staring after him. On the work table she notices his brief case. Apprehension grows in her eyes. Now she has run to the door and is calling wildly for Franc. A moment later she has gathered her painting things together and thrown them into a paintbox.

Daisy is going away, alone. Franc is the only one she can trust to tell. She knows now she must get out. And no one must know where she has gone to. Tom has left his brief case. He is certain to come back for it. If she sees him for one minute Daisy will be lost.

"He loves you, Daisy—" There is an implied question in Franc's tone.

"I don't know. I don't believe he knows," answers Daisy. "But oh, Franc—he's so young! . . . All slim and brown and sandy! . . . He'll always be like that, even when he's old. I know!"

Daisy is not altogether sure where she is going or how she'll get there. Sail from Boston, she thinks. And when her paintings come back from the gallery will Franc take out No. 7 and send it to Tom—at the Bantam Press?

And will Franc please remember that she is lunching with Tom tomorrow—at the old place, at one o'clock? . . . And when she sees Tom will she kiss him for Daisy—

There is a sound of the buzzer. With a wild scramble Daisy hurries into the bedroom. Franc follows and closes the door. A moment later Tom has burst into the room, calling loudly, hopefully—

"Daisy!" He finds the brief case. "Daisy!"

"Hello!" Daisy's answer comes painly from in back of the bedroom door.

"I forgot my case. It's all right. I've got it!"

At the door he turns again. "Don't be late tomorrow! Remember! Twelve-thirty!"

Tom is whistling his way downstairs as the curtain falls.

ACT III

At Tom Collier's six months later, it being a fine bright Sunday morning, Cecelia Collier, Owen Arthur and Grace Macomber have come down to a ten o'clock breakfast.

The library has finally been made over into a chaste dining-room. "Now, at last, Tom's house is Cecelia's house—the House in Good Taste."

There has been a party the night before—a birthday party for Tom. The guests included Daisy Sage, Joe Fisk and Franc Schmidt, invited by Cecelia as a surprise to please Tom. Daisy is just back from six months in Nova Scotia.

There are little straws in the wind indicating some lack of harmony in the Collier home. Tom is not nearly as enthusiastic about the changes Cecelia has made in the house as he might be. Just now there is a discussion on as to whether there should be a white roof or not. Also Tom is consistently reluctant about accepting favors from his father—checks principally—even on his birthday. This continues to distress Cecelia.

Regan is back, too. Tom had found Red without a job and ill in town and asked Cecelia if he could come out for a day or two. But Tom has at least promised to teach him manners.

Tom is a trifle white and wan when he comes in from his room. His memory of what happened at the party, particularly what happened to Tom, is none too clear. From what Grace says it sounds as though he had "put on an act."

Daisy and Joe are back from a walk to the station with Franc Schmidt. Talk turns to the new activities of the Bantam Press, of its new building, its new magazine and its increased success. The Williamson and Warren crowd is seriously suggesting some sort of merger.

Now Tom has gone to drive Grace home in Joe's Ford, Daisy has gone to her room to look over the proofs of Tom's new magazine, and Owen and Cecelia have a chance to compare notes. Cecelia is interested in getting Owen's reaction to Daisy. Why had Daisy accepted the invitation to the party, after first refusing it? And why has she been so watchful of Cecelia ever since she came? Cecelia is no longer jealous of her. Merely interested. She has come to think that it would be quite all right for Tom and Daisy to be good friends—just as good friends as she and Owen are.

There is another thing: Owen can help put through the Williamson deal if he will. Tom has put the price on Bantam Press high hoping to discourage Williamson, but Cecelia knows they will buy if Owen, who is their legal adviser, will merely hint to them that it might be a good thing to do. There is such a thing as legal ethics, as Owen points out. But there is also such a thing as friendship—and Cecelia is hopeful Owen is still interested in her friendship. He only has to telephone Williamson one little word—

Daisy's appearance on the stairs, with the magazine proofs, is timed to hear Owen's and Cecelia's conversation suddenly turned to the advantage it would be to Tom if the Bantam Press were combined with the Williamson interests. They hasten away to the telephone, passing Joe coming in.

Daisy has decided to leave. She wants to get out of that house and quickly. She would have Joe attend to his packing at once, so they will be ready. Joe understands. It is the change in Tom. He was awful at the party.

"And all those pitiful second-hand opinions," continues Joe "I've never known such a change in a person in my life. What's *happened* to him? What do you suppose has done it, for God's sake?"

"That's what I came to find out," admits Daisy.

"Have you?"

"Yes."

"What?"

"The most pitiful thing that can happen to any man."

"But what?"

"Go and pack, Joe."

"It won't take a minute. . . . It certainly can't be C. I thin she's a fine girl, don't you? I talked with her for quite a whi last night. She made great sense. I think she's a damned nic attractive woman."

"So was Delilah."

Tom is back, with a drink in his hand. He is not particularly surprised to hear that they are going. Nor particularly moved when Joe reminds him that he used to be in favor of moderate drinking.

"So solemn . . . *all so solemn,*" he mutters, as Joe leaves them to do his packing. "I'm sorry you don't like my friends."

"Your *what?*" counters Daisy.

TOM—They are, however. Did you read the magazine?

DAISY—Most of it.

TOM—Couldn't finish it, eh?

DAISY—No. I didn't care for it.

TOM—Why not?

DAISY—It seemed to me that *one* oh-so-bright weekly was enough, without more of the same.

TOM—Not sufficiently solemn. I see.

DAISY—Not half!—And so *cheap,* Tom! Oh, how can you?

TOM (*a moment. Then*)—You can't please everybody.

DAISY—Never mind. It doesn't matter.

TOM—Doesn't it, Daisy?

DAISY—Tom, ever since I got home I've heard from all sides how you'd changed. I couldn't believe. I came here to find out if it was true, and if so why.

TOM—Well, is it?

DAISY (*turning away*)—Tom—

TOM (*puts down glass*)—And if so why? Why?

DAISY (*a sudden cry*)—Oh, Tom—I pity you with all my heart! (*He rises and is at her side in an instant, her wrists in his hands.*)

TOM—*Pity me!* What are you talking about?

DAISY—I came to find out. I've found out. Now I'm going. (*She calls.*) Joe!

TOM—Found out what? Pity me, why?

DAISY (*looks down at her wrists*)—Would you mind? (*He releases her. A moment. They gaze at each other. Her eyes soften.*) And love you, Tom—love you with all my heart, as well. Remember that.

TOM (*brokenly*)—Daisy I— (*He recovers himself, and with the recovery the cynical smile returns. He flicks the collar of the dress with his hand as he says*): Give us a kiss, Daisy.

Daisy has stepped back from Tom in horror. Her call to Joe to discover whether or not he is ready is almost a scream. Cecelia joins them quickly, thinking someone might have summoned her.

Cecelia is evidently surprised that Daisy and Joe are leaving and perfunctorily insistent that they should reconsider. Surely they can stay until after lunch. No? She *is* sorry. But there probably is nothing that can be done about it.

"Good-by, Tom," says Daisy.

"Once I wouldn't say it, would I?" he recalls.

"Once you wouldn't—"

"Well— Good-by."

"This time you do."

"Good-by!"

Daisy gestures helplessly and goes. For a moment Tom is alone. Then Cecelia rejoins him.

"Honestly! If that wasn't the rudest thing!" she says. Tom does not answer. "I presume you agree, don't you?"

"I don't know what it was." He is staring straight in front of him. Cecelia looks at him intently for a moment.

"Well—if we're going to Grace's—"

"I'll get my hat."

He is moving toward the door when the curtain falls.

At ten o'clock that night, when Tom returns from the Williamsons', he finds the dining-room dimly lighted, a small fire burning and a cold supper on the serving table. In the center of the room a card table, with places for two, is set up. There a champagne glass at each place, and two armchairs are drawn up.

The scene reminds Tom of some place, but he cannot place it. The supper idea was Cecelia's. She thought he might be hungry. She is anxious to know if everything went all right, and pleased when he tells her that the Williamsons have signed and the deal will be completed when he adds his signature with that of a notary.

Tom thinks perhaps something has happened to his nervous system. He feels so awfully light. He is having visions. He would rather hold to the visions than believe, as Cecelia does, that he is just tired and hungry.

Regan is in to pour the wine. Cecelia had thought perhaps Tom would feel like celebrating. Suddenly Tom recalls what is of which the room reminds him. The wine suggested it. It was the Florentine! Flora Connover's place! The best twenty-guinea house in London!

"Rather expensive, wasn't it?" Cecelia suggests, not certain what Tom is talking about.

"But one went to Flora's to celebrate," explains Tom. "The food was good, the waiter discreet, the wines excellent, the lady most artful."

"Tom! How revolting!"

"But we must send the boys back happy, you know."

"I don't care to hear about it, thank you."

Cecelia would know more of the deal with the Williamsons. Tom got his own terms, save that the Williamsons reserved the right to pass on his selections, he reports. And he had insisted on changing the wording of the announcement they had prepared for the papers. They had made it read: "Williamson, Warren and Company have absorbed the Bantam Press, formerly owned by—" Tom had substituted "bought a controlling interest in" for "absorbed."

"Poor little Bantam—poor little plucked capon!" Tom sighs. Nor will he admit that the deal is a grand thing for him—with all its "increased scope," and "perfect distribution facilities."

But Cecelia is sweet tonight. Tom is beginning to notice her particularly with his second or third glass of champagne. She had locked her door against him the night before. Why? Because sometimes she was afraid? That he does not believe. But he would like her to know that locked doors aren't necessary ever. Suddenly he presses her for an explanation.

Tom—Why was it? Tell me *instantly* why it was.

Cecelia—Is that an order?

Tom—Tell me. (*She tries to meet his gaze but cannot.*)

Cecelia (*with difficulty*)—You mean—why I—why I didn't want you near me—

Tom—Yes.

Cecelia—And you don't know—

Tom—No.

Cecelia—Well, if you don't, you ought to.

Tom—Tell me, I say.

Cecelia—You'd been so—consistently disagreeable, that's all.

Tom—About what? Wanting Regan back?

Cecelia—No.

Tom—What then?

Cecelia—Your father chiefly. . . . He telephoned this afternoon. . . . He wanted to know if you got the birthday check. I told him that you had, and had tried to call him. Well, I had to say something.

Tom—I don't know whether to send it back, or just not to cash it. (*He takes his wallet from his coat pocket.*)

Cecelia—Of course, you simply can't allow yourself to show any kind of graciousness toward him.

Tom—No. (*He takes a check from the wallet.*)

Cecelia—As a way of telling you how pleased with you he is, he sends you a small check, and you have the extraordinary bad taste to— (*He holds out the check before her, leaning over the table. Her eyes widen.*) What! (*She reseats herself.*) Good Heavens—I don't believe it!

Tom—There it is.

Cecelia—But there isn't that much money in the world!

Tom—In Father's world, there is. He feels he can afford it to get us to come live with him.

Cecelia—Of course, I don't understand your attitude about that either.

Tom—Don't you, C?

Cecelia—He knows how inconvenient it is here in Winter, and having that great, huge, lovely house in town, it's perfectly sweet and natural of him to—to, well, to ask—

Tom—Yes—you, to preside night after night at his deadly dinners, me to listen eternally to his delphic advice on what to do and how to live—in short, to allow him to own us. Of course, he's willing to pay. He always is.

Cecelia—Oh, how ridiculous you are, really! His whole life long he's tried to help you, to do things for you—

Tom—In order to own me. I tell you I know him.

Cecelia—You're the only child he's got, and he's an old man and a very lonely man. I think it's horrible beyond belief, the way you treat him. How you can be so hard, I don't know.

Tom—Hard? I'm not hard enough—that's the trouble with me. I never have been. I was brought up to dodge any truth—if it was unpleasant. In myself or anyone else—always be the little gentleman, Tommy—charming and agreeable at all costs—give no pain, Tommy.

Cecelia—You seem to have outgrown it nicely.

Tom—Not yet, I haven't. No, not by a long shot. The inclination's still there, all right. Still going strong.

Cecelia—Don't be discouraged.

Tom—All right, C.

It is Tom's self-consciousness about money that stands in the way of their contentment, Cecelia insists. It could all be s pleasant if he would only try being the fine, kind, generous man he ought to be. He could, if he would, start with being kind to his father, by accepting the check and going to live with him.

"It's only for a few months," persists Cecelia, following her advantage. "And I think to refuse his present would be extremely bad manners—just about in a class of those of your little lady of easy virtue, this morning. If—"

Cecelia sees from Tom's expression that she has gone too far and is quick to apologize. "I'm sorry to have said that about her," she adds, hurriedly. It is an apology that Tom accepts a little wearily.

Now his manner suggests a certain conciliation. Suppose he were to do as she wants him to do about his father. Would she like him much better? She would. And there would be no more locked doors? Not one—ever. That, agrees Tom, sounds most inviting. Suddenly he is beginning to see "with an awful clearness," and Cecelia is thrilled.

"I want so to feel—I don't know—together again, as we used to be," said Cecelia, as she moves closer to him.

"You're very pretty, you know."

"Why, thank you, sir."

"Very exciting, too." Tom's manner has changed.

"I don't know whether it is you or the wine speaking," smiles Cecelia.

"Me—through the wine," insists Tom.

They ring for Regan and order another small bottle. Cecelia is happy. Tom is free with his praise of her beauty. He finds her not only very attractive, but very seductive as well. Cecelia is flattered. . . . Now Regan has gone and they have raised their glasses to drink Tom's toast.

"To the pleasant *ways* of life."

"Such pleasant ways," agrees Cecelia.

TOM—Good, isn't it?

CECELIA—So good. I'm feeling it a little.

TOM—That's what it's for, eh?

CECELIA—It must be.

TOM (*holds up his glass*)—Champagne, the friend of lovers—

CECELIA (*her face inclines toward him, then she averts her head. Softly*)—No—not yet—

TOM—Artful child.

CECELIA—You think?

Tom—Lovely, alluring thing—

Cecelia—I like you too, now.

Tom—Pleasant here, isn't it?

Cecelia—So pleasant. (*She pours from bottle into her glass and sees that* Tom's *glass is still filled and says*): But you aren't taking any.

Tom—It makes me see almost *too clearly.*

Cecelia—Take a little more, and everything will get so—lovely and vague and—the way I feel now.

Tom—A good feeling, is it?—Is it, you lovely thing?

Cecelia (*a whisper*)—Delicious— (*She lowers her glass to the table. Then gropes for his hand, holds it against her breast.*) Oh—Tom— (*He looks at her.*)

Tom—One last toast?

Cecelia—Do we dare? (*He rises and draws her to her feet. He then hands her her glass and then picks up his own.*) But to what?—What to?

Tom—You name it.

Cecelia—To love—

Tom raises his glass to his lips but does not drink. Cecelia has drunk her wine and moved over to him. Her head is on his breast, her arms around his neck. His arms have remained motionless at his sides. Cecelia is sure now that he is going to be an angel about everything. She has moved slowly toward the stairs and turned to urge him not to be long. He blows a kiss in her direction. When she has disappeared he turns to ring for Regan.

Red is not quick to answer the summons, nor in pleasant mood when he comes. He is quitting again and this time for good. That is all right with Tom. Red can go immediately, but he had better look in to say good-by before he leaves.

Tom has taken his father's check, written an endorsement on its back, folded it carefully and placed it on the mantelpiece under a vase. . . .

Regan is back with a suitcase. Tom also wants his hat and coat. Regan is puzzled by this. He does not want Tom to drive him to the station. He can walk. But Tom has other plans. They will drive in together.

"*We* will—" Red doesn't understand.

"I'm going back to my wife, Red," says Tom, very gently.

"To your—?"

"To my wife, I said!"

Regan goes on ahead with his suitcase. "Tom looks once around him, draws a deep breath of smoke from his cigarette, exhales it slowly, then turns and follows Regan and closes the door gently behind him."

THE CURTAIN FALLS

THE LEFT BANK

A Comedy in Three Acts

By Elmer Rice

The theatre season of 1931-32 began slowly in late August and came through September without much to boast of in the way of new plays. Usually some far-seeing producer has held over from his early spring tryouts a potentially popular success with which to surprise the eager firstnighters.

In late September the Theatre Guild, which had failed with "He," was represented by its associates of the Group Theatre, Inc., in the production of Paul Green's "The House of Connelly," but this promised to be no more than what is often referred to witheringly as a "critics' success."

It remained for Elmer Rice to score the first definite dramatic success of the new season with his "The Left Bank," produced and staged by the author October 5 at the Little Theatre.

Mr. Rice had, since his sweeping success with "Street Scene," 1928-29, given much of his time to motion pictures and had spent several months in Europe. The effects of the trip abroad, added to impressions and memories of other trips abroad, are shown in "The Left Bank."

Mr. Rice herein considers the case of youthful seekers after freedom of thought and action in a foreign country. He has taken the left bank of the Seine as his locale, and drawn his people from the radical younger set of expatriate Americans seeking to break down the natural barriers of the Latin Quarter and become an integral part of the life of "the most civilized country that there is in the world today." Their discussions and reactions are literate and human.

It is after 10 o'clock of a spring morning in Paris as "The Left Bank" opens. The room occupied by John and Claire Shelby in "a small, third-rate hotel on the Boulevard Montparnasse" is still in comparative darkness.

The Shelbys are abed in that room. It is the ringing of a bell in the foyer that arouses them. At least it arouses Claire. She sits bolt upright in bed, shakes her head, as though to clear it and staggers out to the phone.

Photo by White Studio, New York.

"THE LEFT BANK"

Now Susie has come to comfort him. Isn't he glad Susie is going to get a divorce and live in Paris? And wouldn't he like to come now and keep her company while she gets dressed?

(Alfred A. Hessé, Millicent Green and Horace Braham)

A moment later she is back. The call is for her husband who refuses for a moment to care much whether it is or not. He had a lot rather bury a tired and aching head in the pillow and stay there. They will have to quit going to parties for a while, John mentions, in passing from the bed to his bathrobe and slippers.

With the drawing of the heavy window draperies the Shelbys' room is revealed as being large and fairly second-class. "The furniture is not bad, but rather decrepit and in a state of disrepair. . . . The wall paper bears a vivid pattern of black and orange." There is "a lavabo" at back, hung with chintz curtains, carpeted with a strip of linoleum, behind which Claire retires to wash her face and hands and brush her teeth.

John's message brought from the telephone, is that Waldo and Susie Lynde are in Paris, at the Gare du Nord, and coming over. They have just arrived from Calais, are on their way south, and have decided to stop at the same hotel with the Shelbys. It would be just like Susie Lynde to prefer something romantic—"a charming little hotel on the left bank, my dear. The quaintest little place you can imagine," resents Claire.

John is also considerably distressed at the prospect of having the Lyndes so near. "God, you know, it's funny!" explodes John, in the midst of a general disagreement with everything else that is happening this morning. "I never fail to be amazed by the obtuseness of people. Apparently, it doesn't occur to them that I might not enjoy having them right here, in the next room."

It is John's idea that they had better fly to the Pyrenees, or to Spain, if their privacy is to be continually invaded by casuals from Calais. Claire, on the other hand, would like to stay put somewhere for a little while. She is fair sick of packing and unpacking.

In the mail there is a check for five hundred francs, less commission, for the sale of one of John's articles. That will help entertain the Lyndes. And a letter from McAndrews, the head master of Teddy's school in England, announcing that Waldo Lynde has been there to visit the boy. Also protesting that it was his, McAndrew's, understanding when he took Teddy that there was to be no visiting or interference of any kind.

The Shelbys are not in complete agreement, either as to the qualifications of McAndrews or the advisability of Teddy having been sent to his school for six months. John is convinced that it is the best thing for Teddy, who is, to John, suffering from a definite neurosis. But Claire is sorry she ever agreed to the six months' experiment that has separated her from her son.

"I think he's a perfectly healthy, normal boy," says Claire. "And I think it was a great mistake putting him in with a lot of queer abnormal children."

A knock on the door announces a visitor, presently revealed as Alan Foster, a handsome youth in his middle twenties, who has come to invite them to tea. The coming of the Lyndes will interfere with their going, John and Claire explain. Susie Lynde is the daughter of Claire's brother Robert and it is brother Robert, recently deceased, whose "Life and Letters" John is hoping to put into a biography as soon as he can acquire a little privacy and an opportunity to do concentrated work.

John has gone to take his bath and Alan takes advantage of the moment to press his interest in Claire. He would like to know why she did not keep an appointment to go to lunch with him. He would also like to know when she is going to give him another sitting for the head he is doing of her.

Claire is afraid she must have forgotten the luncheon engagement and she is more or less definite about not wanting to sit for Alan again. She may have the perfectly formed torso he continues to assure her she has, but it happens that she does not like being mauled, an attitude which irritates Alan considerably.

"Where do you get off, high-hatting me, I'd like to know?" demands Alan.

"There doesn't seem to be any other way of making you understand that I'm not interested," Claire replies.

"All right; if you're not interested, you're not interested. But you don't have to be high-hat about it."

"There's nothing high-hat about me, and you know it. You can be charming and very amusing, as long as you keep off the subject of sex. On that subject, you're just as boring as everybody else."

John, back from his bath, is still grouchy. The water was not hot. The croissants brought with the coffee are not fresh. The butter is rancid. He dislikes the service, he dislikes the hotel. He would prefer an apartment, even though Claire, trying to hurry him that she may have the room straightened before the Lyndes arrive, again points out their inability, on present income, to increase their expenses. John also resents that reference.

"I know that we're hard up, Claire. There's nothing to be gained by reminding me of it constantly."

"I just don't want to increase our expenses, that's all."

JOHN—Well, then let's find another hotel.

CLAIRE—No hotel we could afford would be any better than this. We've tried enough of them. I'll tell you what I think, John, if you really want to know.

JOHN—Of course I want to know.

CLAIRE—Well, I think we should go back to America.

JOHN—Are you serious?

CLAIRE—Yes. Very serious.

JOHN—I hope you'll excuse me. I have a terrible head this morning and perhaps I'm just a little dull. Perhaps that's why I find it just a little difficult to understand what it is that you're proposing.

CLAIRE—It doesn't seem to me to be very difficult to understand. I'm proposing that we go back to America.

JOHN—For what purpose?

CLAIRE—To live.

JOHN—Live where and how? In Greenwich Village? One could endure the kept women, I suppose. But the Indiana poets and the interior decorators and the advertising men—!

CLAIRE—I wasn't thinking of the Village, particularly. We could live outside New York, somewhere.

JOHN—In Westport, with the illustrators, perhaps. Or in Croton-on-Hudson with the uplifters.

CLAIRE—I can't see that they differ very much from the people we play around with here.

JOHN—Are you comparing Paris to Forest Hills?

CLAIRE—You've been complaining bitterly about Paris, all morning. No privacy; no hot water. Stale croissants and rancid butter. You'd get fresh butter even in Forest Hills.

JOHN—Feminine logic can obscure any issue.

CLAIRE—I'm sorry I'm not capable of masculine logic. And I'd like to know what you call the issue.

JOHN—You know very well what the issue is. It's that no civilized man can live decently in America.

CLAIRE—Well, perhaps I'm not civilized. But I know I'd rather like the idea of a shack some place, where we could have Teddy with us and where he'd find some healthy, normal little dumbbells to run around with.

JOHN—Teddy is where he belongs; in the hands of a trained specialist. When McAndrews has finished straightening him out, we'll send him to a boarding school in Switzerland, where he can improve his French.

CLAIRE—I think it's more important that he should be with us.

JOHN—That's because you take a sentimental and not a rational view of his education.

CLAIRE—There's nothing sentimental about wanting to see one's own child, occasionally.

JOHN—You do see him occasionally.

CLAIRE—I haven't seen him in nearly three months. Besides, what right have we to deprive him of contact with his own country?

JOHN—Contact with Woolworth and Ford and the Y.M.C.A. and the American Legion? Is that what you mean?

CLAIRE—I mean with America. He was born in America and so were most of his ancestors for three or four generations. What do you want to make of him—an Englishman or a Frenchman or what?

JOHN—I don't want to make anything of him but a civilized man.

CLAIRE—He might prefer to be a happy one.

JOHN—An epigram.

CLAIRE—Forgive me if I have infringed your rights.

John insists it would cost more money to live in America. Claire counters with the suggestion that they would also make more. John is convinced that man needs more than physical sustenance. He must also have spiritual sustenance.

"A man can't create in a spiritual vacuum, in an atmosphere that's esthetically sterile," he protests with fervor. "And that is exactly what America is: a spiritual vacuum, a cultural desert."

"I've never been as convinced of that as you are," Claire reminds him.

"It's not a matter of conviction. It's a matter of feeling—of sensitivity. No cultivated person can long survive in a country that has no traditions and no standards of taste, in a country that is wholly absorbed in the problem of material organization, in a country where leisure is unknown and—"

Claire is quite familiar with John's views on that subject. And also his concluding contention that the only living that's important is the life of the spirit.

"We used to agree about that when we were in college," Claire recalls. "It was different, then. We were adolescents, with a lot of bad upbringing to live down. We felt that we had to get away, to escape from our past, if we were ever to make anything of ourselves. That's really why we came over here—we had so many things to run away from. But, now—I don't know. I find that what concerns me chiefly is that I'm not packing next week and that tomorrow's dinner is provided for."

Waldo and Susie Lynde arrive with some bustle and the usual hand luggage. "Waldo is a typical college-bred, fairly well-to-do American professional man of about thirty. Susie is five or six years younger, slender, attractive, sinuous and expensively dressed."

There are kisses all around, and the usual comparisons of the more recent adventures with weather and health.

Susie is delighted with the Shelbys' hotel. She has always been looking for just such an adventure and has always been dragged to the expensive places. Waldo, for his part, is free to confess that he likes his comfort.

Waldo's report on Teddy is not too cheering. He found the boy brown and sturdy, running about half naked with the other boys. But it was not easy to tell exactly how he was otherwise. McAndrews would not permit him to talk with Waldo alone. Teddy had seemed glad to see Waldo and had sent his love to— both of them.

"I'm sure he didn't send his love to me," John is quick to interpose. "He hates me at present."

"I always hated both my parents," agrees Susie. "I think most children do."

"He has a violent mother fixation and can't endure having me about," explains John. "That's one reason we had to send him away."

Soon the Lyndes are installed in the only double room that's vacant, which happens to be next to that of the Shelbys, with a connecting door. That's fine for the Lyndes, and the Shelbys try to appear pleased. Susie is for having the connecting door unlocked at once. It will be so clubby. . . .

Adjustments are normal, after Susie has found out where everything is, including the bath-room, and Waldo has borrowed a razor blade. Susie continues to be thrilled, and Waldo to accept the situation as graciously as possible. Still, Waldo cannot quite understand why anyone living in Paris would prefer the Boulevard Montparnasse to the other side of the river, where the shops and theatres are, and the Champs Élysées.

"That's the point of view of the American tourist," ventures John.

"Sure it is. But that's what I am—just an American tourist," admits Waldo. "And I like to be where things are going on."

JOHN—Well, if you like the kind of things that go on along the boulevards and the Rue de la Paix, you're welcome to them. But that's not the real Paris: the real Paris is over here.

WALDO—Why is this more real than the other?

JOHN—Because this is the Paris that is Paris: the soul and the meaning of the city that for ten centuries has worn civilization like a jewel upon her brow. Saint Germaine des Pres. The Rue Saint Jacques. The Sorbonne. The Cluny, Saint Etienne du Mont. The Beaux Arts. Saint Julien le Pauvre. The streets around Saint Severin, where Dante and François Villon walked. That's Paris.

WALDO—But that's all dead, isn't it?

JOHN—Dead? It's eternally alive. It will be remembered when all this jerry-built, machine-made Americanized world is forgotten.

WALDO—Maybe. But it seems to me we've got to live with the things that are going on, now. I don't know, maybe it's just lack of imagination, but I think you've got to go whichever way the world is going, not where it came from.

JOHN—It's that sort of laissez-faire philosophy that makes America the cultural Dead Sea that it is. Climb on the band-wagon. Follow the crowd. Root for the home team. Boost, don't knock. Smile, smile, smile. And what is the result? A nation unequaled in all history, both for its material wealth and its spiritual poverty.

WALDO—It's a stern indictment, but if all the rest of us are guilty, I'll have to plead guilty, too. I'd feel a little embarrassed having the only well-fed soul among a hundred and twenty million spiritual paupers. (*As* CLAIRE *enters*): Only I wish I had a little more of the material wealth.

CLAIRE—What material wealth?

WALDO—The kind that goes with being a soulless American.

CLAIRE—Oh, that! Yes, so do I. John, what about the post office?

JOHN—That's the tenth time you've reminded me of it.

CLAIRE—I'm sorry.

JOHN—Where there is no vision, the people perish. America, in the midst of plenty, is dying of esthetic and emotional starvation. I'll be back in ten minutes.

Claire is anxious to hear Waldo's real report on Teddy the moment they are alone, and Waldo is a bit reluctant to give it for fear he, knowing little of modern psychology, did not quite un derstand. Waldo is fond of children, Teddy is a favorite of his, and he is quite sure Teddy is all right

Susie is back from her investigations, still thrilled with everything. She is only sorry they will not be able to stay longer. But they just have to go visit Susie's female parent in order to get father's estate settled up.

Susie is not too happy about anything, but she is certainly glad she has no kids to worry about. That's one of the things she and Waldo are not agreed upon. In fact Susie finds Waldo pretty difficult at times—so "middle of the road, both feet on the ground, nose to the grindstone." Susie likes excitement. Even now she is trying to talk Waldo into letting her stay in Paris for six months or a year and study modeling. Perhaps if Claire were to suggest it—

The busy Claude has called Claire to her bath. Susie has had a minute to inspect the room surreptitiously, to satisfy herself as to the state of Claire's things. Waldo is finished with his dressing and it has occurred to Susie that it would be a fine idea if Waldo were to close her father's estate alone. But, as Waldo reminds her, she is the one who will have to decide about the distribution of pictures and things.

Then, suggests Susie, why not take John and Claire down with them. After all, John is as much concerned with the closing of the estate as they are. But probably Claire wouldn't go—

Susie has another idea—that she should stay in Paris a year and study. Even to that one Waldo does not rise with any particular enthusiasm. Having a wife in Paris while he is in America trying to hold on to his clients and his business is not exactly his idea of marriage.

Claire, back from her bath and slipped into a dress, continues her job as guide by taking Waldo down stairs to the bureau to telephone. It's pretty hard getting a telephone number in Paris alone.

When John comes back from the bank he finds Susie becomingly draped in the armchair, her legs crossed to improve their display and her nose in a book. She is, she pretends, quite surprised at John's return and is quick to readjust her skirts to hide her knees.

Susie is pleased to discover, too, that John thinks she has developed in the two years since he has seen her. Susie was afraid he would still think her quite inconsequential. It is nice to know that he doesn't, and she will have a cigarette—and a light—if he will get them.

John has noticed that Susie has lovely hair. He is sorry she feels so strongly about going to her mother. Mother is at Vence, isn't she? It's a lovely place, in the Alps Maritimes, only about an hour from Nice. It would be nice if he and Claire could go with them, as she suggests. He could get some new material for the biography—but, John fears, that is out of the question. Claire probably would not want to go, and, anyway, he is expecting his sister the next week.

Susie is so disappointed she takes another cigarette and another light. This time she notices that John's hands are really quite remarkable. Some day she hopes she will develop enough talent to model them. And John's palm! That's interesting, too. With a sharp break right there in the heart-line. Of course, Susie doesn't believe in such silly stuff but it is interesting to play around with.

As John thinks things over he decides to speak to Claire about the trip to Vence. Claire would not necessarily have to go. He could go alone and Claire could stay in Paris.

"Oh, please don't suggest anything like that," protests Susie, with a startled frown. "I wouldn't want Claire to get the idea, even for a moment, that I had influenced you to go."

"You are a little naïve, aren't you?"

"You see; that's what you think of me! I knew it."

"Now don't be offended! I think you're charming," protests John, taking Susie by the shoulders.

"You don't at all. You think I'm very stupid."

"Nothing of the sort. I love that youthful unspoiled directness in you. (*Patting her cheek.*) But don't worry about Claire. She knows by now that nobody can influence me."

"You know, that's what I admire most about you, John. The way you go straight ahead, living your own life and doing whatever you want to do."

"It's the only way that an intelligent civilized man can live, Susie, if he's to remain intelligent and civilized. That's why we minority men come to France, because here one can live the good life and yet not be a social outcast."

"Don't you think you'll ever go back?"

"No, never."

Claire is back and as soon as Waldo has finished telephoning they will start for lunch at the Medicis' Grill. They can have a cocktail at the d'Harcourts first, John suggests.

Then John casually presents the suggestion to Claire that he go with Waldo and Susie to Vence. He could help close up the estate and at the same time get a lot of new material for the biography. He also could write the article for the *London Mercury*, of which Claire reminds him, as easy in Vence as he could in Paris and he would only have to be gone four or five days, which would not interfere materially with his sister's visit.

CLAIRE—Well, why not go, if you want to?

JOHN—Yes, I think I'll go.

SUSIE—You'll come, too, Claire?

CLAIRE—No, thank you, Susie. Your mother isn't one of my enthusiasms. I'm not traveling down to the Midi to see her.

SUSIE—No, I don't think that's right. I don't think you should leave Claire here alone, John.

CLAIRE—That's all right, Susie. No American is ever alone in Paris for long.

JOHN—You see, we have many friends here.

WALDO (*entering*)—The Bensons have gone to Brussels, Susie.

SUSIE—Well, they mean very little in my life. John is thinking of going to Vence with us, Waldo.

WALDO—Fine.

SUSIE—But Claire doesn't want to go and I don't think it's right to leave her stranded here, do you?

CLAIRE—I've told you I don't mind, Susie.

WALDO—You don't want to come, Claire?

CLAIRE—No.

WALDO—Well, I can hardly blame you.

SUSIE—Poor Waldo wishes he didn't have to go, either.

JOHN—If I can do anything to relieve you of the responsibility, Waldo—

WALDO—Well, there's really nothing that I could do, that you couldn't do equally well. The point is that Susie has to arrange with her mother about the distribution of all those chattels.

JOHN—Then why not let me go, and you stay here and enjoy Paris?

WALDO—Well, that's an idea.

JOHN—It will give me a chance to get some additional material for Robert's biography. And anyhow, I'll be glad to get away from Paris for a few days.

SUSIE—Yes, but what about me?

JOHN—You'll come with me.

SUSIE—And leave Waldo here?

JOHN—Yes, why not—since Waldo doesn't want to go? It's all perfectly simply. *You* must go, and I feel that I *should*. Waldo would rather not, and feels that he needn't. So *he* stays and *we* go.

WALDO—Sure.

SUSIE—I don't know. It looks funny.

JOHN—In what way?

SUSIE—Of course, if we arranged it that way, Claire would have Waldo to keep her company.

CLAIRE—Susie, child, you must *learn* to stop worrying about Claire.

WALDO—How do you know Claire wants Waldo to keep her company?

CLAIRE—This is getting frightfully involved. I suggest lunch.

SUSIE—Yes. We can discuss it later. Come on, Waldo, let's get our hats. (*She and* WALDO *go to other room.* CLAIRE *gets her hat.*)

JOHN—I think that Susie has outgrown Waldo, don't you?

CLAIRE—I haven't thought about it. It costs money to ride to Vence.

JOHN—I'll get Waldo to advance it. He can charge it to the administration costs of the estate.

CLAIRE—Did you cash the money order?

JOHN—Yes, of course I did.

CLAIRE—I suggested the Medicis' for lunch because it's fairly cheap. So please don't order a fifty-franc wine. (SUSIE *and* WALDO *enter.*)

SUSIE—We're ready. And I warn you that I'm going to order everything on the card. My first meal in Paris is always an event.

JOHN—Well, we'll try not to disappoint you. Come along! (*He links his arm in hers and they exit.*)

WALDO—Does a Frenchman have just as much trouble getting a telephone number?

CLAIRE—Yes, just as much. Go ahead, I must lock the door. (WALDO *exits followed by* CLAIRE.)

THE CURTAIN FALLS

ACT II

The night of the fourteenth of July Claire and Waldo are in the Shelby room listening to the noise of the celebration in the boulevard outside. It is a hot night, the windows are open and the sounds of the shouting crowds below, mixed with much muddled dance music, most of it American Jazz, come floating upward. It is a familiar scene to Claire, but new to Waldo.

They have just finished dinner. Claire is still at table. Waldo, looking down from the window, is amused to see the taxis stop until the crowd is finished dancing. That, Claire points out to him, is one of the grand things about Paris: the city belongs to the people.

"No, I guess this couldn't go on in New York, could it?" Waldo ruminates.

"It wouldn't be true in New York," Claire points out. "We're pretty sadly lacking in the graces, don't you think? And we don't know very much about enjoying the simple things of life: eating and drinking and love-making—and dancing in the streets.

WALDO—Why is that? Is it because we're so busy making a living that we haven't time for anything else?

CLAIRE—I don't think that has much to do with it. Everybody is absorbed in making a living. The French care much more about money than we do.

WALDO—Then what is it?—why don't we know how to enjoy ourselves?

CLAIRE—I don't know. I think perhaps it's because we're essentially a Christian people. We've been taught for centuries to believe in the mortification of the flesh and to look for heaven anywhere except on earth. You can't enjoy the good things of life if you're ashamed of your appetites and have to be a little furtive about satisfying them.

WALDO—Well, an awful lot of us seem to be trying to get over it.

CLAIRE—Yes, I know. Kicking off the lid and making whoopee. But most of that is nothing more than putting your morality in reverse. To be a real pagan, you have to swap your conscience for a palate.

WALDO—How do you go about doing that?

CLAIRE—Ah, that's the problem we emancipated Puritans are all trying to solve. I'm beginning to suspect that it can't be done. I think that maybe you have to be born with the palate—and without the conscience.

WALDO—Well, that's what I think. Why try to be something that you're not? If you're born a Latin, be a Latin. And if you're born an American, be an American. I can't see this business of suddenly cutting loose and running wild. What's the sense of a plodding, middle-of-the-road fellow like me putting vine-leaves in his hair and trying to pretend he's a Casanova?

CLAIRE—I think you'd look rather sweet, Waldo, with vine-leaves in your hair.

WALDO—Well, I'll get some, tomorrow, and try them on for you.

CLAIRE—You're so good to me. Still, don't you think, Waldo, that there's a middle ground somewhere? I mean, we Americans are such extremists. We either murder people to emphasize our belief in the Eighteenth Amendment or else we devote ourselves to acquiring delirium tremens. And apparently the only alternative to chastity is to take a different bed-fellow every night.

WALDO—But is it to go on like this? Or is the pendulum going to swing back all the way?

CLAIRE—My guess is no. How about some more coffee?

Claire is willing to admit, however, that although the old world's opinion of America must have been largely influenced by our contributions of "jazz, plumbing and Charlie Chaplin," America's opinion of the old world is pretty generally founded on first-hand knowledge.

"We're a nation of travelers," she points out. "Say what you will about us, you can't deny that we travel. There's not a hamlet in Oklahoma that hasn't sent its quota of pilgrims to the tomb of Napoleon and the Café de la Paix. Go to any lumber-camp in the great Northwest and you'll find a lithograph of the Mona Lisa. And, at this very minute, ten million of us are dancing in front of the Dome."

The celebration goes on. Now it sweeps in with a roar. Now it dies down to an echo. Claire thinks Waldo should be a part of it, and not be spending his time sitting around helping her nurse a sprained ankle. But Waldo is content. Then, if he will insist on staying, Claire thinks they might at least have a drink. So Claire has a glass of cognac and Waldo tries the Cointreau.

The talk turns to the absent John and Susie. It is too bad they could not have got back for the celebration, thinks John. But Claire is satisfied they are having a very good time where they are. Especially Susie.

They have cleared away the dinner dishes, made themselves comfortable and taken another drink. Waldo, with his collar off, because of the heat, is practicing his French and waiting on Claire with all the airs of a valet de chambre. Now, with his work done, he sits down beside her and takes her hand.

"You know, I think perhaps I'm a little sentimental about you," he confesses.

"Well, I don't object to a little sentimentality, now and then," admits Claire.

WALDO—I think you're mighty nice.

CLAIRE—You're not so bad, yourself.

WALDO—It's sort of funny, isn't it, our being thrown together like this?

CLAIRE—Yes, it is.

WALDO—Perhaps I should have gone to Vence with Susie and John.

CLAIRE—Why?

WALDO—Well, I don't know—

CLAIRE—Do you think you'd have had a better time?

WALDO—You know that wasn't what I meant. It's only—

CLAIRE—Are you afraid that you'll be compromised? Or are you chivalrously thinking of me?

WALDO—Well, I don't blame you for making fun of me. I suppose I am a pretty conventional sort of person.

CLAIRE—I'm not making fun of you, my dear. I was just being a little playful. Have I gone and hurt your feelings?

WALDO—No, no, of course not. As a matter of fact, I wasn't thinking about us at all.

CLAIRE—Well, as far as Susie and John are concerned, there isn't any doubt that they are having a better time, the way things are.

WALDO—Yes, I suppose they really didn't want me along, did they?

CLAIRE—Why, Waldo, you didn't ever think they did, did you?

WALDO—No, I suppose not.

CLAIRE—You don't mean to say that you've ever had any doubt about it!

WALDO—Well, I don't know—

CLAIRE—I really don't see how they could have made the thing more obvious.

WALDO—You see, my mind works pretty slowly. I've wanted to talk to you about it, ever since they left, but somehow or other—

CLAIRE—But, Waldo, I took it for granted all along that you accepted the situation for what it is. I had no idea. (*As* WALDO *rises abruptly and walks away.*) Oh, Waldo, my dear, I'm so sorry.

WALDO—I suppose I'm pretty conventional.

CLAIRE—I'm frightfully sorry that it disturbs you so.

WALDO—Doesn't it disturb you?

CLAIRE—Well, not a great deal. I'm not a great believer in the importance of sexual fidelity. And I'm not terribly possessive—or, at any rate, I've learned to behave as though I'm not. You see, I'm rather used to this sort of thing.

WALDO—You mean it happens all the time?

CLAIRE—Well—often enough.

WALDO—And you don't mind?

CLAIRE—Well, I suppose I do. But not very much, really. I used to; but one gets accustomed to everything. Besides, my views have changed, too, I suppose.

WALDO—But doesn't the marriage relationship mean anything to you?

CLAIRE—Yes, I think it does—I know it does. But don't ask me what. It's one of the things I'm profoundly puzzled about—along with a lot of other people, apparently. But I'm sure I don't think it means anything as simple as a man and woman sleeping exclusively together.

WALDO—No, I suppose I don't either. But—well, theories are one thing and facts another.

Claire is distressed that Waldo feels as he does, and a little regretful that she had not done something to prevent John and Susie putting over their plan. But it was all so elaborately arranged, she was convinced that he, too, saw through it. And, in fairness to John, Claire thinks Susie was the chief instigator.

"I recognize the technique," she explains to the less alert Waldo. "I've seen it work before. Don't think I'm trying to whitewash John, but this is getting to be a fairly familiar story. John likes to think of himself as an expert seducer; but actually he's fair game for any moderately clever female."

Waldo does not think this sort of thing has ever happened before with Susie. Anyway, it is something he has preferred not to think about.

"It isn't that I believe particularly in monogamy," declares Waldo. "It's that—well, it's an emotional reaction rather than a moral one. When you care for somebody—"

"Yes, I know what you mean. But, at bottom, it's really possessiveness, isn't it?"

"Maybe it is. But if you happen to have a possessive nature—"

"Don't you think it is more civilized not to have?"

"Perhaps I'm not civilized. But all these civilized people

around here—are they so much better off?"

"Perhaps they are not really civilized, either," Claire admits. "Perhaps it's just a thin surface layer. That's what I'm beginning to think. You see, Waldo, to me all this—this escapade of John's and Susie's—all this sex business and the way we all talk and think and carry on, nowadays, is all part of a larger problem, a basic problem of adjustment and self-realization."

A knock on the door is followed by the announcement from Madame that she has a telegram for Claire. Claire thinks that it is probably from John announcing that his biographical researches will detain him and Susie a few days longer. But it isn't. It is from Lillian, John's sister, and she has further complicated matters at the McAndrews school by visiting Teddy. Now McAndrews insists the boy be taken away.

Waldo is convinced it would be much the best thing to do, but Claire can think of nothing to do with Teddy. Teddy and John simply cannot get along together.

"You see, Waldo," she explains, "ever since I've known John he's been in revolt against his own patterned upbringing. And from the moment Teddy was born, John has insisted that the child should be left free, that John's own educational process should be completely reversed. I can't tell you how difficult it's been."

Waldo has an idea that perhaps he might help, but before he can explain what is in his mind Lillian Garfield has arrived. Walked in on them, in fact, having been told by the concierge to go right up. Waldo explains that if he is not very presentable it is only because he is trying to keep cool, and Claire adds quickly that both she and Waldo have just been idling by the window watching the crowds on the boulevard.

"I sprained my ankle the other day, and I don't dare go out in the crowded streets," she explains.

"Oh, I'm sorry to hear it," sympathizes Lillian. "How do you get up and down these stairs?"

"I don't. I've been having my meals in. Waldo's been a perfect dear. He's waited on me and kept me company. John's away, you see. He and Susie have gone down to Vence to see my sister-in-law about the settlement of my brother's estate. Susie is his daughter and Waldo's wife and—"

"Yes, I know. I must say I'm very much disappointed not to find John here. I wrote that I was coming."

There is nothing to do about Lillian's disappointment but make the best of it. But there is something to be done about taking

Teddy away from that awful school, Lillian thinks. She can well understand why such a man as McAndrews would insist that there shall be no visiting, even if he can boast an international reputation as an educator. She found Teddy running around about half naked and using such language as no child of John's should know anything about.

CLAIRE—It was John's idea to send him to McAndrews.

LILLIAN—Yes, John has changed too, in more ways than one, since he left home. To think of a man with his talents and his background, living here like this, year after year! It's not the kind of life I planned for him.

CLAIRE—It's difficult to plan other people's lives for them, Lillian.

LILLIAN—He could have had a brilliant career, if he'd listened to me. What has he made of himself? A gypsy, an outcast! It's not what I hoped and prayed for, I can tell you that. And now, to see his child neglected, uncared for—

CLAIRE—He's not being neglected, Lillian. We simply haven't the same ideas about education, that's all.

LILLIAN—Yes, I know. I know about these ideas that people have nowadays. Just to live for oneself, to think of nothing but one's own comfort and selfish pleasures. And the children— God knows what's to become of them! I can tell you that if I were fortunate enough to have a child of my own, I'd give my whole life to it; I'd devote myself to it every minute, day and night.

CLAIRE—I'm sorry you haven't a child, Lillian, since you've always wanted one so much. But, after all, you can't expect everyone to take the same view of things that you do.

LILLIAN—Yes—everything is changed nowadays. People have different ideas about marriage, too. I was taught to believe that marriage is a sacred thing; that when a woman gives herself to a man in marriage, she forms a bond that only death can break. But, nowadays, nothing is sacred and married women no longer respect either their husbands or themselves.

CLAIRE—Lillian, I think your trip has made you awfully tired and upset. I think that you should really get a good night's rest. Have you found a place to stay?

LILLIAN—I know that I'm intruding. I suppose it was tactless of me, to walk in, unannounced. I'm very sorry. You see, I'm not used to the modern way of doing things.

Lillian has barely had time to pull herself together when Alan Foster dashes into the room. He, too, had been told to come right up. Alan is the forerunner for a crowd of celebrants, friends of Claire's and John's, who are at the moment waiting in the boulevard below to hear whether or not the Shelbys have any liquor.

Being assured by the flustered Claire that there is a little liquor, the crowd starts up. It is quite beyond Lillian how anyone with Claire's background can live like that. The revelation is so overwhelming that Lillian is in tears by the time the party arrives. They are held outside the door until she is able to dab her eyes dry and strengthen her resistance with a gulp of cognac.

The crowd barges in and there is a variety of greetings, mostly osculatory and all vociferous. They are having a grand time, all of them, and are in such spirits it is perfectly simple for them to make themselves at home, not only with Claire's room and her liquor, but with her friends as well.

The talk is free and, to an outsider, a trifle scandalous. Frequently it concerns this one's affair with that one, and the other's conviction that all life should be gay and free.

Lillian stands it as well as she can, refusing the drinks and trying not to be shocked by the conversation, until she hears Miriam assure Joe that when he says he had the story about the two fish peddlers from Wienie Frankfurter he is a goddam liar—

Then Lillian thinks she will be going and goes, despite all their efforts to detain her.

"She doesn't understand la vie de Bohême," explains Claire, when she returns from the hall.

The party goes on, gathering momentum with the drinks and the free spirit of the crowd. Now Joe does a Russian dance. Now Charlie has arrived at the point at which he grows classical and insists on reciting Horace. When Willard suggests that it may be Virgil Charlie is profoundly upset.

"Good God," demands Charlie, with emphasis, "how can a man go through life and not know Horace?"

"Four out of five over forty do," ventures Willard.

"Ah knowed a waiter in Charleston by de name ob Horace," adds Joe.

"That's American education for you," shouts Charlie. "No wonder the country is run by demagogues and shoe-salesmen. No wonder we're a nation of barbarians without any sense of values."

"What is being able to spout Horace got to do with a sense of values?" demands Willard.

"Everything. How can a man have any perspective if he isn't grounded in the classics? That's the trouble with all you fellows who call yourselves modernists. You're nothing but a lot of illiterate journalists who think the world was made by Sinclair Lewis."

"Oh, God, they're starting on humanism again!" explodes Dorothy.

Now they are in the thick of the argument, waving glasses and metaphors, pillows and declarations, until they get down past the point where "what America needs is discipline and regimentation" to say nothing of "an established church and a hereditary monarchy." At about which time Dorothy again arises to insist that, this having been reported to be the fourteenth of July she, for one, purposes continuing on to the boulevards. Joe would even push on to the Bastille.

"We have nothing to lose but our chains!" insists Joe. Now that the liquor's all gone that seems a good idea, too.

They try to take Waldo with them. At least Dorothy tries to take Waldo with her. And Alan offers to stay and keep Claire company. But Waldo and Claire manage to be rid of them finally. There is some kissing and a lot of "good nights," Gus and Sonia are rescued from the next room, and the party is on its way.

"Well, thank heaven the liquor gave out," sighs Claire. "We'd have had Madame up here in another five minutes. It's all Alan's fault. I'm sure they never would have come here if he hadn't suggested it."

Claire wonders why Waldo did not go with them, particularly in view of Dorothy's urging, but Waldo had much rather be with Claire, helping clean up the mess and waiting on her. He even is interested in hearing all Claire's troubles. Interested now in hearing of the scene with Lillian, who is quite sure to think the worst of everything she has seen and heard.

Lillian, Claire explains, has always hated her. Never forgiven her for marrying John. But, for that matter, Lillian would have felt the same about anybody who took John from her.

"All her frustrated maternity spent itself on John," Claire explains; "and now that he's escaped her it's turned to bitterness."

"Rather tragic, isn't it?"

"I suppose it is. But I'm getting pretty tired of feeling sorry for frustrated people, especially when they use their frustration as a weapon for attacking others. . . . As a matter of fact, John married me largely because he wanted to get away from Lillian.

She was swamping him so with maternal solicitude that he felt
himself going under."

Waldo feels that he can sympathize with the person who wants
children and can't have them. And that brings him back to the
idea he had for meeting the problem of Teddy: Why not let him
take the boy for a year or so? Take him back to America with
him. Sort of keep an eye on him—

Claire is pleased at the thought of Teddy's being with Waldo,
but wonders what Susie would think about it.

"I thought of that, too," Waldo admits. "But as far as Susie
is concerned, Claire, she's been wanting to stay over here for
a while anyhow, and—

CLAIRE—I thought you were opposed to the idea.

WALDO—Well, I have been. But Susie seems to think that her
happiness depends upon her being here for a while. And, in a
way, it's selfish of me not to let her stay if she really wants to.
So, all things considered—

CLAIRE—You really are a sweet and generous person, Waldo.

WALDO (*embarrassed*)—Why no, I'm not—not a bit.

CLAIRE—Yes, indeed you are. And I shan't ever forget it,
either.

WALDO—Would you be willing to trust me with Teddy?

CLAIRE—Without a moment's hesitation, Waldo. But it would
be useless to try to persuade John.

WALDO—I'm afraid John doesn't think much of my intelligence.

CLAIRE—It's entirely a question of jealousy. He'd be too afraid
that you'd win Teddy away from him.

WALDO—Well, it's too much for me.

CLAIRE—Yes, and it's getting to be almost too much for me.
(*Going to him.*) Waldo, you're a lovely person and I can't tell
you how much I appreciate all your kindness.

WALDO—Why, I haven't done anything. But there isn't anything I wouldn't do for you.

CLAIRE—I know it, Waldo; and it's such a nice feeling. I'm
so awfully, awfully fond of you. (*She kisses him swiftly.*) Now,
run along and let me go to bed. I'm terribly tired.

WALDO (*holding her hand*)—I hate to leave you.

CLAIRE—And I hate to have you go. But it's late. And if
I'm going to England on Saturday, there'll be lots to do. Good
night, my dear. (*As* WALDO *tries to take her in his arms.*) No.
Run along now, like a nice boy.

WALDO—All right. Good night. (*He looks at her a moment,*

then exits abruptly to his room and closes the door. CLAIRE *takes a step forward, stretches out her arms and then clasps them to her, in an embrace. Then she sits down and cries quietly.*)

WALDO (*knocking at the door*)—Claire!

CLAIRE (*springing to her feet*)—Yes; what is it?

WALDO—May I come in?

CLAIRE—Yes, come in. What's the matter?

WALDO—I was wondering about your bandage.

CLAIRE—Oh, thanks. But it's really very comfortable. I think I'll just leave it for tonight. Thanks a lot.

WALDO—Are you sure?

CLAIRE—Yes; I want to get right to bed. I'm very tired.

WALDO—You won't get much sleep. It's pretty noisy.

CLAIRE—Yes, and it will be all night.

WALDO—Well, good night.

CLAIRE—Good night, Waldo. (*He starts to go, then, taking her in his arms, kisses her.*)

CLAIRE (*pushing him away*)—Go along now. Please, dear.

WALDO—Do you want me to?

CLAIRE (*almost inaudibly*)—Yes. (*He releases her and is about to go. Then, suddenly and impulsively, he takes her in his arms again and presses his lips to hers. She puts her arms about his neck and responds to his kiss.*)

THE CURTAIN FALLS

ACT III

Two days later Claire's room is in some disorder. There are the remnants of a breakfast on the table, the bed has not yet been made and a half-packed suitcase rests on a chair.

The room is empty when John Shelby and Susie Lynde, followed by Claude with their hand baggage, come in from the hall.

They are undoubtedly surprised at not finding either Claire or Waldo. Susie sinks into a chair with a curious expression on her face. She had quite evidently been all steeled for the meeting and cannot quite adjust herself to the unexpected situation.

She is, John allows, a funny child. He would comfort her with a caress, but Susie is in no mood for caresses at the moment. She is dead tired and much in need of sleep. It isn't easy for John to understand why Susie should be so anxious as to the whereabouts of Waldo and Claire. What difference does it make where **they are?** The fact that Claire's suitcase is only partly packed indicates that she will be back before she starts for Calais. Why should she be self-conscious about them?

"After all, we're adult and presumably civilized individuals, aren't we?" demands John.

"Yes, that's all very true," admits Susie. "But still I don't see how you can help feeling a little funny about it."

"That's because you haven't fully grown up yet, my dear."

"You mean I haven't your wealth of experience."

"Exactly. You're still having growing pains. Our moral heritage dies hard.

"Oh, who gives a damn about morals!"

Susie is not in a pleasant mood. She can't help but wonder about Claire and Waldo. Nor is she at all satisfied with John's conviction that probably nothing at all has happened. Waldo is not the type in whom Claire would be interested. "Claire," says John, "has grown accustomed to a rather more stimulating kind of contact. After all, our friend Waldo—"

"Yes, I know what you mean," admits Susie. "All the same, I'd trust him sooner than I would Claire."

Now Susie has gone into the other room, just out of natural curiosity. And when John accuses her of wanting to make sure which of the beds had been slept in, her feelings are hurt and she will not be made up with easily.

"You're tired," that's John's conclusion. "Why don't you go in and—"

SUSIE—Yes, I am tired. Tired and worried.

JOHN—Why are you worried?

SUSIE—Well, good heavens, there'll have to be some sort of explanation, won't there? We can't go on acting as though nothing had happened.

JOHN—Why not?

SUSIE—Because we can't, that's why not. Waldo isn't as stupid as all that. And even if he doesn't suspect us, you may be pretty sure that Claire does.

JOHN—Claire has long since grown accustomed to the fact that I'm not a monogamist.

SUSIE—Yes, that's all very pretty. But it's not going to endear me to her, you may be sure of that. She happens to be a woman and so do I.

JOHN—But you already dislike each other.

SUSIE—Yes, but at least we're polite to each other.

JOHN—Then go on being polite.

Susie—It's easy enough to say—

John—Claire leaves for England in an hour. Surely, you can be polite for an hour. I'm just wondering— (*He breaks off.*)

Susie—What?

John—I don't know whether I should go to England with Claire or not.

Susie—Why do you want to go to England with her?

John—I don't want to. But, after all, I have some responsibility for Teddy.

Susie—And what about me? Are you just going to walk off and leave me stranded here?

John—But, I don't see—with Waldo here—

Susie—So you're just going to hand me back to Waldo, is that it?

John—That's hardly a fair way of putting it.

Susie—All it means to you is a gay week-end.

John—Susie, Susie, you know that isn't true.

Susie—Then how can you talk about leaving me?

John—But you must realize that I have certain responsibilities—

Susie—Don't you think you have some responsibility to me? Don't you? Don't you think I'm entitled to a little consideration too? What kind of a girl do you think I am, anyhow? (*She begins to cry.*)

John (*kneeling beside her*)—Don't cry, darling. Please don' go on like this. There's nothing to be gained by it.

Susie—I thought you really cared for me.

John—I do care for you. You know I do. I adore you Only—

Susie—Oh, I can't bear the thought of it being all over! Jus a few short days and then— (*Clinging to him.*) Oh, John dea don't leave me!

John—But, Susie, dear—

Susie—I'll be so miserable if you go to England. Please don go.

John—All right, I won't go. There, now are you satisfied

Susie (*embracing him*)—You sweet thing! (*Stroking h hair.*) I wish I knew what you see in me—a man like you.

John—Why, that's absurd, Susie dear. You have a great de to give me—a great deal. Your youth, your freshness, your u spoiled simplicity—

Susie—Oh, I hope it's true! Oh, John, you're so wonderful— Kiss me, darling!

Their passionate embrace is interrupted by another knock at the door. This time it is Lillian Garfield. Susie has barely time to powder her nose before Lillian opens the door.

John's greeting to his sister is perfunctory but friendly. He and Susie are just back from Vence, he explains. Claire must have gone to the bank or somewhere.

At Lillian's suggestion Susie leaves them. Lillian wants to talk to John about Teddy. John cannot quite understand why she should be so worried about Teddy, and is inclined to resent her interference. Whatever Lillian's opinion may be, McAndrews is "a brilliant educator with a psycho-analytic approach, whose methods are quite unintelligible to the layman."

There are doubtless a great many things that Lillian does not understand, she admits, but she does know when a child is being neglected and ill-treated. As for Teddy's going to another school, that thought is also disturbing to Lillian. She wishes John would let her take Teddy.

"I'll engage the best doctors or psychologists or whatever you want," promises Lillian. "And you could pick out any tutor or governess that suited you. I'll do anything you say, only let me have him. Just for a year, John—just let me try it for one year."

John considers the suggestion absurd. In his opinion Lillian is quite unqualified to bring up a child.

"I brought you up," answers Lillian, mortally wounded.

"Yes, exactly," replies John. "And I've had to spend twenty years of my life undoing the results of your upbringing."

LILLIAN—How can you talk to me like that, John? How can you say such things to me? I don't see how you can say such things. You were everything to me—my whole life. I had no other thought in life but you. I just lived for you. And now you tell me—! Oh, I don't deserve this. No, I don't. As God is my judge, I don't deserve it.

JOHN—I haven't meant to reproach you, Lillian. But you don't seem ever to have realized that I've outgrown my childhood—that you can't go managing my life, forever.

LILLIAN—Yes, I realize it. I realize everything. I realize that my whole life has been wasted.

JOHN—You exaggerate everything.

LILLIAN—Yes, wasted—utterly wasted. The best I had to give gave to you—and you hate me for it.

JOHN—But I don't hate you, Lillian.

LILLIAN—What's my life been? Nothing but disappointment.

I wanted a child. More than anything else, I wanted a child of my own. Well, that was denied me, too. And what has my marriage been? Nothing but misery and humiliation. You don't know what I've had to endure. My husband lives openly with a common little whore—and I must pretend not to know it. And now you—

JOHN—I urged you ten years ago to divorce him.

LILLIAN—Yes, that's easy enough to say. But I have different ideas about marriage. I believe that marriage is a sacred thing. But nowadays people look at things differently. You and your friends—you have other ideas. Yes, and your wife, your wonderful wife—!

JOHN—What has Claire to do with this?

LILLIAN—Everything. She turned you against me from the beginning. She poisoned your mind against me—

JOHN—You're talking nonsense, Lillian.

LILLIAN—Don't try to tell me. I'm not such a fool as you seem to think I am. I know all about these wonderful modern ideas. I suppose she's a fit person to bring up a child—a woman who turns over her baby to a savage ruffian, so that she can carry on, undisturbed—

JOHN—Just what do you mean by that?

LILLIAN—Oh, there's a lot I haven't told you—there's a lot I haven't opened your eyes to. I haven't told you how I came here the other night and—

JOHN—All right, Lillian. That's enough of that. You have no right to come here spying on Claire. You'd better understand that.

LILLIAN—You're letting her lead you to ruin, that's what you're doing. A boy with your genius and your opportunities—drifting like this, living here like this. John, why don't you give this up? Why don't you come back home and lead a normal respectable life? I'll give you a house and enough to live on; and you could take up some profession—

JOHN—So you want a whore to keep too, do you? Well, understand this: you can't make a prostitute of me. It was to escape your dull, sodden, complacent world that I came here. Go back and live on your husks? No, thank you! I prefer to starve decently in freedom. That's a word you've never learned—freedom! Freedom and self-respect! Individuality!

Claire is back. She kisses John perfunctorily and mutters practically indistinct "Hello" to Lillian, who promptly leaves

Lillian will not have it said that she ever came between husband and wife.

Claire and Waldo have been to the telegraph office to notify McAndrews that Claire is coming for Teddy. For the present it will be necessary for Madame to put a cot in the room for him to sleep on, she announces, because she does not intend sending him away to any more faddish schools. She wonders if John would object very much if Waldo were to take Teddy back to America with him.

The idea is, to John, quite astonishing. She must be aware that Waldo "is utterly incapable of taking care of Teddy."

Claire is not at all aware of that, and as for John's counter suggestion that if anyone is going to take charge of Teddy he had rather his sister Lillian should have him, that is something that will never, never happen.

Waldo is back from the telegraph office. He and John greet each other perfunctorily, perhaps a shade suspiciously. Is John going to England with Claire? No. Is Waldo? No. Waldo does not know what his plans are until he sees Susie. And Susie has plans of her own; as she is pleased to tell them all when she is summoned.

Susie has come to an important decision. Quite suddenly, while she was changing her clothes, she had decided to get a divorce. She wants to stay on in Paris and go ahead with her sculpture. Furthermore she does not think she would ever be content to go back to the stuffy life she and Waldo had been leading in New York. Also she has thought for a long time that she and Waldo were mismated.

"We're just incompatible, that's all," Susie tells Waldo. "You don't mean to cramp my style, but you do. And, as far as you're concerned, you'd be much better off with a different type of woman—well, say somebody like Claire."

It is Waldo's opinion that, after all, marriage is marriage, and while he will not try to hold Susie against her will—

"It isn't that I'm not fond of you, and all that, Waldo," Susie explains; "but—well, I'd rather have my freedom."

Susie has gone to the bath. John is glad Waldo has taken everything so sensibly, and Waldo, his temper rising, is admittedly tempted to lay violent hands on John. Claire stops him.

Claire finds it difficult to talk to John when they are alone. But she has definitely made up her mind to one thing: she is going back to America and she is going to take Teddy with her. For how long? She does not know. Perhaps indefinitely. Perhaps for ever.

"So you've turned chauvinist, have you?" sneers John.

"You know I haven't," Claire answers. "You know it's not because I believe that America is any better than France. It's
simply that my roots are there. I want to go and live in my own
country, among my own people. I'm tired of being an exile; tired
of drifting—of this aimless wandering existence that we live here."

JOHN—We are living in the most civilized country that there
is in the world today—and you call it living in exile!

CLAIRE—Yes, that's just it! We're living in the midst of it
without ever becoming part of it. We're aliens here and we'll
never be anything else. And all the people we know; they're all
aliens too—playing around on the outside of something they can
never make their own. We're like a lot of hungry little children,
pressing our noses against a shop-window and crying for delicacies
that we can never touch. I've had enough of it. I want to go
home and dig for turnips in my own garden.

JOHN—I'm not impressed by your gastronomic metaphors.
France is my spiritual home, whatever the accidents of my birth.
The imagination does not confine itself within national boundaries.
There is no tariff upon intelligence. Good taste recognizes no flag.
I happen to be a sensitive individual, who prefers civilization to
barbarism; cultivated speech and manners to the buffooneries of a
plutocracy; intellectual and spiritual freedom to slavery—and the
wines of Burgundy to even the most delectable Kansas turnips.

CLAIRE—Yes. I know. I've heard it all before—many—too
many times. It sounds well over the liqueurs and looks well in
the pages of the highbrow quarterlies. But in the terms of daily
living, it all comes down to wild parties and futile little love-
affairs, to hand-to-mouth living and hack-work to make ends meet.

JOHN—You're suggesting tactfully, I take it, that I am not a
best-seller.

CLAIRE—I mean you're not really happy here, not really satisfied. You scorn America, but you're bitterly resentful because
you're not recognized as one of her major prophets. Oh, I don't
mean to reproach you or discourage you. If it's what you want
to do, why go on doing it. But not I; I've had enough. I'm going back.

JOHN—What it all comes down to is that you're leaving me,
isn't it?

CLAIRE—I'm going back! If you want to come along, come.

JOHN—You know I'll never go back.

CLAIRE—Then perhaps it's you who are leaving me.

JOHN—I don't intend to surrender my convictions to your romantic notions of life in America.

CLAIRE—I don't think my notions are romantic. I don't expect to find America an earthly Paradise. I'm merely trying to face the realities of my life, instead of running away from them.

JOHN—The long and short of it is that you prefer life in America without me, to life with me, here. Isn't that it?

CLAIRE—Well, yes, if you insist upon putting it that way. Especially when life with you here cuts me off from my child.

JOHN—Yes, yes, I understand. There's no need to qualify and explain. So this is the end, is it? This is what's become of all that fine fervor and enthusiasm of yours, is it?—all that splendid revolt and fine appetite for freedom? You've done with it; you're going back to the old, crippling patterns that we came here to escape from.

CLAIRE—We were half-grown then and youth is the time for rebellion. But I don't want to be a rebel all my life. I'm through fighting ghosts—shadows that were only projections of our own fears. As for freedom—well, I've long since stopped believing that freedom is a matter of geography. John, the spirit has gone out of our marriage. Why should we go on—

Waldo has come back. He wants to apologize to both of them. And he will be glad to take Claire to the station. He takes her bag and goes on ahead.

So, it is for Waldo that Claire is leaving him, John charges. It isn't, Claire answers, but Waldo can have her if he wants her. Which is utterly incredible to John. That, after all their years together, after all their lives have meant, Claire should be willing to throw herself away on a "grinning nit-wit—" But, let her go. John doesn't need her.

Claire has gone. They will each have to work out things for himself, she is convinced. For a moment John has thrown himself despairingly on the bed. But now Susie has come to comfort him. Isn't he glad Susie is going to get a divorce and live in Paris? And wouldn't he like to come now and keep her company while she gets dressed?

Susie has John by the hand and is leading him into the other room. Claude, making up the bed, looks after them.

"Ah, ces Americaines!" he mutters, with a shrug. Then he bursts into song as

THE CURTAIN FALLS

BRIEF MOMENT

A Comedy in Three Acts

BY S. N. BEHRMAN

THE production of S. N. Behrman's "Brief Moment" in early November was attended by items of some local significance. Katharine Cornell had taken a lease on the Belasco Theatre, following David Belasco's death, and this was the first attraction offered under her management, with her husband, Guthrie McClintic, acting as director.

Alexander Woollcott, who had attained eminence as a New York dramatic critic, accepted Mr. McClintic's offer to turn actor and play a part in the comedy—a part which Mr. Behrman had confessedly written with the critic in mind.

Celebration of both events was achieved without undue excitement but with complete success. Miss Cornell was generously felicitated upon her selection of a first play for her business venture as an actress-manageress, and Mr. Woollcott was acclaimed by his former colleagues as a comedian of good address and an amusing girth.

Mr. Behrman had made friends with the New York playgoers with two previous plays, "The Second Man," produced successfully by the Theatre Guild in 1927, and "Serena Blandish," produced less successfully by Jed Harris in 1929. His gift is for a pleasant wit and incisive characterization. His comedies have excited favorable reactions because of the pungency of their comment on modern life rather than because of the emotional force of their situations.

"Brief Moment" is distinctly modern. In fact there is something more than a suggestion that its story is deliberately based on the marital adventure of a certain rich man's son who tried unsuccessfully to compose his rather confused life by marrying a musical comedy actress.

The sitting-room of Roderick Deane's roof apartment, the scene of the first act, overlooks the East River in New York. It is on the second floor of a triplex apartment and gives onto a glass-enclosed veranda from which the best view of the river is to be had.

"BRIEF MOMENT"

Abby: All right, I'll reform. No more tricks. I'll lead the simple life.

Roderick: Abby, dare I believe you? Oh, Abby, can I ever make an honest woman out of you?

(*Francine Larrimore and Robert Douglas*)

On the particular afternoon that "Brief Moment" opens there
are two young men in the living-room. They have been playing
backgammon. They are young Mr. Deane and his friend Harold
Sigrift, known pretty generally as "Sig" and given to the frequent
utterance of those wise and witty sayings called epigrams above
stairs and wisecracks below.

"Sigrift is very fat, about thirty years old and lies down whenever possible. He somewhat resembles Alexander Woollcott, who
conceivably might play him," reads the author's description of
this character.

Deane is a personable young man in his middle twenties, slim
and volatile, blessed with an alert mind, and a fairly broad but
not too comprehensive education.

Sigrift, stretched out on a chaise-longue, manages when urged,
to roll over, prop himself on one elbow and throw the dice in
order that the game, which apparently has been interfering with
the conversation, may be finished.

The topic under discussion, however, will not be put aside. It
is concerned directly with a certain young woman whom Roderick
is apparently determined to marry, to the implied dismay of most
of his friends and the quite evident distress of Mr. Sigrift.

It is quite all right for Roderick to adore this young woman,
Sigrift admits, but it is not necessary for him to take out a license
for that.

With no particular subtlety Sigrift would warn his young
friend about what he is letting himself in for. This girl, this Abby
Fane, if that is her real name, is no more than a blues singer in a
night club.

Well, what's the matter with that? counters Roderick. What is
he, Sigrift? A snob?

"The girl's magnificent," he announces, with fervor. "Her
vitality is magnificent. After all, who the hell am I? A millionaire's son. Well, what of it? The town's lousy with them. I've
been a failure at everything. . . ."

"At twenty-five?"

RODERICK—My God, if you're not a success when you're 25,
when will you be? I play a saxophone—do I do it as well as
Bunny Weifel, who's 22? I ran a jazz band—did I make a hit of
it? I am a composer. Not so hot. Aviation—well, I got my
license, but who hasn't? Among artists, I'm tolerated because
I'm rich. And don't think I don't know it.

SIGRIFT—Will the prima donna of the Hotsy Totsy change all

that?

RODERICK—I don't say she will. All I say is, it's no concession for me to marry her. The very assumption is arrogant. She may turn me down flat. (SIGRIFT *just whistles*.) Well, she may!

SIGRIFT—If she turns you down, my blossom—then I'm Skippy.

RODERICK—She's lovely. She's got freshness, high spirits, vitality. She's unspoiled—

SIGRIFT—My God, you don't think *that!*

RODERICK—No, I don't give a damn. I mean she's unspoiled by civilization.

SIGRIFT—Unspoiled by it? She hasn't encountered it yet.

RODERICK—She transforms that dirty little night club. Those banal words she sings—they become something—

SIGRIFT—What do they become?

RODERICK—She has glamor. She has poetry.

SIGRIFT—I'm reluctant to blight this dewy romance.

RODERICK—Blight your head off.

SIGRIFT—Let me tell you something about vitality, my chuck. It's fatiguing to live with. I lived with a girl once who had vitality. She wore me out. Nowadays I go in for languor.

RODERICK—That's why you're so trim and athletic looking.

SIGRIFT—What is this mania for flat stomachs anyway? I think they're insipid.

RODERICK—You're a Roman Emperor, Sig—misplaced. . . .

SIGRIFT—I'm sensible, that's all. I'm not a mass of whimpering complaints. I'm comfortable.

RODERICK—That's it! I'm not. Damn it!

SIGRIFT—You might write a tune—"I've Got Those Maladjusted Blues"—and get your girl friend to sing it in the Hotsy Totsy.

Does Roderick happen to know Manny Walsh, Sigrift wonders. Manny is the owner of the Hotsy Totsy, where Abby sings. He is also the most powerful racketeer in town. And he loves Abby Fane. Then there is also that distinguished polo player, Cass Worthing—

The arrival of Roderick Deane's sister Kay interrupts the discussion. Kay is an attractive young woman, consciously, happily alive in the spirit of the time. She has come to meet her brother's girl friend and is impatiently anxious. She has seen and heard Abby at the Hotsy Totsy the night before and is simply crazy about her. The girl's wonderful, thinks Kay. Some showman is bound to discover her, and when he does Abby will "wow" everybody. If Rod wants to marry her, according to his sister, he is showing damned good taste. Nor does she think if Sigrift should cable the news to her father it would do any good. Father would probably want to back a show for Abby. . . .

Manny Walsh is calling. That causes some excitement. Sigrift is amused that Roderick should be thus honored. Kay is thrilled. The papers are full of Manny.

"A nice companion for your little sister," ventures Sigrift.

"I'd trust her with Walsh rather than with you any day," announces Roderick with more than a suggestion of conviction. "Abby tells me he looks after the girls in the night club like a father. Takes care of them when they are sick—writes to their mothers—"

Walsh is tall, broad-shouldered, good looking and slightly ivoried as to complexion in the night-life tradition. He is neither quite at ease, nor perceptibly flustered by his reception. He will not have a cocktail, nor a high-ball, because he makes it a rule never to drink in the daytime. He has come to speak with Mr. Deane, and he would like to see him alone. Sigrift is annoyed at that request. It forces him to move.

"Surely, Manny, you can talk in front of baby," he protests. "You could spell out the big words."

"Sorry! It's personal." Manny is quite serious.

With the others gone Manny comes quickly to the subject in mind. He has come to talk with Roderick about Abby. That little girl means a lot to Manny, though he knows she will give him holy hell if she learns he has been there.

"Abby's the first dame that ever got the best of me," confesses Manny.

"How?"

MANNY—That's it. Don't know. But I feel she knows everything I'm thinking, but that I don't know a damn thing she's thinking.

RODERICK—Do you find Abby mysterious? That's funny—I've always thought her transparent. Am I wrong?

MANNY—No, you're right, but she buffaloes me. It's foolish, because I know her from way back. She comes from where I come from. And I've gone much farther than she has. You wouldn't believe me if I told you what my income is. The newspapers say it's $1,000 a day. Well, it's more than that.

RODERICK—Understatement in the newspapers! What a relief.

MANNY—I've worked myself up, and in my racket that's not

so simple. Besides brains you've got to have physical courage.

RODERICK—I'm sure of it.

MANNY—It's funny, Deane, I've handled the God-damnedest things in my time—right now I'm in the thick of a muddle—you've seen the papers—

RODERICK—Yes. Aren't you frightened at all these revelations?

MANNY—No. All this agitation don't mean anything. Nobody gives a damn. . . . But this is what I came to tell you. I don't know what you've heard about me and Abby.

RODERICK—I haven't heard anything.

MANNY—I understand. You're a gentleman. But I just wanted to tell you this—the reason Abby and me ain't married is because she won't marry me. I've asked her a thousand times.

RODERICK—Did she give any reason?

MANNY—The God-damnedest reason.

RODERICK—What?

MANNY—She says I'm too serious. Can you beat it? And the funny thing is everything I've done, I've done for Abby. She's been—my inspiration. I think most everything a man does he has got some little girl in the back of his mind. Don't you?

RODERICK—Sometimes I think it's even more pervasive than that.

MANNY—Sure. Now I'm on top, I can't get the one thing I want.

RODERICK—That's life, isn't it? Always ironic. . . .

MANNY—Don't misunderstand me. I'm going right on—Abby or no Abby.

RODERICK—I'm sure you will.

When Abby Fane arrives Kay is there to meet her with Manny and Roderick. Abby is a pretty girl, blonde, petite and smartly gowned. Her manner is easy and she is blessed with more grace and more observation than a majority of her kind. Abby is plainly pleased by the warmth of Kay's greeting, and quite surprised to find Manny Walsh there. She is also a little concerned to discover that Manny has just decided, on this unusual occasion, to break from his established rule and take a drink. This is one of the days Manny should leave drink alone, seeing that he is being indicted all over the place.

Kay has asked Manny to drive her home. That, she considers, should be an experience—to be taken home in an armored car by a man with forty-seven indictments!

Alone with Roderick Abby is impressed by many things. By
an apartment to reach which you ride up thirty floors and then
walk two. By the friendly attitude of Rod's sister Kay.

She is glad Rod likes Manny. She is proud of Manny, too.
She has been intending to tell Rod about him. She wants to have
it all straight about them.

"Manny's one guy I'm not going to stop seeing," she warns.

"I wouldn't give him up for worlds," Rod assures her.

ABBY—I've known him ever since I was a little girl. He knew
my father in Pittsburgh. He drove a taxi. That's what my
father did. Manny blew to New York. I decided one morning—
I was waitress in a bum restaurant—that I wanted to go to New
York too—try the stage. I didn't know what it was all about,
but I wanted to. Manny sent me the money. He gave me a
job in his night club. No one—my own father couldn't have been
sweeter. For some reason he wants to marry me. Always has,
he says. But you know—there'd be no point in marrying Manny.
What would marriage give us we haven't got now? (*Hastily.*)
You know what I mean . . .

RODERICK—Well—vaguely—

ABBY—What I mean is we're just good friends. We don't have
to be married to be good friends. There's nothing more between
Manny and me. Not that I'm a virgin or anything like that—

RODERICK (*murmuring*)—Who is?

ABBY—It's funny—I've known him for so long, and I've known
you so little, and yet I couldn't possibly talk to him as frankly as
I do to you. Why is it? He puts me on a pedestal. He'd be terribly shocked if he heard me talk like this. Manny is so respectable.

RODERICK—Perhaps he's a little inflexible.

ABBY—Yeh—he's got a single-track mind.

RODERICK—That's probably why he's so eminent in his profession. Men of action seldom have complicated minds.

ABBY—Is your mind complicated?

RODERICK—It's often divided.

ABBY—Is it divided about me?

RODERICK—That's curious—it's not divided about you.

ABBY—Thought maybe you wanted to back out.

RODERICK—No, I have a feeling of absolute certainty about
you.

ABBY—Sometimes I feel you're kidding—the way you talk—
not about me alone—in general—

RODERICK—That's a defense.

ABBY—Why do you want to marry me? It was the surprise of my young life when you asked me. If you'd asked me to live with you I'd have said okay. Maybe you'd rather—

RODERICK—No! I have a feeling that sort of thing is rather complicated.

ABBY—You have a feeling. Don't you know?

RODERICK—Only theoretically.

ABBY—Gee, I thought that all rich men—

RODERICK—You mustn't generalize—even about rich men.

ABBY—Mustn't I? O.K., Chief. That's out. You see I'm prepared to be an obedient wife.

Abby is signing for the "Scandals." She thinks perhaps Roderick had rather she would not go on with that, but he sees no reason why she should not. That surprises her a little, but she is pleased. Again Roderick would reassure her of his affection for her and his admiration. She has a grip on reality which he lacks. Abby cannot understand that. To her he has everything in the world to make him happy. The fact that he finds himself incurably introspective and unhappy is puzzling to her.

"I think of myself in relation to the outside world—and I seem to myself to be so highly—dispensable," Rod tries to explain. "I mean to say—I've never had anything in my life that was intimate, personal—a part of me. I am surrounded by successful people, all of them much more talented than I am. I've tried Art. I've tried writing songs—"

"Well, what the hell of it! Tin Pan Alley! If you knew the mugs I know who're hits in Tin Pan Alley!"

"No, that isn't the point," Rod answers, seriously. "The point is that Tin Pan Alley does express them. I'm unemployed spiritually. (*A sound from* ABBY.) I have in a way an unfortunate heritage. My father is an overbearing man who impressed it on me early in life that I must justify my existence. He shifted the burden of proof onto me. (*She doesn't quite get that.*) I simply want to convey to you that you are marrying a failure."

"Don't be like that, honey. Whenever you get blue—leave it to mamma. She'll— (*With a whistle and a pass of her hand.*) just whistle the blues away. You'll be a success with me, honey."

A moment later Abby has again taken stock of the situation and decided that she cannot go through with it. She thought she could, but she can't marry Rod. She has nothing to offer him.

"You must let me be the judge of that," he suggests.

ABBY—I'm not in love with you.

RODERICK—Well, you're fond of me, aren't you?

ABBY—I adore you. You're too good to be true.

RODERICK—I'll take that for a start.

ABBY—No. It's more than that. It's that—I don't want to fall in love again. As far as that sort of thing is concerned, I'm willing to call it a day. You see, Rod—I've been in love once—terribly.

RODERICK—Did you have bad luck?

ABBY—I had the damnedest time. Well, I got over it. It nearly killed me, but I finally did. I thought—when I met you—well, you seemed so nice. I didn't know there were men like you—I thought: well, this is a way out for me. Security. Independence. Nice life. That's what I thought—that's the low-down, Rod. But, hell—you're too nice for that. You can do better than that. I advise you to pass it up.

RODERICK—Do you?

ABBY—Well, you don't have to take my advice if you don't want to.

RODERICK—This love affair—is it over?

ABBY—Over.

RODERICK—Really over? Are you sure?

ABBY—Say, you get to a point you don't feel anything any more.

RODERICK—I don't think you're jaded somehow. I'm glad you told me this. But since you say it's over—suppose you don't mention it again.

ABBY—Okay. I guess you mean that I—

RODERICK—I don't see quite how I could expect you to organize your past as a kind of prelude to my appearance—a kind of prolonged entrance music. It would be immensely flattering but I could scarcely expect it. If we can organize the future—we'll be doing pretty well.

ABBY—You'll take a chance, then? (ROD *embraces her—kisses her.*)

RODERICK—This is the wisest thing I've ever done—closer than I've ever been—

Harold Sigrift, plainly disturbed, returns to announce that this is a hell of a house. "Bootleggers chase you out of one room and butlers out of another." Sigrift is coldly charmed to meet Miss Fane, but it does not improve his temper, even though he is warned that before he says anything insulting Roderick would like him to know that he and Miss Fane are to be married.

Sigrift finds the statement hard to credit. If it is publicity Miss Fane is looking for she will get none of it. And if, as she says, she is willing to bet that he (Sig) and she are going to be great friends she is suffering from delusions of grandeur. Sigrift frankly disapproves of Abby as a fiancée although he admits that he has found her quite exciting in her night club.

"In a night club I appreciate you," he tells her. "I appreciate you as a symbol of our raucous and mechanical age. But when you invade the home—"

"Oh, come now, Sig, a profligate like you defending the home—" protests Roderick.

"And when your racketeering, bootlegging friend—who shouldn't be allowed in the house, except to deliver his wares with the other tradesmen—comes swaggering in the front door, meets us on a plane of equality—takes home our sister—"

"Manny's all right," interrupts Abby.

"By what standards, young lady? Tell me that. By what standards?"

"Oh, nuts to you!" replies Miss Fane. For the moment Sigrift is vanquished. He is muttering something that sounds like "washed in poetry, bathed in glamor," as he disappears.

With some spirit Abby tears up the list of words she had decided not to use in this society. She will have a collection of longer ones when next she meets Mr. Sigrift.

Sig, Rod repeats, is really a kindly person underneath.

"Oh, I think he's swell," agrees Abby, with exaggerated enthusiasm.

"And I think you're wonderful," enthuses Roderick. "Gosh, what fun you'll be! Just be yourself, Abby—that's all I ask."

ABBY—Oh, I'll be much better than that.

RODERICK—Have you any idea how totally unsuited we are to each other?

ABBY—I'm just getting the idea.

RODERICK—We have absolutely nothing in common. It should be an exciting marriage. Think of the thrill of discovery.

ABBY—Don't think I don't know what a great break this is for me. I'll make it up to you. I'll do you justice. You won't be ashamed of me, honey. You know I'm a wonderful mimic. I can imitate anybody. I'll imitate your friends.

RODERICK—Will you?

ABBY—Watch me, honey. In six months—honest, Rod, I promise you—I'll do a better act than they do. What time is it, darling? (*Looks at his wrist watch.*) Got to go.

RODERICK—I thought you were staying for dinner.

ABBY—Mm—Mm! You've had enough of me for one day—besides, I've got a rehearsal.

RODERICK—Cut the rehearsal.

ABBY—No, sir. Can't do that. It's going to be a grand number. Wait till you hear it. You'll be mad about it.

RODERICK—I'll go with you—

ABBY (*stopping him*)—No. I want to go alone. Just this once, honey.

RODERICK—Why?

ABBY—Got a lot to think about—Okay, sweet?

RODERICK—Okay, darling. When will I see you?

ABBY—I'll see what I can do for you, Mr. Deane. May have a spare fifteen minutes late in January. (*She kisses him.*) I'll call you in an hour. Bye, darling.

THE CURTAIN FALLS

ACT II

Eighteen months later, in the same penthouse living-room of the Deane's, Abby Fane Deane, becomingly arrayed in a lovely tea gown, is serving tea to Sergei Voloschin, "a stocky, black-haired, genial" Russian motion picture director.

Abby has always been interested in Russia, and Sergei, whose interest at the moment is Abby herself, would be glad to take her back to his country if she would say the word. True, he is headed for Hollywood, but he would willingly cancel that agreement.

Abby is stirred by the suggestion but discouraged by its impracticability. There are not only the transportation problems, there is also a husband to be considered. A husband Abby is pleased to consider rather important.

"My country has the only civilized divorce laws," Sergei insists, with some force. "There—once a marriage has outlasted its spiritual significance—you have only to ask for a divorce to get it."

Reduced to a discussion of his real passion, Sergei is free to admit that it is men in the mass. "It is an age of mass," he insists. "What is the French Revolution compared to our revolution? The individual no longer counts. He has been relegated to oblivion by modern science and by modern philosophy, also."

As his thought sweeps on Sergei admits that Abby is not for him. "The gulf is too much between us," he concludes. "I am a simple peasant. What am I doing here?"

"What am I?" Abby is also curious.

"You are the exquisite product of a luxurious aristocracy," insists Sergei.

The butler has announced Mr. Cass Worthing. Mr. Worthing is convinced that Abby's tea is a relay race with other entrants to follow him. He is not pleased with what he has seen of Sergei, taking his elaborate leave with hand kissings and protests of affection. He does not understand how even a nut like Roderick Deane can stand for him and his kind.

Mr. Worthing is also hurt because Abby had left him standing alone at the place they had appointed for a rendezvous the day before, and because she now finds that she will be unable to see him this evening. It appears to "Cass" that Abby has "gone lady" on him. She was much more amusing in the old days.

The old days, as Abby recalls, were also much more amusing to Cass than they were to her. His attitude toward her then was quite casual. She has not forgotten that. Nor is she convinced that he has changed greatly, or that he will ever be able to make her think so. Still, Cass is persistent.

"Abby—you know I mean more to you than anybody—husband or no husband," he says.

"Why?"

CASS—Because you know what we were to each other.

ABBY—Hardly remember.

CASS—You're a liar.

ABBY—Another life, Cass dear.

CASS—You're my kind. You're more like me than anybody.

ABBY—Why do so many men say that to me? The only man I ever knew who didn't was Manny. He acknowledges a certain difference—all in his favor. So does Rod, as a matter of fact—all in my favor.

CASS—Saw Manny last night.

ABBY—He will be here tonight.

CASS—Dropped in at the Hotsy Totsy. Old place isn't the same.

ABBY (*mockingly*)—That's nice.

CASS (*furious that his romantic suggestions meet an ironic response*)—What the devil's the matter with you anyway? (*She laughs.*) What the hell are you laughing at?

ABBY—Your line, Cass. It's so transparent. Trying to look wistful over your memories of the Hotsy Totsy. Old Heidelberg. Old Lang Syne. Old stuff. (*He gets up in a rage.*) What a temper you have! It's becoming to you.

CASS—What's your game?

ABBY—My what, Cass?

CASS—Why do you see me? Why do you make dates with me? Why do you break them? If you're no longer interested, say so and I'll clear out.

ABBY—All right, I'm no longer interested.

CASS—You lie like hell.

ABBY—Mr. Worthing!

CASS—Abby—

ABBY—Yes?

CASS—The other day—in the restaurant—when I ran into you for the first time since—when you looked at me—

ABBY—What happened when I looked at you?

CASS—When our hands touched—

ABBY—My dear—I said hello, and we shook hands. What of it?

CASS—I know you so well, Abby.

ABBY—Do you?

CASS—I know—and you know—that it is the same.

ABBY—Oh, much better, I think, Cass. (*Pause.*) I believe— if I remember—I think—I just began to bore you a little bit. But I'll never bore you again, Cass. I promise. You're going to find me much more entertaining.

CASS—The other day when I saw you—I said to myself—

ABBY—That's what I want to know! What did you say to yourself? How did I look to you?

CASS—I said to myself, "Why, she's radiant—she's—

ABBY—Life in the old girl yet, eh? Well, what did you expect— I grieved for a bit, but—life must go on, you know.

CASS—I'll make it up to you, Abby.

ABBY—Will you? Do you think you can?

CASS—Yes, I think I can.

ABBY—I'm afraid, Mr. Worthing, that the old spark's not there any more.

CASS—It isn't, eh?

Cass has taken Abby in his arms and is kissing her with passion when Harold Sigrift comes into the room. His "Good God!"

exclamation is less startling to Cass and Abby than might have been expected. Mr. Worthing rises, wipes his lips with his handkerchief and proceeds toward the door. Abby meets the situation calmly.

"You see, Cass, how utterly absurd it is to attempt rape here," she says. "Completely impractical."

Roderick Deane has followed Sigrift into the room. He passes and greets Cass on his way out. This is what used to be known as a "situation," Sigrift admits, but nothing comes of it now.

Roderick finds himself affectionately greeted by Abby, is soon telling of his afternoon spent, of all places, at the public library, where he has been looking up references to justify his social attitude that the aristocrats were always pioneers in revolution.

"The amazing thing to me," Rod reports, "was that vast room with hundreds of people sitting there, intent, concentrated, this island of silence in the clangor of the city. I got a pile of books in front of me and began to read. But I couldn't follow. I got lost. I realized that I wasn't equipped, even to argue with Sig. I tried another tack—but those immense vistas of reference, those interlocked roads, stretching into infinity, terrified me. I gave it up. But the girl sitting across from me hadn't moved. She looked up at me over the edge of her book, impersonally. None of the people there had moved. They were sitting there intent, concentrated. I imagine they are sitting there still. They'll sit there forever. . . ."

"And none the wiser," concludes Sigrift.

Cass Worthing is a man to envy, Roderick continues, because Cass is thoroughly self-sufficient.

"Occasionally he requires—coöperation," ventures Sigrift, with a slight leer in the direction of Abby.

"Oh, Sig, Sig," explains Abby, meeting the leer with a shake of her head; "if you were a woman what a bitch you would have made. . . . I'll explain to you, Rod, the meaning of that innuendo. It is this: that when Sig came into the room, he saw Worthing kissing me. But he did it without encouragement. It was *not* coöperative."

SIG—It's always better to hear about these things from your wife than from your best friend.

ROD (*he is affected but he can't bear to show it*)—I started to say—I envy Worthing—and I envied him even without knowing that Abby kissed him.

SIG—He kissed Abby.

ABBY (*rises*)—Thank you, Sig.

SIG—Well, well, well! What country started the Great War?

ROD (*annoyed*)—Stop chattering, Sig. I envy him because he isn't troubled by anybody—never thinks about anything, but his own pleasure. The world is a background for his sporting instincts, all his instincts. I don't blame you, Abby—Mercutio!

SIG—A Mercutio with a few minor exceptions. A Mercutio without wit or loyalty or courage. A moron-Mercutio.

ROD—He flies to Havana.

SIG—Courage of a kind. After all, Rod, cowardice is a kind of imagination. Worthing's safe.

ROD—Nevertheless—I envy him. I wish I were like him.

SIG—Do you know, Abby—the chief difference between Rod and me is that he envies all the attributes he hasn't got. I despise all the attributes I haven't got.

ABBY—That's why you're fat and Rod's thin. (*A moment's pause.*) What time is it?

ROD—Six-thirty.

ABBY—It isn't! I've got to be thinking about dressing for dinner.

SIG—Who've you got sitting next to me?

ABBY—Dr. Lehman. She's a psycho-analyst. She's very well known.

SIG—Has it ever occurred to you, Rod, that Abby is a celebrity glutton?

ABBY—Not at all. Dr. Lehman is coming to meet Dr. Vick from Vienna. He's a great man, Dr. Vick.

SIG—Everybody from Vienna is a great man. A considerate hostess would have put me next to a chorus girl.

ABBY—Not if she were considerate of the chorus girl.

With Sigrift gone Abby has called Roderick to the sofa beside her and is driving his blues away with her familiar feminine wave of the hand. Her report of the day's activities brings in Sergei and the tea. Abby, admitting that she is only a mimic at heart, has come to adore her success with her new life. She adores the thought of all the people who are at that particular moment dressing to come to her house to dine. She gets an awful kick out of that.

Parvenue? Of course she's a parvenue. "There is nothing in the world so delicious as being a parvenue," she says. "I'm sorry for you because you can't be one. Why, when I go into the Hotsy Totsy now I feel like a great lady visiting the poor. I'd like to have the Prince of Wales and Lindbergh here to dine—not because I'm hot about those two boys but simply as an indication of the social distance I've traveled."

"You're incredible," declares Roderick. "You know I get some kind of thrill out of it too, when I see you babbling away at dinner—I hear scraps of your conversation sometimes—all sorts of odds and ends of art chatter—even science—I feel like an impresario who's put over a brilliant hoax."

Roderick is also worried. Can this sort of thing last? It is, after all, a little second rate. What is it, he wonders, that Abby does to men like Dr. Vick and the others. The same thing she did to him, Abby laughs. She laughs, too, at the memory of Sergei declaring her to be "the exquisite flower of a complicated aristocracy." That's a good one. Abby makes mental notes of jokes like that to tell them to her sweetheart.

Still, Roderick is not made happy. This sort of thing is merely a by-product of Abby's coquetry. She has, he has noticed, the faculty of making each man she talks to think she is profoundly interested in him. And if Abby enjoys her conquests Roderick wearies with following after them. He gets nothing from her dinner parties. Even if he is "taken out of himself," as she reasons, what is he taken into? Certainly nothing better.

"Why escape from oneself? Why get out of oneself? Why not cultivate oneself instead of a lot of chattering mediocrities?" Roderick demands.

"That's not true," Abby replies, with spirit. "The most distinguished people in town come to my house."

RODERICK—Like hell they do.

ABBY—Dr. Leopold Vick—

RODERICK—I don't know Dr. Leopold Vick. Maybe he's distinguished. I don't know. But if he is, you don't get his distinction. All you get is his parlor talk. I'm not saying one or two first-raters don't occasionally drift in here. Must on the theory of averages. But they're not first-rate while they are here. They're just stuffed shirts. Of all the indoor sports, celebrity-hunting is the tamest and the most fatuous. The biggest this and the most celebrated that. It's vulgar.

ABBY—Why should I be refined? It's nothing but a damn bore.

RODERICK—You pick up every argot, you're mixed up in a hundred sets. Underneath these layers of adaptive coloring—what are you? I thought I married a simple person. My God, I married a Grand Duchess.

ABBY—What made you think I was a simple person? Just because I sang in a Night Club? Why didn't you wait to discover? I'm not any more simple than you are. We're both complicated—in different ways. But if you want me to chuck all this—all right, I will. After this week no one will step in the house—except your friend Sig, of course—we'll dine alone every night, the three of us!

RODERICK—I won't subject you to that extremity of boredom.

ABBY—What do you expect? I admit I am ravenous—do you know what my youth was? Perhaps I'll get tired of this. Just now I get a kick out of it. What of it? I thought it amused you to see me playing a rôle and getting away with it. Well, it seems it doesn't. You've been harboring secret bitterness. All right. I'll cut it out. I'll cut everything out you want me to cut out. Let's go up in the North Woods somewhere and build an igloo and discover each other.

RODERICK—When I said you made every man you talk to feel that you are profoundly interested in him I should have excluded myself.

ABBY (*overcome with contrition*)—Oh, darling—I'm a beast.

RODERICK—Let's not quarrel, Abby. You know it's like war—I couldn't survive victory.

ABBY (*glibly*)—And neither could I.

RODERICK—You agree to readily. You could survive anything.

ABBY—Do you know what the trouble is?

RODERICK—What?

ABBY—The trouble is you don't love me.

RODERICK—Is that the trouble?

ABBY—Yes, it is. You married—not me—you married an ideal. Simple, elemental—God knows what. Not me.

RODERICK—The trouble is, I utterly adore you.

ABBY—And I you. You foolish boy! What are you worrying about? What are you worrying about?

RODERICK—We're so different.

ABBY—You always knew that.

RODERICK—At first the difference stimulated me, now—

ABBY—Now?

RODERICK—I want to bridge it—to be close to you—I can't. I don't know how. I—

ABBY—You don't have to do anything. Don't you think I know what you've done for me? Don't you think I know how precious you are, and sensitive, and dear? Other men are just crude beside you—just crocks. Darling, I love you.

RODERICK—I love you. (*They embrace.*)

ABBY (*pulling away*)—It must be shockingly late. I hate to dress quickly. I like to linger over it.

RODERICK (*holding her hand*)—Let them wait.

ABBY (*pulling away*)—No, that's too obvious. That's just what they'd expect from me. Is it all right? All blown away? (*She makes the familiar gesture.*)

RODERICK—All blown away.

ABBY—You won't be jealous any more?

RODERICK—Jealous!

ABBY—Of course. That's what all this is about. That silly Sigrift. But what I told you, honey, is absolutely true. Worthing kissed *me!* It was his idea—not mine. 'By, darling! (*She turns off, blowing him a kiss. Everything abruptly goes dead on him.*)

RODERICK (*devastated*)—Damn! Damn! Damn!

The curtain falls.

There is dancing below stairs in the penthouse. Sounds of music rise to the living-room. It is around one o'clock in the morning. Cass Worthing, followed by Abby Fane, come from the dance. Cass has been drinking. He is angry, both with himself and with Abby. Angry with himself because he has found, after leaving Abby, that he still cannot get along without her. He has been trying all afternoon to become interested in other things—in a workout at the club, in liquor, in a couple of girls he and Winnie Dashiell called up and were entertaining. Nothing was any good. He must have Abby. He must have her that night, and he is willing to marry her if necessary. Goddamit, let her give up her pose and be herself. Let her fly with him to Florida, as they had often planned to do in the old days.

Abby is indifferent. Wherever did Cass get the impression that she could not live without him? Abby is doing very well as she is. Nor can anything he recalls of the old days when they meant something to each other change her now. Abby hates reminiscence and is not overfond of the past. Let him go sail fishing in Florida by himself. She may see him there, she and Rod. Will she see him tomorrow? He had better call first. Will she see him later tonight? Perhaps. For an hour? For a drive in the park? All right! With Cass it is a date. . . .

Manny Walsh is looking for Abby. He also wants to talk with her—privately. He will wait until Cass goes. Now he must also wait until Kay Deane goes. Kay has followed Manny from the dance floor. She has been following him all evening. Sometimes Kay is almost convinced that Manny is avoiding her. She is beginning to doubt her sex appeal. Which she needn't, as Manny sees it. "I consider like you're in the family," explains Mr. Walsh. "I wouldn't touch anybody in the family."

"It must be awful to live in the underworld," sighs Kay, as she follows Cass to the bar. "One has to observe such a strict code."

It is about Cass that Manny has come to talk with Abby. Manny knows what's going on; knows that Abby is playing around with Cass and doesn't like it. It isn't fair to Rod. It's dangerous. Worthing's been talking about it, too. Talking loud at the bar with Winnie Dashiell. It is Manny's idea that he should take Cass aside and advise him to pick up his friend Dashiell and get out. Abby won't have that. She can handle Worthing herself. . . .

Sigrift and Roderick have come up from the dance floor. Cass Worthing has barged back to demand that Abby shall come and dance with him. Abby has gone, leaving Manny Walsh, Rod and Sig contemplating the situation with varying degrees of irritation. From below the orchestra swells into "I'm All at Sea—Can This Be Love?"

SIG—That music is an invitation to sex—

RODERICK—More than an invitation—practically a command.

MANNY (*annoyed at this lubrication—bluntly*)—It's a popular song.

RODERICK (*they listen for a moment longer*)—Well, Sig, how did you come out with your blonde?

SIG—She's one of those illiterate girls who expect a flowery approach. I didn't feel up to it so I left her with a *Saturday Evening Post* reader whose success is inevitable.

MANNY—My God, you fellows make too much fuss about sex. Don't you ever think about anything else?

SIG—I think about food a good deal. What do you think about, Manny?

MANNY—Well, I'm a busy man. (*He goes out.*)

SIG—Isn't he elfin?

RODERICK—Enjoying our little party?

SIG—Ha! What a clatter at dinner! Opinions. Epigrams. I could hardly digest. I thought to myself: Multiply this clatter a thousand times and what do you get? The intelligentsia. Dear God, *must* Abby cultivate celebrities? Doesn't she know any obscure people?

RODERICK—You're hard on her, Sig—there's a lot to be said for lion-hunting. Why not? It's a kind of education by specialists. After all, it's better than having the house full of snobs and rich men—especially for a girl like Abby.

SIG—Is it?

RODERICK—I think so.

SIG—I overheard the psycho-analyst from Vienna talking to Abby—on the dance floor, mind you—about bed-wetting and thumb-sucking in infants. And Abby seemed interested. A little more of this bits-and-pieces education and she will blossom forth with an outline of something or other. Why not?

RODERICK—I still insist. It's some kind of intellectual interest. Better than backgammon and gossip.

SIG—Not much.

RODERICK—At least—it's understandable. Besides, who's better?

SIG—Nobody.

RODERICK—What house that you know is better?

SIG—My dear boy, all I'm saying is that Abby isn't an anomaly. She's conventional. Out of a night club you might have expected something different.

RODERICK—It's all right for you and me to lie around making generalizations. We've never had anything to worry about but our states of mind. Abby is different. This sort of thing's fun for her. Why not? The extraordinary thing is—

SIG—What?

RODERICK—Abby is so enormously—adaptable. Whatever environment she falls into—she belongs. In a Night Club. Here. It makes no difference. Whereas I feel like an outsider. Why is that?

SIG—Ask Dr. Leopold Vick. He'll tell you—in sixty lessons. A wonderful discovery—psycho-analysis. Makes quite simple people feel they're complex.

RODERICK—Sig, don't you get a sense sometimes, especially lately, of things disintegrating, crumbling—some enormous transition—the final flicker of civilization—apres-nous-le-deluge?

SIG—My boy, le deluge is here. That mob downstairs is le deluge.

RODERICK—Is this the end of us? Are we in at the death? Rather dramatic. Were people aware when Rome fell? That it was about to fall? Did they get a kick out of it?

SIG—No. They just went on wondering what they were having for dinner and who was sleeping with whom—their chief pre-occupations, I imagine, were gustatory and phallic.

RODERICK—Even as you and I!

SIG—Even as Adam and Eve.

RODERICK—I suppose it's immature not to be casual about everything. I must be adolescent, Sig.

SIG—No, you're an eternal type. You search around for an absolute as men used to search for the fountain of youth or a gold-formula.

RODERICK—The absolute— What the devil are we talking about, Sig?

SIG—It doesn't matter. It's very pleasant.

Roderick is seriously worried. Even Sigrift is forced to admit that. It is a worry based on jealousy. Rod is now ready to admit that. He had always known that there had been a man in Abby's life, but so long as he did not know who he was it was different. Now he is tormented with flares of rage, of indignation—

"Would you like to assassinate Worthing?" inquires Sig, calmly.

"Only momentarily," admits Roderick. "How does one sustain a hate? I have moments of lucidity—rather awful, when I'm overcome with a sense of the triviality of this little intrigue— Abby's rather childish conquests—that saturnine Worthing employing his moment of eternity, swinging a mallet—my own jealousy—a brief moment of petulance against the whole background of life—all of us lost in it. My indignation vanishes. My hate simmers down. That's abnormal, isn't it, to feel like that? (*Head in hands.*) What's the matter with me? What shall I do?"

"You can't do anything. You're Hamlet married to a career woman."

"I might have known you'd think the worst of Abby," declares Rod, dejectedly. "You never did like her."

"On the contrary, I'm secretly in love with her," protests Sig. "She's got that—what did that song writer chap call it—oh, yes— that thing. She's one of those women."

Manny and Cass Worthing come from the bar. They are locked arm in arm, with Manny bearing the heavier part of the burden. Worthing has had plenty of liquor, but he is accustomed to handling it in quantities. It is Manny's idea that both Rod and Sigrift should leave while he tells Worthing the things he has brought him there to tell him. Cass will not have it that way.

Let Manny say what he has to say in front of everybody.

A moment later, when Abby joins the group, Worthing repeats his challenge. He does not care to be under cover any longer. He wants Rod to know that he (Cass) and Abby were lovers once and are lovers now—

The blow that Manny aims at Worthing lands quickly and solidly. Cass goes down and lies for a second where he strikes.

"Is he dead?" cheerfully calls Sigrift.

"No such luck," Manny is forced to admit. "But that kisser of his won't be so handsome in the morning."

Cass has struggled to his feet. He is subdued but defiant. He sees no reason why he should explain to Rod that what he said about Abby was a lie, because, anyway, she has promised to meet him later.

Abby has a different idea. So far as she is concerned this is good-by for Cass. He can wait for her at his place, as he threatens, but she will not be there. . . .

Cass and Sigrift have both gone. Abby has stretched herself out on the sofa. Suddenly she feels all in. . . . Abby is sorry Rod couldn't get to the party. He would have had so much more fun drinking, dancing and flirting downstairs than he had upstairs talking with Sig.

One thing has happened to Abby this night. She has had an illusion shattered. "Would you believe it, Rod," she says, "that I used to think Cass Worthing mysterious? Honest, I did. I used to look at him—I used to study that face—that handsome, impenetrable, regulation face, I used to say to myself: My God, what's going on? What's he thinking? Have I displeased him? Is he angry? He gave me the run-around and I stood for it. When I think what I stood for. Well, now the tables are turned. I'm giving him the run-around. God, it's wonderful!"

"Why don't you keep your engagement?"

"No, thanks. I told you—I never meant to."

"Your operations are too involved for me."

"He used to make engagements with me—and break them. That was a favorite trick of his. He would call me and ask to take me to dinner. Well, I'd wait till six, seven, eight, nine, ten—till it was time to go to the Club. Didn't dare to go out to eat for fear I'd miss him. One night I fainted. Simple starvation. First love. That beautiful first love."

"This is nothing then but an exercise in revenge?"

"Nothing else but! If I were going to deceive you it wouldn't be with Cass Worthing."

Rod is not convinced. Cass Worthing is quite evidently still in love with Abby, and if she were not still in love with him she would not have bothered so about him. With all her technical conversations with Dr. Vick, doesn't she suspect the true motive of this elaborate revenge?

The suggestion angers Abby. She would warn Rod that it would be unwise to put ideas into her head. She has felt ever since she met Cass Worthing casually at the Ritz, after not having seen him for a long time, that she has been in complete command of herself—

"No matter what you say, it was revenge and it was sweeter than sweet," she says. "I've been putting him through it. Not what he made me go through, because he hasn't the capacity for feeling that I have and he isn't in love—just wants me—although, you know, just now, when he went out—I felt he was rather touched—I felt rather sorry for him."

RODERICK—Oh, I'm pretty sure that your hatred is tempered by sympathy.

ABBY—Say, what are you trying to do, anyway? You're making something out of nothing—

RODERICK—I think it would be honest to establish your integrity in one respect, at least—and keep your engagement.

ABBY—God, how jealous you are!

RODERICK—You have the happy faculty of bringing out the worst in me—this pretense of insincerity with Worthing is the most profound confession. You think it exonerates you?

ABBY—Am I on trial?

RODERICK—It's part of everything else—this fake household, this imitation culture—this second-rate intrigue. This story doesn't convince me, even if it does convince you. Is it necessary to flirt with a fellow like Cass Worthing? Do you have to play an elaborate game with him too? Of course, that's absurd. (*Turns away.*) If what I had to offer you was enough, you wouldn't have the time for this kind of childish intrigue. Evidently it isn't. Well, I'm sorry. It didn't work out. Well, that's that.

ABBY—Rod, I swear to you I was just playing a game with Cass—perhaps I shouldn't. I'm terribly sorry.

RODERICK—I appreciate your trying to spare my feelings. Well, you needn't spare them. Perhaps I'm less sensitive than you think.

ABBY (*really touched*)—Rod, I'm terribly sorry—I can't say

any more.

RODERICK—No, it's vulgar and stupid, the whole thing—I'm fed up with it—thoroughly. I'm not interested.

ABBY—Are you dismissing me?

RODERICK—I'm making it possible for you to express yourself. There's no hope for us. I see now, clearly, there never was.

ABBY (*suddenly cold with deadly calm*)—All right! What do you want me to do?

RODERICK—I want you not to spare my feelings! (*Cold too.*) I want you to keep your engagement with Worthing.

ABBY (*seeing through him*)—What a capacity you have for torturing yourself.

RODERICK—You told me once you were a mimic at heart. You seem to be able to imitate anything but honesty.

ABBY—Oh, don't be so damn superior. Honesty! Honesty! What does it all mean?

RODERICK—I'm not surprised that you ask.

ABBY—It's easy for you to be honest—you don't want anything, and what you want you have.

RODERICK—There is very little that I want, that I have.

ABBY—That's a pose.

RODERICK—Very well. It's a pose.

ABBY—My God, I'm not a plaster saint. I'm a human being. When I married you I didn't promise to sit in the corner and twiddle my thumbs.

RODERICK—If we're not careful this will degenerate into a vulgar quarrel.

ABBY—Well, God damn it, I'll be vulgar if I feel like it. I tell you, the trouble with you—if you had any guts—Manny was right—if you had any guts—if you gave a damn about me—when Cass said what he did you'd have laid him out—

RODERICK—Well, you see, I'm cold. I'm heartless. I'm not an emotional type like Manny—or yourself—I don't lay people out. I don't think it solves any problems.

ABBY—Oh, I'm sick of hearing about your problems. You've never been up against a real problem in your life. You're just a self-centered weakling, lying around and dribbling while other people work and struggle and suffer. What the hell are you, anyway? What the hell do you stand for? Anybody can go around picking out flaws in things if they've got nothing else to worry about! Why, it's like living with a hypochondriac telling you about his ailments all the time! The truth is—you're damn ineffectual and you take it out on me because I'm not.

RODERICK—Well, Cass Worthing meets your requirements, doesn't he? Why don't you go to him?

ABBY—If you say that again I will go to him.

RODERICK—Why don't you? He's waiting.

ABBY—Do you mean that?

RODERICK—Yes! At best your fidelity is only technical.

ABBY—You'll let me?

RODERICK—I urge you.

ABBY—Very well. I *will!* Why not? And that will be that! (*She goes out, slamming the door behind her.*)

RODERICK (*after a moment—to himself*)—Costly—gesture!

THE CURTAIN FALLS

ACT III

Three weeks later Rod and Sigrift are back from a dinner. Sigrift has bought most of the early editions of the tabloids and is interested to discover that Abby and Rod are no longer "front page stuff."

They both miss Abby, though only Sigrift is in a mood to admit it. At least Abby's dinner parties were never stuffy, Sig admits. And Rod remembers how she could whistle and wave away the vapors when he was heavy spirited.

Rod thinks perhaps he may go to Russia. Or somewhere. If he is to save himself he will have to be about it. Then Manny Walsh calls.

Manny has come to discover exactly how matters stand with Rod and Abby. Things can't go on the way they have been going, with the papers full of stuff and Abby running around like a headless chicken. That rumor about Abby and Worthing, too—that's all wrong. What's Rod going to do?

Rod thinks probably he and Abby will have to be divorced. As for starting an action, or getting a lawyer, he will do anything Abby suggests. Manny has an idea that if Rod is certain about getting a divorce that there may still be some chance for him with Abby. He plans to take the matter up with her again, and he plans also to lead so different a life that he thinks he will be able to interest her. Business has become so organized for Manny now that he will be able to devote a lot more time to reading and developing himself in other ways. He already has invested in the five-foot shelf and a couple of thousand dollars' worth of other volumes. . . .

Rod has gone to the door with Manny when Abby comes into the living-room. Abby still has her key. Her room, she has noticed on the way up, is just as she left it.

"Hear you're getting married again," Sig offers, conversationally.

"You know all the gossip, don't you, Sig," Abby counters.

"This time I congratulate you. Worthing is perfect for you. . . . You'll be able to deceive him with impunity."

"From that point of view the perfect person would be you," answers Abby.

It is nice to be in that house again, Abby admits. She is finding her hotel suite, with its genteel, green-tinted walls, its discreet decorators' furnishings, rather trying.

"Can you imagine?" she confesses. "When I came to New York first I'd have thought that suite I was in now was Heaven. . . . What the devil I acquired taste for, I don't know. No earthly good to me . . ."

Abby is sitting stretched out comfortably in one of the larger chairs when Rod comes back. Their greeting is casual and a little strained. Sigrift would fill in the awkward waits with light conversation.

"Tell us your early experiences," Sig suggests, affectedly, to Abby. "You must have had an interesting life."

ABBY—Oh, yes! I ran the gamut from rags to riches—I had my moment of glory—and now— I'm a Sunday Supplement Heroine. As a matter of fact one of the papers is actually pestering me to write my biography.

SIG (*pleading*)—Put me in it, Abby. . . .

ABBY—Then it would be suppressed.

ROD (*after a moment*)—It just occurred to me—it's the last time probably we'll ever be in this room together—the three of us. . . .

ABBY—What do you mean?

ROD—I'm giving up this apartment.

ABBY (*really shocked*)—Really!

ROD—Yes. Part of the ballast.

SIG—Rod'll end in some monastery in Tibet wearing a hairshirt and moodily contemplating his navel. (*Pause.*) Well, I think I'll blow. (*He lumbers up.* ABBY *rises.* ROD *rises.*) Now Abby, no matter whom you marry, I hope you'll ask me to dine occasionally. It'll be good for you to have a simple, obscure non-publicized person like myself once in a while for contrast.

ABBY—What a baby you are!

SIG—You can't be a dream-princess to everybody.

ROD—Lunch tomorrow?

SIG—O.K. (*With* MANNY's *voice and gesture.*)

ABBY—Sig, if Rod goes to Tibet, will you call me up sometimes?

SIG—What! That old mad game over again? I couldn't stand it! (*He goes out.*)

ABBY (*crossing to her old place on the sofa*)—Glad to see me?

ROD—Of course.

ABBY—Have you really given up this apartment?

ROD—Yes.

ABBY—Rod—come here and sit beside me. (*He does.*) What've you been doing?

ROD—Thinking.

ABBY—Anything else?

ROD—I've been getting over being sensitive. What with surtax and one thing and another, I can't afford luxuries like that.

ABBY—If I'd been sensitive, I'd been dead long ago.

ROD—What are you doing here now?

ABBY—Well, I was going to supper with Cass and I suddenly decided, I think, that I've done a mad thing, Rod.

ROD—What?

ABBY—I promised to marry Cass Worthing.

ROD—Good idea.

ABBY—Oh, you think so, do you?

ROD—Yes, I think so.

ABBY—Well, I'm glad we have your blessing.

ROD—I should think Cass'd be quite perfect for you.

ABBY—Because he'll set me up in the style to which I've been accustomed. Rod—you've ruined me. You know that—you've ruined me. You and Sig both—you've been bad for me.

ROD—How?

ABBY—I don't know. You've made me dissatisfied and unsure. You've made me suspect myself. (*A moment—she goes on.*) Things don't seem to be any more—quite good enough. Before you, that never occurred to me. Bad! The night clubs, the town, the people I meet—second ratish—something brushed off them—all of them. Is it age? Is it disillusion? What is it? It upsets me—I used to think I was pretty good—you know that, I guess—I used to think everything was pretty grand. I was healthy—had an aptitude for conquest. Not now—not any more. Bad! Your fault, Rod. You shouldn't have done it. You should have let me be. Sore at you!

Rod—My dear Abby, I refuse to feel contrition. If you've come out of this worse than I have—well, that's the chance you took.

Rod sees no reason why Abby should have been assured against disaster, and her feeling sorry for herself is absurd. If he has grown hard it is probably because he is achieving maturity. Abby liked him better, she discovers, as an adolescent, but that Rod also denies. "You married me for your own purposes, without loving me," he says bitterly, "and then you walked all over me."

Abby makes no answer to this charge. She lets Rod light a cigarette for her and frankly admits a feeling of comfort. She is, as Rod has said, just a cat. She can curl up anywhere and go to sleep. But she cannot quite get over the fact that she is meeting a new Rod, a changed Rod.

Abby is interested in Rod's plan to go to Russia. Perhaps he will take her with him. She wouldn't mind if he's not traveling de luxe. Besides, he's going to be fearfully disappointed in those Russian peasant women. . . .

Abby—Can't you say something nice to me? You know you could win me over if you used the right method. All I want is wooing—just a little skillful wooing and I'm yours.

Roderick—You know you're incorrigible.

Abby—You know—you'll never have the fun with anybody you had with me.

Roderick—Some truth in that.

Abby—Well, then. . . .

Roderick—I had to pay too heavily for the fun I had with you . . . Do you know why our marriage was a failure? Because it was based on a false assumption that one can derive from someone else a strength that one hasn't oneself. It can't be done. In our marriage I became an adjunct to you, because you had the vitality to go after what you wanted and I didn't.

Abby—What do you want?

Roderick—I want—

Abby—What?

Roderick—If you must know, I'm sick of my life, heartily sick of it. It isn't my life at all, it's a carbon copy of hundred of other parasitic lives around me. I want to discover my place in the world.

ABBY—Well, how are you going to do it?

RODERICK—As a necessary first step—a stimulus to future endeavor, I've given up all my money—

ABBY—You've done what?

RODERICK—I've left myself barely enough to live on. Not too comfortably at that.

ABBY—Who did you give the money to?

RODERICK—That was amusing. Having decided to give away this fortune, I found that I wasn't equipped even to be generous. It appears that the distribution of money is a profession in itself. I finally had to give it to a group of specialists who will decide what to do with it.

ABBY—A group of specialists. Rod! Rod! If you had been as poor as I have been, if you knew how hard money is to get—as I do—

RODERICK—I never earned a penny of it. I never had any fun out of it.

ABBY—Well, your father will leave you a lot so I guess that will be all right.

RODERICK—I'll cross that bridge when I come to it. People will say I'm eccentric.

ABBY—Coo-coo.

RODERICK—As you so charmingly call it, coo-coo. What of it? What does it matter compared to the fact that tomorrow I walk out of here for the first time in my life—free—

ABBY—Free?

RODERICK—Yes. Miraculously free, Abby. I can't tell you—

ABBY—Free of me, I suppose.

RODERICK—Of all sorts of encumbrances.

ABBY—Thank you.

RODERICK—Sorry, Abby, but that's what I'm going to do. And I'm going to do it alone.

Rod's tone has a note of finality in it that leaves Abby completely devastated. Nor does Rod try to soften the blow. It has taken him a month to come to the decision. With a sigh Abby agrees that she will probably be able to accept the situation. For the first time she believes in the reality of their separation.

Cass Worthing is announced. Rod insists on leaving Abby and her friend alone. Cass is puzzled. He has found a note Abby left for him, but he still does not understand. To Cass everything was settled and Abby was satisfied. What is wrong with her now? Hasn't she any code at all?

Cass would save himself a lot of trouble if he would just drop
her, Abby insists. She is more trouble than she is worth. He is
only interested in her now because he has discovered that someone else wants her. She used to think he was God. Then she discovered the truth. It is too late now for him to make it up to
her, even though he is willing to marry her and do all those things
for her she once had craved, give her all those things she has
missed all her life. She wants something Cass cannot give her.

Abby is in love. In love with Rod. She knows that now.
Knows that she was in love with him even when she was telling
Cass that she would marry him.

"You can't fake being in love, Cass," she tells him. "I married Rod without loving him—you were still in the back of my
mind—and it didn't work—it wasn't good enough. I can't go
on making the same mistake—over and over—"

"Listen, Abby—once you and I are married everything will be
all right," Cass pleads. "We have a tremendous lot in common.
Only here there's no chance for us. I must get you away. I can
make you happy."

"You can't. You mean nothing to me, do you understand that?
Not one single thing in the world. You never will."

Cass, reluctantly, has left Abby. After all, it would be rotten
bad taste for him to spoil a party. And there are other women.
Thank God, there is always the good old address book. . . .

Rod has come, in response to Abby's call. He is surprised to
learn that she has given Cass his dismissal, but he still believes she
will be calling him next day.

No, Abby insists, there will be no more of that. "The minute
I know a man is all mine," Abby explains, "without reservation,
no unexplored region in his mind—all sincerity and nothing more
beyond—I know it's an awful thing to admit—but I lose interest. . . . Well, I've got rid of Cass—you've got rid of me—now
what?"

"Doubtless you'll manipulate your freedom."

ABBY—Freedom? That's what it is for you—for me it's just
being adrift. Well, that's no novelty for me. I've been adrift
before. No novelty to be poor either. Why, of all the men in
the world, did I have to marry you? Will you please tell me?
What have you done to me, Mr. Deane? Perhaps our mistake
lay in marrying. If I'd been your mistress—instead of your wife
—if my position had been—unofficial—I'd have been kept in my
own routine—the things I was used to and knew and could man

age. Perhaps that's the solution for me, Rod, to divorce you and become your mistress.

RODERICK—Don't be flippant.

ABBY—I'm not. You're not going entirely monkish—as Sig suggests. You'll want somebody, I suppose. Might as well be me. You're used to me, after all—a little bit—

RODERICK—This humility of yours is a bit excessive—I suspect it. I can't see you, somehow, in the rôle of Ruth following meekly the man of your dreams.

ABBY—I might—for a while—

RODERICK—I thought so.

ABBY—Well, do you expect eternal adoration—eternal obedience? How can I promise that? All I can tell you is that at this moment I'd rather go to Russia with you than to Florida with Cass. I may change again, damn it all; look how you've changed.

RODERICK—Thanks to you. Don't think I'm not grateful. I am. Profoundly grateful. The night we parted, you said certain things to me—

ABBY—Oh, Rod, I was angry—

RODERICK—Nevertheless, they were home truths. Weakling—hypochondriac—ineffectual—they rang in my ears. I'll never forget what you said to me that night.

ABBY—I'll never forget the thing you did to me that night. You were no longer interested—you dismissed me. You sent me to Cass.

RODERICK—And you went, didn't you?

ABBY—So that's it.

RODERICK—Yes, that's it.

ABBY—Yes. I went to him. I was so furious. I said to myself he wants me—he can take me. When I got there I could not go through with it. I didn't. Then— I waited for you to call me. A day—two—I knew by the way I had hurt you that you loved me. I pictured you struggling not to call me. You didn't and I waited a week—two weeks—you didn't call me. Then I said to myself, "This isn't control, this is anemia."

RODERICK—Did you! (*Grasps her by the arms.*) Did you! Did you!

ABBY—Well, maybe I was wrong!

RODERICK (*with his arms about her*)—You were, damn it—I wish you weren't. You—you—and to think that only five minutes ago I was boasting that I'd got rid of you.

ABBY—No such luck. What are you resenting? The fact that you belong to the human race?

RODERICK—No, the fact that you do.

ABBY—I may be an evil but I'm necessary.

RODERICK—I wish to God I could find an antidote for you.

ABBY—All right, I'll reform. No more tricks. I'll lead the simple life.

RODERICK—Abby, dare I believe you? Oh, Abby, can I ever make an honest woman out of you?

ABBY—No, dear—nobody could ever make an honest woman out of me.

RODERICK—That's true.

ABBY—Aren't you glad?

RODERICK—Don't get coy on me.

ABBY—I'm not. I'm in love with you.

RODERICK—That's a loose expression. It permits you too much latitude. I derive no comfort from it.

ABBY—You will, honey.

RODERICK—You trollop!

ABBY—You missionary!

RODERICK—I'll convert you if it's the last thing I ever do.

ABBY—All right. Convert me. It's so late, Rod, I think I'll spend the night here. Isn't it awful to think—that it's perfectly legal?

RODERICK—I don't know. There is, about you, the eternal glamor of the illicit.

ABBY—Where did you learn to say things like that? In the morning I'll get hold of the group of specialists and get your money back to you.

RODERICK—Now look here, young lady—

ABBY—No, for your own good, darling. I want you to have a career—with the money and me there's no reason you couldn't do anything you like—be an ambassador or something—anything.

RODERICK—I don't want to be an ambassador. We're going to be poor and out of the limelight—and you're going to like it!

ABBY—Oh, Rod, now be reasonable. If you insist on being an idealist you might as well be a successful one.

RODERICK (*hand on her throat*)—Some day, sweetheart, I'll probably murder you.

ABBY—O.K., Chief. (*He takes her in his arms—kissing her passionately.*)

THE CURTAIN FALLS

ANOTHER LANGUAGE

A Play in Three Acts

By Rose Franken

IT was late April before Mrs. Franken's play arrived. On the twenty-fifth of that month it was put forward more or less tentatively at the Booth Theatre by Arthur J. Beckhard, who had previously given it production during a suburban stock company season.

The players engaged, realizing that Mr. Beckhard was taking a showman's chance without even an anemic bankroll to sustain him, agreed to accept a minimum playing wage in case the play's receipts were no more than enough to cover its basic costs of production. Mr. Beckhard, on his part, also agreed to pay them their regular salaries in the event the play did prove a success.

The first night reception of "Another Language" was of that friendly type that might easily have been the subject of suspicion if it had been less persistently sustained. It is not difficult for an astute producer to see to it that his first audience is dominated by friends of the author and the management. But in this instance the apparent joy of those present and their repeated endorsement of the individual players, were greatly in the play's favor. "Another Language" played successfully through the spring and summer.

This late-season success can, I believe, be taken as further proof that honest achievement in the theatre, either in the matter of writing or playing, can be depended upon to inspire an equally honest reaction upon the part of the theatre's patrons.

"Another Language" is a simple domestic comedy declaring neither novelty in plot or character nor exceptional brilliance in composition. But there is no part of it nor any character in it either essentially cheap or obviously false. The play was a success because it is soundly builded on a foundation of human plausibility.

It is a Tuesday evening in October at the Hallams', as "Another Language" opens. Tuesday evenings at the Hallams' have become

267

a sort of accepted obligation on the part of all the Hallam sons and their wives. Mother Hallam rather insists upon them. Through her Tuesday evenings she retains some little part of her former hold on her boys and keeps track of the way in which their wives are taking care of them.

The scene is "the basement dining-room of a high-stoop private house on one of the side-streets of Manhattan. The furnishings bespeak the middle-class opulence of a period thirty years past— a heavily carved dining-set, a Morris chair, and a leather couch of the kind that slants upward for the head and has no sides."

Mrs. Hallam is at the buffet, arranging glassware and silverware for the cold supper she is to serve. "She is under seventy, but she walks with the slow uncertain step of age, as if she wears, with a kind of pride, the becoming mantle of her years. Outwardly, she presents the picture of a sweet and appealing old lady, but one gradually becomes aware of the incessant functioning of an alert mind, a quick discernment, and an indomitable will."

Mr. Hallam, doing his part to help with the preparations, is bringing down an extra chair from the parlor because he has heard that Stella is coming. Stella is Victor Hallam's wife and from Mrs. Hallam's reaction to the extra chair it is evident that she does not place much confidence in Stella. Stella is the kind that winds husbands round her little finger, and she has been absent from many more Tuesday nights than she has attended. She may have brains, Mrs. Hallam concedes, but brainy women do not always make the best wives.

The Hallams begin to troop in. Harry and Helen are the first to arrive. "He is a rather heavy-set man in the early forties, pleasant-faced, dependable and dull. Helen has gone to fat only in one place, around the hips, and looks a little like a horse. She is a small-town American against her husband's rather Teutonic solidity, and is capable of getting pleasantly excited over nothing at all."

Harry has had a hard day. Mother Hallam can see that, even if Helen has overlooked it. Helen, however, has brought a cake she made from a *Ladies' Home Journal* recipe and is pleasantly conscious of having done her duty. Helen and Harry are a bit pecky. Helen thinks Mother Hallam is foolish to stay on in so big a house when she could live much more simply in an apartment and Harry would have Helen know that his mother would not be happy in an apartment. It is apparently an old and worn argument.

Photo by White Studio, New York.

"ANOTHER LANGUAGE"

Mr. Hallam gallantly urges Mother Hallam to tread a few measures. Mother is soon out of breath . . .

*(Dorothy Stickney, Hal K. Dawson, Margaret Wycherley, Wyrley
Birch, William Pike, Irene Cattell and Margaret Hamilton)*

"Everybody coming tonight, Grandma?" asks Helen, finally ignoring her husband.

"My sons never forget Tuesday nights," proudly answers Mrs. Hallam.

HELEN—Listen. What's the matter with your sons' wives?

MRS. HALLAM—I always say my sons' wives are very good to me also. (*Sighs faintly.*) All except Stella—we are not high-toned enough for Stella.

HELEN (*with a trace of envy*)—She certainly gets away with murder the way she hardly ever shows up.

HARRY—I blame Vick.

MRS. HALLAM—Victor tries, poor boy, but what can he do? . . . Well, he said she would be here with him tonight.

HELEN—I'll believe it when I see her.

MRS. HALLAM—She will probably be too tired to come or something—

HELEN—Tired! From what, I'd like to know?

MRS. HALLAM (*too sweetly*)—Art school, perhaps.

HARRY (*an easy ally*)—She certainly does do crazy things.

HELEN—Wasn't it last year she wanted to take a job or something?

MRS. HALLAM (*exercised*)—Yes, and it was all I could do to make Victor put his foot down. "Victor," I told him, "your wife does not have to support you; it is more important for her to make you a good home and bear you children."

HARRY—You said it—

HELEN—That's dumb. If she can't have any, just staying home isn't going to do the trick.

MRS. HALLAM—I feel very sorry for Victor, that is all I can say.

HARRY—Well, he's a grown man; you mustn't worry about him.

MRS. HALLAM (*with spirit*)—He is my youngest, and I am entitled to worry. (*As she speaks,* WALTER *suddenly appears tiptoe at the hall door, a dapper and slightly younger edition of* HARRY. *A puffiness beneath the eyes, and a deeply engraved line from nose to chin marks him definitely as a Hallam. In the family, he is considered a great cut-up. Now the fun simply beams out of his eyes as he makes his way cautiously behind his mother and covers her eyes with his hands. She emits a delighted little scream.*) It is Walter!—Always up to something, such a boy! (*They kiss.*)

HELEN—Hello, Wallie! Where's your wife?

WALTER—Me wiff? (*Looks under the table.*)

GRACE (*from the hall*)—When your wife drops something, you might at least help her find it!

WALTER—Bring it here, sweetness, and I'll pick it up for you!

Grace "is forty, fat, good-natured and literal. She is given to long silences from which she wakes abruptly at the hint of food, gossip or entertainment." At the moment she is concerned with two things: Helen owes her fifty-three cents and her last year's coat has to last her through the winter, unless there is a good sale before Christmas. Otherwise there is nothing new in her life.

Family gossip runs on. Paul Hallam has put his son, Jerry, into his office against the wishes of both Jerry and Etta, his mother. Jerry wanted to study architecture, and Etta was willing. But Paul and Grandma Hallam were against it. Anyway, three years of college is enough for anyone, thinks Uncle Walter. It's more than any of the other Hallam boys had, except Vickie. And they're not so bad.

Grace's maid is going to be fired. The nervy thing, she ate three eggs for breakfast. And Etta, Paul's wife, has got a new pin that someone says cost eight hundred. Which, seeing Paul's business is good again, she'd be a fool if she didn't take.

Now Paul and Etta have let themselves in through the open grill gate and filled the scene with their greetings. "Paul is the oldest Hallam; a little grayer around the temples and more sure of himself in a tense, reserved fashion. Etta is a well-preserved woman of about forty-three, punctiliously dressed in black satin, and round pearl earrings. She wears her husband's success with an air."

Mrs. Hallam, "with her genius for making each of her sons feel himself the favorite," has been waiting to shower an affectionate greeting on Paul, but she is slightly peeved because Etta is late.

Etta is tired. She's had the bridge club and she would have liked a good long night's sleep. Grace isn't very happy, either. Tuesday nights seem a week long to Grace. But there is a promise of some little breaking of the routine this week! Stella may come! There's a report that Vickie is bringing her. Stella coming! Think of that! Helen hasn't seen Stella since she went to the hospital with her miscarriage. Etta didn't even go to the hospital. Neither did Grace, but she sent a basket of fruit, with grapefruit in the bottom to fill it up quickly.

"I'm glad I didn't bother," confesses Etta. "She doesn't kill herself for any of us."

"Yes, and I hand it to her," declares Helen, unexpectedly. The other women are quite surprised at Helen, and it probably is a good thing the men are all over in the corner playing pinochle with Pop. "She made up her mind from the start not to have the family on her neck every second, and she's stuck to it," continues Helen.

GRACE (*bitterly*)—Only you forget Vickie hasn't got the family feeling the others have—

ETTA (*with equal bitterness*)—Ummm—

HELEN (*deliberately*)—I'm not so sure about that. Vickie may be different in a lot of things, but when it comes right down to it he's a Hallam first and last.

ETTA (*going out to hall with her coat*)—Then how does Stella get away with it I'd like to know?

GRACE (*with a wealth of ironical resentment*)—He's crazy about her, that's why.

ETTA—I don't know what holds him. She's not even pretty.

HELEN—Her hair's cute, but that's not enough.

GRACE—I asked Walter once if he thought she had sex.

HELEN—Aren't you terrible?

ETTA (*as she comes back into the room*)—What did he say, Grace? (*Sits at table.*)

GRACE (*complacently*)—He said not for him she didn't. (MRS. HALLAM, PAUL *and* WALTER *enter from hall.* HARRY *and* MR. HALLAM *are still engaged in their game.* WALTER *goes to Morris chair and* PAUL *approaches card table.*)

MRS. HALLAM (*joining her daughters-in-law*)—Paul was telling me that Jerry is catching on very nicely to the business.

ETTA—He's not happy down there, no matter what Paul says.

GRACE (*mischief-making*)—You were willing to let him go abroad to study, weren't you, Etta?

ETTA—I wanted him to—but I'm only his mother.

MRS. HALLAM—I do not want to take my son's part, but Paul was perfectly right. A young boy shouldn't be away from home.

GRACE—He could get in trouble with women and everything, Etta. You know how Paris is.

ETTA—Oh, don't be silly—

HELEN—Etta would like to brag she has a son in Europe studying architecture.

ETTA—Is that so? Well, wait till your children grow up and see how you like all this family interference.

PAUL (*from card table*)—That's enough, Etta, please.

MRS. HALLAM—Children, children— (*A whistle sounds in the*

areaway. MRS. HALLAM *rises quickly.*) Victor! That's Victor! Come in! Come in! (*Voices sound in the hall.*)

HELEN (*straining*)—Listen—I think she's with him!

ETTA—Sounds like her—

GRACE—Well for goodness' sake!

WALTER (*overhearing from the Morris chair*)—Oh, go on, you females are jealous because Stella's ten years younger than you and has a shape.

Victor and Stella Hallam are carrying a long florist's box between them, and laughing at the time they have negotiating the areaway with it, when they arrive. "Stella is about thirty. Because she is very slender she looks even younger. She is pretty in a fragile spiritual way. Her manner becomes a little shy, even timid, as if the crowded, smoke-filled room suddenly takes her breath away. Victor is a Hallam, a young Hallam, but unmistakably of the family in the distinguishing line from nose to mouth. He is not so heavy as his brothers, and has only just begun to lose his shock of thick wavy hair. He is about thirty-five."

The family greetings are hearty, and so lightly strained that only the family is really conscious of it. Stella is glad to be with them all and they are all greatly surprised that she could and did come. Only Father Hallam was sure.

The flowers that Vickie and Stella have brought are six huge chrysanthemums, with stems so long that no one knows what to do with them. Mrs. Hallam is delighted with them, of course, but she questions whether Stella should let her husband spend his money that way. There just isn't a vase in the house that will hold them, and Stella protests earnestly Grace's suggestion that they be cut.

"I told you it was silly to get chrysanthemums like that, Stella," protests Vickie; "next time, listen."

"Oh, Vickie, you liar, you know you had as good a time as I did buying them—and they're so beautiful—"

"So's an oak tree but what are you going to do with it?"

Stella thinks she can put the flowers in the umbrella stand. And she can, agrees Mrs. Hallam, only people do not use umbrella stands for flowers. Stella thinks she will try it, anyway, and lugs in the stand. In it the flowers make a brave display, and Mrs. Hallam agrees it would be quite nice if it weren't meant for umbrellas.

There is some talk that Jerry Hallam may drop in during the evening. It is time that Tuesday nights should begin to mean

something to Jerry, Mrs. Hallam thinks. He's old enough now—
But Jerry wants to be with young people, protests Father Hallam, and the aunts and uncles are divided on the question of Jerry's rights in the matter. After all, he is a Hallam—

Stella can't remember when she has seen Jerry last. At her wedding? It doesn't seem possible. And since then he has become a grown-up man, all of a sudden, to Etta. It's hard for even her, his mother, to believe. And Jerry, she adds, is very mature for twenty-one.

There is some question, it appears, as to whether or not Jerry looks a good deal as his uncle looked when he, Vickie, was younger and before he began to put on flesh. Eleven pounds in one year is what Vickie put on, Stella teasingly reports. Mother Hallam thinks that quite wonderful of Vickie. People should eat plenty and never mind their looks, that's Mrs. Hallam's advice.

"That's right," agrees Vickie. "You tell that to Stella. She's positively starving me."

"Oh, Vickie! Mother actually believes it!" protests Stella, going to him.

"No, she's pretty good to me, my wife is," admits Vickie, putting his arm affectionately around Stella.

"And I guess you are pretty good to her," ventures Mother Hallam. "All my boys are good husbands."

Now it has been decided that it is time to eat and everybody insists on taking a hand in setting the table and bringing in the food.

At table the subject of Vickie and Stella's moving to the West Side is brought up. There is a report, Helen admits, that they are sick of "artists and cockroaches," and Etta is decidedly of the opinion that the East River does not compare with the Hudson. Vickie is not inclined to discuss the matter, but admits that he will be ready any time Stella says the word. Which interests Paul. Vickie pays the rent, doesn't he?

Stella has been moving about and is still not sitting down with the others. It is noticed that she hasn't even taken off her hat. Such a pretty hat, too. She can take it off now. They've all seen it, Helen suggests. They would try it on, those who can get it on, and they are all simply stunned when they discover that Stella had made it herself.

It is nice that Stella has the time to sew for herself, Mrs. Hallam agrees. She hasn't the worries Grace has with her three growing children. And if she wants children, as she says she does, she should not run around so much.

"Yes," puts in the comical Walter, "stay home a day, Stella, and see what the stork brings you."

STELLA—But, Mother, I don't run around, I never make a date. I don't go out of the house hardly.

MRS. HALLAM—Yah, yah, but you have so much always on your mind—that's what wears you out.

STELLA—I have so much on my mind . . . ? (*The women are arrested, sensing a small crisis.*)

MRS. HALLAM—Victor says you go to an art school, now.

STELLA—Oh—that! That's only twice a week for an hour.

MRS. HALLAM—It's twice a week too much when you are run down.

STELLA—Oh, but, Mother, that doesn't hurt me, it does me good. I love it.

HARRY—What do you do there, anyway?

HELEN—What do you think she does, scrub floors?

STELLA—I'm taking a course in sculpturing.

WALTER—What do you sculp?—Nudes?

STELLA—Heads only—

ETTA—What do you do with them when they're finished?

STELLA (*nonplused*)—Why—nothing! (*Laughs.*)

MRS. HALLAM—You see—there is no sense to it.

STELLA—Maybe you're right—but—I think I'd go crazy if I didn't do *something*—

MRS. HALLAM—But you have something to do. Make a good home for your husband and have children.

VICKIE—Mamma means you should get yourself in good condition, Stella, and she's right. Lord knows I'm tired of talking to you on the subject.

GRACE—I only wish someone would invite me to rest up.

MRS. HALLAM—I'm afraid Stella doesn't believe we are talking for her own good.

STELLA—Yes, I do, Mother, but—

VICKIE—But what—?

STELLA—I think everyone knows the thing that is best for himself—

HELEN—And that's polite for "mind your own business."

WALTER—Who should mind their own business?

VICKIE (*half in earnest*)—Oh, we're just trying to put some sense into my wife's head but it looks like a hopeless job.

STELLA—Oh, Vickie—

MRS. HALLAM—Victor is right.

VICKIE (*playing up to the approbation in his mother's eyes. Not unpleasantly but with bravado*)—Yes, and one of these days I'm going to put my foot down, young lady!

WALTER—That's the way to treat 'em!

PAUL—He's only talking!

HELEN—What's the expression you always use, Gran'ma? Stella has him wound around her little finger!

HARRY—Hen-peck makes it clearer! (*There is a general laugh from family.*)

VICKIE (*with a new, harsh note in his voice*)—Oh, so I'm a Hen-peck, eh?

STELLA (*sensing his conflict*)—Oh, please leave us alone—all of you!

GRACE—Stella's mad now!

MRS. HALLAM—No, it is Victor who is angry. He does not like to hear the truth.

WALTER—Gee, I started something!

PAUL—You started something, all right! (*More laughter and comment from family.*)

MR. HALLAM—Children, children, stop it now—please—

The meal is over. The things are cleared away. The men have returned to their cards. The women are beginning to think of dragging the men home. And then Jerry comes barging through the area gate and into the room. "He is young and fresh and clean, and looks amazingly like a youthful Vickie."

For a moment there is considerable renewed excitement, with Jerry kissing all the aunts and acknowledging the hellos of all the uncles. Stella has been working in the kitchen. Now she comes into the room and as Jerry catches sight of her they stand for a second staring wonderingly at each other. Jerry is confused and uncertain until his mother confirms his thought that this is his Aunt Stella.

"Oh, he does remind me of the way Vickie used to be," gasps Stella, in a kind of wonder.

"Why, sure, I remember Aunt Stella," Jerry blurts out. "How do, Aunt Stella."

"*Aunt* Stella. This makes me feel very old," she protests, as Jerry bends to kiss her.

"But, if I don't call you Aunt I can't kiss you," explains Jerry. "Besides, you're not a bit like an aunt—I mean you're not a bit old—or—"

Now the other aunts are up and at him and he is confused again.

"He even puts his foot in it the way Vickie used to," laughs Stella.

Grandma Hallam has brought in a plate heaping with food for Jerry and he manages to set to eating it with a good deal of enthusiasm, protesting that his grandmother should not have gone to all the trouble she did.

They talk with him as he eats, demanding to know when he went into business and how he likes it, and how the business likes it, and is it true that they are not going to have an architect in the family after all—

"Did you really want to study architecture?" asks Stella, suddenly arrested by the conversation.

"Gee, I was crazy to," admits Jerry. "Still want to, about more than anything else in the world."

"Tell me about it."

"Come eat, Jerry," interrupts Mrs. Hallam.

"Yes, Jerry—have a piece of this cake, I made it," interjects Helen.

They have taken over the conversation again, all the relatives. Etta remembers that she can hardly keep her eyes open. Helen remembers that she ought to wash her hair. Grace remembers the last cute movie she saw.

Stella has been standing back of Vickie's chair at the card table, but when he objects that she is keeping the light off his cards she moves over near the stand of flowers. Jerry, watching her, puts his cake plate aside now and joins Stella.

JERRY (*touching the flowers admiringly*)—Gee, I noticed them when I came in. They're gorgeous. Who brought 'em?

STELLA—Uncle Vickie and I.

JERRY—I might have known it.

STELLA—Why?

JERRY—I don't know. I guess because Mother usually brings calf's foot jelly or something. (*They laugh.*)

STELLA (*gravely*)—Jerry, I think I should have brought calf's foot jelly—or something, too. (*They laugh again, a little guiltily.*)

JERRY (*boyishly*)—You couldn't bring calf's foot jelly—because—you don't seem to belong to these Tuesday evenings. Look, aren't they awful? You just have to sit around and jaw over things that aren't important and eat—and eat— (*As* STELLA *smiles.*) Oh, I'm not so crazy about eating as I seem, but I know it tickles Grandma when we eat a lot—

STELLA—You gave a most remarkable performance.

JERRY—No, I mean it, Aunt Stella.

STELLA—I know just how you feel, Jerry.

JERRY—Do you honestly? Before, you know, I was starting to tell you about—

STELLA (*with quick interest*)—Oh, yes, about going abroad—go on—what happened?

ETTA (*rousing herself with an effort*)—What are you two hob-nobbing about?

JERRY (*continuing to* STELLA, *without turning*)—Well, first Dad said he'd think it over, and then the family—I don't know, sort of got him out of it—

ETTA (*petulantly*)—Jerry, I'm talking to you.

JERRY (*annoyed at interruption*)—What?

HELEN—You'd think they were long lost friends—

MRS. HALLAM (*who has risen from card table*)—I only hope Stella was not putting ideas into his head.

JERRY (*angrily*)—What do you mean? Can't anybody even—

PAUL (*sternly*)—Careful, Jerry. You're talking to your grand-mother.

MRS. HALLAM (*crossing to* JERRY)—Well, come over, don't be like company, sit down—

The demands of those who want to go home become more in-sistent. There are excuses. The men should have their rest. To-morrow will be a hard day. Still, the men are hard to move.

Finding themselves together again Jerry and Stella try to take up their conversation where it was interrupted. Jerry wants to tell his Aunt Stella more of the hopes he had at one time.

Stella has taken off an antique pendant she is wearing, a set-ting of moonstone and jade, and this strikes Jerry as being very beautiful. Their heads are drawn quite close together as they examine the delicate workmanship of the pendant. Suddenly Jerry is aware of the perfume Stella is wearing. It smells like violets, he tells her, and she is pleased that he recognized the scent, for that is what it is—Mes Belle Violettes—

"Mes Belle Violettes—Pardonnez moi—je ne polly vous Fran-çaise so velly good. Je never went to college!" It is Uncle Walter, the clown, who, having overheard Jerry and Stella, is puting his compliments.

"You crazy loon—just listen to him—say that over again, Wally," shrieks Grace.

JERRY (*against her silly laughter*)—Aunt Stella, I'd like to see you sometime, when we can talk by ourselves. I mean I want to ask you about paintings and things. Maybe you know of some good exhibitions I could go to. There's nobody much I can talk to—

STELLA—Why, of course, Jerry—any time— (*Thinks a moment, then motions to* VICKIE.) Vickie, just a minute, dear—

VICKIE (*pausing on his way to hall*)—What?

STELLA—Vickie, couldn't everyone come down to our place next Tuesday evening?

VICKIE—That's an idea—you ask 'em, Stella! (VICKIE *raises his hand for attention against the mounting talk.*) Look here people—Stella has something to suggest! Attention! (*Claps* GRACE *on shoulder, quite in* WALTER'S *manner, dislodging her pocketbook from under her arm.*)

WALTER (*struggling into his coat and making a great noise about it*)—Friends, Romans, Countrymen! Lend me your ears—

GRACE—Oh, behave you—and pick up my pocket-book, please

STELLA (*trying to be heard*)—I want you all to come over to our place next Tuesday evening—Jerry's coming too.

MRS. HALLAM (*instantly*)—No, no, that is too big a trip for an old lady like me. Perhaps if you lived nearer, yes—

MR. HALLAM—Come, Mamma, just this once won't tire you—it's a nice idea of Stella's.

ETTA—Yes, Jerry, you ought to say "thank you" to Aunt Stella for inviting you. (JERRY *says nothing.*)

STELLA—Then you will come, all of you?

HELEN—I'm willing if the rest are.

GRACE—I'll go— (*Adds to* HELEN *in an undertone.*) Anything for a change.

HELEN—Way I feel about it.

VICKIE—Fine! Then it's all settled. Our place next Tuesday

MRS. HALLAM (*firmly*)—I am an old lady. It is better for you young people to come to me.

VICKIE (*coaxingly*)—Come on, Mamma dear. I'll blow you a taxi.

JERRY (*to* STELLA)—I meant I wanted to talk to you alone Aunt Stella, not with the whole gang around.

STELLA—Why then—any time, Jerry—just drop in and have dinner with us.

VICKIE (*with his own and* STELLA'S *coats across his arm*)—Get a move on, Stel'. Here's your coat. Catch. (*Throws her coat.* STELLA *catches it. Starts to put it on.* JERRY *moves swift* to her side, and takes it gently from her.)

JERRY—Allow me, Aunt Stella.

STELLA—Thank you, Jerry. (JERRY *holds the coat for her.* STELLA *turns to put her arms into the sleeves. But* WALTER *slips between them, and runs his finger down her spine, with his shrill whistle, as he did earlier to* GRACE *and* HELEN. STELLA *makes no outcry, but starts painfully. The others laugh.*)

VICKIE—He got you that time, Stel'!

JERRY (*dropping the coat on sofa, and facing* WALTER *with blazing eyes*)—That's a damn fool trick! You want to watch out what you're doing, do you hear? (*The others are stunned at the outburst.*)

MRS. HALLAM—What's gotten into you, Jerry, to talk that way?

PAUL (*sternly*)—Apologize to your uncle this instant! (JERRY *is silent.*)

ETTA (*coming down toward* JERRY)—Go on, Jerry, say "Excuse me, Uncle Walter"—you were very fresh, really.

JERRY (*desperately, sullenly*)—I apologize, Uncle Walter. (*Snatches his hat and coat and leaves abruptly.*)

WALTER (*as he exits*)—Don't mention it, my boy. I know our business troubles make you irritable! (*The others indulge in a little strained laughter, glad that the tension is broken. They file out.*)

VICKIE (*looking back toward* STELLA)—Well, come on, Stel', get your coat on, let's move. (STELLA *very slowly puts her coat on and starts toward the door as the curtain slowly falls.*)

ACT II

A week later, again on a Tuesday evening, Vickie and Stella Hallam are preparing to receive the rest of the Hallams at their home near Beekman Place in New York. At least Stella is preparing. At the moment Vickie is asleep in a large armchair in the living-room.

"The living-room is large and square, with high ceiling and old-fashioned trim. It has a gracious lived-in quality, and is furnished with taste and individuality without being in the least bizarre. There are plenty of books, some fine old pieces of English furniture, a lovely hanging, mellow with age, and a Sheraton gate-leg table at right angles to the fireplace, with a large wing-chair opposite."

The ringing of the telephone awakens Vickie. The first call is

for a Mr. Jones, which is wrong. But a second call is from Jerry
Hallam, and he wants to come over before the rest of the family
arrives. Jerry seems upset about something. It is Stella's idea
that he wants to talk with them.

The boy probably wants to do more belly-aching about his work
at the factory. That's Vickie's opinion. And he does not intend
to take any part in that discussion. As regards Jerry and the
family Vickie will mind his own business and he will insist that
Stella do likewise.

Stella is convinced Vickie's attitude is all wrong. Paul has
enough money to let Jerry at least try to find himself. "Putting
him in business now, when there is so much in him that wants to
come out, that's waste," Stella insists.

"Well, if that's the stuff he's been handing out to you, no wonder he's been hanging around here the past week—"

"Once for tea and once to return a book."

"And Saturday, you told me—"

"I didn't expect him," insists Stella, smiling a little at the
recollection. "That was to return another book, and I was leaving
for the exhibition so I took him along."

Apparently Vickie is a little tired of hearing of how Jerry rose
to the beauties of the exhibition and how Stella is convinced that
he has the makings of a great artist. That's all bologney to Vickie.
She must be wanting to make a fairy out of Jerry, favoring his
hanging around art galleries all the time.

Stella is equally disappointed that Vickie will not understand.
It is not like him to express "the kind of mentality that ridicules
what it doesn't understand."

"Sometimes, if I close my eyes, I think it is Harry or Walt
talking," she tells him, and his anger flares as he warns her, as
he has done before, to leave her opinion of his family out of their
discussions.

"But it isn't the family," persists Stella. "It's *you*. If you're
so blind you can't see that Jerry ought to get away to find himself, then . . . (*Pauses and goes on with an effort.*) Something
in you that's always been very dear and precious to me has died
without my knowing it—"

Stella admits that she is fond of Jerry. She would be fond of
all the other Hallams if they would let her. But the Hallams resent her. Stella knows that. They have always resented her.
And she can't understand their hatred.

"I just want more out of life than waking up in the morning and
going to bed at night. Oh, I want a great deal more than that

Vickie— (*She goes to him.*) And I want a great deal more of marriage than the mere routine of a man and woman living together. Because that doesn't have to happen, it shouldn't happen —especially when two people began by loving each other the way we did—"

"You did used to love me—"

"I still do, more than anything else in the world—"

"Like fun you do—"

Vickie tries to hide his real feelings by making light of them. If Stella loved him, he insists, she would give up some of the fads she is following. The art school for instance. That isn't getting her anywhere. She's just plain garden variety romantic, that is what's the matter with her. She expects a honeymoon to last forever. It can't. It's bound to wear off and something a lot better take its place—

"I know this, Vickie," Stella answers, quite seriously, "nothing can ever take the place of tenderness and respect—and chivalry. You just stand still without them, or you keep going down, and down, and down—"

"Bunk, Stella. Honestly, bunk. I'm going to call you Romantic Susie. Come on, kiss me, Romantic Susie—"

A moment later she is in his arms, a little against her will. She would have their talk out. That is what they need. To talk things out. She feels no response to Vickie's quick desire. That sort of thing doesn't mean anything in her present mood.

"God, I don't know what you want," snaps Vickie, repulsed and hurt. "You're just all balled up—love, reason, sex—all balled up—"

Then, veering away from further discussion, Vickie would change the subject to the expected arrival of the family. A moment later they are laughing and happy again, with Stella close in Vickie's arms.

"Ah, Vickie," Stella confesses, "every night I pray this prayer —Dear God, bless Vickie, whom I love— (*She makes a little face.*) And all my dear in-laws—"

The doorbell announces Jerry. Stella has not had time to change from the soft white house dress that, Vickie insists, the folks will think is a nightgown. Now Vickie has dashed into the bathroom to shave, with a parting warning that Stella is not to encourage Jerry in any foolishness about going abroad. Which puts them right back where they started.

Jerry is a little excited. For a second he stands in the doorway staring at Stella and holding a wrapped package awkwardly in his hand. Stella would have him come in and be comfortable while she goes to change her dress, but Jerry would like to have her stay as she is, at least until he has shown her what he has brought. He doesn't want to wait until everyone's there.

"I kept imagining on the way down, me walking in, and you here by yourself—I didn't think it would happen—but it has—so you can't just go in and change your dress—"

Jerry is fumbling with the package and Stella, aware of his overwrought condition, is trying to keep the scene casual. Now he is trying to tell her all that their meeting Saturday and going to the art exhibition had meant to him.

". . . I remember every word you said—and how you looked when you said it," he reports, eagerly.

"Jerry, this is dreadful. You sound like a detective!"

JERRY—No, I'm not fooling. Being with you that day made everything different and wonderful—but all it meant to you was —going to an exhibition, I guess.

STELLA—Oh, no, it didn't, it meant more than that, Jerry. Because I enjoyed seeing the pictures with you—it was nice being with someone for a change.—It was awfully nice. (*There is a wistful unguarded note in her voice as she adds the last sentence. JERRY is arrested by it; he searches her eyes eagerly. But STELLA's face has suddenly become a mask. She turns a friendly impersonal smile upon him. It quenches JERRY's fire. When he speaks again, the timbre has gone from his voice.*)

JERRY—Oh. Well. I see, sure. (*Turns away in disappointment.*) I'm just crazy, I guess. Forget it, will you, Stella? I came in here, just sort of crazy, that's all—

STELLA (*not disputing it*)—What was it you wanted to show me, Jerry?

JERRY (*very young, with his back to her*)—Nothing. I wouldn't mean anything to you. Never mind. (*Turns half toward her, twanging the string of his package, as if he wished she'd take it from him.*)

STELLA (*smiling*)—Is this it? (*Takes the package.*)

JERRY (*in his throat*)—Umm.

STELLA (*uncertain*)—Shall I open it?

JERRY (*inarticulate*)—Sure. If—if you want.

STELLA—It's—soft! (*A beautiful little grin comes over JERRY tense young features.*)

JERRY—Go ahead. See what it is. (*STELLA unwraps it, an brings to light an enchanting English puppy made of plush.*

is at once nonsensical and appealing.)

STELLA (*taken unawares*)—Oh!

JERRY (*his face transfigured*)—Do you remember it?

STELLA—Of course I remember it— (*She has forgotten* JERRY, *forgotten the dog; her mind is in some hinterland of space.*) We were walking over Fifty-seventh Street—after the exhibition—it was in a shop window—

JERRY (*taking it swiftly and with laughter*)—And you were like a little kid, the way you stopped and laughed at it—

STELLA—I've always had a weakness for toy-stores—

JERRY (*his voice trembling with happiness*)—And you said— "Oh, Jerry, look! Isn't it adorable!"—and I knew right away that I'd have to surprise you with it!

STELLA (*turning her eyes upon him as if she has come back from a long distance; speaking slowly*)—But you shouldn't have done it, Jerry—

JERRY—D-don't you like it?

STELLA—I love it. It's one of the sweetest things that ever happened to me, your surprising me this way. But it won't do, you see. (*She tries to smile.*) It just won't do.

JERRY—Why, you're crying!

STELLA—Nonsense! Why should I cry—over a funny little dog?

JERRY (*at a loss; his eyes wide*)—I don't *know!*

STELLA (*starting to wrap it up again*)—Neither do I.

Jerry is afraid Stella will not keep his gift, and she is not sure she should. For one thing she does not want him to spend his money on her, and for another she is his aunt and "little boys oughtn't to buy things for their aunts."

But she is not his aunt, not really, Jerry insists. And he doesn't want her to try to influence the family in favor of his going abroad. He does not want to go if it would mean that he cannot see her any more. And he doesn't want her to treat him like a child.

"Gosh, I didn't know I was going to feel this way about you," he says, earnestly. "Even when I bought the dog, it was only fun, surprising you— And then I went into a phone booth to see if I could come right over with it. It must have happened then— because—when I heard your voice—such a funny feeling came over me that—that I couldn't talk—I lost my breath sort of—so I said, "Is Mr. Jones there—""

Vickie is calling from the bedroom. He is in a temper as he comes through the door. He cannot find his clothes-brush. For a moment he does not notice Jerry, who is secretly fuming with rage at his uncle's attitude toward Stella. Vickie takes Jerry's scowl as proof that he has come to the party to belly-ache about his job, and grouching won't help that any.

Stella has found the clothes-brush where Vickie had left it and he is raging again as he bolts back into the room with it.

JERRY—I'd like to kill him, treating you like that!

STELLA (*with an effort*)—Jerry, don't be silly. (*Pause.*) Uncle Vickie and I love each other very dearly—we—we're not romantic any more— (*She stops, then goes on bravely, repeating* VICKIE'S *words of earlier in the evening.*) But romance doesn't mean anything. It wears off and something much better comes in its place—

JERRY—I don't believe that. And you don't believe it either! It's just that he doesn't understand things about you—he doesn't know how to make you happy.

STELLA (*with finality*)—I am very happy—

JERRY (*gropingly*)—Then—Saturday was all a dream—I mean I only imagined that—

STELLA (*her feelings get the better of her*)—No, you didn't imagine it, Jerry. It was wonderful. I *did* love it. Oh, but I must have been mad—I was under a spell, as if Time had gone back seven years— It wasn't *you* I was happy with, Jerry, it was Uncle Vickie—don't you see?

JERRY (*trying to take it all in*)—Then there isn't any place for me at all—

STELLA—No, Jerry. (*There is a deep silence, while* JERRY *turns away, struggling with his heart-break.* STELLA *goes to him.*) Jerry. Listen to me. You're not in love with me the way you think. (*He wheels in denial.*) Oh, no, you're not! I'm just taking the place of the girl you will love some day. Now you're—lonely I guess—and you're dazzled by the experience of talking to someone who understands the things you want to say—

JERRY—Would that make me suffer the way I'm suffering now?

STELLA (*simply*)—I think so—

JERRY (*with sudden overwhelming penetration*)—Would make *you* suffer the way you're suffering—?

STELLA—Jerry! Stop it!

JERRY (*wildly, triumphantly*)—I won't stop it! I know what you're doing! You're treating me like a child because you're afraid! You're afraid of yourself, and you're afraid of me!

STELLA (*struggling against him*)—Jerry—

JERRY (*pleading*)—Ah, Stella, there's nothing wrong about it, Stella—we didn't ask it to come—it just happened—like something natural and beautiful—

STELLA (*hoarsely*)—Jerry, don't—leave me alone—please— (*She realizes that his touch spells peril for her. Blindly, she picks up a book, and puts it in a book-case, trying to conquer herself. VICKIE enters from bedroom, drawing on his coat. He is fresh and spruce and satisfied with himself.*)

VICKIE (*smugly*)—Here we are—

STELLA (*with too much composure in her voice*)—Did you leave the room tidy, Vickie—in case the folks go in there—?

VICKIE—It's all right— (*Catches sight of the partially wrapped dog on the chair. Picks it up, looks at it, and chuckles.*) They certainly can make stuff these days—where'd it come from? (*He looks from JERRY to STELLA. JERRY doesn't answer.*)

STELLA—Jerry bought it for his girl. He opened it for me to see.

She takes the dog and is wrapping it up again as Vickie, in high spirits, continues riding Jerry about his girl and remembering that he once had bought Stella something or other like a plush dog.

It was a kitten with a blue ribbon about its neck. Stella remembers. She still has it. And he is not to tease Jerry any more, but to help him go away. He must change his mind about Jerry, for her sake—

There are voices in the hall. The Hallams are coming. Jerry, about to bolt the room, hysterically, is stopped before he can get away. A moment later a chorus of greetings herald the arrival of the family.

They are all there except Etta and Paul. Jerry'd forgotten to tell Vickie and Stella that they weren't coming. Etta's sister has been rushed to the hospital with a ruptured appendix. Jerry should have remembered—but they are not to scold him, says Vickie. The kid's in love. He's got a girl.

Stella succeeds in diverting their minds to the task of hanging up their wraps. Then she turns to help Mrs. Hallam, who is giving some slight indication of fainting after her climb of the stairs. It takes the whole family and a bottle of smelling salts to restore Mrs. Hallam before she is able to walk into the bedroom flanked on four sides by her solicitous sons.

"But it was only one flight up, and she's used to stairs in a private house," protests Stella.

"She made up her mind last week already that these particular stairs would be too much for her," explains Helen.

Grace and Helen find Stella's apartment interesting and the sandwiches which they sample in the kitchen delicious. With Stella out of the room for a moment they are quick to observe also that the furniture doesn't match and that whatever kind of dress it is that Stella is wearing it isn't anything either of them would wear.

The best laugh is the plaster cast of Vickie's head on which Stella has been working. It might be Harry. In fact Helen decides it is Harry. Her husband's head on Stella's table. Might mean something. But she needn't flatter Harry, Vickie soon corrects her. He is the subject.

Now Mrs. Hallam has recovered sufficient strength to come back to the living-room, assisted by Papa and the boys. The old lady is interested in Stella's house, though she would never think of using one room for both a living-room and a dining-room. They do frequently use their dining-room as a sitting-room at home, Mrs. Hallam admits, but they have a parlor, too.

Walter has found what he comically calls a small Vickie-to-rola and has started it playing a record. It happens to be something by Beethoven and Grace doesn't like it. She would have him put on something good. Helen finds "The Wedding of the Painted Doll," and is delighted. So are they all. Soon the urge to dance is creeping over them.

Now Helen has pushed her Harry forward and is trying to make him waltz. It is not much of a success. Then fat Grace and Walter try it and do a little better, but not much. There are calls now for Vickie and Stella, but Vickie is soon out of step and covering his awkwardness by accusing Stella of trying to lead. Stella and Vickie used to dance well together. Helen remembers them dancing at their wedding. Vickie held Stella tight enough that night.

Mr. Hallam gallantly urges Mother Hallam to tread a few measures. Mother is soon out of breath. Then Mrs. Hallam suggests that Jerry should dance with one of his aunts, and Vickie pushes Stella forward as a partner. "The two youngest ought to be able to give a pretty good performance," ventures Uncle Harry.

Stella holds back. "Her breath comes quickly; her eyes are a little dilated with fear; she is afraid to trust Jerry and herself to the situation."

The urging of the family continues. Walter shoves Jerry toward Stella, and Vickie impatiently bids her dance. "Why do you have to spoil the fun all the time?" he demands.

Jerry has been standing near the book shelves, motionless, watching Stella. "Now he slowly puts the book he has been holding upon the table, and quietly crosses the room. Deliberately, and without saying a word, he holds out his arms to her, and as if mesmerized by the crowding, expectant faces around her, she takes a forward step, and drifts into his waiting embrace. Smoothly, beautifully, they glide into the rhythm. He holds her tenderly, reverently, his eyes closed, their faces touching in a wordless kiss. This that they are doing becomes more than a dance. It is a fulfillment of dreams and longing, a touching of the rainbow, a brief paradise of ecstasy. If the others gradually become aware of something strange, unreal—it comes through to them only as a distilled, disturbing beauty. They watch in silence, not untinged with awe, and are satisfied to call it 'fine.' A spell is on the room. Stella and Jerry, wrapped in oblivion, linger in each other's arms, their cheeks still touching—and no one says a word. Then Walter, not knowing what it is all about, becomes uncomfortable."

"Well, they win the dance," agrees Walter.

"They ought to get a loving cup," adds Harry.

Grace and Walter start a search for something that will serve. Walter finally hits upon the cast of Vickie. That's hollow, just like Vick's head, he laughs.

The family finds this extremely funny. "Their feelings, so unwontedly stimulated, find relief in delirious laughter, and thus Jerry is shaken out of his heaven by the harsh shrieks, and opens his eyes to find the clay head of Vickie thrust, like a mocking symbol, into his hands. He stares at it for an instant, swept by emotions too complex for him to handle. Then he dashes it to the ground, where it smashes in little pieces.

"Damn you!" shouts Jerry, sweeping them all in a single violent gesture. "Damn all of you!"

With that he has pushed by Walter and is gone, the hall door slamming behind him.

Walter is sputtering with indignation. "This is the second time he's done that to me!" he declares, angrily.

"We oughtn't to let him get away with it. I'll get him back," adds Harry.

Stella is trying to stop them. The cast was only a bit of practice work anyway. Let Jerry go. He didn't know what he was doing.

Helen (*shrewdly*)—I bet anything Stella knows what ails him— (*They are diverted from* Jerry's *exit and turn to look at* Stella *in quick suspicion.*)

Stella (*fencing*)—Yes—yes, I do—! He's terribly unhappy—

Vickie (*angrily, breaking in before she can excuse him*)—Hell, no excuse for this, he's just a damn sore pup because he can't get his own way—

Harry (*to* Vickie)—What's eating him?

Vickie (*generalizing with a large sweep*)—Ach, you know— he's dissatisfied over at the factory. . . .

Grace—Carrying on for *that*, imagine!

Mrs. Hallam (*in great agitation*)—I blame Etta. She gives in to him—she spoils him—

Walter—He ought to be thrashed—

Harry—And Paul ought to see that he gets it good and plenty—

Stella—Oh, you fools! You damn fools!

Mrs. Hallam—I thought so. Stella has been encouraging him for all she is worth—

Stella—And if I have, is it any worse than what you've done?

Vickie (*starting forward*)—What are you saying . . .

Mrs. Hallam (*shaking with indignation*)—One minute, Vickie, I would like to hear what it is that we have done— (*She rises with difficulty, and faces* Stella. *It is at last an open declaration between them.*)

Stella (*she looks at Vickie but he turns away*)—If you really want to know I'll tell you— You're all so sure of yourselves! You're trying to mold Jerry's life to fit your own and it's wrong! I know what I'm talking about because you've done the same to Vickie and me and you *mustn't!* You've got to let the three of us alone— You've got to let Vickie and me keep our marriage the way it started out— It's the only thing that'll save us. . . .

Mrs. Hallam (*breaking in*)—Enough, please—I have heard enough. (*She feels for her chair and sinks into it with a little moan, resorting to her one sure weapon.*)

Harry (*furiously to* Vickie)—I think your wife's lost her mind.

Walter (*to* Grace)—Get a little water for Mamma— (Grace *goes into the kitchen, reluctant to miss the excitement.*)

Stella (*seeking the refuge of* Vickie's *arms*)—Vickie, you see what I'm driving at, you know I'm right—make them see it—

Vickie (*ignoring her plea, his nostrils dilated with anger*)— Shut up, can't you!—Look what you've done! (*Rushes to his*

mother's side, then wheels back to STELLA.) Make some excuse
for your actions, can't you—

STELLA (*through dead lips*)—No—

Stella goes quickly into her bedroom and closes the door. Mrs.
Hallam rises to declare that she is going home. She cannot stay
after such insults, even in response to Vickie's distressed pleading.
She always knew Stella was that kind. The others are for staying, after the money they have spent on the taxi getting there.
And all those sandwiches in the kitchen! But Mrs. Hallam is
obdurate. Her coat adjusted she kisses Vickie.

"Good-by, my boy," she says; "I know it is not your fault.
Come up soon; your mother is always happy to have you—"

"Sure," answers Vickie; "I'll phone—or something—later."

They are gone now, filing out one after the other. Vickie tries
to put as good a face on the situation as he can, but his anger and
humiliation flare up as he views "the desolate battlefield." He
stalks to the bedroom door and flings it open. "You can come out
now— They've gone," he calls.

Stella stands at the threshold for a moment, very still. Then,
quietly, she says: "Don't use that tone to me, Vickie."

She has nothing to explain, she continues, when he suggests that
she is lucky to have a chance to explain. She needed him and he
did not love her enough to know about it. She is sorry for what
has happened, but perhaps it is best that they should know
where they stand.

So far as Vickie is concerned he knows where they stand, and
will stand. Stella will do as he says in the future. She has
made a monkey of him long enough. They have reached the
turning point in their affairs, and while he is gone she will have
time to think that over. He is going to join his folks.

"Vickie, if you go up there now we'll never get back to where
we were," Stella pleads.

"You've got the cart before the horse, my dear," he answers,
proud of himself. "It's up to you now to make the first move
to get back to where we were. My slate's clean. I've been as
good a husband as any man could be to any woman—"

"Have you, Vickie?" The fire is gone from her. "The weary
droop of her shoulders, and the dry sorrow in her eyes gives the
look of one who is with her dead." To Stella, it is suddenly over.

"And haven't I—? Haven't I, I ask you?" he demands, expanding again. "I've given you everything you ever wanted.
I don't gamble, I don't drink, I don't cheat— Good God, I don't

know that other women even exist— (*The bell rings. He breaks off.*) Who the devil's that—?"

Jerry brushes by Vickie at the door. He is looking for his Aunt Stella. He has come back to admit that what he did was rotten of him. Vickie mustn't blame Stella. Stella didn't have anything to do with it. And Vickie shan't accuse her of anything.

"Oh, Jerry, keep quiet—get out—go away—I don't want you here!" pleads Stella.

"You stay right where you are, Jerry," orders Vickie, in a tone of authority. If his nephew has the decency to come back and say he's sorry, Stella will have the decency to hear him out. Vickie has stood as much family insult as he is going to stand!

STELLA—But Jerry and I have nothing more to say to each other—he has nothing to do with what's happened between us— it's you and I who need to talk—

VICKIE (*with the upper hand*)—Oh, no, we don't—I told you, I've said my say—I'm *through* until you come to your senses! (*Swoops up his hat and coat with a gesture and starts for the door.*)

JERRY (*aghast*)—Gee, Uncle Vick, you can't do this to Aunt Stella—

VICKIE (*for STELLA's benefit*)—It's all right, your aunt and I understand each other perfectly— (*Directly to STELLA.*) And as for Jerry you might try as long as he's here, to undo a little of the mischief you began— Let him see where a lot of idiotic notions land you! Good night! (*Turns on his heel, goes out of the door, and closes it firmly behind him.*)

JERRY—I'm going to get him back! He's *crazy!*

STELLA (*wearily, picking up pieces of the plaster head*)—No, Jerry— Let him go. You go too.—I want to be alone—

JERRY—But you oughtn't to be alone now— God, the way they all walk out on you—and it's their fault, too!—God, it's *funny!* It's their fault, and they all walk out on *you!*

STELLA—Don't worry about it, Jerry— Just go home and forget everything you've seen and heard tonight—between Uncle Vickie and me— (*She rises and puts the broken pieces on the table.*) Such an ugly death—to something that was so—beautiful— (*Sinks into the chair.*)

JERRY—Oh, but gee, Stella, I can't leave you like this—gee your eyes, Stella, I can't stand the pain in them. I just want to do anything for you, I don't care what it is—I want to do some thing to take that look out of your eyes— (*He is on his knees before her.*)

STELLA (*closing her eyes against him*)—Then go home, Jerry— go home—

JERRY (*pleading, but curiously free of self and passion*)—Oh, but, Stella, I can't go home, and leave you like this—I love you and that gives me the right to stay when everybody else walks out on you—I *belong* here—just because I love you, see?

STELLA (*fighting against him like a drug*)—Jerry—don't—I'm too tired to scold you the way I ought—

JERRY (*still kneeling*)—Ah, Stella, you don't want to scold me— (*He draws her to him.*)

STELLA—I—must— (*She tries to unlock his arms, but he is stronger than she is, and slowly, gently, he brings her head closer to his upturned face. His lips touch hers. There is beauty in his reverence, and beauty in her acceptance.—But the kiss climbs slowly from reverence to passion, as the curtain falls.*)

ACT III

Early next morning, in the Hallam dining-room, Helen is setting a place at table for her husband Harry's breakfast. Father Hallam, carrying a glass and a bottle of medicine, has just gone upstairs.

It is soon apparent that Mother Hallam has had a fainting spell in the night and that Harry and Helen have been called to take over the morning routine. They are both fairly upset about it. With Harry the upset is rationalized by his sense of family loyalty. With Helen it is resented as one of those additional burdens for which she let herself in when she married a Hallam.

Vickie Hallam has spent the night at his mother's, and that is cause for interesting speculation on Helen's part. Why is Vickie there? What has happened between him and Stella? Did Vickie walk out and leave Stella?

"I wonder if he'd have stayed away from her all night if Gran'-ma hadn't gotten sick!" wonders Helen.

"You've got your worries, haven't you?" sneers Harry.

"Well, it's sort of interesting to watch them panning out like all the rest of us," says Helen.

"What?"

"Oh, I knew it couldn't last. I always said Vickie's no different from all you boys—he only stayed in love a little longer, that's all."

Helen is also willing to bet that this is going to be a showdown between Stella and Vickie. Harry hopes it will be. It is about time Vickie was putting his foot down. If Stella wants to leave him let her go. Good riddance to bad rubbish. That's Harry's opinion.

Vickie comes from upstairs, looking fagged and tense. To find his brother and sister-in-law picking on each other as usual does not improve his mood. His mother is awake, Vickie reports, and Harry can go up if he likes. The doctor said the spell was a case of nerves and excitement. Most likely from the scene of the night before.

Stella? Stella's coming over, Vickie announces. As soon as he had telephoned her she had agreed to come over and sort of apologize to Mother Hallam to make her feel good.

"I don't believe it," says Helen, with conviction.

"Well, contrary to what you and the rest think, she hasn't got me wound round her little finger, has she?" answers Vickie, with satisfaction. If Helen had any idea that what's happened could bust things up between Stella and him she's silly. Stella's not a child. . . .

Harry has gone to business. Vickie hears Stella coming and shoos Helen out of the room. He greets her shyly, a little in doubt. Stella is "quiet and remote." When she speaks her voice is colorless.

Vickie does not have to thank her for coming, Stella says. She came because she wanted to. "I did not want to hurt Mother, and if it will make her feel better for me to say so, it would be stupid to stay away."

VICKIE—Know you haven't said "Good morning" to me yet?

STELLA—In the hall I did—when I came in. (*Makes no further move toward him.*)

VICKIE (*gruffly, sheepishly*)—Not what I call "Good morning!" (*Looks at her in slow realization that there is still a rift between them.*) Look here, Stella. You still mad, or what?

STELLA (*with the still resignation that comes from hours of inner battle.*)—Why should I be mad? You act a certain way because you're you, I act a certain way because I'm me.—And that's all there is to it.

VICKIE (*hiding his discomfort with insolent humor*)—Now suppose you tell it to me in English.

STELLA—I can't tell it to you any more plainly, Vickie. And you wouldn't want to understand me anyway—so what's the sense of hashing everything all over again. It won't do any good.

VICKIE (*with alacrity and magnanimity*)—All right, let's for-get. You did wrong last night but you can't do more than say you're sorry. I did wrong, maybe, by leaving you alone, and—*I'm* sorry.—Didn't sleep a damn wink, you little devil. First time we ever slept apart, you know it?

STELLA—Yes.

VICKIE—What you needed though, young lady. Now come on, wasn't it?

STELLA (*with her first trace of real emotion*)—No, Vickie, it wasn't.

VICKIE—Get the woozies, being by yourself?

STELLA (*very quietly*)—I wasn't by myself very long—

VICKIE (*comically*)—Hunh?

STELLA (*without a break, looking straight at him*)—Jerry didn't leave until almost three.

VICKIE (*remembering*)—Oh, Jerry— (*Laughs a little.*) What'd he do, talk your ear off?—You should have pitched him out, you're too soft with him, Stel'.

STELLA (*with innuendo*)—I wasn't soft with him.

VICKIE—Talk some sense into him?

STELLA (*on a breath*)—I hope so.

VICKIE—Good.—Now let's kiss and make up.

STELLA (*somehow evading him and leaving him emotionally groping*)—I wish it were as simple as that. But it isn't. There's no use to our kissing and making up. It would only be the same thing over again—

VICKIE—What d'you want me to do, Romantic Susie, bring a pound of candy and a bunch of roses home tonight?

STELLA (*undramatically*)—I won't be there, Vickie.

Not be there? The statement startles Vickie. To cover his feelings he "adopts an attitude of indifferent defiance." Where does she think she's going? Does she expect to get a separation or something?

Stella plans nothing so spectacular. She just wants to be alone for a little while to think things through. She thinks Vickie should be doing the same thing. He'll probably want to stay on at his mother's. As for what the folks will think—Stella doesn't care. Yes, she is willing to admit that the Hallams are all right, sane, and level-headed—

"And I believe also that all the Hallams in all the world are always right," she adds, turning on Vickie almost vindictively.

"They think they know what you are, until their very knowing almost *makes* you what they think you are. And then—God help you—if you're not strong enough to help yourself—"

"Honestly, Stel', you're all upset over nothing—I don't see what you're driving at—"

"There's so much you don't see, Vickie, that it—almost breaks my heart—" she says.

Now, to prove that he is master, and that she cannot leave him, Vickie has drawn Stella roughly into his arms and kissed her upon the lips "as if wanting to fire her with the old, easy passion." She remains limp in his arms and he is worried.

"God, Stella—limber up—inside, I mean," he says. "I got a feeling I just can't get *at* you! (*His anger turns to a kind of baffled pleading.*) Here I am, all ready to take you in my arms, and—I can't find you— That's the way I sort of feel—"

"And it's the loneliest feeling in the world, isn't it, Vickie—"

"There is a quick, deep silence. He meets her eyes. This is his first moment of dawning comprehension. Then Helen enters from upstairs carrying an empty glass and a medicine dropper, and shatters the moment completely."

Stella goes upstairs to see Mrs. Hallam—goes alone, at Helen's suggestion—and Vickie is left to do what he can to convince Helen that all is quite as it should be between him and Stella.

Now Paul and Etta have arrived in a state of agitation. Not because of Mrs. Hallam, but because of Jerry. Their son has not been home all night and they cannot understand it. Etta, at the verge of hysterics, is sure something terrible has happened; Jerry is in some hospital! Nor does the suggestion that if he were they would have had word of him allay her fear. Even Helen is agreed that there is cause for grave excitement, considering the mood Jerry was in at Stella's—

"What mood?" demands Paul.

"Kid was upset—family sort of got his goat, I guess—" Vickie explains.

That might explain it, Etta thinks. She knows Jerry has been unhappy in the business. But Paul is still firm that Jerry shall adjust himself to his work.

The only other thing Vickie can think of is that the kid is in love. They were teasing him about that, too. Stella knew, but Stella wouldn't tell who the girl was.

If Jerry is in love, that might explain to Paul his staying out all night. He may have been with the girl. But Etta is sure her son is much too sweet and innocent for that sort of adventure.

Besides, no decent girl would allow such a thing—

At that moment Jerry comes down the area-way stairs. "He walks as if in a daze, his shoulders sagging a little, his eyes filled with pain."

A simple explanation of what has kept him out is all that his relieved mother would have, but his father is firm and demands a complete account of everything.

Jerry is sorry. He must have just forgot them. He has spent the night walking, mostly. As for the rest of it, it is no affair of theirs. Let them leave him alone. Why can't they leave him alone? Yes, if they must know, he is in love! But with whom he is in love he will not say.

"Jerry, darling," pleads Etta, "if she's a nice girl and comes from a nice family, I want to meet her. Why shouldn't I?"

"Certainly," adds Paul, "why shouldn't your mother meet her? Bring her up."

JERRY—I—I can't bring her up—

PAUL—Why not?

JERRY—Oh, leave me *alone,* for Christ's sake! (VICKIE, *working on a socket with a screw driver, is arrested by the boy's reluctance.*)

PAUL—Is she someone you'd be ashamed to let your mother meet?

JERRY—No, she isn't! She's the most wonderful person in the world!

ETTA—Well, all the more reason, darling! Bring her up.

JERRY—I—can't!

PAUL—*Why* can't you? That's what I want to know! And I'll know it before I'm through with you.

JERRY—She's . . . married. (VICKIE *says nothing. But sitting there in the chair, he knows. As if his hands had become numb and useless, the screw driver slips to his lap.*)

ETTA—Oh, my God!

HELEN (*in an incredulous whisper*)—Married!

PAUL (*compressing his lips*)—So that's it! So that's the story. (*As if getting down to a loathsome but necessary task.*) Well, where did you pick her up?

JERRY—In heaven! That's where!

PAUL (*handling the thing admirably from his point of view*)— Yes, we know all about that. One more question. Did you spend the night with her—(*with thick irony*) in heaven? (*Before* JERRY *can speak* VICKIE *is on his feet, too afraid to hear*

the answer. His voice is a cry of repressed anguish.)
        VICKIE—It's enough! Let him alone, now, can't you?
        PAUL (*confronting* VICKIE)—Let him alone, when he's mixed
up with some—bum! (VICKIE *recoils. It is his instinctive impulse to throttle the word in* PAUL'S *throat, but in a flash he
realizes that to react thus would be to expose* STELLA. JERRY,
however, flies at his father with all the fierce gallantry of youth.)
        JERRY—You use that word about her and I'll kill you!
        PAUL—I'll call her by her right name and that'll be a damn
sight worse—
        VICKIE (*beside himself*)—Lay off, I tell you, for God's sake—
        PAUL (*turning to* VICKIE)—Let *me* manage this, will you?
        VICKIE (*drawing a red herring*)—Well, this is no place for a
scene with Mamma sick upstairs, what's the matter with you!

There is a step on the stair. A second later Stella appears.
"Her eyes travel mutely from Jerry's tear-stained tragic face to
Vickie's stricken agony. It is as if the three of them were alone
in the room."
        Stella goes first to Jerry. She is worried by his appearance.
What is the matter?
        Before anyone else can speak, Paul volunteers the answer.
Jerry has been running around with a married woman; a married woman who is probably trying to frame something on him—
        The woman's not framing anything on him, Stella assures them.
She knows. She might tell how she knows if Jerry did not plead
so earnestly for her not to bare a story that, he says, is so beautiful that none of them could understand it.
        Again Paul is beside himself with anger. It is his right to
know everything there is to know, and he will. "There has never
been a scandal in the Hallam family and my son won't be the first
to start one," boasts Paul. He'll buy the woman off, if necessary.
And he'll ship Jerry out of the country on the next boat.
        Paul has turned to Stella again. Perhaps she doesn't know
that Jerry, the young fool, had not been home all night. What
time had he left her house?
        It was three o'clock. Vickie answers the query. But that is
all he can tell. Where did Jerry go after he left Stella's at three
o'clock? He walked—and walked, repeats Jerry.
        That's a lie, Paul declares. Jerry is lying and Stella is trying
to shield him. Did he spend the night with this bum? If so,
what's her game? How long has this been going on?
        Now Jerry, grown desperate, has turned to Stella for permis-

sion to tell.

"I'd like to tell 'em," he shouts, his voice breaking raucously. "Honest, I want to tell 'em—I'm proud of loving you—" He faces them with a lift of his head. "D'you get that, all of you? I'm proud of loving her!"

In an instant Paul has turned upon Stella, but Vickie is before him.

"Stop it! I've heard enough," Vickie shouts.

"You poor deluded fool—no wonder you've heard enough!" sneers Paul. "So this is the sort of stuff she does behind your back—"

"Who says it's behind my back?" demands Vickie, his voice a bellow, his bravado increasing as he sees they begin to believe him. "What do you take me for? Don't you suppose I've known about it all along— Didn't you hear me say I knew he'd been down at the apartment until three o'clock— Does that look like Stella was doing anything behind my back?"

What would have been the good of making a fuss? How could anybody take such a tempest in a teapot seriously, demands Vickie.

PAUL (*with stiff lips*)—When did this begin with him—

VICKIE—Guess it began that night at the folks' last week. We got home and Stella said, "I think I made a hit with your nephew." (STELLA *wheels toward* VICKEY.) We laughed ourselves sick over it—"

JERRY (*stricken; turning to* STELLA *in desperate unbelief*)—Stella!—You laughed! (STELLA *is completely bowled over at this unexpected twist to the story. She can find no words, merely looks at* JERRY *in a wordless denial.* VICKIE *takes it up loudly, aggressively.*)

VICKIE—What'd you think we'd do, kid, sit down and bust out crying over it?

JERRY (*ignoring him. Slowly, gropingly, to* STELLA)—You—laughed—

STELLA—Jerry! Jerry! *No!*

VICKIE (*grabbing* STELLA'S *arm, and breaking in again*)—And a damned lucky thing for you that we did take it as a joke—

PAUL (*angrily*)—Your uncle's right, you impudent pup, you!

ETTA—The idea. A big boy like you making such a spectacle of yourself. You ought to go right over and say, "I apologize, Aunt Stella!"

JERRY (*his eyes burning into* STELLA'S, *his face twisted and old with disillusion*)—I—apologize—Aunt Stella— (*Feels blindly for his hat on the table and exits.*)

STELLA (*after him*)—Jerry! No! Don't believe it! Come back!

VICKIE (*sharply*)—Let him go!

PAUL (*blocking her way*)—He needs a jolt to bring him to his senses—

STELLA (*flinging all her strength against* PAUL's)—But you can't let him go that way; he believed it!

The area-gate has slammed. Stella is powerless in Paul's hands. Both he and Vickie are urging her to let things stay as they are. What happens now is none of her business—

"But it is my business," she pleads, facing Vickie. "That boy loves me, and if it's the last decent thing I do, I won't let you destroy something that's been beautiful to both of us—"

Now they have rounded upon her again. Paul and Etta. She faces them with the truth. Vickie has lied to them. She had never made fun of Jerry. And Vickie had not lied to save her, but to save the family.

"You made a gesture for me, Vickie, I admit it," she says. "But it wasn't good enough. You were afraid for them to know that I was this bum they were talking about, so you made a joke of it and hid behind it like a coward—and you didn't care what you did to Jerry as long as you were safe—"

"That's a good story," sneers Paul, ironically.

VICKIE—She's telling you the truth! Don't you know it when you hear it?

PAUL—Not from her, I don't, or from you either!

VICKIE—Well, you're going to hear it now whether you like it or not. She's right.—I didn't have the guts to face the truth before the family because for seven years you've been waiting to say, "I told you so"— Now go ahead and say it!

PAUL (*with strong, incredulous contempt*)—And you're going to let her get away with it—

VICKIE (*violently*)—No. I'm not going to let her get away with anything. I don't have to. (*Approaches* STELLA. *He is suddenly quiet and controlled.*) When you came in here this morning you said you wanted to go away. Well, you listen to what I have to say first, and then you can go if you want—I won't keep you— (*He grabs her arms roughly, not caring that he hurts her.*) I'm not even going to ask you if you spent the night with him. I'm going to tell you— (*There is a tense silence before he goes on.*) You didn't—do you understand that—you didn't! I know you didn't—*because I know it!* (*As his voice mounts in a mad triumph of conviction,* MRS. HALLAM *is heard on the stairs. She enters in her bathrobe and slippers, with* MR. HALLAM *close behind her. He has not wanted her to come down, but she is indomitable even in her weakness. She knows that something is the matter.*)

MRS. HALLAM (*her old chant*)—Children—children— (VICKIE'S *hands drop to his side as he releases* STELLA. ETTA *and* PAUL *try to look casual, as if their very hearts hadn't stopped beating at the old lady's entrance at this crucial moment. But* MRS. HALLAM *pierces them all, even* HELEN, *who for once in her life has become a mute outsider to passions which have gone beyond her ken. She continues with a tinge of reproach.*) Excitement again—excitement—I couldn't rest—

STELLA (*as no one else speaks*)—I'm sorry, Mother—

MRS. HALLAM (*in a feeble but inexorable voice as* MR. HALLAM *helps her to the Morris chair*)—Where did Jerry go—? (HELEN *and* ETTA *exchange glances of apprehension.*)

PAUL (*fencing for time*)—Jerry—?

MRS. HALLAM (*forestalling denial*)—Yes. He was down here. I heard him.—Why couldn't he come up to see his grandmother—after last night—(*She looks at* VICKIE, *inviting his championship.*) What is the matter with him? (VICTOR *remains silent.* STELLA *crosses to couch to get her coat. The old lady's eyes follow her. And all at once, she knows who is at the bottom of this trouble. Again she turns to* VICKIE *and commands him.*) Victor! I asked you something. What is wrong with Jerry now?

VICKIE (*after a pause full of conflict*)—Nothing wrong with him, Mom. Poor kid, he needs a break—that's all. (*As he speaks, he moves toward* STELLA, *and takes her coat and holds it for her. His hands rest for the space of a moment on her shoulders. This is a new gesture for* VICKIE, *implicit with the beginning of many things.*)

STELLA (*knowing and accepting all that he is trying to offer*)— Thank you, Vickie— (*Slowly, involuntarily, she lifts her hand to cover his, as the curtain falls.*)

THE DEVIL PASSES

A Comedy in Prologue and Three Acts

By Benn W. Levy

THE London censor refused to pass Benn Levy's "religious comedy," "The Devil," and still holds to that decision. The play was given a private performance at the Arts Theatre in London in January, 1930, and acquired shortly after by Arch Selwyn for America.

Mr. Selwyn recalled that a Molnar comedy bearing the same title had been much talked about in this country twenty odd years ago. Because of some copyright mix-up at that time this Molnar "Devil" was simultaneously produced by rival managers, George Arliss being the star of a Harrison Grey Fiske production and Henry E. Dixey heading a Shubert company.

For fear there would be confusion in the public mind Mr. Selwyn changed the title of the Levy play to "The Devil Passes." Two of the players in the London experiment were brought over with the play, Diana Wynyard to play the heroine and Ernest Thesinger for the rôle of Cosmo Penny, author. To give weight to the cast Arthur Byron, Robert Loraine, Basil Rathbone, Cecilia Loftus and Mary Nash were engaged.

There is no more than a light suggestion of fantasy in the playing of "The Devil Passes." The Prince of Darkness, in Mr. Levy's conceit, assumes the pleasing shape of a young curate passing through an English parish and pausing to expose the virtues rather than to stimulate the sins of certain muddled souls with whom he comes in contact. He is a reasonably likable young man, and his actions and reactions are at least ninety-five per cent normal.

As the curtain rises on the prologue of the play, the snap of an electric switch in the hall of D. C. Magnus' London apartment gives light enough to reveal the sitting-room as rather small and intimate and "packed tight with good things; especially pictures. A Goya, a Monet, a John are the most conspicuous. One or two fine Tang and Han figures are there also, and a majolica plate and a pretty Victorian sampler; so that we conclude that Mr. Magnus' tastes are a little fashionable as well as catholic and

Photo by White Studio, New York.

"THE DEVIL PASSES"

A week later, on a sunny Sunday afternoon, Nicholas Lucy and Paul Robinson are discovered "locked tight and immobile in each other's arms." It is an attitude so satisfying to them that they remain as they are "just long enough for us to be slightly embarrassed."

(Basil Rathbone and Diana Wynyard)

cultured."

Entering the room a second later are Mr. Magnus himself, "a large man in his early fifties, a fine looking fellow in an unorthodox way," and a girl. "Strongly individual she is, if a little self-consciously so. She carries a black sombrero and wears a stiff, heavy black cloth cloak that reaches almost to the ground. Her hair is straight and severe; she is very beautiful."

The girl comes in slowly, being held by the discovery of the treasures about her. She is quick to note an attractive Cézanne and she adores the Empire clock, even though it does remind her that there is such a thing as time to be considered. It was half after one when they left the Jevinsons.

"I got there just after ten," Magnus recalls, "met you at a quarter-past and began talking to you at half-past: so that you can calculate, if your arithmetic is up to it, that we chattered almost solidly for not less than three hours! Good God!"

"And apparently we haven't finished yet."

THE GIRL (*accepting a whiskey and soda*)—It's been rather an amazing evening, hasn't it?

MAGNUS—Why?

THE GIRL—Well, do you usually go to a party and spend the entire evening talking, talking, talking to someone you've never met before in your life?

MAGNUS—Sometimes.

THE GIRL—And do attractive young women frequently seek you out and devote their entire evening to you, as I did?

MAGNUS—As frequently as I let 'em.

THE GIRL—I suppose so. People are such snobs.

MAGNUS—You're not a snob, I think. So why did you?

THE GIRL—Seek you out?

MAGNUS—Yes.

THE GIRL—Partly because you're a celebrity, and I like celebrities, especially the less modish ones. I like them not for snobbish reasons, but because on the whole—though not always—they're more interesting than nonentities. Otherwise they'd *be* nonentities.

MAGNUS—The theory's all right. Still, for my quiet tastes, give me nonentities every time.

THE GIRL—That's mere inverted snobbery. In practice are your friends nonentities?

MAGNUS (*amused*)—No.

THE GIRL—Very well, then.

MAGNUS—Was fame my only attraction? Don't humiliate me so.

THE GIRL—No. I was interested by what I knew of you.

MAGNUS—Yet you've never read a line I've written?

THE GIRL (*smiling gently*)—No. That rankles, does it?

MAGNUS—No. It does an author good to meet an illiterate, say once a month.

THE GIRL—I'm extremely well read.

MAGNUS—I notice gaps in your reading.

THE GIRL—They shall be filled up. Don't forget, you're going to give me a copy of "The Distant Drum."

MAGNUS—I have it here. Read it, and you will be more interested in me than ever.

THE GIRL—Lawrence once told me that with the possible exception of Norton Douglas, you're the wickedest old scamp in Europe.

MAGNUS—I protest. He does me an injustice. I'll swear I'm wickeder than Douglas.

THE GIRL—You haven't told me yet why you were content to spend three hours with *me*. Was it simply your preference for nonentities?

MAGNUS—Not only that.

THE GIRL—Then what was the attraction?

MAGNUS (*teasing her*)—Physical.

THE GIRL—Of course: but only that?

MAGNUS—Othello liked Desdemona because she listened to him patiently while he showed off to her.

THE GIRL—Doesn't my brain or personality interest you at all?

MAGNUS—Very much. But it wouldn't if you were ugly.

THE GIRL (*good-humoredly*)—I see. Well, I suppose I should be satisfied with that.

Continuing revelations establish Magnus as a divorcee. "She was very good, and I was very wicked. So she left me." That is his explanation.

His chief surviving relative is his Aunt Laura Magnus, to whom he has dedicated a book. Aunt Laura is eighty-six, an invalid, has five thousand a year and he is her only living relative. She did not read the book, but the dedication so pleased her that she immediately altered her will in his favor.

Magnus does not feel that he sets too much store by money, as his visitor now charges, but he does hope that he has a proper respect for it. He lives by his writings. Fortunately the cinema has been better than fairly kind these last few years, so he can live well.

"Why can't somebody find a film magnate for me?" wonders the girl. "People shouldn't be selfish over such things. I'd be quite satisfied with even a share in one."

MAGNUS—Have *you* got any money?

THE GIRL—Not a penny.

MAGNUS—How do you live?

THE GIRL (*shrugs*)—Like a cat. Odds and ends. Anything that turns up.

MAGNUS—I thought you were some sort of an artist.

THE GIRL—So I am: some sort of a one. As a matter of fact I was rather promising. But I couldn't afford to study.

MAGNUS—And so?

THE GIRL—And so I do what I can.

MAGNUS—Don't you paint at all now?

THE GIRL—Oh, yes: a few scraps of commercial work. Occasional book-jackets, now and then a menu card for the Savoy, and so on. But I'm not too good at it.

MAGNUS—But that doesn't keep you?

THE GIRL—No: I sit occasionally too. (*He raises his eyebrows.*) I don't mind, really. I'm rather vain of my figure.

MAGNUS (*with a glance of disapproval at his own*)—Enviable state of mind!

THE GIRL—Then I get photographed in other people's furs and pearls for the advertisements. That brings in a bit. Then the Jevinsons are sweet to me. They're always putting odd jobs of work in my way when they can: and when they can't (*She grins.*) a good square meal. He even lets me work at his place sometimes. Backwash of the studios, a dear friend once called me. The description's as good as any other.

MAGNUS—What a dismal existence. How old are you?

THE GIRL—Twenty-four.

MAGNUS—Twenty-seven years younger than I. What's going to become of you?

THE GIRL—I make it a rule never to look more than a day ahead.

MAGNUS (*gravely*)—The wise virgin!

THE GIRL (*after a slight brooding pause*)—Do you think I am?

MAGNUS—What? Wise?

THE GIRL (*also gravely*)—No.

MAGNUS (*respectfully echoing her seriousness*)—At first I

wasn't sure. Now I think you are.

THE GIRL—People often ask me, but they never believe me
when I tell them. You're quite right.

MAGNUS—Miraculous!

THE GIRL (*laughing happily*)—I suppose you think it's foolish
of me?

MAGNUS—Very. Unless you lack the inclination.

THE GIRL—I wish to Heaven I did.

MAGNUS—Then why?

THE GIRL—Oh, a variety of reasons.

MAGNUS—Moral ones? Religious ones?

THE GIRL—Good Heavens, no. I see God as Hardy sees him:
an opponent who holds all the trumps in his hand, who loves to
tease you and trick you and bait you and make you caper for his
inane sardonic amusement.

MAGNUS (*shaking his head*)—It's not worth being bitter about.

THE GIRL—I'm not bitter. But if that's what God is, why
should I owe him anything? Why should I waste time trying to
be good? Well, I don't. I live *my* life, not his. And when
every now and again he drops a thunderbolt on me, I just scramble
on to my feet again as best I can, snap my fingers and trudge
along till the next one drops. I find that thunderbolts are less
painful if you treat them like that.

His visitor's philosophy reminds Magnus that he knows someone with a God pretty much like hers. He is the Vicar of
Magnus' parish in the country, and he is frankly bitter.

"He happens to have been struck by more than the usual
number of thunderbolts; one tragedy after another," explains
Magnus. "His first wife died of ptomaine poisoning on their
honeymoon; and his second wife didn't. Calamity affected him
that way, that's all. First he became an ordinary respectable
atheist. Then his atheism gave way to the need for some First
Cause that he could actively hate. He went half-mad really
and grew to hate God with a kind of maniac sincerity. It was
then that he took Holy Orders."

"How horrible! Why?"

"He wants to betray God. He thinks he can do it better as
a clergyman."

Strange as it may seem, this rebellious Vicar's parishioners
adore him; he is a fine preacher and a first-class theologian, and
because of the work he is doing his wife prays for him steadily
and is as content as circumstances permit.

The talk turns again to themselves, to that matter of the girl's unexpected inhibition, in view of her definite attitude toward God and life.

"It's difficult to explain," she admits. "Just as some people hoard up their money for their children, so I hoard up my—my purity for the man I shall fall in love with. It sounds rather romantic and high-school when you put it into words. And perhaps it is. (*She shrugs.*)

"Ah, take the cash and let the credit go," quotes Magnus.

"You're probably right. Do you do that?"

"I do," Magnus answers, with conviction. "That's why your sardonic, teasing God doesn't worry me. I don't know what he wants or what he doesn't want, what I *should* do or what I *shouldn't* do, what to expect or what not to expect, but I do know that Goya painted good pictures (*He jerks his head toward one.*) that Wren built good buildings, that Mozart made good music, that Cortot can play good music, that, though I may not have heard the heavenly angels sing, the Vatican choir is pretty good to go on with; that there are some very good books in this vale of tears, that there are good brains to wrestle happily with one's own, that friendship is good and laughter is good and women's kisses are good and color and form and sleep are good and food is good and drink is very good and life, life is good; and, for all I know to the contrary, so is death. In short, God has made me a very good universe. I couldn't have done it better myself."

His is the pagan's creed, charges the girl, which Magnus is content to admit. Now he is wondering whether or not she considers fifty-one a very ripe old age, and she has assured him that she does not; that, in fact, she does not care very much for young men.

Magnus has written inscriptions on the fly leaves of two of his books, that she may make a choice between them. It is then that he learns her name for the first time. Her parents had called her Elsie, but, refusing to believe she even looks like an Elsie, she had rechristened herself Paul—Paul Robinson.

"To my friend, Paul," then, is the inscription in the first book. And "A ma chere amie Paul" in the second. It is not necessary that she should make a hurried choice, Magnus suggests. Let her think it over. But Paul sees no reason for delay. She is sorry, but she thinks she will take the first book, simply as a friend.

"But it's not because I think you're too old," she is quick to add.

"My dear, you needn't excuse yourself!"

PAUL—Aren't you curious to know why?

MAGNUS—Why, I draw the obvious conclusion.

PAUL—Then you're wrong. I do like you enormously: yes, physically as well as mentally. And I love being with you. You're terribly companionable; and somehow—reassuring. And I love talking to you. But . . . (*She stops at a loss.*)

MAGNUS—But what?

PAUL—Upon my honor, I don't know. I'm probably being a fool and throwing away something good. But there it is. What you call my unexpected inhibition, I suppose. I'd better go. It's nearly two. Can I have my book?

MAGNUS—Yes. (*He hands it to her and then changes his mind.*) No, I'm going to write something else in it first. (*He turns to his desk.*)

PAUL—A poem? (*Unseen by her he takes a check-form from a drawer and begins to write.*)

MAGNUS—The loveliest in the world. (*She puts on her cloak and picks up her hat.*) You must promise not to read it till you get home.

PAUL—I promise. (*He blots the check, folds it in the fly-leaf and hands her the book.*)

MAGNUS (*after regarding her for a moment in friendly silence*)—Don't you ever put your hat *on?*

PAUL—Yes; but not this one, if I can possibly help it. It's a bit too big in the crown!

MAGNUS—It's a fine, gallant affair.

PAUL—I suppose you think that's another childishness?

MAGNUS—Well, there is something about a black sombrero that seems to—er—go to an artist's head.

PAUL (*offering her hand*)—Good night. (*The movement means putting book and hat into the same hand. The book falls. she picks it up; but the check is disclosed. She reads it slowly.*) That's a very large check.

MAGNUS—It's larger than I can afford.

PAUL—Have I by any chance got hold of the wrong book?

MAGNUS—I don't think so. Make sure.

PAUL (*reading*)—"To my friend Paul."

MAGNUS—The right book.

PAUL—Have we misunderstood each other?

MAGNUS—I don't think so.

PAUL—Then what's this for?

MAGNUS—For my friend Paul.

PAUL—For nothing at all?

MAGNUS—For over three delightful hours. This is precisely the kind of sentimental fatuity that you would expect from a man of fifty-one. Good night. (*He offers his hand.*)

PAUL (*taking it a little absent-mindedly*)—Good night. (*She goes slowly towards the door. And there she stops. Then making up her mind, she comes back deliberately, drops her cloak again and hands him the book.*) Please may I have the other copy?

MAGNUS—You've changed your mind?

PAUL—Yes.

MAGNUS—What made you?

PAUL—Your darling check. It nearly made me cry. (*He gives her a long, slow, wicked, friendly wink.*)

MAGNUS—It was meant to! (*The impudence of it nearly takes her breath away, but she manages, as a point of honor, to recover, and laughs back at him with a good humor and camaraderie equal to his own.*)

THE CURTAIN FALLS

ACT I

On a September evening about two months later, D. C. Magnus, clad in an old camel-hair dressing gown, is sleeping comfortably in one of the easiest chairs in the living-room of the converted farmhouse which is his cottage in the country. "This room is also well stocked with covetable possessions."

Paul Robinson, "dressed for dinner in a long-sleeved, long-skirted, long-bodiced, tight-fitting black velvet dress, high-necked at the back but cut low and square in front," brings in a letter with which she wakens Magnus by tapping him playfully on the nose with it. It is time for him to be dressing for dinner.

Magnus cannot dress until Dorothy Lister is finished with the bathroom. Dorothy and Louis, her husband, are friends of Paul's. She has known Louis for years, Dorothy for an hour. Dorothy is an actress; one of the best actresses, Magnus is willing to concede, and certain to be heard from.

Other guests include Cosmo Penny. Cosmo is a novelist, and a friend of Magnus'. A novelist one might naturally expect to write something rather precious, but whose work is, to the contrary, fairly solid; the style suggests Conrad more than anyone else. Cosmo, thinks Magnus, is the victim of a vicious circle—he is not successful because he lacks self-confidence and he lacks self-confidence because he is not successful. . . .

There is news in the mail that Magnus is opening. Aunt Laura is dead. And if Paul wants to enjoy the laugh she said she would have if Aunt Laura disappointed Magnus in her will, now is her time to laugh. Magnus has been cut off!

The news does not come as a surprise to Magnus, however. Aunt Laura had warned him. Either he had to give up Paul or he had to give up all hope of the legacy.

"Aunt Laura was old fashioned," he explained; "she disapproved of sin."

"Then why didn't you tell me? I should have left you."

"That's *why* I didn't tell you."

PAUL—But how did she know?
MAGNUS—I suppose somebody told her.
PAUL—Who?
MAGNUS—I don't know. Does it matter?
PAUL—It was Mrs. Messiter. I know she thinks we're living together.
MAGNUS—Does she? What a nasty-minded old lady!
PAUL—She can't stand me.
MAGNUS—She always seems very polite to you.
PAUL—Only because the Bible tells her to be polite to sinners.
MAGNUS—Anyway it wasn't Mrs. Messiter. She doesn't know my aunt. To think that an obscure Nonconformist charity should benefit to the tune of nearly one hundred thousand pounds from your immorality!
PAUL—But, darling, what are you going to do?
MAGNUS—Why, nothing. I haven't the chance now. Don't be so solemn about it.
PAUL—Had you the chance three weeks ago?
MAGNUS—Oh, yes, the old lady was fair. She suggested forcibly that I should give you up. She asked me whether I wouldn't rather become her sole legatee than remain a forsaken profligate. I thought it over very carefully, and finally decided that I would rather remain a forsaken profligate. (*She turns her eyes away for she is touched.*)
PAUL—Oh. D. C., you are a dear.
MAGNUS—Nothing of the kind. I wasn't thinking of you. I

simply asked myself quite selfishly which I wanted most, you or five thousand a year.

PAUL (*almost shyly*)—Wasn't there a—a third alternative?

MAGNUS—You mean I might have married you? (*She nods.*) I thought of that. To have suggested marriage when a legacy was at stake, but not before, struck me as rather a poor compliment to you.

PAUL—You're a very nice man.

MAGNUS—You mustn't say things like that; you'll destroy my reputation. By the way, *will* you marry me? Five thousand a year no longer stands between us.

PAUL (*when she recovers power of speech*)—Do you want me to?

MAGNUS—Very much, if *you* want to.

PAUL—You once said a married man was like a kite with a tail of lead.

MAGNUS—Did I ever make as bad an epigram as that?

PAUL—You meant it for more than a mere epigram. (*There is a silence while she looks about her strangely.*) When a girl's not married, marriage seems like a haven of rest and safety. I wonder what the haven seems like when you're in it.

MAGNUS—Well, are you inclined to try?

PAUL (*coming at length to a decision, she shakes her head*)—No, darling.

MAGNUS—Thank God!

PAUL—You took a risk.

MAGNUS—A very small risk. I trusted your intelligence.

PAUL—Still, you'd have had to go through with it.

MAGNUS—Worse things have happened to me than that.

PAUL—Why did you ask me?

MAGNUS—Politeness.

PAUL—I'm sorry, but you *are* a nice man.

MAGNUS—I tell you quite sincerely I'm nothing of the kind. I serve no one's interest but my own. The moment I cease to derive a childish pleasure from paying you that kind of compliment, I shall immediately discontinue the practice.

The guests are gathering for dinner. Dorothy Lister, Cosmo Penny and Louis Kisch, Dorothy's husband, are in. Dorothy is "an attractive woman of a not easily guessable age, though probably in her early thirties. Cosmo, who is rather less than that, is clearly a man who spends some pains and imagination on his appearance. . . . Kisch is an ugly little chap, with coarse, unruly hair, and a face either morose or beaming."

Paul has gone to mix the cocktails. Dorothy has fallen to wondering whether or not Paul is living with Magnus. True, as her husband reminds her, although Paul has been staying at the Magnus cottage two months, there have always been other guests in the house.

"You may be right," Dorothy admits. "Post-war morals are very strange. As far as I can gather people nowadays frequently go away together for a week-end and then forget why."

It appears that most people are convinced that Paul is straight, except a Mrs. Messiter, the wife of the rector. But Mrs. Messiter's opinion is not to be taken too seriously since they are agreed that she is censorious, smug, self-righteous, Pharisaical, dutiful and plain. In fine, Louis insists, Mrs. Messiter is a horrible woman.

Now Paul is back with the cocktails, and a moment later the Messiters arrive. "She is a prim, dowdy, middle-aged little woman; and he is a strange, maladroit man—perhaps slightly her junior—with an unconciliatory, fanatical eye."

The Messiters do not have too easy a time fitting in with the activities of the group. They are not interested in the cocktails, and when Cosmo brings out one of Louis Kisch's pictures Mrs. Messiter, who paints a little herself, is rather critical of that. She finds the left arm of the lady in the center of the picture certainly half a foot longer than the right, and the woman in front is, as Mrs. Messiter sees her, plainly knock-kneed.

Mr. Kisch explains amiably, that as everyone naturally has his preferences, his happens to be for women with abnormally long left arms. And as for the other lady, explains the artist, "Alas, she was born knock-kneed. And what God has joined together who am I to put asunder?"

Then Magnus comes down full of apologies for being late. He is quickly forgiven. The Messiters were probably a little early, Mrs. Messiter agrees, and, in any event, Mr. Lucy isn't there yet.

MAGNUS—Oh, no, I forgot. The famous new curate.

MRS. MESSITER—We were going to bring him with us, but he said he might have to be a minue or two late.

MESSITER (*smiling unamiably*)—He was finishing his sermon for tomorrow.

PAUL—D. C. has been exciting my curiosity about him.

MESSITER—How?

PAUL—Mainly by telling me nothing.

MESSITER—What a shame! And there is so much, too, to tell!

MAGNUS—So you continually say.

DOROTHY—But what can be so mysterious about a new curate?

MESSITER—Nothing, I assure you, Miss Lister. I merely happened to mention to D. C. that when Mr. Lucy climbed the pulpit to preach his first sermon a number of the congregation immediately rose and left the church.

MAGNUS—But you also refused to mention why.

DOROTHY—Was he drunk?

MESSITER—He was sober.

MRS. MESSITER—He's quite a nice young man really. Herbert, I don't think you should give the impression that he isn't.

MESSITER—I, my dear? Why, he's my very pride, the present joy of my life. I revel in him.

MAGNUS—That is precisely why I expect something eccentric.

DOROTHY—Let's guess. I say he's a chronic drunkard.

PAUL—I say he's a kind of "private secretary," complete with bath-bun and glass of milk.

COSMO—I say he's an escaped convict with pale blue ears. Louis?

LOUIS—I say— (*But the door opens and* ELLEN, *a maidservant, comes in.*)

ELLEN—The Reverend Nicholas Lucy. (*There is a pause, while* MESSITER, *almost leering, watches greedily for the effect that his new curate is about to make upon the company. Some of them catch a sight of him before his entrance and these are vaguely, faintly startled. But before we see the gentleman himself the curtain falls.*)

Dinner is over. In the living-room, sitting before the fire, Mrs. Messiter, Dorothy Lister and Paul Robinson are trying desperately to keep each other interested pending the arrival of the men, who are still talking in the dining-room.

Mrs. Messiter is full of idle community small talk, and both her listeners try politely to supply the queries expected of them. It is not until Mr. Lucy's name comes into the conversation that there is an awakening of interest. Dorothy is not at all sure that she likes Mr. Lucy, and Paul is quite positive in thinking the dinner dreadful. She is ready to pray that Magnus will not ask Mr. Lucy again.

"I really don't see that he did any harm to you," Mrs. Messiter objects.

"He didn't," admits Paul. "He just oppressed me. I don't know why."

Dorothy was also conscious of the oppression. And yet, it appears, it was nothing Mr. Lucy did. He hardly opened his mouth once.

Laughter from the dining-room indicates that the gentlemen are enjoying themselves. A moment later they have joined the ladies. Now the provocative Lucy comes into the group. Soon he is sitting "elegantly erect on a stiff, high-backed chair that he has set midway between the other six. He is a man of about thirty with clerical clothes exquisitely cut to encase his exquisite figure. His hands are beautiful; his features are lean, delicate, pallid and aquiline. But apart from the fact that the assurance and poise of his bearing are almost breathlessly fascinating to behold there is no very easily definable reason why he should have made the faintly discomforting impression that he did."

The conversation continues to swirl aimlessly around Mr. Lucy. Dorothy Lister, drawn out by Magnus, is telling of an outburst of temperament that made her ill. Cosmo is fencing a little heavily with Mrs. Messiter, who is still disturbed by the free speech of these professional friends. She has a feeling, too, that they are making fun of her, for which Cosmo is quick to offer apology.

Back to Dorothy's temperamental reactions the cause is disclosed as being her disappointment at losing her big opportunity Granville-Barker is to do "Macbeth" at Albert Hall and Dorothy might have had the rôle of Lady Macbeth if she were not bound by contract to an unpromising play called "Priscilla or Charybdis," which is not likely to run more than a fortnight at most.

Dorothy could chuck the "Priscilla or Charybdis" part, and would, even though the young author had written it especially for her. Dorothy is not sentimental. She is an artist. But she is bound hand and foot by her contract. A statement that inspires Messiter to applause.

"What I like about D. C.'s parties is the absence of hypocrisy," says Messiter. "All his friends are unprincipled on principle. That's so comfortable. . . . A circle of distinguished blackguards."

"Not blackguards, Messiter," corrects Magnus. "The modern term is realists."

Nicholas Lucy speaks for the first time. In a voice that "rich, deliberate and courteous" he suggests that they play the game of Truths.

"If we do I shall leave the room," insists Paul, who thinks Truths a hateful game.

MRS. MESSITER—Is this some new game?

DOROTHY—So new, Mrs. Messiter, that since the world began it has never really been played properly yet. And I love it.

COSMO—So do I. The most enchanting form of exhibitionism ever invented.

MESSITER—How is it played?

MAGNUS—It's not an easy game.

MRS. MESSITER—But somebody must explain.

NICHOLAS—It merely consists, Mrs. Messiter. in telling the truth.

MRS. MESSITER—Well, really, you know, that doesn't sound very difficult.

NICHOLAS—It will surprise you.

LOUIS—For example, Mrs. Messiter. If you had to go away tomorrow and spend a fortnight's honeymoon with one of the men present, not including your husband, which of us would you choose?

MRS. MESSITER—Well, really, Mr. Kisch; you see, that's so personal.

DOROTHY—Oh, no; not in the least.

MRS. MESSITER—Oh, I think it is, really.

MAGNUS—But personal questions are permissible.

COSMO—And you haven't answered, Mrs. Messiter. Which of us, now?

MRS. MESSITER—Well, you see, I haven't got to go away with one of you.

PAUL—But supposing you had.

MRS. MESSITER—But, you see, I never *would* have to.

PAUL—But just suppose.

MRS. MESSITER—Well, one can't really suppose a thing like that.

MESSITER (*dryly*)—Beatrice is trying to say that it's a very difficult question.

MRS. MESSITER—Supposing I ask Miss Robinson that question.

PAUL (*amiably*)—Then I should refuse to answer it.

NICHOLAS—Let us try.

PAUL—If it is clearly understood that I shall answer no awkward questions.

COSMO—No, I protest. There are a number of awkward, intimate and extremely impertinent questions that I particularly want to ask you.

PAUL—You'll be disappointed; the truth is much less romantic than your imagination.

COSMO—But I adore the sordid.

DOROTHY—Cosmo!

NICHOLAS—We will play it in a specialized form. Listen.

PAUL—Very well; but firelight only.

DOROTHY—Yes; Cosmo, the lights. (COSMO *turns out all lights save for a reading lamp. . . . Their faces are lit up with an orange topsy-turvy chiaroscuro from the fire.*)

NICHOLAS—We will all answer one question, the same question, in turn. A nice, comprehensive question.

DOROTHY—My teeth are chattering already.

NICHOLAS—Let us go from left to right. Mr. Kisch, we will begin with you. The truth, the dead truth, the whole truth, so help us all God. It is agreed?

MESSITER—Agreed.

DOROTHY—Agreed.

THE REST (*more or less simultaneously*)—Agreed.

Louis has little trouble answering Nicholas' first question, once it is sufficiently amplified so he understands it.

"What, above all else, is your innermost heart's desire?" Nicholas asks. "Or, by implication, what do you believe? If you had to sacrifice all your aspirations, which one would you sacrifice last?"

Louis, after puffing for a moment at his pipe, answers seriously.

"I want in the long run only one thing," he says. "I want to paint beautiful pictures. And then more beautiful pictures."

That, agrees Dorothy, is a true answer, and when it comes her turn, which is next, she tries to be equally truthful. Her want is the "most blatantly inglorious in the world." She wants to hear that special kind of music which is applause. She always has as long as she can remember.

"The greatest thrill of my life was the first time I heard a stranger in the street whisper, 'Look, that's Dorothy Lister!'" confesses Dorothy. "And it thrills me almost as much now To be talked about, read about, written about, listened to, looked at, to be important, noticed, applauded: there's my poor, miserable little heaven. Not very noble, but there you are. It's kind of incurable disease. That's why I've been literally sick and ill, physically ill like an angry child, about missing Macbeth."

Mr. Lucy thinks perhaps he will be able to help Dorothy. He read a little law before he took Holy Orders, and it is just possible he may find that Dorothy's contract is not water-tight.

Cosmo Penny is next. All his flippancy has departed as he announces his answer.

"I want clapping hands, too, though not for the same reason as Dorothy," says he. "I don't want it for it's own sake. I want it because I think the position of the Unsuccessful Author is a humiliating one. One is liable to become either what is known as a 'disappointed man,' a literary hanger-on, or a Micawber. The character of each strikes me as undignified to the point of nightmare. I want success mainly to rid me of my own doubts— doubts about my competence, I mean. My perpetual bogey is that my work is merely tripe, if I only knew it, and that the praises of my friends are merely charity, if I could only see through them. I believe if ever I were completely and permanently convinced that for all these years I have been taking myself with such ludicrous seriousness, but really have been more suitably, less laughably employed as a respectable insurance broker, I believe then that—from genuine shame, not for effectiveness—I should commit suicide. I quite realize that success is not a final criterion, but it's the most concrete and tangible one we have. That's why I want it. That's the bogey I want to get rid of."

Now Mrs. Messiter must state her heart's desire and she does so quickly and pridefully.

"I want what I confess I thought we all should have chosen. I just want to do my duty."

Now it is Paul's turn. She never moves her eyes from the fire as she answers.

"I—I want love," admits Paul. "Just like the kitchenmaid; her choice also, probably."

"And Dante's," Magnus reminds her.

PAUL—But I want the kind the kitchenmaid wants. That is to say the kind that probably doesn't exist.

MAGNUS—The kind that Dante wanted.

PAUL (*still gazing into the fire*)—D. C., you're an angel from Heaven.

DOROTHY—But you must have had it? You're grown-up and beautiful.

PAUL—Oh, I've had it in a way often enough: but never without a fly or several flies in the ointment. I have even had it once in a far—well, sweeter fashion than I deserve. (*She is sitting by* MAGNUS' *feet, and at this point, unseen by the others, presses one of them affectionately with her hand.*) But I want to lose myself completely and recklessly in some unfortunate man, and him to lose himself completely and recklessly in me. I want everything else and everyone else to become mere shadows. And I even want it to be wise and right for us to be like that, instead of foolish. I want no prosaic buts. I don't want reality to come poking its nose in in odd ways to jeer at us. I want circumstances to mold themselves easily to our love, and not our love to be modified and straight-jacketed by circumstances. In other words, I want the moon and the stars. I've finished. D. C., it's your turn.

MAGNUS—Mine? Well, I don't want to produce beauty, I don't want applause, I don't want recognition, I don't want idyllic love, and I certainly don't want to do my duty: though I quite appreciate the value of all these things. There happens to be something I want still more. I want to be comfortable.

DOROTHY—D. C., you're shirking. Play fair. The truth.

MAGNUS—On my honor. Heaven and earth may rot—they probably will. But provided that I don't, it won't worry me. In other words, I want to be comfortable. I, me, myself. I'm a professional egotist. If you, Dorothy dear, fell downstairs tomorrow and broke your neck, I shouldn't mind in the slightest—

DOROTHY—Oh, D. C.!

MAGNUS (*ignoring her*)—Except in so far as it would deprive me personally of the pleasure of your company. For your sake or for Louis' I shouldn't care a rap. For my own I should. Selfishness seems to me the one thing insisted upon by common sense. I repeat I want to be comfortable. I am an ignorant savage: every man is. And though I don't know what is before or behind or above or below or beside me, I do know that I have my senses. And I want them, therefore, to be utilized and satisfied to the greatest possible degree. I ask no more than to be a pig in clover. I repeat, I want to be comfortable.

When, at the last, it comes Mr. Messiter's turn, it is Mrs. Messiter who is the more concerned of the two. She wishes they would not ask Mr. Messiter. Truths is not a nice game for a minister. He might get excited, and—

Mr. Messiter will not be bullied, even politely, and he promises to try not to be violent. First of all, Mr. Messiter wants the living of St. Anthony's at Greenlake, whose encumbent, having but recently suffered a stroke, encumbers it no longer. St. Anthony's, Mr. Messiter is convinced, is a stepping stone to preferment. No less than four Archdeacons have been appointed from there in the last nine years. Secondly, Mr. Messiter wants his ambition satisfied, his gigantic ambition:

"I want to rise in the church, to rise and rise," declares Mr. Messiter, with something like hysteria. "I want to be one of its leading dignitaries, perhaps even its chief dignitary. Suppose, only suppose, that from that high pinnacle I could—expose God! (*He is carried away and speaking as if to himself.*) What a glorious, cracking, crashing exposure! The archbishop himself laughs and declares God to be the mad, malignant bully that he is. Wouldn't that set God's institutions tottering?"

Mrs. Messiter is showing visible signs of distress. Mr. Messiter should not say such things, she contends, even in fun.

Nicholas, however, is greatly interested. He thinks, perhaps, he may be able to help Mr. Messiter, too. It happens that Bishop Morris in whose diocese Greenlake falls, is his uncle. At Nicholas' suggestion the Bishop has expressed a desire to hear Mr. Messiter preach.

"It is possible he may come over and stay with me next week-end," says Mr. Lucy. "Shall I ask him?"

"Yes, ask him," Messiter replies, quietly.

Now they have all answered save Nicholas, and Paul is for stopping the game. She is, she admits, strangely afraid of what Mr. Lucy may say. But the others insist there shall be no exceptions.

"I—I must confess that I am something of a skeptic," Nicholas begins. "By temperament I am only able to believe what I see pushed immediately under my nose. I have no sense of the future or of the past: only of the present. I am no metaphysician: I can only believe in the one simple obvious reality. In short, I believe in God."

Cosmo—Possibly then you also believe in the Devil?

Nicholas—But certainly. The Devil, after all, is only God's advertising agent: the Devil's complete failure being proof of God's success.

Magnus—But what of the Devil's complete successes?

Nicholas—With all possible respect to the Devil, for whose skill and industry I have the sincerest admiration, I am forced to disclose a secret: he has had none.

Messiter—No complete successes? My dear Lucy, I protest,

you're discourteous. What about me?

NICHOLAS (*with deference*)—I am rebuked. I seem to have fallen into the pitfall of a generalization. (*Yet somehow the polite withdrawal is not convincing.*)

DOROTHY—But doesn't it beg the question to say you believe in God? Do we know what the word means? I don't.

PAUL—What do *you* mean by God?

NICHOLAS (*smiling faintly*)—You shall see.

THE CURTAIN FALLS

ACT II

A week later, on a sunny Sunday afternoon, Nicholas Lucy and Paul Robinson are discovered in the center of D. C. Magnus' living-room "locked tight and immobile in each other's arms." It is an attitude so satisfying to them that they remain as they are "just long enough for us to be slightly embarrassed." Then Paul, with evident reluctance, pushes Mr. Lucy from her. It is time, she says, for them to come back from heaven.

"I love you and I love you and I love you," Nicholas repeats, with ardor.

"It's not true. It couldn't be true," disbelieves Paul.

"Why, my heart? Why?"

"Because I love you too: so much, so much."

They must compose themselves, insists Paul. There are things that must be thought out, even though no one should come in. There is something that Nicholas will have to know: She has been living with Magnus. Not since she met Nicholas, but before. What does he think about that?

Nicholas is, of course, jealous. He is naturally greedy of Paul. But it makes no real difference to him. True, a Christian clergyman might think such a thing very dreadful, but—

"I didn't fall in love with a standard of morals," declares Nicholas. "I fell in love with Paul."

"And I fell in love with Nicholas," repeats Paul, feelingly.

"I suppose you loved him?"

"I supposed so, too, until I met you. D. C. and I walked: you and I fly. That's the difference."

"It was a big price to pay for a walk."

Still, Paul would not have Nicholas doubt the sincerity of her affection for Magnus. She was lonely when they met and Magnus was ideally companionable. "He's the dearest person in the world," she insists, and Nicholas understands.

They are still beaming upon each other when Magnus comes in. He has some papers in his hand and is looking for Cosmo Penny. Nicholas, however, will do for the moment. Magnus wants him to witness his signature.

Magnus is also interested in knowing how it is Nicholas is able to leave his uncle, the Bishop. It appears the Bishop is having tea with the Messiters. Messiter is in a pretty bad state of nerves. His preparations for his sermon on Sunday have taken a lot out of him. In this state he has decided that he will not permit any of his intimate friends to come into the church Sunday except Magnus. Not even Mrs. Messiter is to be admitted.

Nicholas has gone into the garden in search of Cosmo, and Magnus has taken up the matter of the papers with Paul. They represent a life settlement which he has been making upon her. He would like to have Louis Kisch serve as trustee, if Paul is satisfied.

Paul is visibly moved at any suggestion of settlement. She does not want a settlement, she insists, almost violently. She will not have a settlement. Nor is she being merely sentimental about it, as Magnus charges.

"It flatters my vanity to know that you are economically free to leave me tomorrow, and that you don't," he says with a touch of tenderness that adds to rather than takes from Paul's agitation. . . .

Nicholas has been seeking a meeting with Cosmo because he has wanted to talk with Cosmo about the prospect of his doing another book. Cosmo is not at all sanguine. Just now he is filling in with "sixpenny journalism; the higher criticism at the lower wages." The similarity of his prose style to that of Conrad's may be, as critics insist, quite remarkable, but "on the question of sales the dissimilarity between us remains equally curious."

Nicholas, it now appears, was a great friend of the late Joseph Conrad. So close a friend, in fact, that just before Conrad died he had sent to Nicholas an unpublished manuscript which he had written on a long holiday and of which no one, not even Mrs. Conrad, suspected the existence. Nicholas is in need of advice as to what should be done with this manuscript. He would like to have Cosmo read it that they may later confer. Cosmo is lightly curious about all the mystery, but takes the manuscript. . . .

Dorothy Lister has arrived without Louis Kisch. Louis has evidently missed another train. Nicholas also has good news for Dorothy. He has been looking over the contract she sent him and he thinks that, by taking advantage of Clause 7 in that document, she will be able to break it. At least it offers a loophole.

Dorothy is quite dumbfounded. Reading Clause 7 now it is perfectly plain that she can get out of her agreement, and the part of Lady Macbeth, she happens to know, is still open to her. But when it comes to hurrying off a letter to the management of "Priscilla or Charybdis" on the next post she hesitates. With all of Nicholas' assurance that she is amply protected against suit for breach of contract, and even though he personally agrees to pay damages that may be assessed against her, Dorothy still hesitates. After all, there is that misguided young author to be considered. Yes, and the rest of the cast, who would be thrown out of their jobs. On the other hand, there is an understudy who might take her place. And that wonderful chance in Macbeth—

Dorothy is at the desk writing the letter that will break her contract four days before the play's opening. Nicholas has obligingly agreed to send in the maid that the letter may be hurried to the post.

But when the maid arrives, though the letter is finished, Dorothy has come to a new decision.

She slowly tears the letter across twice and drops the pieces in the wastepaper basket as the curtain falls.

In the distance church bells can be heard. It is Sunday morning and in the Magnus living-room Cosmo Penny is just finishing the Conrad manuscript. Nicholas Lucy joins him from the garden.

Cosmo is enthusiastic about the Conrad story. "My considered opinion is that every other book he ever wrote, even 'Lord Jim,' seems literally amateurish by comparison," declares Cosmo.

Nicholas is pleased with Cosmo's reaction. He is also free to predict that one day Cosmo will write such a book. When he does, as Louis Kisch has said, all that he has written before will immediately be in great demand, and this will spur him to go on writing better books.

Furthermore Nicholas is possessed of an idea. Why should not Cosmo publish this Conrad manuscript under his own name?

"Are you stark, staring mad?" demands Cosmo.

"I don't think so, but I may not be the best judge," quietly answers Nicholas. "You seem surprised at my proposal."

Cosmo—Did you suppose it was precisely what I might have expected from a Christian priest?

Nicholas—But why not? Is it not for us to set the example of Christian charity, of helping as best we can all whom we may encounter by the wayside?

Cosmo—Of robbing Peter to pay Paul? Is that Christianity?

Nicholas—Pauline Christianity perhaps. But that is not what I am doing. Aren't you forgetting that Conrad is dead? How, therefore, could my friend possibly benefit by the publication of this book in his name?

Cosmo—His reputation can benefit.

Nicholas—His reputation! What do you imagine he cares for his reputation now? And you once chid Miss Lister for sentimentality! I confess, Mr. Penny, I had expected to find you more of a realist.

Cosmo—D. C. defined that as alternative term for a blackguard.

Nicholas—May I leave the term and withdraw the offense?

Cosmo—Your only offense lay in ever supposing that I would purloin another man's work, and therefore his royalties, at the expense of his legatees. Surely not even a realist would define that as a Christian act?

Nicholas—Don't you scuttle rather suddenly to Christianity for shelter as soon as your sentimental shibboleths are threatened with dispassionate examination? No doubt you will regard it as a cruel, heartless question if I ask you what possible moral claim an author's legatees can lay to his royalties. Did they do his work or did he?

Cosmo—Do his wishes constitute no claim?

Nicholas—None whatever. These legatees have a moral claim not to be left in poverty; but not because of his wishes: merely because they are human beings, and every human being has that moral claim. The question of poverty, however, does not enter into our case. It is simply a question of a few hundred pounds more or less. And do you seriously imagine that Joseph Conrad would not have bequeathed to you a few hundred pounds, had he known that your work and therefore English letters in general would benefit? Which after all is what we are assuming.

Cosmo—A rather handsome assumption.

Nicholas—That may or may not be. But even if we are wrong, how much harm will have been done?

Cosmo—Well, for a start I should probably find myself in jail for fraud. What guarantees have I against exposure?

NICHOLAS—Ah! (*He beams at him, then claps him gently on the shoulder.*) Spoken like a realist!

COSMO—Very likely, but that's not an answer.

NICHOLAS—Guarantees? How can you be exposed when nobody in the world save you and I know that this work exists?

COSMO—For all I know that may be a lie. Or alternatively when the thing is out you might doublecross me, blackmail me.

NICHOLAS—Which would involve me as an accomplice before the fact. Besides, I am a rich man, you are a poor one. But I can give you an even more concrete proof that I am telling you the truth. When could you come to my house?

COSMO—I suppose I could come tonight, or—

Mrs. Messiter, Dorothy and Paul have returned from a walk. Mrs. Messiter is greatly worried about what is happening in the church, and the worry has brought on her neuralgia. Mrs. Messiter is naturally anxious that the rector should succeed, and she is pleased that Nicholas is able to report the excellent impression Mr. Messiter has made on his uncle, the Bishop. But Mr. Messiter is not at all well, and— Well, Mrs. Messiter wishes Mr. Messiter could be satisfied with a small parish. She wants nothing for herself.

Nicholas is pleased to find Mrs. Messiter so forgetful of self. He knows another. Having found and pieced together the letter Dorothy did not send to her managers, Nicholas would compliment her also upon her sentimental consideration of others.

Dorothy not only resents Nicholas "nosing in other people's dust-bins," but would acquaint her friends with exactly what has happened. Nicholas, she tells them, has been urging her to take advantage of a paltry technical error in her agreement, at whatever cost to her associates, so that she might play Lady Macbeth. She is quite incensed at the thought now, and she is not sentimental.

Cosmo Penny, too, suffers a new burst of indignation in the light of Dorothy's experience. If Nicholas had any thought that he (Cosmo) ever intended using the Conrad manuscript he is vastly mistaken. Cosmo also insists on informing the other guests of the proposals that Nicholas had made.

"We must sometimes sacrifice others as well as ourselves in order to achieve what we believe to be right," declares Nicholas in explanation of his attitude. "Miss Lister, I understand, is a great artist. So also is Mr. Penny; even though at present he lacks due recognition. Is their art not worth some sacrifice? Besides Art, we are constantly told in this enlightened century, transcends mere Morality. It is the one point on which artists appear to be agreed. Art and Morals have nothing to do with each other. Isn't that the maxim? (*With irony.*) I seem to have heard it. For myself I should reply, then so much the worse for Art. But a priest must sometimes try and see the other man's point of view."

"You're a clever devil, aren't you?" sneers Dorothy.

"It's very kind of you, but I believe no cleverer than any other devil," calmly replies Nicholas.

Paul is the only one of the group who is willing to side with Nicholas against the "sentimental angels." Paul believes that Nicholas had the courage of Dorothy's and Cosmo's convictions. That is what rankles.

Now Magnus is back from early church service and visibly upset. Mrs. Messiter is quick to notice this and is hysterically apprehensive. Magnus tries to reassure Mrs. Messiter, but is frank to admit that something has happened.

In the garden doorway Messiter suddenly appears. He is hatless. His face is dead white, his eyes smoldering.

"Poor people, who were not at the church," he begins, with a slow, sardonic glance at his listeners. "They missed the Great Exhibition. They missed the fun. And all my fault. I would not let them come! . . . They shall have a special private performance."

Grinning repellently he has moved over to a chair which he mounts "and stands there a moment, his hands clasping his lapels, a lumbering, boorish figure." Again Mrs. Messiter would stop him, but he must go on.

"In the name of the Father, and of the Son, and of the Holy Ghost," he intones, quietly.

"Amen," responds Nicholas, calmly. "He is the only person present who is in no way discomfited."

"The twenty-first chapter of the gospel according to St. John," resumes Messiter, "the twenty-ninth verse: 'Jesus saith unto him, Thomas, because thou hast seen me thou hast believed; blessed are they that have not seen and yet have believed.' My friends, that verse refers, as you may remember, to the incident when our Lord appeared in person to Thomas after the Resurrection, because Thomas had found it hard to believe the story of the Resurrection at all as related to him by the other apostles."

Mrs. Messiter would cry out but he silences her abruptly.

"Now, according to the other three gospels not only Thomas

but his fellow apostles also were unable to believe in the Resurrection," continues Messiter, with mounting vehemence. "Now why does St. John's gospel differ from the others on this point? Surely it is because St. John claimed himself to be one of the apostles; Matthew, Mark and Luke did not—"

For John to have admitted that all twelve doubted would have been to include himself, runs the argument, and so John preferred to make Thomas the scapegoat. . . .

Again Mrs. Messiter cries out in an effort to stop her husband from further embarrassment, but he will not be stopped. The truly wonderful thing, he is reasoning, is not that the four chronicles should differ so much, but that they should differ so little. . . .

"Consider for a moment the four evangelists and their widely different temperaments and upbringing. St. John is the best educated and the strongest in argument and he, as we might expect, draws our Lord as a tireless and first-rate debater. Luke, the artist, the romantic, embellished his tale with every kind of literary fancy and displays the born story-teller's relish for all the miracles and parables. Matthew gives us a Jesus who is rough-tongued, combative, provocative; but Luke softens this portrait till certain sentimental Victorians were tempted to go yet a step farther and create the quite unwarrantable and, I think, uninspiring fiction of a 'Gentle Jesus, meek and mild.'"

"Oh, don't; please, stop, please," pleads Mrs. Messiter, whimpering pitiably.

MESSITER (*roughly*)—Stop sniveling, Beatrice. (*He says it without so much as looking at her, and continues in his earnest pulpit manner.*) My friends, ask yourselves could any other biography in the world, written by four such different men in such haphazard circumstances, exhibit so little inconsistency as this? Is not this reflection an incomparable support to us in our belief? But here is the question that I beg you earnestly to consider today. There are several kinds of belief. Which shall be yours? "Blessed are they that have not seen and yet have believed." We are told that seeing is believing. Yes, but such belief is too easy: it is faith in its lowest form. Ask yourselves, dear friends, each one of you, how far can you believe *without* seeing. There is the true test of your faith. (*His voice now rises in an infectious rhetorical crescendo.*) Can you believe without seeing, without seeing object, reason or cause? Can you see poverty, disease, misery, sin and death all about you and still believe that God is good, that God is omnipotent, that God is omnipresent? "Blessed are they that have not seen and yet have believed." (*Suddenly he stops dead. Not a sound is heard but* Mrs. Messiter's *whimpering. When he speaks again, still addressing himself to no one in particular, seeing no one, his speech is scarcely above a whisper.*) Then I heard a voice speaking and sounding—like *my* voice. It said: I don't believe. Do you hear? I don't believe. It's all fiddlededee. Fiddlededee. Rank fiddlededee. A malicious tale invented to enslave us. (*His voice rises again, but this time with something very like frenzy.*) "Behold, thy King cometh, sitting on an ass's colt." Well, I at least am not that ass's colt. Do you hear? And I won't be. Go on, God; strike me dead! You heard me: you heard me!

Mrs. Messiter—Herbert, Herbert: stop, please!

Messiter (*turning on her with a falsetto scream, the tears streaming down his face*)—Shut up! Shut up! Do you want to spoil the fun? Have you no sense of humor? Can't you see I'm the King's Jester, The King of Heaven's? Can't you let God's Fool cut his capers in peace? Can't you— (*But suddenly he interrupts himself, pressing his sleeve impetuously to his mouth. He moves not very steadily to the garden-door, of which the lower half only is closed. He leans over it, swaying slightly, and there* Magnus *goes to him.*)

Cosmo (*after a moment, to* Magnus)—Can I do anything?

Magnus (*preoccupied with* Messiter)—No, it's all right. He's just—he's just being sick. (Mrs. Messiter *still whimpers.*)

THE CURTAIN FALLS

ACT III

Next morning the week-end party is breaking up. Dorothy Lister and Cosmo Penny are in the living-room with their hand-bags. Magnus is at his desk going over his Monday letters.

"Well, D. C., many thanks for the week-end," calls Dorothy. "It's been simply horrible."

"It's been dreadful," echoes Cosmo.

"It has," agrees Magnus. "But you must blame the Prince of Darkness for that. He seems to bring his own atmosphere with him."

Mrs. Messiter has come to inquire pitifully about her husband. She is not at all surprised to learn that Mr. Messiter is quite himself again, after a long solid sleep. . . .

Magnus has gone to the station with Cosmo and Dorothy when Mr. Messiter comes down. "He is heavy-footed, dull-eyed. Almost he seems shrunken, like a pricked bladder. At his appearance Mrs. Messiter braces herself gallantly to a pathetic brightness, but her husband's eye only rests on her for a dull moment."

Mrs. Messiter chatters along cheerfully about a variety of trivial matters, the weather principally. Nor will she allow herself to be crushed by Mr. Messiter's doleful predictions as to what is most likely to happen to them. What if he should be kicked out of the church, as he is certain he will be, there are lots of ways of leading a useful holy life outside the church. What if he did, as he says, make an exhibition of himself—we're all human, we all make mistakes. Even St. Peter denied the Lord thrice.

"Peter did it for Peter's sake. I did it for God's sake," says Messiter. "I had nothing to gain. Can't you see? Your God tricked me. I was like a squib that went off too soon. And now he's laughing at me."

"Now, Herbert," she cautions, "you're not to get excited again."

He has sat down beside her and taken her hand, which he presses to his brow, and she, delighted, has drawn his head down onto her shoulder and is comforting him. What's done is done, she tells him, and it wasn't any of it really his fault. It was that creepy Mr. Lucy, Mrs. Messiter thinks. Ever since he has been there Mr. Messiter has been jumpy like.

"We'll find somewhere to go all right, and something to do," she promises, rocking him gently to and fro. "It'll be quite a —well, adventure, to start afresh. And, after all, you know I'm not so very old. (*She giggles.*) What is it they say? There's life in the old girl yet?"

She is still giggling when Mr. Lucy appears in the doorway, but the sight of the curate causes her to straighten up quickly and push Mr. Messiter's head back from her shoulder.

Nicholas' greeting is genial. He has come, he tells them, with a message. He has had a long talk with his uncle and his news will interest Mrs. Messiter, he thinks, even though Mr. Messiter insists he does not want to hear it.

"My news, quite briefly, is that you will not be remaining much longer in this parish," Nicholas continues, "and that your appointment to the parish of St. Anthony in Greenlake will be published very shortly."

"Is that—is that a dreadful joke?" demands Mrs. Messiter.

"It is a kind of joke, isn't it?" admits Nicholas. "I admire your sense of humor."

"What's your game?" demands Messiter, sullenly.

"Is it really so surprising?" smiles Nicholas. "I conclude that you are thinking of yesterday's sermon. We discussed that point, the Bishop and I, at some length. I presumed to call his attention to the moral of that unfortunate episode, as it presented itself to me. Here, I said, is a man who believes so strongly in God that he could not bear to pretend to believe in him when he didn't! How ardent, I said, must be the faith of a man who would rather destroy himself than affirm a faith that he did not hold. A man who would publicly proclaim his hate of God rather than achieve his own heart's desire, must love God well indeed. Such a man, I said, is surely a true servant of God, of his conscience, of his sense of right, of truth. My uncle is a wise old gentleman. The argument had already occurred to him. My advocacy was unnecessary. He would have decided on your appointment even without me." (*He smiles on them triumphantly.*)

Mr. Messiter is still unconvinced as he turns to go home. His glance is sullen and his manner mystified and grim as he demands:

"Who *are* you?"

"*I?* Why, just a poor devil striving to do his appointed work."

The Messiters are gone, Mrs. Messiter bustling and happy, Mr. Messiter with his arm about her shoulders, Mrs. Messiter calling a cheery "Good morning, Mr. Lucy" as they pass into the garden.

A moment later Paul Robinson has come into the room. She is buoyantly happy, and her happiness is echoed by Nicholas. They are, he feels, ideally in love and so thrilled in each other's arms, with their very blood singing for joy, that Nicholas finds it hard to understand why Paul suddenly should insist that all they have dreamed of being to each other can never be more than a dream.

"A short, silly dream," insists Paul, gravely. "I lay awake till five o'clock this morning thinking about it; crying most of the time."

"I don't understand."

"Don't you?" And then, after a pause, she adds: "D. C."

NICHOLAS—But he can't keep you if you want to come to me.

PAUL—Want to! (*She laughs harshly again.*) God, how I want to!

NICHOLAS—Well?

PAUL—But he wants *me*.

NICHOLAS—And don't I? I want to *marry* you.

PAUL—He offered to.

NICHOLAS—Then it's for you to choose. Is it so hard?

PAUL—He's made a big settlement on me: unconditionally. He sacrificed five thousand a year for me. He even offered to marry me. That's how much he wants me. How can I leave him flat?

NICHOLAS—Wouldn't I do as much?

PAUL—Yes, dear. And through him I met you. It's the old story: when it comes to the point, free love is bondage.

NICHOLAS—But listen: you love me.

PAUL—How I love you!

NICHOLAS—Then how could you bear to continue with him?

PAUL—I don't know how I shall. It will be hell. Poor D. C.

NICHOLAS—You shall not. (*He walks up and down the room, thinking. Then, his mind made up, he halts in front of her.*) Listen: the conviction has just crossed the back of my mind that you must act at once. You must speak to Magnus. (*She opens her mouth to speak, but he overbears her.*) No, hear what I say. We are faced with a simple problem in arithmetic: your happiness and mine against his; two to one. We each have forty or fifty years before us, he has twenty or twenty-five. Eighty years are just four times as important as twenty. You must tell him the truth: quite simply.

PAUL—I can't, I can't.

NICHOLAS—You spoke yesterday about realism.

PAUL—I should feel such a beast: ashamed for the rest of my life.

NICHOLAS—And proud if you prostituted yourself and me for a romantic scruple?

PAUL—It would hurt him so much, so much.

NICHOLAS—Do you think I love you?

PAUL—I never doubted it.

NICHOLAS—And do you love me? (*She merely laughs.*) Very well then; you must be strong.

PAUL—I can't, I can't.

NICHOLAS—Kiss me.

PAUL (*in terror*)—No! Don't touch me: I should give way.

NICHOLAS—Would you?   (*Overcoming her resistance, he kisses her.*) Say you will.

PAUL (*very low*)—I will.   (*He puts her hands to his lips reverently.*) Oh, darling, don't.

NICHOLAS—Today? This morning?

PAUL—Can't I have a little time?

NICHOLAS—It will only be the harder.

Now Magnus joins them. This is the time, thinks Nicholas, that Paul will want to tell Magnus of her plans. Once or twice she starts to speak and fails. Then, without looking at either of them she finds the courage.

"D. C., dear, I want to ask you something," she says. There is a long pause before she can go on. "Will you . . . I want you to take me away somewhere: to Sicily—or anywhere."

"Do you, indeed?" he answers, mildly surprised.

"I'd like to go as soon as possible," Paul goes on, a little confusedly. "I'd . . ."

She can say no more. Without raising her eyes from the ground she goes into the garden. It seems to Magnus that she is crying, and he can't quite understand.

Nicholas explains. Paul is in love with him, he says. He has asked her to marry him and she has said that she would like to. Whether she does or not depends on Magnus. Just now she was going to announce her engagement to Nicholas, when her courage failed her. It is possible that if Magnus would offer Paul her release—

But Magnus is no Sidney Carton. As a professional egotist self-denial is as much opposed to his temperament as to his principles. Nor would he permit Nicholas to call Paul back to make another plea, if he could help it.

Paul is constrained and plainly unhappy. She repeats her desire to get away, and she does not want to wait. It may be just a silly fit of nerves, but she is tired of everybody there and of herself.

"I only know I want to get away somewhere: just we two," she hurries on, without ever raising her eyes to look at him. "Travel if you like. I've never been anywhere. Perhaps it's just that I'm not really a sociable animal. We're all right together, you and I. I like that. I'm at my worst in crowds."

"That's a bad trait."

"Never mind whether it's good or bad. Just let's go."

For a moment Magnus silently paces the room. Then, having

arrived at a decision, "he takes a rather menacing stance in front of her."

"You're a disgusting little liar!" he says, sternly. "Why don't you tell the truth?"

PAUL—What on earth are you talking about?

MAGNUS—You know quite well what I'm talking about. I'm talking about your nasty affair with that scallawag of a parson.

PAUL (*controlling herself*)—So he told you, did he?

MAGNUS—Yes, *he* told me, as you hadn't the courage to. Love, he called it: I think that was his euphemism.

PAUL (*her temper rising too*)—And love it is. I meant to spare you, but now I'm not sorry. I didn't expect to be abused like a pickpocket.

MAGNUS—Perhaps you expected me to appreciate the joke? Meant to spare me! You should have thought of that earlier.

PAUL—Do you suppose we can control these things?

MAGNUS—I know tomcats can't control their passions.

PAUL (*in a fury*)—God, D. C.! (*Senseless with rage, she throws herself at him, but he catches her wrists.*)

MAGNUS—And I know tomcats can scratch. But you shan't scratch me. So that's why you heroically refused my offer of marriage, is it?

PAUL—Let go my wrists, you swine!

MAGNUS—Thank God, it was only a mistress who betrayed me and not a wife. That much is only according to the rules. (*He lets her go contemptuously.*)

PAUL (*nearly inarticulate with rage*)—Oh, if I could only betray you a thousand times a day!

MAGNUS—I don't doubt but that you've tried! Love! So you've found your kitchenmaid's dream at last, eh?

PAUL—Don't talk about love, you! You only understand adultery, prostitution.

MAGNUS—Very likely. Still I shan't ask for my money back. The settlement stands.

PAUL—Do you suppose I'll touch it?

MAGNUS—If Lucy lets you! Now be off. Ellen will help you pack.

PAUL—I've nothing to pack. It all belongs to you. Besides, you may find it useful later. (*Her whole frame shivering with temper, she goes to the door. Then suddenly she turns and looks at him. His back is towards her. Suddenly, unexpectedly, she 'bursts into peal upon peal of laughter, but the laughter is not far from tears. He stares at her in amazement.*)

MAGNUS (*at length*)—What's the matter with *you?* (*She does not stop.*) Stop that, for God's sake!

PAUL (*with a touch of hysteria*)—Dear D. C.! Dear D. C.!

MAGNUS—Now, what the devil?

PAUL (*between her laughter*)—You're a rotten actor, D. C.

MAGNUS—Have you gone raving mad?

PAUL—A rotten actor, a rotten actor!

MAGNUS—I haven't the faintest idea what you're talking about. Have you?

PAUL—You needn't keep it up any longer. I call your bluff. (*She goes to him gently with a smiling mouth but brimming eyes and takes his arm affectionately in her two hands.*) Fancy my being deceived for a moment! (*He throws off her hands roughly; but, unperturbed, she presses his arm to her again.*) Fancy my thinking that you genuinely meant all the harsh, vulgar, nightmare things you said! Forgive me, D. C.

MAGNUS (*less convincingly*)—I meant every one of them.

PAUL—Baby, baby! Give in, D. C. dear. Confess. (*He looks at her sullenly for a moment.*)

MAGNUS—I give in. (*She squeezes his arm fondly. She presses her cheek silently against his shoulder.*)

PAUL (*quietly*)—Why so elaborate, D. C.?

MAGNUS—I thought there might be some trouble in making you go otherwise. You're a good loyal little beast.

PAUL—There would have been.

MAGNUS—Secondly, the prospect of a scene of sentimental renunciation filled me with horror. And also it occurred to me that if I behaved like a novelette husband, you might have no remorse when you *had* gone.

PAUL (*when she can speak*)—You're just an angel; you're just an angel.

Their parting now is cheerful, even playful. Paul has re-iterated her love for Nicholas and Magnus, for all he thinks it damned silly, is content. Let her marry her parson, if she will. He will send Nicholas in to her and she can tell him.

Nicholas is neither surprised nor apparently excited by the news. Now that Paul is free to marry him he is ready to go away. He has work to do elsewhere. And he is not coming back.

There is a long silence. Paul finally finds her voice, though now it is a strangely shrill voice.

"But—aren't you going to marry me?" she asks.

"Young lady, look at me," he answers, without feeling. "Do I look like a marrying man?"

PAUL (*suffocating*)—But you—you *asked* me to marry you.

NICHOLAS—Did I? Very likely. (*Then as if in explanation.*) You see, I have my work to do.

PAUL—Work? I don't know what you're saying. What work?

NICHOLAS—God's work.

PAUL—Were you doing—God's work when you asked me to marry you? (*His slight shrug again.*)

NICHOLAS—God moves in a mysterious way his wonders to perform.

PAUL (*wildly*)—But there was no point! It was just—pointless, pointless cruelty!

NICHOLAS—In time to come, when you are cooler, you will see the point.

PAUL (*screaming*)—Then you admit it! It was all humbug. All your love, all humbug.

NICHOLAS (*imperturbable*)—All humbug.

PAUL—Oh, you're—you're . . . (*But a fit of violent sobbing interrupts her.*) You're wicked, wicked! Can't you see? You're the wickedest man in the world! You care for nothing at all except your God.

NICHOLAS—For nothing else at all. Is that wicked?

PAUL—For your wicked God! I see it all now. (*Hysterically.*) You must be the Devil himself, do you hear! The Devil himself! You look like him! You wanted Dorothy to ruin that poor young author, you wanted Cosmo to steal a dead man's work, and me to betray D. C. and D. C. to imprison me, and Messiter to profit by a blasphemous hypocrisy.

NICHOLAS (*quite unemotionally, almost inhumanly*)—Yes; and you all thought you could do it. I offered you all what you thought you wanted most in the world. But you found you had made a mistake. You found to your surprise and humiliation that you all wanted to serve God more. You set your poor, little silly-clever selves up against God and thought you could get away with it. I merely showed you that you couldn't. That is my work.

PAUL (*still sobbing bitterly*)—If there were a God, he wouldn't let you draw another breath.

NICHOLAS (*continuing smoothly*)—When you are told that God is omnipotent, it merely means that in the long run he has you all on the end of a string. He may hold some on a longer, looser string than the others, but the string is there, always there. It is a mistake to strain at it: it only hurts. That much I think I have been able to demonstrate. A circle of distinguished blackguards, Messiter said. Poor little blackguards! Mrs. Messiter's is the only wise head among you. That, you see, is the point, the whole point. Mrs. Messiter's is the only wise head among you.

PAUL (*breaking out again*)—I say your God is a cruel, malicious God!

NICHOLAS—That is what people always say when they pull too hard against the string.

PAUL—Has he no pity, no compassion?

NICHOLAS—Certainly not. He is not a person. What vanity is it that tempts you to invest him with your own little human attributes?

PAUL (*banging her fists madly against the desk she has been crying on*)—I tell you my heart is broken: broken, do you hear? Does it mean nothing to you?

NICHOLAS—Nothing: less than nothing. Every little tinpot philosopher has been able to see that fame and money are blind alleys; but it took a Plato to discover that so also is beauty; and a Jesus of Nazareth to point out that personal love is a mere wasteful, distracting nuisance.

PAUL (*crying wearily*)—My heart is broken, my heart is broken!

NICHOLAS (*unmoved*)—A broken heart. How grotesquely trivial! Think what I have given you instead; a vision of God, a vision of God. No less. (*For a little while longer she cries. He takes no heed. Presently her tears grow less. At last she collects herself.*)

PAUL—Is that . . . I suppose that's really all you have to say.

NICHOLAS—Isn't it a great deal? (*She moves about the room, while her composure returns. In front of the mirror she halts.*)

PAUL (*very nearly achieving the normal tone of her voice*)— My nose is all swollen with crying.

NICHOLAS—Your eyes are a little bit pink too.

PAUL—Yes, I think I'll go and bathe them in cold water.

NICHOLAS—Warm water is better.

PAUL—I suppose we shan't meet again.

NICHOLAS—Not if you're lucky.

PAUL—Good-by. (*And then—for she has the soul of a gentleman—she goes to him and offers her hand.*)

NICHOLAS (*taking it*)—Good-by.

PAUL (*not too easily*)—I hope your—work prospers.

NICHOLAS—Do you say that—in malice or in earnest?

PAUL (*ever so slightly reluctant*)—I'm not quite sure. I believe—in earnest.

NICHOLAS—I'm glad.

PAUL—Good-by.

NICHOLAS—Good-by. (*Then as she goes out.*) Remember, *warm* water.

Nicholas Lucy, his face utterly without expression, takes up his hat and is about to leave when Louis Kisch comes in at the door, carrying a suitcase and an overcoat. He is, Louis fears, a little late, having been expected Friday. But Nicholas is glad he came. There is a little matter he has been wanting to talk to Louis about.

"Do you remember last week-end we played a silly game called Truths?"

"I do."

"Do you remember also declaring yourself that your one desire in life was to create beauty?"

"I do."

"I have been thinking about that; and frankly the idea *has* just flitted across the back of my mind that . . . Now how exactly shall I put it? (*But before he can put it any way the curtain has hidden them both from sight.*)

CYNARA

A Drama in Prologue, Three Acts and an Epilogue

By H. M. Harwood and R. Gore-Browne

ONE of the comparatively few imported dramas to achieve a
definite popularity in the New York theatre during the early
season of 1931-32 was "Cynara," adapted from a novel by
R. Gore-Browne called "An Imperfect Lover," and put into play
form by H. M. Harwood and Mr. Browne.

In London, the summer of 1930, "Cynara" achieved a similar
popularity when played by Gerald Du Maurier and Gladys
Cooper. In America the cast was headed by Philip Merivale,
the English actor whose recent successes have been earned this
side the Atlantic, and Phœbe Foster.

The play restored a note of sentimental romance to a theatre
that has for several seasons last passed been rather completely
wedded to a less attractive realism. This undoubtedly accounts
in part for its success. In structure and content "Cynara" falls
into familiar and conventional grooves. Peopled with interesting
humans who have also acquired ease and skill in the actors' job
it becomes an always interesting and frequently moving romance.
Its theme is taken from Ernest Dowson's poem bearing the
lengthy Latin title, "Non Sum Qualis Eram Bonæ Sub Regno
Cynaræ."

"Cynara" starts with a prologue. The Warlocks, Jim and
Clemency, are out on the balcony of a private suite in a Capri
hotel. It is August and fearfully hot. Clemency, an attractive
wife in semi-negligee, has been trying to doze off. Jim, a handsome fellow in old gray flannels and a tennis shirt, in his middle
thirties, is sitting on the stone balustrade alternately gazing out
over the blue sea and observing his pretty wife.

They might, the authors are agreed, represent a honeymoon
couple in these idyllic surroundings, save for the fact that there
is noticeably a sense of strain in their conversation. Jim
moves about restlessly. Clemency, when she opens her eyes,
talks pleasantly and naturally enough but—"You get the impression that both are talking from fear of silence rather than
because they have anything to say. They talk as one talks to

335

the sick, as though afraid of uncovering a tender place."

Jim finds it hot and difficult to sleep. Clemency is ready to move on to Switzerland, or any other place that Jim wants to go. Even back to London. But Jim doesn't want that.

Jim could, if he liked, consider a Tanganyika offer from an old friend of his named Tring, but he knows the place is being offered him, not because he is the man for it, but rather from a sense of loyalty and friendship. Still, if there were nothing else—

CLEMENCY—You're sure that it's absolutely over—at home? There wouldn't be any chance?

JIM—None; and I don't want to try. I don't want that kind of life any more. It was all right—with you—but—

CLEMENCY—You mean—?

JIM (*he leans over and just touches her hand*)—It won't work. You know that—it's not your fault. It was good of you to try.

CLEMENCY—You mean—I can't help you?

JIM—There's only one way to help me. And you can't do that. You've been terribly good. Don't think I'm not grateful. But it isn't any use.

CLEMENCY—Jim, if I could only understand—

JIM—I know.

CLEMENCY—Jim, if you could *tell me* something more! You've never really told me. I have to imagine everything. And that's much worse.

JIM—What do you want to know? You heard all the facts.

CLEMENCY—Just that it happened. That's all. What happened to *you?* That's what I want to know. Inside you, I mean. Mightn't it help you, too—to talk about it?

JIM—Modern psychology?

CLEMENCY—Yes—two thousand years or so. Don't, if you don't want to.

JIM—I don't mind.

CLEMENCY—Suppose I hadn't gone away? (*He shrugs his shoulders.*) When did it start?

JIM—The night you left—in a way.

CLEMENCY—The same night?

JIM—That began it. You remember when I came up to your room and found Merton packing? You'd asked Tring to dine and hadn't put him off. I didn't want him—alone at home. We went to Soho, a place he knew. I thought I was in for a damned dull evening. (*Laughs.*) If you hadn't gone that particular

"CYNARA"

Jim: I warned you. We knew it couldn't last. You knew that from the beginning.
Doris: Yes, I know. I'm cheating.

(Philip Merivale and Adrianne Allen)

night—that's what I keep wondering—what would have happened then? Is the whole thing just chance? Doesn't it matter *what* we do ourselves? I dream of it every night— (*The lights begin to fade.*) coming into your room, seeing Merton and the luggage and Gorla. I go through the whole business over and over. I wake up with that man's voice in my ears—

The scene fades out.

As the lights come on we are in Clemency Warlock's bedroom in Montagu Square. It is the evening of the 19th of the previous May. It is an attractive bedroom, the walls and curtains done in silver gray. There are suitcases about and a bit of hurried packing going on by Merton, Mrs. Warlock's maid.

Warlock, home from the office, is surprised and a little irritated when he finds that his wife and her sister, Gorla, are planning to catch the eight o'clock train from Fenchurch Street. They are on their way to Paris, and then to Aix, Merton explains. She thought Mrs. Warlock had telephoned.

Gorla, dressed for traveling, a lively and attractive young woman of twenty-two, shortly proves a better source of information. Clemency, insists Gorla, is responsible for the whole thing. Gorla is being saved again. For herself, she had much rather not be saved. She would much prefer to carry out her original plan of going to Paris for a week-end with Tristram Stone, the aviator. But Clemency will not have it.

How did the Tristram affair come up? Well, according to Gorla, Tristram, being a parachutist, and engaged in a film called "The Price of Passion," had jumped from his cockpit to escape a mad baron and landed in the pig-sty on the Kentish estate. Gorla had fallen in love with Tristram immediately.

"I don't know where you get it from," sighs Jim.

"No," frankly agrees Gorla, "Clemency would never do that."

JIM—I should hope not.

GORLA—Well, that's all right for you, isn't it? Lucky I've got all the bad blood in the family. You like safety, don't you?

JIM—Safety! And this—acrobat—! Does he want to marry you?

GORLA—Oh, no. Nothing of that sort.

JIM—What does he want?

GORLA—Well—Jim—

JIM—Why doesn't he want to?

GORLA—Three reasons—a wife and twins.

JIM—Twins! Good God! Haven't you any sense of humor?

GORLA—I don't think twins are funny. I haven't got a music-hall mind. No one thought Romulus and Remus particularly funny. I'm awfully sorry, for your sake, Jim.

JIM—Sorry!

GORLA—Yes, really. I can see that it's a frightful bore for you having your well-ordered existence broken into. It's entirely Clemency's fault—being stuffy and elder-sisterly, and all that. Like a fool I promised always to tell her whenever I felt like doing anything drastic—what she calls drastic. It would have been far less trouble for me to have gone off quietly—as I wanted; but I'd promised, and so I rang her up. She made me come up here. And now I've promised to wait a month.

Tristram, to Jim, is obviously a swine. Nor can he see why Gorla can't find someone decent and marry him. But Gorla does not want to marry. If they would just stop agonizing about her virtue and let her go on such an experience—she might come back a perfect paragon, "a female version of the Albert Memorial."

It is all right for Clemency and Jim to be staid and happy— if they are happy—but Gorla believes in at least keeping her soul alive.

"I'm not such a fool as you think," she insists. "I don't think love affairs are the only things in life."

"They seem to occupy a good deal of your attention," Jim reminds her.

"Only because other people make them difficult—butting in. And anyhow, sex is important."

Of course, a man of Jim's type could never understand that, agrees Gorla, although she is convinced that if she did not know him so well she might find him quite interesting. As for Jim's boast of contentment and happiness in his marriage, Gorla doesn't quite see how he can be so sure. He has never put his happiness to the test.

When Clemency comes, dressed for her journey, she is anxious that Jim should understand that everything had to be decided at once, even over Gorla's protest. There was nothing else to do. And after Gorla goes, still protesting that if they think Aix can wash away love they are silly, Clemency reveals her further plans. Clemency knows Gorla. In a few weeks she will have forgotten all about her aviator and probably have settled on someone else.

"If Gorla wants to behave like Pauline Bonaparte, I should let her," Jim insists, peevishly. "How you come to have a sister like that I don't know. Besides, it is all talk. Probably she wouldn't do anything at all."

"She would," declares Clemency. "She has natural bad taste in men, and she thinks this sort of thing romantic and interesting."

Hearing Gorla's opinion of them from Jim—that they are "sunk in slothful comfort and complacency"—Clemency is suddenly also a little anxious about Jim.

"I've never been away for four weeks before, have I?" she asks. "Never," solemnly answers Jim.

CLEMENCY—Perhaps it'll be a good thing for you, Jim. You must seize the opportunity.

JIM—Opportunity? For what?

CLEMENCY—Oh, I don't know. Whatever husbands do when they're left in London. One always hears about grass widowers.

JIM—Widows.

CLEMENCY—Isn't there any chance of your coming out?

JIM—In term? Not a hope. What time is this damned train?

CLEMENCY—Eight o'clock.

JIM—Why Fenchurch Street?

CLEMENCY—I wanted to go tonight. It's the best way.

JIM—Why won't tomorrow do?

CLEMENCY—She'd change her mind. It'll be a filthy journey, but we'll get the day in Paris. Don't come to the station.

JIM—Oh, yes.

CLEMENCY—No, it'll make you cross. You hate stations. Besides, you're dining with John Tring, or rather he's dining with you.

JIM—Why is he?

CLEMENCY—Don't you remember—he was coming here? I didn't put him off. I thought he'd be company for you.

JIM—I don't want him.

CLEMENCY—Oh, yes. He's an amusing old thing, and he knew your father. You can try the 1908 Cockburn. It's quite ready.

JIM—I don't think I want to dine here alone with old Tring.

CLEMENCY—Well, go out somewhere. Be boys together. But Mrs. Woods has got quite a nice dinner for you.

JIM—I won't be pacified with food and drink—blast and damn! (*He throws on the bed a package which he has been holding in his hand.*)

CLEMENCY—What's that, Jim? (*She picks it up.*) What's

this?

JIM—Nothing that matters.

CLEMENCY—It's a box. Why, it's from Dows! What is it? Can I open it?

JIM (*sulkily*)—If you like.

CLEMENCY—Jim! It's jade—oh! For me?

JIM—It was. You've forgotten, I suppose.

CLEMENCY—Tomorrow? Of course I hadn't. It's maddening. I cried a little.

JIM—I'd got the corner table at the Berkeley—the same one.

CLEMENCY (*holding him*)—It's too maddening!

JIM—Don't go. Let her take her chance.

CLEMENCY—No. We mustn't. I do feel responsible.

JIM—Rot! Your father's responsible, if anyone is. Why doesn't he look after her?

CLEMENCY—He would—if she were a sow.

JIM—I can fix this fellow all right. He won't trouble us.

CLEMENCY—That's no good. Gorla has to be diverted. You can't extinguish her.

JIM—Well—my God! If she's like that—!

CLEMENCY—You're fond of her, Jim. You don't want her to do something she'd be sorry for.

JIM—Would she?

CLEMENCY—Of course. She doesn't understand. I feel I *must* help. I've been so lucky.

JIM—Lucky?

CLEMENCY—With you.

JIM—Ordinary decency.

CLEMENCY—You think that, because you're like that.

JIM—Gorla thinks I'm a dull dog. (*She laughs.*) I daresay. I've got work to do. I've no time to be temperamental. All this sex business. Tiresome nonsense. If she'd get a job of work—

Merton has come to call Clemency. There isn't much time, and the chauffeur thinks the traffic may be heavy.

Jim has decided to go out to dinner after all. He can't spend the evening at home listening to Tring prosing. As a final warning, Gorla considers Clemency quite courageous in trusting Jim. "Suppose he goes bad on you?" she says. "I should hate anyone to trust me as much as that."

But Clemency is sure of Jim. "Go out and see people," is her last word of advice to her husband.

"I'm waiting until you've gone to ring up all the people I

know," he warns.

"Yes, do, darling." Clemency has followed Gorla out. The cutain falls.

A few hours later Jim Warlock and his friend, John Tring, a man some years Jim's senior but secretly reluctant to acknowledge either his age or its handicaps, are at dinner in a small Italian restaurant in Soho. They are seated at a table in a half booth at back, near the end of the dining-room.

The restaurant, run by a genial, portly Italian named Joseph, is at the moment sparsely filled, though voices may be heard from adjoining wings. A young American and a French girl are just finishing their supper in another booth and contemplating with some eagerness the evening's adventures to follow.

The restaurant has been Tring's choice. It is not well known, which is fortunate. "When they get known, up go prices and down goes cooking," sententiously remarks Tring. "Dress clothes have been the death of dining."

The conversation has turned to marriage. It has been seven years for Jim and Clemency.

"Jacob and Leah! Then Rachel!" mutters Tring, ruminatively. "Good ideas those fellows had! They say our bodies are entirely renewed every seven years. . . . Concentration is the secret of life. Never mix your wines or your women. Polygamy should be consecutive, not contemporaneous. . . . Change, variety, as often as you like, but not at the same time. No man can serve two mistresses!"

Tring is off on a flood of memories. "Dear dead women," he quotes, "with such hair, too. What's become of all the gold that used to hang and brush their bosoms?"

Jim is not responsive. The American and the French girl have paid their reckoning and hurried on. Two shop girls, Doris Lea and Milly Miles, have taken the vacated table. They are attractive girls in their early twenties and dressed with such becoming smartness as to catch the eye of Tring. None of his "dear dead ladies" was turned out as these girls are. Nor would they have been found in a restaurant in Soho unescorted twenty years ago. "They'd have been going home to high tea with mother," admits Tring, "and wearing feather boas."

"The dark one's nice looking," casually ventures Jim. But he disapproves quickly of Tring's suggestion that the young women be asked to join them.

"No, no, you can't do that," protests Jim. "They're respectable girls—"

"Call no woman respectable until she's dead," soberly counters
Tring. "Death is the supreme achievement of respectability.
Temperance—modesty—chastity—Death! England's contribu-
tion to modern morality. Shades of Drake and Hawkins!"

"Well, what's your cardinal virtue?"

"Courage! That's what makes these girls admirable. There's
nothing between them and poverty but the next week's wages.
No security but their own health and energy—and they're not
afraid. They're gay and light-hearted because they're independent. Respectable? By God, yes! It would do you good
to meet them!"

Doris and Milly are in the midst of a light debate concerning
a boy who suggests nothing half so much to Doris as "a bolster
and a bowler hat." To prove a point she has, at Milly's daring,
reached over to the hatrack in the corner and taken Jim's bowler
hat. Putting it on she makes what Tring is pleased to remark,
a charming picture. Doris is slightly flustered at the discovery
of the hat's owner so close at hand, and is free with her apologies.

The friendship flourishes. With some hesitancy on the part
of Jim and Doris, and a little maneuvering on the part of Tring
and Milly, the girls are finally prevailed upon to share a bowl
of peaches with their new friends, after Tring's formal assurance
of his and Jim's innocence.

"We're immensely respectable," says Tring. "My friend is a
barrister."

"Oh, and what are you?" Milly wants to know.

"I, my dear, am an old man. . . . Tring is my name. This is
Mr. Warlock."

Coffee is ordered. And brandies for the men. Acquaintance
ripens slowly. Particularly between Doris and Jim.

"Mr. Warlock has to acclimatize himself. These surrounding
are strange to him," explains Tring.

DORIS—You don't come here regularly?

JIM—This is the first time.

DORIS—Where do you go generally?

JIM—Oh, different places. I'm usually at home, working.

TRING—Don't be afraid, Warlock. We'll make allowance
for your plutocratic weaknesses.—He goes to the Ritz and the
Berkeley, and so forth!

DORIS—Oh, those places? Why do you come here, then?

TRING—I brought him. We're celebrating his grass-widowe

hood.

DORIS—Oh, you're married? (JIM *nods.*) Been married long?

JIM—Seven years.

MILLY—Coming up for air soon, I suppose?

TRING—No—he's not amphibious.

MILLY—What's that? Left-handed? (JOSEPH *brings in the coffee and the brandy and withdraws.*)

TRING—Amphibians lead a double life—air and water. Mr. Warlock is definitely a deep-sea monster.

DORIS—You do go on, don't you? I met another married man last week—

TRING—Yes—it's epidemic.

DORIS—He said his wife didn't understand him.

MILLY—Said she was cold, I suppose? They always say that.

DORIS—Does your wife understand you?

JIM—I shouldn't wonder. I'm very easy.

DORIS—Any kids?

JIM—No.

MILLY (*to* TRING)—She's soppy about kids!

TRING—A very laudable enthusiasm.

MILLY—That's all right for you, I daresay. A fat lot of good to girls like us!

DORIS—I wouldn't like to be married. Fancy telling anyone whatever you did! I had a fiancé once, but I gave him the bird!

JIM—Why?

DORIS—Oh, well, I hate meanness, don't you? I had to buy my own chocolates at the pictures! And then there were parcels. If I asked him to carry a parcel he got ever so mad. I don't think a man who can't carry a parcel is much use, do you?

JIM— I suppose not.

TRING—Obviously no good at all!

DORIS—You're a barrister, aren't you? Where do you work?

JIM—At Chambers and at the Law Courts.

It further transpires that Doris and Milly are manikins; that they are employed by Mme. Ducette who can supply Rue de la Paix models at half price; that they live together in Farmer's Green, twenty-five minutes by tube; that Doris' people are dead. As people, Doris adds, they were all right, but not to live with.

Near the door Milly and Tring have found a gambling machine and Milly, with one shilling, has won a handful of shillings.

She refuses to keep the money, however. It was Tring's shilling, and therefore the winnings are his. The girls will not even stay to help spend the money.

Besides, Doris and Milly are due at the Plaza to see Lily Damita in a picture. And they cannot accept company because two boys are to meet them there. Tring is the only one of the four who is confident that they will all meet again. To him it has already been arranged. They will meet at Farmer's Green.

The girls are doubtful, but interested in the suggestion. Especially Doris. Not until they are gone does Tring explain.

It appears that a nephew of Tring's has Parliamentary ambitions and that Farmer's Green is in his district. He has given a swimming bath to the district and there are to be dedicatory exercises the following Saturday week. The nephew happens to be in a nursing home, and has prevailed upon his Uncle John to take charge of the ceremonies and make the dedicatory speech.

This is a job that Tring purposes to turn over to Jim. Being a barrister Warlock is used to public speaking and could do it handsomely. Especially now that there are these new friends to consider—

"What about Miss Doris Lea?" demands Tring, despite Jim's laughing denials. "It's a bond, undoubtedly. Don't despise coincidence. An hour ago you'd never heard of Farmer's Green. Now, from two entirely different points of the compass it swims into your ken. Obviously you must get to know the place better. Probably our friends will be there. She will see you in your glory—and what a charming girl! You had a success there!"

JIM—Rot!

TRING—But she is charming, isn't she? The other one's got the brains, but your Doris has emotion.

JIM—My Doris!

TRING—I speak comparatively. And what a lovely figure. Don't you think so?

JIM—I didn't notice.

TRING—I begin to fear that you are destined for the Bench.

JIM—She seemed intelligent, but it's difficult to talk to girls like that. There's no common ground—

TRING—No common ground? God, man! there's the earth on which we live! (*He calls.*) Joseph! No common ground? A girl with a figure like that? You're an amazing fellow. (JOSEPH *appears.*) Joseph, two more Armagnacs.

JIM—No, no, no—!

TRING—Yes, yes! You really need it!
The curtain falls.

Ten days later the Public Baths at Farmer's Green are officially opened with a bathing beauty contest. On this side of the pool there are four dressing rooms and a small ante-room letting into the pool. In the ante-room several of the contestants are gathered in their bathing suits when Mr. Boot, the organizing secretary, ushers in the committee to meet the Chairman, Mr. Tring.

John Tring and Jim Warlock arrive a moment later and are duly presented. The exercises are to be brief, it is explained. The Chairman will make the usual opening remarks, followed by a song by Mrs. Councillor Apted, who has chosen "Good-by, You Daffodils" as her number. The beauty parade, a purely local affair, will follow around the edge of the pool. Mr. Warlock will then give his decision and present the winning lady with the prize—"a silver 'aypern'."

Jim is somewhat taken by surprise to find himself a judge of the beauty contest as well as the principal speaker. He has, he feels, no talent for the job. Mr. Tring is much better qualified—

But the committee has already been taken by the tireless Mr. Boots to the seats awarded them. Jim is holding back, hoping to learn some facts about Farmer's Green with which to point his speech, when one of the dressing-room doors opens and Doris Lea appears.

Doris is wearing the bathing costume of a contestant with a wrap thrown across her shoulders. She is greatly surprised to meet Mr. Warlock again, and made laughingly nervous by the further announcement that he is to be the judge of the beauties. She hopes he likes her suit. She hopes he will give her the prize. Jim, joining in the laugh, warns Doris that he cannot be bribed.

Now Jim has been furnished with information dating back to the days when Farmer's Green was no more than a green field and there were buses every twenty minutes to a tube station two miles away. Today there is a bus to Charing Cross every four minutes and a population of twelve thousand, half of whom are blessed with telephones and at least two thousand with radio sets. . . .

Now the girls are lined up for the grand entrée. None of this group is eager to go first, so Milly nobly takes that place. The others follow after, several being advised by their mothers as to how to put their best attractions forward.

"Keep your stomach in, dearie, and walk easy from the hips,"

Mrs. Day warns daughter Olive.

Doris is the last in line, and, according to Mr. Boot, an easy winner. Mrs. Day is not convinced.

"A deal too thin, to my mind," ventures she. "In my day a man wouldn't have turned round to look at a girl like that."

A moment later the voice of Speaker Warlock can be heard from the pool. "With so much beauty it is difficult to judge," he is saying; "but I award the prize to the young lady on the extreme right, in the black and green dress."

"The winner of the competition is Miss Doris Lea!" announces Mr. Boot. . . . "Will Miss Lea please come forward?"

There is a slight wait followed by the crash of falling chairs. In a moment echoes of a confusing accident are heard. Mr. Boot is urging the crowd please to keep its seats. A moment later he holds open the door and Jim Warlock, supporting a limp and pale Doris Lea, comes through.

Helped to a chair Doris is all apologies and Warlock all anxiety. Her ankle has been turned, but so far as Jim's hurried examination can tell there are no broken bones. Milly has run in, a little cross that Doris should have been so clumsy.

Now how is Doris to get home? Jim is considerably concerned about that too, and John Tring shares the agitation.

TRING—I hope she isn't badly hurt?

JIM—No. But I'm wondering how she is going to get home.

TRING—That's easy. Take her in your car. I'll go by tube.

DORIS—Oh, no, I couldn't.

TRING—Yes, yes, certainly! Beauty in distress.

JIM—We couldn't all get in?

TRING—Not with the epergne. You mustn't leave that behind!

MILLY (*appearing in the doorway*)—All right, Mr. Warlock, I'll get a taxi.

JIM—That's all right. (*To* DORIS.) I'll drive you home. You get your clothes on. I shan't be long.

DORIS—Thanks ever so. It is kind of you—

BOOT (*appearing at the swing-doors*)—We're waiting for you, Mr. Warlock. (JIM *and* TRING *follow him out of sight.*)

MILLY—Dorrie, we don't want to bother him. I'll get a taxi.

DORIS—But you're meeting Fred at five.

MILLY—He can wait.

DORIS—No, no—why should you? I shall be all right.

MILLY—And what about the stairs?

DORIS—I daresay Mr. Warlock will help me.

MILLY—I daresay he will. Is the old man going?

DORIS—No, it's a two-seater. I saw it come up. It's lovely—black and yellow. I do think it's kind of him!

MILLY—Kind of him? Soppy little fool! I know his sort.

DORIS—I don't know what you mean! He said I really won. He said he couldn't help himself!

MILLY—I shouldn't wonder. They often can't.

The curtain falls.

About three weeks later, the evening of Derby Day, Doris Lea lets herself into her modest flat in Farmer's Green and turns on a light. "The room is neither very tidy nor very comfortable; the furnishing and decoration nondescript." Jim Warlock is standing in the doorway. Field glasses are slung across his shoulder.

Jim is surprised to find no one there. Milly, he was quite sure, would be there to meet them and ready to give him another going over. Jim feels that he is not at all popular with Milly. She has spent a good part of the time at the races warning him off Doris, which Doris rather resents. Doris feels that she is quite able to take care of herself.

This, Doris is happily agreed, has been a perfect day. That she has won a bundle of notes on a forty-to-one shot adds something, but not much. A Gypsy fortune teller told her she was going to be happy. Money is nice to have, of course. But it isn't happiness. . . .

Jim thinks perhaps he had better be going. He knows Doris must be tired and—well—he'd better be going. For one thing, he has left the taxi-man waiting and if he sends him away now, as Doris suggests, it is sure to create a wrong impression. Even that does not discourage Doris. She should care what a taxi-man thinks!

Besides, how can Doris believe that Jim has had a good day, or that he doesn't think her flat both common and sordid, if he won't stay a bit? Why is it he is always so eager to leave her? Why is he so worried about what Milly might think? Doris can look after herself, if she has to—and she hasn't had to, particularly, tonight.

"You mean I haven't tried to kiss you?" suggests Jim, bluntly. "You probably haven't wanted to."

"I didn't want to spoil it. We've had such a good day."

"Of course, if that's the way you feel about it—"

"No, but—if I did that Milly would be right."

"I think it's a pity we lost her, if you think so much of her opinion."

"Now you're being thoroughly naughty. It isn't that I don't want to."

"Well, *how* does one know?"

Jim, on the defensive, cites the awarding of the bathing beauty prize as one sign of his regard. If he started citing others it would take him too long. Perhaps he had better send the taxi away—but he can't stay more than ten minutes at most. Not even if the tube does run until twelve o'clock! . . .

Doris has found a bottle of whiskey, some water and a couple of glasses by the time Jim gets back. He doesn't want a drink, though he is willing to take one to be sociable. His thought is not on the drink, however. Or on Doris. A lot of things are rushing through his mind.

Presently his serious mood breaks through Doris' reserve. What is wrong with him? Or with her? Does he think she has the plague? Why, feeling as he does, did he come after her in the first place? Why did he let her know where he was to be so they could meet?

Jim is puzzled by this attack. He had made no appointment to meet Doris. He was as much surprised as she when she and Milly walked in. It must have been Tring who arranged that. Tring, the old scoundrel!

Now, Doris, still in temper and almost in tears, is insisting that Jim shall take the bank notes which are his winnings, and his hat, and go. It is all spoilt, now. Everything is spoilt.

"I thought you had planned it all," she is saying, between suppressed sobs, as his arms go around her. "I thought you'd meant me to come. That you wanted me."

"I did want you," protests Jim. "If I'd thought of it—"

Doris (*shaking her head*)—No, no. It's not the same. You must have hated seeing us there. Such a bore for you.

Jim—Damned nonsense! (*He shakes her.*)

Doris—I'm so ashamed.

Jim—For God's sake, be sensible. I didn't know you were coming. I never thought about it. God knows why Tring did it. But I'm damned glad he did. I was delighted when you turned up, and I've had the best day I've ever had in my life. There! (*He kisses her, not passionately, but he holds her still in his arms.*) Now I'm off.

Doris (*not moving*)—Not yet.

JIM—Yes, yes.

DORIS (*under her breath*)—Just a minute. Only a minute. (*She looks up at him.*) It hasn't spoiled it, has it? (*He shakes his head. She lifts herself toward him, and kisses him. He gently disengages himself.*)

JIM—Doris, I must go. (*She doesn't move.*) You must let me go.

DORIS—Do you want to?

JIM—I must. Can't you see? It isn't fair.

DORIS—To your wife?

JIM—To you. I'm no good to you. It couldn't last.

DORIS—That's my lookout.

JIM—No, it isn't. It's mine. You don't know what you're doing. I do.

DORIS—How do you know I don't?

JIM—Of course you don't.

DORIS (*slowly*)—You mean—you're afraid—of being the first? (*Pause.*) You needn't be afraid. You wouldn't be.

JIM—What!

DORIS—I suppose I'm a fool to tell you. It was years ago. I was seventeen. I'd just started work. There was a man, not very old, about thirty. He used to take me out to restaurants and theatres—stalls. He was quite rich. There didn't seem any harm in it. Then one day he told me what he wanted. I'd never dreamt of anything like that. I was green then, if you like. He'd always been so respectful. I told him I couldn't, really, and then he cried.

JIM—And you were sorry for him?

DORIS—I thought perhaps it didn't matter much. I don't think it does. Do you?—if you're fond of anyone? But you've got to be—both of you—fond. That's what I found. I felt dreadful after. I thought I'd have a baby, and have to tell Aunt Maud. I was living with her then.

JIM—And what happened—to him?

DORIS—Oh, I told him I couldn't ever see him again. I couldn't have, either. So, you see, I'm quite a bad girl, really. I suppose I oughtn't to have told you. You won't like me any more now.

JIM—My dear!

DORIS—I expect you hate me for it. Milly says you shouldn't ever tell men things like that.

JIM—And since then, haven't you met anyone—anyone you cared for?

Doris—No. There are the boys I go out with, to dances and pictures, but I don't really care for them. They're common really. I haven't let anyone kiss me since I was engaged. I haven't wanted to. So, you see, you needn't be so particular. I've always dreamed of someone like you. (*Low.*) And you needn't be afraid. I shouldn't ever be a nuisance. I'd go away whenever you told me. You do like me, don't you?

Jim—Too much.

Doris—No, no. Not too much. You mustn't say that. You mustn't. (*He suddenly takes her in his arms and kisses her passionately. There is a long pause, and she draws her head back and looks at him.*) Darling! Darling!

The scene fades out.

Ten days later, in the garden of a country inn near London, Jim Warlock and Doris Lea are finishing dinner at a table under a plane tree. Only the light over the table softens the surrounding darkness, save for the faint lights in a couple of windows of the hotel some fifty yards away.

It is not cold, but Doris is worried for Jim. She thinks she had better fetch his coat. Her solicitude amuses him. Still, Doris insists, he might catch cold—and she couldn't even come and nurse him. She would not like to have him really ill, as he suspects. But, if he were just a little ill, and she could be with him, she wouldn't mind.

"Women are morbid," insists Jim. ". . . They'd rather have a sick man in the house than a healthy one out of it."

Doris (*kissing his hand*)—Oh, I wish time would stop sometimes.

Jim—All right if you can choose your own time.

Doris—I'd choose now. Nothing better than this can happen. I'll always remember this place.

Jim—It's lovely, isn't it?

Doris—I've never liked the country before. It frightens me rather.

Jim—Little cockney.

Doris—But I like it with you.

Jim—A month out of London would do you all the good in the world. You ought to take a holiday.

Doris—I'd love to. Where'd we go?

Jim—I? I can't do that sort of thing, I've got to work.

Doris—I wouldn't go without you. (*Pause.*) Must we go

back tomorrow?

JIM—Afraid so.

DORIS—Not another night? Oh, wouldn't that be lovely? Can we come next week?

JIM—Next week? Well, I'm not sure about that.

DORIS—Do let's.

JIM—I'm not sure how I shall be fixed.

DORIS (*after a pause*)—Do you mean your wife will be back?

JIM—She's a week overdue now.

DORIS—Jim! You won't stop seeing me, will you? You won't? I couldn't bear it.

JIM—Naturally, it won't be so easy.

DORIS—You mean we won't be able to go away together?

JIM—Certainly not that, I'm afraid.

DORIS—But you will see me? (*There is no answer.*) You must. You couldn't do that.

JIM (*slowly*)—My dear, you know I told you.—I warned you, didn't I?

DORIS—I know, but that was different.—That was before.

JIM—Nothing's altered, you know.

DORIS—Oh, yes. Everything's different now. I love you so much more. I couldn't get on without you now. (*Violently.*) I'd rather die.

JIM—Don't talk like that, it's silly.

DORIS—But I would. Why should it make any difference? It isn't as if you loved her.

JIM—But I do, Doris. I've told you.

DORIS—You can't. Not like this. If you did, you wouldn't be here—would you?

JIM—Yes. That sounds simple enough.

DORIS—What's she like? Is she very lovely?

JIM—I think so.

DORIS—Prettier than me?

JIM—It's different—quite different.

DORIS—She can't love you like I do. If she did, she wouldn't have gone away.

JIM—You don't understand. Don't you see, it's all part of me, my life with her?

DORIS—But I'm part of you, too. I am, aren't I?

JIM—Of course.

DORIS—The best part?

JIM—In one way—yes—the last of my youth—adventure—romance.

Doris—You'll never be sorry, will you?
Jim—No.
Doris—Promise? (*He nods.*) I'll never be sorry either; whatever happens. I want you to remember that. This is what the Gypsy meant. She said I'd be happy while it lasted, and I have.

The servant has come to clear the things and ask what time Madame wishes to be called in the morning. The wedding ring on Doris' hand has not been worn in vain. The servant's "Madame" proves that. It makes Doris feel very grown up.

It is time for them to go in, but for a little Doris must linger in the shadows to take her leave of the garden.

"I wonder if it knows?" she muses. "The garden? The house? All of it. I wonder if it knows that people come here to be happy? I should think it must."

"Funny child."

"I always think places *must* know, and be glad when people come again. I felt yesterday that it knew us again and was glad we'd come back. It must be dreadful for it when people don't come back. It must wonder what has happened."

"Don't, Doris," protests Jim, rising suddenly.

"Jim!"

"You make it feel like a charnel house," he adds, violently.

"Jim!"

"Darling, I'm sorry! I didn't mean that."

They have drifted into the darkness. Trailing back Doris' voice can be heard.

"We'll come back, won't we?" she is asking, pleadingly, as the curtain falls.

A week later Clemency Warlock's bedroom in Montagu Square is littered with half-unpacked suitcases and odd garments. Clemency herself is in the bath and calling through the door to her sister Gorla that she is about to emerge.

Jim Warlock is up from the drawing-room where he has been talking to Gorla's newest intended, a young man named Joe she had met at Aix and in whom at the moment she is terribly interested. Gorla is grateful now that Jim had taken the stand he did about Tristram, the aviator.

"It's terrible fun being engaged," confesses Gorla. "If I'd gone to Paris with Tristram it wouldn't have been nearly such fun now, would it? You were so terribly right about that, darling, and I thought you such a sop! . . . I'm a changed woman, Jim; I'm simply devoted to the idea of matrimony. I want Joe and me to be just like you and Clemency—'The world forgetting by the world forgot.' I do hope Joe won't say anything to upset me about it. (*Gets up.*) Anyhow, thank you ever so for letting Clemency take me. I know now how hellish it must have been for you. Joe will never let me go off for six weeks—at least, I hope he won't. (*Going to* CLEMENCY.) Good night, darling, and thank you a thousand times for everything."

Gorla has gone and Jim and Clemency are alone. It was easy to steer Gorla into safe waters once Joe appeared on the scene at Aix, Clemency reports. But she did have to stay the extra week not to spoil it. And now, what about Jim? What has he been doing? Has Mrs. Woods looked after him all right? Has he seen anyone interesting? Not that Clemency expects to hear everything at once—but—

Also, there is one common task that he has overlooked. He has forgotton to kiss her. That, Jim is quick to deny. He had kissed her at the station.

"At the station?" repeats Clemency, with a significant pause. "Oh, well! How do you think I'm looking?"

"Lovely—as always."

"No, no. Same old face, same old wife," smiles Clemency, taking Jim's hand and holding it against her cheek.

For a second Jim's hand rests affectionately against Clemency's face, but he does not kiss her. When he speaks it is to inquire what sort of fellow it is that Gorla has taken on. Joe, Clemency reports, was a Rugby international. He is "British and reliable." And that is what one wants in a husband.

"Does Gorla want that?" demands Jim.

"Every woman does," Clemency answers, quickly. "Reliability—that's the husband's long suit. The Colman-Menjou business is all very well, but not for marriage. Life would be simply hell if you couldn't trust a man. Every time he went out, wondering where he was going—and how many of your friends knew? Suppose you couldn't trust me?"

"You?"

CLEMENCY—Yes. Supposing you didn't really believe me about Aix. That you thought it wasn't really Gorla at all who kept me there?

JIM—That never occurred to me.

CLEMENCY—Exactly. That's where you're lucky—where we're

both lucky—perhaps. You probably don't even think that I have any chances.

Jim—Chances?

Clemency—Yes. Of affairs—little romances.

Jim—Do you know, I never thought about it.

Clemency—It's disgusting of you. And all conceit.

Jim—Would you like me not to trust you?

Clemency—No, but I don't want you to think that I couldn't if I wanted to. As a matter of fact, I could have lots of dishonorable proposals if I wanted them. That's where you're so maddeningly right. I don't want them, and so they don't happen. As a matter of fact, I did have one at Aix.

Jim—What?

Clemency—There! You see.

Jim—Who was it?

Clemency—An Italian officer.

Jim—Oh! Italian. That's automatic.

Clemency—Don't be rude. He liked me.

Jim—I'm sure he did.

Clemency—And he was divinely beautiful. And said the most wonderful things.

Jim—Well, why didn't you?

Clemency—Jim! You don't really think I could. (*Looks at him.*) What's the matter?

Jim—Why do you want to talk of all this? It's not us, all that sort of thing.

Clemency—I was only joking.

Jim—I know.

Clemency—Sometimes I wonder. *Ought* one to be so sure? (*The telephone by the bedside rings.*) Who on earth is that, at this time of night?

Jim (*at the telephone*)—Yes, who is it?—Mr. Warlock speaking. Oh, it's you.—Yes, it's me.—Where are you speaking from? Well, what is it?—No, I told you—I'll let you know—I can't be sure.—No, that's impossible. Yes, tonight—going to turn in, yes.—Good night.

Jim's voice is noticeably irritable as he explains that the telephone call was only from someone in Chelsea. There is to be a party and someone wants to know if he is going! . . .

Now Jim has decided that there are many letters that have to be written. He hurries toward his dressing-room. Clemency is at some loss to understand his attitude as she slowly crosses

the room, switches off the lights and gets into bed. Only the bed
light is burning when Jim returns rather soberly to warn her from
the doorway that there is something that she ought to be told.
Something rather important. Which sets Clemency's voice shaking a little, as she suggests that perhaps it can wait until the
next day.

"It's about those copper shares I bought for you," Jim admits,
finally, as Clemency stares blankly at him. "Moxon rang up
after you'd gone and said that—"

But Clemency has burst into laughter.

CLEMENCY—Oh, Jim, you ass!

JIM—Why?

CLEMENCY—What did you frighten me for?

JIM—Frighten you?

CLEMENCY—I thought it was something really important.

JIM—Well, they've gone to one-and-fourpence.

CLEMENCY—I don't care if they're a ha'penny. Really!
(*She is half laughing and half crying. He comes over to her and
puts his hand on her shoulder.*)

JIM—Well, I must say. You're tired—better go to sleep
now.

CLEMENCY—I'm not tired. (*She draws down his head and
kisses him.*)

JIM (*slowly withdrawing himself*)—Yes, you are. If you're
not, you ought to be. Got everything you want? (*He tucks
her in, full of care and kindness, and everything is at the moment
of no particular use to her. She remains motionless, following
him with her eyes.*) There. I won't wake you tomorrow. Have
your sleep out. (*He kisses her gently and goes to his room,
closing the door.*)

Two days later, in Kensington Gardens, Jim Warlock is waiting
impatiently on a park bench. It has been raining. The collar of
his light raincoat is turned up and a soft hat is pulled over his
eyes. Presently he rises, looks at his watch, and starts down the
path.

A second later Doris Lea rushes in. She is out of breath and
pretty wet. She had had some trouble getting away from the
shop and a crowded bus had forced her to ride on top. But she
doesn't mind. If Jim can come home with her she will soon be
in dry clothes. Fortunately Milly has gone out.

Jim cannot do that. He has another engagement, as he had told her on the telephone. Which reminds him Doris must never call him at his house again. That is too dangerous.

Doris is all apologies, but she had not seen him for three days and was terribly anxious. When can they go on another week-end? Doris will not go for a holiday by herself, as he suggests. She couldn't afford it for one thing. She has just been sacked at Ducette's. She was making too many mistakes. Couldn't keep her mind on her work. Couldn't keep her mind on anything but Jim. Why can't they go on as they were before? *She* needn't know. And nothing that she doesn't know can hurt her. They don't have to go out. They can meet in Doris' flat—

"Other people do it," Doris concludes, earnestly.

"Lies. All the time, lies," mutters Jim.

"If you loved me, you wouldn't mind. You can't give me up, Jim. You can't."

"I warned you. You knew it couldn't last. You knew that from the beginning."

"Yes, I know. I'm cheating."

"You know what you said yourself?"

"That I'd go away when you wanted?" Doris remembers that. "I'd have said anything then. Oh, God! What am I to do? Do you mean I'm not to see you again? Ever?"

"No, no," quickly protests Jim. "I don't mean that. But it can't be the same. Of course we'll meet again."

Jim can't say just when he can arrange another meeting. Not for a day or two, anyway. Perhaps Wednesday. He'll try to make it Wednesday—

DORIS— . . . Aren't you going to kiss me? There's no one here. (*He kisses her rather hurriedly.*) You'll have forgotten all about me in half an hour. I wish I'd never gone to that restaurant, then we wouldn't have met. No, that isn't true. It's been worth it. It has, hasn't it?

JIM—It's been wonderful. I'll never forget you, Doris.

DORIS—Do you remember the Gypsy? She said I'd be happy while my luck lasted. And I was, indeed I was.

JIM—You'll be happy again.

DORIS—And lucky when my happiness went, she said. I wonder what she meant. (*She looks him in the face.*) It's gone now, all right. (*She turns and hurries away.* JIM *stands looking after her as the lights fade out.*)

CYNARA

The following Thursday Jim and Clemency Warlock are in the Warlock library. It is shortly before dinner. They are to dine with John Tring at Claridge's, but neither is dressed. They are just back from a walk through the park. Clemency had gone to meet Jim at his chambers and walked home with him.

There are several minor questions to be answered. Will they or will they not go to Constance's for a week-end? Will Clemency wear her jade green, or her new fringed white dress she got in Paris? And where will they go in August, after Term?

Clemency would like to find some place that is really quiet. She knows that Jim is tired. He has not been very nice to her since she came home from Aix. She still regrets that she had not asked him about going. She knows, as he says, that asking was not necessary. But she is that kind of wife. Anything her husband does not want her to do Clemency finds no joy in doing.

"I'm a modern woman, Jim," she confesses. "If I'm given my head I keep looking for the bridle."

John Tring has arrived ahead of time. Clemency goes to dress. Jim is finishing up a note or two at the desk. The talk turns to recent experiences. Tring knows that Jim has been seeing a good deal of Doris Lea. Tring has seen Milly Miles! And Milly has had plenty to say.

Now Jim would ask his friend's advice. Tring has, in his time, had his serious love affairs. And they have come to an end.

"Did you ever leave someone whom you still wanted, and who wanted you?" Jim asks.

"Indeed, yes!"

JIM—Well, why did you do it?

TRING—Why not? There are more reasons for leaving someone you want than there are for leaving someone you don't want. It's people who are indifferent who stay together. If you're going to make a bonfire you want something to strike a match on!

JIM—And if the house catches fire, and there's someone who won't leave it?

TRING—Yes, that's the trouble. Women may have no sense of time, but they have a mighty strong sense of eternity!

JIM—They're not all alike!

TRING—They are to the same man. Just as all men are alike to some woman. It's what *you* are that matters, not what *they* are. A man always thinks: "Ah! If I'd chosen someone different!—Illusion! To him every woman would be the same. That's Don Juan's tragedy. He can only hear one tune. Every woman he meets knows that. If she can't sing it, she passes him by. We're all tuned in to a certain wave-length. We only pick up what we're tuned into. Your little Doris—you think if she had been different, less romantic, less serious, things would be easier? But you would have got the same reaction in the end with any Sunday school teacher! No, it's all very painful. She's going to suffer, and it's because you are what you are. You're that kind of man—kind-hearted, sympathetic, gentle. The sort that's bound to make hell of somebody's life!

JIM—Surely, if you're fond of someone you want to be kind?

TRING—You may want to, but you mustn't unless you want to damn them utterly!

JIM—The least one owes is a little consideration!

TRING—Consideration? When you're telling a woman you don't want her?—It's like brushing a man's hair the morning you hang him!

JIM—She *knew*—she knew I was married! I told her it couldn't last. She agreed, absolutely!

TRING—Of course she agreed. A woman in love! She would tear up Magna Carta! You must face facts. What a woman says *before* isn't evidence!

JIM—Don't they ever mean what they say?

TRING—Certainly they mean it. But what they don't know is what it's going to mean to them! That's where they have the bulge on us. We do stay put. If a girl marries a man, thinking she's got hold of Casanova, it's a hundred to one that she won't find in a few weeks she's drawn John Knox. But a man may easily start his honeymoon with Helen of Troy and find himself landed with a vestal virgin!

JIM—Or vice versa.

TRING—Exactly! That's the trouble about marriage. Women always hope it's going to change the husband. Men always hope it won't change their wives—and both are disappointed! (*He gets up.*) Never if you can help it be a woman's first lover—unless, of course, you've got the explorer's temperament. As for your little trouble—get out of it, quick! It's not your line of country.

JIM—Yes, but how?

TRING—It doesn't matter how, so long as you don't try to behave like a gentleman. That's always fatal.

A moment later the butler has announced a young woman to see Mr. Warlock. Her name is Miles. Tring thinks perhaps he had better go out through the dining-room.

Milly is defiantly belligerent. She has come to tell Mr. Warlock what she thinks of him. She is there without Doris' knowledge. She has come to learn what Jim purposes doing about Doris. A gentleman would put his hand in his pocket, that's what a gentleman would do, whether the girl wanted him to or not. And perhaps if Milly were to tell Mrs. Warlock what she knows—

Mrs. Warlock, Jim informs her, is at the moment upstairs. He has no intention of stopping Milly telling anything she wants to. But by the time she has finished talking with Mrs. Warlock there will be a policeman in the house. A threat of extortion is frequently called blackmail, and the penalty for blackmail is likely to be severe. Nor is Jim fearful lest the story be spread over the newspapers. His name would not appear in it. Milly is beside herself with rage.

MILLY—You damned swine! All right! You're too clever for me! I'll go. No wonder you've broken her heart! My God!

JIM (*stopping her*)—Where is she?

MILLY—She's at home, cleaning a dress—and crying.

JIM—She'll have got my letter now.

MILLY—That will be a treat for her! (*Violently.*) What the hell did you want, butting in? She was happy enough!

JIM (*disturbed*)—Wait a minute, wait a minute. (*He goes to the table and starts to write a letter. The* BUTLER *appears.*)

BUTLER—If you please, sir, there's a police officer would like to speak to you.

JIM—Oh?

MILLY (*wildly*)—Look here, what's the game? You've got nothing on me!

JIM—Please, please! This has nothing to do with you. (*To the* BUTLER.) What does he want?

BUTLER—He didn't say, sir. It's an inspector.

JIM—Oh! Well, let him come in. (*The* BUTLER *withdraws.* CLEMENCY'S *voice is heard.*)

CLEMENCY (*invisible*)—Gorla, we're ready! (*She comes in from the left, followed by* TRING.) Jim dear, do you know what the time is? (*She sees* MILLY.) Oh— (*The door on the right opens and a police inspector comes in. He addresses* TRING.)

INSPECTOR—Mr. James Warlock?

JIM—Yes.

TRING (*indicating* JIM)—That is Mr. Warlock.

INSPECTOR—Could I have a word with you, sir?

JIM—Well, what is it?

INSPECTOR—Are you acquainted with a young woman of the name of Lea?

JIM (*startled*)—Who?

INSPECTOR—Doris Emily Lea, of Gresham Mansions, Farmer's Green.

JIM—Why do you ask me that?

INSPECTOR—A letter from you was found at her rooms.

JIM—Well?

INSPECTOR—Well, sir, would you be surprised to hear that the young woman is—dead?

JIM—What—?

INSPECTOR—Dead.

JIM—When—when did you say—?

INSPECTOR—Two o'clock they found her. Suicide, I should say.

JIM—Oh, my God!

MILLY (*rousing herself from her frozen horror*)—Now perhaps you're satisfied? Damn you—damn you to hell! You bloody gentlemen! (*She falls sobbing on the chair.* CLEMENCY *stares aghast at* JIM.)

THE CURTAIN FALLS

ACT III

In a Coroner's court in North London Jim Warlock, Milly Miles, Mme. Ducette and other witnesses are seated on a long bench to the left of the Coroner's desk. Facing them are the jury and reporters. At the back a small group of interested citizens, among them John Tring, is gathered.

A police officer on the stand is completing his evidence. He had entered the bedroom of Doris Lea's flat and found the young woman lying on the floor near the bed. By the side of the body was a small bottle of salts of lemon—

"Salts of lemon is the common name for the chemical which the Police Surgeon who gave the evidence just now called potassium superoxylate," the Coroner explains to the jury. "As you know, it is used for cleaning clothes."

The lips, mouth and throat of the dead girl were burned by the acid, the police officer continues. He had afterward searched the flat and found a letter in the mailbox that had come by afternoon post. It was written from a house in Montagu Square and in it the writer had explained why he had been unable to meet the deceased the evening before. It was signed "Jim."

The Foreman of the Jury would like to know if the officer had found any money in the flat? The officer had. "There was one shilling and three-pence in the deceased's purse."

Mme. Ducette is the next witness. She testifies that Doris Lea had been one of her employees and that, up to two weeks before, she had been a good worker. Suddenly Doris had lost interest in her work, and when, finally, she had come late on a Monday morning and could do nothing but "sit and look at the past with big eyes," Mme. Ducette saw that something had to be done.

The girls offered Doris a cup of tea, and when she carelessly spilled this over a new Paris model, Mme. Ducette discharged her and told her to take the dress home and clean it. She had given Doris the salts of lemon for the cleaning, after calling her attention to the "Poison" sign on the bottle.

The Coroner next calls Milly Miles. Milly had last seen Doris Lea on Thursday morning. They had quarreled that morning over Jim Warlock. Warlock had known Doris about six weeks, Milly relates, after she and Doris had met him and a friend in a restaurant.

"It wasn't an ordinary 'pick-up,' " insists Milly. "He had an old man with him—old enough to know better. They looked respectable enough. They kept sending us fruit. Well, we had to say 'thank you,' didn't we?"

The meetings at Farmer's Green beauty show, and afterward at the Derby, are recalled. It was after the Derby, when Doris and Jim had given Milly and Tring the slip, that the affair really started. Milly had stayed with her mother that night.

CORONER—Now I want you to think carefully before you answer my next question. (*Pause.*) Have you any reason to suppose that there have been improper relations? (*There is a rustle of pleasurable anticipation in the court.*)

MILLY—Well, I ask you. What else does a gentleman like him want with girls like us? (*A roar of applause from the crowd.*)

VOICES OF THE CROWD—Ther dirty swine. That's 'im at the end of the row. Pleased with 'imself, ain't 'e?

CORONER—I will not allow these interruptions. (*To* MILLY.) Your friend was in love with Mr. Warlock?

MILLY—She was soppy about him. Used to sleep with his picture under her pillow. Once she bought a book of poetry. I warned her then what would be the end. And didn't I get a telling off! But I was right. *As* she found out on Monday.

CORONER—What happened on Monday?

MILLY—He gave her the chuck. I'd been to the pictures. I came home and found her in her wet things lying on the bed. She told me it was all over.

CORONER (*writing*)—Monday, the seventh.

MILLY—Wednesday evening she went out to see him. For the last time, she said. He never turned up.

VOICES—What a shame! I never! The dirty swine!

MILLY—I told her at breakfast next morning I was going to see Mr. J. W. That's how we quarreled. Said she wouldn't have anything hurt him. Said she'd love him all her life. If I went to Montagu Square she'd never speak to me again. (*Pause.*) She won't, either.

CORONER—Did you go?

MILLY—I left the flat in a temper. I went to the shop. At six o'clock I took the Baker Street bus. I told Mr. Jim what I thought of him.

CORONER—What attitude did he take?

MILLY—He? He threatened to put the police on me!

CORONER—Have the Jury any questions to put to this witness?

AN AGED JUROR—I should like to ask the young lady one rather delicate question. (*To* MILLY.) I should like to ask if you knew of any trouble Miss Lea was in?

MILLY—Jim Warlock's trouble enough for any girl.

AGED JUROR—You don't understand the point of my question. I will have to make myself clearer. Was Miss Lea expecting—er—to be a mother?

MILLY—Girls aren't as simple as they were in your day!

Milly is excused. Jim Warlock is called. "There is a buzz of expectancy as Jim leaves his seat and crosses to the witness box." The crowd mutters vicious criticisms as he is being sworn.

Jim's face is drawn, his voice low. He admits his acquaintance with Doris, admits that she was his mistress. As to the cause of her death, he had told her that they could not go on meeting as they had been doing and she appeared distressed.

Forced to answer the Coroner's inquiry as to why he had

terminated the relationship Jim admits it was because of his wife. Yes, Doris had known that he was married; had known it from the first.

"Did you not think that a married man who persuaded a girl in her early twenties to enter into an illicit relationship incurs a very heavy responsibility?" demands the Coroner.

"I think so now," answers Jim.

Jim had told Doris on Monday that he would have to give her up; that he would try to see her on Wednesday. He was unable to keep that appointment because he had to take Mrs. Warlock to a cocktail party. He had tried to telephone Doris and, when he could not reach her, had written the note in evidence.

That, admits the Coroner, is all he wants to know. The Foreman of the Jury, however, would like to find out something about the witness' financial status and whether or not he had made any provision for the girl. Jim had tried to arrange something, he explains, but it was not easy. He did not want to hurt Doris' feelings.

The Foreman is not impressed. Neither is a Jurywoman who, speaking as a mother, would like to know whether or not Doris, at the time of her meeting with Jim, was a good girl. Jim prefers not to answer that question. The Coroner warns him significantly that the Jury will naturally draw its own conclusions.

The Coroner will call no more witnesses. The testimony presented, he feels, has "elucidated this deplorable case."

"You have been impaneled to return a verdict as to the manner in which Doris Lea met her death," sums up the Coroner. "In view of the very straightforward nature of the medical and police evidence, you will have no difficulty in deciding that point. You have then to consider the state of mind of the deceased when she took the fatal step. You have heard that she quarreled with the girl she lived with. That she had lost her employment. That by an unfortunate chance a poisonous chemical was put in her hands. That she had no money. You have also heard that the married man on whom she had set her affections had recently broken off the guilty relation between them in a manner that I can only describe as brutal. I think you will have little doubt that there is to be found the deciding factor. Ladies and gentlemen of the jury, you will now consider your verdict."

There are more vicious remarks from the crowd. One man would call the crime murder. Another would hang the likes of Jim Warlock. . . . John Tring makes his way through the crowd to Jim's side. Jim is grateful for, but little moved by, Tring's sympathy. Clemency had wanted to come, too; to show that she was standing by loyally. Jim would not have that. For the future Jim has not made any plans. The Bar's finished, of course. . . .

The Jury is ready to report. The verdict is unanimous. The finding is that Doris Emily Lea came to her death as a deliberate suicide. The Jury wishes to add a rider to the verdict "expressing in the strongest terms our disgust at the conduct of Mr. Warlock."

"I entirely agree with the verdict and the rider," booms the Coroner. "When a married man of mature years—"

The lights are fading. Through the gathering darkness the voice of the Coroner is heard continuing—

"—of excellent education and a good station in life entangles a young girl of an inferior class in an irregular union, quite apart from the breach of the moral law, he assumes a very grave responsibility. In addition to this, Mr. Warlock, by his refusal to answer an important leading question, has chosen to cast reflections on the previous character of this dead girl. The Jury have, I think, taken their own view of his attempt to screen himself by what is, in effect, an attack on the character of a girl who is no longer here to speak for herself. I do not think I need comment further on that. Mr. Warlock seems to have acted throughout with a levity as cynical as it has proved disastrous. If he had shown a little less selfishness, a little more restraint, a little more kindness, this unfortunate young woman would have been alive today."

On the balcony of the hotel at Capri Jim Warlock is concluding his recital of the story to Clemency.

"That's what I hear every night. It goes on and on and on," Jim is saying.

Clemency looks up slowly. There is dull pain in her eyes, not untouched with pity.

"Then you weren't the first?" she asks.

"No."

"Why did you let them think you were? They asked you."

"I know."

"That made a difference, didn't it? If the Coroner had known that—?"

"Yes, I suppose so."

"Why didn't you say?"

"I couldn't. It was her secret. She needn't have told me."

Clemency still is not satisfied. Nor can she understand. How could Jim make such a sacrifice for someone he didn't really care for? He is quick to answer that.

"I never said that. I did care. I don't want you to think that—that it didn't matter."

"You're frank, aren't you?" There is a shade of bitterness in Clemency's tone.

"It's too late to be anything else. That's all I've got left now. That I don't have to lie about it."

Again Clemency must go on. Was there love-making between Jim and Doris after she (Clemency) had come home? Did Jim still want Doris then? Did he ever think of her when he was with Doris?

"Would you have thought of her while you were with me?" Clemency demands, hesitantly.

"I don't think so," Jim answers, as one convinced. "You know, that sort of thing doesn't mean so much to men. Tring's right about that."

CLEMENCY—Then why were you giving her up, if it meant so little? And for something that meant only that, you risked everything—everything we'd built up—our happiness. Didn't all that mean *anything* to you?

JIM—It meant everything. It *does* mean everything. More than I knew. I've learnt that, anyway.

CLEMENCY—That horrible old man. And I thought him amusing. Things that make amusing conversation aren't so funny in one's own life.

JIM—I'm afraid it hasn't helped you much—my telling you.

CLEMENCY—Yes, it has. I'm glad to know.

JIM—If you could have seen her—perhaps. I think you'd have understood in a way— (*A pause.*)

CLEMENCY—I did see her.

JIM—What?

CLEMENCY—I went to look at her in the mortuary.

JIM—Clemency!

CLEMENCY—I thought I ought to see what she was like. I wanted to understand. I said I was a relation. In a way, that seemed to be true. (*A pause.*) She was pretty. And so young. (JIM *covers his face.*) It seemed so strange that *you* should have done that—you, so kind and gentle.

JIM—Kind—yes—that's just it. Well, that's all. (*He looks at her.*) I'll go down to the port, the afternoon boat's in. I'll see what's going on.

CLEMENCY—Yes. Thank you for telling me, Jim. (*He looks at her almost eagerly.*) I'm glad I know.

John Tring has seen Jim leaving the house, but has let him go. Tring has arrived on the afternoon boat and he wants to talk to Clemency before he sees Jim. Tring feels that he is in disgrace with Clemency—he is the Mephistopheles of the story. And he is guilty.

"I did take him to Joseph's. I did speak to the girls. And, of course, I did nudge the laws of chance a bit about Epsom," Tring admits. "Yes, so far as Fate ever has one eye open, I suppose I'm guilty. . . . I suppose I thought it might be good for him. . . . And he put me on my mettle—something he said. . . . He said he couldn't talk to girls like that—that he'd nothing in common with them. That's a dangerous thing to say of any fellow creature. No man should be as sure of himself as that. Mischievous of me, of course. But to offer a man a cocktail isn't to ask him to get drunk."

CLEMENCY—Perhaps you think it *has* been good for him.

TRING—Who can say?

CLEMENCY—I can.

TRING—You think he's a worse man than he was?

CLEMENCY—He's a different one.

TRING—Yes. He was a successful, honorable, upright Englishman. Now he's an outcast, a liar, a seducer of women. Also he's a man who has suffered. Isn't he more human? I'd rather have him as he is now.

CLEMENCY—I suppose it doesn't matter that his career has gone? That our whole life is smashed up?

TRING—If you'd seen as many careers as I have, you wouldn't shed many tears over that. Is it such a privilege to spend your life in the sordid quarrels of other people?

CLEMENCY—He liked it. And he'd have gone into politics.

TRING—To be dragged in chains at the rump of the mob—a leader of democracy! Well, he can join the Labor Party. At least they've that much sense. *They* don't think that sexual morality is the measure of a good citizen.

CLEMENCY—You think it doesn't count, I know.

TRING—Well, wouldn't it be better if it counted less? Nature thinks so. She doesn't worry about a little superfluous energy.

CLEMENCY—Is that the latest word for adultery?

Tring—Oh—if you're going to bombard me with the Commandments?

Clemency—No. I'm not thinking about morality.

Tring—Thank God for that.

Clemency—It's personal. I don't pretend it isn't. Something's gone. The thing that was us. I can't find it.

Tring—Don't take the senses too seriously. After all—between you and him—what did passion count for?

Clemency—It kept the rest alive.

Tring (nodding)—The yeast in the household bread. And unleavened bread is no good?

Clemency—Not to me.

Tring—It never touched his love for you.

Clemency—That's where I'm lost. Supposing I'd done it—what would *he* have thought? What *could* he have thought? I *couldn't* do it unless I'd changed to him.

Tring—Ah! There's the great gulf fixed. Monogamy is the woman's invention. Men don't really believe in it.

Clemency—They believe in it for us.

Tring—Yes, you've talked them into it. Women capitalized chastity, and got us to subscribe for the shares. It's paid them well enough, too. Now the bottom's out of the market. Women don't like a man who isn't jealous. It brings monopoly value down with a run.

Tring is interested in making out a case for himself, but he also is eager to help Clemency if he can. He does not blame her for the way she feels. One feels as one can. Clemency, he is willing to admit, is in the right unequivocally—and that ought to help. But it is not argument that she can look to for help. Nor is pity for Jim of much use. It is a matter of her heart. She must try her imagination. Let her suppose, for a moment, that she is never going to see Jim again. Suppose he were not to come back—

Clemency is disturbed by the thought. Surely, Jim will be back. He isn't that sort of coward.

"There are plenty of reasons why we never see people again," ventures Tring. "It's always happening. Just say to yourself, 'I shan't ever see him again. That's over!' Say it."

"No."

Tring—What would the world look like? That's what you want to know. (*There is a pause, then* Jim's *voice*.)

Jim—Hello, you *here!* Did you come on the boat?

Tring—Yes, I must have just missed you. You got my letter?

Jim—Today. You've not lost much time.

Tring—I thought you might like to talk things over. Not that I can tell you much. I've not been there myself.

Jim—Can I be of any use there?

Tring—Well, you'll have to find that out.

Jim—I can't even pot geraniums.

Tring—Geraniums grow there like weeds.

Jim—It tempts me. It's very good of you, Tring.

Tring—My dear fellow! Well, when will you go? You'll want to go back to London.

Jim—London? What for? Can't I get what I want out there?

Tring—I should think so.

Jim—I should like to go at once.

Tring—Good. There's an Orient boat from Naples on Sunday. You can pick up an East Coast boat at Port Said or Suez.

Jim—Sunday? That'll do. You'll cable Thorburn I'm coming?

Tring—Yes. He expects you, anyway.

Jim (*looking at him curiously*)—Does he? (*He laughs a little bitterly.*) You're sure he won't mind?

Tring—Why should he? You won't alter the climate. The African sun is impervious to these great moral issues. It'll go on shining just the same.

Jim—You'll get me a berth?

Tring—To Port Said?

Jim—Yes, you'll want some money. Will you pay everything? We'll settle later. (*He goes off to get the money.*)

Tring (*to* Clemency)—So you won't need your imagination?

Clemency (*who has listened to the previous conversation as one who has been pushed out of a game*)—No.

Jim (*coming back*)—Here's five thousand lire. We can settle up later.

Tring—Yes, I shall see you off. (*The boat's siren sounds.*) That gives me ten minutes. (*He takes up his hat.*) Till Sunday, then. You'll be over in the morning? They may sail early. (*He turns to take* Clemency's *hand.*) I shall see you?

Clemency—Remember, we want an outside cabin—on the port side. It'll be hot.

Tring (*startled, then delighted*)—I'll remember. (*He pats her hand, nods to* Jim *and goes out.*)

Jim—What do you mean? You're not coming.

CLEMENCY—You don't want me?

JIM—Why are you coming?

CLEMENCY—I won't if you don't want me to.

JIM—That's not it. You know all about that. You know whether I want you or not. It's this: What's done is done. She's paid her bill, and I've paid mine—part of it! I can't go on always being sorry, feeling there's something I ought to be ashamed of. I don't say it's easy for you to forget—I don't say it's possible—but if you can't, it isn't any good to me. And don't come with me because you're sorry for me—that's no good to me any more! If you come, it must be because—well, not because I want you. It's got to be because you want me! You understand? (*There is a pause.*)

CLEMENCY—I understand. It's all right, Jim. (*She takes his hand.*) You needn't be afraid!

THE CURTAIN FALLS

THE PLAYS AND THEIR AUTHORS

"Of Thee I Sing." By George S. Kaufman and Morrie Ryskind; music by George Gershwin; lyrics by Ira Gershwin. Copyright, 1931, 1932, by the authors. Copyright and published, 1932, by Alfred Knopf, New York.

George S. Kaufman continues as practically an annual contributor to these volumes of Best Plays, but this is his first appearance as a winner of the Pulitzer prize. He was born, as reference to previous volumes will disclose, in Pennsylvania, was a newspaper columnist before he took to play writing and shared his early successes with Marc Connelly as collaborator. He has also written plays with Edna Ferber and Moss Hart, was for many years dramatic editor of the New York *Times,* and is now one of the wealthiest and one of the most popular of playwrights.

Morrie Ryskind has been a Kaufman collaborator in the writing of other musical comedies. They worked together on "Strike Up the Band" and "Animal Crackers" as well as "Of Thee I Sing." Ryskind was born on New York's east side, went through the public schools to Columbia University, and was fired from college six weeks before he would have graduated because of an anti-war editorial he wrote for the school paper. He had the last laugh over that incident when Columbia, which is the custodian of the Pulitzer awards, gave "Of Thee I Sing" this year's prize. Ryskind wrote the picture, "Palmy Days," for Eddie Cantor, and has published two or three volumes of light verse, the latest entitled "Diary of an Ex-President."

Ira Gershwin, whose lyrics have been called Gilbertian on occasion, contributed his bit to the success of "Of Thee I Sing." He, too, is an east side boy, born in 1896, making him, as may easily be computed, two years older than his brother George. He advanced, not too smartly, through public school to City College, which he left when he discovered that he was still taking first-year mathematics in his second year. A try at medicine, a variety of jobs and finally the inspiration to be as good a lyricist as George was a composer assailed him. He wrote under the pseudonym of Arthur Francis at first, so as not to climb on George's reputation, and his first set of lyrics were written for

370

Vincent Youman's and Paul Lannin's "Two Little Girls in Blue." That was in 1921. In the ten years that have followed he has written practically all his brother's lyrics and many for other composers.

George Gershwin, whose music cannot be dismissed in any consideration of "Of Thee I Sing," even though the award was made on the literary content of the play, was born in 1898 in Brooklyn. Through school he cared little for music, but when the family acquired a second-hand upright, his biographer, Isaac Goldberg records, George (né Jacob) was fascinated by the keyboard and his career was started. He wrote his first score, that for "La, La, Lucille," in 1919, and did the scores for all of George White's "Scandals" the next five years. He achieved the "Rhapsody in Blue" in 1923 and his fame as a composer has mounted steadily since then.

"Mourning Becomes Electra." A trilogy in fourteen scenes by Eugene O'Neill. Copyright, 1931, by the author. Copyright and published, 1931, by Horace Liveright, Inc., New York.

Eugene O'Neill's last appearance in this record was in the volume devoted to the season of 1927-28, when he won the Pulitzer prize with "Strange Interlude." The next three years he devoted for the most part to the writing of "Mourning Becomes Electra," which has quite frequently been called his masterpiece. He has won the Pulitzer prize for his "Beyond the Horizon," "Anna Christie," and "Strange Interlude." He was born in New York in 1888 and gained a first step-up when the Provincetown Players produced his one-act plays of the sea.

"Reunion in Vienna." A comedy in three acts by Robert Emmet Sherwood. Copyright, 1931, by the author. Copyright and published, 1932, by Charles Scribner's Sons, New York.

Robert E. Sherwood's first success in the theatre was earned with the comedy called "The Road to Rome," which was included in "The Best Plays of 1926-27." He was born in 1896 in New Rochelle, N. Y., and after graduating from Harvard in 1918 he went to war. Two years later he was on the staff of *Vanity Fair,* later editor of *Life,* and is now on the editorial staff of *Scribner's Magazine,* doing book reviews when he is not attending editorial conferences or writing plays. "The Queen's

Husband," "This Is New York" and "Waterloo Bridge" are also his.

"The House of Connelly." A drama in two acts by Paul Green. Copyright, 1931, by the author. Copyright and published, 1931, by Samuel French, New York.

Paul Green won the Pulitzer prize the season of 1926-27 with "Abraham's Bosom," which was duly included in this record at that time. He was born on a farm near Lillington, N. C., laboriously worked his way through school, graduating from Blue Creek Academy in 1914. He was attending the University of North Carolina when the war called him away. He came back and graduated in 1921. He is now a member of the faculty of the University, employing his spare time in playwriting. Several volumes of his plays have been published by Samuel French.

"The Animal Kingdom." A comedy in three acts by Philip Barry. Copyright, 1931, by the author. Copyright and published, 1932, by Samuel French, New York.

Philip Barry is also a frequent contributor to the pages of this "Best Plays" series. "The Animal Kingdom" represents his sixth appearance since his first success, "You and I," was included in the issue of 1922-23. Our constant readers, therefore, are pretty well acquainted with the facts of his biography. Born in Rochester, N. Y.; graduated from Yale; studied drama at Harvard with Professor Baker. He was an attaché of the American embassy at London for a time, and was trying to like being a writer of advertising copy when he was able to escape into playwriting.

"The Left Bank." A comedy in three acts by Elmer Rice. Copyright, 1930, 1931, by the author. Copyright and published, 1931, by Samuel French, New York.

Elmer Rice won the Pulitzer prize the season of 1928-29 with "Street Scene," and after it had been running the better part of a year bundled up his family and left for European parts determined not to come home until he had written another play or two. When he did come back he brought the manuscripts of "The Left Bank" and "Counsellor-at-Law," and proceeded to produce them himself. "The Left Bank" came first and was a success. "Counsellor-at-Law," with Paul Muni, followed a month or so later and was even more popular. Which was something of a record for the young man. Rice was born in New York in 1892. He tried the law and did not like it. He tried playwriting and produced "On Trial," which set a fashion in flash-back dramas. He has written several other plays, "Wake Up, Jonathan," for Mrs. Fiske, "The Adding Machine," etc.

"Another Language." A comedy in three acts by Rose Franken. Copyright, 1931, by the author. Copyright and published, 1931, by Samuel French, New York.

A new name in the list of best-play playwrights is that of Rose Franken, whose "Another Language" bounded into an overnight success in New York last spring. It is Mrs. Franken's first play to be produced. She wrote another called "Fortnight" some years ago, and when that failed of production, after promises, she was so irritated she sat down, worked her temper off on the typewriter, and wrote another. This one, originally called "Hallam Wives," lay around producers' offices for a few months and was finally taken out by Arthur J. Beckhard, a concert manager eager to try the drama. He produced "Another Language" with a stock company in Woodstock, N. Y., later changed the title and managed a production for it on Broadway. Mrs. Franken is the wife of Dr. Sigmund Franken, an oral surgeon of more than local standing; the mother of three children and a born housewife. She writes better when she cooks and keeps house and lets the maid go, she says. She was born in Dallas, Texas.

"Brief Moment." A comedy in three acts by S. N. Behrman. Copyright, 1931, by the author. Copyright and published, 1932, by Farrar & Rinehart, New York.

S. N. Behrman (Sam to his friends; Samuel Nathaniel to his mother) came to Broadway notice with the production of a smart comedy called "The Second Man," which the Theatre Guild produced a matter of five years back. Before that he had attended to the matter of being born in Worcester, Mass., in 1893, and being educated at public schools, Clark College, Harvard University (where he studied drama with Prof. George Pierce Baker and got an A.B.), and Columbia University (where he took his M.A.). After that Behrman was a book reviewer on the New York *Times,* a press agent on Broadway and a working collaborator with Kenyon Nicholson, who also writes plays. Together they did several pieces, best known of them being "Love Is Like That." He wrote "The Man Who Forgot" with Owen Davis, "Serena Blandish" by himself, and has toyed with the movies.

"The Devil Passes." A drama in three acts by Benn W. Levy. Copyright, 1930, by the author. Copyright and published, 1930, by Martin Secker, London.

Benn W. Levy's name has appeared on the local hoardings with increasing frequency since that year (1926 it was) when an adventuring producer of plays named Dr. Louis Sunshine offered "This Woman Business" to Broadway. It was not a success, but other Levy plays that have followed have been. These include the immensely popular "Mrs. Moonlight," the quite popular "Springtime for Henry" and the "Art and Mrs. Bottle" that served Jane Cowl well two seasons ago. Mr. Levy was born in London in 1900, the son of a wool merchant and a nephew of the late Jacob Schiff. He was for a time managing director of Jerrolds, London publishers. He was educated at Repton and Oxford, and the last few years has been flirting rather successfully with the cinema in Hollywood.

"Cynara." A drama in three acts by H. M. Harwood and R. F. Gore-Browne. Copyright, 1930, by the authors. Copyright and published, 1931, by Samuel French, New York.

Harold Marsh Harwood has been writing plays in England for these many years, several of them in collaboration with his wife F. Tennyson Jesse. He expected, however, to be a doctor, having taken his degree in medicine at Cambridge in 1900. He practiced for some time thereafter. When the theatre got into his blood stream, however, he went in for management as well as writing and adapting plays, being the lessee of the Ambassador Theatre in London. "Billeted," which Margaret Anglin played in America in wartime, was his; also "The Mask," "A Social Convenience" and others.

Robert Gore-Browne is a British novelist of standing and was from his novel, "An Imperfect Lover," that the play "Cynara" was evolved.

PLAYS PRODUCED IN NEW YORK
JUNE 15, 1931—JUNE 18, 1932
(Plays marked with asterisk were still playing June 18, 1932)

THAIS

(4 performances)

A drama in three acts, adapted by Ellison Harvey from the novel of Anatole France. Produced by Drama Repertoire Players, Inc., at the President Theatre, New York, June 19, 1931.

Cast of characters—

A Cairene peddler	Richard Garrick
A Bedaween	Thomas H. Kiely
Paysol	Gordon Fallows
Nicias	M. Manisoff
Dorian	Richard Garrick
Chareas	Thomas H. Kiely
Zenothemis	Adrian Krisberg
Crobyle	Gene Woods
Myrtale	Eda Reis
Thais	Dorothy Deer Horn
Helen	Ann Rutledge
Drose	Rivkah Baselidrosa
Nadito	Joseph Reller
Selah	Dorothy Tannen
Albina	Gertrude Magill
Maria Pai	Gene Woods

Staged by Dorothy Deer Horn.

The dramatic story of the strenuous efforts made by a courtesan of Alexandria to keep a perfectly good Cenobite monk from continuing faithfully in the work of the Lord. She was no more than temporarily successful.

THE WOODEN SOLDIER

(32 performances)

A comedy in three acts by Alexander Carr. Produced by Lesser Productions, Inc., at the Biltmore Theatre, New York, June 2, 1931.

Cast of characters—

Maggie	Valerie Valaire
Benny	David Begleiter
Jennie	Mara Kevall

```
Sarah Kaufman...............................Jennie Moscowitz
Jake...............................................Sam Bennett
Sylvia.............................................Billie Mae
Moses Kaufman..............................Robert Leonard
Arthur.......................................Waldo E. Edwards
David...........................................Alexander Carr
Butler..........................................Bert Henderson
Simon Von Gartenbaum.........................Victor Morley
Sheriff............................................W. A. Norton
    Acts I, II and III.—Living-room in Kaufman Home.
    Staged by Victor Morley.
```

David Kaufman, gassed in the war, takes to drink. After years of wandering through the jails of the world he returns to the home of his brother, Moses, who has cheated him out of his part of a legacy. David, whose Gentile sweetheart had died after bearing him an illegitimate son, finds his boy also in love with a Gentile girl. He continues his drinking, but manages to bring his cheating brother to book and to make things easy for his son and the girl.

PAID COMPANIONS

(8 performances)

A comedy in three acts by Bernard J. McOwen. Produced by Seecil Productions, Inc., at the Masque Theatre, New York, June 22, 1931.

```
Cast of characters—
Penelope Forrest...............................Ida Anderson
Lila Vaughn......................................Lee Smith
Bruce Reynolds...............................Hal Clarendon
Mona Monte..............................Georgine Cleveland
Patricia Harford...............................Cecil Spooner
Thomas Clay Dayton...........................Don Costello
Policeman........................................George Clark
House Detective..............................William Nelson
    Acts I, II and III.—The Living-room of Lila Vaughn's Pent-house
Apartment.
    Staged by Dan Malloy.
```

Lila Vaughn, having come from the West to New York in the hope of having her voice cultivated, is sick and lonesome. She appeals for help to a casual acquaintance who happens to be in the business of providing companions for lonesome gentlemen able to pay handsomely for the service. The lady sells Lila to Bruce Reynolds, an engineer recently returned from the African jungle for six months at $1,000 a month. Lila loathes Bruce and the new life and when her western sweetheart hunts her out and wants to marry her despite everything she suffers an attack of hysteria during which she shoots the engineer. The friendly detectives call it suicide.

PIRATES OF PENZANCE

(24 performances)

An operetta by W. S. Gilbert, music by Arthur Sullivan. Revived by the Civic Light Opera Company at Erlanger's Theatre, New York, June 29, 1931.

Cast of characters—

Richard	Herbert Waterous
Samuel	Sano Marco
Frederick	Howard Marsh
Major-General Stanley	Frank Moulan
Edward	William Danforth
Mabel	Vivian Hart
Kate	Georgina Dieter
Edith	Frances Moore
Isabel	Frances Baviello
Ruth	Anne Yago

General Stanley's Daughters, Pirates, Policemen, etc.: Olga Schumacher, Roslyn Shaw, Patricia Clark, Edith Artley, Eleanor Gilmore, Gertrude Walden, Frances Baviello, Mabel Thompson, Helen Hosp, Isabel Norwood, Rosa Rubenstein, Mary Joe Matthews, Marie Pittman, Marynia Apel, Julia Reid, Adele Story and Charlotte LaRose. Edward Taylor, Bert Melrose, Hobson Young, Charles Maduro, Edward Lambert, Felix Noonan, Allan Ware, Frank Murray, Martin Lilienfield, Frank Dowling, Harrison Fuller, Francis Clark, Ramon Recalde, John Cardini, Bernard Lane and Lee Talbot.

Synopsis: Act I.—Rocky Seashore off Cornwall. Act II.—Ruined Abbey.

Staged by Milton Aborn.

"The Pirates of Penzance" was revived December 6, 1926, by Winthrop Ames at the Plymouth Theatre, New York. Ernest Lawford was then the Major General, William Williams the Frederick and Ruth Thomas the Mabel. And again the following year November 24, with the late Fred Wright, the English comedian, as the Major General, Williams again the Frederick and Lois Bennett the Mabel. It was repeated October 19, 1931, for eight performances with the above list of principals.

ZIEGFELD FOLLIES, 1931

(165 performances)

A revue assembled by Florenz Ziegfeld. Produced at the Ziegfeld Theatre, New York, July 1, 1931.

Contributors of words and music—

Gene Buck	Dave Stamper
Mark Hellinger	Hugo Reisenfeld
J. P. Murray	Mack Gordon
Barry Trivers	Harry Revel
Ben Oakland	Dmitri Tiomkin
Walter Donaldson	

Principals engaged—

Harry Richman
Jack Pearl
Albert Carroll
Hal Le Roy
Arthur Campbell
John Daly Murphy
Earl Oxford
Frank and Milt Britton
Buck and Bubbles

Ruth Etting
Helen Morgan
Gladys Glad
Faith Bacon
Mitzi Mayfair
Dorothy Dell
Collette sisters
Reri
Ethel Borden

Staged by Florenz Ziegfeld, Gene Buck; dances by Bobby Connelly and Albertina Rasch.

IOLANTHE

(24 performances)

An operetta by W. S. Gilbert, music by Arthur Sullivan. Revived by the Civic Light Opera Company at Erlanger's Theatre, New York, July 13, 1931.

Cast of characters—

Lord Chancellor..................................Frank Moulan
Earl of Mountararat...........................Frederick Persson
Earl of Tolloller.................................Howard Marsh
Private Willis..................................Herbert Waterous
Strephon......................................Joseph Macaulay
Queen of the Fairies..............................Vera Ross
Iolanthe...Dean Dickens
Celia...Georgina Dieter
Leila..Gertrude Waldon
Fleta..Eleanor Gilmore
Phyllis...Vivian Hart
Fairies: Misses Olga Schumacher, Roslyn Shaw, Patricia Clark, Edith Artley, Eleanor Gilmore, Gertrude Waldon, Frances Baviello, Mabel Thompson, Helen Hosp, Isabel Norwood, Rosa Rubenstein, Mary Joe Matthews, Marie Pittman, Marynia Apel, Julia Reid, Adele Story and Charlotte LaRose.
Dukes, Marquises, Earls, Viscounts, Lords, Barons, Peers: Messrs. Edward Taylor, Bert Melrose, Hobson Young, Felix Noonan, Allan Ware, Frank Murray, Martin Lilienfield, Frank Dowling, Harrison Fuller, Francis Clark, Ramon Recalde, John Cardini, Bernard Lane, Lee Talbot.
Act I.—An Arcadian Landscape. Act II.—Palace Yard, Westminster. Date: Between 1700 and 1882.
Staged by Milton Aborn.

"Iolanthe, or The Peer and the Peri," was last revived by Winthrop Ames in the spring of 1926, with Ernest Lawford as the Lord Chancellor, John Barclay as Lord Mountararat, William Williams as Strephon, Adele Sanderson as Iolanthe and Vera Ross the Queen of the Fairies. It was repeated January 4 for eight performances.

SHOOT THE WORKS

(87 performances)

A revue assembled by Heywood Broun and Milton Raison: Produced at the George M. Cohan Theatre, New York, July 21, 1931.

Contributors of words and music—

Heywood Broun
H. I. Phillips
Peter Arno
Sig Herzig
Edward J. McNamara
Michael H. Cleary
Philip Chagrig
Jay Gorney
Dorothy Fields
Ira Gershwin
Alexander Williams
Robert Stolz
A. Robinson

Dorothy Parker
Nunnally Johnson
E. B. White
Jack Hazzard
Irving Berlin
Max Lief
Nathaniel Lief
E. Y. Harburg
Jimmie MacHugh
Vernon Duke
Herbert Goode
Walter Reisch

Principals engaged—

Heywood Broun
William O'Neal
Johnny Boyle
George Murphy
Jack Hazzard
Edward J. McNamara
Al Gold
Percy Helton
Edgar Nelson

Julie Johnson
Imogene Coca
Frances Dewey
Margot Riley
Frances Nevins
Virginia Smith
Lee Brody
Lela Manor
Lila Manor

"Shoot the Works" was a coöperative revue organized by Heywood Broun for the purpose of giving a hundred or more out-of-work actors temporary jobs.

TRIAL BY JURY

(16 performances)

Operetta in one act by W. S. Gilbert, music by Arthur Sullivan. Revived by the Civic Light Opera Company, at Erlanger Theatre, New York, July 27, 1931.

Cast of characters—

The Learned Judge.............................Frank Moulan
Foreman of the Jury..........................Frederick Persson
Defendant.......................................Howard Marsh
Counsel.......................................Joseph Macaulay
Usher...William Danforth
Plaintiff.......................................Theo. Pennington
Jurors: Bert Melrose, Hobson Young, Felix Noonan, Allan Ware, Frank Murray, Martin Lilienfield, Frank Dowling, Harrison Fuller, Francis Clark, John Cardini, Bernard Lane and Patrick Quinton.
Bridesmaids: Frances Moore, Olga Schumacher, Roslyn Shaw, Patricia Clark, Gertrude Waldon, Frances Baviello, Mabel Thompson, Isabel Norwood, Rosa Rubenstein, Mary Joe Matthews, Marynia Apel, Adele Story, Harriet Gottlieb, Marie Kelley, Lillian Koniver, Katherine Calle and Mary Harper.
Scene—Court of Exchequer.

Followed by—

H.M.S. PINAFORE

Cast of characters—

The Right Hon. Sir Joseph Porter, K.C.B..........Frank Moulan
Capt. Corcoran, Commander of H.M.S. *Pinafore*....Joseph Macaulay
Ralph Rackstraw..................................Howard Marsh
Dick Deadeye.....................................William Danforth
Bill Bobstay.....................................Frederick Persson
Josephine..Theo. Pennington
Little Buttercup (Mrs. Cripps)...................Fay Templeton
Hebe...Ethel Clark
Sailors: Bert Melrose, Hobson Young, Felix Noonan, Allan Ware,
    Frank Murray, Martin Lilienfield, Frank Dowling, Harrison Ful-
    ler, Francis Clark, John Cardini, Bernard Lane, Harold Raymond,
    Carroll Godwin.
First Lord's Sisters, His Cousins and His Aunts: Misses Frances
    Moore, Olga Schumacher, Roslyn Shaw, Patricia Clark, Ger-
    trude Waldon, Frances Baviello, Mabel Thompson, Isabel Nor-
    wood, Rosa Rubenstein, Mary Joe Matthews, Marynia Apel,
    Adele Story, Harriet Gottlieb, Marie Kelley, Lillian Koniver,
    Katherine Calle, and Mary Harper.
Scene—Deck of H.M.S. *Pinafore,* off Portsmouth, England.
Staged by Milton Aborn.

"Trial by Jury" was last revived in New York by W. A. Brady in May, 1915. It was sung then on the same bill with "The Sorcerer." DeWolf Hopper was the Judge, Arthur Aldridge Defendant, Gladys Caldwell Plaintiff, Herbert Waterous Foreman of the Jury and William Danforth Usher. In the cast of "The Sorcerer" the veteran Digby Bell made a brief reappearance on the stage as Doctor Daly. . . . "Pinafore," with Fay Templeton coming on from Pittsburgh to sing Buttercup, was revived in May, 1931, with the above principals. The opera was first sung in London in 1878 and in America the same year. A notable revival was staged at the Century Theatre, New York, in 1926, with John Hazzard as Porter, Marguerite Namara as Josephine, Danforth as Deadeye and Miss Templeton as Buttercup.

RUDDIGORE

(16 performances)

Operetta in two acts by W. S. Gilbert, music by Arthur Sullivan. Revived by the Civic Light Opera Company at Erlanger's Theatre, New York, August 10, 1931.

Cast of characters—

Robin Oakapple....................................Frank Moulan
Richard Dauntless.................................Craig Campbell
Sir Despard Murgatroyd............................William Danforth
Old Adam Goodheart................................Sano Marco
Rose Maybud.......................................Ethel Clark
Mad Margaret......................................Ann Carey
Dame Hannah.......................................Sarah Edwards

Zorah...Frances Moore
Ruth..Frances Baviello

Ghosts

Sir Rupert Murgatroyd...........................Hobson Young
Sir Joseph Murgatroyd..............................Allan Ware
Sir Lionel Murgatroyd............................Felix Noonan
Sir Conrad Murgatroyd.........................Harrison Fuller
Sir Desmond Murgatroyd........................Frank Dowling
Sir Gilbert Murgatroyd...........................Francis Clark
Sir Mervyn Murgatroyd........................Patrick Quinton
Sir Roderic Murgatroyd.......................Herbert Waterous
   Act I.—Fishing Village of Rederring, in Cornwall. Act II.—
Picture Gallery in Ruddigore Castle.   Time—Early in the 18th
Century.
   Staged by Milton Aborn.

"Ruddigore" was revived in May, 1927, by Lawrence J. Anhalt
at the Cosmopolitan Theatre, New York. On that occasion Alexander Clark was the Oakapple, Craig Campbell the Dauntless,
William Danforth the Sir Despard Murgatroyd, Violet Carlson the
Rose Maybud, and Herbert Waterous the Sir Roderic.

THE MIKADO

(32 performances)

Operetta in two acts by W. S. Gilbert, music by Arthur Sullivan.
Revived by the Civic Light Opera Company at Erlanger's Theatre,
New York, August 24, 1931.

Cast of characters—

The Mikado of Japan..........................William Danforth
Nanki-Poo.......................................Howard Marsh
Ko-Ko...Frank Moulan
Pooh-Bah.....................................Herbert Waterous
Pish-Tush..Allen Waterous
Yum Yum...Hizi Koyke
Pitti-Sing..................................... Ethel Clark
Peep-Bo......................................Eleanor Gilmore
Katisha...Vera Ross
   Act I.—Courtyard of Ko-Ko's Official Residence. Act II.—Ko-
Ko's Garden.
   Staged by Milton Aborn.

For the seventeenth and eighteenth weeks of the Gilbert and
Sullivan season Mr. Aborn repeated the performances of "The
Mikado" with which he had begun the season in May. Allen
Waterous and Eleanor Gilmore were the only changes in the
original cast.

"The Mikado" was repeated October 26 for eight performances
and December 25 for twelve performances with the same cast.

THREE TIMES THE HOUR

(23 performances)

A melodrama in three acts by Valentine Davies. Produced by Brock Pemberton at the Avon Theatre, New York, August 25, 1931.

Cast of characters—

John	Harold Heaton
Sylvia Jordan	Linda Carlon
Tom Crane	James Shelburne
Roger Hurlburt	Allen Ramsay
Colonel Beauchamp	Francis Stewart
Joan Porter	Anne Reynolds
Angus McKee	Charles C. Wilson
Dey	Hal K. Dawson
Haskins	Byron Russell
Cooper	Sam Levene
Jack Reed	Del Cleveland
Ramon Delgado	Pierre Mario
Linda Reed	Aleta Freel
Jeanne	Elvira Trabert
Mrs. Lawrence M. Blake	Katharine Warren
Mrs. Roger Hurlburt	Vira Rial
Henri	Jack Bohn
Robert Phillips	Ben Lackland
Postal Messenger	Harry Blythe
Anna D'Asti	Francesca Braggiotti
Smith	Philip Van Tassel
Hildah Lovering	Gertrude Flynn
Dr. Elliott	Horace Pollock
Davis	Jack Winne
Lawrence M. Blake	Robert Strange
Albert	Hamilton Brooks

Acts I, II and III.—The Fifth Avenue Residence of Lawrence M. Blake.

Staged by Antoinette Perry and Brock Pemberton.

Mrs. Lawrence M. Blake has invited a large crowd to a dancing party in the Blake home on Fifth Avenue. On the third floor her husband, Lawrence M. Blake the banker, is keeping in seclusion, guarded by detectives, because of a threatening letter he has received. Unless he does something about a bank that has closed its doors he will be shot by midnight. Despite the guards a would-be killer is admitted to the house and dashes upstairs to the Blake study. Later it is revealed that the killing plot was partly arranged by Blake himself to help him with a financial deal of international importance. The action, beginning on the first floor and continuing upward, one act to the floor, is theoretically simultaneous.

AFTER TOMORROW

(77 performances)

A drama in three acts by Hugh Stange and John Golden. Produced by John Golden at the Golden Theatre, New York, August 26, 1931.

Cast of characters—

Willie Taylor	Donald Meek
Elsie Taylor	Marjorie Garrett
Sidney Taylor	Barbara Robbins
Malcolm Jarvis	Joseph Sweeney
Pete Piper	Ross Alexander
Mrs. Piper	Josephine Hull
Florence Blandy	Edythe Elliott
Ruth Jacobs	Eleanor King
Alice Reilly	Angela Atwell
Dr. Sullivan	Ross Hertz

Acts I, II and III.—Living-room of the Taylors' Basement Apartment on Washington Heights, New York City.
Staged by John Golden and Hugh Stange.

Sidney Taylor and Pete Piper have been saving a marriage fund. They have $400 the week Pete gets a new job at $40 the week and decide on immediate marriage. The day before the ceremony Sidney's mother, disgusted with poverty, runs away with a roomer, Malcolm Jarvis, and her father, a plodding, lovable incompetent, suffers a stroke. The marriage fund goes to the doctors. A month later the eloping Mrs. Taylor sends back a thousand-dollar bond of her paramour's money. Pa Taylor turns it over to Sidney and Pete, swearing he saved it, and dies.

EARL CARROLL'S VANITIES

(278 performances)

A revue in two acts, dialogue by Ralph Spence and Eddie Welch; music and lyrics by Harold Adamson and Burton Lane. Produced by Earl Carroll at the Earl Carroll Theatre, New York, August 27, 1931.

Principals engaged—

Will Mahoney	Lillian Roth
William Demarest	Helen Lynd
Frank Mitchell	Olive Olsen
Jack Durant	Irene Ahlberg
Woods Miller	Lucille Page
Milton Watson	Beryl Wallace
Al Norman	Helen Arlen
Slade Brothers	Doris Andress
Rooney Ensemble	Olive Disen
Thermein Ensemble	Eileen Wenzel

Staged by Earl Carroll.

Principal songs—"Good-night, Sweetheart," "It's Great to be in Love" and "Tonight or Never."

FRIENDSHIP

(24 performances)

A comedy in three acts by George M. Cohan. Produced by Mr. Cohan at the Fulton Theatre, New York, August 31, 1931.

Cast of characters—

Joe Townsend	George M. Cohan
Jenny	Marjorie Dalton
Stephen West	Minor Watson
Louise Dale	Lee Patrick
Mrs. Steinert	Beatrice Moreland
Cecil	Clifford Jones
Sully	Howard Hull Gibson
Rudolph Steinert	Robert C. Fischer
Joan	Helen F. Cohan
Alfred	Thomas Gillen

Acts I and III.—Louise Dale's Home on the East Side, New York. Act II.—Stephen West's Bachelor Apartment.
Staged by George M. Cohan.

Joe Townsend, widower, has supported Louise Dale, a night club hostess, in comfort for three years in a New York apartment. Louise, achieving an education and culture, decides that Joe does not love her, but looks upon her merely as an interesting experiment. She decides to become a writer, marry Cecil Steinert, who also hopes to write, and pay Joe back all that she owes him. Cecil's father seeks to save his son from the alliance and comes to a clash of tempers with Townsend, who is trying to protect Louise. In the end Cecil is sent back to his mother and Louise is glad to return to and marry Joe Townsend.

CLOUDY WITH SHOWERS

(71 performances)

A comedy in three acts by Floyd Dell and Thomas Mitchell. Produced by Patterson McNutt at the Morosco Theatre, New York, September 1, 1931.

Cast of characters—

Peter Hammill	Thomas Mitchell
Miss Blake	Viola Ilma
Miss Jackman	Cyrena Smith
Miss Munn	Florence Hastings
Miss Pedrick	Joyce Hill
Miss Stearns	Charlotte Orr
Miss Thornhill	Helen Moore
Miss Critchlow	Rachel Hartzell

```
Miss Smith.......................................Lois  Brown
Dr. Grey......................................William  Walcott
Dr. Whipple.................................Clarence  Bellair
Reporter.........................................Barton  Adams
Alfredo...........................................Adrian  Rosley
O'Keefe............................................Victor  Killian
Short Man.........................................Owen  Martin
1st Trooper.....................................Richard  Abbott
2nd Trooper.......................................Tom  Dillon
Johnny..........................................Neil  Buckley
    Synopsis: Act I.—A Room at Quiller College. An Afternoon in
April.  Act II.—A Room in Alfredo's Cottage.  A Few Hours Later.
(The Curtain Is Lowered During Act II to Denote Passing of
Time.)  Act III.—Dr. Grey's Study.  That Night.
    Staged by Thomas Mitchell.
```

Peter Hammill, English professor at Quiller College, takes to task "Cricket" Critchlow, a member of his class, for having written a paper entitled "The Sex Life of the Modern Women." The paper, says the professor, is both untrue and in bad taste. Miss Critchlow argues the point with him, insisting that he not only does not know what he is talking about, but that he is prejudiced because he knows nothing of women and is actually afraid of the sex. He would be afraid, for instance, to have it known that he had taken her for a ride in his Ford. Accepting the dare, Hammill takes Cricket for a ride. They are wrecked in a storm near a roadhouse, and when they seek shelter run into a gangster murder and complications. They marry and avoid scandal.

THE MERRY WIDOW

(32 performances)

A musical comedy in three acts by Victor Leon and Leo Stein; music by Franz Lehar. Revived by the Civic Light Opera Company at the Erlanger Theatre, New York, September 7, 1931.

Cast of characters—

```
Popoff, Marsovian Ambassador.......................Hal  Forde
Natalie........................................Manilla  Powers
Prince Danilo...................................Donald  Brian
Sonia............................................Alice  McKenzie
Camille DeJolidon.................................Roy  Cropper
Marquis Cascada...................................Sano  Marco
Raoul De St. Brioche...........................Milton  Tully
Khadja.........................................Edward  Orchard
Nova Kovich....................................William  White
Olgo..............................................Dean  Dickens
Nish..............................................Will  Philbrick
Head Waiter...................................Walter  Franklyn
Zo-Zo..........................................Frances  Baviello
Fifi............................................Theo  Van Tassell
Lo-Lo...........................................Olga  Schumacher
Frou-Frou.......................................Dorothy  Duncan
Clo-Clo............................................Therese  Hyle
Margot.............................................Mary  Moss
Zu-Zu..........................................Dhenise  Delehente
Sapho...........................................Frances  Moore
```

aa

Guests, Servants, etc.: Frances Baldwin, Sylvia Gans, Mary Rysz, Kathryn Curl, Dorothy Shaw, Vera Muller, Irene Hubert, Marie Dolan, Cryilla Tuite, Theo Van Tassell, Dhenise Delehante, Frances Moore, Mary Adeline Moss, Frances Baviello, Dorothy Duncan, Therese Hyle, Olga Schumacher, June Yorkin, Walter Franklyn, Lloyd Ericsson, Rudy Glaisek, Siegfried Langer, August Loring, Sigmund Glukoff, Serge Ury, Mario Pichler, Otis Holwerk, Thomas Green.

Act I.—The Marsovian Embassy, Salon of the Ambassador. Act II.—Gardens of Sonia's Residence, in Paris. Act III.—Café Maxim, Paris.

Staged by Milton Aborn.

"The Merry Widow," originally produced at the New Amsterdam Theatre, New York, in 1907, was revived in 1921 by Henry W. Savage with Reginald Pasch as the Danilo and Lydia Lipkowska as Sonia, and again in 1929 by the Jolson Theatre Musical Comedy Company with Evan Thomas as the Danilo and Beppe De Vries as the Sonia. Donald Brian was the original Danilo. "The Merry Widow" was repeated February 22 for sixteen performances, with Beppe De Vries singing Sonia and Sara Blair the Natalie.

JUST TO REMIND YOU

(16 performances)

A drama in three acts by Owen Davis. Produced by Sam H. Harris at the Broadhurst Theatre, New York, September 7, 1931.

Cast of characters—

Dick Tanner	Tom Fadden
Irma Tanner	Isabel Baring
Jimmie Alden	Paul Kelly
Doris Sabin	Sylvia Field
Nettie Pierce	Peg Entwistle
John	Charles Fang
Miss Fallen	Genevieve Bowman
Jennie	Gladys Hurlbut
Mrs. Robins	Jessie Graham
Ben Fairchild	Jerome Cowan
Austin Jones	Harold Healy
Judge Higgins	Edward H. Robins
Eddie Mason	Owen Davis, Jr.
Dave Morris	Calvin Thomas
Dan Costigan	Frank Shannon
Tony	Frank McDonald
Jake	Charles Richards
Nolan	Charles Slattery
Mack	Henry Shelvey
Bill	Charles Naughton

Acts I, II and III.—Jimmie Alden's Laundry in New York City.

Staged by Melville Burke.

Jimmie Alden puts his savings into a laundry business in West Fifty-seventh Street, New York. Opening day he is visited by representatives of neighborhood gangs and advised to chip in $100 a month for protection. Jimmie refuses to be shaken down.

That night the front of his laundry is blown out. Still he refuses. Acid is put in his tubs. Jimmie stands firm until he is shot in the back. The day he is shot a grafting politician, Judge Higgins, is reading Lincoln's Gettysburg speech at a school dedication across the street. He has just reached the "of the people, by the people, for the people" line when Jimmie goes down.

FREE FOR ALL

(15 performances)

A musical comedy by Oscar Hammerstein 2d and Laurence Schwab; music by Richard A. Whiting. Produced by Schwab and Mandel at the Manhattan Theatre, New York, September 8, 1931.

Cast of characters—

Tom	Peter Lang
Stephen Potter, Sr.	Edward Emery
Joe Butler	David Hutcheson
Gracie Maynard	Thelma Tipson
Anita Allen	Vera Marsh
Michael Byrne	Peter Higgins
Marishka Tarasov	Tamara
Andy Bradford	Don Tomkins
Joan Sumner	Dorris Groday
Steve Potter, Jr.	Jack Haley
Marie Sinnot	Lilian Bond
Miss Gibbs	Dorothy Knapp
Dr. Raymond Allen	Philip Lord
Mr. Vergil Murgatroyd	Charles Althoff
Mrs. Ida Jones	Jeannette Loff
Pete Weber	Seth Arnold
Miners	Gus Howard, Clair Kramer, John Donahue
Terence Canavan	G. Pat Collins
Jim Allison	Harry Shannon
Silver Dollar Kate	Grace Johnston
Divorcees	Dorothea James, Olive Bayes, Julia Chandler
Digger Watkins	Al Downing
A Reporter	Robert Randall
A Nurse	Rae Powell
Mr. Preston	E. Saulpaugh
A Judge	Edward Walters

Act I.—Scene 1—Dining Room of Stephen Potter's Home. 2—Office of Dr. Raymond Allen. 3—Rambler Copper Mine. 4—"Free For All" Community Houses. Act II.—Scene 1—"Silver Dollar Kate's." 2—Top of the Shaft. 3—In the Mine. 4—Square in New Leaf Corners.

Staged by Oscar Hammerstein 2d; dances by Bobby Connelly.

Steve Potter, Jr., rich and worthless, even as an amateur magician, gets mixed up with a group of young communists led by Marie Sinnot, editor of a radical newspaper. Old Man Potter sends the crowd of them west to run one of his copper mines. The experience runs into money and music and Steve marries Marie at the curtain.

Principal song—"When Your Boy Becomes a Man."

LADIES OF CREATION

(72 performances)

A comedy by Gladys Unger. Produced by Raymond Moore at the Cort Theatre, New York, September 8, 1931.

Cast of characters—

```
Mr. Dinkle........................................Fred Stewart
Tessie Wade.....................................Paula Trueman
Sam Hannigan....................................John B. Litel
Sibyl Vanderlyn.................................Chrystal Herne
Mr. Abel........................................Frank Monroe
Idora Day......................................Dorothy MacKaye
Bruce Bellamy.................................Charles Campbell
Orme Willington.............................Charles Trowbridge
Florence Willington............................Spring Byington
    Synopsis: Act I.—Autumn.  Act II.—Winter.  Act III.—Spring.
    Acts I, II and III.—Private Office of Sibyl Vanderlyn, Inc.
    Staged by George Somnes.
```

Sibyl Vanderlyn, interior decorator, decides that her career is much more important to her than men. She uses sex appeal as a saleswoman, and vamps her general manager, Sam Hannigan. When Sam would take her seriously she fires him. When the business goes to pot Sibyl is forced to send for Sam, who refuses to return unless she agrees to marry him, which she does.

THE MAN ON STILTS

(6 performances)

A comedy in three acts by Edwin and Albert Barker. Produced by Arthur Hopkins at the Plymouth Theatre, New York, September 9, 1931.

Cast of characters—

```
A Radio Announcer............................James MacDonald
A Radio Engineer.................................Garland Kerr
First Porter.......................................Jack Tyler
Second Porter..................................William Layden
Third Porter.......................................James Bruce
Fourth Porter..................................Harold Enright
Joe Day........................................Raymond Bramley
A Bellboy........................................Bruce Duncan
Miss Tousey.....................................Eda Heinemann
Policeman Doyle.................................James T. Ford
Georgia Van Allen................................Helen Dodge
Mrs. Van Allen...................................Flora Zabelle
Mark Van Allen...................................Harry Knapp
Senator Abner Tarbotton......................Robert Cummings
Godfrey Block...................................Harry Ellerbe
Rufus Blindloss...............................George Pembroke
Heine Clabber.................................Harold Kennedy
Ted Sensibull................................Chas. P. Thompson
Englehouse Verbena Coffypopper.....................Paul Porter
Minnie Schmaltz..................................Maud Burns
```

```
A Song Plugger...........................Chas. F. O'Connor
An Accordion Player...............................Len Doig
McGann...............................Hobart Cavanaugh
Phœbe Smith...........................Madeline King
A. L. Fishel...............................Mel Tyler
B. J. Goldfoyle.........................Samuel Schneider
Miss Tabloid...............................Helen Dudley
Mr. White Sheet...........................Elmer Cornell
Mr. Pink Sheet.............................Jack Daniels
Mr. Yellow Sheet........................Arthur Marlowe
"Honey" Callahan.......................Lillian Emerson
Cleary...............................Kirk Brown, Jr.
A Detective...............................Owen Coll
A Magazine Man.........................Pascal Cowan
The Human Fly..........................Frank Layton
    Acts I, II and III.—Suite in the Belshazzar Hotel, New York.
    Staged by Arthur Hopkins.
```

Godfrey Block, working on a street paving job in San Francisco, seizes the steam roller to cover the amount of salary due him. Playfully he starts running his property east. A drunken newspaper man writes a story describing the adventure of the first leg of a cross-country tour. A self-seeking senator fastens on the stunt as an aid to his good roads campaign. Within a week Godfrey is a nationally publicized character. Arriving in New York, he is disgusted with the fuss that has been made over him and publicly denounces the scheme and all its backers. Which, in the news columns, makes him a bigger hero than ever.

THE SINGING RABBI

(4 performances)

A musical comedy in three acts by Bores and Harry Thomashefsky; music by J. Rumshinsky and Harry Lubin. Produced by Harry Thomashefsky at the Selwyn Theatre, New York, September 10, 1931.

Cast of characters—

```
Rifka ...............................Winifred Wee Griffin
Miriam...............................Edna Archer Crawford
Yankele...............................Florenz Ames
Jacob...............................Will Claire
The Widow Sheindel.....................Regina Zuckerberg
Shloima...............................Philip Ryder
Nuchem...............................Sam Ash
Regina...............................Flora LeBreton
Gidalia...............................Bores Thomashefsky
Padula...............................Tino Valenti
Bianca...............................Frances Dumas
Baron Koch.............................Adolph Lyons
Madame Dodee...........................Gertrude Mudge
Bettie...............................Donna Fairchild
Jean...............................Robert Rhodes
The Captain...........................Harry Pierson
First Mate...........................Russell Harvey
Miss Van Buren........................Betty Keyes
    Act I.—Home of the Widow Sheindel in Galicia. Act II.—Aboard
```

Steamer En Route to New York.   Act III.—The Widow Sheindel's
Home in New York.
Staged by William E. Morris.

Shloima, Nuchem, Jacob and Gidalia Sheindel, returning to
their old home in Galicia after having won success in various
parts of the world, decide to center their future activities in New
York and take their beloved mother, the Widow Sheindel, with
them.   On the way over their niece, Regina, falls in love with a
worthless aristocrat but is saved this side of the gangplank.   The
venture in New York is entirely satisfactory.

GEORGE WHITE'S SCANDALS

(202 performances)

A revue in two acts, sketches by George White, Lew Brown
and Irving Caesar; music by Lew Brown and Ray Henderson.
Assembled and produced by Mr. White at the Apollo Theatre,
New York, September 14, 1931.

Principals engaged—

Willie Howard	Ethel Merman
Everett Marshall	Barbara Blair
Rudy Vallée	Ethel Barrymore Colt
Ray Bolger	Jane Alden
Ross McLean	Gale Quadruplets
Fred Manatt	Joan Abbott
Peggy Mosely	Loomis Sisters
Alice Frohman	Hazel Boffinger

Staged by George White.

Principal songs—"Life Is Just a Bowl of Cherries," "That's
Why Darkies Are Born," "This Is the Missus," "My Song" and
"The Thrill Is Gone."

THE CONSTANT SISTER

(64 performances)

A comedy in three acts by Mae West.   Produced by Constant
Productions, Inc., at the Royale Theatre, New York, September
14, 1931.

Cast of characters—

Cokey Jenny	Adele Gilbert
Harry	Donald Kirke
Lou	Jack McKee
Joe Malone	Walter Glass
Bearcat Delaney	Russell Hardie
Buck	Ralph Sanford
Babe Gordon	Mae West
Charlie Yates	Arthur R. Vinton

```
Bellhop.........................................James  Dunmore
Man-in-the-Booth............................Bernard  Thornton
Mr.  Gay.......................................Rudolph  Toombs
Liverlips..........................................Robert  Rains
Money Johnson...................................George  Givet
Headwaiter.....................................Lorenzo  Tucker
Waiter...........................................Hubert  Brown
Wayne  Baldwin..................................Walter  Petrie
Leonard  Colton.....................................Paul  Huber
Barry Washburn.................................William  Daly
Entertainer  ("African  Strut").......................Paul  Meers
Detective-Sergeant...............................Joseph  Holicky
Annette..........................................Leona  Love
Clara...........................................Ollie  Burgoyne
Liza.............................................Trixie  Smith
Defense  Attorney...................................Paul  Huber
White  Characters:  Adele  Gilbert,  Grey  Patrick,  Christine  Wagner,
    Cora  Olsen,  George  Bush,  Harry  Howard,  George  Bloom,  Billy
    Kohut,  Billy  Rapp.
Colored  Characters:  Marie  Remsen,  Florence  Lee,  Allen  Cohen,
    George  Williams,  Henry  Matthews,  Harry  Owens.
    Acts  I,  II  and  III.—In  the  streets,  hotels,  apartment  houses  and
speakeasies  of  Harlem,  New  York.
```

The adventures of Babe Gordon include her affair with Bearcat
Delaney, whom she ruins as a prizefighter; Money Johnson, the
black boss of a colored resort in Harlem, and Wayne Baldwin,
proprietor of a department store. In the end she returns to Bearcat Delaney to protect him against a charge of murder, but retains her side interest in Baldwin. The play is a dramatization of
Miss West's novel of the same title.

OLD MAN MURPHY

(48 performances)

A comedy in three acts by Patrick Kearney and Harry Wagstaffe Gribble. Revived by Robert V. Newman at the Hudson
Theatre, New York, September 14, 1931.

Cast of characters—

```
Dudley  Weatherbee.............................Walter  Vaughn
Margaret  Murfree..............................Gertrude  Fowler
Elinor  Murfree...................................Peggy  Conklin
Hopkins........................................St.  Clair  Bayfield
Charles  Murfree................................Henry  O'Neill
Mike  Donovan..................................Henry  Wadsworth
Henry  Stonehill.............................William  R.  Randall
Patrick  Murphy.................................Arthur  Sinclair
Widow  Donovan..................................Marie  O'Neill
Larry  Heffernan..................................Leo  Curley
    Act  I.—Murfree Home.  Acts  II  and  III.—Widow  Donovan's.
    Staged  by  Harry  Wagstaffe  Gribble  and  Lawrence  Bolton.
```

Produced originally at the Royale Theatre, New York. "Old
Man Murphy" ran from May 18 to June 6, was transferred to
the Fulton, where it played until July 11, 1931. See "Best Plays
of 1930-31."

FAST AND FURIOUS

(7 performances)

A colored revue in two acts. Assembled and produced by Forbes Randolph at the New Yorker Theatre, New York, September 15, 1931.

Principals engaged—

Tim Moore	Baby Goins
Clinton (Dusty) Fletcher	Grace Smith
Melva Boden	Neeka Shaw
Helmsley Winfield	Lois Deppe
Juano Hernandez	Emma Maitland
Al Richard	Edna Guy
Aurelia Wheeldin	Etta Moten
Jackie Mabley	Midgie Lane

Forbes Randolph Choir

Staged by Forbes Randolph.

SINGIN' THE BLUES

(45 performances)

A Negro melodrama by John McGowan. Produced by Alex Aarons and Vinton Freedley at the Liberty Theatre, New York, September 16, 1931.

Cast of characters—

"Potato-Eyes" Johnson	Ashley Cooper
"Knuckles" Lincoln	Mantan Moreland
Jim Williams	Frank Wilson
"Bad Alley" Joe	John Sims
Dooley	James Young
Colored Policeman	Joe Byrd
Rocky	Johnny Reid
Eddie	Shirley Jordon
Mazie	Jennie Sammons
Jay	S. W. Warren
Dave Crocker	Jack Carter
Edith	Estelle Bernier
Sam Mason	Ralph Theodore
"Whitey" Henderson	Millard Mitchell
Tod	C. C. Gill
Sid	Percy Wade
Susan Blake	Isabell Washington
Elise Joyce	Fredi Washington
Jack Wilson	Percy Verwayne
"Sizzles" Brown	Maud Russell
Officer Frank	James Stark
A Singer	Susaye Brown

The Lindy Hoppers: Shorty and Esalene, Jordon and Jordon, George and Betty.

The Four Flash Devils; Bruce Johnson's Washboard Serenaders; Wen Talbert's Choir; Eubie Blake and His Orchestra.

Act I.—Scene 1—Johnson's Pool Room, Chicago.   2—Chicago Street.   3—Crocker's Place, Harlem.   Act II.—Scene 1—Susan's Room.   2—Magnolia Club.   Act III.—Magnolia club, police station and Crocker's office.

Staged by Bertram Harrison; dances by Sammy Lee.

Jim Williams, shooting his way out of a Chicago crap game, accidentally kills a policeman. Fleeing to New York Jim meets Susan Blake in a night club, falls in love on sight, and thereafter hides from the police, mostly in Susan's room. Chased through a couple of night clubs where Susan works Jim manages to get away. Susan may follow him South.

I LOVE AN ACTRESS

(20 performances)

A comedy in three acts, adapted by Chester Erskin from the Hungarian of Lazlo Fodor. Produced by Chester Erskin at the Times Square Theatre, New York, September 17, 1931.

Cast of characters—

Valentin..John Dunn
Mr. Revesz...David Leonard
Mr. Keleman..................................William Franklin
Felix...John Williams
Marianne......................................Dorothy Mathews
Mr. Franks.....................................Percy Woodley
Eva Sandor....................................Muriel Kirkland
George..Walter Abel
Willie Strauss.............................Ernest Glendinning
Boske..Ellen Lowe
Caroline.................................Alice Belmore Cliffe
The Doctor.......................................Fuller Mellish
The Nervous Gentleman......................Etienne Girardot
Mother of the Bride..............................Maude Nolan
The Bride...Lora Hays
The Groom.......................................Robert Bowen
First Porter.......................................E. A. Treco
Second Porter..................................Albert Sherwin
Shoppers and Travelers: Maude Sinclair, Lillian Ross, Gene Powell, Frank Ross, Charlotte Weinstein, Gail Barrington, Fred Steinway, Edward Van Danaker, Jane Hamilton, Jean Mann, Jean Belle Kook, Louise Kay, Augusta B. Scott and Beatrice Punsly.
Pages: Herbert Schwartz, Jackie Winston and Bernard Punsly.
Act I.—Interior of a Fashionable Department Store in Buda-Pesth. Act II.—Reception Room in Eva Sandor's Villa in the Svabhegy Mountains. Act III.—Salon of Eva Sandor. Act IV.—At One of the Gates in the Eastern Terminal, Buda-Pesth.
Staged by Chester Erskin.

George, a young engineer, falls desperately in love with Eva, the favorite actress of Budapest, and follows her everywhere, even into her home. George's persistence is about to be rewarded by Eva when Willie Strauss, the richest man in Hungary, proposes marriage. Eva is about to run away with Willie when George appears at the railway station and is the cause of her missing the train.

HE

(40 performances)

A comedy in three acts by Alfred Savoir, adapted by Chester
Erskin. Produced by the Theatre Guild at the Guild Theatre,
New York, September 21, 1931.

Cast of characters—

Bartender	Leslie Hunt
Elevator Man	Claude Rains
Monsieur Matard, Hotel Proprietor	Cecil Yapp
Professor Coq	Eugene Powers
The Invalid, His Daughter	Viola Frayne
Miss Scoville	Edith Meiser
Commander Trafalgar	Edward Rigby
He	Tom Powers
Princess	Violet Kemble Cooper
Bell Boy	Lester Salkow
Monsieur Ping	William Gargan
Hotel Doctor	Le Roy Brown
First Porter	Lawrence Hurdle, Jr.
Second Porter	Charles W. Adams
Doctor	Robert Le Sueur

Acts I, II and III.—The Bar of a Hotel in the Bernese Alps of
Switzerland.

Staged by Chester Erskin.

He appears in the bar of a hotel in the Bernese Alps just after
a convention of free thinkers has voted to abolish God. He introduces himself as God. He is accepted lightly by the delegates
to the convention. When certain happenings, including an unexpected change in the weather, a small avalanche that passes over
yet does not harm an old lady, and a vicious prizefighter who is
completely upset by the visiting deity, He is viewed with some
alarm. They try imprisonment, but are forced to release the visitor when the help strikes and a glacier embraces the hotel. He
helps them dig their way out, with the aid of a Napoleonic elevator
man and a whip, and goes peacefully back to the sanitarium when
the keeper comes for him.

THE CHOCOLATE SOLDIER

(16 performances)

A musical comedy in three acts adapted by Stanislaus Stange
from the original of Bernauer and Jacobson; music by Franz
Lehar. Revived by the Civic Light Opera Company at Erlanger's
Theatre, New York, September 21, 1931.

Cast of characters—

Nadina...Vivienne Segal
Aurelia...Ann Carey
Mascha...Vivian Hart
Bummerli.......................................Charles Purcell
Capt. Massakroff................................Detmar Poppen
Col. Casimir Popoff...............................Hal Forde
Maj. Alexis Sparidoff............................Roy Cropper
A Dancer.....................................Theo. Van Tassel
　　Act I.—Nadina's Sleeping Apartment in Popoff's House. Acts II
and III.—Garden of Popoff's House.
　　Staged by Milton Aborn.

Two previous revivals of "The Chocolate Soldier," based on George Bernard Shaw's "Arms and the Man," were made in the season of 1921-22 and that of 1929-30. The first was sponsored by the Messrs. Shubert at the Century Theatre, and had Tessa Kosta as the Nadina and Donald Brian as Bummerli. Last season's revival was made by the Jolson Theatre Musical Comedy Company, at the Jolson Theatre, under the direction of Milton Aborn. Alice Mackenzie was the Nadina and Charles Purcell the Bummerli.

THE BREADWINNER

(55 performances)

A comedy in three acts by Somerset Maugham. Produced by Messmore Kendall at the Booth Theatre, New York, September 22, 1931.

Cast of characters—

Charles Battle..................................A. E. Matthews
Margery...Marie Lohr
Judy..Betty Linley
Patrick..Angus Macleod
Alfred Granger....................................Eric Cowley
Dorothy.......................................Eleanor Woodruff
Diana..Irene Blair
Timothy..Charley Powers
　　Acts I, II and III.—Drawing room of the Battles' House at Golders
Green.
　　Staged by A. E. Matthews.

Charles Battle, facing bankruptcy on the London stock exchange, unnerved by worry and disgusted with the attitude of his wife and children, who regard him as no more than a good provider, refuses the help of his friends and permits himself to be hammered out of the exchange. Reactions of the family run true to Battle's expectations. He gives them three-fourths of what he has saved from the smash and goes his way.

DID I SAY NO?

(15 performances)

A comedy in three acts by Elizabeth Miele. Produced by Hamilton Productions, Inc., at the Forty-eighth Street Theatre, New York, September 22, 1931.

Cast of characters—

Irving Greenberg	Herbert Rudley
Sophia Greenberg	Miriam Stuart
Courtney Travers	Coburn Goodwin
Sam Goldstein	Martin Wolfson
Patrick Goldstein	John McNulty
Rebecca Greenberg	Anna Appel
Judge Louis Levine	Maurice Freeman
Mrs. Mollie Hoffman	Helen Salinger
Mrs. Michael Murphy	Maida Lea
Philomena Sorrento	June Mullin
Joe Collins	Samuel Dockrell
Mrs. Fred Brighton	Helen Appel
Hugh Carrington	Thomas M. Reynolds
Officer McKee	Gordon Hamilton
Judge Warren	Edward Poland
Prosecutor Berkley	Thomas V. Morrison
Court Clerk	George Wilhelm
Court Reporter	Samuel Pierce

Staged by Priestley Morrison.

Rebecca Greenberg, proprietress of an auction room, has trouble keeping her son and daughter, Irving and Sophia, out of trouble. Sophia quit her fiancé, Sam Goldstein, having been lured by a slick crook. Irving, in the shop when Policeman Murphy accidentally kills himself, is accused of the crime. Rebecca makes a successful mother-plea for Irving before the jury and Sophia is saved from the crook.

IF I WERE YOU

(77 performances)

A comedy in a prologue and three acts by Sholem Aleichem. Produced by Messrs. Shubert at the Ambassador Theatre, New York, September 23, 1931.

Cast of characters—

Ivanoff	Edward Leiter
First Student	Martin Cravath
Second Student	Arnold Emanuel
Third Student	Charles Davis
Fourth Student	Antonio Passy
Schneyerson	Harry Mervis
Siomka	Jack Marcus
Sarah	Fernanda Eliscu
Betty	Natalie Browning

```
David Shapiro.............................Maurice Schwartz
                                        ⎧  Joan Claire
Betty's Schoolmates.......................⎨  Istar Barzel
                                        ⎩  Estelle Kamins
Greensberg........................................Harry Worth
Hourwitch...................................Charles Livingstone
Katz..............................................Meyer Levin
Chief of Gendarmes................................George Nash
Janitor............................................Sam Lerer
Students. Gendarmes: Charles Davis, Louis Pennewell, Zack Rosen,
    Constantin Krummel, Antonio Passy, Martin Cravath, Arnold
    Emanuel.
    Prologue—Suite in a Fashionable Hotel. Acts I, II and III.—
Home of David Shapiro in a Russian City Outside the Jewish Pale.
Staged by Maurice Schwartz.
```

During a students' reunion Ivanoff, an aristocrat, offers to trade identities for a year with Schneyerson, a Jew, to prove there is no real racial discrimination in Russia. The change is made. Ivanoff, armed with Schneyerson's papers, goes to a strange city. He rooms at the home of David Shapiro and falls in love with Shapiro's daughter Betty. Schneyerson, visiting Ivanoff, also loves Betty and would break his word rather than see her tricked into marriage with a Christian under an assumed name. Ivanoff and Schneyerson are arrested, their respective identities reëstablished. Schneyerson gets Betty.

PEOPLE ON THE HILL

(5 performances)

A drama in three acts by Torvald Liljencrantz. Produced by the Midtown Producers, Inc., at the Comedy Theatre, New York, September 25, 1931.

Cast of characters—

```
Barry Michaels...............................Alden Chase
Wick Martin...............................Burgess Meredith
Madge Davis......................................Jane Kim
Coralie Martin................................Elaine Temple
Packy Davis...................................Grover Burgess
Fan Arndt....................................Claudia Morgan
Chrystal Martin................................Helen Coburn
Laura Martin...................................Irene Shirley
Hugh Henery................................Murray Stephens
Miss Rogers..................................Elizabeth Tyler
Mr. Milliken..................................Warren Murray
    Acts I, II and III.—By a lone cypress on a hilltop and at Laura
Martin's.
    Staged by Jerome Mayer.
```

A group of young liberals, including Barry Michaels and Coralie Martin, are spending the summer together. They assert their right to accept life unconventionally, subscribing to its laws and regulations according to individual discretion. Barry and Coralie decide to marry. Barry is drowned in the surf. Coralie admits that she is pregnant. Her younger sister Chrystal, also in love with Barry, begs for a chance to share the responsibility of rearing Barry's baby. Coralie's older sister, Laura, insists that Coralie shall protect her child's name by marrying a man she doesn't love. The infant dies before Coralie's wedding. Chrystal jumps with the body into the sea to join Barry. The group goes to Paris.

THE HOUSE OF CONNELLY

(91 performances)

A drama in two acts by Paul Green. Produced by the Group Theatre, Inc., under the auspices of the Theatre Guild, at the Martin Beck Theatre, New York, September 28, 1931.

Cast of characters—

Big Sis...Fanny De Knight
Big Sue..Rose McClendon
Patsy Tate....................................Margaret Barker
Will Connelly....................................Franchot Tone
Jesse Tate...Art Smith
Geraldine Connelly...............................Stella Adler
Evelyn Connelly...............................Eunice Stoddard
Robert Connelly..............................Morris Carnovsky
Mrs. Connelly.....................................Mary Morris
Duffy..J. E. Bromberg
Virginia Buchanan.............................Dorothy Patten
Essie...Ruth Nelson
Charlie..Walter Coy
Jodie..William Challee
Alec.......................................Clement Wilenchick
Ransom...Philip Robinson
Reuben..Clifford Odetts
Isaac..Friendly Ford
Tyler...Gerrit Kraber
Alf..Robert Lewis
Henry..Herbert Ratner
Serenaders: Phœbe Brand, Walter Coy, William Challee, Virginia
  Farmer, Friendly Ford, Sylvia Feningston, Gerrit Kraber,
  Lewis Leverett, Gertrude Maynard, Paula Miller, Robert Lewis,
  Clifford Odetts, Philip Robinson, Clement Wilenchick.
  Act I.—Scene 1—Field on the Connelly Plantation. 2—Dining-
room in Connelly Hall. 3—Ruined Garden of Connelly Hall. Act
II.—Dining-room.
  Staged by Lee Strasberg and Cheryl Crawford.

See page 145. See page 145.

NIKKI

(39 performances)

A musical comedy in two acts by John Monk Saunders, music by Philip Charig. Produced by Harrison Hall at the Longacre Theatre, New York, September 29, 1931.

Cast of characters—

```
Shepard (Shep) Lambert....................Douglass Montgomery
Nikki...................................................Fay Wray
Francis (The Washout)............................John Brooke
William (Bill) Talbot.........................Nathaniel Wagner
Cary Lockwood.....................................Archie Leach
Willard (Wiffie) Crouch.......................Louis Jean Heydt
Kiss-Me-Quick.................................Bobbie Tremaine
Benj...........................................Rudolfo Badaloni
Additional characters and entertainers: Marcel Rosseau, Albert Fon-
    taine, Louis Sterner, Modesca and Michael, Bobbie Tremaine,
    Edith Murray, the De Limas, Page Innes, Frank Chapman,
    Delphine Dawn, Julia Barron.
Acts I and II.—Bars in Paris and a bullring in Lisbon.
Staged by William B. Friedlander.
```

Shep, Francis, Bill and Wiffie, aviators out of the war, still shaken and striving to forget with the help of liquor and liquorish adventures, meet Nikki holding a gentleman's false teeth in a Paris bar. The boys become devoted to Nikki and take her on a tour of the Paris bars and afterward to Lisbon to see a bullfight.

Principal song—"Taking Off."

WASHINGTON HEIGHTS

(7 performances)

A drama in three acts by Vincent Lawrence. Produced by Philip Goodman at the Maxine Elliott Theatre, New York, September 29, 1931.

Cast of characters—

```
Jim Grove...................................William Harrigan
Mary Grove......................................Joanna Roos
Louise Boley................................Constance McKay
Joe Boley.......................................Clay Clement
Beatrice Gaynor.................................Jane Bramley
The Policeman.................................William Crane
The Child.......................................Drew Price
Acts I, II and III.—Living-dining Room of the Grove Apartment
in Washington Heights, New York.
Staged by Philip Goodman.
```

Jim and Mary Grove, living a hand-to-mouth existence in an uptown New York apartment, are nerve-frayed and restless. Jim, prodded by a sex-crazed neighbor, suffers an obsession culminating in his attack upon a visiting niece, who falls from a fire-escape and is killed.

PAYMENT DEFERRED

(70 performances)

A drama in prologue, three acts and epilogue, adapted by Jeffrey Dell from a novel by C. S. Forester. Produced by Gilbert Miller at the Lyceum Theatre, New York, September 30, 1931.

Cast of characters—

Hammond.......................................S. Victor Stanley
A Prospective Tenant...........................Horace Sinclair
William Marble.................................Charles Laughton
Annie Marble......................................Cicely Oates
Winnie Marble..................................Elsa Lanchester
Jim Medland.......................................Paul Longuet
Charlie Hammond.............................S. Victor Stanley
Madame Collins.................................Dorice Fordred
Doctor Atkinson....................................Lionel Pape
Harry Gentle..................................Stanley Harrison
Bert Bricketts....................................Malcolm Soltan
    Acts I, II and III.—Living Room at 3, Malcolm Road, Dulwich.
    Staged by H. K. Ayliff.

William Marble, a bank clerk in fear of his creditors, murders his nephew, Jim Medland, newly come from Australia and without friends or acquaintances in London, and buries the body in the garden. Marble, haunted by conscience, spends the money the crime nets him, but brings nothing but successive disasters upon himself and his family. In the end he seems likely to be charged with the murder of his wife, who has taken poison after learning her husband's guilty secret and discovering his unfaithfulness.

THE GOOD COMPANIONS

(68 performances)

A comedy in two parts adapted by J. B. Priestley and Edward Knoblock from Mr. Priestley's novel of the same title. Produced by Lee Shubert at the Forty-fourth Street Theatre, New York, October 1, 1931.

Cast of characters—

Mrs. Oakroyd...................................Mildred Cottell
Sam Oglethorpe...............................Matthew Boulton
Leonard Oakroyd..............................Robert Harrigan
Albert Tuggeridge..................................Max Kirby
Jess Oakroyd....................................George Carney
Elizabeth Trant...................................Valerie Taylor
The Landlord at Tumbleby..........................Frank Petley
Effie Longstaffe...............................Norah Wyn Clare
Inigo Jollifant...................................Hugh Sinclair
Fauntley..J. C. Aubrey
Susie Dean..Vera Lennox
Morton Mitcham.................................Henry Hallatt
Mrs. Tarvin......................................Isobel Ohmead

```
Mr. Tarvin....................................Wallace Evennett
Joby Jackson....................................Ernest Jay
Professor Miro................................Robert Harrigan
Linoleum Man................................Matthew Boulton
Envelope Man....................................Frank Petley
Summers..........................................Roy Emerton
The Ginger Policeman............................J. C. Aubrey
Jimmy Nunn...................................Wallace Evennett
Elsie Longstaffe..............................Norah Wyn Clare
Joe Brundit.......................................Roy Emerton
Mrs. Joe.........................................Isobel Ohmead
Jerry Jerningham..................................Max Kirby
Mrs. Mounders...........................Lillian Brennard Tonge
A Waiter..........................................James Jolly
Mr. Dulver.......................................Basil Hanbury
                                              ( Boyd Gilmour
                                              | Philip Tonge
The Dulver Family.............................{ Walter Plinge
                                              | Minnie Pine
                                              ( Ann Pinner
A Photographer................................Robert Harrigan
A Reporter....................................Matthew Boulton
Landlord of the Crown, Gatford.....................James Jolly
Lady Partlit...................................Mildred Cottell
Ridvers...........................................Frank Petley
Mr. Pitzner........................................Ernest Jay
Ethel Georgia................................Marcella Swanson
Monte Mortimer..................................James Baber
Mr. Gooch.........................................J. C. Aubrey
Railway Porter..................................Basil Hanbury
    Acts I and II.—On the English highroad; at Rawsley, Gatford, and
Bruddersford.
    Staged by Julian Wylie.
```

Jess Oakroyd, having lost his job and quarreled with his wife, takes to the road. Elizabeth Trant, being restless and eager to know life, goes motoring. Inigo Jollifant, getting more fun out of composing popular songs than teaching, quits his job at the Washbury school to go adventuring with Morton Mitcham and Susie Dean, showfolk. They all meet in Rawsley, where Miss Trant agrees to finance a reorganization of the Dinky-Do Concert Party and call it the Good Companions. Six months later the Good Companions are a going concern, but are temporarily put out of business by a hoodlum riot at Gatford.

THE CAMELS ARE COMING

(11 performances)

A comedy in three acts by Don Mullally. Produced by Mr. Mullally at the President Theatre, New York, October 2, 1931.

Cast of characters—

```
Terry Tracy..................................J. Anthony Hughes
Bobby Marchante................................Shirley Booth
Bell Boy..........................................Clyde Stone
Jim Waldrone....................................Earl Simmons
Milton Markowitz...........................Joseph Greenwald
Sylvia Markowitz...............................Gita Zucker
Manny Manoff..................................Guido Alexander
```

```
Alice Buckley.....................................Rose Mary King
Eddie Collins........................................Lionel Dante
Glenn Thomas.......................................Bill Vaughn
Millicent Bryant.............................Caroline Humphries
William Wallace................................Anthony Pawley
Matty Wolfe..................................Thomas McQuillan
Clay Farrell.......................................Edward Marr
Charlie Evans.........................................Jack Reed
Frank Smith...........................................Joe Gerson
    Acts I and II.—Hotel Sitting Room of Terry Tracy's Suite.  Act
III.—Stage of a Theatre.
    Staged by Don Mullally.
```

Terry Tracy, playwright, is urged by his fiancée, Bobby Marchante, to quit drinking and get back to writing plays, and by his pal and adviser, Jim Waldrone, to accept the offer of Milton Markowitz, who offers to finance a play by Terry if Terry will put on paper a play he, Markowitz, has in his head. Terry finally accepts the Markowitz offer and thereafter fights desperately to preserve his art from being violated by the well-meaning but low-caste Markowitz who, among other things, insists upon putting a herd of camels in his drama.

THE LEFT BANK

(242 performances)

A drama in three acts by Elmer Rice. Produced by Mr. Rice at the Little Theatre, New York, October 5, 1931.

Cast of characters—

```
Claire Shelby.............................Katherine Alexander
John Shelby........................................Horace Braham
Alan Foster.......................................Cledge Roberts
Claude..........................................Alfred A. Hesse
Waldo Lynde..................................Donald Macdonald
Susie Lynde.....................................Millicent Green
Lillian Garfield..................................Merle Maddern
Charlie Miller.....................................Fred Herrick
Joe Klein...........................................Murray Alper
Dorothy Miller.....................................Rose Lerner
Gustave Jensen.................................A. L. Bartolot
Sonya Darachek...................................Tamara Nicoll
Miriam Van Diesen.............................M. Dorothy Day
Willard Simmons................................Edward Downes
Mary Adams...........................................Janet Cool
    Acts I, II and III.—Bedroom in a Hotel on the Boulevard Mont-
parnasse, Paris.
```

See page 208.

ENEMY WITHIN

(8 performances)

A drama in three acts by Will Piper and Lois Howell. Produced by Roy Walling at the Hudson Theatre, New York, October 5, 1931.

Cast of characters—

Regan...George MacQuarrie
Pete...Royal C. Stout
Lily McNab....................................Eleanor Williams
Izzy Rabinowitz................................Milton Wallace
Kenneth Mason...................................Edwin Whitner
Frank Henderson......................................Lew Eckels
Selma Wolfe..Anne Forrest
"Uncle" Wolfe....................................Arthur S. Ross
Don Candler....................................Walter N. Greaza
Jim Moran..Sam J. Park
Leslie Van Ingen...............................Wilbur DeRouge
Edgar "Count" Muller.......................Herbert Ashton, Jr.
Qualino...Ricardo Bengali
Judge Gibbons..................................Ben MacQuarrie
Nicoletti.....................................Edward Colebrook

   Act I.—Scene 1—Speakers' Rostrum at Madison Square Garden.
2—Reception Room in the Regan Club. Act II.—Private Room at the
"Count's." Act III.—Scene 1—Reception Room. 2—Judge Gibbons'
Court.

   Staged by Roy Walling.

Selma Wolfe, whose father is thick with the political crook of his
district, one Regan, has been decently brought up but becomes
involved in a murder when she is tricked into driving the murder
car. She is willing to testify against the gang, but Attorney
Don Candler, who loves her, saves her the disgrace. A bullet
intended for Candler is deflected and kills Regan.

THE GEISHA

(16 performances)

A musical comedy in two acts by Owen Hall, music by Sidney
Jones, lyrics by Harry Greenbank. Revived by the Civic Light
Opera Company at Erlanger's Theatre, New York, October 5,
1931.

Cast of characters—

O Mimosa San.......................................Hizi Koyke
Juliette Diamont....................................Ethel Clark
Nami (Wave of the Sea)......................Theo. Van Tassell
O Kiku San (Chrysanthemum)..................Dhoris Delehante
A Mana San (Blossom).........................Margaret Walker
O Kinkoto San (Golden Harp)..................Olga Schumacher
Komurasaki (Little Violet)...........................Mary Moss
Lady Constance Wynne..............................Ann Carey
Miss Mari Worthington............................Cyrilla Tuite
Miss Ethel Hurst...................................Irene Hubert
Miss Mabel Grant................................Kathryn Curl
Miss Molly Seamore................................Rella Winn
Reginald Fairfax...................................Roy Cropper
Dick Cunningham..................................Sano Marco
Arthur Cuddy...................................S. Otis Wolwerk
George Grimson.................................August Loring
Captain Katana...................................Milton Tully
Takemine..Edw. Orchard
Wun Hi...James T. Powers
The Marquis Imari............................Detmar Poppen

Act I.—House of Ten Thousand Joys. Act II.—Chrysanthemum
Fête in the Palm Garden.
Staged by Milton Aborn.

"The Geisha" was a hit of the season of 1896-97. It was revived by Arthur Hammerstein and the Messrs. Shubert in March,
1913, with Jimmie Powers singing his original rôle of Wun Hi,
surrounded by an all-star cast that included Alice Zeppilli as O
Mimosa San, Lina Abarbanell as Molly Seamore, Frank Pollock
as Capt. Katana, Carl Gantvoort as Fairfax, Charles King as
Cunningham and Pauline Hall as Lady Constance.

THE STREETS OF NEW YORK, OR POVERTY IS NO CRIME

(87 performances)

A melodrama in five acts by Dion Boucicault. Revived by the
New York Repertory Company at the Forty-eighth Street Theatre,
New York, October 6, 1931.

Cast of characters—

Lucy Fairweather (The Heroine).....................Dorothy Gish
Mark Livingstone (The Hero).......................Rollo Peters
Badger...Romney Brent
Gideon Bloodgood (The Villain)...................Moffat Johnston
Alida Bloodgood..................................Fania Marinoff
Mrs. Puffy..Jessie Busley
Puffy..Frank Conlan
Paul Fairweather..................................Sam Wren
Captain Fairweather...............................A. P. Kaye
Mrs. Fairweather..............................Winifred Johnston
Dan Puffy......................................Mervin Williams
Daniels..Jock Munro
The Duke of Calcavella........................Anton Bundsmann
Edwards..Robert Turney
Maid..Eleanor Shaler
Gentlemen and Ladies, Laborers and Unemployed Persons: Messrs.
	Russell Rhodes, Alvin Barrett, Ronald Jones, Jock Munro and
	the Misses Barbara Childs, Ann Tewksbury, Cecilia Lenihan and
	Nancy McKnight.
	Synopsis: Act I.—The Panic of 1837. The Office of Bloodgood,
the Banker. "His Hand Does Not Tremble—Not a Muscle Moves.
What a Magnificent Robber." Act II.—Scene 1—The Panic of 1857.
The Park, Near Fourteenth Street. "Beware, Mr. Livingstone, How
You Seek to Renew Our Acquaintance." Scene 2—Bloodgood's
Office. "If This Panic Do But Last, I Shall Double My Fortune."
Scene 3—A Room in Puffy's House. "Heaven Help Us! I Fear the
Worst Is Not Come." Act III.—A Room in Bloodgood's House.
"Keep Your Gold! It Would Soil My Poverty." Act IV.—Scene
1—Union Square. "It Is My Wedding Ring." Scene 2—The Ves-
tibule of The Academy of Music. "I Wonder They Permit Such
Vagabonds to Hang About the Opera." Scene 3—The Antics at No.
19½ Cross Street, Five Points. "A Bullet Is a Good Argument."
Act V.—Scene 1—Brooklyn Heights. Three Months Later. "Look
in His Face and Confess the Infernal Scheme by Which Alida Blood-
good Compelled You to Renounce Your Love." Scene 2—The Exterior of No. 19½ Cross Street, Five Points. "Now, Badger—Do
Your Worst! I Am Safe." Scene 3—Bloodgood's House. "More
Than One Mask Must Fall." *Virtue Triumphant!*
Staged by Knowles Entrikin.

The Fairweathers lost their money in the panic of 1837. The Livingstones lost theirs in the panic of 1857. This kept Mark Livingstone, who was proud, and Lucy Fairweather, who was even prouder, apart for many months. Having lived through snow-storms and fires, with stage effects, they are finally united the same week that Gideon Bloodgood, the dishonest banker who stole the Fairweather money, is run to earth by Badger, who tried to be a crook but couldn't quite make it. The play was first performed in New York in December, 1857.

THE GUEST ROOM

(67 performances)

A comedy in three acts by Arthur Wilmurt. Produced by Carol Sax at the Biltmore Theatre, New York, October 6, 1931.

Cast of characters—

Janet Fairley	Joan Kenyon
Mrs. Martin	Beverly Sitgreaves
Willard Simms	Otto Hulett
Charlotte Powers	Helen Lowell
Mrs. Lessing	Joan Gordon
Mr. Lessing	Herbert Warren
Mary	Edmonia Nolley

Act I.—Dining Room, Mrs. Elton's House. Act II.—Drawing Room, Mrs. Martin's. Act III.—Living Room, the Simms' Apartment.

Staged by Carol Sax.

Charlotte Powers, being homeless following the death of her sister, fastens herself on Mrs. Martin, an old friend, moves into Mrs. Martin's guest room and refuses to take any hint that she has outstayed her welcome. After a year she is politely ejected and proceeds to break up her niece Janet's home by moving in there. Forced to choose between her husband and her aunt Janet decides in the husband's favor and Miss Powers moves in with another old and unsuspecting friend.

DIVORCE ME, DEAR

(7 performances)

A comedy in three acts by Katherine Roberts. Produced by Sidney M. Biddell at the Avon Theatre, New York, October 5, 1931.

Cast of characters—

Mary Adams	Francesca Bruning
Cheever	Robert Vivian
Geoffrey Lawrence	Richie Ling

Veronica Vare....................................Violet Heming
Eleanor Lawrence..............................Anne Sutherland
Kenneth Gardner.............................G. P. Huntley, Jr.
Peter Vare.......................................Reginald Mason
Celeste...Andree Corday
Andre Guigue...................................Gustave Rolland
    Act I.—Living Room of the Vare Residence. Act II.—Peter's Villa, St. Cloud, Environs of Paris. Act III.—Veronica's Boudoir.
    Staged by Antoinette Perry.

Veronica Vare, become so used to her husband, Peter, that she is certain she needs a change, insists upon a divorce. Peter, being wise, permits Veronica to file her papers in Paris and wait six months. When the degree is about to be granted Peter goes to Paris, apparently eager for freedom, which hurts Veronica's vanity. She gets her divorce, but wants to marry Peter all over again, having found out that Kenneth Gardner, the man she thought she wanted, is not the man she wants at all.

THE FATHER

(20 performances)

A tragedy in three acts by August Strindberg. Revived by Lee Shubert at the Forty-ninth Street Theatre, New York, October 8, 1931.

Cast of characters—

Adolph...Robert Loraine
Pastor...Reyner Barton
Orderly..Jan Linbermann
Nojd...Barrie Livesay
Laura ....Dorothy Dix
Dr. Ostermark..................................Lawrence Hanray
Margaret...Haidee Wright
Bertha...Maisie Darrell
    Adolph's House in a Swedish Town.

Preceded by

BARBARA'S WEDDING

A comedy in one act by J. M. Barrie.

Cast of characters—

The Colonel......................................Robert Loraine
Dering...Barrie Livesay
Barbara..Winifred Wynne
Karl...Bruce Moir
Billy..Colin Cardew
Granny...Haidee Wright
    Staged by Robert Loraine and Malcolm Morley.

Strindberg's "The Father" was previously revived by Warner Oland in April, 1912, when Rosalind Ivan played the Laura, an by Robert Whittier in May, 1928, when Mr. Whittier played the captain and Florence Johns was the Laura. It will be recalled as the story of the unhappy misogynist who is driven temporarily insane by the subtle suggestion of his wife that he is not the father of their child.

Barrie's one-act play, "Barbara's Wedding," is a fantasy going back to war benefit days. A veteran of the Indian campaigns wanders in his mind trying to keep hold of the facts of the great war.

TWO SECONDS

(59 performances)

A tragedy in prologue, two acts and epilogue, by Elliott Lester. Produced by Irving Lande and William Stephens at the Ritz Theatre, New York, October 9, 1931.

Cast of characters—

Warden	James Marr
2nd Reporter	Victor Morgan
1st Reporter	Paul Stewart
Student	Joseph Kramm
Screw	Harold Shackman
Prison Doctor	Leonard Jerome
Minister	Joe Graham
John Allen	Edward Pawley
Bud Clark	Preston Foster
Lizzie	Rhea Martin
A Bookie	Phil M. Sheridan
1st Girl	Katherine McHugh
2nd Girl	Ann Williams
Annie	Dale Gardner
A Fat Girl	Edna Howard
Tony Scafidi	Harold Huber
Shirley Day	Blyth Daly
A Tough Guy	Gordon McCracken
Justice of Peace	J. Gordon Kelly
Doctor Walton	J. Gordon Kelly
1st Detective	Victor Morgan
2nd Detective	Paul Stewart
District Attorney	William Green
A Judge	Frank Miller

(Note: The Play Consists of a Prologue—20 Scenes—and an Epilogue. There Will be One Intermission of 15 Minutes.)
Prologue and Epilogue—In prison. Acts I and II.—In and around a large city.
Staged by Egon Brecher and Alexander Leftwich.

During the two seconds elapsing between the time they strap him in the electric chair and his execution John Allen, murderer, mentally reviews those events in his life which have brought him to this end. He recalls his meeting with Shirley Day, a dance hall girl; his getting drunk and being married to her late at night; his quarrel with his pal, Bud Clark, over Shirley; his discovery that Shirley is cheating with the dance hall proprietor to whom she returns; his winning money to pay the dance hall man; his shooting of Shirley to redeem his own tortured soul and rid the world of one not fit to live; his trial and conviction. Then the current is turned on.

A CHURCH MOUSE

(164 performances)

A comedy in three acts by Ladilaus Fodor. Produced by William A. Brady, Ltd., at the Playhouse, New York, October 12, 1931.

Cast of characters—

Chapple...John Gray
Baron Thomas Von Ullrich...........................Bert Lytell
Olly Frey...Louise Kirtland
Count Von Talheim.............................Wallace Erskine
Jackson...Charles Abbe
Baron Frank Von Ullrich.....................Charles Campbell
Susie Sachs...Ruth Gordon

Act I.—Private Office of the President of the Vienna Universal Bank. Vienna. Acts II and III.—Apartment in a Fashionable Hotel in Paris.

Staged by Melville Burke.

Baron Thomas Von Ullrich, Vienna's greatest banker, is forced to discharge his secretary, Olly Frey, because she persists in capitalizing her physical charms in the office. Olly is dismissed as a secretary and reëngaged as a prospective mistress. Susie Sachs, a starving suburbanite, hears of Olly's dismissal and applies for the job by sneaking past the outer guards and getting into the Baron's office. Susie dares the Baron to test her competence and wins the place. Taken to Paris for a conference Susie secretly works to keep the Baron away from Olly and finally dresses herself up as a counter attraction. The Baron is impressed, dismisses his mistress and takes Susie to wife. Also to the Café de Paris.

LEAN HARVEST

(31 performances)

A drama in three acts by Ronald Jeans. Produced by Kenneth Macgowan and Joseph Verner Reed at the Forrest Theatre, New York, October 13, 1931.

Cast of characters—

Mrs. Trent..Molly Pearson
Steven...Leonard Mudie
Anne..Patricia Calvert
Gladys..Lillian Bronson

```
Nigel..............................................Leslie Banks
Celia Hardman......................................Vera Allen
Mr. A. Tellworthy..........................Fothringham Lysons
Mrs. Tellworthy.....................................Ada Potter
Philip Downes......................................Nigel Bruce
Miss Moggs......................................Lillian Bronson
Duckitt..........................................Charles Esdale
Ann...............................................Evelyn Mills
Richard...........................................Edwin Mills
Tommy............................................Warren Mills
Dr. Plumtree....................................John Hoysradt
Leila Perrett..................................Peggy Hovenden
Jack Crabb......................................Alfred Flanders
Carmen Bracegirdle..........................Paula Bauersmith
Dr. Fisher..................................Fothringham Lysons
Mr. Featherstone...............................Harry Sothern
Mr. McGowan..................................John Hoysradt
Porteous.........................................Joaquin Souther
```
Act I.—Scene 1—The Trents' House at Chipping Hanbury. 2—Subway Platform in London. 3—Celia's Flat in Bedford Square. Act II.—Scene 1—Nigel's Library at Rutland Gate. 2—Nigel's Bedroom. 3—Sitting Room. Chipping Hanbury. 4—Nigel's Bedroom. Act III.—Study in Nigel's House in Park Street.
Staged by Leslie Banks.

Nigel Trent is ambitious but selective. Though his family is hard pressed he refuses to take a job until he can get one that promises him a future, causing Anne, his fiancé, to break her engagement. Finding the job he wants, Nigel marries Celia Hardman. Together they achieve a great success, but Celia eventually tires of Nigel's neglect of her in the interest of his business and runs away with Philip Downes. Nigel thereupon suffers a stroke, loses his mind and leaves all his fortune to his brother Steven, who has married Anne, Nigel's first sweetheart.

EVERYBODY'S WELCOME

(139 performances)

A musical comedy in a prologue and two acts by Harold Atteridge, music by Sammy Fain, based on the comedy, "Up Pops the Devil," by Frances Goodrich and Albert Hackett. Produced by the Messrs. Shubert at the Shubert Theatre, New York, October 13, 1931.

Cast of characters—
```
"Biny" Hatfield...................................Harry Ritz
George Kent..........................................Al Ritz
Polly Bascom..................................Frances Williams
Ann Cathway...................................Harriette Lake
Gilbert Morrell...................................Roy Roberts
Steve Herrick.....................................Oscar Shaw
Jimmy Blair..........................................Jim Ritz
"Artie".......................................Charles McClelland
Mrs. George Kent...............................Jean Newcombe
A Drunk.........................................Thomas Harty
Kelly.............................................Jack Ross
Louella May Carroll..........................Ann Pennington
```

Laundryman.....................................Spencer Barnes
Mr. Platt...Charles Garland
Mrs. Platt.......................................Lucille Osborne
Jane..Elsie Duffy
Helen...Edna Hedin
Dora..Mary Brooks
Trixie...Naida Pahl
Premier Dancer...................................Ruth Reiter
Specialty Dancers: Andrew and Louise Carr.
    Prologue—Rehearsal Hall in "Biny" Hatfield's Dancing Academy,
N. Y.   Act I.—Studio Apartment of the Merricks' in Greenwich
Village.   Act II.—At the Merrick Apartment and on the stage of
Proxy's Theatre.
    Staged by William Mollison.

Ann Cathway and Steve Herrick have been housekeeping in
Greenwich Village for a year, but Steve's writing has gone to pot.
Ann proposes that she go back to her old job on the stage while
Steve takes on the housework and gets back to his typewriter.
Steve tries this, but soon rebels. He and Ann separate, but are
drawn together when Ann discovers that she is going to have a
baby and Steve hears about it.
    Principal songs—"As Time Goes By," "Nature Played a Dirty
Trick On You" and "Even as You and I."

THE PILLARS OF SOCIETY

(2 performances)

A drama in three acts by Henrik Ibsen. Revived by the New
York Repertory Company at the Forty-eighth Street Theatre, New
York, October 14, 1931.

Cast of characters—

Consul Bernick....................................Moffat Johnston
Mrs. Bernick...Ann Dere
Olaf...Richard Jack
Martha Bernick..................................Fania Marinoff
Johan Tonnesen....................................Rollo Peters
Lona Hessel.....................................Armina Marshall
Hilmar Tonnesen...................................Romney Brent
Rector Rorlund.................................Knowles Entrikin
Dina Dorf...Dorothy Gish
Krap...Edgar Stehli
Shipbuilder Aune..................................Frank Conlan
Mrs. Rummel.......................................Jessie Busley
Mrs. Postmaster Holt............................Eleanor Shaler
Mrs. Doctor Lynge..............................Ann Tewksbury
Miss Rummel......................................Barbara Child
Miss Holt..Cecilia Lenihan
Rummel...Robert Lowe
Vigeland..Dudley Hawley
Sandstad..Sam Wren
Townspeople and Others: Russell Rhodes, Anton Bundsmann, Alvin
    Barrett, Robert Turney, Mervin Williams, Ronald Jones, Jock
    Munro, Virginia Volland and Nancy McKnight.
    Acts I, II and III.—The Sun Room of Consul Bernick's House in
a Small Norwegian Coast-town. The Summer of 1876.
    Staged by Winifred Lenihan.

Consul Bernick, a pillar of society, a model of rectitude in a small Norwegian town, has had an affair with an actress and, being threatened with discovery, has shifted the blame to his younger brother, who has sailed for America. Later he lets it appear that the brother also has taken a considerable sum of the firm's money, the Consul's excuse being that the firm's credit is threatened, and the time gained by the reported theft will save it. Even a pillar of society is justified in lying for the community good. The accused brother returns unexpectedly from America, the truth must finally be told and Consul Bernick courageously makes confession to his townspeople the night they are giving him a grand birthday party.

*THE CAT AND THE FIDDLE

(284 performances)

A musical comedy in two acts by Jerome Kern and Otto Harbach. Produced by Max Gordon at the Globe Theatre, New York, October 15, 1931.

Cast of characters—

Book Vendor	George Kirk
Mme. Abajoue	Lucette Valsy
Alexander Sheridan	Eddie Foy, Jr.
Shirley Sheridan	Bettina Hall
Pompineau	George Meader
Victor Florescu	Georges Metaxa
Angie Sheridan	Doris Carson
A Waiter	George Magis
Odette	Odette Myrtil
Constance Carrington	Margaret Adams
Chester Biddlesby	Fred Walton
Major Sir George Wilfred Chatterly	Lawrence Grossmith
Clement Daudet	Jose Ruben
Maizie Gripps	Flora Le Breton
Jean Colbert	Peter Chambers
Claudine	Lucette Valsy

Act I.—Scene 1—Quay in Brussels. 2—Entrance to "La Petite Maison." 3—Victor's Rooms. 4—Entrance to "La Petite Maison." 5—Shirley's Apartment. 6—Limousine. 7, 8—Theatre in Louvain. Act II.—Scene 1—Daudet's Apartment in Brussels. 2—Street Under Daudet's Window. 3—Victor's Rooms. 4—Phantasy. 5—Dressing room. 6—Exterior of "La Petite Maison." 7—Al Fresco Café of "La Petite Maison."

Staged by Jose Ruben.

Shirley Sheridan, American music student at the Conservatoire in Brussels, has long admired Victor Florescu, a fellow student, from a distance. They meet at the quay and are mutually thrilled. Victor has composed "The Passionate Pilgrim." The producer considers the score too heavy. He hears Shirley playing some of her own American songs. Insists she shall write something to be interpolated in Victor's opera, which makes Victor furious. Particularly as he believes that Shirley goes to the producer with the songs. It takes considerable singing and a bit of explanation to get the young composers harmoniously mated by 11.15.

Principal songs—"She Didn't Say Yes, She Didn't Say No," "The Night Was Made for Love," "The Love Parade" and "Try to Forget."

MELO

(8 performances)

A drama in three acts by Henri Bernstein, adapted by Arthur Pollock. Revived by Lee Shubert in association with A. H. Woods at the Maxine Elliott Theatre, New York, October 19, 1931.

Cast of characters—

Romaine Belcroix	Helen Flint
Marcel Blanc	Walter Armitage
Pierre Belcroix	Sebastian Shaw
Christiane	Margaret Delamere
Jeanne	Fanny Davenport
Dr. Remy	Harry Davenport
A Priest	Robert Harrison
François	Guy Cunningham
A Professional Dancer	Jan Marquand
A Maitre D'Hôtel	Jean Villon
A Man	Stapleton Kent
Another Man	John Prescott
A Woman	Agnes Craven

Act I.—Scene 1—Garden of Pierre and Romaine Belcroix's Home Near Paris. 2—Corner of Marcel Blanc's Studio, Paris. 3—Russian Cabaret. 4—Marcel Blanc's Studio. Act II.—Scene 1—Living-room of the Belcroix Home. 2—Studio. 3—Pierre's Bedroom. 4—Café Terrace. Act III.—At a Cemetery, in the Home of a Priest and in Marcel's Studio.
Staged by Marcel Varnel.

See "The Best Plays of 1930-31."

THE SEX FABLE

(33 performances)

A comedy in three acts by Edouard Bourdet, English text by Jane Hinton. Produced by Gilbert Miller at the Henry Miller Theatre, October 20, 1931.

Cast of characters—

Louise	Mary Chippendale
A Porter	Joseph Walton
Nicole Martin	Anne Teeman
Jimmy Leroy-Gomez	Derek Williams

Isabelle Leroy-Gomez.............................Helen Haye
Manuel Leroy-Gomez.............................Allen Tower
Lili Leroy-Gomez...............................Leona Maricle
Clarisse Lee-Gomez.............................Margaret Dale
Antoine..Ronald Squire
Philippe Leroy-Gomez..........................Anthony Ireland
Christina Leroy-Gomez...........................Helena D'Algy
Carlos Pinto......................................Rafael Corio
A Page...Jack Kilfeather
1st American Girl.............................Constance Trevor
2nd American Girl...........................Consuelo Flowerton
An American Man................................Wylie Adams
A Spaniard.....................................Ernesto Guiterrez
A Spanish Lady...................................Audrey Davis
1st Maharajah..................................W. Wana Singh
2nd Maharajah......................................John Henry
A Waiter..William Horne
Jules...E. J. De Varny
Inez...Lita Lope
Another Waiter...............................Morris Morrison
Countess Polaki.........................Mrs. Patrick Campbell
Dorothy Freeman....................................Lora Baxter
    Act I.—Sitting Room of Mme. Leroy-Gomez' Apartment in a Paris
Hotel. Acts II and III.—Hall of the Hotel.
    Staged by Gilbert Miller.

Isabelle Leroy-Gomez, mother of a considerable family of Argentinians and a widow, is considerably exercised over the task of providing rich and marriageable mates for her boys, who have not been brought up to work, and keeping them married after suitable mates have been found. She manages affairs with a fairly high hand, and in the end sees Philippe and his rich Christina detached from their respective lovers and returned to each other; her youngest son, Jimmy, engaged to Dorothy Freeman, rich American, whom he is forced to marry because of the liberal allowance promised, and her daughter Lili successful in a business which permits her to take an option on Carlos Pinto, a Spanish gigolo.

NEW CHAUVE-SOURIS

(29 performances)

A mixed revue assembled by Nikita Balieff. Produced by Morris Gest at the Ambassador Theatre, New York, October 21, 1931.

Principals engaged—

M. Balieff
Mme. Diakonova
Mme. Nikitina
Mlle. Ryaboushinskaya
Boris Romanoff
M. Dolinoff
Mme. Poliakova
Mme. Komisarjevskaya
M. Vetchor
Mme. Cortis
M. Zotoff
George Hayes

K. Moyeensko
Norman Duggan
Gordon Weld
Irina Hicks Antarova
Alexei Tcherkassky
Nicholas Moyessenko
William Whitehead
William Home
Geoffrey King
Helen Kingstead
Mary Ault

The program of this Russian-English entertainment was divided into two parts. Part I, a ballet, "A Romantic Adventure of an Italian Ballerina and a Marquis," Part II, a fantastic drama after the story by Alexander Pushkin, with incidental music by Alexei Archangelsky, called "The Queen of Spades," and Part III, a musical buffonade inspired by airs of Offenbach and Lecocq, "1860, or An Interrupted Festival."

NO MORE FRONTIER

(28 performances)

A drama in prologue and three acts by Talbot Jennings. Produced by Shepard Traube and Max Sonino at the Provincetown Theatre, New York, October 22, 1931.

Cast of characters—

PROLOGUE

Capt. Jack Bailey	Gibbs Penrose
George Bailey	Charles Thompson
Hannah Bailey	Dorothy Bordon
Mordecai Bailey	Charles Blake
Gail Carlton	Ruth Gillmore
Flint Bailey	Cameron King

ACT I

Jim Steele	Forrest Berkeley-Boone
Flint Bailey	Cameron King
Last Star	Cyrus Staehle
Chaplain Ashworth	Graham Velsey
Gail Bailey	Ruth Gillmore
A trooper	Edwin Clare
Sue McCarty	Julia McMahon

ACT II

Colonel Purdum	H. S. Wilson
Idaho Red	Edwin Clare
Shadow	Gibbs Penrose
Flint Bailey	Cameron King
George Bailey, 2nd	Kermit Murdock
Mord Bailey, 2nd	William Castle
Rev. Mr. Ashworth	Graham Velsey
Jim Steele	Forrest Berkeley-Boone
Cal Smith	Louis Peters
Gail Bailey	Ruth Gillmore
Margaret Steele Bailey	Irene Homer
Jim Bailey	Jackie Kelk
Flint Bailey, 2nd } as children	Charles Belin
Bob Ashworth	Lyle Blake

ACT III

Margaret Steele Bailey	Irene Homer
George Bailey, 2nd	Kermit Murdock
Jim Bailey	Pascal Cowan
Gail Bailey	Barbara Pearson
Howard Cameron	Arne Boesen
Flint Bailey	Cameron King
Flint Bailey, 2nd	John Beal
Mord Bailey	William Castle
Jack Bailey, 2nd	Charles Walters

Jim Steele.................................Forrest Berkeley-Boone
    Prologue—Bailey Home, Indiana, 1875. Act I.—Idaho Cabin,
1877. Act II.—Golden Eagle Bar, Alturas, 1899. 2—Bailey Ranch
House. Act III.—George Bailey Home, Alturas.
    Staged by Shepard Traube.

Flint Bailey, born in Indiana of a family of pioneers, hears the
call of the West and goes cattle raising in Idaho. Gail Carlton,
his fiancée, follows him and they rear a family. Their children
also insist on pushing out beyond the horizon. Third generation
Baileys are interested in airships and submarines, and the fourth
takes to speculating on the possibility of getting in touch with
Mars.

WONDER BOY

(44 performances)

A comedy in three acts by Edward Chodorov and Arthur Barton. Produced by Jed Harris at the Alvin Theatre, New York, October 22, 1931.

Cast of characters—

Joe Glick...Allen Jenkins
Peter Hinkle.................................'...William Challee
A Porter..Donald Heywood
Tatyana Mirova...............................Barbara Bulgakova
Miss Manheim.....................................Hallie Manning
Office Boy...Eddie Craven
Phil Mashkin......... ....Gregory Ratoff
Sam Bernfeld....................................Robert Leonard
George Kelly.......................................Henry O'Neill
Schwartz..Sam Levene
Max Benowitz.................................James R. Waters
Frances Reis......................................Jeanne Greene
Mac...Cecil Holm
Tony... Ross Hertz
Kelly's Secretary.................................Estelle Scheer
Montague Levy......................................Maurice Cass
Miss Reis' Secretary...............................Eva Franklin
A Fireman..James Kearney
Charlie Horton.......................................Matt Briggs
A Girl..Constance Almy
Sol Griffith..................................Bruce MacFarlane
A Reporter......................................Horace McMahon
Another Reporter...................................Vincent York
A Camera Man.....................................Arnold Preston
Another Camera Man............................Herman Shapiro
A Tailor...Jacob Bleifer
A Hatter...Max Beck
A Station Master..................................D. J. Hamilton
A Red Cross Woman...........................Margaret Meyers
An Apple Seller....................................Joseph Ploski
A Youth..Thomas Fisher
A Bellboy...Frank Carter
A Page Boy...Arnold Moss
Commodore Cohen...............................Bernard Gorcey
Harry Rich..David Burns
Mabel Fenton......................................Hazel Dawn
    Act I.—Scene 1—Pullman Car. 2—Office of Phil Mashkin, President Paragon Picture Corporation. 3—Office of George Kelly, Publicity Director. 4—Office of Miss Reis. 5—Office of Max Benowitz.

6—Mashkin's Office.   7—Flashes.   8—A Room in Sylvania Hotel, Philadelphia.   9—Pullman Car.   Act II.—Scene 1—Sherry-Netherlands Hotel.   2—Backstage at Capitol Theatre.   3—Commodore Cohen's Suite.   Act. III.—Mashkin's Office.
Staged by Jed Harris.

Peter Hinkle, ambitious to study dentistry in New York, takes a job with the picture star, Mabel Fenton, in Los Angeles to raise funds. Starting for New York, he is halted en route by Paragon Picture agents, at the behest of Phil Mashkin, Paragon overlord, who, seeing the picture in the New York projection room, decides Peter and not Miss Fenton will be the star sensation of the showing. Peter protests that he wants to be a dentist, not a picture actor, but is bullied into signing a contract and making a personal appearance with the picture, which is a flop. Paragon reverses its trickeries in an effort to be rid of Peter and recover the good will of the abused Miss Fenton.

THE UNKNOWN WARRIOR

(4 performances)

A drama in three acts translated by Cecil Lewis from Paul Reynal's "Le Tombeau Sous l'Arc de Triomphe." Revived by James B. Pond at the Morosco Theatre, New York, the afternoon of October 22, 1931.

Cast of characters—

Soldier...Maurice Browne
Father..Daniel Reed
Betrothed ....Rosalinde Fuller
    Acts I, II and III—A house in the country a day's ride from Paris.

A soldier on leave has his time cut from four days to four hours. The disillusionments of war have embittered his soul. The discovery that his father and his sweetheart have also become accustomed to getting along very pleasantly, even happily, without him adds to his misery of mind. After a night with his betrothed he returns to the front to lead a forlorn hope. "The Unknown Warrior" was first produced in America by Charles Hopkins at the Hopkins Theatre, New York, October 29, 1928. It was then withdrawn after eight performances.

MOURNING BECOMES ELECTRA

(150 performances)

A trilogy by Eugene O'Neill. Produced by the Theatre Guild at the Guild Theatre, New York, October 26, 1931.

Cast of characters—

HOMECOMING

Seth Beckwith.....................................Arthur Hughes
Amos Ames...Jack Byrne
Louisa..Bernice Elliott
Minnie..Emily Lorraine
Christine...Alla Nazimova
Lavinia Mannon....................................Alice Brady
Capt. Peter Niles, U. S. Artillery................Philip Foster
Hazel Niles.......................................Mary Arbenz
Captain Adam Brant................................Thomas Chalmers
Brigadier-General Ezra Mannon.....................Lee Baker
     Scene 1.—Exterior of the Mannon House in New England, 1865.
2.—Ezra Mannon's Study. 3.—Exterior of the House. 4.—Ezra
Mannon's Bedroom.

THE HUNTED

Mrs. Josiah Borden................................Augusta Durgeon
Mrs. Everett Hills................................Janet Young
Dr. Joseph Blake..................................Erskin Sanford
Josiah Borden.....................................James Boshell
Everett Hills, D.D................................Oliver Putnam
Christine Mannon..................................Alla Nazimova
Hazel Niles.......................................Mary Arbenz
Peter Niles.......................................Philip Foster
Lavinia Mannon....................................Alice Brady
Orin Mannon.......................................Earle Larimore
A Chantyman.......................................John Hendricks
Captain Adam Brant................................Thomas Chalmers
     Scene 1.—Exterior of the Mannon House. 2.—Sitting Room. 3.—
Ezra Mannon's Study. 4.—Clipper Ship "Flying Trades," East
Boston. 5.—Exterior of the Mannon House.

THE HAUNTED

Abner Small.......................................Erskin Sanford
Ira Mackel..Oliver Putnam
Joe Silva...Grant Gordon
Amos Ames...Jack Byrne
Seth Beckwith.....................................Arthur Hughes
Peter Niles.......................................Philip Foster
Hazel Niles.......................................Mary Arbenz
Lavinia Mannon....................................Alice Brady
Orin Mannon.......................................Earle Larimore
     Scene 1.—Exterior of the Mannon House, 1866. 2.—Sitting Room.
3.—Study. 4.—Sitting Room. 5.—Exterior of Mannon House.
     Staged by Philip Moeller.

See page 65.

EAST WIND

(23 performances)

A musical comedy by Oscar Hammerstein 2d and Frank Mandel, music by Sigmund Romberg. Produced by Laurence Schwab and Frank Mandel at the Manhattan Theatre, New York, October 27, 1931.

Cast of characters—

Monsieur Granier	Greek Evans
Jacques	Vance Elliott
Gabrielle	Betty Junod
Julie	Francis Markey
Claudette Fortier	Charlotte Lansing
Réné Beauvais	William Williams
Claire	Rose Mullen
Mimi	Sherry Pelham
Lorraine Fortier	Dennie Moore
Marie Martel	Vera Marsh
Capt. Paul Beauvais	J. Harold Murray
Capt. Dejan	Thomas Chadwick
Taxi Driver	I. Anchong
A Tourist	Gus Howard
Pierre Fortier	Jules Epailly
Victor Cliquot	Joe Penner
Tsoi Tsing	Ahi
King of Luang-Prabang	Ivan Izmailov
His Interpreter	Y. Y. Hsu
King of Cambodia	Frank Dobert
His Interpreter	S. Wong
Hop Sing	J. C. Donsu
Capt. Gervais	Gladstone Waldrip
Papa Gouli	Raymond Bramley
Violinist	Evelyn Klein
Cellist	Blanche Stepner
Pianist	John Tomney
A Maid	Marjorie Dille
The Stage Manager	O. J. Vanasse
The Compére	Emile Ladoux
The McNulty Sisters	{ Lorraine Pearl / Leatrice Pearl
King in Ballet	Alex Yakovleff
Prince in Ballet	Aron Tomaroff
Dr. Duval	George Chapell

Act I.—Scene 1—Country Fair, Near Marseilles. 2—On Board Ship. 3—Pierre Fortier's Casino, Saigon, Indo-China. 4-6—Elephant Enclosure. 5—Pierre Fortier's Home. 7—Along the River Front, Saigon. Act II.—Scene 1—Restaurant "Aux Belles Poules," Paris. 2—Gare de Lyons. 3—Papa Gouli's Apartment. 4—Stage of a Music Hall. 5—M. Granier's Study. 6—Lorraine's Wine Shop, Marseilles

Staged by Oscar Hammerstein 2d, dances by Bobby Connelly.

Claudette Fortier, rejoining her father, Pierre, in Saigon, Indo-China, after years at school in France, meets, loves and marries Réné Beauvais, who leaves her for a dancing girl. Réné's better brother Paul, a captain of the French army stationed at Saigon, also loves Claudette. After both she and Réné go to the bad as a result of their mismating, Capt. Paul finds Claudette and marries her.

Principal songs—"East Wind" and "You Are My Woman."

THE ROOF

(28 performances)

A drama in seven scenes by John Galsworthy. Produced by Charles Hopkins at the Hopkins Theatre, New York, October 30, 1931.

Cast of characters—

Gustave...Edouard La Roche
The Hon. Reggie Fanning.................Blade Stanhope Conway
Major Moulteney...............................William Sauter
Baker..Austin Fairman
Brice..Vernon Kelso
Mr. Beeton....................................Ernest Cossart
Mrs. Beeton................................Charlotte Granville
Henry Lennox..................................Vernon Steele
Evelyn Lennox...............................Charlotte Walker
Diana..Helen Rowland
Brye..Frances Tannehill
A Nurse.......................................Selena Royle
A Young Man...................................Henry Hull
A Young Woman.................................Anne Forrest
Froba...Hajop Boyajian
Two Pompiers...................Ralph Cataly, Jaques C. Dancy
     Scene 1—Ground Floor. 2—First Floor. 3, 4, 5, 6—Second Floor. 7—the Roof.
     Staged by Charles Hopkins.

Guests in a small residential hotel in Paris are aroused at midnight by a fire that has been started in the kitchen by a tipsy person named Brice to be even with a waiter over an imagined affront. The guests aroused on various floors make their way to the roof, from where they are severally rescued. All escape save the chap who started the fire.

THE VENETIAN

(9 performances)

A drama by Clifford Bax. Produced by Maurice Browne in association with the Messrs. Shubert at the Masque Theatre, New York, October 31, 1931.

Cast of characters—

Piere Buonaventuri...........................Howard Bailey
Tessa..Marian Litenius
Antonia......................................Catherine Lacey
Scipio.......................................Patrick Glasgow
Emilia..Phoebe Coyne
Bianca Cappello.............................Margaret Rawlings
A Baker's Boy................................Patrick Glasgow
A Major-Domo.................................Edward Broadley
Consini......................................Roland Hogue
Cardinal Ferdinando de' Medici................Alaistair Sim
Francesco de' Medici, Duke of Tuscany...........Wilfred Walter

Giovanna of Austria, Duchess of Tuscany..............Lea Penman
Vettora... Kemble Knight
Julia... Catherine Lacey
Celio Malespini.................................Gregory Robins
Marietta... May Ediss
A Lady-in-Waiting............................. Marian Litenius
Another....................................... Helen Glenn
A Servitor.......................................Frank Woodruff
Another...................................... Charles Crompton

Scene 1—Corner of Venice: April, 1574. 2—Room in the Pitti Palace: July, 1574. 3, 4, 5—Room in Bianca's House in Florence: April, 1575. 6—Courtyard in the Pitti Palace: September, 1578. 7—Garden at Cajano: September, 1578.

staged by Ellen Van Volkenburg.

Bianca Cappello, having married a commoner in Italy of the sixteenth century, is brought before Francesco de' Medici for sentence. Francesco, becoming interested in Bianca, pardons her husband who is later killed. Bianca thereupon marries Francesco who adopts her son. Cardinal Ferdinand de' Medici, eager to inherit Francesco's throne, plans the son's abduction. Bianca hopes to thwart Ferdinand by poisoning him. When the wily Cardinal refuses the wine, Francesco, to prove his loyalty to his wife, drinks it. Bianca thereupon finishes the drink and they die together.

THE LAUGH PARADE

(231 performances)

A revue in two acts by Ed Wynn and Ed Preble, music by Harry Warren. Produced by Mr. Wynn at the Imperial Theatre, New York, November 2, 1931.

Principals engaged—

Ed Wynn	Jeanne Aubert
Lawrence Gray	Eunice Healey
Bartlett Simmons	Sara Jane
Al Barron	Frieda Mierse
Eddie Cheney	Kathryn Bryan
Jack Powell	Madeline Dunbar
Jerry Rogers	Amelia De Gatano
Wilbur Hall	Levenoria Sabalis
Harry Seaman	De Gatanos

Staged by Ed Wynn; dances by Albertina Rasch.

Principal songs—"Ooh, That Kiss" and "You're My Everything."

CYNARA

(210 performances)

A drama in three acts by H. M. Harwood and R. F. Gore-Browne, adapted from Mr. Gore-Browne's novel, "An Imperfect

Lover." Produced by Lee Shubert at the Morosco Theatre, New York, November 2, 1931.

Cast of characters—

Clemency Warlock	Phoebe Foster
Jim Warlock	Philip Merivale
Hotel Attendant	Peter Barbier
Merton	Gladys Bell
Gorla Kentish	Miriam Jordan
Hon. John Tring	Henry Stephenson
Joseph	Joe Romantini
Waiter	Peter Barbier
A Customer	Jean Derayville
Mildred Miles	Mary Newnham-Davis
Doris Lea	Adrianne Allen
Rev. Harold Dringer	Hannam Clark
Marjorie	Marguerite Martin
Katherine	Kathryn O'Neill
Polly	Mary Williamson
Mrs. Day	Mary Scott Seton
Olive Day	Edna Bennett
Miss Dringer	Gladys Bell
Mr. Caraway	Thomas Bate
Mr. Boot	A. P. Kaye
Grace Boot	Vera Fuller Mellish
Alice Boot	Linda Eder
Miss Trix	Shirley Gale
Mr. Small	Mario Majeroni
Sergeant of Police	Paul Hanson
Coroner	A. P. Kaye
Clerk of the Court	Clement O'Loghlen
Mrs. Mott	Gladys Bell
Madam Ducette	Alice Marin
Foreman of the Jury	Hannam Clark
Juryman	Mary Scott Seton

Prologue—Balcony of the Warlocks' Private Suite, Capri. Act I.—Warlocks' Bedroom. 2—Restaurant in Soho. 3—Farmer's Green. 4—Farmer's Green. Act II.—Scene 1—In Surrey. 2—Warlocks' Bedroom. 3—Kensington Gardens. 4—Jim Warlock's Study. Act III.—Coroner's Court. Epilogue—Capri.

Staged by Harry Wagstaffe Gribble.

See page 335.

THE CHIMES OF NORMANDY

(16 performances)

A comic opera by Robert Planquette. Revived by the Civic Light Opera Company at Erlanger's Theatre, New York, November 2, 1931.

Cast of characters—

Serpolette	Vivian Hart
Germaine	Vera Myers
Gertrude	Ann Johnson
Jeanne	Dhoris Delehante
Nanette	Theo. Van Tassel
Suzanne	Georgine Dieter
Henri, Marquis of Corneville	Edward Nell, Jr.
Jean Grenicheux	Roy Cropper
Gaspard	Herbert Gould

The Bailli...Detmar Poppen
Notary...Robert Capron
The Ensemble: Mary Hennessy, Keitha Gillette, Dhoris Delehante,
    Georgina Deiter, Ann Abbott, Mary St. John, Mitzi Eder, June
    B. Clarke, Winefred McClary, Doris Colman, Vera Mueller,
    Lauretta Brislin, Olga Schumacher, Maria Julian, Theo. Van
    Tassel, Cyrilla Tuitt and Gertrude Rittenhouse, Lloyd Ericsson,
    Alexander Black, Rudy Glaisek, Hudson James, A. Otis Holwerk,
    Siegfried Langer, August Loring, Paul Graham, George Koenig,
    Buck Williams and Robert Dawson.
    Act I.—Scene 1—Fishing Village on the Coast of Corneville. 2—
On the Way to the Fair. 3—Fair at Corneville. Act II.—Interior
of the Chateau of Corneville. Act III.—Grounds of the Chateau.
Staged by Milton Aborn.

The last previous revival of "The Chimes of Normandy" in
New York was that of the Van Den Berg-Conger Opera Company in May, 1915. The revival was staged at the Standard
Theatre, Ninetieth Street and Broadway. Arthur Cunningham
was the Marquis, Carrie Reynolds the Serpolette and Fred Frear,
a veteran comedian, the bailiff.

HERE GOES THE BRIDE

(7 performances)

A musical comedy in two acts by Peter Arno, music by John
W. Green and Richard Myers. Produced by Mr. Arno at
Chanin's Forty-sixth Street Theatre, New York, November 3,
1931.

Cast of characters—

Roddy Trotwood.....................................Eric Blore
Tarkington..Joseph Spree
Etta Fish...Colletta Ryan
Diddles Stuyvesant................................Dorothy Dare
Bubbles Stuyvesant..............................Pauline Gaskins
Doddles Stuyvesant...................................Ann Roth
Toodles Stuyvesant.............................Roberta Robinson
Roger Loring.....................................John Gallaudet
Betty Fish.......................................Grace Brinkley
Tony Doyle..Paul Frawley
June Doyle....................................Victoria Cummings
Hives...Bobby Clark
Blodgett..Paul McCullough
June's Maid.......................................Norma Taylor
Eloise Bess.......................................Mary Pettis
Judge Humphrey.................................Dudley Clements
Taxi Drivers............................Al and Ray Samuels
Hotel Clerk.....................................Bruce Carrington
Flossie...Chick & Andy
Baroness Von Ga Ga..........................Charlotte Homann
Rose..Frances Langford
Sparker...Harry Holbrook
House Detective....................................Philip Lord
Clerk of the Court.................................Gordon Clark
June's Attorney..................................Harry Holbrook
    Act I.—Scene 1—Scandal Sheet. 2—Trotwood's Penthouse. 3—
Reno Station. 4—Hotel Riverview Lobby. 5—Hotel Promenade.
6—Ross Alley. Act II.—Scene 7—Corridor in the Hotel. 8—Two

Bedrooms.   9—Hotel   Garden.   10—Divorce   Court.   11—Cal-Neva
Lodge.
     Staged by Edward Clarke Lilley, dances by Russell Markert.

Betty Fish loves Tony Doyle. Tony is married to June, who loves Roger Loring. So they all go to Reno and are straightened out in a handy divorce court. Hives and Blodgett go along, Hives as valet to Mr. Doyle and Blodgett as valet to Hives.

Principal songs—"Music in My Fingers," and "My Sweetheart, 'Tis of Thee."

CAUGHT WET

(13 performances)

A comedy in three acts by Rachel Crothers. Produced by John Golden at the Golden Theatre, New York, November 4, 1931.

Cast of characters—

Clifford Vanderstyle.............................Michael Milan
Julia Vanderstyle............................Dortha Duckworth
Peter Smeed...................................Bertram Thorn
Tommy Jones..................................Geoffrey Bryant
Michael Meer.....................................Robert Lowes
Dolores Winthrop............................Gertrude Michael
Elizabeth Betts...................................Sylvia Field
Stanley..Joseph King
Brewster...Allan Hale
Peterson...Robert Bruce
A Watchman..................................... James Davey
     Acts I, II and III—Corner of the Living Room in the Country
House of Clifford Vanderstyle.
     Staged by Rachel Crothers.

The Vanderstyles are giving a house party up the Hudson. The guests find themselves stormbound and restless. Elizabeth Betts, the most restless of them all, proposes that they pretend to steal the Vanderstyle pearls, famed for their $250,000 value, and, when the fun is all over, give them back. The trick works, but the pearls actually disappear. There is much mystery, a lot of questioning and finally a proper explanation.

HAMLET

(28 performances)

A tragedy by William Shakespeare. Produced by the New York Producing Association, Inc., at the Broadhurst Theatre, New York, November 5, 1931.

Cast of characters—

Claudius, King of Denmark........................David Horne
Gertrude, Queen of Denmark......................Mary Servoss
Hamlet, Prince of Denmark....................Raymond Massey
Polonius..John Daly Murphy
Laertes....................................Colin Keith-Johnston
Ophelia...Celia Johnson
Horatio.......................................Leon Quartermaine
Ghost of Hamlet's Father........................Burton McEvilly
Rosencrantz.......................................Robert Lowing
Guildenstern...Frank Rothe
Marcellus...H. H. McCollum
Bernardo...Bernard Savage
Francisco..George Cotton
First Grave Digger..................................George Carr
Second Grave Digger........................Clifford Heckinger
First Player.....................................Herbert Ranson
Player King...John Holmes
Player Queen......................................Ilse Gronau
Poisoner...Jerome Andrews
Priest...Charles T. Lewis
Pages: John Glenn, Wyman Kane, Sydney Smith, Jack White.
Ladies of the Court: Gloria Braggiotti, Gladys Burch, Helene Fred-
    eric, Edith Gresham, Marcia Linya, Catherine Meredith, Kitty
    Reese, Felicia Terry, L. M. Tice, Anne Wessman.
Gentlemen of the Court: Guy Collins, Tom Dougall, James Duffus,
    Ernest Howard, Stanley Howard, Irving Jackson, Leopold Lane,
    Edmund Tabell, Edward Wright.
Acts I, II and III.—The Castle of Elsinore.
Staged by Norman Bel Geddes.

An emended version of the Shakespeare play, bringing it down
to two and a half hours of playing time by telescoping certain
scenes and playing it in three acts and one set.

* COUNSELLOR-AT-LAW

(258 performances)

A drama in three acts by Elmer Rice. Produced by Mr. Rice
at the Plymouth Theatre, New York, November 6, 1931.

Cast of characters—

Bessie Green...............................Constance McKay
Henry Susskind...................................Lester Salkow
Sarah Becker....................................Malka Kornstein
A Tall Man..Victor Wolfson
A Stout Man..Jack Collins
A Postman...Ned Glass
Zedorah Chapman..............................Gladys Feldman
Goldie Rindskopf................................Angela Jacobs
Charles McFadden.........................J. Hammond Dailey
John P. Tedesco....................................Sam Bonnell
A Bootblack.......................................William Vaughn
Regina Gordon.....................................Anna Kostant
Herbert Howard Weinberg........................Marvin Kline
Arthur Sandler.............................Conway Washburne
Lillian Larue....................................Dorothy Dodge
An Errand Boy...................................Buddy Proctor
Roy Darwin..Jack Leslie
George Simon...Paul Muni
Cora Simon......................................Louise Prussing
A Woman..Jane Hamilton

```
Lena Simon......................................Jennie  Moscowitz
Peter J. Malone...................................T. H.  Manning
Johann  Breitstein.............................John M.  Qualen
David Simon......................................... Ned  Glass
Harry Becker...................................Martin  Wolfson
Richard Dwight, Jr..............................David  Vivian
Dorothy  Dwight....................................June  Cox
Charles Francis Baird.............................Elmer  Brown
    Acts I, II and III.—Suite of Law-Offices in the Mid-Town Section
in New York.
    Staged by Elmer Rice.
```

George Simon, born of poor parents on the east side of New York, raises himself by night school and work in a lawyer's office to a position of prominence among lawyers. After thirteen years of success he marries an aristocratic divorcee, whose case he handled. Five years later he is threatened with disbarment when one of the blue bloods of the Bar Association uncovers a framed alibi used by Simon when he was struggling upward. Mrs. Simon at the same time decides she has stood George as long as she can and sails for Europe with an old friend. George beats his Bar Association enemy and will probably marry his sympathetic secretary, Regina Gordon.

HOT MONEY

(9 performances)

A comedy in three acts by Aben Kandel. Produced by James W. Elliott at the George M. Cohan Theatre, New York, November 7, 1931.

Cast of characters—

```
A Waiter...........................................Al Rauh
Boy.......................................... Roger  Girod
Girl.........................................Sandy  Goodwin
Mike Donahey..............................Hobart  Cavanaugh
Mr. Ginsberg...............................Robert C. Fischer
Gar Evans.....................................Leo  Donnelly
Stanislaus....................................Morton  Ullman
Oscar Brown......................................Jack  Winne
Clifford  Grey................................Willard  Dashiell
Helen  Wilson..................................Peggy  Conklin
First Girl........................................Jane M. Jonson
Second Girl....................................May  Wood
Messenger  Boy....................................Joe  Neale
Gus  Vanderbilt.................................Martin  Tarby
Colombo.......................................Arthur  Albro
First Workman.................................George  Rogers
Second Workman................................R. Le  Page
Poppolos....................................Alexis  M.  Polianov
Robert Moore.................................Robert  W.  Craig
Geoffry Weston...............................Clark  Twelvetrees
Francine  Drake...............................Dorothy  Vernon
A Salesman....................................Leo  Daschbach
Millie........................................ Allys  Dwyer
Chippie.....................................Elaine  Staggers
```

Mrs. Miller.....................................Suzanne Jackson
Dr. Pfeiffer....................................Harold Kennedy
Salvatora Pachinelli............................William E. Blake
Mrs. Pachinelli.................................Alma Ross
Pasquale Pachinelli.............................Roy Lemay
Mr. Christanopolos..............................Henry DeKoven
Warren..Albert R. Berg
Wm. Hastings....................................Ed. Redding
Jerome Banks....................................Leo Kennedy
    Act I.—Scene 1—Speakeasy on 52nd Street. 2—Dressing Room
in a Turkish Bath. 3—Loft on 5th Avenue. Acts II and III.—
Offices of the Golden Gate Rubber Company.
    Staged by Bertram Harrison.

Gar Evans, promoter, is dragged out of a speakeasy, sobered up
in a Turkish bath and given a job exploiting an artificial rubber
patent. Mr. Ginsberg, who knows the inventor, raises $25,000
"front money" and Evans hires expensive offices and a high pressure selling staff. Within a few weeks sucker money is pouring
in, but the inventor has disappeared. Bankruptcy and court
action threatened, Evans sells out to the Rubber Trust. The
trust did not want the business but had to be rid of the nuisance.

BRIEF MOMENT

(129 performances)

A comedy in three acts by S. N. Behrman. Produced by
Guthrie McClintic at the Belasco Theatre, New York, November
9, 1931.

Cast of characters—

Roderick Dean...................................Robert Douglas
Harold Sigrift..................................Alexander Woollcott
Kathryn Dean....................................Frances Rich
Manny Walsh.....................................Paul Harvey
Abby Fane.......................................Francine Larrimore
Sergei Voloschyn................................Boris Marshalov
Cass Worthing...................................Louis Calhern
Butler..Edwin Morse
Maid..Helen Walpole
    Acts I, II and III.—Sitting Room in Roderick Dean's Roof-
Apartment, New York City.
    Staged by Guthrie McClintic.

See page 236.

THE SOCIAL REGISTER

(97 performances)

A comedy in three acts by Anita Loos and John Emerson.
Produced by Erlanger Productions, Inc., at the Fulton Theatre,
New York, November 9, 1931.

Cast of characters—

```
Gloria Hall..........................................Betty Garde
Mr. Jones.........................................Wilfred Clarke
Lula............................................Elizabeth Taylor
Patsy Shaw.........................................Lenore Ulric
An Electrician.....................................William Boag
Kay Wilson........................................Helen Tucker
Ruth Prescott.....................................Lenore Sorsby
Lester Trout.......................................Alan Edwards
Claude...........................................Donald Stewart
Charlie Breene..................................Sidney Blackmer
Chris..............................................Hans Hansen
Mr. Breene........................................Oswald Yorke
Mrs. Breene..............................Teresa Maxwell-Conover
Mr. Wiggins.................................George Henry Trader
Muriel Devenant.............................Hilda Heywood Howe
Mrs. Sherrard..................................Madeleine Gray
Mrs. Vandervent....................................Jane Farrell
A Debutante...........................................Vera Krug
Duc De Renan..............................Marcel Journet, Jr.
Prince Alexis......................................Sidney Elliot
Lady Sharpley....................................Andree Villars
Ronald........................................... Alan Wallace
Lady Singer.....................................Winifred Martin
Gentleman Singer....................................Tom Burton
    Acts I, II and III.—Gloria's Apartment and the Breene Home.
    Staged by John Emerson and Anita Loos.
```

Patsy Shaw, a "Vanities" girl, is afflicted with a mothering instinct that impels her to be nice to stray and unhappy men, including Charlie Breene, one of the Breenes, and wealthy. Trying to make good with Charlie's family at a party which the snooty Mrs. Breene has organized to expose Patsy our heroine gets a little squiffy on champagne, balls out the family and successfully turns a swell musical into a penthouse jazz dance. She and Charlie quarrel over Patsy's attentions to Lester Trout, but make it up when Charlie threatens to go bad in Paris if Patsy does not take him back.

PETER FLIES HIGH

(8 performances)

A comedy in three acts by Myron C. Fagan. Produced by Leonard Bergman at the Gaiety Theatre, New York, November 9, 1931.

Cast of characters—

```
Jim Walker.........................................Ivan Miller
Judy Walker........................................Mary Loane
Kate Walker.......................................Eileen Wilson
Mrs. Turner.....................................Adelaide Hibbard
Bill Curdy........................................Brian Donlevy
Irma Brooks.......................................Dulcie Cooper
Peter Turner........................................John Hole
Express Man.....................................Charles Gabest
George Brooks.....................................Burke Clarke
```

```
Judge Michael O'Brien............................Henry Crosby
Mrs. Brooks.....................................Kathryn Givney
Mrs. O'Brien.......................................Ida Backus
Sheriff...........................................Thomas Stone
Mr. Barrett........................................Forrest Orr
    Acts I, II and III.—Living Room of Peter Turner's Home in
Rosedale, N. J.
```

Peter Turner, having great confidence in himself, leaves home with the avowed intention of coming back a great success. Aided by tall talk and the gullibility of the New Jersey natives he is able to put across a deal that saves his face after threatened failure.

THE SCHOOL FOR SCANDALS

(23 performances)

A comedy in five acts by Richard Brinsley Sheridan. Revived by Lee Shubert at the Ethel Barrymore Theatre, New York, Nov. 10, 1931.

Cast of characters—

```
Lady Sneerwell..................................Beatrice Terry
Snake........................................... Ernest Rowan
Lady Sneerwell's Servant.........................Albert Froom
Joseph Surface..................................McKay Morris
Maria.........................................Anne Seymour
Mrs. Candour.....................................Anita Rothe
Crabtree......................................William Kershaw
Sir Benjamin Backbite.........................Arthur Treacher
Lady Teazle...................................Ethel Barrymore
Sir Peter Teazle.........................Charles H. Croker-King
Lady Teazle's Servant.............................Erna Rowan
Rowley.........................................Ralph Roberts
Sir Oliver Surface.............................Harry Plimmer
Moses..........................................A. G. Andrews
Trip..............................................Marcel Dill
Charles Surface................................Walter Gilbert
Careless......................................Charles Romano
Sir Harry Bumper..............................John Drew Colt
Joseph's Servant..............................William Tannen
    Tableau I.—At Lady Sneerwell's House.  Tableau II.—At Sir
Peter Teazle's House.  Tableau III.—At Charles Surface's House.
Tableau IV.—At Joseph Surface's House.  Tableau V.—At Sir
Peter Teazle's House.  At Joseph Surface's House.
    Staged by E. M. Blyth.
```

The last previous revivals of "The School for Scandal" were staged in New York during the season of 1925-26. In October Mrs. Samuel Insull (Gladys Wallis) brought to Broadway the production with which she had raised $100,000 for charity in Chicago. Herbert Druce was her Sir Peter. In December George C. Tyler and Basil Dean revived the comedy at the Knickerbocker Theatre with May Collins as the Lady Teazle and O. P. Heggie as the Sir Peter.

MARRIAGE FOR THREE

(5 performances)

A comedy in three acts by Elmer Harris. Produced by Lee Shubert at the Bijou Theatre, New York, November 11, 1931.

Cast of characters—

Marie... Claudia Morgan
March.. Thomas Reynolds
Judge Hall....................................Frederick Perry
Grace Trainor............................Jessie Royce Landis
Tom Trainor...................................Terence Neill
Peggy Howard.................................Verree Teasdale
Miss Austin................................Marjorie Ezequelle
    Acts I, II and III.—Living Room of the Trainor Home.
    Staged by Stanley Logan.

Grace Trainor, having undergone a major operation that precludes the possibility of her continuing as a normal wife to Tom Trainor, is called east by the illness of an aged aunt. She leaves Peggy Howard, an attractive house guest, to run the home for Tom. When she returns a month later she learns that Tom and Peggy have not devoted all their time to golf. Learning later that Peggy is to bear Tom a child Grace proposes that Peggy have the baby and that she (Grace) adopt it and bring it up as her own. Peggy agrees, but balks at the signing of the papers.

LOUDER, PLEASE

(68 performances)

A comedy in three acts by Norman Krasna. Produced by A. L. Jones at the Masque Theatre, New York, November 12, 1931.

Cast of characters—

Allen West....................................Buford Armitage
Ruth... Mildred Wall
Kathryn Block.....................................Aleta Freel
Herbert White.......................................Lee Tracy
Eddie Maney.....................................Millard Mitchell
Snitz Gumble....................................Percy Kilbride
Polly Madison...................................Louise Brooks
Bernie..J. H. Stoddard
George Brody....................................Charles Laite
Frederick Garrett ....Charles Brokaw
Charlie Harris......................................Allen Nagle
Kendall King.....................................Frank Thomas
Bailey....................................... Robert Gleckler
Herman Schneider............................Charles G. Wilson
Santa Claus.....................................Henry Sherwood
    Acts I, II and III.—Publicity Offices of Criterion Pictures, Hollywood.
    Staged by George Abbott.

Herbert White, head of the press department of Criterion Pictures, being called to account for his failure to put over Polly Madison, star, conceives the scheme of having her disappear in a rowboat during a Malibu beach party. The police and the press accept the story that Polly has been lost at sea, and a great search is organized. Chief Bailey of the Police grows increasingly suspicious, decides to investigate and finally makes it extremely warm for the conspirators.

SING HIGH, SING LOW

(68 performances)

A comedy in two acts by Murdock Pemberton and David Boehm. Produced by Walker Towne, Inc., at the Sam H. Harris Theatre, New York, November 12, 1931.

Cast of characters—

Doaks	Frank Vergun
Willie Norworth	Ben Lackland
Pop	Frank Andrews
Julius Speiger	Herbert Goode
Wiener	Con MacSunday
Roberts	Ifor Thomas
Magnolia Jackson Wainwright	Barbara Willison
Antoinette Ranconi	Lorna Elliott
Adolf	Lynn Root
Corbett West	Albert Vees
Hugo Winthrop Adams	Ralph Locke
Arthur Warren	Don Beddoe
Gregory Townsend	William Lynn
Adelina Drebelli	Hilda Kutsukian
Emilio Amalfi	Giuseppe Sterni
Scene Painter	Cornelius Vezin
Another Scene Painter	George Higginbottom
Craig	Fred House
Stagehand	S. K. Binyon
Another Stagehand	Rudolph Gratz
Madame Elsa	Josephine Deffrey
Rudolph Krauskopf	John Taylor
Harry	Vernon Howard
Weaver	J. S. McLaughlin
Stein	James Seymour
Thompson	Richard Galli
Wallace	Spencer Kimbell

Principals of Corps de Ballet: Grace Lydon, Jean Kayson, Katherine Eyles, Elinor James, Jean Walton, Vera Volkenau, Ina Korsch, Mary D. Smith.

Acts I and II.—In and about the Cosmopolitan Opera House, New York. August. Scene 2—The Same. Late September. Scene 3—Studio of the Director, Signor Amalfi, a Few Moments Later. Scene 4—Stage of the Cosmopolitan Opera House, a Few Weeks Later. Act II.—Scene 1—Incidents During the Premiere of "The Unhappy Princess." (a) Interlude Before the Last Act of the Opera, Seen from the Front. (b) Back-Stage Toward the Close of the Opera. Scene 2—The Director's Studio, Immediately Following. Scene 3—The Press Room. Next Morning.

Staged by Clarence Derwent.

Magnolia Jackson Wainwright, winning a singing contest in the southern town that is her birthplace, comes to New York to embark on a career at the Cosmopolitan Opera House. She is favored first by Willie Norworth, the sub-press agent; second by Hugo Adams, the Mæcenas of the opera, and third, by Emelio Amalfi, the impresario. Adams, being the money man, forces the début of "Jackie," whereupon she turns for sympathetic support to Signor Amalfi, the impresario, and finally elopes with Willie, the press agent.

IF LOVE WERE ALL

(11 performances)

A comedy in three acts by Cutler Hatch. Produced by the Actor-Managers, Inc., at the Booth Theatre, New York, November 13, 1931.

Cast of characters—

Dr. Philip Bryce................................Walter Kingsford
Margaret Bryce................................Aline MacMahon
Janet Bryce..................................Margaret Sullavan
Frank Grayson....................................Hugh Buckler
Alice Grayson....................................Mabel Moore
Ronald Grayson...............................Donald Blackwell
George Manning..................................Marc Loebell
John..John M. Troughton
Emil..Jules Bennett
    Acts I, II and III.—At the Bryce's. At the Grayson's. A farm in the country and a restaurant on the east side.
    Staged by Agnes Morgan.

Janet Bryce discovers that her mother is in love with Frank Grayson. She consults with Ronald Grayson, Frank's son, in her search for a way to stop the affair before her father, Dr. Bryce, eminent psychologist, and Ronald's invalid mother are hurt. Janet and Ronald decide that the adult lovers should be left together for a summer in the hope their passion may burn itself out. They arrange such a summer. At the end of that time the Grayson-Bryce affair is more set than ever. Bringing their guilty parents together for a final showdown the children are amazed to discover that the situation as it exists has been known to both Mrs. Grayson and Dr. Bryce from the first.

THE WIVES OF HENRY VIII

(69 performances)

A series of character sketches by Cornelia Otis Skinner. Presented by James B. Pond at the Avon Theatre, New York, November 15, 1931.

"THE WIVES OF HENRY VIII"

1. Catharine of Aragon Scene, 1525.
2. Anne Boleyn Scene, The Tower of London, May 19, 1536.
3. Jane Seymour Scene, Gardens of Hampton Court, October, 1537.
4. Anne of Cleves Scene, The Arrival of Anne at Rochester, 1540.
5. Katheryn Howard Scene, York, During a Royal Progress, 1542.
6. Katherine Parr Scene, Whitehall, January 26, 1547.

Miss Skinner also revived several of her character sketches formerly given in New York, including:

A Picnic in Kentucky.
In a Telephone Booth.
The Eve of Departure.
On the Beach at Barbados.
A Lady Explorer.
A Southern Girl in the Sistine Chapel.
In a Gondola.
Homework.

* REUNION IN VIENNA

(248 performances)

A comedy in three acts by Robert Emmet Sherwood. Produced by the Theatre Guild, Inc., at the Martin Beck Theatre, New York, November 16, 1931.

Cast of characters—

Kathie	Mary Gildea
Laundryman	Stanley Wood
Elena	Lynn Fontanne
Dr. Anton Krug	Minor Watson
Ilse	Phyllis Connard
Emil	Lloyd Nolan
Herr Krug	Henry Travers
Frau Lucher	Helen Westley
Countess Von Stainz	Virginia Chauvenet
Count Von Stainz	Edward Fielding
Poffy	Edouardo Ciannelli
Bredzi	Bela Lublov
Strup	Otis Sheridan
Torlini	Bjorn Koefoed
Police Inspector	Murray Stevens
Chef	Joseph Allen
Rudolf Maximilian Von Hapsburg	Alfred Lunt
Baroness Von Krett	Cynthia Townsend
General Hoetzler	Frank Kingdon
Talisz	Owen Meech
Sophia	Justina Wayne
Koeppke	William R. Randall
Valet	Joseph Allenton
Bellboy	Noel Taylor

THE BEST PLAYS OF 1931-32   433

Busboys..........................Ben Kranz, Hendrik Booraem
Waiters......................Charles E. Douglass, George Lewis
  Acts I and III.—Drawing-Room in the House of Doctor Anton
Krug, Vienna. Act II.—Ante-Room of the Imperial Suite, Hotel
Lucher.
  Staged by Worthington Miner.

See page 118.

THE MERCHANT OF VENICE

(6 performances)

A comedy in five acts by William Shakespeare. Revived by
the Chicago Civic Shakespeare Society at the Royale Theatre,
New York, November 16, 1931.

Cast of characters—

The Duke of Venice..............................Tyrone Power
The Prince of Morocco.........................Gordon Burby
The Prince of Arragon.........................France Bendtsen
Antonio.......................................William Faversham
Bassanio...................................Pedro de Cordoba
Salanio.. Lionel Ince
Salarino.......................................Thayer Roberts
Gratiano...Hart Jenks
Salerio....................................... Ralph Menzing
Lorenzo...John Bryan
Shylock..Fritz Leiber
Tubal..John Burke
Launcelot Gobbo..............................Whitford Kane
Old Gobbo.......................................Frank Peters
Leonardo...................................... Claudius Mintz
Clerk of the Court...............................John Forrest
Balthasar...................................... Dorothy Martin
Portia....................................... Helen Menken
Nerissa.. Viola Roache
Jessica......................................Virginia Stevens
Dance of Revelers in Act II by...................Dorothy Martin
  Act I.—Scene I—Street in Venice. 2—Portia's House at Belmont.
Act II.—Scene 1—Before Shylock's House. 2—The Same. Act
III.—Portia's House. Act IV.—Court of Justice. Act V.—Partly
at Venice, and Partly at Belmont.
  Staged by George Vivian.

During this engagement the Chicago Society also revived
Shakespeare's "Julius Cæsar," "Hamlet."

NAUGHTY MARIETTA

(24 performances)

A musical comedy by Rida Johnson Young, music by Victor
Herbert. Revived by Milton Aborn at Erlanger's Theatre, New
York, November 16, 1931.

434

THE BEST PLAYS OF 1931-32

Cast of characters—

```
Captain Richard Warrington..........................Roy Cropper
Lieutenant Governor Grandet......................Detmar Poppen
Etienne Grandet, Son of Lieut. Gov..............Louis Templeman
Sir Harry Blake, an Irish Adventurer..............Leslie McCloud
Rudolfo, Keeper of Marionette Theatre.............James Murray
Florenze, Secretary to Lieut. Gov.....................Tom Collins
Lizette, a Casket Girl.............................Eulalie Young
Adah, a Quadroon......................................Ann Carey
Silas Slick, Capt. Dick's Servant....................Robert Capron
Nanette........................................Theo. Van Tassel
Felice.............................................Ann Johnson
Fanchon........................................Dhoris Delehante
Night Watchman................................Buck Williams
Pirate..............................................Paul Graham
Indian..............................................Paul Graham
Marietta D'Altena..................................Ilse Marvenga
The Ensemble: Mary Hennessy, Dhoris Delehante, Georgina Deiter
    Mitzi Eder, Winefred McClary, Doris Colman, Vera Muller,
    Laurette Brislin, Olga Schumacher, Maria Julian, Theo. Van Tas-
    sel, Gertrude Rittenhouse, Ethel Sheridan, Muriel Day, Elsie
    Frank, Deborah Ledger and Bella Girard. Lloyd Ericsson,
    Alexander Black, Rudy Glaisek, Hudson James, S. Otis Holwerk,
    Siegfried Langer, August Loring, Paul Graham, George Koenig,
    Buck Williams and Lowell Handshaw.
    Act I.—Place D'Armes—New Orleans, 1780.  Act II.—Scene 1—
Marionette Theatre.  2—Ballroom of the Jeunesse Doree Club.
    Staged by Milton Aborn.
```

The last previous revival of "Naughty Marietta" in New York was made by the Jolson Theatre Musical Comedy Company, of which Milton Aborn was also the inspiration, in October, 1929. In that cast Ilse Marvenga was also the heroine and Roy Cropper the Captain Richard. "Naughty Marietta" was repeated December 7 for 8 performances.

FAST SERVICE

(7 performances)

A comedy in three acts by Elliott and J. C. Nugent. Produced by Edgar Selwyn at the Selwyn Theatre, New York, November 17, 1931.

Cast of characters—

```
"Bing" Allen.....................................Elliott Nugent
Neila Anderson..................................Muriel Kirkland
Doris Borden...................................Florence Shirley
M. De Stael........................................Rene Roberti
"Flaming" Varick..............................Millicent Hanley
John Blair..........................................J. C. Nugent
Gordon McIlvaine.....................................Jack Raine
Tommy Mullen...................................Edmond Breon
A French Reporter..................................Rene Roberti
Second French Reporter...........................Howard Lane
Waiter...........................................Kenneth Dana
Pedro.............................................Tino Valenti
Dr. Balch.........................................Harold Woolf
Bell Boy..........................................Howard Lane
Pablo...........................................Joey Montague
```

A Man...Jed Cogut
His Wife..Jean Mann
    Act I.—Scene 1—Garden of a Washington Country Club. 2—
Modiste Shop in New York.   3—Locker Room.   Rolland Garros
Stadium, Paris. 4, 5—Living Room of "Bing's" Apartment.   Act
II.—Scene 1—Patio of the Conquistador Hotel, Baja California, Mex-
ico. 2—Neila's Bedroom. Act III.—Patio.
    Staged by Edgar Selwyn.

"Bing" Allen, national tennis champion, meets and loves Neila
Anderson at a dance. Neila, doubting Bing's sincerity, decides
she cannot risk life with a popular champion and is about to
marry John Blair, an aging millionaire. Bing prevails upon her
to spend the night at his hotel. Next day Neila, hearing further
of Bing's irresponsibility, does marry Blair. Bing, disheartened,
goes to Lower California and would turn professional and open a
hotel. He meets Mrs. Blair, who is unhappy, and a reconciliation, divorce and second marriage of Bing and Neila is made
possible.

STEEL

(14 performances)

A drama in three acts by John Wexley. Produced by Richard
Geist, Inc., at the Times Square Theatre, New York, November
17, 1931.

Cast of characters—

Daniel Raldny.....................................Egon Brecher
William Summers (Called Skinny)....................Seth Arnold
Betty Dugan..Lili Zehner
Melania Dugan (Called Mela)....................Eleanor Phelps
Steve Dugan...................................Barton MacLane
Joe Raldny.......................... ....Paul Guilfoyle
Jim Nelson.....................................Byron MacGrath
Charley Yart...Frank Ray
Paul Salitski...................................Truman Quevli
Nick Dablonski..................................Hubert Courtney
Tony Jarrouse..................................George Colan
Pat..Daniel Royal
Bill Anderson....................................Edgar Stehli
Doctor Fields...................................Clarence Chase
Detective Johnson................................Lewis Eckels
Detective Donovan..........................Royal Dana Tracy
Beatty..Everett Jonas
Trooper......................................David S. Lifson
    Acts I, II and III.—Home of Daniel Raldny in the Milltown of
Ironton, U. S. A.
    Staged by John Wexley.

Daniel Raldny has scrimped and saved that his son may go
to college. Daniel is working in the rolling mills of Ironton.
When he discovers that his son, while grateful, hates the steel
works and all they mean; is, in fact, definitely radical, he dies of
a stroke. The son, Joe, bitterly carries on. Incidentally he

seduces Betty Dugan, his sister-in-law, who dies in childbirth, and organizes a union that calls a strike. Joe is beaten by the State Troopers. When one of these comes to arrest him and he is further mistreated his sister, Melania, shoots the trooper and goes to jail charged with murder.

THE LADY WITH A LAMP

(12 performances)

A drama in three acts by Reginald Berkeley. Produced by Kenneth Macgowan and Joseph Verner Reed at the Maxine Elliott Theatre, New York, November 19, 1931.

ACT I

Scenes 1 and 2—Embley Park, Hampshire

William Nightingale.................................Edgar Kent
Lord Palmerston....................................J. W. Austin
Sidney Herbert.....................................Leslie Barrie
Mrs. Nightingale...................................Nellie Malcolm
Elizabeth Herbert..............................Patricia Collinge
Henry Tremayne.....................................Stuart Casey
Selina Bracebridge.................................Jane Savile
Florence Nightingale...............................Edith Evans

Scene 3—Harley Street, London, 1854

Lady Heritage.....................................Hilda Plowright
Mrs. Calder.......................................Barbara Allen
Lady Christabel Deane...........................Barbara Bruce
Miss Pelt..Anne Revere
Elizabeth Herbert..............................Patricia Collinge
Mrs. Nightingale...................................Nellie Malcolm
Henry Tremayne.....................................Stuart Casey
Sidney Herbert.....................................Leslie Barrie
Lord Palmerston....................................J. W. Austin
Dr. Smith..Langdon Bruce
Nurse..Ann Lynwood
Florence Nightingale...............................Edith Evans

ACT II

Scutari. Winter, 1855

Surgeon..Philip Tonge
Selina Bracebridge.................................Jane Savile
Corporal Jones.....................................Leslie Barrie
Mrs. Williams......................................Virginia Tracey
Mr. Bamford..Joaquin Souther
Dr. Cumming..Edgar Kent
Mr. MacDonald......................................Langdon Bruce
Dr. Sutherland..................................St. Clair Bayfield
Nurse Bates.....................................Betty Upthegrove
Henry Tremayne.....................................Stuart Casey
Nurse..Frances Simon
Orderly..David Hughes
Stretcher Bearers....................Harry E. Allen, Peter Martin
Florence Nightingale...............................Edith Evans

ACT III

Scenes 1 and 2—A Room in Old Burlington Street, London

Dr. Sutherland..................................St. Clair Bayfield
Maid..Betty Upthegrove

Elizabeth Herbert	Patricia Collinge
Sidney Herbert	Leslie Barrie
Mrs. Nightingale	Nellie Malcolm
Lord Palmerston	J. W. Austin
Florence Nightingale	Edith Evans

Scene 3—A Bedroom in South Street, London

A Nurse	Anne Revere
Dr. Sutherland	St. Clair Bayfield
Elizabeth Herbert	Patricia Collinge
Florence Nightingale	Edith Evans

Scene 4—The Drawing Room, South Street

Pressman	Harry Sothern
Nurse	Anne Revere
Tankerton	Philip Tonge
"The Times" Representative	James Barrow
Pursuivant	Edgar Kent
The Secretary of State for War	Arthur Metcalf
Lord Mayor of London	H. Langdon Bruce
President of the American Red Cross	Joaquin Souther
German Diplomat	Frank Carew
Court Chamberlain	Leslie Barrie
Mother	Barbara Bruce
Little Girl	Frances Simon
Elizabeth Herbert	Patricia Collinge
First Lady	Barbara Allen
Second Lady	Ann Lynwood

Nurses: Alix Holland, Elizabeth Farrar, Mary Kemble, Helene Willard

Veterans: Joseph Kennedy, James Milaidy, Frank Munnell, David Hughes, Harry E. Allen and Wilbur Young

Florence Nightingale	Edith Evans

Staged by Leslie Banks.

A biography in drama covering the highlights of Florence Nightingale's life. She is discovered in her twenty-eighth year, when she has decided on a career of service to humanity as a nurse. She is followed through the Crimean campaign, in which she reorganized a decidedly inefficient hospital service; her later reforms in London, and brought up to 1907, three years before she died, when she is invested with the Order of Merit by the British government. On this occasion, being confined to a wheel chair, she is also given the keys to the City of London by the Lord Mayor.

THE DEVIL'S HOST

(28 Performances)

A drama in three acts by Carl Glick. Produced at the Forrest Theatre, New York, November 19, 1931.

Cast of characters—

Lawrence Austin	A. Trevor Bland
Peters	George Le Soir
Julia Carrington	Edna Archer Crawford
Allison Barker	Bob Roltner
Howard Chandler	Daniel Moyles
Molly Easton	Ami de Cerami

```
Jack Randall.......................................Robert Perry
Hank Summers.......................................Leo Fields
Paul Morrison...............................Richard Thornton
Madge Carson.....................................Claire Devine
M. Duvall.......................................Gilbert Douglas
George Bullard..................................Edward Cutler
    Acts I, II and III.—The Drawing Room of the New York Home
of M. Duvall.
    Staged by Bernard Steele.
```

M. Duvall, the greatest practical joker of them all, seeing that he is the Devil, invites a selected group to assemble at his house. Having them there he appears mysteriously and suavely unmasks the lot of them—the banker who would bribe a politician; the politician waiting to be bribed; a Broadway playboy who would seduce a pure girl and a couple of people with pasts, including an actress. The actress shoots the Devil, but he doesn't mind.

A WIDOW IN GREEN

(27 performances)

A comedy in three acts by Lea Freeman. Produced by James W. Elliott at the Cort Theatre, New York, November 20, 1931.

Cast of characters—

```
Sue..............................................Claiborne Foster
Henry.............................................David Higgins
Angelica.........................................Cecelia Loftus
Mrs. J. Stephen Van Studdiford................Katherine Emmet
Mrs. Liddy...................................Perita West Gardner
Louise...........................................Peggy Allenby
Lady Rumley....................................Florence Edney
Mr. Heddlety....................................Johnnie Brewer
The Whitford Boy...........................Maury Tuckerman
The Harkness Girl...........................Lucille Lisle
Tommy Shannon..............................Ernest Glendinning
    Act 1.—Scene 1—Drawing Room of the Old Johnson Home, River-
side Drive, New York. 2—Living Room in Sue's Cottage at Brinsley
Village, England.  Act II.—Sue's Cottage at Brinsley.  Act III.—
Drawing Room of Johnson Home in New York.
    Staged by A. H. Van Buren.
```

Sue, living quietly as a romance-starved spinster in Brinsley Village, England, meets Tommy Shannon, roving American, in the teashop and timidly invites him to her cottage to supper. Tommy, charmed by the naïveté of Sue, is graciously attentive. Sue assumes that he shortly will propose marriage, and is forehanded in announcing her engagement to the inquisitive neighbors. Tommy suddenly decides to continue roving as far as Africa. Sue, sensitively hurt, continues her make believe marriage. When she hears Tommy has been drowned in Africa she holds funeral services over his ashes. Tommy unexpectedly walks in on the ceremonies. Later he makes good his proposal

IN TIMES SQUARE

(8 performances)

A comedy in three acts by Dodson L. Mitchell and Clyde North. Produced by Barry Macollum and Maurice Greet at the Longacre Theatre, New York, November 23, 1931.

Cast of characters—

Cokey Davis	Barry Macollum
The Stage Manager	Wyrley Birch
Sally Stewart	Thelma Ritter
Jack Logan	John S. Butler
David Benson	Dodson L. Mitchell
Rose Hobarth	May McCabe
Chick Rivers	Frank Shannon
J. Wilbur Craig	Reginald Mason
Gladys Earle	Ninon Bunyea
Hamilton Hart	Frederick G. Lewis
Austin Jewett	Walter N. Greaza
A Stranger	Harvey Walters
Cameraman	James Anderson

Acts I, II and III.—Stage of the Stuyvesant Theatre, New York. Staged by Clyde North.

J. Wilbur Craig owns a theatre and is in love with Gladys Earle, a leading acress. A play is being rehearsed in the theatre for which Gladys' former husband, Austin Jewett, is engaged as leading man after he has come through a spell of dissipation. The stage manager of the theatre, Chick Rivers, is running dope, using the theatre basement as a cache and killing off those pals he fears will betray him. Chick manages to fit his murders into the plot of the rehearsed play and suspicion falls on Austin Jewett after the discovery of a body in a trunk. J. Wilbur is finally revealed as an aid to the law and the coke peddler is killed.

THE GOOD FAIRY

(151 performances)

A comedy in three acts by Ferenc Molnar, English text by Jane Hinton, produced by Gilbert Miller at the Henry Miller Theatre, New York, November 24, 1931.

Cast of characters—

The Head Waiter	Paul McGrath
Underwaiter	Salo Douday
Konrad	Evelyn Roberts
Lu	Helen Hayes
Dr. Metz	Douglas Wood
Dr. Sporum	Walter Connolly
Karoline	Ruth Hammond
Law Clerk	Jack Lynds

Act I.—Private Dining Room.   Acts II and III.—Max Sporum's Office.
Staged by Gilbert Miller.

Lu, an usherette in a motion picture theatre, is greatly influenced by picture plots. She conceives it her duty to make life brighter for both herself and as many others as possible. She will sell her body to the amorous business man, Konrad, who is pursuing her, but she will also do good by making Konrad pay for his happiness by helping others. Posing as a married woman, the wife of a poor lawyer, and promised that her husband shall be given a fine position by Konrad, she selects a lawyer at random from the telephone book. He turns out to be Dr. Sporum, middle aged and poor. Konrad promises him everything. Then Lu runs away with a headwaiter and the contract is broken. An epilogue reveals Lu married ten years later to Dr. Metz, a diplomat, whom nobody suspected of being eligible.

MISS GULLIVER TRAVELS

(21 performances)

A comedy in three acts by George Ford and Ethel Taylor. Produced by George Ford at the Hudson Theatre, New York, November 25, 1931.

Cast of characters—

Ned Gulliver	P. J. Kelly
Julia Gulliver	Ethel Taylor
Hermoine Dracey	Evelyn Beresford
Kendle Dracey	Robert Noble
Rowley Ruggles	Harry Ratcliffe
Sidney Spoonbill	Arthur Bowyer
Lily Dale	Josie Heather
Lem Fink	Harold de Becker
Peter Dracey	Vernon Rich
Tom Scroggins	Leslie Hunt
Matthew Bottlejohn	James Mullin
Sir George Beresford	H. Cooper-Cliffe
Henry Breckenridge	Craig Ward
John Crump	Lewis Douglass
Norman Guffy	James Mullin
Alfred Clayton Lunk	Al Ochs
Scipio Johnson	Doe Doe Green
Cariolanus	Richard Kane
Robert Smythe	Donald Macmillan
Kickapoo Waddlepop	James Benton
Otto	By Himself

Act I.—Scene 1—Interior of the White Hart Inn, Albany, N. Y. 2—In a Woods at Cherry Valley. Act II.—Interior of an Old Barn at Aberdeen, Ohio. Act III.—Scenes 1 and 2—Greenroom of the Theatre at Washington, D. C. 3—Stage of the Theatre.
Staged by Ethel Taylor.

Ned Gulliver, managing director of "Gulliver's Thespians," a company of English actors stranded in Albany, N. Y., in 1811 takes the $200 sent from England for the transportation of his daughter, Julia, back to the home of her grandparent, Sir George Beresford, buys a couple of wagons and starts for Louisville, Ky., where he hears there is a new and empty theatre. After touring experiences Julia is reclaimd by Sir George and the Thespians land in Washington, D. C. Four years later Julia returns from England and marries the love interest, Kendle Dracey.

COASTWISE

(37 performances)

A drama in three acts by H. A. Archibald and Donn Mullalley. Produced by Edward F. Gardner at the Provincetown Theatre, New York, November 30, 1931.

Cast of characters—

Annie Duval	Shirley Booth
Nelson	Gordon Hamilton
Marty	Thomas McQuillan
Alan Farquhar	Richard Stevenson
Alec MacDonald	Charles Gibney
Minnie	Priscilla Knowles
Roberts	Alexander Campbell
Mrs. Farquhar	Lucia Moore

Acts I, II and III.—Farquhar's cabin in Northwestern Canada. Staged by Donn Mullalley.

Coastwise Annie worked the boats in and out of Vancouver, gambling and sinning. The night she won $300 from Nelson she had to run for her life and hid in the cellar of Alan Farquhar's cabin. Farquhar, being drunk, didn't mind until he sobered up and then, being an English gentleman, he would throw Annie out. Agreed to let her stay a week to protect her from Nelson. Annie stayed on and made a man of Farquhar. He offered to take her to England, but she wouldn't go. She stayed in Canada, but she didn't go back to the boats.

THE FIREFLY

(8 performances)

A musical comedy in three acts by Otto Harbach, music by Rodolph Friml. Revived by the Civic Light Opera Company at Erlanger's Theatre, New York, November 30, 1931.

Cast of characters—

Sybil Vandare	Miss Atkins
Suzette	Eulalie Young

```
Pietro.............................................Leslie McCloud
Geraldine Vandare..................................Miss Colburn
Jack Travers.......................................Roy Cropper
John Thurston..............................Louis Templeman
Mrs. Oglesby Vandare................ .........Mrs. Herbert Waterous
Jenkins............................................Robert Capron
Herr Franz.........................................Detmar Poppen
Nina...............................................Ilse Marvenga
Antonio Columbo...............................Georgina Dieter
Correlli...........................................Siegfried Langer
```
The Ensemble: Mary Hennessy, Dhoris Delehante, Georgina Dieter, Mitzi Eder, Winefred McClary, Doris Colman, Vera Muller, Laurette Brislin, Olga Schumacher, Maria Julian, Theo. Van Tassel, Gertrude Rittenhouse, Ethel Sheridan, Muriel Day, Elena Frank, Deborah Ledger and Bella Girard, Lloyd Ericsson, Alexander Black, Rudy Glaisek, Hudson James, S. Otis Holwerk, Siegfried Langer, August Loring, Paul Graham, George Koenig, Buck Williams and Lowell Handshaw.

Act I.—Recreation Pier, New York. Act II.—Vandare Estate, Bermuda. Act III.—Vandare Home, New York.

Staged by Milton Aborn.

"The Firefly" was produced originally the season of 1912-13, with Emma Trentini the star. Nina, a street singer, is induced to adopt the costume of a boy and ship as a cabin boy on a boat Bermuda bound. Returned to New York later, after a season of study in Europe, she electrifies the social somebodies and marries the rich young man who had been haunted for years by her firefly smile. The trick being to smile like a firefly.

AFTER ALL

(20 performances)

A comedy in three acts by John Van Druten. Produced by Dwight Deere Wiman at the Booth Theatre, New York, December 3, 1931.

Cast of characters—

```
Mrs. Thomas.......................................Helen Haye
Mr. Thomas....................................Walter Kingsford
Ralph.............................................Edmund George
Phyl..............................................Margaret Perry
Mrs. Melville.....................................Minna Phillips
Alice.............................................Lillian B. Tonge
Mr. Melville......................................Philip Leigh
Duff Wilson...................................Humphrey Bogart
Greta.............................................Dorothy Mathews
Cyril Greenwood...............................J. Kerby Hawkes
Doris Melville....................................Patricia Calvert
```
Acts I and II.—The Thomas Home in Kensington. Act III.—Scene 1—Studio in Chelsea. 2—House Near Regent's Park.

Staged by Auriol Lee.

Ralph Thomas, 24, wishes to go on his own, leave his home and share lodgings with a friend. His parents are hurt but resigned. Phyllis Thomas, 20, following her brother, also breaks home ties and takes a flat, confessing frankly that she wishes to be near her

true love, who is unhappily married to an invalid wife. Father
Thomas dies. Mother Thomas carries on. Ralph marries a
dancing nymph and is unhappy. Phyl marries her married man,
when his wife dies, and presents him with four children in three
years, including twins. Both Phyl and Ralph find themselves
in their thirties reverting to the home standards of their parents
which they flouted in the beginning.

BLOODY LAUGHTER

(35 performances)

A drama in three acts by Ernst Toller, adapted by Forrest
Wilson and William Schack. Produced by Maurice Schwartz at
the Forty-ninth Street Theatre, New York, December 4, 1931.

Cast of characters—

Greta..Helen MacKellar
Egon Hinkemann...............................Maurice Schwartz
Paul...L. Byron Shores
Barker...Edmund Elton
Stone Mason....................................Richard Clarke
Bricklayer.....................................Ernest Anderson
Max Knotch.....................................Harry Mervis
Professor Musicus..............................Antonio Passy
Kraft..Milton Tighe
Michael Unbeshwert.............................Fred Eric
Singengott.....................................Charles Livingstone
Peter Immergleich..............................George R. Wilhelm
Bartender......................................Charles Davis
The Boy..Herman Block
Peppi..Marie Adels
Applicants for Freak-show, Soldiers, etc.: W. Flatley, Louis Panne-
    well, Frederic Berest, Joseph Olney, Morton Ullman, Harold
    Tenbrook, Arnold Emanuel, Walter Lissom, Elton Boswell
    Smedley Rovington, Harcourt Bauer.
Figures in the Dream Scene: Deniston Wilson, Jackobina Caro, Ida
    Strongin, Theodosia Busanne, Enid Shaw, Ann Schultz, Judith
    Abarbanel, Lilly Karen, Estelle Kamins, Grace Grey.
    Act I.—Scene 1—Home of Egon Hinkemann. 2—Barker's Office.
3—Paul's Room. 4—In Front of the Freak-show. Act II.—Scene 1
—In a Park. 2—A Beerhall. Act III.—Scene 1—In Front of the
Freak-show. 2—Hinkemann's Home.
    Staged by Maurice Schwartz.

Egon Hinkemann, returned from the war permanently crippled
and incapacitated for normal domestic life, seeks fitfully to carry
on. In fear of losing his wife's love, as well as her respect, he
takes the only job he can find, that of a freak in a street show
in which he is advertised to tear the flesh of animals with his teeth.
Later, made aware of his wife's unfaithfulness, he bitterly up-
braids her until she kills herself in despair. Egon then hangs
himself.

LITTLE WOMEN

(17 performances)

A drama in four acts by Marian de Forest, based on the story by Louisa May Alcott. Revived by William A. Brady at the Playhouse, New York, December 7, 1931.

Cast of characters—

Mr. March	Burr Carruth
Mrs. March	Marie Curtis
Meg	Lee Patrick
Jo	Jessie Royce Landis
Beth	Joanna Roos
Amy	Peg Entwistle
Aunt March	Jane Corcoran
Mr. Laurence	Carson Davenport
Laurie	Lee Crowe
Professor Frederick Bhaer	Arthur Donaldson
John Brooke	Harry Worth
Hannah Mullett	Caroline Newcombe

Acts I, II and III.—Sitting Room of the March Home in Concord, Mass. Act IV.—Apple Orchard, Plumfield.

Staged by Wm. A. Brady, Jr.

The March family, including the four March girls, Meg, Jo, Beth and Amy, passes through the several crises of having their chaplain father reported seriously ill at Washington after he has joined the army; the marriage of Meg to John Brooke; the marriage of Jo to Prof. Bhaer; the birth of Meg's twins and the death of Beth. The play was originally produced in 1912, when it was staged for Mr. Brady by Jessie Bonstelle. Alice Brady was the Meg of that production, Marie Pavey the Jo, Gladys Hulette the Beth and Beverley West the Amy.

THE PASSING PRESENT

(16 performances)

A drama in three acts by Gretchen Damrosch. Produced by Arthur Hopkins at the Ethel Barrymore Theatre, New York, December 7, 1931.

Cast of characters—

Jenny	Marjorie Dalton
Aunt Hallie	Helen Strickland
Lansing French	Morgan Farley
James Simpson	Neil McFee
Ridgley French	Cyril Scott
Kathie French	Josephine Brown
Page French	Hope Williams
Orloff	Jose Alessandro
Fraülein	Maria Ouspenskaya
Doctor Henry	E. J. Ballantine

Maud French.....................................Lillian Emerson
Laura Tobey.....................................Lynn Beranger
Brock Tobey....................................Douglas Gilmore
Luke Bodey....................................... Herbert Duffy
Mr. Lerner.......................................Louis La Bey
A Girl...Elizabeth Goddard
A Man..Thaddeus Clancy
     Acts I, II and III.—The Center Hall of the French House in New
York.
     Staged by Arthur Hopkins.

Page French, the most dependable of the Frenches, is faced
with a family crisis when her brother Lansing confesses that he
has invested money that did not belong to him in a stock deal
and has otherwise put himself in the way of being jailed by the
government. Page agrees to raise the money needed to square
Lansing by borrowing it from her cousin Laura's husband, whom
she knows to be in love with her. Lansing's confession, however,
reaches his father's ears. The old French home is sold to meet
the boy's obligations and the family is broken up.

THE SECOND COMIN'

(8 performances)

A drama in three acts by George Bryant. Produced by Jerome
H. Wallace at the Provincetown Theatre, New York, December 8,
1931.

Cast of characters—

Wilbur...Irving Hopkins
Nicodemus...................................A. B. Comethiere
Helen..Lillian Butler
Glory..Enid Raphael
Elaine..Ruth Peterson
Dr. Evans......................................Gordon Fallows
Manny...Alice Ramsey
Sam...Hayes Pryor
Old Joe..Lloyd Russell
Fanny..Maggie Elliott
Susie...Anis Davis
     Acts I, II and III.—A corner before the pulpit in a colored church
in the deep South.

Rev. Wilbur, penetrating an all-Negro section of the deep
South, makes progress as a missionary among the colored re-
ligionists until Nicodemus, the chief doubter of the community,
dares him to perform a miracle that shall indicate the Lord's
trust in him. Let the Lord send a black Jesus the colored people
can recognize. To save his tottering church, Wilbur conceives
the idea of hypnotizing Glory, Nicodemus' pure sweetheart, and
convincing her that she is to become the mother of a miraculously
begotten son. When Glory's boy is born next Christmas day he

is white and looks too much like the preacher to satisfy Nicodemus. There is a fight, in the midst of which the Rev. Wilbur dies of a stroke.

SPRINGTIME FOR HENRY

(199 performances)

A comedy in three acts by Benn W. Levy. Produced by Kenneth Macgowan and Joseph Verner Reed at the Bijou Theatre, New York, December 9, 1931.

Cast of characters—

Miss Jones	Edith Atwater
Mr. Henry Dewlip	Leslie Banks
Mr. Johnny Jelliwell	Nigel Bruce
Mrs. Julia Jelliwell	Frieda Inescort
Miss Smith	Helen Chandler

Acts I, II and III.—Sitting Room of Mr. Dewlip's Flat, London. Staged by Arthur Sircom.

Henry Dewlip, a rich young idler, having fired the last of his secretaries, engages Miss Smith through an agency. She turns out to be a puritanically minded young woman living in the same apartment building. Miss Smith's innocence and charm fascinate both Henry and his best friend, Johnny Jelliwell, and irritate Mrs. Jelliwell, who was also anticipating an affair with Henry. Miss Smith finally confesses that she has been married, that she has a small son and that she was compelled to shoot her husband. This discourages Henry but not Jelliwell. So Henry takes Mrs. Jelliwell.

1931–

(12 performances)

A drama in fourteen scenes by Claire and Paul Sifton. Produced by the Group Theatre Company at the Mansfield Theatre, New York, December 10, 1931.

Principals engaged—

Franchot Tone	Friendly Ford
J. E. Bromberg	Lewis Leverett
Morris Carnovsky	Gerrit Kraber
Clement Wilenchick	Art Smith
Stanford Meisner	Walter Coy
William Challee	Grover Burgess
Clifford Odets	Byron McGrath
Harry Bellaver	Phœbe Brand
Philip Robinson	Mary Morris
Robert Louis	Virginia Farmer

Gertrude Maynard   Sylvia Pennington
Stella Adler   Eunice Stoddard
Ruth Nelson
    Staged by Lee Strasberg.

Adam quarrels with his foreman and quits his job as a truck-man in a warehouse. He tries to get another job and fails. He breaks his engagement to marry The Girl. He is put out of his furnished room. He sinks to panhandling. He tries robbery, but can't quite stick it. He looks up The Girl again and in their mutual lonesomeness they give way to their love. The Girl loses her job and is driven to the streets. Adam has six weeks in a hospital. He finally lands a $12-a-week job in a Union Square restaurant. The Girl comes in. When he wants her to go with him she confesses that her body has become disease-ridden. To-gether they go into the square to join the Reds.

JACK AND THE BEANSTALK

(16 performances)

A fairy opera in three acts by John Erskine, music by Louis Gruenberg. Produced by George Bye at the Forty-fourth Street Theatre, New York, December 21, 1931.

Cast of characters—

Jack......................Mary Katherine Akins, Alma Milstead
Mother...........................Beatrice Hegt, Marion Selee
Princess..........................Pearl Besuner, Ruby Mercer
Cow..............................Roderic Cross, George Newton
Giant.......................Raymond Middleton, Julius Huehn
Locksmith...Willard Young
Butcher........................Roy Nichols, Mordecai Bauman
Tanner..John Barr
Barker...Roland Partridge
    Act I.—Scenes 1 and 5—Outside Jack's House. 2 and 4—On the Road. 3—Country Market. Act II.—Scenes 1, 3, 5 and 7—Near Giant's Castle. 2, 4 and 6—Kitchen in Castle. Act III.—Outside Jack's House.

Jack, hearing of the Giant who had robbed his father of his dearest possessions—the hen that laid the golden egg, the harp that played by itself and a bag of gold—sells his talking cow to a Fairy Princess disguised as an old lady at the fair. Given a handful of seeds he impatiently casts them on the ground and they straightway grow into a huge beanstalk. Jack climbs into the Giant's country, recovers his property and takes over the Princess as well. The Juilliard School of Music sponsored the holiday production.

COLD IN SABLES

(15 performances)

A comedy by Doris Anderson and Joseph Jackson. Produced by Arthur Greville Collins at the Cort Theatre, New York, December 23, 1931.

Cast of characters—

John Hammond....................................Taylor Holmes
Victoria Hammond...........................Olive Reeves-Smith
Julia...Dorothy Lord
Grace......................................Jessimine Newcombe
Janet..Kate Roemer
Lilly La Mar..................................Dorothy Mackaye
Douglas West..................................Brandon Peters
Mobelia...Francis Grant
Detective..William Green
    Acts I and III.—Living Room of the Hammond Apartment in New
York. Act II.—Lilly La Mar's Apartment.
    Staged by Arthur Greville Collins.

Victoria Hammond discovers that John, her husband, is keeping Lilly La Mar in an apartment, if not in luxury. Her method of being even is to force John to buy her sables when he buys Lilly sables, and to flirt with Douglas West by way of conquering her loneliness. In the end Victoria is triumphant and Lilly La Mar is convinced she had rather be a wife than a mistress.

IT NEVER RAINS

(20 performances)

A comedy in three acts by Aurania Rouverol. Revived at the New Yorker Theatre, New York, December 24, 1931.

Cast of characters—

Mabel Rogers....................................Elwyn Harvey
Savannah.......................................Beatrice White
Henry Rogers....................................Jack Bennett
Jimmy Rogers.....................................Carl Julius
Norleen Sears................................Marjorie Warfield
Clara Donavan...............................Annabelle Williams
Walter Donavan...................................James Kelso
Dorothy Donavan................................Julie Hornaday
Dane Lawson....................................Abram Gillette
Gale...Beatrice White
Margaret......................................Dorothy Lawson
Mary...Ivy Keith
    Acts I, II and III.—Living Room of the Rogers' Bungalow, Los
Angeles, Cal.
    Staged by J. J. White.

Produced originally in November, 1929, "It Never Rains" ran for 185 performances at the Republic Theatre, New York. See "The Best Plays of 1929-30." Henry Rogers involves an eastern friend in a California real estate deal which looks crooked but turns out a good investment.

TOM SAWYER

(6 performances)

A comedy in four acts dramatized by Paul Kester from the story by Mark Twain. Produced by the National Junior Theatre at the Alvin Theatre, New York, December 25, 1931.

Cast of characters—

Widow Douglas	Kate Conway
Aunt Polly	Alice John
Mrs. Harper	Dorothy Stewart
Walter Potter	William Lovejoy
Mary Rogers	Mary Cullinan
Dr. Robinson	George Lee
Becky Thatcher	Mary Buckner
Sid Sawyer	Ezra Stone
Muff Potter	Melvin Fox
Gracie Miller	Katherine Rolin
Tom Sawyer	Preston Dawson, Jr.
Joe Harper	Robert de Lany
Injun Joe	John Shellie
Ben Rogers	William L. Keen
Huckleberry Finn	Clifford Adams
Alfred Temple	Adelbert Stephenson
Amy Laurence	Frances Fulton
Reverend Sprague	Richard Enbach
Sheriff Jones	Arthur de Angelis
Judge Thatcher	L'Estrange Millman

Act I.—Village Street. Act II.—Village School. Act III.—Aunt Polly's House. Act IV.—Scene 1—Jackson's Island. 2—Street. Staged by Katherine Brown and Glenna Tinnin.

The adventures of Tom Sawyer and Huck Finn, beginning with the whitewashing of Aunt Polly's fence and including the witnessing of Indian Joe's murder of Dr. Robinson, the flight to the island and the freeing of the wrongfully accused Muff Potter. . . . The National Junior Theatre's repertory on this visit also included Jules Eckert Goodman's dramatization of Stevenson's "Treasure Island," produced originally by Charles Hopkins at the Punch and Judy Theatre, New York, December, 1915.

FATA MORGANA

(27 performances)

A comedy in three acts by Ernest Vajda, translated by James L. A. Burrell. Revived by Jimmie Cooper at the Royale Theatre, New York, December 25, 1931.

Cast of characters—

George.....................................Douglass Montgomery
His Mother.................................Grace Van Auker
Annie......................................Lillian Savin
His Father.................................William Ingersoll
Peter......................................James Jolley
Rosalie....................................Claire Grenville
Blazy......................................Edward Butler
Mrs. Blazy.................................Antoinette Rochte
Therese....................................Doris Lauray
Katherine..................................Margaret Mullen
Henry......................................Kemble Knight
Franciska..................................Dorothy Slaytor
Charles Blazy..............................Richard Spencer
Mathilda Fay...............................Ara Gerald
Gabriel Fay................................Richard Temple
    Acts I, II and III.—George's home on the Great Hungarian Plain
Known as the Puszta.

"Fata Morgana" was first produced by the Theatre Guild at
the Garrick Theatre, New York, March 3, 1923. See "The
Best Plays of 1923-24." George, left at home when the family
goes to a village celebration, is rather deliberately seduced by
Mathilda Fay, a married cousin. George accepts his obligations
and would have Mathilda divorce her husband and marry him.
Mathilda convinces George that she needs the money and position her husband guarantees her.

SENTINELS

(11 performances)

A drama in three acts by Lulu Vollmer. Produced by Walter
Batchelor, Daniel Dare and Louise Carpenter at the Biltmore
Theatre, New York, December 25, 1931.

Cast of characters—

John Hathaway..............................Burke Clark
Sara Hathaway..............................Katherine Tracy
Mallie.....................................Laura Bowman
Hester.....................................Dorothy West
George Hathaway............................Ben Smith
Tom Hathaway...............................Owen Davis, Jr.
Thunder....................................Wayland Rudd
Edith Redfern..............................Elizabeth Love
The Reverend Doctor Carroll................Sayre Crawley
Abbey Howe.................................Jane Wheatley
Officer....................................Milano Tilden
James Stanley..............................Orrin Burke
    Acts I, II and III.—Home of the Hathaway Family in a Southern
City.
    Staged by Priestley Morrison.

George Hathaway knows of a forged marriage certificate in
Edith Redfern's past. When Edith is to be married to his brother,
Tom, and an enemy of the family seems likely to make use of the

scandal, George goes to the bank to try to recover the evidence. In a scuffle he shoots and kills the enemy. Mallie, the Hathaways' colored servant who has practically brought up the Hathaway boys along with her own son, Thunder, senses the crime. Realizing George's danger, she determines to sacrifice her own son for the honor of the Hathaways. When Thunder is threatened with lynching George confesses.

SUGAR HILL

(11 performances)

A musical comedy by Charles Tazewell; music by Jimmy Johnson; lyrics by Jo Trent. Produced by the Moving Day Company, Inc., at the Forrest Theatre, New York, December 25, 1931.

Cast of characters—

Sister Huff	Carrie Huff
Matilda Small	Margerite Lee
Steve Jenkins	Flournoy Miller
Sam Peck	Aubry Lyles
Loucinda	Junita Stinette
Jasper	Chappy Chapelle
Gyp Penrose	Broadway Jones
Joe	Albert Chester
Mitzie	Kay Mason
Cleo	Edna Moten
Tress	Tressa Mitchell
Uncle Henry	Harrison Blackburn
Officer Brown	Andrew Copeland
Cleo's Mother	Ina Duncan
Parson Johnson	J. Louis Johnson

Girls—Lela Brogden, Laura Duncan, Jennie Day, Edna Ellington, Aurora Edwards, Thelma Green, Inez Gray, May Haygood, Josephine Heathman, Alberta Lowery, Catherine Noizette, Gussie Williams, Bobby Smith, Charle Downs, Noma Alderonte.
Boys—Joe Loomis, Maurice Ellis, Pedro Turner, Hallie Howard, E. A. Midleton, Adolph Henderson, Geo. Mason, James Moses, Richard Shopsire, Dewit Davis, Alfred Anderson and Pagasusth-Mule, Himself.
Acts I and II.—Sugar Hill.

A story of the Negro colony in Harlem having to do with recent activities of colored racketeers.

*OF THEE I SING

(201 performances)

A musical comedy in two acts by George S. Kaufman and Morrie Ryskind; music by George Gershwin; lyrics by Ira Gershwin. Produced by Sam H. Harris at the Music Box, New York, December 26, 1931.

Cast of characters—

Louis Lippman......................................Sam Mann
Francis X. Gilhooley............................Harold Moffet
Maid...Vivian Barry
Matthew Arnold Fulton.......................Dudley Clements
Senator Robert E. Lyons........................George E. Mack
Senator Carver Jones.........................Edward H. Robins
Alexander Throttlebottom..........................Victor Moore
John P. Wintergreen............................William Gaxton
Sam Jenkins....................................George Murphy
Diana Devereaux................................Grace Brinkley
Mary Turner..Lois Moran
Miss Benson..June O'Dea
Vladimir Vidovitch..................................Tom Draak
Yussef Yussevitch..............................Sulo Hevonpaa
The Chief Justice...................................Ralph Riggs
Nora..Leslie Bingham
The French Ambassador...........................Florenz Ames
Senate Clerk.......................................Martin Leroy
   Acts I and II.—In and around New York, Washington and At-
lantic City.
   Staged by George Kaufman; dances by Chester Hale.

See page 29.

THE BRIDE THE SUN SHINES ON

(77 performances)

A comedy in three acts by Will Cotton. Produced by the New
York Repertory Company at the Fulton Theatre, New York,
December 26, 1931.

Cast of characters—

Mrs. Marbury....................................Jessie Busley
Treloar..Russell Rhodes
Everett Marbury................................Dudley Hawley
Mrs. Lane......................................Fania Marinoff
Hubert Burnet......................................Henry Hull
Alfred Satterlee....................................Sam Wren
Psyche Marbury.................................Dorothy Gish
Meredith Lane......................................Nicholas Joy
Dorine..Armina Marshall
Dr. Blair...Frank Conlan
Gloria Fawcett..................................Eleanor Shaler
Harry James..................................Mervin Williams
Bridesmaids: Ann Tewksbury, Anita Heller, Barbara Child, Helen
   Dedens, Janet Langhorne, Muriel Chase.
Wedding Guests: Alvin Barrett, Anton Bundsmann, Ronald Jones,
   Jock Munro, Robert Turney
   Acts I, II and III.—Everett Marbury's Country House, West-
chester.
   Staged by Knowles Entrikin.

Psyche Marbury is to be married to Albert Satterlee, dumb but
sincere, at three o'clock. At two o'clock Hubert Burnet, musician,
arrives to play the organ. Psyche has long nursed a secret passion
for Hubert. Hubert has long been in love with Psyche, but afraid
if he acknowledged it she would marry and dominate him. Now
Psyche and Hubert discover each other and are miserable. The

wedding goes on, but it is Hubert and not Albert who goes away with the bride.

ADAMS' WIFE

(8 performances)

A drama in three acts by Theodore St. John. Produced by William A. Brady at the Ritz Theatre, New York, December 28, 1931.

Cast of characters—

Red Hitchcock	Arthur C. Morris
Chris Nelson	Ernest Pollock
Jennie Adams	Sylvia Field
Jim Adams	Victor Kilian
Tom Bach	Ralph Urmy
Peter Barrett	Eric Dressler
Joe	Alonzo Thayer

Acts I, II and III.—Living Room in Jim Adam's Ranch House, Kansas.

Peter Barrett, working through the threshing season in Kansas to make college money, finds Jennie Adams the loyal wife and drudge of Jim Adams, her kindly meant but thoughtless husband. Neighbors are strongly influenced by the K.K.K. When Peter's and Jennie's acknowledged love for each other becomes apparent the neighbors would take them out and flog them. Jim, sensing that his wife's love for another man is nothing she should be whipped for, holds up the mob until Peter and Jennie escape.

HAY FEVER

(95 performances)

A comedy in three acts by Noel Coward. Revived by Patterson McNutt at the Avon Theatre, New York, December 29, 1931.

Cast of characters—

Sorel Bliss	Betty Linley
Simon Bliss	Anthony Kemble-Cooper
Clara	Alice Belmore Cliffe
Judith Bliss	Constance Collier
David Bliss	Eric Cowley
Sandy Tyrell	Terence Neill
Myra Arundel	Julia Hoyt
Richard Greatham	Edward Cooper
Jackie Coryton	Valerie Cossart

Acts I, II and III.—The Hall of the Bliss House at Cookham. Staged by Constance Collier.

First produced in New York in October, 1925, with Laura Hope Crews playing the chief rôle. Judith Bliss, an actress who has retired, is living with her somewhat erratic family near London. An unexpected assembling of week-end guests gives Judith an audience before which she performs variously, it being her weakness to dramatize her every adventure. The guests stand it as long as they can and then escape back to London.

PAPAVERT

(13 performances)

A comedy in three acts by Charles K. Gordon, based on a suggestion by George Froeschel. Produced by Joe Zelli at the Vanderbilt Theatre, New York, December 29, 1931.

Cast of characters—

Meussel	Jules Epailly
Wismuth	Charles La Torre
Hilda Papavert	Alice Reinheart
1st Comrade	Eileen Myers
2nd Comrade	Dorothy Miller
Mrs. Papavert	Lotta Linthicum
Max Lazar	Edward Leiter
Commissioner Conolly	William Roselle
Dr. Mullins	James Malaidy
Warden Flannigan	Hugh Cameron
Willi Papavert	Edgar Stehli
A Convict	Milton Roberts
A Guard	George Vinton
Mrs. Weinstein	Stella Unger
Siegbert Moses	Max Figman
Jules Bavache	Herbert Corthell
Inspector Vieth	Willard Dashiell
Captain Schrager	Jack Klendon
Officer Lawson	D. J. Hamilton
Officer Butler	Arthur Hebert
1st Bookbinder	Bert Wittly
2nd Bookbinder	David Hughes

Act I.—Scene 1—Anteroom of the Meeting Hall. 2—Office of the Warden. Act II.—Papaverts' Home. Act III.—Scene 1—Police Station. 2—Papaverts' Home.
Staged by Charles K. Gordon.

Willi Papavert, having been sent to prison for a murder he did not commit, is adopted by the local Communist leaders as a martyr. When he is pardoned by the governor he comes back to his home to find it the headquarters for Communist activities, with his wife also afflicted with the Red urge. Willi only asks that he be permitted to get back his old job as a bookbinder. Failing this he would like to be returned to the nice, quiet, dependable jail from which he has been freed. Willi's gentleness wins a kind of peace for him in the end.

EXPERIENCE UNNECESSARY

(45 performances)

A comedy in three acts, adapted by Gladys Unger from the German of Wilhelm Sterck. Produced by the Messrs. Shubert at the Longacre Theatre, New York, December 30, 1931.

Cast of characters—

```
Gus.............................................Leo  Needham
Miss Musgrave...................................Patricia Calvert
Theda Thompson.................................Verree Teasdale
Winthrop Allen..................................Rex  O'Malley
Frank  Cameron...................................Walter  Woolf
The Steward..................................Rudolph Badaloni
The Visitor..................................Frederick Stewart
The Porter.........................................Albert West
The Bride.........................................Sheila  Barrett
The Groom......................................Milton Le Roy
    Acts I and III.—Frank Cameron's Private Office. Act II.—Bridal
Suite on the S.S. Saturnalia.
    Staged by H. C. Potter.
```

Frank Cameron is in the habit of advertising annually for a traveling companion, female, interested in a European trip. Theda Thompson, his secretary and secretly in love with Cameron, takes on the job one year and manages both to elude her employer's too ardent advances during the trip and to excite him into a proposal of honorable marriage when they get home.

A return engagement of "Experience Unnecessary" was played for twenty-five performances at the National Theatre, New York, beginning March 26, 1932. Eva Leonard Boyne was substituted for Patricia Calvert; G. P. Huntley, Jr., for Rex O'Malley; John Junior for Frederick Stewart; Eleanor Audley for Sheila Barrett.

BERLIN

(26 performances)

A drama in three acts by Valentine Williams and Alice Crawford. Produced by Raymond Moore and Carl Reed at the George M. Cohan Theatre, New York, December 30, 1931.

Cast of characters—

```
Frau von  Hentsch..............................Ethel Strickland
Dr. von Hentsch..................................Charles Richman
Major Von Ungemach..........................Walter  Wilson
Johann........................................William  Franklyn
Olivia  Dunbar...................................Helen  Vinson
Abbott...................................G. P. Huntley, Jr.
Ilsa Von Wiltsche..............................Peggy Hovenden
Rudi Von Linz.......................................David  Morris
Dr. Grundt......................................Sydney  Greenstreet
```

Hedwig..Aileen Poe
Nigel Druce.................................G. P. Huntley, Jr.
Floria Von Pelligrini.........................Katherine Wilson
Vogel...Jacob Bleifer
Bauer...Curtiss Karpe
Prince Karl...................................Moffat Johnston
Frau Hulda.................................Charlotte Granville
Freda...Helena Rapport
Mitzi...Sue Moore
Hans...William Howard
Schlier.......................................Arthur Kaskal
Cloak Room Attendant..........................Mary Orr
Head Waiter.................................E. J. DeVarney
Baron Von Robe.................................Albert Hayes
Count Papenfels.................................Walter Harris
Major Von Ritemeister..........................John Feistel
    Act I.—Scene 1—Front of Dr. von Hentsch's House. 2—Dr. von
Hentsch's Study. Act II.—Scene 1—Street. 2—Floria's Apartment.
3—Café Zur Nelke. 4—Schippke's Cloak Room. 5—Schippke's Res-
taurant. Act III.—Scene 1—Room at Dr. Grundt's. 2—An Attic.
    Staged by Fritz Feld.

Nigel Druce, posing as Abbott, is an English secret service
operative working in Berlin in July, 1914. Being jailed as a
political prisoner, he escapes. On his way to liberty he meets
Olivia Dunbar, an English typist serving as secretary to Dr. Von
Hentsch. Enlisting Olivia's services in the recovery of papers
hidden in Berlin, Nigel meets the girl later and the two of them
are chased from one danger to another by Dr. Grundt, head of
the Kaiser's secret service. They finally escape with the papers.

SOCIETY GIRL

(13 performances)

A comedy in three acts by John Larkin, Jr. Produced by
William Brandt at the Booth Theatre, New York, December 30,
1931.

Cast of characters—

Watkins...Edna West
Miss Halloway.................................Hallie Manning
Judy Gelett...................................Claire Luce
Ronnie Carb...................................Robert Allen
Luke...John Taylor
Briscoe.......................................Brian Donlevy
Johnny Malloy.................................Russell Hardie
Tom Warburton.................................Gordon Richards
Zoe Van Ruyl..................................Helen Shipman
Peter Bragdon.................................Tom Rutherford
Matagalpa.....................................Charles Palazzi
    Act I.—Living Room in Judy Gelett's Penthouse. Act II.—Scene
1—Hampton Bays. Johnny Malloy's Training Quarters. 2—Sutton
Place. Act III.—Scene 1—Sutton Place. 2—Hampton Bays.
    Staged by Stanley Logan.

Judy Gelett, fed up with the monotonous routine of her life as
a society girl, adventures with Johnny Malloy, prize fighter.
Johnny takes Judy more seriously than she expected to be taken.

When she would call the whole thing off he smacks her soundly, knocking her quite cold, and carries her away to his training camp, where he makes a woman of her by forcing her to do a woman's job of cooking and waiting on him until she is physically in trim again. Then he marries her.

THE LANCASHIRE LASS

(21 performances)

A melodrama in five acts by Henry J. Byron. Produced by Walter Hartwig at the President Theatre, New York, December 30, 1932.

Cast of characters—

```
Robert Redburn...............................Carl Benton Reid
Ned Clayton......................................Herbert Ranson
A Party of the Name of Johnson.................Barlowe Borland
Spotty.........................................Bernard Jukes
Mr. Gregory Danville..............................John Boone
Farmer Kirby..................................Joseph Lazarovici
Jellick.........................................Edward M. Favor
Sergeant Donovan.............................Jack C. Connelly
Milder.......................................Charles P. Thompson
Inspector Kitely..................................Colin Hunter
Phil Andrews.......................................John Hilton
A Postman.......................................James Lindsay
Ruth Kirby....................................Mercedes Desmore
Kate Garstone..................................Bernard Ostertag
Fanny Danville....................................Barbara Allen
Mrs. Agatha Bootle...............................Cecile Wulff
A Flower Girl.......................................Laura Grey
    Act I.—In the Fields and at Farmer Kirby's Cottage. Act II.—In
Danville's Office and the Drawing Room of Danville's House. Act
III.—A Street and a Wharf in Liverpool. Act IV.—At Farmer
Kirby's and in a Prison. Act V.—An Australian Farmhouse.
    Staged by Walter Hartwig.
```

This "powerful emotional melodrama of home life in the days of Queen Victoria" was first produced in London in 1868, "with Henry Irving in the cast." It was later shown in New York at the old Wallack's Theatre with J. W. Wallack and a company of New York actors assigned to the various rôles. The story has to do with the trouble Ruth Kirby got into before she was properly married to Ned Clayton.

SAVAGE RHYTHM

(12 performances)

A drama in three acts by Harry Hamilton and Norman Foster. Produced by John Golden at the John Golden Theatre, New York, December 31, 1931.

Cast of characters—

Conjur-woman..Mamie Cartier
Another...Georgette Harvey
Star... Vivian Baber
Waitress.......................................Venezuela Jones
Great-Grandchildren........................... { Joe Sobers
                                              { Raymond Bishop
Sweetback................................ Ernest R. Whitman
Flirt...Olive Wanamaker
Roustabout.....................................Juano Hernandez
Boy Neighbor....................................John Robinson
Sweetback's Wife..................................Inez Clough
Parson..J. W. Mobley
Barbecue Man......................................Al F. Watts
Fighting Boy......................................James Daniels
Another...Alvin Childress
Old Church Man......................................Fred Miller
    Acts I, II and III.—A Small Community in the Lower Mississippi
Swamplands.
    Staged by Robert Burton.

Orchid (a Star) revisits her home in the deep South after having achieved some success as a dancing girl in a New York musical comedy. She finds her people quite as unenlightened, so far as modern civilization goes, as they were when she left them. Her grandmammy is still a conjur-woman. Her mother has inherited the power. Her roustabout sweetheart considers that she still is his girl. The wife of a "sweetback," jealous both of Orchid and her sister, stabs the sister. The conjur-women are called to bring the dead woman's soul back to name her murderer. They fail. Orchid feels the power. In a trance she denounces the "sweetback" as being the real cause of the murder. By tribal custom he is sent into the swamp to die.

THE DEVIL PASSES

(96 performances)

A comedy in three acts by Benn W. Levy. Produced by Arch Selwyn at the Selwyn Theatre, New York, January 4, 1932.

Cast of characters—

D. C. Magnus.......................................Arthur Byron
Paul Robinson....................................Diana Wynyard
Dorothy Lister....................................Mary Nash
Cosmo Penny....................................Ernest Thesiger
Louis Kisch..Ernest Cossart
Beatrice Messiter..................................Cecilia Loftus
Rev. Herbert Messiter............................Robert Loraine
Ellen..Gwen Day Burroughs
Rev. Nicholas Lucy................................Basil Rathbone
    Prologue—Mr. Magnus' Flat in London. Acts I, II and III.—
Mr. Magnus' Cottage in the Country.
    Staged by Benn W. Levy.

See page 300.

LOST BOY

(15 performances)

A drama in three acts by T. C. Upham. Produced by Burton Harfod at the Mansfield Theatre, New York, January 5, 1932.

Cast of characters—

Joe Hebert	Edgar Barrier
Toivo	Mooney Diamond
Francis Demarco	Elisha Cook, Jr.
Mrs. Demarco	Ruth Chorpenning
Aggie Demarco	Ann Thomas
Mr. Demarco	George Colan
Mr. Gilkey	William Balfour
Gould	Ralph Chambers
Judge Donnelly	George Price
Dr. Stewart	Clyde Franklin
Court Stenographer	Peter Xantho
Bill	Jules Garfield
Dick	Charles Berre
Albert	Richard Ross
Mr. Bullock	Joseph Eggenton
Mrs. Hazelton	Carrie Weller
Mr. Felch	George Rogers
Jimmy	Gilbert Squarey
Policeman	Alexander Smith

Act I.—Scene 1—A Freightyard in a Small Town in New England. 2—Demarco Home. 3—Judge's Chamber. Act II.—County Training School. Act III.—Demarco Home.
Staged by James Light.

Francis Demarco, 15, a chronic truant, is suspected of a railroad yard crime and arrested. Through the kindly offices of the truant officer, Mr. Gilkey, and a friendly psychiatrist, Dr. Stewart, the Judge is prevailed upon to send Francis to the County Training School in place of jail. Francis, convinced the world is against him, sets out to make a record as the worst boy in the school in order to get even with everybody. The psychiatrist prevails upon the boy to mend his ways and has him well on the way to recovery when the superintendent, Mr. Bullock, interferes and attempts to beat Francis back into line. Francis fells Bullock, steals his revolver and kills three guards in making his escape. Surrounded at home, he kills himself.

WOLVES

(29 performances)

A drama in three acts by Romain Rolland. Translation by Barrett H. Clark. Produced by Maurice Schwartz at the Forty-ninth Street Theatre, New York, January 6, 1932.

Cast of characters—

Quesnel.. Charles Dalton
Verrat... Fred Eric
D'Oyron... Leslie Austin
Teulier.. Maurice Schwartz
Chapelas... Ernest Anderson
Buquet.......................................L. Byron Shores
Vidalot.......................................George R. Wilhelm
First Officer.....................................Herbert Delmar
Second Officer...............................Owen Cunningham
Jean-Amable............................... Charles Livingstone
A Soldier...Antonio Passy
Yakob Gabel ....Harry Mervis
Innkeeper Rifel...................................Richard Clark
Soldiers: Raymond O'Brien, Orlin Crawford, Jack Morgan, Edward
    Wright, Henry Schafer, Joe Bodell, Elmer Barleb, Lionel Rose,
    Morton Ulman, Louis Pannewell, Fred Berest.
Acts I, II and III.—Mayence, 1793, a Hotel Which Serves as
General Staff Headquarters.
Staged by Maurice Schwartz.

A group of officers of the Revolutionary Army are headquartered in Mayence. Like a pack of wolves they are beset by personal quarrels, hates, jealousies and suspicions. D'Oyron, the aristocrat among them, is accused in a letter taken from a spy, of being of service to the enemy. He alleges a conspiracy and is defended by Teulier, a scientist and academician. The snarling generals refuse to hearken to Teulier's plea for justice and send D'Oyron to the guillotine and Teulier to trial before the Committee for Safety. A drama inspired by the Dreyfus case.

NEVER NO MORE

(12 performances)

A tragedy in three acts by James Knox Millen. Produced at the Hudson Theatre, New York, January 7, 1932.

Cast of characters—

Mammy.. Rose McClendon
                (HER CHILDREN)
Tom... Morris McKenney
Joe... William L. Andrews
Milly..Enid Raphael
Ike........ ....James Dunmore
Laura... Viola Dean
Solomon....................................... Rudolph Toombs
Susie..Dorothy Paul
                (THE OTHERS)
Deacon... Lew Payton
Neighbor... Leigh Whipper
Acts I, II and III.—Outside Mammy's Cabin on a Southern
Plantation.
Staged by Chester Erskin.

Mammy, living with her six children and daughter-in-law in a cabin on the plantation, is counting her blessings the day Solomon, her last born and her only wild boy, is trailed by bloodhounds to her door. Solomon, in panic, has strangled a white girl who screamed when he touched her. The mob with the dogs catches Solomon, after Mammy has locked him out of the cabin, and burns him outside the door. When the leader of the mob would burn out the family as well, Mammy, with a dynamite bomb used in the clearing, threatens to blow up the lot of them if they make a move.

ELECTRA

(6 performances)

A tragedy in one scene by Sophocles. Translation by J. T. Sheppard. Revived by Robert Henderson at the Selwyn Theatre, New York, January 8, 1932.

Cast of characters—

```
An Old Servant..............................Charles Waldron
Orestes......................................John Buckler
Pylades..................................Robert Schnitzer
Electra.................................... Blanche Yurka
The Chorus: Anna Duncan, Alma Kruger, Doris Rich, Charlotte
    Orr, Ann Lynwood, Elizabeth Farrar, Alice Dalton, Mary Stuart,
    Eleanor Goodrich, Ruth Guiterman, Wendy Atkin and Miriam
    Schiller.
Chrysothemis...............................Joyce Carey
Clytaemnestra.......................Mrs. Patrick Campbell
Her Attendants.................Janet Lawton, Marie Lavezzo
Aegisthos................................. Robert Henderson
His Attendants................William Kline, George Stearns
    Outside the Palace Gates at Mycenæ. The Action of "Electra" is
Continuous.
    Chorus Directed by Anna Duncan; Music by Richard Malaby.
```

The last previous revival of Sophocles' "Electra" was made by Carl Reed and Elizabeth Marbury for the Greek actress, Marika Cotopouli, at the New Yorker Theatre in December, 1930. Margaret Anglin read the Edward Plumptre version with the Symphony Society of New York, Walter Damrosch conducting, at Carnegie Hall in February, 1918, and again at the Metropolitan Opera House at two benefit performances in 1927.

THE GONDOLIERS

(8 performances)

An operetta in two acts by W. S. Gilbert and Arthur Sullivan. Revived by the Civic Light Opera Company at Erlanger's Theatre, New York, January 11, 1932.

Cast of characters—

The Duke of Plaza-Toro...........................Frank Moulan
Luiz...Dudsworth Fraser
Don Alhambra Del Bolero......................William Danforth
Marco Palmieri................................Howard Marsh
Giuseppe Palmieri...............................Allen Waterous
Antonio...Bobby Fuller
Francesco.. Sano Marco
The Duchess of Plaza-Toro...........................Vera Ross
Casilda... Ruth Altman
Gianetti..Vivian Hart
Tessa..Cecilia Branz
Fiametta..Frances Moore
Vittoria......................................Mabel Thompson
Giulia..Rosa Rubenstein
Inez.. Belle Flower
    Act I.—The Piazetta, Venice. Act II.—Pavilion in the Palace of
Barataria. Year 1750.
    Staged by Milton Aborn.

"The Gondoliers" was first revived by Mr. Aborn in June, 1931.
This repeated performance carried the same cast of principals with
the exception of Joseph Macauley, who was replaced by Allen
Waterous.

THE BLACK TOWER

(72 performances)

A melodrama in three acts by Ralph Murphy and Lora Baxter.
Produced by Ben Stein at the Sam H. Harris Theatre, New York,
January 11, 1932.

Cast of characters—

Dr. Eugene Ludlow...........................Walter Kingsford
Inspector Quirk..............................Raymond Bramley
Sylvia Knight...................................Mabel Grainger
Nick Rumsey...............................J. Anthony Hughes
Professor Steiffitz............................John F. Hamilton
Duffy... Thomas Blake
Mona.. Katherine Squire
Moran...Clay Cody
    Prologue—Lonely Spot in Central Park. Acts I, II and III.—
Tower Room of Dr. Ludlow's Country House.
    Staged by Sidney Salkow.

Dr. Eugene Ludlow, fanatic, has an idea he can achieve perfection in sculpture that will satisfy even the critics by stealing handsome humans and turning them into statues by a patented style of
embalming. He tries the experiment on a young woman who has
appealed to him for work, or would have tried it if the detectives
had not ferreted out his Black Tower laboratory up the Hudson
and put him out of business. The play is based on a short story,
"The Wine of Anubis," by Crittenden Marriott.

THREE MEN AND A WOMAN

(8 performances)

A comedy in three acts by Frank Harvey. Produced by David Productions, Ltd., at the Lyceum Theatre, New York, January 11, 1932.

Cast of characters—

PROLOGUE

Eileen Kell	Franc Hale
Rangei	Carl H. Vose
Gordon Kingsley	Barrie O'Daniels

THE PLAY

William Kell	William Desmond
Harry Cass	Walker Whiteside
Eileen	Franc Hale
Rangei	Carl H. Vose
Gordon Kingsley	Barrie O'Daniels
A Government Inspector	Edward Carson

Acts I, II and III—Living Room of a Lighthouse on Cape Forlorn, off the Coast of New Zealand.

Staged by Walker Whiteside and Lee C. Millar.

Harry Cass is serving as mate to "Skipper" Kell, in charge of a lighthouse off Cape Forlorn, New Zealand. The Skipper's wife, Eileen, being young and restless, philanders with Harry a matter of two years, and then quits him the day a handsomer lad, Gordon Kingsley, is washed up on the rocks of the lighthouse in a disabled motor boat. Cass' jealousy, plus the Skipper's suspicion, brings about a crisis in which Kingsley is exposed as an embezzler of building association funds. Kingsley jumps into the ocean, Eileen is sent ashore, the Skipper and Harry go on tending the lights.

THE ANIMAL KINGDOM

(183 performances)

A comedy in three acts by Philip Barry. Produced by Gilbert Miller and Leslie Howard at the Broadhurst Theatre, New York, January 12, 1932.

Cast of characters—

Owen Arthur	G. Albert Smith
Rufus Collier	Frederick Forrester
Cecelia Henry	Lora Baxter
Richard Regan	William Gargan
Tom Collier	Leslie Howard
Franc Schmidt	Betty Lynne
Joe Fisk	Harvey Stephens
Daisy Sage	Frances Fuller
Grace Macomber	Ilka Chase

Acts I, II and III.—At Tom Collier's, in Connecticut and Daisy
Sage's Apartment in 38th Street, New York.
Staged by Gilbert Miller.

See page 179.

JEWEL ROBBERY

(54 performances)

A comedy in three acts adapted by Bertram Bloch from the
Hungarian of Lazlo Fodor. Produced by Paul Streger at the
Booth Theatre, New York, January 13, 1932.

Cast of characters—

Hollander.. Robert Vivian
Leopold..Harold Johnsrud
Marianne...................................... Cora Witherspoon
Count Rehberger..............................Frederick Roland
Lenz..Lionel Braham
Teri... Mary Ellis
Franz...Clarence Derwent
Paul.. Stuart Casey
Customer..Basil Sydney
His Friend......................................Louis M. Simon
Berta...Hazel Nagley
Detective...................................... Eugene Powers
Act I.—22 Kartner Strasse.   Act II.—10 Argentinier Strasse.
Act III.—37 Grueneberg Strasse, Vienna.
Staged by Paul Streger.

Teri, wife of Franz, is in the Hollander jewelry shop in Kartner
Strasse when a gang of holdup men, led by a supposed customer
(Basil Sydney) robs the place. Teri is thrilled and interested in
the robber, who afterward breaks into Teri's room to test her
interest and, kidnaping her, takes her to his own apartment. Teri
escapes from there, but not until a rendezvous has been arranged
for Nice.

DISTANT DRUMS

(40 performances)

A drama in three acts by Dan Totheroh. Produced by Guthrie
McClintic at the Belasco Theatre, New York, January 18, 1932.

Cast of characters—

Quincey Briddleman............................. Edward Ellis
Philip Allen.....................................Maurice McRae
Jay Pike..Thomas B. Findlay
Bill Shaw...Leo Curley
Nathan Pike....................................Edward Potter
Mrs. Pike....................................... Beulah Bondi
Mrs. Shaw.......................................Mabel Colcord
Mrs. Sawyer.....................................Eda Heinemann
Mrs. Williams...............................Margherita Sargent
Jason Allenby....................................Edward Pawley
Doctor Tracy....................................John Ravold

```
Joe Clemens....................................William Lawson
Harris Wolfhill...................................Arthur Hohl
Eunice Wolfhill..................................Pauline Lord
Reverend Williams..........................James P. Houston
Grandma Briggs...... ...........................Kate Morgan
Mrs. Clemens....................................Mary Michael
J. Plinge.........................................Charles Kuhn
Harrison Lee....................................Richard Cubitt
    Acts I, II and III.—Scene 1—On a Foot-Hill Meadow in the
Snake Indian Country and in the Mountains of Idaho.
    Staged by Guthrie McClintic.
```

Eunice Wolfhill, wife of Harris Wolfhill, leader of a party of pioneers traveling by ox train over the Oregon trail in 1848, is beset with strange visions and prophecies which she accounts for by the fact that her great-grandmother had been a witch. Eunice is not in love with, but faithfully loyal to, her husband, whom she married to help him claim 300 additional acres of land when they reached Oregon. Eunice is loved by Jason Allenby, a young wagoner, arousing the suspicions of her husband. When the party is lost in the Idaho mountains, and the Snake Indians who have been camping on their trail offer to show them the pass if they will give Eunice to their chief, Wolfhill agrees. Eunice accepts the sacrifice as her foreordained destiny.

A LITTLE RACKETEER

(48 performances)

A musical comedy in two acts adapted by Harry Clarke from the German of F. Kalbfuss and R. Wilde; music by Haskell Brown; lyrics by Edward Eliscu. Produced by the Messrs. Shubert at the Forty-fourth Street Theatre, New York, January 18, 1932.

Cast of characters—

```
Donnie Parker....................................Carl Randall
Mr. Knoblock....................................John Perkins
Frank Leave....................................George Marshall
Alberta Lawrence............................Barbara Newberry
Ethel Pierson....................................Grace Hayes
Dick Barrison.................................... John Garrick
Head Waiter..................................George Del Rigo
Flossie..........................................Kay Simmons
May............................................Evelyn Reide
Donovan.....................................Daniel J. Sullivan
Jay Slump........................................William Kent
Dixie............................................Queenie Smith
Mrs. Alameda Snook..........................Lorraine Weimar
Henry........................................Hamtree Harrington
Grayson..................................... Walter Johnson
The Ghost Priest...........................Khalil Oglou Mazini
Yo Hay Tong.............................Princess Yo Hay Tong
Show Girls—Leone Sousa, Julia Barker, Eleanor Arden, Jerry
    Rogers, Dorothy Drum, Bobby Hamilton, Marion Gillon, Agatha
    Phillips.
```

Dancers—Marjorie Crane, Madeline Eubanks, Elsie St. Clair, Billy
Joy, Martha Pacini, Colleen Ward, Snookie Gordon, Inez Goetz,
Joan Abbey, Gertrude Medwin.
Gentlemen—John Perkins, George Del Rigo, Harold Offer, Kai Han-
sen, Al. Berl, Steve Mikol, Ned Lynn, Jimmie Corke, Stanley
Ledman, George Marshall.
Specialty Dancers—Tom and Betty Wonder.
Acts I and II.—In and Around the Central Park Casino, and
Dick's Apartment.
Staged by William Caryl; dances by Albertina Rasch.

Dixie, a big city waif, falls into the habit of pretending to
fall asleep in the tonneaus of parked automobiles in front of
fashionable cafés and night clubs.   Usually the owners of the
cars, mellowed by their evening's experiences, take pity on the
poor little thing and tip her generously.   Dick Barrison, finding
Dixie in his car, goes farther.   He takes her home with him and,
learning her racket and that she is adventure-crazy, he pretends
to be a society burglar on his own account and conspires with
Dixie to burglarize his own house.   When all is discovered they
agree to get married.

WHISTLING IN THE DARK

(143 performances)

A melodramatic farce by Laurence Gross and Edward Childs
Carpenter.   Produced by Alexander McKaig at the Ethel Barrymore Theatre, New York, January 19, 1932.

Cast of characters—

Joe Salvatore.....................................Ralph Theadore
Slim Scanlon......................................S. Henry Norell
Hilda...Martha Mayo
Herman Lefkowitz..............................Joseph Kleema
Charlie Shaw..................................Arthur R. Vinton
Jacob Dillon...................................Edward Arnold
The Cossack.................................Charles McClelland
Benny..Jack Stone
Wallace Porter...................................Ernest Truex
Toby VanBuren....................................Claire Trevor
Pratt...John Kearney
Cap O'Rourke..................................Horace Cooper
Miriam..Helen Mehrmann
Ray..John Kane
Doggy..John S. Irwin
Police Sergeant.............................Charles McClelland
Policeman.....................................Arthur T. Hebert
Acts I, II and III.—Living Room in Jacob Dillon's House Near
Spuyten Duyvil.
Staged by Frank Craven.

Wallace Porter, a writer of crime fiction and an amateur crimi-
nologist, looking for a house to rent comes upon one with a sign
on it overlooking the Hudson.   Venturing inside he finds himself
in the hideout of a gang of hijackers and assorted crooks.   Learn-

ing his profession the leader of the gang, Jacob Dillon, determines
to hold Porter prisoner until he has thought up a murder plan
by which the crooks can be rid of a certain eminent citizen and
leave no trace of the murder for police to work on. To delay a
search for Porter they send for his fiancée, Toby VanBuren,
and lock her up, too. Porter evolves a perfect crime and then
tries to block it before the murder can be done. His knowledge of radio helps him out.

TEN NIGHTS IN A BARROOM

(37 performances)

A drama in three acts by William W. Pratt, adapted from a
novel by T. S. Arthur. Produced by George E. Wintz at the
John Golden Theatre, New York, January 20, 1932.

Cast of characters—

Mr. Romaine—A Philanthropist	Carl H. Carlton
Sample Swichel—A Yankee Tippler	Billy Bryant
Simon Slade—Landlord of the "Sickle & Sheaf Inn"	Sam Bryant
Harvey Green—A Villainous Gambler	Clyde Shafer
Frank Slade—The Inn Keeper's Son	Frank Anton
Willie Hammond—Judge Hammond's Son	Mack Frank
Mrs. Slade—The Inn Keeper's Good Wife	Joan Meyer
Joe Morgan—A Drunkard	Carl H. Carlton
Mary Morgan—The Drunkard's Daughter	Betty Bryant
Mehitable Cartright—The Gal Who Never Had a Beau	Florence Reynolds
Mrs. Morgan	Josephine Bryant
Fiddler Joe	Vic Faust
Harmonica Pete	Paul Robinson

Acts I, II and III.—In and Around the Sickle & Sheaf Hotel
and Joe Morgan's Home.
Staged by Billy Bryant.

A favorite of the 'fifties detailing the home tragedies resulting from Joe Morgan's drinking and the gambling of Willie Hammond, the Judge's son. A revival was staged by Katherine Kirk-
wood in a Greenwich Village theatre in April, 1928. Mr. Bryant's
company also gave a few performances of "East Lynne" during
this engagement.

ADAM HAD TWO SONS

(5 performances)

A play in three acts by John McDermott. Produced by Aarons
and Freedley at the Alvin Theatre, New York, January 20, 1932.

Cast of characters—

Joe.. Alex Cross
Ed... Jay Adair
Matt..Paul Kelly
Kid... Raymond Hackett
Pablo... Edward LaRoche
Teresa...Raquel Torres
Leary... Preston Foster
Jim..John Junior
Ted.. James Young
Leo... Frank Horton
Luisa...Regine Valdy
Derelict... Marshall Hale
The Guy With a Wife in Scranton.....................Harry Klint
Mate.. Herbert Belmore
The Fat Girl...Pilar Arcos
Sister Teresa....................................Constance Kerr
Maizie.. Evelyn Downing
The Argentine................................Aristide DeLeoni
The Russian....................................Daniel Marenko
Pedro.. Harry DeKoven
Doctor..Franklin Munnell
Sailor..Walter Farrell
Hostesses: Lola Bazan, Gilberti Fray, Johanne Douglas, Genevieve
   Frizzell, Helen Glenn, Muriel Campbell.
Don Pedro Via Orchestra.
   Act I.—Scene 1—A Prison Road Camp, Near San Francisco.
Scene 2—The "Siesta Hour" at the Bolivar Café on the Outskirts
of Panama.   Act II.—The Bolivar Café.   Act III.—Pedro Miguel
Lock, Panama Canal.
   Staged by Melville Burke.

Matt and his brother, "Kid," are wild boys who did not get a
break at home.   To avenge a grudge they sneak out of a prison
camp between the watchman's rounds, murder a doctor, and sneak
back.   When they escape to the Canal Zone later they are trailed
by the detective who suspects their prison camp alibi.   They
also both fall in love with the same Mexican beauty, fight it out
on a couple of boats and when Matt is wounded he shoots himself in the presence of witnesses to prevent his kid brother being
accused of his murder.

THE WELL OF THE SAINTS

(5 performances)

A drama by John Millington Synge.   Revived by the Irish
Theatre at the Barbizon Theatre, New York, January 21, 1932.

Cast of characters—

Martin Doul.................................Augustin Duncan
Mary Doul...................................Agnes McGrail
Timmy.......................................Maurice Redmond
Mollie Byrne....................................Betty Murray
Bride...Grania O'Malley
Mat Simon.......................................Sean Dillon
The Saint..P. J. Kelly
The Girls.......................Julia, Mary and Peggy Gallagher

Martin and Mary Doul, blind beggars, recover their sight with the aid of drops of water drawn from a sacred well. After looking upon the ugliness of themselves and being disappointed in the world they are content to be "dark" for the rest of their lives.

THE HOUSE OF DOOM

(8 performances)

A drama in three acts by Charles K. Champlin. Produced by J. J. White at the Masque Theatre, New York, January 25, 1932.

Cast of characters—

John Penbrook	William Melville
Jack Hillard	Frank Brooks
Oscar Small	Walter Deluna
Silas Manning	Willard Dashiell
Paul	Etienne Girardot
Dorothy Manning	June Justice
Dr. Horace Luther	Robert Brister
Maxine Dumond	Francesca Hill
Lionel Manning	Chas. K. Champlin
The Beast	Ray Earles
Budda Abdullah Kahn	Edward Keane
Clara	Ruth Edell

Acts I and III.—Home of the Mannings. Act II.—Dr. Luther's Laboratory.

Staged by George L. Graves.

Lionel Manning, suffering a nervous breakdown, is being treated by Dr. Luther, who lives next door. Dr. Luther has invented a naturescope by the operation of which he believes he can transfer the soul of one person to the body of another. He is eager to try it on Lionel. He also plans to marry Lionel's sister, who will inherit the Manning money if anything happens to Lionel. Dr. Luther is aided by an Indian hypnotist, Abdullah Kahn. Lionel is forced into the naturescope with a lunatic and goes quite mad. At which point Dr. Kahn awakens Lionel from his trance and the mystery is solved. Lionel was only dreaming.

EAST OF BROADWAY

(39 performances)

A comedy in three acts by T. Reginald Arkell and Charles Wagenheim. Produced by Charles Rowe at the Belmont Theatre, New York, January 26, 1932.

Cast of characters—

Ida Soloman	Betty Worth
Lester King	Joseph Striker

```
Mrs. Soloman..................................Maude Elliott
Willie Posner................................Paul Stewart
Benny Soloman...............................Alfred Corn
Herschel Soloman.........................James R. Waters
Leibkeh Markowitz............................Abe Sincoff
Mike Mulligan..................................Jack Williams
Lora McDonald..........................Paula Bauersmith
Abie Soloman.........................William McFadden
McWhite...........................................Teddy Hart
Viola Dean....................................Vesper Nelson
Gloria Simpson.............................Hattie Koehler
Supovich..........................................Al Raymond
Vera...............................................Ann Caruth
Two Old Men.................................{ Edward Murray
                                            { J. K. Brown
```
    Acts I, II and III.—Home of Herschel Soloman. Act II.—Scene
2—Parablin Studio.
    Staged by Lew Levenson.

Herschel Soloman, an honest Jewish peddler, is living with his
wife, his daughter Ida, a manicurist, and his son Benny, a news-
boy, on the east side of New York. Benny innocently becomes
involved with a dope-peddling gang; Ida is threatened with
seduction. Herschel, to raise $250 to help Benny, accepts a job
with a moving picture company to play a Jewish type part.
Benny is cleared. Ida is married. Mamma is happy.

LADY WINDERMERE'S FAN

(4 performances)

A comedy in four acts by Oscar Wilde. Revived by the Afternoon Theatre at the Recital Theatre (Daly's West 63rd Street),
New York, January 26, 1932.

Cast of characters—

```
Lord Windermere..........................Richard Stevenson
Lord Darlington...............................Sherling Oliver
Lord Augustus Lorton.........................Herbert Standing
Mr. Hopper.........................................Carl Emory
Lady Windermere.................................Ellis Baker
Duchess of Berwick.................................Essex Dane
Lady Agatha Carlisle........................Florence Williams
Mrs. Erlynne.......................Theresa Maxwell Conover
```
    Acts I, II and IV.—A Room in Lord Windermere's House. Act
III.—Lord Darlington's Rooms.
    Staged by Arthur William Row.

Written in 1891 and popular in its day, "Lady Windermere's
Fan" was last revived by Margaret Anglin in 1914, with Sarah
Cowell LeMoyne, Arthur Byron, Pedro de Cordoba, Sidney
Greenstreet and Margery Maude in the cast.

ROBIN HOOD

(29 performances)

A romantic opera in three acts by Harry B. Smith; music by Reginald De Koven. Revived by the Civic Light Opera Company at Erlanger's Theatre, New York, January 27, 1932.

Cast of characters—

Alan-a-Dale	Eleanor La Mance
Little John	Allen Waterous
Will Scarlet	Fred Patton
Annabel	Vivian Hart
Friar Tuck	Frank Lalor
Dame Durden	Helen Bertram
Robert of Huntington (Afterwards Robin Hood)	Howard Marsh
Lady Marian Fitzwater	Charlotte Lansing
Sheriff of Nottingham	William Danforth
Sir Guy Gisborne	John Cherry
Herald	John Eaton
Jailer	Pat Quinton
Sexton	Frank Clark

Act I.—A Market Place in Nottingham. Act II.—Sherwood Forest. Act III.—Courtyard at Sheriff's Castle.
Staged by Milton Aborn.

Milton Aborn last staged a revival of "Robin Hood," first produced by the Bostonians on June 9th, 1890, in November, 1929, under the auspices of the Jolson Theatre Musical Comedy Company, a Shubert organization. Roy Cropper sang the title rôle, Danforth was the sheriff, Greek Evans the Little John, Charles Gallagher the Will Scarlet, Muriel Alcock the Alan-a-Dale, Olga Steck the Maid Marian and Dorothy Seegar the Annabel. In a May, 1912, revival George B. Frothingham was drafted for the rôle of Friar Tuck, which he created. Florence Wickham was the Alan-a-Dale, Basil Ruysendael the Will Scarlet, Carl Grantvoort the Little John, Ann Swinburne the Annabel, Bella Alten the Maid Marian, Pauline Hall the Dame Durden.

THROUGH THE YEARS

(20 performances)

A romantic musical play by Brian Hooker, based on Jane Cowl's drama, "Smilin' Through"; music by Vincent Youmans. Produced by Vincent Youmans at the Manhattan Theatre, New York, Jan 28, 1932.

Cast of characters—

Kathleen	Natalie Hall
Kenneth	Michael Bartlett

Ellen..Marion Ballou
Dr. Owen Harding...........................Charles Winninger
John Carteret...................................Reginald Owen
Willie Ainley.....................................Nick Long, Jr.
Penelope...Caryl Bergman
Betty Fallow....................................Martha Mason
Captain Moreau.................................Gregory Gaye
Lucy..Leone Neumann
Mary Clare.......................................Audrey Davis
Jeremiah Wayne...............................Michael Bartlett
Moonyeen...Natalie Hall
Arabella..Martha Mason
Roger..Nick Long, Jr.
Mrs. Ainley......................................Lelane Rivera
Singing Girls: Kay Adams, Dee Collins, Adline Forbes, Mildred
    Gethins, Estelle Malin, Marie Valot, Anna Worth, Leone Neu-
    mann.
Dancing Girls: Peggy Andre, Gloria Beaumont, Emilie Burton, Evelyn
    Hannons, Ann Hardman, Gertrude Lowe, Dolly Martinez,
    Evelyn Monte, Sonny Nelson, Peggy Schenck, Winnie Torney,
    Paulette Winston, Patricia Francis.
Boys: Frank Barron, John Frederick, Ray Thomas, Ivan Sokoloff,
    Jack Lawrence, Anton Luksor, Irving Pichler, Norman Van
    Emburgh.
Act I.—Carteret Garden, in 1914. Act II.—Scene 1—The Carteret
Garden, 40 Years Before Act I. Scene 2—The Carteret Garden,
Again in 1914. Act III.—(This Act Takes Place in 1919.) Scene 1
—The Hedge Corner on the Ainley Estate. Scene 2—The Carteret
Garden, Same Evening.
    Staged by Edgar McGregor; dances by Jack Haskell and Max
Scheck.

Kathleen and Kenneth want to marry. They are opposed violently by Kathleen's uncle and guardian, John Carteret, because
Kenneth's Uncle John, in a fit of jealousy, had shot and killed
Carteret's sweetheart, Moonyeen, on her wedding night forty
years before. The spirit of Moonyeen appears to Carteret and
convinces him he should not stand in the way of the young
people's happiness.

Principal songs—"Drums in My Heart," "Kinda Like You,"
"Through the Years," and "Kathleen Mine."

THE MARRIAGE OF CANA

(2 performances)

A comedy in three acts by Julian L. McDonald. Produced at
the Provincetown Playhouse, New York, February 2, 1932.

Cast of characters—

Isabell (Bell) White..........................Marjorie Lorraine
James Duncan High...........................Juano Hernandez
Granny White.....................................Alice Ramsey
Willy Barnes.......................................Hayes Pryor
Whyoming Hurtt.................................Wayland Rudd
Sarah Barnes......................................Alice Gorgas
Rube James.......................................James E. Downs
Reverend Jones....................................Albert Watts
Lily Rice...Vi Jones

Wedding Guests........Ellen Bailen, James Peebles, Beatrice Joyce
Staged by Anatol Bendukov.

Isabell White, tired of working in a laundry, wants to marry a reliable savin' man. She is wooed violently by James Duncan White, barber and gambler, but she rather prefers Whyoming Hurtt, bricklayer and steady. Whyoming is unable to make progress until he takes several shots of gin and learns that women like to be lied to. He makes himself out a money-making hero and wins Isabell. White appears at the wedding and exposes Hurtt, who would run away in shame. But Isabell and her Granny are satisfied and hold Whyoming to his bargain.

IF BOOTH HAD MISSED

(21 performances)

A drama in three acts by Arthur Goodman. Produced by Walter Hartwig, in association with William A. Brady, at the Maxine Elliott Theatre, New York, February 4, 1932.

Cast of characters—

Abraham Lincoln....................................Daniel Poole
Thaddeus Stevens...............................John Nicholson
Edwin M. Stanton.............................Royal Dana Tracy
Gen. U. S. Grant.................................Aubrey Beattie
Benjamin Butler....................................Earl Mitchell
Mrs. Lincoln....................................Catherine Proctor
Mrs. Jefferson Davis...........................Charlotte Walker
Sambo..Morris McKenney
John Wilkes Booth....................................Fred Eric
Francis Hilton.......................................John Burke
Tad Lincoln..Robert Ober
John Hay...Robert Toms
John Nicolay...................................Richard Barrows
Gideon Welles..................................A. C. Henderson
William Seward................................Thurlow Bergen
Henry Stanberry..................................Howard Kyle
Chief Justice Chase................................Orrin Burke
Andrew Johnson..................................Ernest Pollock
Benjamin F. Wade................................H. A. Wilson
Henry W. Davis.....................................Doan Borup
Major Rathbone..................................Hayden Rorke
Call Boy...Samuel Bunyan
Hugh McCullough................................Frank Kettrick
William Dennison...........................George W. Williams
Major Reed.......................................John Maroney
Captain Smiley..................................Anthony Pawley
Senator Wickers...............................William McRobie
Senator Bayard...................................John C. Davis
W. M. Evarts....................................Thomas Murphy
Senator Grimes................................George H. Sinclair
A Lieutenant...................................Charles Crumpton
First Orderly...................................George Mantell
Second Orderly.......................................Paul Dorn
A Soldier...Lionel Dante
A Messenger...................................Lawrence DeGaun
    Act I.—Scene 1—Passageway Behind the Boxes in Ford's Theatre, Washington. 2—Secretary Stanton's Office in the War Department.

Act II.—President's Office. Act III.—Scene 1—U. S. Senate Chamber. 2—Epilogue.
Staged by Milton Smith.

John Wilkes Booth's attempt on the life of Abraham Lincoln is frustrated when Sambo, a Ford's Theatre attendant, throws up the arm of the would-be murderer as he pulls the trigger. Lincoln thereafter assumes responsibility for his own policies, which were in fact inherited by Andrew Johnson. Lincoln's humaneness in dealing with the conquered Southern states infuriates the politicians. Party leaders finally conspire successfully for the president's impeachment. When the necessary two-thirds majority is lacking and Lincoln is acquitted he is shot down by Francis Hilton, an embittered newspaper editor.

THE FATAL ALIBI

(24 performances)

A drama in three acts by Michael Morton, based on Agatha Christie's novel, "The Murder of Roger Ackroyd." Produced by Jed Harris at the Booth Theatre, New York, February 8, 1932.

Cast of characters—

Geoffrey Raymond	Edward Crandall
Mrs. Ackroyd	Effie Shannon
Major Blunt	Kenneth Hunter
Flora	Jane Wyatt
Parker	Donald Randolph
Caryl Sheppard	Helen Vinson
Hercule Poirot	Charles Laughton
Ursula Bourne	Jane Bramley
Sir Roger Ackroyd	Lionel Pape
Captain Ralph Paton	Lowell Gilmore
Dr. Sheppard	Moffat Johnston
Inspector Davies	Lawrence H. Cecil
Mr. Hammond	Fothringham Lysons
Margot	Andree Corday

Acts I and II.—Hall at Sir Roger Ackroyd's, Fernly Park. Act III.—Hercule Poirot's Cottage.
Staged by Charles Laughton.

After voices have been heard issuing from his study Sir Roger Ackroyd is found stabbed to death. Hercule Poirot, famous French detective, is given the case and, after many investigations, fastens the crime on the little suspected Dr. Sheppard who had, it appears, been blackmailing Sir Roger and hoped to benefit from his passing. The voices had been produced by a planted dictaphone, which Dr. Sheppard had smuggled out of the house.

MAURICE CHEVALIER

(17 performances)

French comedian in an intimate song recital. Presented at the Fulton Theatre by Charles B. Dillingham, February 9, 1932.

Fray and Braggiotti play a medley of popular Chevalier's Songs.

Maurice Chevalier recites a prologue.

Fray and Braggiotti play "Dark Eyes" (Impression of a Russian Orchestra with Cymbalum), "Gershwiana" and "Bolero" by M. Ravel.

Maurice Chevalier sings "Little Hunka Love," "C'Etait Moi" (It Was Me), "Oh! That Mitzi," "Mon Petit Tom" (Love story of Mr. and Mrs. Elephant). Impersonation of: Dorville, Boucot, Mayol, famous French comedians, singing "You Brought a New Kind of Love to Me," "Hello, Beautiful," "Oh! That Mitzi."

Fray and Braggiotti play a medley of popular Chevalier's songs: Fantasy on "Dancing in the Dark," "Yankee Doodle": variations, (1) à la Chopin, (2) à la Gershwin.

Maurice Chevalier sings "Ma Reguliere" (My Regular Girl), "What Would You do?," "Dites-moi Ma Mère" (Tell Me, Mother). Imitations of Rudy Vallée and Willie Howard. Imitating him in "All I Want Is Just One," and "Sweeping the Clouds Away," "Valentine" (French popular song), "Louise."

M. Chevalier gave a similar concert in New York during the season of 1929-30 with the Duke Ellington orchestra. On this occasion he was assisted by Jacques Fray and Mario Braggiotti, pianists.

AIR MINDED

(13 performances)

A comedy in three acts by Nathaniel Davis. Produced by Davenport Productions, Inc., at the Ritz Theatre, New York, Feb. 10, 1932.

Cast of characters—

Emma Clements	Belle D'Arcy
Shorty Quinn	Frank Otto
Joyce Cameron	Charlotte Wynters
Freddy Cameron	Edwin Mills
Butch Emery	Pat Collins
Joseph Clements	George MacQuarrie
The Man with a Silk Hat	Edgar Mason
The Man with a Derby Hat	Harry McNaughton
Simon Spring	Bernard Pate
Doctor Mitchell	Bernard Craney

Acts I, II and III.—Lobby of the Valley Green Hotel.
Staged by H. McRae Webster.

Kenneth Vandeveer (the Man with a Silk Hat) is disappointed at the altar in New York and flies west. Landing at an airport in the mountains he finds Joyce Cameron, to whom he takes a fancy, and Freddy Cameron, her inventive young brother. Kenneth decides to stay on at the airport, buy a plane to fly in, help Freddy get his patent and make love to Joyce. When Joyce discovers that he is rich she breaks off their engagement, but when he explains practically everything and gets Freddy his patent, she relents and they become engaged again.

ZOMBIE

(21 performances)

A drama in three acts by Kenneth Webb. Produced at the Biltmore Theatre, New York, Feb. 10, 1932.

Cast of characters—

Dr. Paul Thurlow	Hunter Gardner
Sylvia Clayton	Pauline Starke
Jack Clayton	Robert J. Stanley
Pedro	George Regas
Josephine	Etta Moten
Professor Luke Wallace	Burr Caruth
Martha Wallace	Rose Tapley
Haitian Laborers	{ Peter Clarke { Lackaye Grant
Reed	Jerome Sheldon
Bates	Booth Hagin

Acts I, II and III.—Living Room of a Bungalow in the Mountains of Haiti.

Staged by George Sherwood.

Sylvia Clayton, wife of Jack Clayton, living on a plantation in Haiti where the natives believe it is possible to bring the dead to life, is distressed with doubt as to whether she loves Jack or her friend, Dr. Thurlow, best. Jack drinks a prescription prepared by Thurlow and seemingly dies. Three midnights later he is roused from the dead, a Zombie, and goes stalking about the place scaring the daylights out of everybody. It takes quite a bit of voodoo influence to bring Jack finally back to life.

MONKEY

(28 performances)

A comedy in three acts by Sam Janney. Produced by Robert Sparks at the Mansfield Theatre, New York, Feb. 11, 1932.

Cast of characters—

Robert Kenmore	Wright Kramer
Dr. George Hollins	Frank Wilcox
Greta Kenmore	Charlotte Denniston
Bracker	Roland Hogue
Joe Banning	Clifford L. Jones
Murlen	Houston Richards

Officer McSweeney...........................Edward McNamara
J. Emmelton Stotes.............................Randall O'Neil
Howard Styrman................................John T. Dwyer
Dr. Edward Pomeroy Nichols......................George Lessey
Inspector Monkey Henderson......................Richard Whorf
Medical Examiner Hughes..........................Dan Malloy
Estelle Fenley.................................Nedda Harrigan
   Acts I, II and III.—Apartment of Robert Kenmore.
   Staged by Robert Sparks.

Inspector "Monkey" Henderson of the New York police force is called in to solve the murder of Robert Kenmore, shot dead after he had quarreled with Greta, his daughter, and Joe Banning, her fiancée. "Monkey" craftily eliminates all obvious clews and fastens the murder on the lover of Kenmore's mistress, a Dr. Nichols.

BLESSED EVENT

(115 performances)

A comedy in three acts by Manuel Seff and Forrest Wilson. Produced by Sidney Phillips and Harlan Thompson at the Longacre Theatre, New York, February 12, 1932.

Cast of characters—

Alvin Roberts..................................Roger Pryor
Miss Stevens...................................Mildred Wall
Gladys Price....................................Lee Patrick
George Moxely...............................Charles D. Brown
Louis Miller....................................Ralph Locke
Hanson.....................................George Greenberg
Office Boy......................................Eddie Lynch
Miss Baumann..............................Dorothea Petgen
Herbert Flint...................................Lynn Root
Mr. Moskowitz..............................Milton Wallace
Frankie Wells.................................Allen Jenkins
Mme. Fleurette...............................Ollie Burgoyne
Ulysses......................................Verman Jones
Sylvester....................................Herman Jones
Amelia Romond...............................Thelma Tipson
Dorothy Lane.................................Isabel Jewell
Mrs. Roberts....................................Jean Adair
Bellboy.......................................Robert Allen
Emil..John Robb
Waiter...............................J. Herman Mankiewicz
Sam Gobel.....................................Matt Briggs
Reilly..Frank Rowan
Cooper.......................................Kenneth Dana
Boldt.......................................Walter Kinsella
Louis Demarco.................................David Leonard
Joe Pasquali.................................Herbert Duffy
Policeman.....................................Henry Shelvey
Detective....................................John F. Morrissey
   Prologue and Act I.—Office at *The Daily Express.* Act II.—Living Room of Alvin Roberts' Suite. Act III.—Room at the Chateau Harmony.
   Staged by Harlan Thompson.

Alvin Roberts, working in the mailing department of the *New York Express,* is given a chance to substitute for the editor of the

Broadway Highlights department. Alvin, inventing a language of his own and filling the column with the most intimate and sensational Broadway gossip, specializes in the early announcement of anticipated births, classified as "blessed events." When he publishes that of Dorothy Lane, ruins her reputation and gets himself into a jam with the expectant but raging father, Sam Gobel, Big-Time Racketeer, an attempt is made on the life of Alvin. He escapes bullets and beatings and does what he can to make it up to Dorothy.

THERE'S ALWAYS JULIET

(108 performances)

A comedy in three acts by John Van Druten. Produced by Gilbert Miller at the Empire Theatre, New York, February 15, 1932.

Cast of characters—

Leonora Perrycoste.................................Edna Best
Florence..May Whitty
Dwight Houston..............................Herbert Marshall
Peter Walmsley...................................Cyril Raymond
    Acts I, II and III.—Leonora's Sitting Room in a Flat in the West
End of London.
    Staged by Auriol Lee.

Leonora Perrycoste meets Dwight Houston at a tea in London. They are mutually attracted. Leonora is trying to find out something about Dwight, who is an American architect, when he, uninvited, calls upon her. They break their respective dinner dates for that evening and go to a revue. The next day they motor in the country. The third day Dwight is recalled to America. Discovering they are deeply in love, Leonora agrees to go as far as Southampton and stay the night. Dwight will not permit her to. Dwight wins a three-day respite. Likewise Leonora's agreement to return to America with him.

COLLISION

(7 performances)

A comedy in three acts adapted by John Anderson from the German of Lothar and Sebesi. Produced by Lewis E. Gensler at the Gaiety Theatre, New York, February 16, 1932.

Cast of characters—

Lia	Eva Condon
Honti	Porter Hall
Porter	Stanley Harrison
Klenitsch	Victor Kilian
Milk Woman	Patsy Klein
Olga	June Walker
Passenger	James Hagan
Dr. Gestzi	Geoffrey Kerr
Headwaiter	Ralph Nairn
First Waiter	George Fairchild
Second Waiter	Franklin Munnell
Orchestra Leader	M. Charles Palazzi
Author	Lennox Pawle
Author's Bride	Frances Dade
Bridegroom	Richard Hemingway
His Bride	Joann Castle
A Guest	Anita Murray
Fedor Rozgonyi	P. Yanyst

Act I.—Platform of a Provincial Railway Station in Germany.
Acts II and III.—Dining Room at the Myrten-Krunz.
Staged by Melville Burke.

Olga, in love with the village physician, timid Dr. Gestzi, conspires to bring the medic to the point of proposal. By pretending to be engaged to a pianist arriving by train she excites the doctor's jealousy. When the train is in collision Olga faints. Recovering she pretends to be dazed and to accept Dr. Gestzi as the expected bridegroom. The doctor, fearing the result of a shock, agrees to humor Olga to the point of taking her on a honeymoon. Two days later he is happy to marry her and make her an honest woman.

"WHEN THE BOUGH BREAKS"

(17 performances)

A drama in three acts by Jerome Sackheim. Produced by Arthur Lubin at the Forty-eighth Street Theatre, New York, February 16, 1932.

Cast of characters—

Richard Warren	William Post, Jr.
Lewis Warren	Clyde Franklin
Pritch	Maud Durand
Magma Warren	Pauline Frederick
Walker Maitland	Malcolm Duncan
Jim Hamilton	Louis Jean Heydt
Joan Leonard	Dorothy Libaire

Acts I, II and III.—Living Room of the Warren Home and Joan's Apartment.
Staged by Arthur Lubin.

Dick Warren and his father are pals, somewhat to the distress of Dick's mother. When the father dies Mrs. Warren thinks to have her son to herself. To retain this dominancy of his life she fights off his love affair with Joan Leonard, preferring that he make the girl his mistress rather than his wife, and would defeat his plan to go into business with his chum, Jim Hamilton. In the end Dick declares his independence and leaves his mother.

* FACE THE MUSIC

(141 performances)

A musical comedy in two acts by Irving Berlin and Moss Hart. Produced by Sam H. Harris at the New Amsterdam Theatre, New York, February 17, 1932.

Cast of characters—

Hal Reisman	Andrew Tombes
Kit Baker	Katherine Carrington
Pat Mason, Jr.	J. Harold Murray
Mrs. Mashbesher	Mary Boland
Her Footman	Peter Sargent
Mrs. Meshbesher	Helen Lyons
Martin Van Buren Meshbesher	Hugh O'Connell
Mr. O'Rourke	Edward Gargan
A Sister Team	Aida Conkey and Teddy West
Pickles	Margaret Lee
Joe	Jack Good
Louis	Dave Burns
Mme. Elise	Frances Halliday
Her Assistant	Elizabeth Houston
A Lady of the Evening	Jean Sargent
Postman	Ward Arnold
May	Dorothy Claire
Rodney St. Clair	Joseph Macaulay
Rivington	Oscar Polk
Sheriff	Clyde Fillmore
Mr. Delaney	Martin Shepard
Stage Doorman	Charles Burrows
Detective	Thomas Arace
Clerk of Court	Charles Coleman
Prosecuting Attorney	Joseph Macaulay
Judge Furioso	Vernon Jayson

Albertina Rasch Dancers: Dorissa Nelova, Lead; Vida McLain, Valerie Huff, Alice Kellerman, Kathleen Vannoy, Mary Vannoy, Virginia Bethel.

Staged by Hassard Short and George S. Kaufman; dances by Albertina Rasch.

Hal Reisman, a producer of spectacles stopped by the depression, meets Mrs. Martin Van Buren Meshbesher, whose husband is a sergeant of New York police. The Meshbeshers are "lousy with money," and would love to produce a show if they can be guaranteed that they will lose a lot. Reisman's guarantee is positively sweeping. "The Rhinestone Girl" is produced, is discovered to be terrible, and is sure to lose a fortune when the City of New York goes broke and faces a deficit. By dirtying up "The Rhinestone Girl," and thus attracting the public, the situation is saved.

Principal songs—"Let's Have Another Cup of Coffee," "I Say It's Spinach" and "Manhattan Madness."

TRICK FOR TRICK

(69 performances)

A drama by Vivian Crosby, Shirley Warde and Harry Wagstaffe Gribble. Produced by Robert V. Newman at the Sam H. Harris Theatre, New York, February 18, 1932.

Cast of characters—

John Russell	Burke Clarke
Constance Russell	Eleanor Phelps
Walter Lawrence—Known as "Azrah"	James Rennie
Albert Young	Lawrence Bolton
David Adams	Walter Vaughn
Professor Roland King	Harry Mestayer
Lieutenant Jed Dodson	Granville Bates
George La Tour	Henry O'Neill
Susie Henry	Sascha Beaumont
Dr. Frank Fitzgerald	Halliam Bosworth
Sergeant Pete Dennehy	Robert W. Craig
Joseph Lombard	Averill Harris
Stenographer	Fred Knight
Jim Peabody	Paul Hoover

Acts I, II and III.—House of Walter Lawrence, New York City. Staged by Harry Wagstaffe Gribble.

Walter Lawrence, known as Azrah, the Mystic, accused of having caused the suicide of a magician's assistant, plans a materializing séance at which he will produce the spirit of the dead girl that she may herself name her murderers. George La Tour, for whom the dead girl had worked, seeks to break up the séance. La Tour is found dead with a knife thrust to the heart when the séance is finished. Azrah is accused of having arranged the second killing but is cleared. The Fitzgerald girl's father, a doctor, had stabbed La Tour with a knife blade concealed in a stethoscope.

WILD WAVES

(25 performances)

A comedy in three acts by William Ford Manley. Produced by Doran, Ray and Hewes at the Times Square Theatre, New York, February 19, 1932.

Cast of characters—

Miss Croft	Edith Van Cleve
Tragedian	William Friend

Soprano..Mary Kemble
Basso..Fred Malcolm
Mother..Edith Gravetta
Lover...Larry Jason
Potter..Charles O'Connor
Dr. Podmore....................................Bertram Marburgh
Roy Denny....................................Bruce MacFarlane
Harold...Richard Huey
Control Man......................................Robert Shayne
Prudence Prewitt................................Violet Barney
Brix...Paul Porter
Miss Lehman.......................................Anne Revere
Bogelman...Stuart Brown
Girl..Frances Simon
Page..Edward Craven
Daisy...Mary Robinson
Joe...Frank Verigun
Nancy Hodson...................................Betty Starbuck
Mr. Edward Reiss...................................Joseph King
Mr. Seymour Haverstraw.....................George Graham
Dr. Hammerhoch.................................Maurice Cass
Mitch Gratwick................................Osgood Perkins
John Duffy..John Beal
Whelpley......................................St. Clair Bayfield
Attendant......................................Roger Ramsdell
Scrub Woman...................................Jessie Graham
Mrs. Banfill...Helen Blair
Mr. Peacock...Neil McFee
Saxophone Player...........................Charles Thompson
Mr. Tupperman...................................Dan Charlier
The Battle Sisters...............Tallulah Wesley, Irene Cattel
Ward Heeler..................................Charles O'Connor
Mr. Thwacker...................................Horace Sinclair
Chauffeur..Wallace Acton
Elderly Lady...................................Virginia Tracy
Tony..Jack Rigo
Gus..Horace McMahon
Photographer.......................................Alvin Kerr
Photographer's Assistant..........................Gerald Davis
First Girl.......................................Tallulah Wesley
Second Girl......................................Frances Simon
    Acts I, II and III.—Lobby and Studios of Station WWVW.
    Staged by Worthington Miner.

John Duffy fails to get on in Radio, despite a good voice, because he lacks courage. Nancy Hodson, program arranger for WWVW, with whom John is secretly in love, tries to save him, but without success. Mitch Gratwick, studio manager, takes John in hand, tries to make him bitter and independent, and fails. In an emergency John substitutes for Roy Denny, favorite crooner, and is a great hit. Still he can do nothing for himself. In the conspiracy to put Duffy over all three are fired. Having found themselves and each other, John, Nancy and Mitch are content.

NEW YORK TO CHERBOURG

(3 performances)

A comedy in three acts by H. G. Buller. Produced by Paul E. Martin, for Pilgrim Productions, Inc., at the Forrest Theatre, New York, February 19, 1932.

Cast of characters—

Mabel Torrence	Jocelyn Gordon
Constance Carroll	Natalie Schafer
Floyd Warren	Gerald Kent
Franklin Spence	Taylor Holmes
Atkinson	Edward Broadley
Officer Conroy	Arthur Gould-Porter
Opal Raymond	Eleanor Winslow Williams
Reginald Richie	Edward Lester
Jeremiah Mott	George Christie
Alfredo de Pisza	Edward Raquello
Tom	Isidor Marcil

Act I.—Scene 1—Living Room in Constance Carroll's Apartment, New York City. 2—Suite on Board Steamship *Oceanic*. Act II.—The Suite. Act III.—Section of the Upper Deck Café.

Staged by Paul E. Martin and H. G. Buller.

Franklin Spence, eloping with Constance Carroll, runs into comical obstructions in the persons of Opal Raymond, who wants Franklin, and Floyd Warren, who wants Constance. (Having been called away, our reporter cannot say of his own knowledge who got who.)

THE INSIDE STORY

(24 performances)

A drama in three acts by George Bryant and Francis M. Verdi. Produced by A. H. Woods at the National Theatre, New York, February 22, 1932.

Cast of characters—

Bill McGowan	Frank Camp
Mrs. McGowan	Marie Hunt
Gerald Stockton	Roy Roberts
Nick Lipman	Brian Donlevy
Gus Bernstein	George Pembroke
Bert Teagle	Frank M. Thomas
Rod Guzman	Gage Clark
Louis Corotto	Louis Calhern
Mamie Gillette	Marguerite Churchill
Frank Delaney	Stanley Ridges
Capt. Dan Engle	Paul Everton
House-detective Boynton	Edward Keane
Hotel Maid	Mary Redmond
Detective Symons	Edward Jones
Detective Haight	John Burkell
Elevator Boy	William Goode
Fred Beekman	Harland Tucker
Mrs. Beekman	Harriet MacGibbon
Evelyn Beekman	Frances Tannehill
Tom McIntyre	Edward Ellis
Harry Coates	Fred Irving Lewis
First Prison Guard	Jack Clifford
Second Prison Guard	Alexander Cross
Governor Hazelton	William Courtenay
Warden Bridges	Frank Camp
Father Joseph	W. W. Shuttleworth
Mrs. Stockton	Aphie James

Acts I, II and III.—In a Middle-western City, and at the State Capitol.

Staged by A. H. Van Buren.

Louis Corotto, the "Big Shot" of gangdom, tired of Mamie Gillette, a fighting mistress, seeks to be revenged by framing the boy who loves her and having him sentenced to the electric chair for murder. The boy, Gerald Stockton, walks into the trap. Thereafter every move either the legal department of the state or private attorneys make to help him is defeated by Corotto, whose power reaches even the governor, whose election he has bought. A few minutes before Stockton is to be hanged Mamie shoots and kills Corotto, which revives the governor's courage.

THEY DON'T MEAN ANY HARM

(15 performances)

A comedy in three acts by A. A. Milne. Produced by Charles Hopkins at the Charles Hopkins Theatre, New York, February 23, 1932.

Cast of characters—

Arnold	Gavin Muir
Lola	Marion Burns
Stephen	Vernon Kelso
Meg	Patricia Calvert
Mr. Tilling	O. P. Heggie
John	Ernest Lawford
James	Richie Ling
Gloria	Ruth Vivian
Clare Tilling	Clare St. Clair
Mrs. Tilling	Molly Pearson

Acts I, II and III.—Two Floors of a House in the Neighborhood of Tottenham Court Road.

Staged by Charles Hopkins.

A quartet of flat dwellers, representing the calloused younger set in London, in a spirit of levity take on the pressing problems of the Tillings, a middle-class family living in the flat below. Mr. Tilling is a peddler of books, Mrs. Tilling an invalid, the Tilling daughter an ambitious girl who can find nothing better than addressing envelopes as a job. Lola, the one sincere member of the quartet, arranges with her distinguished brother, Sir John, to operate on Mrs. Tilling, and her other brother, James, the Dean, to do something for Miss Tilling. In the end the interference of the would-be helpers plunges the Tillings from a state of reasonable contentment into one of tragedy. Mrs. Tilling dies, the daughter is shipped away to Canada, Tilling is broken.

RIDDLE ME THIS

(100 performances)

A comedy in three acts by Daniel N. Rubin. Produced by John Golden at the John Golden Theatre, New York, February 25, 1932.

Cast of characters—

Dr. Ernest Tindal............................Charles Richman
Mrs. Ruth Tindal.............................Georgette Spelvin
Detective Capt. McKinley.....................Thomas Mitchell
Dr. Sully....................................James C. Lane
Alcock.......................................Charles Laite
Duffy..Robert Burton
Brown..James Duddy
Mrs. Ward....................................Marjorie Garrett
"Kirk".......................................Frank Craven
Mrs. Alvin...................................Kate McComb
Frank Marsh..................................Robert Lowes
Vera Marsh...................................Erin O'Brien-Moore
Jack Reed....................................Dan Jarrett
Julia Reed...................................Blyth Daly
    Act I.—Mrs. Tindal's Bedroom. Acts II and III.—Office at Police Headquarters.
    Staged by Frank Craven.

Detective Captain McKinley and Kirk of the press are buddies who have worked and drunk together on many murder mysteries. When Mrs. Ruth Tindal was found strangled in her bedroom McKinley got the assignment and Kirk chased along to represent his newspaper. All circumstantial evidence pointed to the guilt of Frank Marsh, a youthful lover of Mrs. Tindal. Marsh persistently denied his guilt, his sister Vera believed him, and Kirk, liking Vera, sided with the Marshes to the disgust of McKinley. They were right. Kirk finally traps Dr. Tindal, the murdered woman's husband, into what amounts to a confession. As the audience knows, the doctor had done the murder and set the trap for young Marsh.

THE MOON IN THE YELLOW RIVER

(40 performances)

A play in three acts by Denis Johnston. Produced by the Theatre Guild, Inc., at the Guild Theatre, New York, February 29, 1932.

Cast of characters—

Agnes..Josephine Williams
Blanaid......................................Gertrude Flynn
Tausch.......................................Egon Brecher

```
Aunt Columba.....................................Alma Kruger
George..........................................Edward Nannary
Captain Potts.................................John Daly Murphy
Dobelle..........................................Claude Rains
Willie..........................................Barry MacCollum
Darrell Blake.......................................Henry Hull
Larry.............................................Wylie Adams
Another of Blake's Men..........................John O'Connor
Commandant..................................William Harrigan
A Soldier.........................................Paul Stevenson
Another Soldier.........................Desmond O'Donnovan
      Acts I and III.—Living Room. Act II.—Armory.
      Staged by Philip Moeller.
```

Tausch, a German electrical engineer, builds a power house on the coast of Ireland and finds himself violently opposed by the Republican army. An unsuccessful attempt is made to blow up the works; Tausch calls for help from the Government forces; the Commandant who responds shoots the leader of the rebels. Tausch protests the legalized murder, in which crisis the works are blown up accidentally. Ireland returns to its local problems. Tausch goes home.

CHILD OF MANHATTAN

(87 performances)

A romantic comedy in three acts by Preston Sturges. Produced by Peggy Fears at the Fulton Theatre, New York, March 1, 1932.

Cast of characters—

```
Miss Sophie Vanderkill........................Helen Strickland
Eggleston........................................Joseph H. Roeder
Otto Paul Vanderkill...........................Reginald Owen
Spyrene...........................................Ralph Sanford
Clifford..........................................Charles Cromer
Flo..................................................Judy Abbot
Madeleine McGonegal...........................Dorothy Hall
Buddy McGonegal............................Jackson Halliday
Mrs. McGonegal..................................Maude Odell
Martha........................................Jacqueline Winston
Lucinda, Limited..............................Franz Bendtsen
Constance........................................Joan Hamilton
Myrtle..............................................Eileen Bach
A Girl.........................................Constance Fuller
Yvette...........................................Louise Sheldon
Lilly...............................................Peggy Fish
Gladys.............................................Mary Orr
Jewel............................................Geraldine Wall
Aunt Minnie.....................................Jessie Ralph
Luthy McGonegal..............................Harriet Russell
Nurse.............................................Alice John
Doctor........................................Alexander Campbell
John Tarantino....................................John Altieri
Charley.......................................Alexander Campbell
Panama C. Kelly.............................Douglass Dumbrille
Cootch Dancer..................................Mercia Marquez
A Piano Player...................................Willie Smith
A Waiter....................................Charles Hubert Brown
```

Adelaide Vanderkill..............................Elizabeth Young
Acts I, II and III.—In Loveland Dance Hall, Madeleine's Home
and a Penthouse.
Staged by Howard Lindsay.

Madeleine McGonegal, hostess in the Loveland Dance Hall, meets Otto Paul Vanderkill of the New York Vanderkills on whose estate the dance hall stands. Otto Paul, a widower with a grown daughter, is greatly charmed by Madeleine and later makes her his mistress. When he discovers that he is to be a father Otto Paul marries Madeleine, but when the infant dies Madeleine insists on divorcing him. Thereafter they resume their original penthouse arrangement.

MARCHING BY

(12 performances)

A musical play in two acts by Ernst Neubach, adapted by Harry Clarke and Harry B. Smith; music by Jean Gilbert, Gordon and Revel. Produced by Messrs. Shubert at Chanin's Forty-sixth Street Theatre, March 3, 1932.

Cast of characters—

PROLOGUE

Elsa..Cornelia Chason
Lieut. Muller.......................................Jack Lee
Butler...Herbert Weber
Hans Von Arnheim...................................Jack Leslie
Lieut. Franz Almasy..............................Guy Robertson
Countess Anna Von Hatfeld.......................Desiree Tabor
Edda Von Goetzen..................................Betty Davis
Captain Goerlich..................................Walter Palm
Sergeant...Kenneth Paige
Lieut. Hauser.....................................Ralph Slear
Colonel Popen.....................................Philip Lord
Eva..Betty Dair

THE PLAY

Captain Von Zedlitz..............................John J. Walsh
Lieut. Kaufman...................................Arthur Singer
Lieut. Donnheim..................................Walter Nagle
Captain Bauer...................................Charles Christie
Lieut. Dorch......................................Roy Vitalis
Lieut. Schantz...................................Victor Young
Sergeant...Kenneth Paige
A Cossack..Herbert Weber
Colonel Popen.....................................Philip Lord
Ilsa...Kathleen Edwardes
Mitzi...Katherine Skidmore
First Girl..Joan Dudley
Second Girl..Betty Dair
Third Girl.......................................Marie Valday
Anton Androssy..................................Victor Casmore
Elias Butterman....................................Solly Ward
Anna..Desiree Tabor
Ilma Sachalow......................................Ethel Norris
Lieut. Franz Almasy..............................Guy Robertson
Sergeant Karloff...................................John Walsh

```
Sasha Sachalow....................................Donald Burr
Colonel Petroff..................................Leonard Ceeley
Ivan Tarnoff........................................Hugh Miller
Major Orloff.......................................Arthur Geary
Orderly............................................Gerald Moore
Nicoli............................................Samuel Krevoff
```
   Prologue—Ballroom in the Chateau of the Countess Von Hatfeld
Near Lemberg, Austria. August 1914. Acts I and II.—Lobby of
the Hotel Imperial, 1915.
   Staged by J. C. Huffman.

Countess Anna Von Hatfeld, in love with Lieut. Franz Almasy
of the Austrian army, finds herself in the Imperial Hotel of Lemberg helping to hide Lieut. Franz when the Russians march in
in 1915. Franz pretends to be a waiter and is forced to look
on while the Russian Colonel Petroff makes violent love to Anna.
But not for long. By 11:10 Franz and Anna are reunited and
in splendid voice.

PARK AVENUE, LTD.

(10 performances)

A play in three acts written and produced by Deborah Beirne
at the Provincetown Playhouse, New York, March 3, 1932.

Cast of characters—

```
Jenny Lewis.......................................Bee Morosco
Maria.............................................Dina Lanzi
Peter Saulisbury.................................Hugh Banks
Bill Keyes........................................Robert Allen
Bobby Gibson...................................Kirk Brown, Jr.
Betty Bradley..................................Mildred Baker
Perry Bradley..................................Gordon Nelson
Mrs. Bradley...................................Laura Alberta
Jerry Smith......................................Ray Rawlings
The Doctor }
Watkins    } ....................................Peter Martin
Mack..........................................Wells Richardson
Jimmie Bracken }
Clancy         } ..........................George Wilheim
```
      Staged by Harold Southgate.

Peter Saulisbury has a Tenth Avenue love nest and Maria to
adore him. Betty Bradley is attached to an upper class boy
friend in Park Avenue. Peter has a scheme for a jitters sanitarium for the well-to-do, and sells the idea to Betty. Betty and
Peter are married. Two years later Peter would like to drift back
to Maria and Betty is hungry for her Park Avenue boy, but they
decide to give matrimony another try.

ALICE SIT-BY-THE-FIRE

(32 performances)

A play in three acts by Sir James M. Barrie. Revived by William A. Brady by arrangement with Charles Frohman, Inc., at the Playhouse, New York, March 7, 1932.

Cast of characters—

Colonel Grey....................................Charles Dalton
Mrs. Grey.......................................Laurette Taylor
Amy Grey...Peg Entwistle
Cosmo Grey................................. Maurey Tuckerman
Stephen Rollo................................Robert Harrigan
Leonora Dunbar...................................Lucille Lisle
Nurse..Jane Corcoran
Fanny...Alice May Tuck
Richardson.......................................Nan Sheldon
    Acts I and III.—Grey's Apartment. Act II.—Rollo's Chambers.
    Staged by Stanley Logan.

Ethel Barrymore played "Alice Sit-by-the-Fire" during the season of 1905-06, supported by Bruce McRae.

THE OLD LADY SHOWS HER MEDALS

(32 performances)

A play in one act by Sir James M. Barrie. Revived by William A. Brady by arrangement with Charles Frohman, Inc., at the Playhouse, New York, March 7, 1932.

Cast of characters—

Mrs. Dowey....................................Laurette Taylor
Mrs. Twymley..................................Alice May Tuck
Mrs. Haggerty......................................Nan Sheldon
Mrs. Mickleham................................Jane Corcoran
Private K. Dowey...........................Lawrence Fletcher
Mr. Wilkinson, a Clergyman......................Leslie Austin
    Scene: A Charwoman's Home, London.
    Staged by Stanley Logan.

"The Old Lady Shows Her Medals" was produced originally at the Empire Theatre in New York in May, 1917, with Beryl Mercer in the title rôle. It was also used by the Androssan and Saltcoat Players of England when they won the New York Little Theatre Tournament prize in 1928.

MONEY IN THE AIR

(48 performances)

A play in three acts by Thetta Quay Franks. Produced by Frank Rowland at the Ritz Theatre, New York, March 7, 1932.

Cast of characters—

Rollins...Horace Pollock
Patrick...Frank Harvey
Penelope Worthington..............................Vera Allen
Mrs. Courtney Manners.........................Katherine Stewart
Henry Dale.......................................Joaquin Souther
Colonel Jim Barton..............................Hugh Buckler
Sally Dale.......................................Cynthia Rogers
Larry Derreau...................................Frederic Forman
Arthur Hamilton...............................Gordon Richards
Murphy...John Todd
Billy..Richard Skinner
    Acts I, II and III.—Living Room of the Worthington Home on Long Island.
    Staged by Arthur Sircom.

Penelope Worthington is in love with her lawyer, Col. Jim Barton. Penelope is rich and Col. Barton will not marry her so long as she has money. Penelope tries to find a long-lost nephew, heir to her fortune, that she may leave the money to him and thus be free. She agrees to pay half a million for the nephew's discovery. The man who agrees to deliver the nephew is shot. Many people are suspected. After a wide search the murderer is uncovered.

THE ROUND-UP

(8 performances)

A play in four acts by Edmund Day; incidental music by Margaret Larkin. Revived by Card Reed and A. Wichfeld at the Majestic Theatre, New York, March 7, 1932.

Cast of characters—

Jack Payson......................................Byron Shores
Dick Lane..Frank MacNeills
Bud Lane...Nell Buckley
Jim Allen..Elmer Grandin
Parenthesis......................................Clifford Dunston
Sage Brush Charlie...............................Tex Ritter
Fresno...George Leech
Show Low...James Young
Slim Hoover......................................Herbert Corthell
Buck McKee.......................................Walter Wilson
Peruna...Joseph Garry
Rev. Samuel Price................................Edward M. Favor
Sheriff Wiggins..................................Tex Cooper
Echo Allen.......................................Gertrude Michael
Mrs. Josephine Allen.............................Marie Taylor
Captain Jones....................................Robert Mulligan

Polly Hope..................................Marianne Risdon
    Act I.—Allen Hacienda. Act II.—Living Room. Act III.—Lava
Beds in the Desert. Act IV.—The Round-up.
    Staged by Lawrence Marston.

Echo Allen, giving up her fiancé, Dick Lane, for lost, agrees
to marry Jack Payson. The night of the wedding Lane reappears
but is turned away by Payson. After the wedding Payson, con-
science-stricken, confesses his trick and, to satisfy the hysterical
Echo, goes into the desert in search of Lane. Payson and Lane,
dying of thirst, are surrounded by Apaches and rescued by the
U.S. Artillery. Echo discovers it is her husband she truly loves.

HOT-CHA!

(119 performances)

A musical comedy in two acts by Lew Brown, Ray Henderson,
Mark Hellinger and H. S. Kraft; music by Brown and Hender-
son. Produced by Florenz Ziegfeld at the Ziegfeld Theatre, New
York, March 8, 1932.

Cast of characters—

Jack Whitney......................................Buddy Rogers
Hoffman..Arthur Page
Revenue Man......................................Roy Sedley
José Diaz..Robert Gleckler
Mae Devlin.......................................June MacCloy
Toodles Smith....................................Marjorie White
Dorothy Maxwell..................................June Knight
Alky Schmidt.....................................Bert Lahr
Bus Boy..Nick Basil
Conductor..Jack Daley
Brakeman...Louis Delgardo
Girl in Compartment..............................Rose Louise
Ramon La Grande..................................Tito Coral
Hap Wilson.......................................Lynne Overman
Conchita...Lupe Velez
Store Keeper.....................................Jules Epailly
Three Troubadours........................Hernandez Brothers
Gendarme...John Fulco
Servant..Alma Ross
Lopez..Vic Monroe
Doctor...Chas. La Torre
Ramona...Miriam Battista
Manuel...Jules Epailly
    Act I.—Scene 1—Golden Fleece Club, New York. 2—En Route to
Mexico. 3—A Public Square in Mexico City. 4—Living Quarters
Over José's Café. 5—Training Camp for Matadors. 6—Fiesta. Act
II.—Scene 1—Governor's Party. 2—Street in Mexico City. 3—Out-
side the Arena. 4—Matador's Entrance to the Bull Ring. 5—Court
of José's Café.
    Staged by Edgar McGregor; dances by Bobby Connelly.

The third time the Golden Fleece Night Club is raided the proprietor moves his floor show into Mexico City. Alky Schmidt,
comic waiter, is carried along when he is accidentally locked in
the ladies' washroom of the Pullman. In Mexico, Alky, needing a

job, an American promoter, Hap Wilson, promotes him as a lineal descendant of Mexico's most famous matador, which infuriates the bulls.

Principal songs—"You Can Make My Life a Bed of Roses" and "Say What I Wanna Hear You Say."

NIGHT OVER TAOS

(13 performances)

A play in three acts by Maxwell Anderson. Produced by the Group Theatre, Inc., at the Forty-eighth Street Theatre, New York, March 9, 1932.

Cast of characters—

Indian Slave	Robert Lewis
Doña Vera	Mary Morris
Valeria	Virginia Farmer
Maria	Paula Miller
Raquel	Margaret Barker
Conchita	Gertrude Maynard
Nuña	Phœbe Brand
Lita	Eunice Stoddard
Carlota	Dorothy Patten
Cristina	Sylvia Feningston
Graso	Friendly Ford
Doña Josefa	Stella Adler
Father Martinez	Morris Carnovsky
Diana	Ruth Nelson
Diego	Harry Bellaver
Federico	Franchot Tone
Narciso	Herbert Ratner
Captain Mumford	Art Smith
Don Hermano	Lewis Leverett
Don Miguel	Sanford Meisner
Felipe	Walter Coy
Santos	Gerrit Kraber
Pablo Montoya	J. Edward Bromberg
Andros	Clement Wilenchik
Don Fernando	Luther Adler
Don Mario	Philip Robinson
Mateo	Clifford Odets
2nd Trapper	William Challee
3rd Trapper	Grover Burgess

Acts I, II and III.—Great Hall of the Montoya Hacienda. Taos, New Mexico, 1847.

Staged by Lee Strasberg.

Don Pablo Montoya, the last leader of the Spandish grandees in Taos, New Mexico, in 1847, seeks to rally his people to a defiant defense of their ranches and their ancient feudalism against the encroaching American government from the north. Don Pablo's eldest son, Federico, would betray his father, and is killed. The younger son, Felipe, would marry his father's favorite fiancée. Don Pablo, sick of defeat and a love fever, drinks the poison he had prepared for Federico.

THE WARRIOR'S HUSBAND

(83 performances)

A comedy in three acts by Julian Thompson. Produced by Harry Moses at the Morosco Theatre, New York, March 11, 1932.

Cast of characters—

First Sergeant	Paula Bauersmith
Buria	Virginia Volland
Second Sergeant	Edna Holland
First Sentry	Frances Newbaker
Second Sentry	Avalon Plummer
Third Sentry	Rita Rheinfrank
Caustica	Bertha Belmore
Heroica	Dorothy Walters
Pomposia	Jane Wheatley
Hippolyta	Irby Marshal
Sapiens	Romney Brent
Sapiens Major	Arthur Bowyer
Antiope	Katharine Hepburn
Captain of Archers	Helene Fontaine
Theseus	Colin Keith-Johnston
Homer	Don Beddoe
Runner	Thelma Hardwick
Hercules	Al Ochs
Gaganius, the Herald	Porter Hall
Achilles	Alan Campbell
Ajax	Randolph Leymen

Amazon Sentries and Guards: Eleanor Goodrich, Nina Romano, Agnes George, Eve Bailey, Clara Waring, Dorothy Gillam and Rose Dresser.
Amazon Huntresses: Theodosia Dusanne, Mary Stuart, Miriam Schiller and Barbara Dugan.
Greek Warriors: Thaddeus Clancy, Walter Levin, Arthur Brady and Jerry Feigan.
Act I.—Pontus, Outside Hippolyta's Palace. Act II.—Before Hippolyta's Tent. Act III.—Inside Theseus' Tent.
Staged by Burk Symon.

Theseus is conducting Hercules on his ninth labor, which is to recover from Hippolyta, Queen of the Amazons, the girdle of Diana, secret of the Amazons' power. Meeting Antiope, handsome younger sister of Hippolyta, Theseus falls in love. Antiope, planning to conquer Theseus by kissing, as she had seen the weaker Amazonian men conquered, is amazed at the resistance of the Greek as well as his perfection of the art of osculation. Hippolyta's whole Amazonian army, in fact, is in danger of being conquered by the romantic Greeks. Hippolyta recovers the girdle in time to ward off defeat, but Antiope goes back to Greece, willing captive of Theseus. As a one-act play "The Warrior's Husband" was played as far back as 1921, and was an entry in the Little Theatre Tournament the season of 1923-24.

THE YOUNG IDEA

(3 performances)

A comedy in three acts by Noel Coward. Produced by The Snarks at the Heckscher Theatre, New York, March 18, 1932.

Cast of characters—

George Brent	Robert Le Sueur
Gerda	Margaret G. Brett
Sholto	Andrew J. Fox, Jr.
Jennifer	Lois S. Coffin
Cicely	Eleanor Landon Parker
Priscilla Hartleberry	Muriel Wilson
Claud Eccles	Henry G. Bartol
Julia Cragworthy	Margaret S. Ijams
Eustace Dabbit	Sterling T. Foote
Sibyl Blaithe	Helen Swenson
Rodney Masters	John D. Lodge
Huddle	Katharine D. Harvey
Hiram J. Walkin	Drelincourt M. Martin
Maria	Francesca Braggiotti Lodge

Acts I and II.—Hall of George Brent's House in England. Act III.—Jennifer Brent's Villa in Italy.

Staged by Gene Lockhart.

George and Jennifer Brent have been separated for fourteen years, during which time George has lived with Cicely, his second wife. Gerda and Sholto Brent, children of Brent's first marriage, determine to try and effect a reconciliation of their parents. In England the children find their father restive and unhappy, after his experience with Cicely. They proceed to make him more restless and to irritate their stepmother to such a degree that she is ready to elope with a traveling co-respondent. After which Sholto and Gerda bear papa off in triumph to their mother's home in Italy.

A FEW WILD OATS

(4 performances)

A comedy in three acts by Arthur Hoerl. Produced by Forest Productions, Inc., at the Forrest Theatre, New York, March 24, 1932.

Cast of characters—

Alan Joyce	Lee Crowe
Rosemary Grayson	Mildred VanDorn
Alison	George Le Soir
Leonard Grayson	Ross Chetwyn
Eleanor Grayson	Jane Saville
Janet Maitland	Eileen Ericks
Agnes Lovelace	Marion Ball
Henry Dillowell	John Ross
Gregory	Robert Allen

Acts I, II and III.—Living Room of Grayson Summer bungalow
on Long Island.
Staged by C. W. Keim.

The Leonard Graysons have decided upon a divorce to the disgust and grief of their daughter, Rosemary. Rosemary decides that marriage must be desperately uncertain and that she had better sow her wild oats before rather than after taking a husband. She invites a couple of boys and another girl to help her throw off the moral standard. Before Rosemary's party is well started it is interrupted by Gregory, a neighbor. Rosemary decides Gregory is her mother's gigolo. But Gregory, being a friend in need, determines to save the situation by locking the girls in their room and keeping the boys in the garden. In the end he explains all and wins Rosemary for himself.

HAPPY LANDING

(26 performances)

A play in three acts by John B. Hymer and William E. Barry. Produced by Messrs. Shubert at Chanin's Forty-sixth Street Theatre, New York, March 26, 1932.

Cast of characters—

George Stebbins	Harry Davenport
Sam Taylor	Edwin Redding
Charles Stevens	William Carey
Blin Gardner	Russell Hardie
Phyllis Blair	Margaret Sullavan
Miss Crawford	Marjorie Wood
Russell Whiting	William David
Bellboy	Boris Nicholai
Caso	Griffin Crafts
Hal Herndon	John Butler
Radio Announcer	Nolan Leary
Reporters	Randolph Hale, Harold Bolton, Charles A. Richards, Lady Justine Jordan
News Cameraman	Banfield Taylor
Mrs. Thomas W. Dumont	Lenore Chippendale
Norma Landis	Catherine Dale Owen
Major Green	Thomas Reynolds
Hennesey	Tom Tempest
Miss Bond	Anne Carpenger
Carvello	Pierre Mario
Mr. Platt	Banfield Taylor
Mr. Knobb	Nolan Leary
Luigi Cerrino	Rene Roberti
Ira Thompson	John Parrish
Robert Willis Granville	Harold Heaton

Act I.—Scene 1—Hangar, Old Orchard, Maine. 2—Switchboard in the Lewiston (Me.) Exchange. 3—Suite in a New York Hotel. Act II.—Scene 1—Parlor of a Brooklyn Home. 2—Russell Whiting's Office. 3—Room in Blin Gardner's Apartment. Act III.—Scene 1—Blin's Apartment. 2—Speaker's Platform. 3—Hangar in Old Orchard.

Staged by Lawrence Marston.

Blin Gardner, a garage mechanic at Old Orchard, Me., patents a carburetor for airplane engines and assembles a plane with the help of money advanced by his fiancée, Phyllis Blair, who has received a small inheritance. Blain hops successfully from Old Orchard to Tokio for a $50,000 prize. On his return tricky advertising promoters get hold of him. In a month he is a first-page hero suffering slightly from a swelling ego. Phyllis leaves him and goes home. When Blin realizes what this means he quits his promoters spectacularly at a national radio banquet and flies to Maine to recover Phyllis.

LIFE BEGINS

(8 performances)

A play in three acts by Mary Macdougal Axelson. Produced by Joseph Santley at the Selwyn Theatre, New York, March 28, 1932.

Cast of characters—

Ringer Banks.....................................Edwin Fleming
Miss Bowers............................Elizabeth Von Nardroff
Miss Pinty....................................Mildred Dunnock
Jed Sutton...Alan Bunce
Florette Darian..................................Glenda Farrell
Dr. Lee..Dean Raymond
Dr. Alfred Brett..............................Clayton Collyer
Mrs. Riggs...................................Antoinette Rachte
Grace Sutton.....................................Joanna Roos
Mrs. Paley.......................................Helen Brooks
Mrs. West.......................................Eleanor Hicks
Dr. Cramm..Lewis Martin
Dr. Tubby..Frank Wilcox
Peggy Banks....................................Lucile Charles
Mrs. Brown......................................Jean Fullarton
Rose Lorton...................................Ruthelma Stevens
Mrs. Potter.......................................Elaine Troy
Medical Student............................William McFadden
Rita...Darley Fuller
Tony...Joseph Marra
Mr. Hamby-Smith..........................Douglas MacPherson
Mrs. Hamby-Smith..............................Mary May Bell
Woman in a Purple Kimono.........................Ellen Lowe
Mr. Potter......................................Earl Redding
Mrs. Tubby....................................Winifred Harris
Estelle..Valerie Ziegler
    Medical Students, Patients and Internes, etc.
    Acts I, II and III.—Maternity Ward of a City Hospital and the Hall Adjoining It.
    Staged by Joseph Santley.

Grace Sutton, convicted of murder during a vice squad investigation, is brought to the maternity ward of a city hospital to bear a child. Her devoted husband, Jed, is to wait resignedly and patiently for the infant's birth and turn it over to a foster mother.

It proves a difficult birth. After thirty hours the physicians agree a Cesarian operation is necessary to save the child and will likely result in the death of the mother. Jed demands that the mother be saved at the expense of the child. Grace insists that she take the chance. The operation is ordered, Grace dies, Jed is left with the baby.

INTIMATE RELATIONS

(32 performances)

A comedy in three acts by Earle Crooker. Produced by Henry B. Forbes and Jules Lawren in association with George Martin at the Ambassador Theatre, New York, March 28, 1932.

Cast of characters—

Robert Marshall..............................Joseph McCallion
Marie Marshall...................................Maxine Flood
Remblence....................................Gertrude Quinlan
Elizabeth Marshall................................Renah Homer
Edna Proctor.......................................Ruth Abbott
Hoyte Proctor................................Bruce MacFarlane
Patricia Proctor..................................Marion Burns
Jane Marshall.....................................Blanche Ring
Philip Bradley....................................Robert Vivian
Theodore Elliot..................................Michael Barr
Mrs. Louise Elliot...................................Julie Ring
Maroni...Burton Mallory
Hall..Hugh Rennie
Acts I, II and III.—Living Room of the Marshall Home on Long Island.
Staged by Edward Hartford.

Jane Marshall, after her husband's death, discovers that he has been a cheater. She immediately becomes gay by way of belated revenge and gives a grand party. At the party she meets her husband's illegitimate son and likes him much better than her own offspring. Thereafter she helps the little illegitimate to a happy marriage with her son-in-law's sister.

BORDER-LAND

(23 performances)

A comedy drama in three acts by Crane Wilbur. Produced by Philip Gerton at the Biltmore Theatre, New York, March 29, 1932.

Cast of characters—

Sam Sing......................................Peter Goo Chong
Mrs. Luckner...............................Catharine Doucet

```
Bert Cordovan...................................Alan Campbell
Maureen O'Dare..................................Lenita Lane
Gene Cordovan..................................Robert Lowing
Dr. Wolf Luckner...............................Howard Lang
Hugh Templeton.................................Lester Vail
Brother John...................................Edgar Barrier
Malachi........................................Fuller Mellish
    Acts I, II and III.—Cordovan Hunting Lodge.
    Staged by Frank McCormack.
```

Hugh Templeton, experimenting with spiritualism, develops mediumistic powers. His friends insist on his using them. At a séance held in the Cordovan hunting lodge during a vacation Hugh is apparently controlled by the spirit of a murderer whom the testimony of Bert Cordovan sent to the chair. The spirit tries to strangle Bert. That night Bert is really strangled to death with one of Templeton's neckties. Templeton is sent to an asylum for the criminally insane. A year later he takes part in another séance and forces a confession from the real murderer, Bert's brother.

BLOODSTREAM

(29 performances)

A play in three acts by Frederick Schlick. Produced by Sidney Harmon at the Times Square Theatre, New York, March 30, 1932.

Cast of characters—

```
Adonia Crusoe..................................William Andrews
Juke Taylor....................................Ernest R. Whitman
Moth Anderson..................................Wayland Rudd
Gypsy Kale, alias God..........................Frank Wilson
James Knox.....................................Cecil Holm
Warden Davis...................................Clyde Franklin
Cecil Thurston.................................Hale Norcross
Jim............................................Andrew F. Hutchins
Dewey..........................................Bart Crane
Jack...........................................M. Coates Webster
    Acts I and II.—Tunnel in the Flat Top Mine Prison. Act III.—
    Prison Yard.
    Staged by Sidney Salkow.
```

James Knox, a white sent to work with colored prisoners in a coal mine prison, rebels against the inhuman treatment of the warden. Attacking the warden in a mine tunnel, Knox takes his gun, holds the guards at bay and inadvertently kills one of them. Knox and four involuntary accomplices are hunted in the mine and finally forced to yield. Knox is shot through the shoulder as he emerges and then beaten into insensibility by the warden. Later, while they are in the mine looking for the other prisoners, Gypsy Kale, a demented Negro who believes he is God, blows up a coal pocket, imprisoning himself, Knox and the warden.

BLACK SOULS

(13 performances)

A play in six scenes by Annie Nathan Meyer. Produced by William Stahl at the Provincetown Playhouse, New York, March 30, 1932.

Cast of characters—

Andrew Morgan	Morris McKenney
Phyllis	Rose McClendon
Ettie Boy	Leonia Dawson
Jamie Boy	Carl Crawford
David Lewis	Juano Hernandez
Corinne Thompson	Serena Mason
Ulysses Clark	Hayes Pryor
Senator Verne	Alven Dexter
Luella	Guerita Donneley
Junius Augustus	Sylvester Payne
Governor of the State	Thomas Coffin Cooke

Scenes I, II, IV and VI.—Study of the Principal of Magnolia College. Scene III.—Neighboring Woods. Scene V—Platform in Assembly.

Staged by James Light.

Senator Verne takes an interest in Magnolia College. Andrew Morgan, colored founder of the college, thinks the interest genuine, but his wife knows it is motivated by the senator's physical interest in her. David Lewis, colored professor of literature in the college, also doubts Senator Verne's motives. He had known the Verne daughter intimately in France. When she visits the college and lures Lewis to a cabin in the woods to renew their friendship they are discovered by whites. Lewis nobly insists he dragged Miss Verne there and is lynched.

WE ARE NO LONGER CHILDREN

(12 performances)

A play in three acts by Leopold Marchand, adapted by Ilka Chase and William B. Murray. Produced by William A. Brady, Jr., at the Booth Theatre, New York, March 31, 1932.

Cast of characters—

A Man from the Provinces	George Dill
Waiter	Edward Mendelssohn
Roberte	June Walker
Count de Moreau	Wallace Widdicombe
Paul Verdier	Harold Vermilyea
Jean Servin	Geoffrey Kerr
Aristide Breton	Frederick Roland
Cecile Breton	Freya Leigh
Pierre	H. N. Worth
Mariette	Gertrude Fowler

```
Lisa Duval.....................................Spring Byington
La Vattier..........................................Walter Bonn
Maid..........................................Diana  Bori
    Act I.—A Café in Paris.  Act II.—The Servins' Drawing Room.
Act III.—Hotel Room in Dieppe.
    Staged by William A. Brady, Jr., and Leslie Howard.
```

Roberte and Jean are lovers. Jean, for family reasons, is forced to break up their association and marry Cecile. Years later Roberte, now the wife of a business man, meets Jean at a dinner given in Jean's home. They mutually agree that their respective marriages are unsatisfactory and agree they will try to recapture their old romance. At Dieppe, where they first had been happy, they discover that it is not each other for whom they have been seeking, but for their dead youth. Disillusioned, they return to their families.

LA COMPANIA DRAMATIC ESPAÑOLA

(40 performances)

A repertory from the Spanish Theatre of Madrid, the company headed by Fernando Diaz de Mendoza and Maria Guerrero. Presented by Walter O. Lindsey and Benito Collada at the New Yorker Theatre, New York, April 1, 1932.

Cast of characters—
```
                  PLUMA EN EL VIENTO
                   BY JOAQUIN DICENTA
Mart-Blanca....................................Maria  Guerrero
Andrea.........................................Tarsila Criado
Maruja.........................................Rosario Garcia Ortega
La Senora Rosario..............................Maria Valentin
La Ronca.......................................Josefina Taboada
Un Poeta...........................Fernando Diaz de Mendoza
José Luis......................................Juan Berengola
Miquelon...........................................Fernando Sala
El Cachito de Pan..............................Francisco Fuentes
```

The repertory of the Spanish players also included the Quinteros' "El Genio Alegre," "Los Mosquitos," "Tambor y Cascabel," "Amores y Amorios," and "Mariquilla Terremoto"; Benevente's "La Mariposa Que Volo Sombre el Mar," "No Quiero, No Quiero," "Cuando los Hijos de Eva no son los Hijoz de Adam," "La Malquerida" and "De Muy Buena Familia"; Eduardo Marquina's "El Flandes se ha Puesto el Sol"; Echegaray's "El Gran Galeoto" and "Mancha Que Limpia"; Henri Bernstein's "La Rafaga"; Dicental's "Juan Jose"; Sierra's "Cancion de Cuna"; Lope de Vega's "El Perro del Hortelano" and "La Nina Boba"; Blasco's "Mensajero de Paz"; Zorilla's "Don Juan Tenorio"; Niccodemi's "La Sombra," Codina's "La Dolores"; Astray's "Los Amores de la Nati"; Bourdet's "La Prisionera," "La Malvaloca," and Wilde's "El Abanico de Lady Windermere."

THE DECOY

(8 performances)

A play in three acts by Harrison King. Produced by Frederic Clayton and A. O. Huhn at the Royale Theatre, New York, April 1, 1932.

Cast of characters—

John Kendall	Kirk Brown
Judge Gilbert	Ralph W. Chambers
Joe Wright	Chas. Brokaw
Dr. Hayes	Philip Quin
Mrs. Lawrence	Lorna Elliott
Mrs. Hayes	Madge North
William	James R. Garey
David Kerr	Willard Dashiell
Gloria Kerr	Janet Rathbun
Winthrow	Robert Griffith
Dawes	Joseph Burton
Kit	Mary Emerson
Turkey Ryan	Jerry Lynch
Buck Kelley	Ray Earles
Ella	Lucille Fenton

Acts I, II and III.—Judge Gilbert's Library. Belmont, a Midwestern City.

Staged by A. O. Huhn.

John Kendall, an idealistic newspaper man, fights corruption in his home town of Belmont, exposing David Kerr as a crooked politician but at the same time trying to save Gloria Kerr, whom he loves, from a knowledge of her father's crimes. Gloria loves John enough to stick by him, and this proves so great a shock to her father that he turns decent.

STYLES IN ACTING

A series of character sketches by Dorothy Sands. Presented by James B. Pond at the Booth Theatre, New York, April 3 and 10, 1932.

1. "Millamant" in "The Way of the World," by William Congreve.
2. "Almahide" in "The Conquest of Granada," by John Dryden.
3. "Nellie Hathaway" in "The Silver King," by Henry Arthur Jones.
4. "Candida" in "Candida," by George Bernard Shaw.
5. "Anna Christie" in "Anna Christie," by Eugene O'Neill. (An impersonation of Pauline Lord in her famous rôle.)
6. "Lady Macbeth." The sleep walking scene as it might be portrayed by: a. Haidee Wright, b. Ethel Barrymore, c. Mae West.

BLACKBERRIES OF 1932

(24 performances)

A colored revue in two acts, by Lee Posner, book by Eddie Green, music and lyrics by Donald Heywood and Tom Peluso. Produced by Max Rudnick and Ben Bernard at the Liberty Theatre, New York, April 4, 1932.

Principals engaged—

Eddie Green
Tim Moore
Susaye Brown
Sammy Paige
Johnny Long
Manton Moreland
John Dickens

Alice Harris
Thelma Meers
Harold Norton
Dewey Markham
Gertrude Saunders
Jackie Mabley

Staged by Ben Bernard.

TOO TRUE TO BE GOOD

(57 performances)

A play in three acts by Bernard Shaw. Produced by the Theatre Guild, Inc., at the Guild Theatre, New York, April 4, 1932.

Cast of characters—

The Monster......................................Julius Evans
The Elderly Lady..............................Minna Phillips
The Doctor.............................Alexander Clark, Jr.
The Patient....................................Hope Williams
The Nurse.....................................Beatrice Lillie
The Burglar....................................Hugh Sinclair
Colonel Tallboys, V.C., D.S.O....................Ernest Cossart
Private Meek....................................Leo G. Carrol
Sergeant Fielding................................Frank Shannon
The Elder...Claude Rains

Act I.—Bedroom in Suburban Villa in England. Act II.—Sea Beach in a Mountainous Country. Act III.—Narrow Gap Leading to Beach.

Staged by Leslie Banks.

Patient, ill with the measles, is visited by Monster, an enormous bacillus, and attended by Nurse, a chambermaid turned thief, and Burglar, a rebellious curate. Patient attacks and overpowers her would-be robbers but is overcome by the logic of their arguments that she is wasting her life. For excitement it is agreed they are to kidnap Patient and share the ransom with her. The three go to a remote country, Nurse masquerading as a lady, Patient as her attendant. In the mountains they meet the British army and, after an evening's talk, return to normal.

ANGELS DON'T KISS

(7 performances)

A comedy in three acts by R. B. Lackey. Produced by Allan Cameron Dalzell at the Belmont Theatre, New York, April 5, 1932.

Cast of characters—

Darling Darrow	Sue MacManamy
Henry	Fred Miller
Tivot	Joseph Crehan
John Darrow	Barry Townley
Peter	Billy Quinn
Mary	Marjorie Clarke
Judy	Sally Starr
Cæsar	Hal Clarendon
Partridge	Leo Kennedy
Diane	Joan Clive
Coastguard	Jack Clifford

Acts I, II and III.—John Darrow's Home, Manhasset, Long Island. Staged by H. MacRae Webster.

Darling Darrow is unhappy because she cannot abide her husband's amorous demands and resents his seeking the companionship of other women. When her protests continue to go unheeded, after John has sought to ensnare both her neighbor and her adopted son's fiancée, Darling pretends she is going to kill herself. She sails that night for a Paris divorce and leaves word for her neighbor's husband to come and get her.

HOUSEWARMING

(4 performances)

A play in three acts by Gilbert Emery. Produced by Ann Ayers at the Charles Hopkins Theatre, New York, April 7, 1932.

Cast of characters—

Sarah Fuller	Clare Woodbury
Alfred Joy	Corbet Morris
Anne Gregory	Regina Wallace
Olive Drengle	Eleanor Shaler
Sam Gregory	Richard Hale
Salem Hipple	Frank Conlan
Jane Scott	Beverly Sitgreaves
Edward Sedgwick	Louis Jean Heydt
Mary Sedgwick	Katherine Wilson
Martha Sedgwick	Molly Pearson

Acts I, II and III.—Living Room of the Sedgwick Home and a Corner of Mary's Garden. Staged by Pauline Frederick.

Edward Sedgwick and Mary Wolcott Sedgwick, born in New England, finished in Paris, marry in Paris and return to the old home town of Stoneham to settle down. Edward's aunt, Jane Scott, to whom he owes his education and his chance in the bank, presents bride and groom with a red plush piano, upholstered by the village mortician, as a wedding present. Mary insists it shall be thrown out. Edward feels it should stay in out of respect to Aunt Jane. Mary, seeing no other way out, burns down both house and piano. Edward discovers he likes Mary better even than he does the Sedgwicks.

THE TRUTH ABOUT BLAYDS

(24 performances)

A tragi-comedy in three acts by A. A. Milne. Revived by Guthrie McClintic at the Belasco Theatre, New York, April 11, 1932.

Cast of characters—

Oliver Blayds..	O. P. Heggie
Isobel (his younger daughter)........................	Pauline Lord
Marion Blayds-Conway (his elder daughter).........	Effie Shannon
William Blayds-Conway (his son-in-law).............	Ernest Lawford
Oliver Blayds-Conway } ....his grandchildren.... {	John Griggs
Septima Blayds-Conway } {	Rachel Hartzell
A. L. Royce....................................	Frederic Worlock
Parsons..	Helen Walpole

Acts I, II and III.—Room in Oliver Blayds' House in Portman Square.

Staged by Guthrie McClintic.

Oliver Blayds, famous Victorian poet, confesses on his ninetieth birthday that he has been living a lie for seventy years. Practically all the poetry he has sold under his name was written by a boy named Jenkins, who died when he was twenty. Following the confession Blayds dies. His parisitical family faces the problem of turning over the estate to the heirs of the real poet or keeping the matter secret. Finding an excuse in the discovered will of Jenkins leaving all his writings to Blayds they continue the deception. The play was originally produced by Winthrop Ames at the Booth Theatre, New York, in 1922.

TAKE MY TIP

(16 performances)

A comedy in three acts by Nat N. Dorfman. Produced by Mack Hilliard at the Forty-eighth Street Theatre, New York, April 11, 1932.

Cast of characters—

Mrs. Mary Wells.................................Ethel Remey
Betty Merrill..................................Janet McLeay
Mrs. Merrill...................................Helen Lowell
Henry Merrill..................................Donald Meek
Mollie..Eda Heinemann
Jack Rogers...................................James Spottswood
Mrs. Dolly Browning...........................Florence Shirley
Frank Groves..................................John T. Dwyer
Gilbert Blair.................................William Janney
Wilbur Smith..................................George Christie
George Harvey.................................Frank Andrews
Amy Phillips..................................Marjorie Jarecki
J. Sutton.....................................Gordon Nelson
    Acts I, II and III.—Home of the Merrills in Essex, Conn.
    Staged by Frank Merlin.

Henry Merrill, swept along in the bull market of 1929, loads
up on Triplex Oil stock and drags in his friends and fellow towns-
men. The market breaks, Henry and his friends go broke and
everybody blames Henry. He is less than a worm until he sells
a soap-making invention for a fortune and pays everybody back
what they had lost.

THE TREE

(7 performances)

A drama in three acts by Richard Maibaum. Produced by Ira
Marion at the Park Lane Theatre, New York, April 12, 1932.

Cast of characters—

Ruth..Sylvia Lee
David...Thomas Moseley
Matt..Barton MacLane
Ed..Alexander Cross
Denny...Truman Quevli
Judd..Marc Lawrence
Atwood..Daniel Hamilton
Preston.......................................Perry Norman
Miriam..Laura Bowman
Rachel..Enid Raphael
Sheriff.......................................Leslie M. Hunt
John..Bertram Millar
Ames..William Bonelli
Blake...James J. Coyle
    Acts I, II and III.—A gallows-like tree on a bleak landscape north
of the Mason-Dixon Line.
    Staged by Robert Rossen.

Ruth is to marry Ed. Matt and Denny are both in love with
her. David, a colored boy, also publicly sings her praises. Ruth
is assaulted and strangled to death. David is accused of the
crime and lynched. Matt's conscience drives him to a confession
that he is the guilty man. Denny, who led the mob of lynchers,
is stricken with remorse. To bring peace to their troubled souls
Denny and Matt agree that Matt shall also die by hanging.

FOREIGN AFFAIRS

(22 performances)

A romantic comedy in three acts by Paul Hervey Fox and George Tilton. Produced by B. Franklin Kamsler and Lester Fuller at the Avon Theatre, New York, April 13, 1932.

Cast of characters—

Tito Lanni	Henry Hull
Countess Ilsa Da Cassali	Dorothy Gish
Waiter	Edouard La Roche
Otto Zeigen	Osgood Perkins
Anna	Jean Arthur
Tigani	J. Edward Bromberg
Count Rodolfo Da Cassali	Carl Benton Reid

Acts I, II and III.—Parlor of an Inn in the Italian Tyrol.
Staged by Lester Fuller.

Tito Lanni, diplomat, and the Countess Ilsa da Cassali arrive at an inn in the Tyrol thinking to stay there two weeks. Hearing that the Count Cassali is on their trail they plan to divert his attention from the real situation by pretending to be interested in other affairs. The Countess will flirt with Otto Zeigen and Tito will make up to Anna, the kitchen maid, who happens to be the only other female in the establishment. The Count is reassured, but Tito and the Countess are pretty mad when they discover that they have deceived each other.

ANGELINE MOVES IN

(7 performances)

A comedy drama in three acts by Hale Francisco. Produced by Hale Francisco at the Forrest Theatre, New York, April 19, 1932.

Cast of characters—

Prosper Weems	William Ingersoll
Serina Weems	Antoinette Rochte
Blessington Wells	William Melville
Mrs. Crowley	Mrs. Jacques Martin
Angeline Guertin	Suzanne Caubaye
Naida Weems	Katherine Revner
Digby Struthers	Robert Brister
Jerry Dugan	Gerald Kent

Acts I, II and III.—Living Room of Prosper Weems' Home, Burlington, Vermont.
Staged by J. J. White.

Jerry Dugan ships before the mast in England in order to get back to the United States to claim an inheritance which is to be his on his twenty-fifth birthday if, in the estimation of his father's bankers, he has behaved himself. Otherwise he will have to wait another ten years. Jerry stops off in Montreal, meets a flashing young woman named Angeline Guertin and for three weeks makes violent love to her. Angeline follows Jerry to his home town, where she discovers he is going to marry the banker's daughter, Naida, in order to save his money. Otherwise the banker is likely to declare him unfit. Angeline moves into the banker's house, gets the old boy and herself slightly tight, enlists the coöperation of a gossiping Mrs. Crowley from across the street and finally annexes Jerry for herself.

THE BLUE BIRD

(20 performances)

A Russian revue headed by Yascha Yushny. Produced by S. Hurok at the Cort Theatre, New York, April 21, 1932.

Program included—

St. Petersburg (1825)	With the Gypsies
The Bottle Stoppers	Alkmaar (Cheese Market)
Yugoslavian Washerwomen	Folk Songs and Ballads by Isa Kremer
Volga Boatmen	Yushny's Cossack Chorus
"At the School Gate"	"The Evening Bells"
"The Little Huntsman"	Gossips Around the Samovar
Dance of the Boyars	Russian Marketwomen
Souvenir of Switzerland	Easter Time in Russia

Staged by Yascha Yushny.

MERRY-GO-ROUND

(48 performances)

A play in three acts by Albert Malz and George Sklar. Produced by Michael Blankfort and Walter Hart at the Provincetown Playhouse, New York, April 22, 1932.

Cast of characters—

Sam	Robert Crozier, Jr.
Mike	Jack Bennett
Pete	Joseph Carewe
Ed Martin	Elisha Cook, Jr.
Butch	Harry Bellaver
Stransky	Jean Clarendon
Marge Winters	Ruth Thomas
Jig Zelli	Harold Huber
Maguire	Robert J. Mulligan
Quinn	Frank Layton
Interne	Kempton Race
District Attorney Anderson	Edward Vickery
Assistant District Attorney Wade	Robert H. Gordon
Police Commissioner Garvey	Frank Dae
Mayor Manning	Doan Borup
Dougherty	Lawrence C. O'Brien

The Chief...................................Ian MacLaren
Leonard Collins............................Kermit Murdock
Pegs Martin................................Viola Frayne
John Zelli.................................Mel Tyler
Judge MacMurray...........................Frank Howson
Molly.....................................Nina Melville
Kippy.....................................Dorothy Howard
May.......................................Glorian Gray
Alice.....................................Diane Crystal
Mailman...................................John Bell
Beachley..................................Harry Bellaver
Sergeant..................................Dan Carey
Nurse.....................................Dorothy Braun
Nurse.....................................Glorian Gray
Nurse.....................................Nina Melville
Dr. Koenig................................Thomas F. Tracey
Harry Berger..............................Horace Casselberry
    Staged by Walter Hart.

Stransky, a gangster, is murdered in the Capitol hotel. Ed
Martin, bellboy, sees Jig Zelli do the shooting. Ed is threatened
with being put on the spot by the gangsters if he identifies Zelli,
and threatened with the third degree by the police if he does not.
He sides with the police. Zelli brings his political influence to bear
to get the indictment against him quashed. The governor names
an investigation commission. The police have to have someone to
take Zelli's place and pick on young Martin, beating him into a
confession. When the investigation again draws uncomfortably
close the police get rid of Martin and their problem by arranging
to have the bellboy found hanging in his cell, presumably a suicide.

* ANOTHER LANGUAGE

(64 performances)

A play in three acts by Rose Franken. Produced by Arthur J.
Beckhard at the Booth Theatre, New York, April 25, 1932.

Cast of characters—

Mrs. Hallam...............................Margaret Wycherly
Mr. Hallam................................Wyrley Birch
Harry Hallam..............................William Pike
Helen Hallam..............................Margaret Hamilton
Walter Hallam.............................Hal K. Dawson
Grace Hallam..............................Irene Cattell
Paul Hallam...............................Herbert Duffy
Etta Hallam...............................Maude Allan
Victor Hallam.............................Glenn Anders
Stella Hallam.............................Dorothy Stickney
Jerry Hallam..............................John Beal
    Acts I and III.—The Hallam Home on the West Side. Act II.—
Stella's and Victor's Apartment on the Upper East Side.
    Staged by Arthur Beckhard.

See page 267.

THE MAN WHO CHANGED HIS NAME

(56 performances)

A play in three acts by Edgar Wallace. Produced by Edwal Productions Company at the Broadhurst Theatre, New York, May 2, 1932.

Cast of characters—

Lane... ....Maurice Greet
Mrs. Selby Clive....................................Fay Bainter
Selby Clive..Frank Conroy
The Hon. Frank O'Ryan......................Derek Fairman
Jeremiah Muller............................Reynolds Denniston
Sir Ralph Whitcombe...........................Thomas Louden
Maid... Emily Graham
    Acts I, II and III.—Morning Room at Sunningdale, England.
    Staged by Clifford Brooke.

Mrs. Selby Clive, married to a rich and kindly man some years her senior and grown a little indifferent to his advances, spends an extra night at a hotel in London on her way home from Scotland. In an adjoining room Hon. Frank O'Ryan, her quandom lover, eagerly awaits her opening the intercepting door, which at the test Mrs. Clive fails to unlock. At home Mrs. Clive and O'Ryan, rummaging through Mr. Clive's papers in search of a lease, come upon proof that Clive had, twenty years before, changed his name. Later they learn the original name was that of a notorious murderer who escaped hanging because he had been particular to warn his victims against the things that killed them. Thereafter the theoretically guilty lovers are terrorized by the thought that Clive is also plotting their deaths and misread his every utterance. In the end it is proved that Clive changed his name purposely to escape being taken for the murderer.

BROADWAY BOY

(7 performances)

A play in three acts by Wallace A. Manheimer and Isaac Paul. Produced by Barton Slater at the Forty-eighth Street Theatre, New York, May 3, 1932.

Cast of characters—

Jim...William Balfour
Pat..Jack Irwin
Donald Evans.....................................Maurice Cass
Harry Windham..................................A. J. Herbert
Frank Shelby.......................................Alan Brooks
Begona Durell...................................Roberta Beatty

James Hillery.....................................William Franklin
Edna Harman.......................................Mildred Baker
Helen Ford..Barbara Willison
Bert Flint..Roy Roberts
Jack Chester......................................Murray Alper
Michael Sorley....................................Ben Roberts
Julius Frankel....................................Clarence Derwent
Herbert Bamberger.................................Hans Hansen
Mike..Don Kane
Messenger Boy.....................................William Lobell
Van Elten...Albert Berg

Acts I and II.—Stage of the 47th Street Theatre, New York. Act III.—Scene 2—Flint's Office.

Staged by Jacob A. Weiser.

Bert Flint, a young lawyer, bitten by the theatre bug, yearns to be a Broadway producer. Against his rich Uncle Julius' wishes he tries two plays and scores two failures. The third, and most promising, he brings within a day of production and then faces failure unless he can raise money for the stagehands, the actors and find an understudy for his star, Begona Durell, who shows up drunk. Bert "borrows" a $5,000 Liberty bond from his uncle, is threatened with jail, nearly loses his production to a crafty rival and then scores a success, thanks to the raving notices of suspected critics. This makes it possible for him to marry Edna Harman, the understudy, who saves the show.

BULLS, BEARS AND ASSES

(2 performances)

A play in three acts by Milton Herbert Gropper. Produced at the Playhouse, New York, May 6, 1932.

Cast of characters—

Charwoman...Jessie Graham
Jerry...Huntley Weston
Larry...Clifford Jones
Marino..Salvatore Zito
Belber..Louis Sorin
Merwin..Paul Stewart
Peters..Robert Shayne
Murdock...Howard St. John
Dr. Hollis..Roman Bohnen
Betty Grant.......................................Irene Lee
Charlie Moore.....................................Hobart Cavanaugh
Waters..Len D. Hollister
Decker..Joseph Allen
Manesco...David Manley
Elsie Moore.......................................Sally Bates
Bloom...Lew Welch
Rocco...Ralph Simone
Starr...William Roselle
Mrs. Fisher.......................................Elise Bartlett
Brown...John Daly Murphy
Mrs. Dayton.......................................Olive Reeves-Smith
Lester Kingsley...................................Griffin Crafts
Mrs. Larrabie.....................................Francesca Hill
Delroy..Robert Barrat
Doorman...Frederick Malcolm

```
Columbus.............................................Jack Rigo
Louise...............................................Lillian Savin
Mrs. Espey........................................Virginia Tracy
Gregg.............................................Edward Butler
Mrs. Marino........................................June Mullin
Mrs. Rocco.......................................Arden Benlien
Mrs. Belber..................................Anne Lowenwirth
Kenney...........................................Ashley Cooper
Figbaum......................................Joseph Greenwald
Spencer.......................................Franklyn Munnell
The Baron.........................................Egon Brecher
Chauffeur......................................Frank McDonald
     Acts I, II and III.—Brokerage Office in New York City.
     Staged by Melville Burke.
```

At the peak of the bull market, September, 1929, Elsie Moore insists on taking the $5,000 left her by her aunt and buying stocks with it against the advice of her home-loving husband, Charlie. So infectious does the lure of the gamble become that Charlie also puts in his savings. A month later the crash leaves the Moores flat and blaming each other. For two years they live apart. The depression brings them together. Charlie recovers his lost job. If they work hard and save they may have something to invest in the next bull market.

MOURNING BECOMES ELECTRA

(Second Engagement)

(16 performances)

A trilogy by Eugene O'Neill. Repeated by the Theatre Guild at the Alvin Theatre, New York, May 9, 1932.

Cast of characters—

```
                         HOMECOMING
Abner Small...............................George W. Callahan
Ira Mackel.....................................Forrest Zimmer
Joe Silva........................................Cameron King
Amos Ames....................................Henry Hermsen
Seth Beckwith.....................................Seth Arnold
Peter Niles.....................................Eric Kalkhurst
Hazel Niles...................................Bernice Elliott
Lavinia Mannon..............................Judith Anderson
Orin Mannon.......................................Walter Abel

                         THE HUNTED
Mrs. Josiah Borden.........................Beatrice Moreland
Mrs. Everett Hills.............................Beatrice Maude
Dr. Joseph Blake..........................George W. Callahan
Josiah Borden...................................Harry Hermsen
Everett Hills, D.D.............................Forrest Zimmer
Christine Mannon...............................Florence Reed
Hazel Niles...................................Bernice Elliott
Peter Niles.....................................Eric Kalkhurst
Lavinia Mannon..............................Judith Anderson
Orin Mannon.......................................Walter Abel
A Chantyman....................................Cameron King
Captain Adam Brant............................Crane Wilbur
```

THE HAUNTED

Abner Small.................................George W. Callahan
Ira Mackel......................................Forrest Zimmer
Joe Silva......................................Cameron King
Amos Ames....................................Harry Hermsen
Seth Beckwith....................................Seth Arnold
Peter Niles....................................Eric Kalkhurst
Hazel Niles....................................Bernice Elliott
Lavinia Mannon..............................Judith Anderson
Orin Mannon......................................Walter Abel
    Staged by Philip Moeller.

A two weeks' engagement in New York of the company that
played the O'Neill tragedy on tour.
    See page 65.

THE LADY REMEMBERS

(10 performances)

A farce comedy in three acts by an anonymous writer. Produced by the Graissel Productions Company at the Provincetown Theatre, New York, May 10, 1932.

Cast of characters—

Marya Sontsey....................................Aida Maissel
David Dunstan...............................Frank Conington
Rev. Thaddeus Winton...........................John Francis
Sir Jeremy Frayne............................Gordon Fallows
Emma Winton...................................Marian Leeds
Daniel Frayne.....................................David Shaw
Najda Sontsey..................................Muriel Petersen
Harvey..Eugene Allen
Baroness Von Oom................................Celia Haskell
Fred Tillinghast...............................Joseph Mulhall
    Acts I, II and III.—Living Room in Sir Jeremy Frayne's Home in
England.
    Staged by John F. Grahame.

The Baroness Von Oom, who was Minnie the barmaid in her
younger days, writes her memoirs and includes in the book some
choice references to the Rev. Thaddeus Winton, known as Chicky
when he was an undergraduate at Oxford, and in love with Minnie.

LENIN'S DOWRY

(4 performances)

A comedy-drama in three acts by David Vardi. Produced by
David Vardi at the Chanin Auditorium, New York, May 12, 1932.

Cast of characters—

Maria Sergeyevna Krestovskaya......................Eva Yoalit
Diemyan Krasnov...................................David Vardi
    Acts I, II and III.—Theatre studio in Moscow.
    Staged by David Vardi.

Diemyan is a soldier actor back from the Red army and assigned to a studio theatre in Moscow. His ambition is to play a Red Napoleon. With the help of Maria he gets the part and they are married.

THERE YOU ARE

(8 performances)

A musical play in two acts by Carl Bartfield, music by William Heagney, lyrics by William Heagney and Tom Connell. Produced by Hyman Adler at the George M. Cohan Theatre, New York, May 16, 1932.

Cast of characters—

Chita	Melba Marcel
Pasquale Costeo	Adrian Rosley
Capt. Louis Fidelio	Bruce Norman
Dick Longwood	Robert Capron
Pedro	Arthur Marlowe
Julia Danville	Berta Donn
Carolita Rodriguez	Ilse Marvenga
Peggy Hastings	Peggy O'Connor
Don Jose Gomez	Joseph Lertora
Hidalgo Fernandez Bravo Herrara	Walter Armin
Pancho	Andrew Kellar
Señor Cambro	Hyman Adler
Lloyd Emerson	Roy Cropper
Friar Francesco	Louis Salvo
La Mariposa	Gertrude Stanton

Acts I and II.—Patio of the Inn of "The Blue Dove," Satero, Mexico.

Staged by Horace Sinclair.

Carolita Rodriguez, a Spanish singer, is loved by Lloyd Emerson, as handsome and as daring an aviator without a ship as any of them. Emerson drops in to call and finds Carolita about to suffer a forced marriage to Governor Jose Gomez, a mean hombre if there ever was one. To save Lloyd, Carolita agrees to marry Gov. Jose, but, thanks to Señor Cambra (who is really Diablo the bandit in disguise) she is saved from a fate worse than anything she could think of at the moment.

* SHOW BOAT

(36 performances)

A musical comedy in two acts adapted from Edna Ferber's novel of the same name; book and lyrics by Oscar Hammerstein, II; music by Jerome Kern. Revived by Florenz Ziegfeld at the Casino Theatre, New York, May 19, 1932.

Cast of characters—

Windy..A. Alan Campbell
Steve...Charles Ellis
Pete...James Swift
Queenie.............................Tess Gardell (Aunt Jemima)
Parthy Ann Hawks..........................Edna May Oliver
Cap'n Andy................................Charles Winninger
Elly..Eva Puck
Frank..Sammy White
Rubber Face.............................Francis X. Mahoney
Julie...Helen Morgan
Gaylord Ravenal.................................Dennis King
Vallon..Thomas Gunn
Magnolia...Norma Terris
Joe...Paul Robeson
Faro Dealer................................Gladstone Waldrup
Gambler...Phil Sheridan
Backwoodsman.....................................Jack Daley
Jeb.......................................Gladstone Waldrup
La Belle Fatima...............................Dorothy Denese
Old Sport..James Swift
Landlady...Annie Hart
Ethel..Estelle Floyd
Sister..V. Ann Kaye
Mother Superior.............................Mildred Schwenke
Kim (child).....................................Evelyn Eaton
Mary...Mari Hellgren
Kim (as young woman)...........................Norma Terris
Jake...Robert Faricy
Jim...Jack Daley
Man with Guitar...................................Pat Mann
Charlie......................................J. Lewis Johnson
Lottie.......................................Gertrude Walker
Dolly..Tana Kamp
Hazel...Maurine Holmes
Old Lady on Levee..............................Laura Clairon

Act I.—Scene 1, 8—Levee at Natchez. 2—Kitchen Pantry of the "Cotton Blossom." 3—Outside Gambling Saloon. 4, 6—Auditorium and Stage of the "Cotton Blossom." 5—Box-office. 7—Top Deck.

Act II.—Scene 1—Midway Plaisance, Chicago World's Fair, 1893. 2—Room on Ontario Street, 1904. 3—Rehearsal Room of the Trocadero Music Hall. 4—St. Agatha's Convent. 5—Lobby of Sherman Hotel, Chicago. 6—Trocadero Music Hall. 7—In Front of the Office of *The Natchez Evening Democrat*, 1932. 8—Top deck of the new "Cotton Blossom," 1932. 9—Levee at Natchez.

Produced in December, 1927. "Show Boat" completed a run of 572 performances in New York the season of 1928-29. This revival followed Mr. Ziegfeld's lease of the former Earl Carroll's Theatre and was the first showing of the musical comedy at popular prices.

Principal songs—"Ol' Man River," "Only Make Believe," "Bill," and "Can't Help Lovin' That Man."

ON THE MAKE

(32 performances)

A comedy in three acts by Roger Gray. Produced at the Forty-eighth Street Theatre, New York, May 23, 1932.

Cast of characters—

Eva Dupont.....................................Ruth Fallows
Christine Schroeder...........................Alice Cavanaugh
Vangie Ryan..................................Jeanette Fox-Lee
Bert Gibson..................................John A. Willarde
Danny Martin..................................George Sweet
Mike Caccio.....................................Clyde Veaux
Steve..Billy Barrows
Conroy..Jerome Daley
Duncan.......................................Arthur J. Wood
Asa Sears......................................Harry Short
Agatha Schroeder................................Diana Croye
Oscar Stubbs.........................Worthington L. Romaine
George Larrimore.........................Emmett Shackelford
Henry Gibson..............................Charles Hammond
Wilson...Joseph Burton
Doyle..Phil Hughes
      Acts I, II and III.—Living-room of Chris and Eva's Apartment
on 73rd St., New York.
      Staged by Homer B. Mason.

Christine Schroeder and Eva Dupont are honest stenographers engaged to a couple of aviators, Bert Gibson and Danny Martin. While the boys are up in the air trying for the endurance flight record vice squad crooks force their way into the girls' flat, after Eva has picked up a fellow she hopes to work for a dinner, and who proves a stool pigeon. Christine is arrested and "framed." She buys a suspended sentence for $500. To make back the $500 and get out of debt Christine joins Eva and Vangie Ryan, a neighbor, in the racket of entertaining out-of-town gay boys without sacrificing anything more than her time and social graces. When Bert comes out of the air it takes some explaining to make him believe Christine is still a good girl.

* A THOUSAND SUMMERS

(35 performances)

A play in three acts by Merrill Rogers. Produced by Arch Selwyn and Shepard Traube at the Selwyn Theatre, New York, May 24, 1932.

Cast of characters—

Neil Barton....................................Franchot Tone
Mrs. Hawkins.................................Florence Edney
Mrs. Thompson...............................Josephine Hull
Mr. Thompson...............................Thomas Findlay
Sheila Pennington................................Jane Cowl
Zoe King.....................................Marion Evensen
Tessie..............................Mary Newnham Davis
Laurence Hereford............................Osgood Perkins
      Acts I, II and III.—Sitting-room of Small Hotel in the Lake District of England.
      Staged by Shepard Traube.

Sheila Pennington, widow, has escaped from her rather fast London set for a vacation in the English lake district. At an inn she meets Neil Barton, traveling with his aunt and uncle and on his way to Paris for a year of art. Neil, 21, falls desperately in love with Sheila, 36. It is his first experience with love and Sheila promises his aunt she will take no advantage of his innocence. Sheila dismisses Neil after a hectic encounter. Neil turns to the barmaid Tessie, suffering the disillusionment of his adolescent ideas. Sheila, realizing the possibilities of Neil's further adventuring, lets him go to Paris alone but decides to follow after.

HEIGH-HO, EVERYBODY

(5 performances)

A comedy in three acts by Herbert Polesie and John McGowan. Produced by John T. Adams in association with Arthur Hurley at the Fulton Theatre, New York, May 25, 1932.

Cast of characters—

Buddy Baxter	Joseph Santley
Raymond Henderson	Alfred Kappeler
Dave Frankel	Harry Rosenthal
Kitty Le Voe	Edith Broder
Lottie	Paula MacLean
Pamela Baxter	Sue Conway
Amy Martin	Edna Hibbard
Eddie Clark	Walter Fenner
Gene Gallo	William McFadden
Stoop	Paul Porter
Molly Jones	Elsie Karlin
Ferguson	John R. Hamilton
Fulton	David Herblin
Brown	Edward Emerson
McCormack	Clarence Bellair
Cohen	Maurice Barrett
Mr. Bullock	Edmund Elton
Lena Bullock	Nana Bryant
Miss Ward	Irene Shirley
Dr. Ames	G. Lester Paul
A Remote Control Operator	Austin Coughlin

Prologue. Act I.—Scene 1—Buddy Baxter's Apartment. Scene 2—Ferguson's Office at the Ferguson, Fulton, Brown, McCormack & Cohen Advertising Agency. Act II.—Scene 1—Same as Scene 1, Act I. Scene 2—A Barn in the Berkshires. Act III.—Same as Scene 1, Act I.
Staged by Arthur Hurley.

Buddy Baxter, having made his first hit before the microphone the day he was suffering a severe head cold, is compelled by his manager, Dave Frankel, to sit in draughts and otherwise expose himself to atmospheric conditions that will give his adenoidal tones a certain permanency. Pamela, Buddy's wife, objects to his crooning because it diverts his attention from his home

interests. Buddy is abducted by Eddie Clark, gangster, the day
the Mellow cigarette hour is to be inaugurated with a Baxter program. A physician is about to remove the Baxter tonsils by force
when the crooner is rescued. The home situation is corrected
when Pamela also goes radio and becomes the voice of an imported toilet soap.

YEAH MAN

(4 performances)

A Negro revue in two acts by Leigh Whipper and Billy Mills;
lyrics and music by Al Wilson, Charles Weinberg, and Ken
Macomber. Produced by Walter Campbell and Jesse Wank at
the Park Lane Theatre, New York, May 26, 1932.

Principals engaged—

Mantan Moreland
Rose Henderson
Lily Yuen
Hilda Perleno
Peggy Phillips
Marcus Slayter
Adele Hargraves
"Jarahal"
  Staged by Walter Campbell.

Melodee Four
Eddie Rector
Billy Mills
Leigh Whipper
Walter Brogsdale
Russell Graves
Harry Fiddler

* BRIDAL WISE

(24 performances)

A comedy in three acts by Albert Hackett and Frances Goodrich. Produced by Sigourney Thayer at the Cort Theatre, New
York, May 30, 1932.

Cast of characters—

Tom...Lew Payton
Mary..Ella Gordon
Harry..Victor Beecroft
Peter Burroughs.....................................Jackie Kelk
Sam...Raymond Bishop
Joyce Burroughs.....................................Madge Kennedy
                          (Courtesy Charles L. Wagner)
Gidney Weems..Raymond Walburn
Alan Burroughs......................................James Rennie
Fay Niles...Thelma Marsh
Major Weston..George Wright, Jr.
Gordon..Ben Lackland
Mrs. Chace..Sara Perry
Babe Harrington.....................................Blyth Daly
  Acts I and II.—Courtyard at the Burroughs' Country Place in
Maryland. Act III.—Joyce's Bedroom.
  Staged by Frank Craven.

While Joyce Burroughs has been quarantined with her young
son and the whooping cough her husband, Alan, takes up with

and is taken up by a horsy set in Maryland. Joyce resents Alan's attentions to his new friends and divorce follows a quarrel. Joyce marries her attorney, Gidney Weems, and Alan marries Babe Harrington. The day the new honeymoons are to start the boy, Peter Burroughs, is sent home from school. No one wants Peter on a honeymoon. The Burroughs are forced to stay home and look after him, particularly after he has eaten himself into a fever, and this brings about a reconciliation.

CHRISTOPHER COMES ACROSS

(7 performances)

A farce comedy in three acts by Hawthorne Hurst. Produced by Brock Pemberton at the Royale Theatre, New York, May 31, 1932.

Cast of characters—

Duke of Medinia Sedonia	Kirby Hawkes
Don Alfonso	Ernest Lawford
Isadoro	Patrick Glasgow
King Ferdinand of Spain	Walter Kingsford
Zita	Gilda Oakleaf
Captain Christopher Columbus	Tullio Carminati
Beatriz, The Marchioness of Moya	Fania Marinoff
The Marquis of Moya	Charles Brown
Queen Isabella of Spain	Patricia Calvert
Lady in Waiting	Irene Homer
Don Sebastian De Corazilla	Hamilton Brooks
Prince Otar of Homamb	Gregory Gaye
Dolores De Arana	Betty Laurence
Hernando De Talavero	Gilbert Douglas
A Porter	Clarence Redd
A Sentry	John Gilchrist

Act I.—Anteroom of the Royal Counting House in the Palace of Ferdinand and Isabella. Seville, Spain, 1492. Acts II and III.—The Living-room of Christopher's Apartment in the Palace.
Staged by Antoinette Perry and Brock Pemberton.

Christopher Columbus, having left the court of Portugal for the court's good, trips over to Spain. Spain, being at war with the Moors, is short of able-bodied men at court and Christopher is much sought after by both the ladies in waiting and Isabella, the queen, who is quite willing to pawn her jewels to please him. Christopher has lost interest in his desire to sail west to prove the world is round by coming again to India, but the second or third time King Ferdinand finds the Columbus suite crowded with ladies and Isabella he urges Columbus aboard the Santa Maria.

BLUE MONDAY

(20 performances)

A play in three acts by Benson Inge. Produced by Barnett Warren at the Provincetown Playhouse, New York, June 2, 1932.

Cast of characters—

```
Paul.........................................Theodore St. John
Lucy.................................................Claire Carleton
Frank.............................................Frederic Tozere
Mr. Kampfer................................George M. Clough
Luigi...............................................Bruno Wick
Manny.........................................William Maxwell
Bill Mayes.....................................Burton Mallory
Hogan...........................................Louis E. Miller
Henders.........................................John W. Bayley
Tom-Tom......................................James Dunmore
Antoinette.........................................Mitzi Grill
Regina.............................................Vera Walton
Mamie.........................................Amelia Komptish
Tony................................................Edward D'Oize
Acts I, II and III.—Corner of Factory Room.
  Staged by Barnett Warren.
```

Lucy and Frank, workers in a lampshade factory in New Jersey, are engaged to marry. Lucy comes to question the possibility of happiness with Frank as the wedding day approaches. Paul, an artist from the city, attracts and charms Lucy and she deliberately seeks to attract him. Frank, furiously jealous, kills them both.

HIRED HUSBAND

(19 performances)

A comedy in three acts by August L. Stern. Produced by Robert Sterling at the Bijou Theatre, New York, June 3, 1932.

Cast of characters—

```
Andrew Starr...................................Paul Everton
Edward Gray...............................Herbert Ashton, Jr.
Blodgett.........................................Isadore Marcil
Nina Travis.......................................Terry Carroll
Helen Brooks....................................Flavia Arcaro
Walter Brooks..................................Waldo Edwards
  Acts I, II and III.—Home of Andrew Starr, Gramercy Park, New
York.
  Staged by Alfred White.
```

Because Nina Travis cannot marry Walter Brooks, a sweetheart of her youth, before he is 23, without causing Brooks to sacrifice a large inheritance, and because she is to bear Brooks a child, a temporary husband is engaged for her. Edward Gray, adventuring cattleman from Montana, down and out in New York, agrees to take the job. For three months he is the devoted but distant husband of Nina, falls partly in love with her, but holds to his bargain and disappears at the end of his three months.

* HEY NONNY NONNY!

(16 performances)

A musical revue in two acts by Max and Nathaniel Lief and Michael H. Cleary. Produced by Forrest C. Haring and John H. del Bondio at the Shubert Theatre, New York, June 6, 1932.

Principals engaged—

Frank Morgan
Dorothy McNulty
Richie Craig, Jr.
Ann Seymour
Jack McCauley
Joan Carter-Waddell
Jerry Norris
    Staged by Alexander Leftwich.

Ernest Sharpe
Ralph Sanford
Mildred Tolle
Billie Burns
Frances Maddux
Maurice Brown

Principal songs—"Wouldn't It Be Wonderful?" and "Tell Me Something About Yourself."

TROILUS AND CRESSIDA

(8 performances)

Shakesperian tragedy. Arranged in three acts by Henry Herbert. Produced by the Players Club at the Broadway Theatre, New York, June 6, 1932.

Cast of characters—

Prologue spoken by	Augustin Duncan
Priam	F. Sayre Crawley
Hector	Herbert Ranson
Troilus	Jerome Lawler
Paris	Charles Brokaw
Deiphobus	Alan Campbell
Helenus	Philip Leigh
Margarelon	John Kramer
Aeneas	Leo G. Carrol
Antenor	Gordon Hart
Calchas	Howard Kyle
Pandarus	Eugene Powers
Agamemnon	Eliot Cabot
Menelaus	P. J. Kelly
Achilles	Reynolds Evans
Ajax	Charles Coburn
Ulysses	William Sams
Nestor	Robert Le Sueur
Diomedes	Allyn Joslyn
Patroclus	George Gaul
Thersites	Otis Skinner

Alexander.....................................Burford Hampden
Servant to Paris...............................Ruth Garland
Servant to Diomedes...........................Edwin T. Emery
Helen..Blanche Yurka
Andromache....................................Ivah Coburn
Cassandra.....................................Eileen Huban
Cressida......................................Edith Barrett
Queen Hecuba.................................Margherita Sargent
   Act I.—Scene 1—City of Troy. 2—The Grecian Camp. Act II.—
Scenes 1, 3—Pandarus's Garden. 2—Grecian Camp. Act III.—Scene
1—Grecian Camp. 2—Priam's Palace. 3—The Plains.
   Staged by Henry Herbert.

Shakespeare's satirical fling at the Trojan wars. Save for an
amateur production by the Yale Dramatic Society some years
back this is the only production ever given the tragedy in
America.

THE BOY FRIEND

(15 performances)

A comedy in three acts by John Montague. Produced by Carl
Hunt and George Miller at the Morosco Theatre, New York,
June 7, 1932.

Cast of characters—

Frizzletop....................................Faye Martyn
Goldie..Marcella Swanson
Aunt Belle....................................Gertrude Maitland
Helen...Mary O'Brien
Donnie..Miriam Stuart
The Eel.......................................Brian Donleavy
Roger...Walter Glass
Innocent......................................Jessie James
Hattie..Kathleen Karr
Raincoat......................................Edward Leiter
Daisy...Emily Graham
Pierman.......................................George Probert
Mrs. Pierman..................................Charlotte Walker
Butler..Harold Heaton
Maloney.......................................John Morrissey
Flannery......................................Ronald Hammond
A Man...Eugene Weber
   Acts I, II and III.—Belle's Apartment in the West Fifties, New
York City.
   Staged by Carl Hunt.

Donnie, a chorus girl, living with other girls at Aunt Belle's
boarding house in New York, has succumbed to the blandish-
ments of a cheating booking agent called Raincoat. Daisy, her
friend, has written to Donnie's brother, who turns out to be a
tough customer called the Eel who is wanted by the police. The
Eel comes to New York, threatens to force Raincoat to marry his
sister, after which he will be duly bumped off. In the mix-up
Roger, a small-town reporter trying to make good in the big city
and engaged to Daisy, comes to suspect Daisy when a dead man
is found in the room she shares with Donnie. It turns out that

the dead man is a federal agent chasing Raincoat, who is a dope peddler on the side.

BACK FIRE

(8 performances)

A play in three acts by Jerrold Robert. Produced by the Broome Stagers at the Vanderbilt Theatre, New York, June 13, 1932.

Cast of characters—

Helen..Alice Campbell
Doris Urquehart...Doris Packer
Eugene Breckenridge....................................Donald Gallaher
Betty Davis...Barbara Beals
Arthur Sinclaire..Alexander Stewart
Mrs. Davis...Alice May Tuck
Sally Newton...Mabel Taliaferro
George Davis..Robert Ober
Doctor Norris..Alf Helton
    Acts I, II and III.—At the Davis home.
    Staged by Maurice McRae.

Sally Newton has given herself to her fiancé, Will Davis. Will dies and Sally is wooed by his brother George. Without mentioning names Sally insists on telling George there has been another man. George draws away and later marries Doris Urquehart, who has had many lovers but kept them to herself. George and Doris are unhappy. Sally comes back and comforts George, who eventually finds out about Doris and divorces her so he can marry Sally.

* THAT'S GRATITUDE

(8 performances)

A play in three acts by Frank Craven. Revived by O. E. Wee, Inc., at the Waldorf Theatre, New York, June 16, 1932.

Cast of characters—

Robert Grant...Taylor Holmes
Thomas Maxwell..J. C. Nugent
Dr. Lombard...Howard Hall
Bellboy..Arthur Mack
Lelia Maxwell...Frances McHugh
William North...Warren Ashe
Mrs. Maxwell..Maida Reade
Delia Maxwell...Amy Atkinson
Nora..Helen Mehrmann
Clayton Lorimer.......................................Gerald Kent
    Prologue—Hotel Room in Dana House in Iowa. Acts I, II and III.—Home of the Maxwells, Hutchinson, Kansas.
    Staged by Robert Burton.

This was a popular-priced revival of the Craven comedy that ran originally for 197 performances at the John Golden Theatre, New York, during the season of 1930-31. During that run Mr. Craven played at different times both leading rôles. He started as Robert Grant and later replaced George Barbier as Thomas Maxwell during Mr. Barbier's illness.

STATISTICAL SUMMARY

(LAST SEASON PLAYS WHICH ENDED RUNS AFTER
JUNE 15, 1931)

Plays	Number Performances	Plays	Number Performances
As Husbands Go	148	Old Man Murphy	64
Band Wagon, The	260	Once in a Lifetime	406
Barretts of Wimpole Street, The	370	Patience	16
Crazy Quilt	79	Precedent	184
Ebb Tide	16	Private Lives	256
Gasoline Gypsies	3	Rhapsody in Black	80
Grand Hotel	459	Third Little Show	136
Green Pastures, The	640	Tomorrow and Tomorrow	206
In the Best of Families	159	Unexpected Husband	127
Modern Virgin, A	53	You Said It	192

LONG RUNS ON BROADWAY

To June 15, 1932

Plays	Number Performances	Plays	Number Performances
Abie's Irish Rose	2,532	Kiki	600
Lightnin'	1,291	Blossom Time	592
The Bat	867	Show Boat	572
The Ladder	789	The Show-off	571
The First Year	760	Sally	570
Seventh Heaven	704	The Green Pastures	640
Peg o' My Heart	692	Strictly Dishonorable	557
East Is West	680	Good News	551
Irene	670	The Music Master	540
A Trip to Chinatown	657	The Boomerang	522
Rain	648	Blackbirds	518
Is Zat So	618	Sunny	517
Student Prince	608	The Vagabond King	511
Broadway	603	The New Moon	509
Adonis	603	Shuffle Along	504
Street Scene	601	Bird in Hand	500

PULITZER PRIZE WINNERS

"For the original American play performed in New York which shall best represent the educational value and power of the stage in raising the standard of good morals, good taste and good manners."—The Will of Joseph Pulitzer, dated April 16, 1904.

In 1929 the advisory board, which, according to the terms of the will, "shall have the power in its discretion to suspend or to change any subject or subjects . . . if in the judgment of the board such suspension, changes or substitutions shall be conducive to the public good," decided to eliminate from the above paragraph relating to the prize-winning play the words "in raising the standard of good morals, good taste and good manners."

The committee awards to date have been:

1917-18—Why Marry? by Jesse Lynch Williams
1918-19—None
1919-20—Miss Lulu Bett, by Zona Gale
1920-21—Beyond the Horizon, by Eugene O'Neill
1921-22—Anna Christie, by Eugene O'Neill
1922-23—Icebound, by Owen Davis
1923-24—Hell-bent fer Heaven, by Hatcher Hughes
1924-25—They Knew What They Wanted, by Sidney Howard
1925-26—Craig's Wife, by George Kelly
1926-27—In Abraham's Bosom, by Paul Green
1927-28—Strange Interlude, by Eugene O'Neill
1928-29—Street Scene, by Elmer Rice
1929-30—The Green Pastures, by Marc Connelly
1930-31—Alison's House, by Susan Glaspell
1931-32—Of Thee I Sing, by George S. Kaufman, Morrie Ryskind, Ira and George Gershwin.

PREVIOUS VOLUMES OF BEST PLAYS

Selections of the ten best plays of each season since 1919-1920 in preceding volumes of this Year Book of the Drama are as follows:

1919-1920

"Abraham Lincoln," by John Drinkwater. Published by Houghton Mifflin Co., Boston.
"Clarence," by Booth Tarkington.
"Beyond the Horizon," by Eugene G. O'Neill. Published by Boni & Liveright, Inc., New York.
"Déclassée," by Zoe Akins.
"The Famous Mrs. Fair," by James Forbes.
"The Jest," by Sem Benelli. (American adaptation by Edward Sheldon.)
"Jane Clegg," by St. John Ervine. Published by Henry Holt & Co., New York.
"Mamma's Affair," by Rachel Barton Butler.
"Wedding Bells," by Salisbury Field.
"Adam and Eva," by George Middleton and Guy Bolton.

1920-1921

"Deburau," by H. Granville Barker. Published by G. P. Putnam's Sons, New York.
"The First Year," by Frank Craven.
"Enter Madame," by Gilda Varesi and Dolly Byrne. Published by G. P. Putnam's Sons, New York.
"The Green Goddess," by William Archer. Published by Alfred A. Knopf, New York.
"Liliom," by Ferenc Molnar. Published by Boni & Liveright, New York.
"Mary Rose," by James M. Barrie.
"Nice People," by Rachel Crothers.
"The Bad Man," by Porter Emerson Browne. Published by G. P. Putnam's Sons, New York.
"The Emperor Jones," by Eugene G. O'Neill. Published by Boni & Liveright, New York.

"The Skin Game," by John Galsworthy. Published by Charles Scribner's Sons, New York.

1921-1922

"Anna Christie," by Eugene G. O'Neill. Published by Boni & Liveright, New York.

"A Bill of Divorcement," by Clemence Dane. Published by the Macmillan Company, New York.

"Dulcy," by George S. Kaufman and Marc Connelly. Published by G. P. Putnam's Sons, New York.

"He Who Gets Slapped," by Leonid Andreyev. Published by Brentano's.

"Six Cylinder Love," by William Anthony McGuire.

"The Hero," by Gilbert Emery.

"The Dover Road," by Alan Alexander Milne.

"Ambush," by Arthur Richman.

"The Circle," by William Somerset Maugham.

"The Nest," by Paul Geraldy and Grace George.

1922-1923

"Rain," by John Colton and Clemence Randolph.

"Loyalties," by John Galsworthy. Published by Charles Scribner's Sons, New York.

"Icebound," by Owen Davis. Published by Little, Brown & Company, Boston.

"You and I," by Philip Barry. Published by Brentano's, New York.

"The Fool," by Channing Pollock. Published by Brentano's, New York.

"Merton of the Movies," by George Kaufman and Marc Connelly, based on the novel of the same name by Harry Leon Wilson.

"Why Not?" by Jesse Lynch Williams.

"The Old Soak," by Don Marquis. Published by Doubleday, Page & Company.

"R.U.R.," by Karel Capek. Translated by Paul Selver. Published by Doubleday, Page & Company.

"Mary the 3d," by Rachel Crothers. Published by Brentano's, New York.

1923-1924

"The Swan," by Ferenc Molnar. Published by Boni & Liveright, New York.

"Outward Bound," by Sutton Vane. Published by Boni & Liveright, New York.

"The Show-off," by George Kelly. Published by Little, Brown & Company, Boston.

"The Changelings," by Lee Wilson Dodd. Published by E. P. Dutton & Company, New York.

"Chicken Feed," by Guy Bolton. Published by Samuel French, New York and London.

"Sun-Up," by Lula Vollmer. Published by Brentano's, New York.

"Beggar on Horseback," by George Kaufman and Marc Connelly. Published by Boni & Liveright, New York.

"Tarnish," by Gilbert Emery. Published by Brentano's, New York.

"The Goose Hangs High," by Lewis Beach. Published by Little, Brown & Company, Boston.

"Hell-bent fer Heaven," by Hatcher Hughes. Published by Harper Bros., New York.

1924-1925

"What Price Glory?" by Laurence Stallings and Maxwell Anderson.

"They Knew What They Wanted," by Sidney Howard. Published by Doubleday, Page & Company, New York.

"Desire Under the Elms," by Eugene G. O'Neill. Published by Boni & Liveright, New York.

"The Firebrand," by Edwin Justus Mayer. Published by Boni & Liveright, New York.

"Dancing Mothers," by Edgar Selwyn and Edmund Goulding.

"Mrs. Partridge Presents," by Mary Kennedy and Ruth Warren.

"The Fall Guy," by James Gleason and George Abbott.

"The Youngest," by Philip Barry. Published by Samuel French, New York.

"Minick," by Edna Ferber and George S. Kaufman. Published by Doubleday, Page & Company, New York.

"Wild Birds," by Dan Totheroh. Published by Doubleday, Page & Company, New York.

1925-1926

"Craig's Wife," by George Kelly. Published by Little, Brown & Company, Boston.

"The Great God Brown," by Eugene G. O'Neill. Published by Boni & Liveright, New York.

"The Green Hat," by Michael Arlen.

"The Dybbuk," by S. Ansky, Henry G. Alsberg-Winifred Katzin translation. Published by Boni & Liveright, New York.

"The Enemy," by Channing Pollock. Published by Brentano's, New York.

"The Last of Mrs. Cheyney," by Frederick Lonsdale.

"Bride of the Lamb," by William Hurlbut. Published by Boni & Liveright, New York.

"The Wisdom Tooth," by Marc Connelly. Published by George H. Doran & Company, New York.

"The Butter and Egg Man," by George Kaufman. Published by Boni & Liveright, New York.

"Young Woodley," by John Van Druten. Published by Simon and Schuster, New York.

1926-1927

"Broadway," by Philip Dunning and George Abbott. Published by George H. Doran Company, New York.

"Saturday's Children," by Maxwell Anderson. Published by Longmans, Green & Company, New York.

"Chicago," by Maurine Watkins. Published by Alfred A. Knopf, Inc., New York.

"The Constant Wife," by William Somerset Maugham. Published by George H. Doran Company, New York.

"The Play's the Thing," by Ferenc Molnar and P. G. Wodehouse. Published by Brentano's, New York.

"The Road to Rome," by Robert Emmet Sherwood. Published by Charles Scribner's Sons, New York.

"The Silver Cord," by Sidney Howard. Published by Charles Scribner's Sons, New York.

"The Cradle Song," by John Garrett Underhill. Published by E. P. Dutton & Company.

"Daisy Mayme," by George Kelly. Published by Little, Brown & Company, Boston.

"In Abraham's Bosom," by Paul Green. Published by Robert M. McBride & Company, New York.

1927-1928

"Strange Interlude," by Eugene G. O'Neill. Published by Boni & Liveright, New York.

"The Royal Family," by Edna Ferber and George Kaufman. Published by Doubleday, Doran & Company, New York.

"Burlesque," by George Manker Watters. Published by Doubleday, Doran & Company.

"Coquette," by George Abbott and Ann Bridgers. Published by Longmans, Green & Company, New York, London, Toronto.

"Behold the Bridegroom," by George Kelly. Published by Little, Brown & Company, Boston.

"Porgy," by DuBose Heyward. Published by Doubleday, Doran & Company, New York.

"Paris Bound," by Philip Barry. Published by Samuel French, New York.

"Escape," by John Galsworthy. Published by Charles Scribner's Sons, New York.

"The Racket," by Bartlett Cormack. Published by Samuel French, New York.

"The Plough and the Stars," by Sean O'Casey. Published by the Macmillan Company, New York.

1928-1929

"Street Scene," by Elmer Rice. Published by Samuel French, New York.

"Journey's End," by R. C. Sheriff. Published by Brentano's, New York.

"Wings over Europe," by Robert Nichols and Maurice Browne. Published by Covici-Friede, New York.

"Holiday," by Philip Barry. Published by Samuel French, New York.

"The Front Page," by Ben Hecht and Charles MacArthur. Published by Covici-Friede, New York.

"Let Us Be Gay," by Rachel Crothers. Published by Samuel French, New York.

"Machinal," by Sophie Treadwell.

"Little Accident," by Floyd Dell and Thomas Mitchell.

"Gypsy," by Maxwell Anderson.

"The Kingdom of God," by G. Martinez Sierra. Published by E. P. Dutton & Company, New York.

1929-1930

"The Green Pastures," by Marc Connelly (adapted from "Ol' Man Adam and His Chillun," by Roark Bradford). Published by Farrar & Rinehart, Inc., New York.

"The Criminal Code," by Martin Flavin. Published by Horace Liveright, New York.

"Berkeley Square," by John Balderstone. Published by the Macmillan Company, New York.

"Strictly Dishonorable," by Preston Sturges. Published by Horace Liveright, New York.

"The First Mrs. Fraser," by St. John Ervine. Published by the Macmillan Company, New York.

"The Last Mile," by John Wexley. Published by Samuel French, New York.

"June Moon," by Ring W. Lardner and George S. Kaufman. Published by Charles Scribner's Sons, New York.

"Michael and Mary," by A. A. Milne. Published by Chatto & Windus, London.

"Death Takes a Holiday," by Walter Ferris (adapted from the Italian of Alberto Casella). Published by Samuel French, New York.

"Rebound," by Donald Ogden Stewart. Published by Samuel French, New York.

1931-1932

"Elizabeth the Queen," by Maxwell Anderson. Published by Longmans, Green & Co., New York and London.

"Tomorrow and Tomorrow," by Philip Barry. Published by Samuel French, New York and London.

"Once in a Lifetime," by George S. Kaufman and Moss Hart. Published by Farrar and Rinehart, New York.

"Green Grow the Lilacs," by Lynn Riggs. Published by Samuel French, New York and London.

"As Husbands Go," by Rachel Crothers. Published by Samuel French, New York and London.

"Alison's House," by Susan Glaspell. Published by Samuel French, New York and London.

"Five-Star Final," by Louis Weitzenkorn. Published by Samuel French, New York and London.

"Overture," by William Bolitho. Published by Simon & Shuster, New York.

"The Barretts of Wimpole Street," by Rudolf Besier. Published by Little, Brown & Co., Boston.

"Grand Hotel," by Vicki Baum.

WHERE AND WHEN THEY WERE BORN

Abbott, George ....Hamburg, N. Y. 1895
Adams, Maude ....Salt Lake City, Utah 1872
Aherne, Brian ....King's Norton, England ..1902
Alexander, Katherine ....Arkansas 1901
Allen, Viola ....Huntsville, Ala. 1869
Ames, Robert ....Hartford, Conn. 1893
Ames, Winthrop ....North Easton, Mass. 1871
Anderson, Judith ....Australia 1898
Andrews, Ann ....Los Angeles, Cal. 1895
Anglin, Margaret ....Ottawa, Canada 1876
Anson, A. E. ....London, England 1879
Arliss, George ....London, England 1868
Arthur, Julia ....Hamilton, Ont. 1869
Astaire, Adele ....Omaha, Neb. 1900
Astaire, Fred ....Omaha, Neb. 1899
Atwell, Roy ....Syracuse, N. Y. 1880
Atwill, Lionel ....London, England 1885

Bainter, Fay ....Los Angeles, Cal. 1892
Barbee, Richard ....Lafayette, Ind. 1887
Barrett, Edith ....Roxbury, Mass. 1904
Barrie, James Matthew ....Kirriemuir, N. B. 1860
Barrymore, Ethel ....Philadelphia, Pa. 1879
Barrymore, John ....Philadelphia, Pa. 1882
Barrymore, Lionel ....London, England 1878
Bates, Blanche ....Portland, Ore. 1873
Best, Edna ....England 1901
Beecher, Janet ....Chicago, Ill. 1884
Ben-Ami, Jacob ....Minsk, Russia 1890
Bennett, Richard ....Cass County, Ind. 1873
Bennett, Wilda ....Asbury Park, N. J. 1894
Berlin, Irving ....Russia 1888
Binney, Constance ....Philadelphia, Pa. 1900
Blackmer, Sidney ....Salisbury, N. C. 1896
Boland, Mary ....Detroit, Mich. 1880
Bordoni, Irene ....Paris, France 1895

Brady, Alice ....New York 1892
Brady, William A. ....San Francisco, Cal. 1863
Brian, Donald ....St. Johns, N. F. 1877
Brice, Fannie ....Brooklyn, N. Y. 1891
Broadhurst, George H. ....England 1866
Bryant, Charles ....England 1879
Buchanan, Jack ....England 1892
Buchanan, Thompson ....Louisville, Ky. 1877
Burke, Billie ....Washington, D. C. 1885
Burton, Frederick ....Indiana 1871
Byron, Arthur ....Brooklyn, N. Y. 1872

Cahill, Marie ....Brooklyn, N. Y. 1871
Calhern, Louis ....New York 1895
Cantor, Eddie ....New York 1894
Campbell, Mrs. Patrick ......England 1865
Carle, Richard ....Somerville, Mass. 1871
Carlisle, Alexandra ....Yorkshire, England 1886
Carr, Alexander ....Russia 1878
Carter, Mrs. Leslie ....Lexington, Ky. 1862
Catlett, Walter ....San Francisco, Cal. 1889
Cawthorne, Joseph ....New York 1868
Chaplin, Charles Spencer .....London 1889
Chatterton, Ruth ....New York 1893
Cherry, Charles ....England 1872
Churchill, Burton ....Toronto, Can. 1876
Claire, Ina ....Washington, D. C. 1892
Clarke, Marguerite ....Cincinnati, Ohio 1887
Cliffe, H. Cooper ....England 1862
Clifford, Kathleen ....Charlottesville, Va. 1887
Coburn, Charles ....Macon, Ga. 1877
Coghlan, Gertrude ....England 1879
Coghlan, Rose ....Petersborough, England ...1850
Cohan, George M. ....Providence, R. I. 1878
Cohan, Georgette ....Los Angeles, Cal. 1900
Colbert, Claudette ....Paris 1905
Collier, Constance ....Windsor, England 1882
Collier, William ....New York 1866
Collinge, Patricia ....Dublin, Ireland 1894
Collins, José ....London, England 1896
Connolly, Walter ....Cincinnati, Ohio 1888
Conroy, Frank ....London, England 1885
Cooper, Violet Kemble ......London, England 1890

Cornell, Katharine ....Buffalo, N. Y. 1900
Corrigan, Emmett ....Amsterdam, Holland 1871
Corthell, Herbert ....Boston, Mass. 1875
Courtenay, William ....Worcester, Mass. 1875
Courtleigh, William ....Guelph, Ont. 1869
Coward, Noel ....England 1899
Cowl, Jane ....Boston, Mass. 1887
Craven, Frank ....Boston, Mass. 1880
Crews, Laura Hope ....San Francisco, Cal. 1880
Crosman, Henrietta ....Wheeling, W. Va. 1865
Crothers, Rachel ....Bloomington, Ill. 1878
Cumberland, John ....St. John, N. B. 1880

Dale, Margaret ....Philadelphia, Pa. 1880
Dalton, Charles ....England 1864
Daniels, Frank ....Dayton, Ohio 1860
Dawn, Hazel ....Ogden, Utah 1891
Day, Edith ....Minneapolis, Minn. 1896
De Angelis, Jefferson ....San Francisco, Cal. 1859
Dean, Julia ....St. Paul, Minn. 1880
De Cordoba, Pedro ....New York 1881
Dillingham, Charles B. ....Hartford, Conn. 1868
Dinehart, Allan ....Missoula, Mont. 1889
Dixey, Henry E. ....Boston, Mass. 1859
Dodson, John E. ....London, England 1857
Doro, Marie ....Duncannon, Pa. 1882
D'Orsay, Lawrence ....England 1860
Dressler, Eric ....Brooklyn, N. Y. 1900
Dressler, Marie ....Cobourg, Canada 1869
Drew, Louise ....New York 1884
Dunn, Emma ....England 1875
Dupree, Minnie ....San Francisco, Cal. 1875

Edeson, Robert ....Baltimore, Md. 1868
Eldridge, Florence ....Brooklyn, N. Y. 1901
Ellis, Mary ....New York 1900
Elliston, Grace ....Wheeling, W. Va. 1881
Ellinger, Desirée ....Manchester, Vt. 1895
Elliott, Gertrude ....Rockland, Me. 1874
Elliott, Maxine ....Rockland, Me. 1871
Eltinge, Julian ....Boston, Mass. 1883
Emerson, John ....Sandusky, Ohio 1874
Errol, Leon ....Sydney, Australia 1881

Harris, Sam H. ....New York 1872
Harrison, Richard B. ....London, Ontario 1864
Hayes, Helen ....Washington, D. C. 1900
Hazzard, John E. ....New York 1881
Hedman, Martha ....Sweden 1888
Heggie, O. P. ....Australia 1879
Heming, Violet ....Leeds, England 1893
Herbert, Evelyn ....Brooklyn, N. Y. 1900
Herne, Chrystal ....Dorchester, Mass. 1883
Hodge, William ....Albion, N. Y. 1874
Hopkins, Miriam ....Savannah, Ga. 1907
Hopper, DeWolf ....New York 1858
Hopper, Edna Wallace ....San Francisco, Cal. 1874
Holmes, Taylor ....Newark, N. J. 1872
Howard, Leslie ....London, England 1890
Hull, Henry ....Louisville, Ky. 1893
Hunter, Glenn ....Highland Mills, N. Y. 1896
Huston, Walter ....Toronto 1884

Inescort, Frieda ....Hitchin, Scotland 1905
Irving, Isabel ....Bridgeport, Conn. 1871
Irwin, May ....Whitby, Ont. 1862

Janis, Elsie ....Delaware, Ohio 1889
Joel, Clara ....Jersey City, N. J. 1890
Johann, Zita ....Hungary 1904
Jolson, Al. ....Washington, D. C. 1883

Kaufman, George S. ....Pittsburgh, Pa. 1889
Keane, Doris ....Michigan 1885
Kennedy, Madge ....Chicago, Ill. 1890
Kerrigan, J. M. ....Dublin, Ireland 1885
Kerr, Geoffrey ....London, England 1895
Kershaw, Willette ....Clifton Heights, Mo. 1890
Kosta, Tessa ....Chicago, Ill. 1893
Kruger, Alma ....Pittsburgh, Pa. 1880
Kruger, Otto ....Toledo, Ohio 1895

Lackaye, Wilton ....Virginia 1862
Larrimore, Francine ....Russia 1898
La Rue, Grace ....Kansas City, Mo. 1882
Lauder, Harry ....Portobello, England 1870
Lawton, Thais ....Louisville, Ky. 1881

Nazimova, Alla ....Crimea, Russia 1879
Nielsen, Alice ....Nashville, Tenn. 1876
Nugent, J. C. ....Miles, Ohio 1875
Nugent, Elliott ....Dover, Ohio 1900

O'Connell, Hugh ....New York 1891
Olcott, Chauncey ....Providence, R. I. 1862
O'Neill, Eugene Gladstone ....New York 1888
O'Neil, Nance ....Oakland, Cal. 1875

Painter, Eleanor ....Iowa 1890
Pawle, Lenox ....London, England 1872
Pennington, Ann ....Philadelphia, Pa. 1898
Perkins, Osgood ....Boston, Mass. 1892
Philips, Mary ....New London, Conn. 1901
Pickford, Mary ....Toronto 1893
Post, Guy Bates ....Seattle, Wash. 1875
Power, Tyrone ....London, England 1869
Powers, James T. ....New York 1862
Pryor, Roger ....New York City 1901

Quartermaine, Leon ....Richmond, England 1876

Rambeau, Marjorie ....San Francisco, Cal. 1889
Rathbone, Basil ....Johannesburg 1892
Reed, Florence ....Philadelphia, Pa. 1883
Rennie, James ....Toronto, Canada 1890
Revelle, Hamilton ....Gibraltar 1872
Richman, Charles ....Chicago, Ill. 1870
Ring, Blanche ....Boston, Mass. 1876
Ring, Frances ....New York 1882
Robson, May ....Australia 1868
Ross, Thomas W. ....Boston, Mass. 1875
Royle, Selena ....New York 1905
Ruben, José ....Belgium 1886
Russell, Annie ....Liverpool, England 1864

Sanderson, Julia ....Springfield, Mass. 1887
Sands, Dorothy ....Cambridge, Mass. 1900
Santley, Joseph ....Salt Lake City 1889
Sawyer, Ivy ....London, England 1897
Scheff, Fritzi ....Vienna, Austria 1879
Scott, Cyril ....Ireland 1866

Segal, Vivienne ....Philadelphia, Pa. 1897
Selwyn, Edgar ....Cincinnati, Ohio 1875
Serrano, Vincent ....New York 1870
Shannon, Effie ....Cambridge, Mass. 1867
Shepley, Ruth ....New York 1889
Schildkraut, Joseph ....Bucharest, Roumania 1896
Sherman, Lowell ....San Francisco, Cal. 1885
Sidney, George ....New York 1876
Sidney, Sylvia ....New York 1910
Sinclair, Arthur ....Dublin, Ireland 1883
Sitgreaves, Beverly ....Charleston, S. C. 1867
Skelly, Hal ....Allegheny, Pa. 1891
Skinner, Otis ....Cambridgeport, Mass. 1857
Smith, Ben ....Waxahachie, Texas 1905
Sothern, Edward H. ....New Orleans, La. 1859
Spong, Hilda ....Australia 1875
Stahl, Rose ....Montreal, Canada 1872
Standing, Sir Guy ....London 1873
Starr, Frances ....Oneonta, N. Y. 1886
Stone, Fred ....Denver, Colo. 1873
Stone, Dorothy ....New York 1905
Sydney, Basil ....London 1894

Taliaferro, Edith ....New York 1892
Taliaferro, Mabel ....New York 1887
Tanguay, Eva ....Middletown, Conn. 1878
Taylor, Laurette ....New York 1884
Tell, Alma ....New York 1892
Tell, Olive ....New York 1894
Thomas, Augustus ....St. Louis, Mo. 1859
Thomas, John Charles ....Baltimore, Md. 1887
Tobin, Genevieve ....New York 1901
Tobin, Vivian ....New York 1903
Toler, Sidney ....Warrensburg, Mo. 1874
Truex, Ernest ....Red Hill, Mo. 1890
Tynan, Brandon ....Dublin, Ireland 1879

Ulric, Lenore ....New Ulm, Minn. 1897

Varesi, Gilda ....Milan, Italy 1887
Victor, Josephine ....Hungary 1891

Waldron, Charles ....New York 1877
Walker, June ....New York 1904

NECROLOGY

June 15, 1931—June 15, 1932

Edwin Wallace Dunn, press agent, 73. For 27 years general press representative for Cohan and Harris and for George M. Cohan; once manager for Frank Daniels, Stuart Robson, John Raymond and other stars; well known on Broadway. Born La Crosse, Wis.; died New York City, June 29, 1931.

Horace McVicker, manager, 75. Son of J. H. McVicker, owner of McVicker's Theatre, Chicago; manager of Abbey's and Knickerbocker Theatres, New York; managed Edwin Booth and Ethel Barrymore. Born Chicago; died Sea Bright, N. J., July 30, 1931.

Lester Lonergan, actor, 62. Prominent in support of Mrs. Fiske, Madame Modjeska, John Barrymore and John Drew; played in Western stock companies; first starring venture, "If I Were King"; in later years turned to stage direction; staged "East is West," "The Bad Man," "The Road to Rome," "The Command to Love," and, notably, John Drinkwater's "Abraham Lincoln"; married Amy Ricard, actress. Born Ireland; died Lynn, Mass., August 13, 1931.

Bessie McCoy (Mrs. Richard Harding Davis), comedienne, 45. Best known as one of the McCoy Sisters in the days of Weber and Fields; won fame as creator of Yama-Yama number in "Three Twins." Died Bayonne, France, Aug. 16, 1931.

Sir Hall Caine, playwright and novelist, 78. Wrote "The Christian," "The Eternal City," "The Prodigal Son," "The Bondman," "The Woman Thou Gavest Me," etc.; created Knight of the Order of the British Empire and Companion of Honour. Born Isle of Man; died Isle of Man, August 31, 1931.

Eugene Wyley Presbrey, actor and dramatist, 78. First appearance Boston Theatre, 1874; stage director for many years; plays included "The Courtship of Miles Standish," "A Ward of France," "A Virginia Courtship," "Raffles," "Mary, Mary, Quite Contrary," etc.; twelve years writing scenarios for Paramount and M-G-M; first wife Annie Russell. Born Williamsburg, Mass.; died Hollywood, September 9, 1931.

Lincoln A. Wagenhals, producer, 62. Associated with Collin Kemper in production of "Paid in Full," "Seven Days," "Seven Keys to Baldpate," and "The Bat"; married Hope Latham, actress. Born Columbus, Ohio; died Montrose-on-Hudson, September 11, 1931.

Lawrance d'Orsay (Dorset William Lawrance), actor, 71. Début London, 1877; understudy for Sir John Hare; first appearance in United States 1895 in "An Artist's Model"; supported Annie Russell in "The Royal Family"; starred in "Earl of Pawtucket"; was in all-star revival of "Trelawney of the Wells" with John Drew; was with Paul Robeson in London in "Othello." Born Northamptonshire, England; died London, September 13, 1931.

Arthur Schnitzler, dramatist, 69. Internationally known as dramatist through "Anatol" and other plays. Born Vienna, Austria; died Vienna, October 21, 1931.

Robert Williams, actor, 34. Known in Western stock companies; played in New York with Marjorie Rambeau in "Eyes of Youth"; later in "Abie's Irish Rose," "Friendly Enemies," "The Trial of Mary Dugan" and "Rebound." Born Morgantown, N. C.; died Hollywood, November 3, 1931.

Norma Phillips, actress, 38. Had parts in "The Bat," "Street Scene," and "Come Over Here"; known as "Mutual Girl" in 1914 through series of one-reel pictures. Born Baltimore, Md.; died New York City, November 11, 1931.

Wish Wynn, actress, 49. English comedienne famous for original creation of Cockney girl impersonations; toured world with character songs and sketches; played 600 performances in "The Great Adventure" in London. Born Croydon, England; died London, November 12, 1931.

Fritz Tiden, actor, 54. Member original company "When We Were Twenty-one" with Nat Goodwin and Maxine Elliott; with William Gillette in "Sherlock Holmes"; with Holbrook Blinn in "The Bad Man," and with Otis Skinner in "100 Years Old." Died Liberty, N. Y., November 12, 1931.

Mario Majeroni, actor, 61. Appeared in support of many stars; was playing in "Cynara" the afternoon before his death. Died New York City, November 18, 1931.

Robert Ames, actor, 42. Started with New England stock companies; 12 years with Henry Miller; 3 years with Municipal Stock, Northampton, Mass.; prominently cast in "Nice People," "The Hero," "It's a Boy," and "Icebound"; last ten years alternated between stage and screen; married Vivienne

Segal and later Helen Lambert, both actresses. Born Hartford, Conn.; died New York City, November 27, 1931.

Thomas MacLarnie, actor, 60. Started with James O'Neill in "Count of Monte Cristo" and "Virginius"; with Castle Square company, Boston; well known in both eastern and western stock companies; played "Judge" in "Lightnin' " from 1918 to 1921. Born North Adams, Mass.; died Brighton, Mass., December 1, 1931.

William Elliot, actor and manager, 52. Associated with David Belasco, and later partner of Morris Gest and F. Ray Comstock; started as violinist with Weems Juvenile Concert Party; later played in support of Herbert Kelcey and Elsie Shannon, Mary Shaw, Richard Mansfield, Robert Hilliard and David Warfield; scored success in "Madame X"; off stage four years; came back in "Experience"; married daughter of Belasco and later Mlle. Louise Lagrange of the Comedie Française. Born Boston, Mass.; died Lamb's Club, New York City, December 5, 1931.

J. E. Dodson, actor, 75. Retired in 1909 after active and distinguished service for thirty-three years; came to America with the Kendalls in 1889; joined Charles Frohman's Empire Theatre Co. playing in "The Bauble Shop," "The Masqueraders," etc.; starred in "An American Invasion" (1902), and "The House Next Door," (1909). Born England; died New York City, December 9, 1931.

Clarence Handyside, actor, 77. Fifty years on American stage, after starting in Canada; appeared in support of Julia Marlowe, Richard Mansfield, Elsie Ferguson and Laurette Taylor. Born Montreal, Canada; died Philadelphia, Pa., December 20, 1931.

George Wilson, actor, 82. Veteran comedian; member Boston Museum Stock Co. from 1876 until 1893; toured with Edwin Booth and in support of E. H. Sothern, Eleanor Robson and Annie Russell. Died Boston, Mass., December 24, 1931.

Tyrone Power, actor, 62. Member of illustrious stage family; grandfather of same name famous as interpreter of Irish characters in 19th century; both parents English actors of note; began stage career St. Augustine, Fla., in 1884; later became member of Augustine Daly Comedy Co.; prominent in support of William Faversham, Mrs. Fiske, Julia Marlowe, Mrs. Leslie Carter, Florence Roberts and Henrietta Crosman. Born London; died Hollywood, December 30, 1931.

George W. Monroe, actor, 75. Retired in 1923 after career devoted to Irish women comedy types; appeared with John C.
Rice on variety stage in "My Aunt Bridget" and similar
plays for 12 years. Born Philadelphia, Pa.; died Atlantic
City, N. J., January 29, 1932.

William Hodge, actor and playwright, 57. Popular character
comedian for many years; organized repertory company as
a boy; played with Rogers Bros. in "The Reign of Error";
with James A. Herne in "Sag Harbor"; starred in "The
Man from Home" for five years; wrote and played in "The
Road to Happiness," "Fixing Sister," "The Guest of Honor,"
"Beware of Dogs," "The Judge's Husband," "Inspector
Kennedy," and "The Old Rascal." Born Albion, N. Y.;
died Greenwich, Conn., Jan. 30, 1932.

Herbert Waring, actor, 75. Gave up school teaching to begin
stage career in England; came to America in 1888 with
Mary Anderson; assumed management of Imperial Theatre,
London, 1901; toured with Mrs. Patrick Campbell in "The
Second Mrs. Tanquary," "The Notorious Mrs. Ebbsmith,"
"Magda," etc.; played Iago to Forbes-Robertson's
"Othello"; last American performance with George Arliss
in "The Green Goddess" in 1920. Born St. James Place,
London; died London, Jan. 31, 1932.

Edgar Wallace, playwright, 56. Famous as prolific novelist and
dramatist; had six dramas playing at one time in London;
last play "The Green Pack," opened at Wyndham's Theatre,
London, the night before he died; best known play in America was "On the Spot." Born London; died Hollywood,
Feb. 10, 1932.

Minnie Maddern Fiske, actress, 67. A force in the American
theatre for half a century; first gained fame and stardom as
a comedienne in "Fogg's Ferry," "Caprice," etc.; retired
from stage for five years; came back in "Tess of the
D'Urbervilles"; successfully fought the theatrical trust; organized the Manhattan company for the production of a
series of plays including notably "Leah Kleschna," "Salvation Nell," "The New York Idea," etc.; played a number
of Ibsen heroines including Hedda Gabler, Rebecca West,
and Mrs. Alving; last New York appearance in "Ladies of
the Jury"; was playing "Against the Wind" on tour when
illness forced her retirement; married Legrand White, orchestra leader, and later Harrison Grey Fiske. Born New
Orleans, La.; died Hollis, L. I., Feb. 15, 1932.

George McFarlane, baritone, 55. Prominently cast in many Gilbert and Sullivan revivals; last years devoted to vaudeville and the screen. Born Kingston, Ontario; died Hollywood, Feb. 22, 1932.

Johanna Gadski, operatic soprano, 60. Popular member of Metropolitan Company twenty-two years; sang in vaudeville; in 1930 toured United States and Germany as head of German (Wagner) Opera Company; married Captain Hans Tauscher, officer in Austrian army; considerable trouble when she appeared in United States during and after World War. Born Anclam, Prussia; died Berlin, Feb. 23, 1932.

William J. Guard, publicity director, 70. Formerly Sunday editor of *Morning Telegraph;* last twenty-two years widely known press representative of Metropolitan Opera Company. Born Limerick, Ireland; died New York City, March 3, 1932.

Louis John Bartels, actor, 36. Best known as lead in George Kelly's "Show-off," on stage and screen; played in Western stock companies and with De Lyle Alda in vaudeville. Born Chicago; died Hollywood, March 4, 1932.

John Philip Sousa, composer and bandmaster, 77. Apprenticed to the Marine Band in Washington, D. C., when 14; leader of band at 25; later organized his own band and made annual tours of world for thirty-five years; musical director 6th Army Corps; director musical activities at Great Lakes Naval Station during war; held rank as lieutenant commander; wrote "El Capitan" for De Wolf Hopper; composed "Stars and Stripes," "Semper Fideles," "High School Cadets," etc. Born Washington, D. C.; died Reading, Pa., March 6, 1932.

Bolossy Kiralfy, theatrical producer, 84. Elder of famous Kiralfy brothers, pioneer producers of spectacular ballets and tableaux; came to United States in 1868 to stage "The Deluge," at Niblo's Gardens, for the first time lighted by electricity; staged Barnum and Bailey shows and started Eldorado Park on Hudson; staged spectacles to celebrate anniversaries in many cities. Born Hungary; died London, March 6, 1932.

Chauncey Olcott, actor and singer, 71. Début at Union Square Theatre, New York, in 1886 in "Pepita"; starred in "Terence," "Edmund Burke," "Macushla," "Mavourneen," "Sweet Inniscara," etc.; played in the Red Cross production of "Out There" during the war; popularized "My Wild Irish Rose" and "Mother Machree"; last appearance on stage as Lucius O'Trigger in all star performance of "The Rivals." Born Buffalo, N. Y.; died Monte Carlo, March 18, 1932.

Thomas Jefferson, actor, 76. Son of Joseph Jefferson and sixth in line of famous Jeffersons, beginning in the early 18th century with a Thomas Jefferson who played with David Garrick; played "Rip Van Winkle" (created by his father) for twenty-five years; succeeded Frank Bacon in "Lightnin'"; last eight years in Hollywood. Died Hollywood, April 2, 1932.

Rose Coghlan, actress, 81. An active stage career of more than fifty-two years; retired in 1921; début at the Theatre Royale, Greenock, Scotland; first appearance in London in 1869; came to America with the elder Sothern; first New York appearance at Wallack's in 1872; won fame in the early eighties as leading woman of the Lester Wallack Stock Company; last appearance in 1921 in "Deburau." Born Peterborough, England; died Harrison, N. Y., April 2, 1932.

Johann Andreas Dippel, operatic tenor and manager, 65. Début Stadt Theatre, Bremen, in "Flying Dutchman" 1887; first appearance New York 1890 at Metropolitan in Franchetti's "Asreal"; became permanent member Metropolitan Opera Company, 1898; manager Metropolitan Opera House, New York, 1908-10; director Philadelphia-Chicago Opera Company three years; since 1929 technical sound expert in Hollywood. Born Cassel, Germany; died Hollywood, May 19, 1932.

Augusta, Lady Gregory, dramatist and director, 80. Organized Irish National Theatre; director Abbey Theatre, Dublin; wrote many plays produced at Abbey including "The Workhouse Ward," "The Gaol Gate," "The Rising of the Moon," "Spreading the News"; brought Irish National Players to United States in 1911, '12 and '14; widow of Sir William Gregory, former Governor of Ceylon. Born Galway, Ireland; died Galway, May 23, 1932.

THE DECADES' TOLL

(Players of Outstanding Prominence Who Have Died in Recent Years)

	Born	Died
Bacon, Frank	1864	1922
Belasco, David	1856	1931
Bernhardt, Sarah	1845	1923
Crabtree, Charlotte (Lotta)	1847	1924
Crane, William H.	1845	1928
Drew, John	1853	1927
De Koven, Reginald	1861	1920
De Reszke, Jean	1850	1925
Ditrichstein, Leo	1865	1928
Duse, Eleanora	1859	1924
Goodwin, Nathaniel	1857	1920
Hawtrey, Sir Charles	1858	1923
Herbert, Victor	1859	1924
Mantell, Robert Bruce	1854	1928
Miller, Henry	1858	1926
Morris, Clara	1848	1925
O'Neill, James	1850	1920
Patti, Adelina	1843	1919
Rejane, Gabrielle	1857	1920
Russell, Lillian	1861	1922
Shaw, Mary	1860	1929
Terry, Ellen	1848	1928
Minnie Maddern Fiske	1865	1932
Rose Coghlan	1851	1932

INDEX OF AUTHORS

INDEX OF PLAYS AND CASTS